CENTRAL
ADMINISTRATION
IN BRITAIN

CENTRAL ADMINISTRATION IN BRITAIN

BY
W. J. M. MACKENZIE
*Professor of Government
in the University of Manchester*

AND

J. W. GROVE
*Lecturer in Government
in the University of Manchester*

GREENWOOD PRESS, PUBLISHERS
WESTPORT, CONNECTICUT

Library of Congress Cataloging in Publication Data

Mackenzie, William James Millar, 1909-
  Central administration in Britain.

  Reprint of the ed. published by Longmans, Green, London, New York.
  Bibliography: p.
  Includes index.
  1. Great Britain--Executive departments. 2. Civil service--Great Britain. I. Grove, J. W., joint author.
  II. Title.
  JN321.M24 1975   354'.41   74-33896
  ISBN 0-8371-7996-3

© W.J.M. Mackenzie and J. W. Grove 1957

Originally published in 1957 by Longmans, Green and Co., London, New York

Reprinted with the permission of Longman Group Limited

Reprinted in 1975 by Greenwood Press,
a division of Williamhouse-Regency Inc.

Library of Congress Catalog Card Number 74-33896

ISBN 0-8371-7996-3

Printed in the United States of America

PREFACE

THIS book is primarily a text-book, a systematic exposition of what is already known, and it has no special claim to originality except that this particular body of knowledge has never been surveyed and presented in a unified way before. In imposing unity on our material we have been concerned more with the needs of potential readers than with theories about the nature of the British Constitution or of the modern state. Our main object is to explain the work of the great central Departments of British government, and of the various organs of administration which are directly subordinate to them. The Ministries are familiar, at least in name; and so is the Civil Service. But these fairly simple entities, which lie at the core of central administration, shade off into a complex intermediate zone. The Departments include among their number many small units, unknown to the general public, which are certainly not Ministries: they control directly a great many enterprises which have little to do with administration; it is not much more than accident, in marginal cases, whether a particular service is provided by a Department or by a body which has a different legal form.

It would therefore be absurd to offer here a formal definition of the phrase 'central administration'. Nevertheless, the fact that we approach central administration as if it were a relatively independent part of British government and of British society does imply some general ideas, very hard to work out precisely, about the structure of politics in Britain. The universe of British government (it might be said) consists of a number of worlds, relatively independent, but linked to one another both by constitutional theory and by the practical needs of business. One of these, of course, is that of political parties, Parliament, and Cabinet government; another is that of local government; a third is that of the law, the legal profession, and the courts; a fourth is the relatively new area of semi-public bodies, public corporations, and sponsored associations, which now rules much of our lives. Clearly, central administration stands alongside these as a fifth world, that of central Departments staffed by civil servants; and one could analyse central administration further by separate treatment of the administration of foreign policy, of overseas territories, of the armed forces. We say little of these important subdivisions, we assume knowledge of general theory about the place of central administration in the Constitution, and we deal primarily with the systematic structure of persons, Departments, and forms of procedure, which gives this world its ethos and identity.

The general plan of the book is as follows: We deal first with the Civil Service, the men and women who are the real fabric of the administrative system. In Part II we attempt to explain the traditions and formal rules by which human beings are combined into effective units of administration, the Departments, and the way in which standardised forms of organisation facilitate dealings within central administration. Part III sets out the elements in the system which are specifically concerned with co-ordination and control: the provision of common services, Treasury control, the administrative functions of the Cabinet. Finally, we attempt to set central administration in its context in relation to other parts of British government, treating not of formal organisation, which we must assume to be known to readers from other text-books, but of the ways in which civil servants experience the operation of other worlds of British public life.

Our object throughout has been descriptive rather than critical. Anyone who has lived with British central administration develops a certain affection and respect for it, as the accretion of the wisdom and idiosyncrasies of many generations of able and public-spirited men and women. 'We do it wrong, being so majestical, to offer it the show of violence.' But we do not invite readers 'to venerate what they cannot presently comprehend'. The system has been constructed in great measure by hard thought and vigorous criticism: it cannot live without them in the present period of readjustment to new technical needs and a new educational system. If we are thought at times to have been too complacent, our excuse is that we wish to emphasise that reform is possible only within the context of things as they are, and that reformers are not likely to succeed unless they look first at the system as a whole, and assess coherently the forces which give it stability, strength, and weakness.

Preparation of this book began during the sittings of the latest Royal Commission on the Civil Service, the Priestley Commission, which was appointed in November 1953, and reported in November 1955. The documents submitted to that body, its hearings, and its report make a useful starting-point from which to work. We have, however, attempted to incorporate material about changes made up to the spring of 1957: this material is not always complete, because of time-lags in the publication of details, but we have thought it best to include as much 'stop press news' as possible.

PREFACE

Various friends and colleagues, in the Civil Service and outside it, have helped us greatly by drawing our attention to sources of information and by reading our drafts. We are glad to acknowledge here the help of our academic colleagues in Manchester, Professor Ely Devons, Professor Harry Street, and Mr. Peter Campbell: our friends in the Service must remain (as usual) anonymous. We need hardly say that none of these gentlemen shares responsibility for our opinions or for our errors.

The entire book has been typed and re-typed from various crabbed drafts by Mrs. Kathleen Ashton: we have never ceased to marvel at her tolerance of bad handwriting and her patience in deciphering it.

W. J. M. MACKENZIE
J. W. GROVE

VICTORIA UNIVERSITY OF MANCHESTER
April 1957

ACKNOWLEDGMENTS

WE are indebted to the Controller of H.M. Stationery Office for permission to reproduce material from Government publications, and the map on page 277; and to Messrs. Faber and Faber Ltd. and Messrs. Harcourt, Brace and Company Inc. for an extract from "Difficulties of a Statesman" from *Collected Poems 1909-1935* by T. S. Eliot.

CONTENTS

PART I—THE CIVIL SERVICE

Chapter One—THE GROWTH OF THE SERVICE
1. 'Economic Reform' . . . . . *page* 3
2. Unity in Administration 5
3. The Modern Civil Service 7

Chapter Two—DEFINITION OF THE CIVIL SERVICE
1. Introductory 10
2. The Standard Definition 11
3. Regulation by Law 13

Chapter Three—TERMINOLOGY AND STATISTICS
1. Introductory 15
2. Terminology 15
3. Statistics 21

Chapter Four—THE MANAGEMENT OF THE SERVICE
1. Introductory 32
2. The Basis of Regulation 32
3. The Establishments Divisions of the Treasury . . 34
4. The Civil Service Commission . . . 38

Chapter Five—GENERAL CONDITIONS OF EMPLOYMENT
1. Introductory 44
2. The System of Pay 44
3. Hours of Work 47
4. Annual Leave and Sick Leave 48
5. Differentiation 49
6. Superannuation 50
7. Other Emoluments 54
8. Principles of Pay 54

CONTENTS

Chapter Six—THE GENERAL CLASSES

1. Introductory . . . . *page* 59
2. Historical Development 60
3. The Administrative Class 63
4. The Executive and Related Classes 73
5. The Clerical Class, the Clerical Assistant Class, and the Class of Temporary Clerks 80
6. The Typing Grades and the Machine Operating Class 87
7. The Messengerial Classes and the General Service Class of Cleaners 89
8. The Foreign Service 90
9. The Oversea Civil Service 91

Chapter Seven—THE SPECIALIST CLASSES

1. Introductory 94
2. Classes Generally Present 96
3. Classes Concentrated in a Few Departments . . 101
4. Departmental Classes 114
5. The Post Office 116

Chapter Eight—PROMOTION AND TRAINING

1. Introductory 120
2. Promotion 120
3. Training 124

Chapter Nine—STAFF ASSOCIATIONS AND NEGOTIATING PROCEDURE

1. Introductory 134
2. Staff Associations 134
3. Means of Pressure 140
4. Negotiation 141
5. Conclusion 147

Chapter Ten—PROFESSIONAL STANDARDS OF CONDUCT

1. Disciplinary Procedure 149
2. Probity 151
3. Security 152
4. Political Activity 155

PART II—THE ORGANISATION OF DEPARTMENTS

Introductory . . . . *page* 163

Chapter Eleven—THE HISTORICAL TRADITION

1. Introductory 165
2. The King's Justices 165
3. The Great Officers of State 166
4. The Privy Council 171
5. Secretaries of State and Ministers 173

Chapter Twelve—THE PHYSICAL SETTING 178

Chapter Thirteen—THE PATTERN OF ORGANISATION

1. Introductory 183
2. The Department 183
3. The Permanent Secretary 185
4. The Main Structure 187
5. Private Secretaries 191
6. Central Services 194

Chapter Fourteen—HOW BUSINESS IS DONE

1. Introductory 199
2. Files 201
3. Levels 205
4. Communications 208
5. Allocation and Review of Duties 215

Chapter Fifteen—TYPES OF DEPARTMENT

1. Introductory 222
2. The Commonwealth Relations Office . . . 224
3. The Home Office 228
4. The Air Ministry 232
5. The Ministry of Pensions and National Insurance . 239
6. The Board of Trade 243
7. The Ministry of Agriculture, Fisheries, and Food . 248

Chapter Sixteen—LOCAL AND REGIONAL ORGANISATION

1. Introductory . . . . *page* 260
2. England and Wales 263
3. Wales and Monmouthshire 272
4. Scotland 274
5. Northern Ireland 276
6. The Channel Islands and the Isle of Man . . . 278

PART III—CENTRAL CONTROL OF ADMINISTRATION

Introductory 283

Chapter Seventeen—COMMON SERVICES

1. Introductory 285
2. Agency Services 286
3. Allied Services, Their Scope 287
4. Common Services: Procedure and Controversies . 297

Chapter Eighteen—ACCOUNTING AND FINANCIAL CONTROL

1. Introductory 300
2. The Handling of Public Money 301
3. The Organisations Involved 305
4. The Financial Cycle and the Process of Control . 318
5. The Characteristics of the System 330

Chapter Nineteen—THE ADMINISTRATIVE FUNCTIONS OF THE CABINET

1. Introductory 334
2. Membership of the Cabinet 336
3. Cabinet Procedure and the Cabinet Secretariat . . 338
4. Co-ordination 342
5. Central Direction 349
6. Planning 355
7. Supervision of the Machinery of Government . . 359

PART IV—THE PLACE OF CENTRAL ADMINISTRATION

Introductory . . . . *page* 373

Chapter Twenty—POLITICS AND PARLIAMENT
1. Introductory 376
2. Correspondence and Questions 377
3. Other Parliamentary Business 380

Chapter Twenty-one—THE COURTS OF LAW
1. Introductory 387
2. Lawyers in the Civil Service 388
3. Central Administration and the Organisation of the Courts 389
4. Civil Servants as Legislators 391
5. Civil Servants as Judges 393
6. Civil Servants in Court 398
7. Conclusion 400

Chapter Twenty-two—LOCAL AUTHORITIES
1. Introductory 402
2. Departmental Organisation 406
3. Local Government Organisations 418
4. Individual Authorities 422
5. Conclusion 425

Chapter Twenty-three—INDEPENDENT PUBLIC BODIES
1. Introductory 428
2. General Considerations 429
3. The Nationalised Industries 431
4. The Regional Hospital Boards 439
5. Conclusion 444

Chapter Twenty-four—PUBLICS AND THE PUBLIC
1. Introductory 448
2. The Public as Individuals 449
3. Organised Publics 453
4. Conclusion 464

SELECTED BIBLIOGRAPHY 466

INDEX 471

LIST OF TABLES AND APPENDICES

Table	I. The Growth of the Service . . . *page*	7
	II. The Size of the Civil Service	22
	III. The Size of the Non-Industrial Civil Service 1943 and 1955	23
	IV. Analysis by Departments	24
	V. Established Civil Servants	25
	VI. Percentage of Women in the Main Classes .	26
	VII. The Treasury Classes	26
	VIII. Some Departmental Classes	27
	IX. The Higher Civil Service (some examples) .	29
Appendix	I. The Main Specialist Treasury (or 'General Service') Classes	30
Table	X. The Work of the Civil Service Commissioners	42
	XI. The Administrative Class (Home) . . .	64
	XII. Promotions in the Administrative Class, 1948-1955	69
	XIII. The General Service Executive Class . .	74
	XIV. Entry into Basic Grades of the General Service and Departmental Executive Classes . .	75
	XV. The General Service Clerical Classes and the Class of Temporary Clerks . . .	81
	XVI. Recruitment to the Clerical Class and Related Departmental Classes	84
	XVII. The Foreign Service	91
	XVIII. The Scientific Civil Service	102
	XIX. Distribution of the Works Group and Related Classes	108
	XX. The Works Group of Professional Classes .	109
	XXI. Established Medical Posts	111
	XXII. Post Office Staff	117
Appendix	II. Ministerial Departments existing in 1956, with date of origin of the Department or its main constituent	176

Table XXIII.	Senior Staff in the Commonwealth Relations Office . . . . . . *page*	225
XXIV.	Geographical Location of Established Non-Industrial Civil Servants (Home and Foreign)	260
XXV.	Non-Industrial Staff in Regional Offices . .	261
Map.	Standard Regional Boundaries and Capital Towns	277
Table XXVI.	The Public Services (excluding the armed forces)	403

I
THE CIVIL SERVICE

CHAPTER ONE

THE GROWTH OF THE SERVICE

But remembering the early civility they brought upon these Countrys, and forgetting long passed mischiefs; we mercifully preserve their bones, and pisse not upon their ashes.—Sir THOMAS BROWNE: *Urn Burial.*

OUR purpose is not historical, but so much relating to the Civil Service is defined by past experience that we find it necessary quite frequently to refer to the growth of the Service, of the Departments, and of the system of central control. Little research has been done on the history of the modern Civil Service, and there is a great deal yet to be discovered; but we attempt to present certain fixed points as they are generally understood within the Service and by the limited number of people outside it who take an interest in its affairs. It is perhaps history as it is understood, rather than history as it actually took place, which most influences the ways in which the Service regards itself and in which it is regarded by the public.

By way of introduction we summarise here the most important turning-points in the development of the modern Civil Service. Many of these are of importance because they continue to affect the structure and practice of administration, and we recur to these frequently in later chapters throughout the book.

1. 'ECONOMIC REFORM'

Our starting-point is the failure of the English Crown to assert its authority over Parliament in the seventeenth century, and its related failure to establish an effective system of royal government through centrally organised services, such as prevailed elsewhere in Western Europe. English administration in the eighteenth century was not uniformly inefficient: exploration of history is revealing many corners of government in which strong personalities maintained good order and administered well. But there was no general structure of administration, and the offices that existed were caught up in the working of the society as a whole. A job tended to become a freehold, the property of its occupier. The right to a salary or to the payment of certain fees might be conferred on a political supporter or a family connection: it would generally be held for life and could be bequeathed by will; it could be exercised by deputy or even sold; and it could not be abolished without compensation. If an efficient man had to be appointed in order to get the work done, it was generally possible to find ways and means of appointing and paying him: but there was no regular association between qualifications, appointment, work, and remuneration. This system, which is not wholly comprehensible except in the context of eighteenth-century politics, was attacked in the first place more on grounds of politics than of administration. One wave or current of reform extends from the speeches of Burke in the 1780s to the heyday of Gladstonian finance in the 1850s and 1860s. Its slogan was 'economy': partly in order to check the use of patronage to sustain the position of the government in office, partly in order to reduce taxation and make possible a general reform of the fiscal system.

During this period, and before the Civil Service existed in its modern form at all, there were established five principles which are still of great importance:

(i) Payment from the public purse is to be related to work done. This may seem self-evident today: it only became so because of the rejection of various eighteenth-century assumptions about the nature of public employment. The new principle involved the abolition of sinecures, of all forms of sale of office, of the performance of office by deputy, of a great number of obsolete offices, of remuneration through fees from the public to the official. It is worth noting that this stage of reform was fairly complete by the 1830s, some time before the beginnings of the modern Civil Service.

(ii) The Crown is generally held to have the legal right to dismiss its servants at any time without notice, without compensation, and without cause stated. For a great range of offices this right was not exercised at all in the eighteenth century. Existing officials were not dismissed when a new faction came into power: permanence was a principle established very early, and there was never a 'spoils' system of the old American type, under which a large number of officials are replaced when the government is changed.

(iii) Nevertheless, some exercise of the right to dismiss is necessary if there is to be an attempt to enforce a strict relation between pay and work. A faithful servant may become incapable of work through no fault of his own: it is not then just or reasonable to reward good service by dismissing him from office without compensation. Hence the necessity for a system of pensions. 'Pension' was a word of political ill-omen in the early nineteenth century: 'pensions' were carefully watched by Parliament, and the Superannuation Acts (the first of which was passed in 1810) continue to be the most specific case of Parliamentary intervention in the organisation of the Civil Service (Chapter 5).

(iv) Apart from this, Parliamentary control of organisation is virtually limited to control of finance. The ideal to be achieved was that the number and pay of all servants of the Crown (apart from the judges and a limited number of personal servants of the monarch) should be submitted to Parliament annually for approval in the Estimates of the Departments. What is thus approved is 'the establishment', and in principle no change can be made in it without authority (Chapters 4 and 18).

(v) Control by Parliament means control by the House of Commons. As party discipline grew stronger, control of business in the House of Commons passed to an organised majority supporting a coherent Cabinet, and House of Commons control came to mean Cabinet control. Within the Cabinet, primacy on all matters relating to the Estimates fell naturally to the Chancellor of the Exchequer, and his Department, the Treasury, rose to a position of primacy in central administration through its responsibility for the preparation and management of the Budget (Chapters 4 and 18).

These five points were well established by the middle of the nineteenth century. The final success of the movement for economy in administration can be dated by the Report of the Select Committee on Public Monies in 1856, the creation of the Public Accounts Committee of the House of Commons in 1861, and the Exchequer and Audit Departments Act of 1866. This movement overlaps with another, the movement for centralisation in the interests of efficient administration.

2. Unity in Administration

Centralised administration had been created in Europe not to relieve the taxpayer but for the effective execution of policy. The forms of bureaucratic organisation were familiar before the French Revolution, but gained prestige from the astonishing success of Napoleon's administration in France, and from that of his antagonists in Prussia. One aspect of the Benthamite or Utilitarian movement in England was its demand for the introduction of rational organisation of the same kind into English administration. Such proposals had little chance of political success, for the tendency of the time was hostile to energetic intervention by government, and continental examples were extremely unpopular. Benthamite principles were successful in a few isolated fields, general opinion moved in favour of government action, but 'centralisation' as a principle was defeated and displaced by the principle of 'local self-government'. It is therefore misleading to think of Victorian reform as leading directly to the creation of modern central administration.

Two points serve to illustrate this:

(i) The term 'Civil Service' is one introduced into England from India, where first the East India Company and then the British government carried out a gigantic experiment in centralised administration of the European type. The 'service' of the East India Company was divided into the military service and the civil service. The practice of entry by competitive examination was not fully established until 1853, but from about 1800 the civil service was effectively organised on the basis of systematic training, pay graduated by responsibility, regular promotion, and provision for an adequate pension on retirement. The offices of the old East India Company were a stronghold of Utilitarianism, under the two Mills, father and son; Sir Charles Trevelyan, the permanent head of the Treasury from 1840 to 1859, had made his name in India, and was married to a sister of Lord Macaulay, another great Indian reformer; and the prestige of the Indian Civil Service remained increasingly high throughout the nineteenth century. Even to use the term 'Civil Service' in reference to English administration was at that time somewhat tendentious. There was no 'Civil Service', merely the employees of certain offices or civil establishments, some of which (the Post Office, for instance, and the Customs and Excise) had large staffs and a long history. There were 'civil services', but no 'Civil Service': the question was whether to create one.

(ii) In 1954 the Civil Service celebrated the centenary of the Trevelyan-Northcote Report, which laid down certain principles of extreme importance about what it called 'the Permanent Civil Service of the country'. The only immediate sequel to the Report was the Order-in-Council of 21 May 1855, which is a landmark because it set up a body of three Commissioners to conduct tests for 'the Young Men who may from Time to Time be proposed to be appointed to junior Situations in any of Her Majesty's Civil Establishments'. At first the sole power of the Civil Service Commission was to conduct tests on behalf of Departments. Nevertheless, it was based on the principle that there should be a common channel of entry for all posts on the 'establishment'; and this principle was strengthened by the Superannuation Act of 1859, which made the certificate of the Commissioners necessary for entitlement to a pension on retirement. This Act also appears to contain the first statutory reference to 'the permanent Civil Service of the State', and recognition was strengthened by the Order-in-Council of 4 June 1870, which greatly extended the powers of the Commission and gave it fairly general control over entry, subject to agreement with individual Departments, and with the Treasury (Chapter 4).

In 1867 the primacy of the Treasury was recognised by giving its permanent head the title of Permanent Secretary, with a salary higher than that of other Departmental heads, and it is said that the Lords Commissioners of the Treasury made a Minute conferring on him the title of 'Head of the Civil Service'. If any such Minute was made, it has been lost: certainly it was premature to insist so strongly on the unity of the Service at that time.

3. THE MODERN CIVIL SERVICE

About 1900 there began to be a change in the character of the Service, partly due to the succession of a new generation in administration as well as in politics, and partly to a change of scale. There are no standardised official figures for staff in the earlier periods of expansion, but Table I gives some indication of the rate of growth,

TABLE I
The Growth of the Service

(Sources: H. Finer, *The Theory and Practice of Modern Government* [Revised Edn., New York, 1949], Parliamentary Papers, the Annual Abstract of Statistics)

1797	16,267	1891	79,241
1815	24,598	1901	116,413
1821	27,000	1911	172,352
1832	21,305	1914	280,900
1841	16,750	1922	317,721
1851	39,147	1939	387,400
1861	31,943	1943	710,600
1871	53,874	1950	684,800
1881	50,859		

and emphasises the importance of social reform before 1914 and of experience of war administration. The question of unity was then raised in such a way that it could no longer be evaded, and the present structure of the Service is largely due to those who faced the problems of reconstruction in the period from about 1917 to 1920: it was possible to create it then because of the steady growth of Treasury influence and experience, the establishment of a tradition of entry by examinations of a particular type, the emergence of staff associations representing civil servants as such irrespective of their Departments, and (above all) the immediate pressure of the problems of war and reconstruction. There are three landmarks of the period which should be mentioned here, though it will be necessary to return to them in detail later. These were:

(i) The formal recognition of the general responsibility of the Treasury for the organisation of the Service by the Order-in-Council of 22 July 1920, which gave the Treasury a general power to make regulations 'for controlling the conduct of His Majesty's Civil Establishments'. A little earlier, by a Treasury Minute of 4 September 1919, the Permanent Secretary of the Treasury was officially recognised as Head of the Civil Service: and in a Treasury Circular dated 12 March 1920 it was laid down that the consent of the Prime Minister (whose adviser in these matters is the Head of the Civil Service—since 1956 called the Head of the Home Civil Service) is necessary for the appointment of permanent heads of Departments, their deputies, and their principal finance and establishments officers (Chapter 4).

(ii) The creation by Order-in-Council in 1921 of 'Treasury' classes common to a considerable number of Departments, a long step in a process which had begun earlier (Chapter 6). The first of these classes consisted of civil servants without professional or technical qualifications gained outside the Service.

(iii) The appointment in 1919 of the National Whitley Council, a body which represented both the 'official' side and the 'staff' side of the Service, and so created a central focus for negotiations in all matters affecting the Service. This rested on, and encouraged, the development of strong staff associations, which speak separately for the interests of different sections of the Service, and jointly for the Service as a whole (Chapter 9).

To these should be added, as perhaps the most important developments of the period since 1921:

(iv) The growth of a system of Treasury classes of specialists parallel to the Treasury classes of non-specialists, and not inferior to them in importance (Chapter 7).

(v) The formalisation of a code of professional discipline. Much had been left unsaid previously which was made explicit when the Service grew **large**, but the 'code' (if such it can be called) still leaves a great deal to personal honour and common sense (Chapter 10).

FOR REFERENCE

EMMELINE COHEN: *The Growth of the British Civil Service, 1780-1939* (1941) (contains references to the most important official papers).

The Northcote-Trevelyan Report: (P.P. 1854, XXVII) reprinted in *Public Administration*, Vol. XXXII, p. 1.

E. HUGHES: 'Civil Service Reform, 1853-5', reprinted in the same volume, p. 17; and a postscript by the same author in *Public Administration*, Vol. XXXIII, p. 299.

R. MOSES: *The Civil Service of Great Britain* (New York, 1914). (An early work by a now famous New York City official, which deals with the later nineteenth century.)

S. E. FINER: 'Patronage and the Public Service', *Public Administration*, Vol. XXX, p. 329.

M. ABRAMOVITZ and V. F. ELIASBERG: *The Growth of Public Employment in Great Britain* (Princeton, N.J., 1957).

CHAPTER TWO

DEFINITION OF THE CIVIL SERVICE

Then said they unto him, Say now Shibboleth; and he said Sibboleth: for he could not frame to pronounce it right. Then they took him, and slew him at the passages of Jordan: and there fell at that time of the Ephraimites forty and two thousand.—*Judges*, xii, 6.

1. INTRODUCTORY

WE are met at the outset by the fact that there are no precise criteria, either legal or historical, by which to determine the scope of the Civil Service. There is a central core which is unmistakable, but at the margin no sharp line divides those public servants who are within the Civil Service from those who are not.

In this the Civil Service may be contrasted with the Navy, the Army, and the Air Force. The position of the armed forces is based on statute, and one important effect of such regulating Acts as the Army and Air Force (Annual) Acts, the Naval Enlistment Acts, the Naval Discipline Acts, and the Air Force Constitution Act is to establish for each service a system of naval, military, or air force law. Members of the armed forces are subject to this law as well as to the ordinary law of the land; to make such a system workable there must be a reasonably precise legal definition of the point at which an ordinary citizen enters the forces and becomes subject to military law. Difficult cases arise occasionally, but the line is in general very clear: there is a moment of enlistment and a moment of discharge. The Civil Service, on the other hand, owes its existence not to statute but to the prerogative powers of the Crown, a matter of common law. Common law may be as exact a form of law as statute, if defined by judicial interpretation; but in this instance there has been virtually no judicial interpretation. The Crown does not claim to apply any special form of law to its civilian servants: it disciplines them merely as its servants, as a medieval lord might manage his household or a nineteenth-century industrialist his employees. Its position as master is, however, peculiar, since in law 'it appears that the pay of a Crown servant is not to be considered as a reward for services, but as a payment to enable him to perform his duties'.[1] That is to say, the

[1] Mustoe: *The Law and Organisation of the British Civil Service*, p. 41.

DEFINITION OF THE CIVIL SERVICE 11

Crown cannot be sued on a contract of service: and in consequence questions relating to Crown service have seldom been decided in court.

The British Civil Service may also be contrasted with most other European Civil Services in this respect and in its historical character. In France and Germany *fonctionnaires* and *Beamten* are subject to special codes of law which mark them off from ordinary citizens as definitely as members of the armed forces: there is no ambiguity about status. At the same time, continental Civil Services possess a tradition of unity, stamped on them either by the personality of reforming monarchs, who created their own Crown Service, or by the French Revolution doctrine of the State, one and indivisible, operating through three 'powers', one of which, the executive, is manned largely by civil servants.

The definition of the British Civil Service is therefore partly a matter of tradition and experience; but something can be done to delimit it by reference to a variety of formal sources. We do this here as briefly as possible, since precision has more academic than practical interest.

2. THE STANDARD DEFINITION

The formula generally used is that adopted by the Royal Commission on the Civil Service, 1929-31 (the Tomlin Commission) (Report, para. 9):

> The following is usually taken as the working definition of civil servants, namely, those servants of the Crown, other than holders of political or judicial offices, who are employed in a civil capacity, and whose remuneration is paid wholly and directly out of monies voted by Parliament.

This carefully chosen form of words suggests the following points:

(i) 'Servants of the Crown': this phrase is of little use in deciding marginal cases because there are a number of important public bodies (such as Regional Hospital Boards and some other public corporations) whose statutory position is uncertain and has not yet been (and may never be) cleared up by judicial decision. If it is held that a particular public corporation is a 'servant of the Crown' it will follow that its employees are 'servants of the Crown', and this has certain legal consequences. But it does not follow that they are civil servants.

(ii) 'Holders of political office' can be defined only by reference to the practice of the House of Commons in interpreting clauses in the Regency Act of 1705 and in later Acts which exclude the holders of certain offices from sitting as members of the House of Commons. Offices which do not exclude are political offices. The problem of definition arises only in marginal cases, but it causes difficulty for one or two M.P.s at almost every general election, and it is very desirable that the existing rules should be clarified. A Select Committee of the House of Commons made detailed proposals to this effect in July 1956.

(iii) The phrase 'holders of judicial office' also presents difficulties, since the courts have generally had to decide not 'who is employed as a judge?' but 'when is an employee bound to act judicially?' and the body of law on this point is not very helpful in defining the limits of the Civil Service. The issues involved are of some importance, and are referred to again in Chapter 21.

(iv) 'Employment in a civil capacity' is precise in a negative sense since it means employment otherwise than in the armed forces, which are closely defined for purposes of military, naval, and air force law. Doubtful cases, such as the position of a member of one of the reserve forces not recalled for duties, raise only the same problems for civil servants as they do for other people.

(v) 'Remuneration paid wholly and directly out of monies voted by Parliament.' For practical purposes this is the most important part of the definition, and the theme is one to which we will recur frequently. In effect, civil servants are the employees of such civilian organisations as are subject to Treasury control in the full sense. Treasury control is related to the form of the Estimates presented to the House of Commons and to the appropriation of monies by the House of Commons, a subject discussed fully in Chapter 18.

The two adverbs are both necessary. A 'servant of the Crown' may be remunerated 'directly but not wholly' if he works for a government Department part-time. A man working one day a month for a retaining fee might be in law a 'Crown servant' on that day, but he could scarcely be called a 'part-time civil servant'. Where the line is to be drawn is necessarily uncertain.

The converse possibility, 'wholly but not directly', is of greater general importance. For instance, the British Council is wholly financed by monies provided by Parliament: it is probable (though not certain) that it is a servant of the Crown, and therefore that its employees are servants of the Crown; but they are paid from monies issued as a grant-in-aid and not from the normal form of Parliamentary grant. Hence they are deemed to be paid 'indirectly' and are not 'civil servants'. This is not an isolated case, since it has been part of British practice for a long time to provide public services through semi-independent bodies. Many public servants who would in most European countries be employed directly by the central administration are here employed indirectly, and are not treated as civil servants. Great complexities result, which are referred to further in Chapter 23.

(vi) The Civil Service, as thus defined, has two branches, the Home Civil Service (with which we are mainly concerned) and the Foreign Service. It excludes the old Colonial Civil Service, now the Oversea Service, because its members (though recruited centrally) are remunerated from the budgets of individual colonies, and not out of monies voted by Parliament. A little paradoxically, the Colonial Office is staffed mainly by members of the Home Civil Service, the Foreign Office partly by members of the Foreign Service and partly by the Home Civil Service.

3. Regulation by Law

The absence of a general statutory definition of the Civil Service does not mean that the Civil Service is not regulated by law. Its internal affairs are regulated by Orders-in-Council made under the prerogative powers of the Crown, and by regulations made under these Orders. This framework of regulation is law, but it is law made by the Crown and not by Parliament, and it retains something of the patriarchal and domestic spirit in which the medieval king regulated his household.

In addition to these regulations based on the common law, Parliament is called on from time to time to regulate particular matters by statute: it has intervened in particular in such matters as superannuation, and from year to year in the Appropriation Act it approves the total sums to be spent on the salaries of civil servants employed in each Department.

But Parliament has not created the Civil Service, and in general it does not give powers to civil servants. It gives powers to Ministers (often enormous powers) and it is for the Minister to decide which powers he shall exercise in person, and which through civil servants on the staff of his Department. The Crown and its political servants, the Ministers, still possess in law wide though not unlimited power to regulate the conditions and organisation of the central administration, and in this sense as in others they stand between it and Parliament.

The legal position may be summed up in three propositions, which are formal, but nevertheless have certain practical consequences. First, the internal organisation of the Civil Service is not regulated by Parliament: there is a contrast between the British situation and the American situation, since the Congress habitually interferes in the internal organisation of administrative services; Parliament has legal power to do so but is restrained by tradition and the strength of the Cabinet in office. Secondly, the Service derives its legal unity from the unity of the Crown. This is a traditional bond of some sentimental importance: it also means that much of the law applicable to civil servants is the general common law of Crown service. Thirdly, the Crown has important privileges in law: its servants have not. Indeed, their relation to their employer is weaker than that of an ordinary employee at common law. A civil servant has an informal status of great importance, in that he may have to act on his own responsibility as agent of the Crown: but his legal status is inferior rather than superior to that of the ordinary citizen.

FOR REFERENCE

C. S. EMDEN: *The Civil Servant in the Law and the Constitution* (1923).
N. F. MUSTOE: *The Law and Organisation of the British Civil Service* (1932).
J. A. G. GRIFFITH and H. STREET: *Principles of Administrative Law* (1952).
Special Report from the Select Committee on the House of Commons Disqualification Bill. H.C. 349, 1956.

CHAPTER THREE

TERMINOLOGY AND STATISTICS

The number of the beast: for it is the number of a man; and his number is six hundred threescore and six.—*Revelation*, xiii, 18.

1. INTRODUCTORY

THERE are a number of other rather dry matters of form which it is convenient to insert here, because care in handling them is essential to an understanding of what follows. Our purpose is to give the reader a grasp of the principal terms in use to describe subdivisions of the Service; and to associate with them a summary of Civil Service staff statistics, so presented as to indicate the scale of these subdivisions in relation to one another and to employment outside the Service.

2. TERMINOLOGY

The most important distinctions are those between 'industrial' and 'non-industrial' civil servants; between 'established' and 'unestablished' civil servants; between 'Treasury classes' and 'Departmental classes'; between 'general' and 'specialist'. None of these are precise concepts, but it is possible to give adequate working definitions.

(i) *Industrial and Non-industrial*

This distinction is based on a combination of three factors: type of employment, type of trade union organisation, and procedure for negotiation. Industrial civil servants are manual workers, skilled, semi-skilled, and unskilled, employed in dockyards, ordnance factories, research and other establishments. They are largely organised in the unions appropriate to their trade, and their conditions of service are negotiated through the ordinary machinery of the industry in which they work. Hence a practical definition is that industrial civil servants are (*a*) all home civil servants not covered by the National Whitley Council agreements, and (*b*) the engineering and allied grades of the Post Office. These Post Office grades are within the ambit of the National Whitley Council, and this is appropriate because they are not associated with any recognised trade outside the Civil Service; but the nature of their job is such that they are classified in Civil Service records as 'industrial'.

Non-industrial civil servants can only be defined by reversing this, as (*a*) all home civil servants within the ambit of the National Whitley Council, except for the Post Office engineering and allied grades, and (*b*) the Foreign Service.

These arbitrary definitions represent important differences in practice. Industrial civil servants on the whole are in a position more like that of employees of a nationalised industry or of an old-established private firm than that of participants in the business of central administration. Their problems are of great importance and interest in relation to the debate about nationalisation and private enterprise, but they are largely outside the scope of this book. We cannot, however, make a 'clean cut' between the non-industrial and the industrial Civil Service for two reasons:

First, the distinction between trade organisations does not correspond closely to a distinction between types of skill. The problem is illustrated by the case of the Post Office referred to above. The engineering and allied grades of the Post Office are recognised as industrial, but they are organised in associations of their own: the Post Office Engineering Union for the rank-and-file, the Society of Telecommunication Engineers and the Association of Post Office Controlling Officers for the specialists and supervisors. They therefore come within the ambit of the National Whitley Council, which also deals with the very large non-industrial staff of the Post Office. Such overlapping is common, though it is generally not on so large a scale. Many non-industrial civil servants possess skills and do jobs closely comparable to jobs in industry; many industrial civil servants are in positions of responsibility as foremen, specialists, and supervisors, and could fairly be described as part of the 'administration'.

Secondly, a number of Departments are responsible for the management of establishments manned by industrial civil servants. Part of the job of these Departments is the management of industrial production: their Establishments Divisions contain sections dealing with the employment of industrial workers. In fact, one of the important tasks of central administration is to 'manage' the industrial Civil Service.

(ii) *Established and Unestablished*

Established civil servants are those who are eligible for superannuation benefits under the Superannuation Acts, 1834-1950. Civil servants are eligible if they have received a certificate of qualification from the Civil Service Commissioners and have been appointed to a post 'on the establishment'. A post on the establishment is one which has been approved by the Treasury as central controlling body for the whole Civil Service.

The importance of this formal definition can be seen by contrast with the position of unestablished civil servants, who can be divided into three categories:

(*a*) Those on a genuinely temporary or part-time basis: for instance, extra staff engaged by certain Departments to deal with seasonal rushes of work, academic historians paid a small annual salary so that they may give part of their time to work on the History of the War. In law such people are civil servants within the definition given in Chapter 2, but they do not think of themselves as such, and are not involved in any of the problems of the Civil Service as a career.

(*b*) Unestablished civil servants who are doing a full-time job of a permanent kind, but have no clear prospect of becoming 'established'. The sudden expansion of the Civil Service during the two world wars depended on appointments of this type, most of which terminated at the end of the war. It may also be necessary in peacetime, if there is a shortage of suitably qualified candidates for appointment to established posts, to complete 'the establishment' (perhaps with older people) without there being any necessary intention that those appointed should later qualify for pension by receiving the certificate of the Commissioners.

(*c*) Staff recruited on a temporary basis in the first instance, but with a good prospect of establishment if they complete a probation period satisfactorily and pass some form of simple test. This is the normal practice for some of the Post Office manipulative grades (e.g. postmen and telephonists) and for messengers and other minor grades in other Departments.

The first and third categories raise no general problems of importance: it is the second category which illustrates the contrast between 'established' and 'unestablished' civil servants. The problem is that of the 'permanent temporary' civil servant. The established civil servant has no contractual rights which he can enforce against the Crown, but statute provides for the payment of a pension when he reaches the prescribed age and retires from the Service, and he has a well-founded expectation that he will be employed until that age. Dismissal, or down-grading as an alternative to dismissal, is legally possible at the discretion of the Crown, but such action is extremely rare except as a penalty for serious misconduct. In 1909 it was made rather easier to remove established civil servants without censure by permitting compensation for dismissal on abolition of office or to facilitate reorganisation, but between 1930 and 1939 only thirteen, and between 1949 and 1953 only eleven, Administrative Class officers withdrew under this provision. In 1949, provision was made for retiring civil servants compulsorily on proportionate pension at the age of 50 if this was thought to be necessary on grounds of efficiency. The voluntary retirement of a civil servant over 50 is also permissible if he believes that he has no chance of further promotion or wishes to withdraw for some other reason: but in this case no pension is payable until he reaches the minimum retiring age unless the Treasury is prepared to make an exception on compassionate grounds.

A 'permanent temporary' civil servant is under a serious disadvantage in two respects:

(a) However long his service, he is not entitled to a pension. The largest concession permitted by statute is that a whole-time unestablished civil servant after not less than seven years' continuous service may receive a gratuity on the scale of one week's pay for each year of service.

(b) In the event of a reduction in establishment and consequent redundancy, the burden falls primarily on unestablished civil servants, who are liable to be dismissed on a rough and ready application of the principle: 'last in first out'. Established civil servants also suffer when there is a reduction of staff in their Department, because of loss of prospects of promotion, and the liability to transfer to another Department; but they are very unlikely to lose their jobs.

This situation causes various difficulties in the management of the Service. On the one hand, 'permanent temporary' civil servants may have a real grievance if they work for long periods alongside established civil servants with no greater skill and experience. This has been met from time to time (after much agitation) by the grant of establishment to large blocks of 'temporary' staff. On the other hand, it is out of the question to have a Civil Service which consists (apart from 'transient temporaries') entirely of established civil servants with the expectation of permanency and a pension. This would make it difficult to reduce staff without a breach of faith towards the Service, and would make for great rigidity in administration.

The percentage of unestablished non-industrial staff was brought down from 44 per cent. to 22 per cent. between April 1949 and July 1955. It is doubtful whether it can be reduced much farther without risk of serious inconvenience.

(iii) *Treasury Classes and Departmental Classes*

The former may be defined as classes which are spread over a number of Departments and for the salaries and conditions of service of which the Treasury is directly responsible in negotiation with staff associations and with the Staff Side of the National Whitley Council. Departmental classes are classes each of which is employed only by a single Department: that Department will be responsible for negotiation about conditions of service, subject to the general agreement of the Treasury.

Virtually all non-industrial civil servants fall into one or other of these classes. There are a few individuals who hold appointments on special terms, and there are some groups too small to be recognised as 'classes'. Their numbers are trivial, but their existence serves to emphasise the fact that the classes are the result of standardisation imposed on what was once a highly individual form of employment, and that the tussle between standardisation and differentiation continues.

As examples of Treasury classes we may quote the General Administrative Class (2,596), the General Executive Class (35,493), the Scientific Officer Class (2,878), the Legal Class (536), the Assistant (Scientific) Class (2,612).[1] The following are examples of Departmental classes and grades taken at random: The Tax Inspectorate of the Board of Inland Revenue (2,995), the 'Cadet' grade of the Ministry of Labour (48), the Inspectorate of the Ministry of Education (550), the Examiners and Receivers in the Patent Office under the Board of Trade (237), the officers of the National Agricultural Advisory Service under the Ministry of Agriculture (1,467), the technical staff of the Stationery Office (385).[2]

There are at least 200 distinguishable Departmental classes, ranging in numbers from the manipulative rank-and-file staff of the Post Office (166,625) to small classes such as the Explosive Acts Inspectorate of the Home Office with only five members. About half of all non-industrial civil servants are in Departmental classes or grades.

The trend of policy is from Departmental classes towards Treasury classes, since this makes for greater equity and simplicity in negotiation and improves mobility of staff between Departments. The influence both of the Treasury and of the great 'general' staff associations tells in that direction, but it is never likely to be paramount. Some of the existing Departmental classes have a tradition older than that of the Civil Service itself, and are large enough to afford a satisfactory career for ambitious men even without mobility

[1] Figures from the *Digest of Civil Service Staff Statistics* and the *Report of the Royal Commission on the Civil Service* (Priestley). Cmd. 9613, 1955: as at 1 July 1955. Figures for permanent staff only.

[2] Source: Treasury, Central Staff Records Division. Figures for permanent staff only.

between Departments. Others arise out of the special circumstances of a particular service (the Factory Inspectorate, for instance), and have no parallels outside their own Department. Indeed, such special services continue to develop as the scope of government grows, and new Departmental classes spring up as quickly as old ones disappear.

A useful compromise is the practice of 'linking' Departmental classes to Treasury classes and to one another for purposes of negotiation. These 'links' are very informal and their strength varies, but there are a number of well-recognised groups of classes. For instance, the General Executive Class (35,493) is 'linked' to the main Departmental Executive Classes (28,432).

The Post Office has numerous problems of its own, which are largely outside the scope of this book, since they have more to do with telecommunications and transport than with central administration. But it is desirable to mention it here, as it is much the largest of all Departments and is one of the most complex in its organisation. It employs about 327,000 people altogether, and only about 36,000 of these belong to Treasury classes. Of the rest, about 72,500 are classified as 'industrial', but are within the ambit of the National Whitley Council; about 6,000 are in other industrial classes. The main body, some 212,500, are in non-industrial classes peculiar to the Post Office, which is responsible for negotiations with them.

(iv) *General Classes and Specialist Classes*

Classes may be divided on another basis which cuts across the distinction between Treasury and Departmental classes, and which is of great importance in any analysis of the structure of the Service. No definition is possible except by enumeration, but our distinction is based largely on qualifications at entry into the Service. The general classes are recruited on the basis of general education and personal qualities, without regard to technical qualifications: the specialist classes are recruited from those who have already obtained outside the Service some special qualification relevant to the work for which they are appointed. There are a few exceptions to this generalisation. For instance, the typing grades rank as a general class (though many of their members learnt typing and shorthand outside the Service) presumably because the normal avenue of promotion is into the General Clerical class. Conversely, the machine-operating class and the duplicator operator grades rank as 'specialists', although these techniques are largely taught within the Service. But anomalies do not affect the broad distinction.

TERMINOLOGY AND STATISTICS

The simplest series of classes to enumerate is that of those Treasury classes which are also general classes. These are:

> The General Administrative class
> The General Executive class
> The General Clerical class
> The Typing grades
> The Clerical Assistant class
> The Messengerial grades
> The General Service class of Cleaners.

Many Departmental classes are linked to these, and this framework of general classes (dealt with in Chapter 6) is of great importance. It is not, however, more important than the system of specialist classes, which is less easy to grasp because it is more complex, and therefore attracts less attention. There are at least 180 specialist classes: of these about 50 are Treasury classes, the rest are Departmental classes linked more or less closely to the framework of Treasury classes. The principal specialist Treasury classes are set out in an Appendix at the end of this chapter. They are generally arranged in three main groups:

(*a*) Professional Classes, and Scientific and Technical Staffs I: including qualified doctors and lawyers, graduate scientists (in the Scientific Officer Class), architects, professional engineers and surveyors (in the Works Group).

(*b*) Scientific and Technical Staffs II: in effect, qualified assistants to those enumerated above: medical aides, draughtsmen, experienced laboratory assistants.

(*c*) 'Ancillary Technical and Miscellaneous Supervisory Staffs, and Manipulative Grades other than in the Post Office': a catch-all classification which includes less well-qualified assistants, machine operators of various kinds, canteen managers, supervisors working in industrial establishments but not classified as industrial civil servants. These are all skilled jobs carrying some responsibility. It is perhaps an accident of organisation that they should be classified as 'non-industrial' rather than 'industrial', but it should be remembered that many of them—duplicator operators, photographers, tracers, for instance—are in jobs which are important auxiliaries to 'general' administration as well as to the work of other 'specialists'.

3. STATISTICS

This introduction to the 'grammar' of the Service makes it possible to illustrate its structure and the balance between its parts in a series of Tables,[1] which are given here in as simple a form as possible, with a brief commentary on each. The date chosen is 1 July 1955, the date of the figures used by the Priestley Commission in its Report: our figures do not always correspond to those given by the Commission, as they are drawn from a source (the *Digest of Civil Service Staff Statistics*) which is more comprehensive but does not use exactly the same definitions as those used by the Commission. In the few cases in which we have used Priestley Commission figures, the fact is noted in the Tables. There are minor alterations in the figures from year to year, but the shape of the structure could be altered only by complete reorganisation, a most unlikely event.

(i) *The Size of the Service*

TABLE II

The Size of the Civil Service

	Men	Women	Total
Industrial	377,140	45,620	422,760
Non-industrial	433,336	202,100	635,436
Total	810,476	247,720	1,058,196

The highest recorded total is that of 1943, when the combined figure was 1,448,400. This included 737,800 industrials. The total of the non-industrial Civil Service was then 710,600, and it has therefore fallen only about 10 per cent. below its war-time peak; but this relatively small reduction conceals great changes in the distribution of the Service between groups of Departments, as can be seen in Table III.

The reduction in numbers in both categories is partly due to the switch from war production to peace-time work, and to the gradual abandonment of rationing and other controls. It is also due to the transfer of functions to public bodies outside the Civil Service, such as the National Coal Board, the British Transport Commission, and the Atomic Energy Authority. Many of the public corporations set up since the war have taken over functions from the Civil Service as well as from private industry: in some cases, such as that of the Atomic Energy Authority, a corporation took over duties which had previously been carried out entirely by civil servants, and some 7,000 non-industrial and 10,000 industrial civil servants were then transferred.

[1] Except where otherwise stated, part-time staff are included and are counted as half.

Table III

The Size of the Non-industrial Civil Service 1943 and 1955

(Figures—in thousands—for 1 April in each year:
figures for 1 July 1943 not available)

	1943	1955
Post Office	207·6	247·8
Service and Supply[1]	236·2	134·3
Social Services[2]	36·2	65·9
Revenue[3]	47·3	65·4
Trade[4]	118·9	69·1
Agency[5]	21·7	20·8
Central Government[6]	35·0	23·9
Foreign, etc.[7]	7·7	8·4
Total	710·6	635·6

[1] Admiralty, War Office, Air Ministry, Supply, Aircraft Production (1943 only), etc.
[2] Education, Health, Housing and Local Government, National Assistance Board, National Insurance, Pensions, etc.
[3] Inland Revenue, Customs and Excise.
[4] Agriculture, Food, Forestry Commission, Fuel and Power, Labour and National Service, D.S.I.R., Board of Trade, Civil Aviation, Transport, etc.
[5] Ordnance Survey, Stationery Office, Works, etc.
[6] Home Office, Treasury, Prison Commission, etc.
[7] Foreign Office, Colonial, Commonwealth Relations, etc.

It is probable that, like many other large organisations, the Civil Service could afford some reduction in staff without loss of efficiency, and staff numbers are continually being reviewed. But there are only two things which would permit a large reduction in numbers:

(*a*) A large reduction of the major services to be provided, or the abandonment of some of them. This is at present unlikely, but it is not impossible, if there were (for instance) some dramatic change in the international situation.

(*b*) The transfer of staff and functions from the central administration to other public bodies: it would for instance be possible to give the Post Office the form of a public corporation, or to transform the Ministry of Pensions and National Insurance into a National Insurance Corporation. In one sense, such changes would be no more than paper transactions, since the same people would do the same jobs under a new title; but the central administration has a character of its own, and transfer from it would certainly have some practical effects, good or bad, in each case.

(ii) *Distribution between Departments*

TABLE IV

Analysis by Departments

	Industrial	Non-industrial	Total
Post Office	79,095	247,901	326,996
Admiralty	106,794	33,563	140,357
War Office	76,562	38,872	115,434
Ministry of Supply	71,036	34,444	105,480
Air Ministry	44,321	26,588	70,909
Inland Revenue	*	51,953	51,953
Pensions and National Insurance	*	36,979	36,979
Works	15,588	12,990	28,578
Labour and National Service	*	22,868	22,868
Agriculture and Fisheries and Food	650	17,594	18,244
Forestry Commission	13,302	2,277	15,579
Customs and Excise	*	14,956	14,956
Transport and Civil Aviation	3,070	10,832	13,902
National Assistance Board	*	10,059	10,059
Board of Trade	*	7,179	7,179
Stationery Office	3,763	3,017	6,780
Home Office	2,550	3,340	5,890
Foreign Office	*	5,714	5,714
Health	*	5,700	5,700
Scientific and Industrial Research	995	3,232	4,227
Housing and Local Government	*	2,952	2,952
Education	*	2,883	2,883
Fuel and Power	*	2,105	2,105
Colonial Office	*	1,660	1,660
Treasury	*	1,263	1,263

* Under 500.

Table IV includes all Departments with more than 1,000 non-industrial staff, arranged in order of size, and leaving out of account the Scottish Departments. There will be further reference to this Table in Chapter 15, which deals with types of Departments; it is introduced here in order to illustrate the following points:

(*a*) There is a great difference between the size of Departments, but this difference in size is not a measure of their importance in administration. For instance, two very important Departments, the Colonial Office and the Treasury, come at the bottom of this list, and the list excludes the Commonwealth Relations Office, an important Department with a staff of less than 1,000.

(*b*) The distribution of the industrial Civil Service is quite different from that of the non-industrial Civil Service. The former is concentrated in a limited number of Departments.

(c) Some very large organisations are staffed mainly by non-industrial civil servants: for instance, the Post Office (which is technically a Revenue Department), the two other Revenue Departments (Inland Revenue and Customs and Excise), and the large social service organisations (Pensions and National Insurance, Labour and National Service, National Assistance Board). There is an obvious distinction (though there is no precise line) between these Departments and the smaller non-industrial Departments of great importance, such as the Treasury, the Home Office, or the Ministry of Education.

(iii) *Established Status*

TABLE V

Established Civil Servants

	Established	Unestablished	Total
Industrial:			
Men	171,155	205,985	377,140
Women	4,734	40,886	45,620
Non-Industrial:			
Men	362,126	71,210	433,336
Women	132,693	69,407	202,100
Total	670,708	387,488	1,058,196

Table V illustrates the following points:

(a) The proportion of 'establishment' is quite different in the industrial and in the non-industrial Civil Service: about 40 per cent. in the former, about 78 per cent. in the latter.

The proportion of established to non-established has been increasing ever since the war: in 1945 it was about 40 per cent. for non-industrial civil servants; in 1949 it was still only 56 per cent.

(b) In the industrial Civil Service the proportion of women is quite small: in the non-industrial Civil Service it is about one-third. This proportion, however, exaggerates the relative importance of women civil servants. One indication of the true position is that about five-sixths of the men are established, but less than two-thirds of the women. Another indication is to be found in Table VI, which shows that the proportion of women civil servants is high only in a limited number of classes concerned mainly with routine clerical and ancillary office work.

Table VI

Percentage of Women in the Main Classes, 1 January 1955

(Figures for 1 July 1955 not available)

	per cent.
Administrative (including Foreign)	6
Executive (General and Departmental)	16
Clerical (General and Departmental)	36
Clerical Assistant, etc.	58
Typing	98
Messengers and Cleaners	28
Post Office Manipulatives	27
Professional, Scientific, and Technical, and Inspectorate	7
Technical and Ancillary	32

In all branches of the Service there are a number of women who make careers comparable to those of men civil servants, and who are of great importance in the Service. The proportion cannot be exactly estimated, but it is fairly small, and the career of a woman civil servant is still mainly limited by marriage, or rather by family responsibilities, since there is no marriage bar of any kind. Only 26 per cent. of established male civil servants are below thirty-five, 50 per cent. of women. The 'turn-over' of women civil servants must therefore be much higher than that of men.

(iv) *Treasury Classes and Departmental Classes, General and Specialist*

Table VII

The Treasury Classes

(a) GENERAL (Established and permanent unestablished)[1]

	Men	Women	Total
Administrative (excluding Foreign)	2,401	195	2,596
General Executive	28,273	7,220	35,493
General Clerical	51,274	27,926	79,200
Clerical Assistants	16,300	19,309	35,609
Typing	291	16,184	16,475
Messengers, Porters, etc.	19,436	1,828	21,264
Total	117,975	72,662	190,637

[1] 'Permanent unestablished' civil servants are 'medical rejects': they are employed in established posts and on 'established conditions' except for superannuation and sick leave.

(b) SPECIALIST (some examples) (Established and permanent unestablished)[1]
(Figures from Priestley Commission Report, 1955)

The Scientific Officer Class	2,878
The Works Group	9,488
The Legal Class	536
The Medical Officer Class	384
The Experimental Officer Class	5,064
The Draughtsman Classes	6,098
The Assistant (Scientific) Class	2,612

TABLE VIII

Some Departmental Classes

(Established and permanent unestablished) [1]

	Men	Women	Total
Foreign Service (Branch A) . . .	646	10	656
Departmental Executive Classes . .	25,543	2,889	28,432
Departmental Clerical Classes . .	21,271	8,994	30,265
Inspectorates	2,095	372	2,467
Post Office Manipulatives . . .	128,897	37,728	166,625

[1] See footnote to Table VII.

Tables VII (a) and (b) and VIII illustrate the following points:

(a) *The Balance between Treasury Classes and Departmental Classes.* If the Post Office is put on one side, the Treasury classes now include a large part of the established non-industrial Civil Service, but the preponderance is by no means complete. Even apart from the Post Office, there are a number of non-specialist Departmental classes, such as those of the Inland Revenue, Customs and Excise, and Ministry of Labour, which are strong in numbers and in tradition. There are also a large number of specialist Departmental classes; each of these is small, but each is influential in its own field, and their combined importance is very great.

(b) *The Balance between General and Specialist Classes.* The former greatly outnumber the latter, but a balance stated simply in terms of numbers is misleading. First, the lower general classes (for instance, typists, ancillary staff, and a good many clerks) may work either in general organisations or in specialist organisations on the same kind of 'supporting' job. Secondly, many general civil servants have learnt within the Service techniques and procedures which are as specialised as those of the specialists. The administration, for instance, employs both accountants professionally qualified outside the Service and organised as a specialist Treasury class, and accountants trained within the Service in government accounting, employed solely in that field, but classified as members of the Executive Class. The latter are much more numerous than the former.

(c) *The Foreign Service* is from the point of view of organisation a linked series of Departmental classes: Branch A, Administrative; Branch B, Executive and Clerical; Branch C, Typing; Branch D, messengers and so on at posts overseas. The Foreign Office itself is staffed in part by members of the first three of these Departmental classes, but its staff also includes a good many members of various Treasury classes, and a few of these are to be found in establishments abroad. This position is a result of compromise in a long-drawn battle. It was conceded by the Treasury at the time of the 'Eden' reforms of the Foreign Service in 1943 that a separate Foreign Service exists, apart from the Home Civil Service: the Head of the Home Civil Service is not Head of the Foreign Service and the Treasury is not responsible for higher appointments in the Foreign Office in the same way as in other Departments. On the other hand, Treasury control is applied to the Estimates of the Foreign Office as to those of all Departments; and conditions of service are regulated so as to maintain comparability with those of the Home Civil Service, with proper allowance for the difference of circumstances.

The Colonial Service (known since 1954 as the Oversea Civil Service) is in a different position. The Colonial Office itself is staffed mainly by members of various classes of the Home Civil Service, some of whom may serve abroad for short periods. The Oversea Civil Service provides officials, general and specialist, for the various colonies and protectorates. Their pay is borne on the local budget of the territory where they serve, along with the pay of large numbers of locally recruited officials. The Oversea Service is therefore outside the scope of Treasury control, except in a rather limited sense, and it is recruited in principle by the Colonial Office and not by the Civil Service Commission, although the latter is associated with it in practice (for instance, the First Commissioner or his deputy is *ex officio* chairman of the Oversea Service Appointments Board).

(v) *The Higher Civil Service*

TABLE IX

The Higher Civil Service (*some examples*)

(Source: Priestley Commission Report 1955 and Civil Service Staff Statistics)

	'Highest Ranks of the Civil Service'	Rest of 'Higher Civil Service'	Total 'Higher Civil Service'
Administrative Class	96	887	983
Executive Class	—	138	138
Scientific Civil Service	22	559	581
Works Group	26	602	628
Legal Class	20	100	120
Medical Officer Class	7	496	503
Total	171	2,782	2,953

The Priestley Commission commented on the elements common to the work of all classes of the Civil Service above a certain level of responsibility, and suggested that there should be a special procedure for salary negotiation at this level. They defined 'the Higher Civil Service' as 'all staffs whose salary maximum or whose fixed rate exceeds the maximum of a Principal' (that is, £1,950 on the scales agreed in 1956), and 'the highest ranks of the Civil Service' as all grades carrying a salary above that of Under Secretary (£3,250). In the present context Table IX serves to illustrate the balance between general and specialist classes at the head of the Service. The Table is incomplete because statistics were not given by the Royal Commission for any of the Departmental classes; and salaries are not conclusive evidence about work and status. For instance, the Commission took the view that salaries at the upper end of the Executive Class scale seriously under-estimate the weight of responsibility in managerial posts; and apparently (such is the level of medical salaries) there are no doctors in the Civil Service earning less than about £1,400 a year. Nevertheless, the Table indicates the shares contributed by various classes to the higher management of the Service. In 'the highest ranks' the Administrative Class has no great preponderance in numbers over all other classes combined: nevertheless, it is much the largest single contributor to the Higher Civil Service, and its traditions and influence have great weight.

FOR REFERENCE

There are three regular sources of statistical information about the Civil Service:

(1) The return of *Civil Staffs Employed in Government Departments* made quarterly to Parliament and published as a Command Paper about six weeks after the date to which it refers. This gives a total figure for the non-industrial Civil Service showing the main Departments and the increase or decrease from the preceding quarter.

(2) The *Digest of Civil Service Staff Statistics*, issued annually by the Central Staff Record Division of the Treasury, with quarterly supplements. This gives much fuller, but not comprehensive, information: it is made available to authorised libraries but not to the general public.

(3) The Central Statistical Office's *Annual Abstract of Statistics* (published by H.M.S.O.) contains information based on the foregoing, but it is somewhat less detailed; and total figures for the industrial and non-industrial Civil Service are given (with reference to the beginning of the previous month) in the *Monthly Digest of Statistics*, but they are not in a form which is of much value for the present purpose.

Selections from (1), (2), and (3) are published at regular intervals in the *Whitley Bulletin* (the journal of the Staff Side of the National Whitley Council).

Valuable information is given from time to time in answer to Parliamentary Questions, and in the Reports and Evidence of Commissions of Inquiry. The most valuable recent source is the *Report of the Royal Commission on the Civil Service* (Priestley) (Cmd. 9613) and the *Introductory Factual Memorandum and Supplement* submitted to it by the Treasury.

APPENDIX I

The Main Specialist Treasury (or 'General Service') Classes

Professional Classes, and Scientific and Technical Staffs I

Accountants (Professional)
Actuaries
Legal Staff
Medical Staff
Nursing Staff (Senior Grades)
Psychologists
Scientific Officers:
  (1) Physicists
  (2) Chemists
  (3) Engineers
  (4) Biologists
  (5) General (i.e. not in the specific classes above)

TERMINOLOGY AND STATISTICS

Statisticians (Professional)
Works Group:
  (1) Architects
  (2) General Treasury Class of Engineers:
      (a) Civil Engineers (incl. Structural, Drainage, and Road Engineers)
      (b) Electrical Engineers
      (c) Mechanical Engineers
  (3) Land Officers and Surveyors
  (4) Quantity Surveyors
  (5) Surveyors

Scientific and Technical Staffs II
Assistant (Scientific)
Draughtsmen (Cartographic and Recording)
Draughtsmen (Engineers/Architectural)
Experimental Officers:
  (1) Physicists
  (2) Chemists
  (3) Engineers
  (4) Biologists
  (5) General (i.e. not in the specific classes above)
Illustrators
Librarians (Professional)
Nursing Staff
Occupational Therapists
Pharmacists (incl. Dispensers)
Physiotherapists
Radiographers (incl. Radiotherapists)
Technical Costs Officers
Technical Works, Engineering and Allied Grades

Ancillary Technical and Miscellaneous Supervisory Staffs, and Manipulative Grades other than in the Post Office. (This group includes posts of a supervisory nature in industrial etc. establishments not classified as industrial posts.)

Canteen Managers
Drawing Office Assistants
Duplicator/Machine Operators
Laboratory Attendants
Nursing Staff (minor)
Pharmaceutical Assistants
Photographers
Photoprinters
Telephonists (Blind and Sighted (Non-Post Office))
Teleprinter Operators
Tracers
Wireless Telegraphy Operators

CHAPTER FOUR

THE MANAGEMENT OF THE SERVICE

> And therefore is the glorious planet Sol
> In noble eminence enthron'd and spher'd
> Amidst the other; whose med'cinable eye
> Corrects the ill aspects of planets evil,
> And posts, like the commandment of a king,
> Sans check, to good and bad.
> SHAKESPEARE: *Troilus and Cressida*, I, iii, 89-94.

1. INTRODUCTORY

IN spite of its complexity the non-industrial Civil Service is now treated as a single unit for purposes of personnel management. Much responsibility is decentralised to Departments and within Departments; there is friction and pressure; but it is no longer in dispute that all questions affecting the service of this army of over 600,000 people are interrelated, and that the focus of decision lies in the Treasury. This is due partly to Treasury zeal for economy, backed by pressure from Parliament; but it is also in part the effect of the growth of trade unionism and industrial negotiation within the Service. Skilled officials of the Civil Service trade unions see the importance of a precedent in one section of the Service in its bearing on the deserts of their members in another section of the Service. There is a web of argument, negotiation, and arbitration by which decisions affecting one part of the Service are rapidly transmitted through the whole structure: trade unions and Treasury have a common interest in the maintenance of unity through a relatively small central group of negotiators.

2. THE BASIS OF REGULATION

The formal powers of the Treasury in relation to the Civil Service can be grouped under three headings:
(i) The Crown may under the prerogative regulate all matters relating to its servants, except in so far as the prerogative has been specifically limited by statute. The most formal type of regulation is by an Order-in-Council, made upon the advice of Ministers: in

important matters this will involve the Cabinet as a whole, in lesser matters the Prime Minister as First Lord of the Treasury, and the Chancellor of the Exchequer as working head of the Treasury.

The most important Order-in-Council at present in force is that of 22 July 1920 (revised on 21 November 1950) under which the Treasury has power 'to make regulations for controlling the conduct of Her Majesty's Civil Establishments, and providing for the classification, remuneration and other conditions of service of all persons employed therein, whether permanently or temporarily'. The Treasury therefore has very wide powers, and it is rarely necessary to proceed by Order-in-Council.

In spite of the great power of the Treasury a Minister is still responsible individually for the conduct of his Department. Civil servants are formally appointed to the Service by the Department which first employs them: and a Minister has power under the prerogative to regulate the conduct of his Department, provided that he contravenes no regulation of a more general character.

There is therefore a hierarchy of Orders-in-Council, Treasury Regulations (made formally by a Minute of the Lords Commissioners of the Treasury), Treasury instructions given less formally, Departmental regulations, and Departmental instructions. The general body of rules for the regulation of the Civil Service is contained in the *Estacode*, a large volume which is the bible of all Establishments Officers. Alterations and additions to *Estacode*, if they are to be relatively permanent, are notified to Departments by Establishments Circulars. Matters of transient importance may be dealt with by letter from the appropriate Treasury official to the Establishments Officers concerned. *Estacode* is available to the Civil Service Staff associations, but is not published.

(ii) The Crown may regulate its servants under the prerogative, but it cannot pay them except out of monies provided by Parliament. This position was established in theory in the Revolution Settlement of 1689, but effective procedure for securing Parliamentary control was not devised until the middle of the nineteenth century. The procedure is set out briefly in Chapter 17: its relevance here is that the Estimates for all Departments are formally approved by the House of Commons; to reach the Commons they must be formally approved by the Cabinet; and to reach the Cabinet they must first be submitted to the Treasury, and (except in rare cases) must secure its approval. The Treasury therefore stands guard over all questions of remuneration.

(iii) The Treasury also acts as regulating body under many specific statutes. The most important series is that of the Superannuation

Acts already referred to. These are so important to the Service that they are not likely to be passed or amended by the House of Commons except at the instigation of the Treasury, and they give specific powers of regulation to the Treasury in various respects. In a sense, they also limit the powers of the Treasury, in that certain things may be done only with the consent of the Civil Service Commission: for instance, a pension as defined by the Acts can be paid only to civil servants who have received a certificate from the Commissioners.

In addition, there are many statutes which give individual Departments power to regulate particular subjects with the approval of the Treasury. Few of these statutes refer specifically to the Civil Service; all affect it indirectly; and Treasury approval of Departmental regulations is given only within the general framework of Treasury policy about the powers and duties of civil servants. Moreover, since the First World War every new Department (except new subdivisions of the office of Secretary of State) has been created by statute, and each of these statutes gives the Minister power to appoint (with Treasury consent) such servants as he thinks fit, to be paid such salaries as the Treasury may determine.

3. THE ESTABLISHMENTS DIVISIONS OF THE TREASURY

A word is necessary here to explain in general terms how the Treasury is organised, a subject which is given fuller treatment later (Chapter 18).

There are at present seven Establishments divisions in the Treasury. The focus for the very complicated negotiations about the pay and conditions of service of the non-specialist Treasury classes (a matter discussed more fully in Chapter 9) is the Establishments (General) Division. Recruitment, promotion, and retirement policy is the concern of a second general division, Establishments (Manning). The professional, scientific, and technical classes have their own separate division for all these purposes, Establishments (Professional), which also deals with all matters affecting industrial staff. A fourth division is responsible for Superannuation policy and makes individual pension awards for the whole of the Civil Service (except for the Defence Departments and the Revenue Departments). The fifth division, Establishments (Appointments) deals with the inter-departmental postings of non-specialist staff, and the appointment of individual civil servants to posts outside the Civil Service, including the public corporations.

The control of staff numbers and of the Estimates for staff in certain civil Departments (principally those concerned with the

THE MANAGEMENT OF THE SERVICE

social services, trade and industry, and agriculture and food), and the grading and pay of the Departmental classes employed in them, is the work of a sixth division, Establishments (Departmental). Similar functions are performed for the civilian staffs in the Defence Departments, the Ministry of Supply, and the Department of Scientific and Industrial Research (D.S.I.R.), by the seventh division, Defence (Personnel), which also deals with the pay and allowances of the armed forces. Control of staffing in the remaining Departments (those in the groups designated 'Government and Allied Services', 'Imperial and Foreign', and 'Law and Order') is not separated from other aspects of 'supply', and is dealt with by three so-called 'mixed' divisions.

These 'mixed' divisions belong to the Home Finance and Supply Services Group of divisions, one of the three main groups of divisions in the Treasury, each of which is under a Second Secretary who ranks as a Permanent Secretary of an ordinary Department. The second group of divisions is the Overseas Finance Group, and the third the Establishments and Machinery of Government Group. The latter includes, besides the seven divisions just mentioned: the Organisation and Methods Division, the Training and Education Division, the Establishments Officer's Branch (which is the Treasury's own Establishments Division), and the Machinery of Government Section. The Second Secretary in charge of all this business is assisted by two Third Secretaries (Deputy Secretaries in an ordinary Department) and three Under Secretaries. Each Establishments division is headed by an Assistant Secretary. The whole Group includes (besides clerical staff) about forty senior officials, members of the Administrative Class, and Chief Executive Officers filling Principal posts; and a further fifty to sixty Senior Executive Officers, Higher Executive Officers, and Executive Officers working to Principals.

In Sir Edward (now Lord) Bridges' time a fourth Second Secretary, Sir Bernard Gilbert, acted as Permanent Secretary's Deputy and assisted him especially on matters of economic and financial policy. On the retirement of Sir Edward Bridges and Sir Bernard Gilbert at the end of 1956, Sir Norman Brook and Sir Roger Makins were appointed joint Secretaries of the Treasury. Sir Norman Brook is responsible for supervision of the Cabinet Office and of the Establishments and Machinery of Government Group of Divisions. He reports direct to the Prime Minister on many matters, and has the title of Head of the Home Civil Service. The other Secretary of the Treasury, Sir Roger Makins, works principally with the Chancellor of the Exchequer, and is responsible for the financial and economic side of the Treasury's business.

It is necessary to explain these matters briefly here, although fuller discussion requires consideration of the position of the Treasury within the whole system of central administration, because there has been some controversy about the proper organisation of the higher management of the Civil Service. The theory of the present organisation is that establishments work is closely connected with control of Estimates, with finance in general, and with the development of policy as a whole. In some systems of administration these matters are separated, in the British system they are closely linked. Each division of the Treasury is supposed to have at least a general knowledge of what the other divisions are doing; the staff mixes informally and shares a common 'Treasury attitude', which may change imperceptibly as the situation changes; and (at least at the lower levels) officials are posted freely between divisions. It has been suggested that this traditional system is no longer practicable because of the increase in the range and complexity of Treasury work and the growth in the size of the Department (it now has about 170 members of the Administrative Class as against about 80 in 1938, the largest single group of Administrative Class officials in the Service); and that it does not give sufficient recognition to the dignity of the Service and the complexity of its problems, which require a Minister and a Department for themselves. It is undoubtedly true that the Treasury is a less compact organisation than it was before 1939, and also that the technicality of establishments work continues to increase, so that there is considerable specialisation, and officials who have proved successful tend to stay in it at the higher levels. The present solution is a compromise, which goes some way towards recognising these difficulties: it has developed naturally out of earlier arrangements and attempts to maintain a valuable tradition.

The Treasury Establishments organisation is geared into that of other Departments, because it was laid down in 1919 that each separate Department should have a Principal Establishments Officer, appointed (since the Treasury Circular of 1920) with the consent of the Prime Minister on the advice of the Secretary to the Treasury. The Principal Establishments Officer in a ministerial Department normally is of the rank of Under Secretary; he is the main point of liaison with the Treasury on all establishments matters; and he is responsible for organisation and methods and for training within his Department, matters of some importance which are dealt with separately in later chapters. The Treasury convenes regular conferences of Principal Establishments Officers at which a Third Secretary takes the chair.

This Treasury organisation thus has the last word on all general

THE MANAGEMENT OF THE SERVICE

matters of numbers of staff and conditions of service. It may also influence the careers of individual civil servants. The Minister in charge of a Department is in principle responsible for all appointments in that Department, but this is subject to two important exceptions:

(i) Since 1920 the consent of the Prime Minister has been required for the appointment of Permanent Secretaries, their Deputies, all Principal Finance Officers, and all Principal Establishments Officers. The formal power of appointment remains with the Minister concerned, whose view is bound to carry great weight if it is strongly held; but the Minister is often influenced by the Head of the Home Civil Service, who advises the Prime Minister on the use of his powers.

(ii) Since 1872 each Department has had an Accounting Officer, who is personally responsible to the House of Commons for the observance of correct financial procedure in his Department (Chapter 17), and who is appointed by the Treasury. In practice nowadays the Permanent Secretary is almost invariably appointed to be Accounting Officer, so that this provision raises no separate issues.

In addition, records are kept in the Treasury of the careers of all members of the Administrative Class, and it has an ill-defined responsibility for ensuring equality of opportunity between different Departments. In particular, it has a great deal to do with postings between Departments, including postings to the Cabinet Office and to the Treasury itself, which may be very important steps in an administrative career.

The Treasury has no such general responsibility for careers in the specialist classes. Some important posts always concern the Treasury: for instance that of Secretary of the Department of Scientific and Industrial Research, who is always a scientist, and that of the Procurator-General and Treasury Solicitor, which is the highest post in the legal branch of the Service. But formal responsibility for the most important specialist appointments rests with the Minister concerned, in consultation with his own advisers: the opinion of his Permanent Secretary carries weight, and so does professional opinion within the specialist class concerned.

Below these highest levels the careers of individual civil servants are in the hands of their Departmental chiefs, subject to the observance of the general procedure described in Chapter 8. The Treasury allows complete freedom about individual appointments, including promotions from class to class (except into the Administrative Class), and about the number and grading of posts up to (but not including) the level of Assistant Secretary. A financial limit is settled by the annual Estimates, and total numbers of staff are settled for each

Department as a whole, and sometimes for particular sections of a Department, every six months. Within these limits Departments are allowed freedom of manœuvre.

Departmentalism is therefore as real a factor as centralisation. The opportunities of civil servants of the same rank and capacity may vary considerably from one Department to another according to the pattern of careers and ages. A Department which is stable in numbers or is contracting may suffer badly from a promotion block; a new Department may give opportunities for accelerated promotion. The age-pattern of Departments may vary for particular reasons. A civil servant who feels that he has poor prospects (or poor personal relations) in his own Department has always the right to apply for a transfer; and the system of promotion pools (Ch. 6, below) gives rather better opportunities of evading a Departmental promotion block by transfer. But seniority lists are kept by Departments separately, not for a general service class as a whole. A civil servant transferred at his own request is likely to lose seniority, since he may go to the bottom of his grade in his new Department. When a transfer is made at the request of the Treasury, seniority rights are generally safeguarded, but this is not likely to make a man popular among his new colleagues. If there is so much reduction in the establishment in one Department that there is an actual surplus of established civil servants there, the Treasury may even be forced to offer transfer with the alternative of down-grading or dismissal. In all these matters intervention is difficult, because it may give rise to serious grievances both in the Department that loses staff and in the one to which they are transferred. Treasury powers must therefore be used with great discretion in so far as they directly affect the fate of individuals: they are wide in theory but limited in practice.

4. THE CIVIL SERVICE COMMISSION

The Civil Service Commission is a much older organisation than the Establishments divisions and has a special constitutional position, but it is perhaps most realistic now to treat it as if it were a special organ of the Treasury for a special purpose. Its origin was explained in Chapter 1 (p. 6); its legal powers rest on the Orders-in-Council of 1855 and 1870 as subsequently amended, and on the Superannuation Act of 1859, and later Acts.

The Commission now consists of six Commissioners, who are appointed by Order-in-Council. This method of appointment is unusual and gives a certain dignity to the office; but Commissioners have no formal guarantee of independence or security of tenure, as have (for instance) judges of the High Court, or the Comptroller and Auditor-General. The Commission ranks as an independent Department, not controlled by a Minister, and it is housed in Burlington Gardens, as if to mark its separation from Whitehall; but its expenditure is borne on annual Estimates which must have the approval of the Treasury, and the Commissioners and their staff are career civil servants subject to ordinary Civil Service conditions.

The Commission does not act collectively but as a hierarchical organisation under the direction of the First Commissioner, who ranks as a Deputy Secretary, as do both the Third Secretaries concerned with establishments at the Treasury. It is usual to appoint someone who has had experience of establishments work, and the appointment is seldom a stepping-stone to further promotion so that the First Commissioner is in a position of some independence: but these are rules which easily admit exceptions.

One of the other Commissioners is Secretary to the Commission, Establishments Officer, and generally responsible for administration. Three are, respectively, Director of Examinations (which involves special responsibility for non-specialist recruitment), Scientific Adviser, and Engineering Adviser. The sixth is Chairman of the 'Civil Service Selection Board', the organisation for the conduct of extended interviews, modelled on the War Office Selection Boards. The Commission's staff numbered about 470 in 1956, a big decline from its peak in the period of post-war reconstruction: most of these belong to the general Civil Service classes, but there are a few psychologists and a small Departmental class of 'Assistant Directors of Examinations', about a dozen in all.

The formal rules of recruitment are still based on the principles of 1855 and 1870. A Department may not appoint a candidate to a post on the establishment unless he has received the certificate of the Commissioners. The power of appointment was not transferred to the Commissioners, a step which would have been regarded as extreme in the 1850s, but the Commissioners were given power to see that appointment was used without respect of persons. The formula on which their power was based was that of competitive examination (although they have the authority to dispense with competition under specified conditions), and a Department is not normally at liberty to refuse to appoint an individual who has passed the examination for the appropriate class; for the system rests on the principle that anyone certificated by the Civil Service Commission is fit for duty in the specified class.

It would be unwise to assume that safeguards against the abuse of patronage are now unnecessary, but the atmosphere of patronage has disappeared. Those who possess the power to appoint no longer expect as a matter of course to be flooded with begging letters from candidates and their sponsors: in many branches of work the problem is not to stave off applicants but to go out and find them. Publicity and contacts are at least as important as selection.

The question of qualifications for entry to each class will be dealt with separately in Chapters 6 and 7, and it is necessary here only to describe the main forms of procedure for the grant of a certificate. These may be analysed into qualifying tests, competitive tests, and exceptional cases. Where tests are to be applied they are specified in regulations which are made by the Commissioners with the approval of the Treasury and are available to candidates and to the public. The interpretation of these regulations is a matter for the Commissioners: a court of law might perhaps intervene to ensure that the Commission acted in a judicial manner in interpreting them, but it could not substitute its own interpretation for theirs.

(i) *Qualifying tests.* It was the original expectation in 1855 that in at least some cases the Department should submit the name of an individual to the Commissioners, who would then test him to see if he were suitable for appointment. This procedure was quite frequently used in the earliest days, but it has possibilities of embarrassment and is now used only for certain cases in minor grades where competitive tests are impracticable.

(ii) The usual method of procedure is by *competitive tests.* This was firmly established by the 1870s, but the idea of 'competition' has proved flexible enough to permit great changes. Competitions may be classified in two ways: by entry, which may be open or limited; or by procedure, which may be by examination, by examination and interview, or by interview only. The assumption at first was that competitions would be by written examination only, and would be open to the public by advertisement of the qualifications required, though in practice probably limited to a short list of candidates nominated by the Department concerned. Many variations are now possible, but perhaps the most important are as follows:

(*a*) Open competitions by written examination only are still used for entry into the lower general classes, Clerical and Clerical Assistant, and some others.

(*b*) Open competitions by written examination and interview are usual for the Administrative and Executive classes.

(*c*) Open competitions by interview only are the rule for appointment to the majority of specialist classes. The post or a group of posts is advertised; the qualifications of candidates are investigated; and a short list is prepared for interview.

(*d*) Limited competitions for advancement, open generally to established civil servants within particular age-limits in a particular grade, seeking to advance to another class: for instance from Clerical to Executive, or from Executive to Administrative.

(*e*) Limited competitions for establishment, open generally to temporary civil servants fulfilling certain conditions.

In both (*d*) and (*e*) it is sometimes necessary for the Department concerned to approve candidates before they are examined, and limited competitions may vary in method as do open competitions.

Written examinations range from simple tests of English and arithmetic, such as are set to temporary typists seeking establishment, to examinations at the level of the final Honours examinations of a University. Almost always they are conducted in co-operation with outside examiners, but the final responsibility for the order of merit rests with the Commissioners.

Interviews also vary very much. They may be brief discussions with junior entrants; extended two-day interviews at the offices of the Civil Service Selection Board; interviews with technical candidates designed to assess their capacity as specialists; interviews by a Final Selection Board with the First Commissioner in the chair, giving marks to candidates for the Administrative Class and for the Foreign Service.

(iii) *Exceptional cases* also fall into various categories. It is possible in theory for the Commissioners (in a case where no tests are laid down by the regulations) to devise tests for the individual candidate recommended to them: but this is a procedure so rare as to be unimportant. The important exceptions are those which permit the Commissioners to give their certificate on the recommendation of the Department concerned, with the approval of the Treasury. The regulations are complex, but there are in effect two quite different groups:

(*a*) Recommendations, for instance, 'that the admission of a particular candidate to a specified situation is for special and exceptional reasons justified by the needs of the public service and the proved merits of the candidate'. Particulars of each case must be published in the *London Gazette*, and the numbers are insignificant in relation to the total intake in any year. A sample of those admitted in this way between 1949 and 1952 includes distinguished scientists such as Sir John Cockcroft, an Assistant to Parliamentary Counsel, the Head of the Security Department at the Foreign Office, and the Keeper of the Records of Scotland.

(*b*) Recommendations that candidates or groups of candidates have been employed temporarily on permanent work and that they have proved satisfactory to the Department after a trial period. This is the normal procedure for minor and manipulative grades such as those of postmen, telephonists, and messengers; and many thousands of people are certificated in this way each year.

A simple Table (Table X) drawn from the latest available Report of the Commissioners will indicate the scale of their work, though it is impossible to show all its subdivisions or to suggest the relative burden of different forms of test, some laborious, some very simple.

TABLE X

The Work of the Civil Service Commissioners
(1 April 1955-31 March 1956)

	Number of Competitions	Number of Applications	Number declared successful in Examination and/or Interview	Number certificated for Appointment
Open Competition	208	M 36,168 W 12,888	6,015 4,908	4,536 3,728
Limited Competition	37 (2)	M 7,926 (423) W 7,949	2,053 (268) 4,501	1,840 (266) 3,634
Ordinary Nominations (see iii (*b*) in text)	—	M 30,969 W 8,392	—	27,678 7,071
Special Nomination (see iii (*a*) in text)	—	M 160 W 50	—	132 46

Numbers in round brackets refer to Reconstruction Competitions.

It should be clear from this description that the Civil Service Commission is a less important body than some of the Commissions and Boards in other countries which have taken their names and tradition from 'Burlington Gardens', since these have also absorbed many of the functions of the Establishments divisions of the Treasury. The Commission has, however, moved forward from certification to recruitment, a function of extreme importance in the working of a highly specialised Service which reflects the structure of science, education, and industry in the country. Successful recruitment and selection involve maintenance of contacts with all the bodies responsible for the training and qualification of students, as well as a thorough knowledge of the trends of the market. The Commission is bound to influence the Treasury by interpreting to it the attitudes of those who might enter the Service; it must also attempt to influence the publics most closely concerned by interpreting to them the work of the Service and the careers which it offers. It is difficult politically for the Civil Service to advertise itself except through the Civil Service Commission.

FOR REFERENCE

There are discussions of the management of the Service in many of the books listed in the bibliography.

The most important references in official papers are:

4th Majority Report of the Royal Commission on the Civil Service (MacDonnell), Cd. 7338, 1914.

Report of the Machinery of Government Committee (Haldane). Cd. 9230, 1918 (particularly Part II, Chapter 1).

Final Report of the Committee on the Staffing of Government Offices (Bradbury). Cmd. 62, 1919.

16th Report from the Select Committee on National Expenditure 1941-42 (*Organisation and Control of the Civil Service*), House of Commons paper 120, 1942 (particularly Chapters V, VI and Appendix VI).

'Treasury Establishments Circular 2/49 of 29 July 1949' (reprinted in *Public Administration*, Vol. XXVIII, p. 59).

Reports are issued approximately annually by the Civil Service Commission, occasionally after some delay. The latest available in 1956 was that for 1 April 1955-31 March 1956. The *89th Report of the Civil Service Commissioners for the period 1 April 1954 to 31 March 1955* gives a useful short summary of the powers of the Commission as compared with those it possessed in 1855.

See also:

FREDERIC MILNER: 'Recent Developments in the Work of the Civil Service Commission', *Public Administration*, Vol. XXV, p. 61.

A. P. SINKER: 'What are Public Service Commissions For?', *Public Administration*, Vol. XXXI, p. 201.

CHAPTER FIVE

GENERAL CONDITIONS OF EMPLOYMENT

What shall I cry?
Arthur Edward Cyril Parker is appointed telephone operator
At a salary of one pound ten a week rising by annual increments of
    five shillings
To two pounds a week: with a bonus of thirty shillings at Christmas
And one week's leave a year.—T. S. ELIOT: 'Difficulties of a Statesman.'

1. INTRODUCTORY

IN a sense the whole of this book is concerned with the general conditions of work in the Civil Service. It is convenient, however, to set out separately here some general principles about pay and matters closely related to it, such as hours of work, leave, and superannuation. There is much diversity within the Service, but there are also certain general principles which when taken together distinguish it from any other form of employment in Great Britain.

These principles are historical in origin, and it is only in recent years that the process of negotiation has linked them together into a system or 'package', governed by theories about the proper relation between conditions in the Civil Service and in other employment. The controversy about such general 'formulae' requires some discussion, but it will be most realistic to introduce it at the end of this chapter, after explaining the constituent elements of the system. We describe these primarily on the basis of the report of the Priestley Commission, which completed a thorough review of the position in November 1955.

2. THE SYSTEM OF PAY

Employment in the Civil Service differs from employment in commerce or private industry in that pay depends primarily on grade and on the position reached in a scale of seniority within a grade. In principle no recognition is given either to the special merit of individuals or to the special difficulty of one post rather than another within the scope of a grade. The principle is of great importance, but admits certain exceptions. If a man has to be obtained from outside the Service he may be in a position to strike a bargain on entry which gives some recognition to his special qualifications. Within the Service a limited number of posts (in particular those of Private Secretaries) carry allowances in recognition of additional responsibility.

There is therefore a general resemblance between the system of the Civil Service and that of the armed forces of the Crown, but the working of the former requires a different pattern of scales of pay. This pattern has two features which are of particular importance.

First, the main body of the Service is paid on fairly long incremental scales, with advancement by seniority subject to an efficiency bar. For instance, the London scale for the Clerical Officer grade in 1956 is £240 at the age of 16 with three increments of £30, two of £25, eight of £20, one of £30, and six of £20: that is to say, a maximum of £690 to be reached at about the age of 36, with advancement by seniority subject to an 'efficiency bar' at about the age of 29, which is to be passed only if it is certified that the officer 'is fully competent to perform the highest duties of the grade'. For the Assistant Principal and for the Scientific Officer (normally entering at 23 or 24) the starting salary is £605 with nine increments of £30, two increments of £35, three increments of £30, and one of £20. The notional maximum of the grade is thus £1,055, but it is regarded primarily as a 'cadet' or entry grade, and a competent man would expect to secure promotion into the next grade, which is the 'main grade' for these two classes, before reaching the maximum of the entry grade. The main grade has a long scale of increments: above it is the 'career grade', the level which competent entrants can reasonably expect to reach ultimately and which has a shorter scale.

Secondly, above this level the pyramid is narrower and the higher grades are paid on a principle referred to as 'broadbanding'. There is no particular mystery about this: it means merely that higher grades are paid either on fixed rates or on very short incremental scales. These rates or scales are the same for all posts within the grade, irrespective of differences in responsibility: for instance, all officials graded as Permanent Secretary (except in the Treasury) are paid the same, however big or small their Departments may be.

The resulting structure is summed up by the Treasury as follows[1]:

'(i) Short scales for non-office grades such as messengers, cleaners and Post Office engineering labourers, and some of their super-

[1] Introductory Factual Memorandum presented by the Treasury to the Priestley Commission, p. 39.

visors' (these are technically non-industrial civil servants, but their conditions resemble those in industry);

'(ii) Long scales for many basic or recruitment grades, e.g. the executive officer or works group basic grade' (this is the main body of office staff, general or specialist);

'(iii) Medium-length scales for office staffs in the middle ranges';

'(iv) Short scales for office staffs in the higher ranges—culminating in flat rates at the highest levels' (this is 'broadbanding').

This may be summarised in practical terms as follows, disregarding many proper qualifications. The Civil Service is designed as a career service, offering to entrants a pattern of income covering a lifetime's work. There is stiff selection on entry followed by a period of probation. If this stage is passed (as it usually is), salary will increase for another 12 to 15 years by annual increments, subject to decent competence in the performance of ordinary duties. Beyond that point promotion depends on vacancies in the establishment. There is a policy (perhaps a sentiment rather than a policy) that so far as possible the age-structure of each class and the pyramid of jobs should be such that all competent men can count on promotion one grade above the basic grade of their class (which means generally two grades above the grade of entry). But it is seldom that this works out smoothly: sometimes there is accelerated promotion, sometimes a promotion block, and some classes are so small that there is no effective pyramid. Progress beyond the basic grade is due to a combination of merit, luck, and seniority.

The same thing can be conveyed negatively, by contrast with two other systems of payment for similar work:

(i) Administrative work in commerce and private industry, especially in smaller firms, is often paid on the basis of the rate for the man: a man's salary is a private matter between him and his employer, and the employer is prepared to give a personal bonus for special service. This is impossible in the Civil Service. To quote the Treasury again, 'extra pay will not be given to an officer doing no more than the actual duties of his grade, however proficient may be his performance of them. In the Civil Service such exceptional merit may be recognised rather by accelerated promotion'—or (as the Priestley Commission put it more bluntly) 'outstanding individual merit can be recognised only by accelerated promotion'.[1] Special allowances may be paid for specified extra qualifications or extra duties, but there are general rules even for these exceptions. Rates of pay are made for the Service and not for the individual.

(ii) Some career services attempt to differentiate one job from

[1] Priestley Commission Report, Para. 24.

GENERAL CONDITIONS OF EMPLOYMENT   47

another in considerable detail, in order to relate pay closely to job and job closely to qualifications. The career Civil Service in the U.S.A. is based on a very detailed system of job classification, which breaks down the work of each office into many separate categories, and allocates a man individually to each job at the rate fixed for the job. This is intended to avoid the psychological effects to be expected from a long scale of increments not closely related to efficiency on the job; but it is enormously complicated and has awkward psychological effects of its own. The local government service in Britain also has more detailed classification of jobs than has the Civil Service. This has arisen naturally from the circumstances of local authorities, but it does not seem to have any general advantages worth copying in the Civil Service.

3. Hours of Work

In spite of the legend about the fountains in Trafalgar Square, Civil Service hours are much like those in other forms of office employment. The old Civil Service worked on the basis that if officials were wanted for business they should stay till the business was done: and if there were no business they could go home. Each Department made its own arrangements: '10 to 4' was certainly the official rule in some Departments. But this system (or lack of system) had gone by 1910, when an Order-in-Council prescribed a working day of seven hours, with a half holiday on alternate Saturdays. Since 1910 matters have been made more complicated by variations during the two wars and by an intricate process of negotiation. In 1955 the Priestley Commission recommended (on the basis of outside analogies) that there should be an 84-hour fortnight in London and an 88-hour fortnight in the provinces, including one hour for lunch and no other breaks; that, wherever possible, the Service should adopt the five-day week; and that regular overtime should be abolished. These recommendations were accepted by both Sides after negotiation, and Departments began putting them into effect in 1956.

The cost of overtime was, in 1955, about £20 m. out of a total salary bill of some £450 m., and the Priestley Commission were advised that much of the work could be done in shorter hours without taking on extra staff. It was clear from the protests which followed the Commission's recommendation that many civil servants in the lower grades had come to count on regular overtime, as do many workers at the same income level in industry. The two Sides of the National Whitley Council agreed that there should be no reduction in 'take home pay' at the time the new arrangements came into force, but it seems likely that a substantial number of civil servants will, in future, have opportunity and incentive to add to their incomes by taking part-time work outside the Service after office hours. There is nothing in the regulations to prevent their doing so, provided that their outside work does not 'in any way tend to impair their usefulness as public servants', or conflict with the interests of their Departments (Chapter 10). This is a reasonable arrangement in most forms of employment: the shorter working week means that people can choose either more leisure or extra earnings. But it might be a source of some embarrassment if it were to become usual among civil servants.

4. Annual Leave and Sick Leave

Civil servants are given (normally) nine days a year for public holidays and 'privilege' days (such as the Saturday before Easter Monday), and they also have annual leave beginning at 18 days (3 weeks) and extending to six weeks according to rank and length of service. Leave is not given 'as of right', and a civil servant has no claim to any form of compensation if he is not able to take his leave because of the demands of office business. The practice of giving leave generously was usual long before 'holidays with pay' had been heard of in other walks of life. Although it was not a formal right, it was regarded as one of the attractions of a post in the Civil Service: part of a 'package', which combined relatively low rates of pay with security, some leisure, and the prospect of a pension. The present rates are based on the Priestley Commission recommendation that Civil Service leave should not be 'screwed down precisely and mathematically to commercial practice', but that nevertheless it should come closer to it: so that, while leave remains reasonably good, it is no longer one of the characteristic advantages of the Civil Service in time of peace.

Provision for sick leave is generous, but perhaps not better than in the best outside firms. 'Sick leave may be allowed on full pay for a period not exceeding six months during any twelve months, followed by sick leave on half pay provided that in any period of four years or less the total sick leave does not exceed twelve months.'[1] These arrangements apply to established civil servants: temporary civil servants in regular employment were given similar but less generous concessions in 1948.

[1] Introductory Factual Memorandum, Para. 105.

5. Differentiation

The whole question of 'equal pay for women' was the subject of inquiry by a Royal Commission which reported in October 1946[1]: and in May 1952 the Government announced that it would concede the principle for the Civil Service, but could not implement it until the financial position was easier. After further pressure, agreement was reached with the National Whitley Council, and the Chancellor of the Exchequer announced (on 1 January 1955) that women's pay would be brought up to that of men by stages over a period of seven years. It seems reasonable to hope that this will end an old controversy.

There remains a general differentiation between rates of pay according to place of work. This was accepted in principle by the staff associations represented on the Reorganisation Committee of 1920, presumably because this made it easier for them to relate pay claims to evidence about differences in the cost of living in London and elsewhere. The Service was then largely, though by no means wholly, a central London service: civil servants at headquarters were strongest in the staff associations, and it was not unreasonable that Civil Service pay should be negotiated primarily as a London rate, with a proportionate reduction to allow for lower cost of living and lower rates in outside employment outside London.

The system is now rather complicated, but it is for most civil servants a three-tier system: the top rate is for inner London, the intermediate rate is for outer London and certain large towns, the 'provincial' rate applies everywhere else. The reductions vary according to rank, but in general terms they are now about $2\frac{1}{2}$ to 3 per cent. on intermediate rates, about 5 to 6 per cent. on provincial rates. On 1 July 1955 there were about 167,000 established non-industrial civil servants on the inner London rate, about 119,000 on intermediate, about 202,000 on provincial (the remainder—about 7,000—were serving overseas).

The main staff associations are now strongly opposed to this system. In the first place (they maintain), it is illogical that rates should be negotiated on a basis which applies only to a small part of the Service. Secondly, the Service is now recognised as a 'national' service, not a headquarters service, and it ought as a matter of status to be treated like other similar services. Thirdly, any system of boundary lines is bound to be arbitrary. It will produce anomalies between civil servants who work close together on different sides of

[1] Royal Commission on Equal Pay for Men and Women (Asquith). Report. Cmd. 6937, 1946.

D

a line; or for a man who is posted from an office on one side of the line to an office on the other side, but continues to live at his old address. Such anomalies may have practical effects on mobility within the Service and on readiness to accept promotion involving transfer, and the difficulties are not wholly overcome by making transfer grants for removal expenses, even though these are on quite a generous scale.

The Priestley Commission was committed by the principle of 'fair comparison' (which is discussed below) to maintaining differentials, since it held that they were to be found in outside employment. Otherwise, it accepted part of the argument of the staff associations by proposing that there should now be a two-tier instead of a three-tier system, and that the basic rate should be negotiated for the Civil Service nationally, subject to an inner London differential, to be settled with reference to the rates paid to employees in other London offices. This working compromise has proved acceptable to the Treasury and to the associations after prolonged discussion and is likely to be put into effect in 1957.

6. Superannuation

The question of pension rights is one of great importance in the history of the Civil Service. Most of the statutory provisions affecting the Service are concerned with superannuation, and till quite recently the expectation of a pension on retirement was one of the main features which distinguished permanent employment under the Crown from any form of private employment. The power of the Crown to grant pensions to its servants has been closely limited by statutes, and the series of Superannuation Acts in a sense defines the extent of the permanent Civil Service by defining the limits within which the Treasury may move in the settlement of pensions. These limits are narrowly defined, and there is less freedom of executive action here than in other matters affecting the regulation of the Service. But no statute confers the right to a pension on any employee of the Crown: the Treasury within the limits set has the power to grant or to withhold. In practice the stability of expectation is as great as if pensions were granted by law, but the principle of discretion is of some importance in debates concerning the basis of pensions.

There is thus a combination of detailed statutory regulation with precedents set by Treasury practice in the exercise of discretion. In the course of 150 years the subject has become extremely intricate, and all that can be given here is an elementary summary.

GENERAL CONDITIONS OF EMPLOYMENT 51

The basis of superannuation (as already explained) is establishment, and this depends on certification by the Civil Service Commissioners. The basic scheme is non-contributory, with certain contributory benefits added in recent years. The central point is that any established civil servant who has had 'reckonable service' (a matter requiring careful definition) of at least ten years, and who reaches the minimum retirement age (normally 60), will be granted:

(i) A pension of $\frac{1}{80}$ of his salary[1] for each year of service, subject to a maximum of $\frac{40}{80}$.

(ii) A lump sum (known as the 'additional allowance') of $\frac{3}{80}$ of his salary[1] for each year of service, subject to a maximum of $\frac{120}{80}$.

It will be noticed that this arrangement makes it particularly valuable to secure promotion to a higher grade in the years just before retirement, a matter which is always present in the minds of civil servants and of Establishments Officers. The scheme does, however, avoid the actuarial difficulties of a contributory scheme in a period of inflation, and grants a pension which most people would think fair at the time of retirement.

The basic scheme makes no provision for widows or other dependents, except that the 'additional allowance' (or a gratuity of a year's salary, whichever is the greater) is payable if the civil servant dies before retirement and after not less than five years' 'reckonable service'. There is, however, a contributory scheme for widows and other dependents which is compulsory for all entering the Service after 14 July 1949, optional for others, providing for a widow's pension at one-third of the rate payable to the civil servant, and for proportionate pensions for children under the age of 16. There are two forms of contribution: a regular deduction from salary of $1\frac{1}{4}$ per cent., or a reduction (by $\frac{1}{80}$ for each year of service) in the lump sum payable on retirement or death.

It is now possible for a civil servant to remain at work after the age of 60 in his existing rank, and in an established capacity; or he may formally retire at 60 and then continue, either in his former rank or in a lower rank, in a 'disestablished' capacity. In either case he qualifies for increased pension up to a maximum of $\frac{45}{80}$, and for increased 'additional allowance' up to a maximum of $\frac{135}{80}$.

There are also arrangements for payments on early retirement. Those relating to retirement on grounds of ill-health are uncontroversial except in detail. An issue of principle is involved, however, (on the one hand) in the Treasury's right to 'pension off' a civil servant before the age of 60 if it is in the interests of the Service, and

[1] 'Salary' here means 'salary (or wage) and other pensionable emoluments, averaged over the last three years of service' (Priestley Report, p. 171).

(on the other hand) in the individual civil servant's right to take accrued benefits in some form if he withdraws from the Service in his own interest before that age. When superannuation was introduced, the Crown retained its right to dismiss unsatisfactory servants without pension; but it has naturally been reluctant to exercise the right in cases of mild idleness or inefficiency, where the penalty would be out of proportion to the offence, and would have a bad effect on the morale of the Service generally. Parliament, however, views with suspicion the idea that pensions—'non-effective benefits'—should be granted except on the completion of a career in the Service, and did not like the introduction of provisions for retirement on abolition of office, for voluntary retirement, and for compulsory retirement on grounds of inefficiency. The arrangements first introduced in 1909 (as explained in Chapter 3) have had only slight practical effect. They do, however, represent a change of principle, introduced in the interests of the public service at the expense of individual civil servants; and they therefore improve the case for suggesting that corresponding concessions should be made to individuals who wish to leave the Service in their own interest. It is claimed on behalf of civil servants that pensions should be treated as 'deferred pay' accruing from year to year, and that a civil servant should be able to withdraw, taking with him what has accrued. The Treasury replies that a pension is in one sense deferred pay, because its value should be taken into account in assessing what a job in the Civil Service is worth; but that its amount and conditions are settled by a bargain with the Treasury which represents the interests of the Service. In this bargain one important consideration in the minds of those managing the Service is to secure recruits for a career taken as a whole, and to discourage individuals from taking elsewhere skill and experience that they have gained in the service of the Crown. Hence they are not prepared to grant proportionate pensions on voluntary withdrawal under the age of 50 except to 'approved service'. 'Approval' is given fairly generously, since there are many forms of public service which are outside the scope of the Superannuation Acts only because of accidents of history: even private employment is sometimes 'approved' where the success of the firm is of particular importance to the State.

There are two other matters which arouse a good deal of controversy. First, the difficulties which arise when staff are employed for long periods without being established and therefore without becoming eligible for pension. Large numbers of staff were in this position between 1919 and 1939, and only secured fair treatment after long and rather bitter negotiations. The Priestley Commission

GENERAL CONDITIONS OF EMPLOYMENT

accepted the Treasury's assurance that it was now the policy to establish staff to meet the full needs of permanent employment so far as these could be foreseen. If this is done, the problem should become manageable, although there will always be hard cases due to fluctuation in the size of the Service or to increased recruitment of clerks in their forties or later.

Secondly, there is the falling value of pensions in a period of inflation. It is pointless to argue that retired officials stand to gain because pensions could not be reduced if prices fell: it is not really tolerable in practice that the State should allow faithful servants to fall into poverty through a continuous rise in prices. But no general formula is possible except that which relates pension to salary rates prevailing at the time of retirement. If prices rise, pensions lag behind them until sufficient pressure builds up to secure from the Treasury its agreement to a general increase. Acts for this purpose were passed in 1944, 1947, 1952, and 1956.

Most forms of employment comparable to the Civil Service now have their own superannuation schemes, and eligibility for a pension is no longer the special mark of the Civil Service. The idea of 'career' service has become an ordinary feature of society, and the responsibility of providing for retirement is deemed as a matter of course to fall not on the individual but on the service to which he belongs. Furthermore, the extension of the Civil Service into technical fields means that there is a growing overlap between a career in the Civil Service and careers in fields such as law, medicine, engineering, or scientific research under employers other than the Crown. For instance, a pensionable career as civil servant may overlap with a pensionable career as doctor: it would be awkward if there were no freedom of transfer of doctors' pension rights between the Civil Service and the various branches of the National Health Service.

The national pattern of pension rights is now extremely intricate, and Civil Service pensions are only a part of it. The Priestley Commission suggest that the Civil Service might be reviewed as a whole, in order to consider whether some parts of it are for pension purposes detachable and should be assimilated to schemes in force for professions outside the Service. The matter is perhaps too confused for such a review to be possible, but breaches with tradition are allowed to occur when it seems convenient. For instance, certain established civil servants still remain within the Federated Superannuation System for Universities; the system has been abandoned for permanent staff recruited after 1 January 1953, but temporary staff (mainly scientists) may still opt for the system to facilitate interchange with the University world. These breaches remain rare, and the existence of a unified scheme of pensions is still a great factor of unity in the diversity of the Service.

7. Other Emoluments

In any discussion about Civil Service pay there arises the question of benefits in kind, often tax free, which are given generously by private employers: entertainment allowances, housing allowances, lunch vouchers or special canteen facilities, the use of office cars, large daily allowances while travelling. Such concessions are partly a result of high rates of income tax, and the government cannot take part in what is (in spirit though not in law) a form of tax evasion. If it tried to do so, it would be halted promptly by the House of Commons. There is no topic so dear to Members and to the popular press as that of waste by civil servants on entertainment, free travel, or rides in official cars.

The result is that, in this matter, the Civil Service at all levels is screwed down to standards much below those of a prosperous firm in business. There may be, as in industry, a concealed subsidy to Departmental canteens, in that the price of meals does not bear its full share of the cost of accommodation: but 'free lunch vouchers' are unknown except for members of the staff under 18. Travel allowances are relatively low and individual applications for them are carefully scrutinised. Even the highest officials may not use official cars for travel between home and office except in extreme emergency, and on business they must generally draw upon a pool of cars. No official has a personal entertainment allowance: Departmental funds for entertainment exist, but are carefully guarded.

No other policy is defensible, but this has its effects throughout the Service. At the bottom, Civil Service pay is worth less than an equal salary in business; at the top, there is a feeling of exasperation because an official who has great powers in large matters is given no discretion in small ones.

8. Principles of Pay

Theories about Civil Service pay arise (like many other forms of political theory) from the necessities of debate. The most recent commentary is that of the Priestley Commission, which was appointed largely because confusion and deadlock had arisen through discussion based on the report of the Tomlin Commission, written twenty-five years earlier and in very different circumstances. The principles enunciated by the Priestley Commission have been

GENERAL CONDITIONS OF EMPLOYMENT

accepted by the Treasury and (with some reservations) by the staff associations. A summary of them will serve to set out the points on which agreement has been reached and those which are still at issue.

The Commission stated two main principles:

(i) 'The primary principle of Civil Service pay is fair comparison with the current remuneration of outside staffs employed on broadly comparable work, taking account of differences in other conditions of service.'[1]

This means that comparison is to be made grade by grade and class by class with types of work outside the Service, and that Civil Service pay must be 'fair' by these outside standards. 'Fairness' is construed, with apparent precision, to mean that Civil Service rates should be better than those of the lower half of outside employers, but need not be as good as those of the top quarter. The process of comparison (the Commission suggested) should be carried out by an independent research organisation, using all available techniques of statistical sampling and job analysis. Such an organisation (called the Civil Service Pay Research Unit) has now been set up, with the agreement of both Sides, under the supervision of a special committee of the National Whitley Council. Day-to-day control is vested in a Director (an Under Secretary) appointed by the Prime Minister.

(ii) 'Internal relativities should be used as a supplement to the principle of fair comparison in settling Civil Service rates in detail, and may have to be the first consideration when outside comparisons cannot be made, but they should never be allowed to override the primary principle or to become rigid.'[2]

Relativities may be 'vertical', between one grade and those above and below it; or 'horizontal', between grades in different classes. The Commission attached great importance to vertical relativities, since an adequate step in pay from one grade to the next is the only way to give a financial incentive to seek promotion. They disapproved of all horizontal relativities, on the ground that it would be unfair and inefficient to freeze the relative rates of pay of two classes irrespective of the demand for them outside the Service. Even vertical relativities are to be used with caution; horizontal relativities are to be used only when fair comparison breaks down, as it sometimes must do because the Service employs categories (such as meteorologists) for whom there is virtually no outside employment at all.

These principles seem plain, but are not unchallenged, and they can be set in relief only by discussing the alternatives offered.

[1] Report, Para. 96.
[2] Report, Para. 769 (3).

There is, first, what may be called the 'economic' principle, best expressed in a quotation from a committee under the chairmanship of Sir Alan Anderson which reported in 1923.[1] 'In our view there is only one principle in which all the factors of responsibility, cost of living, marriage, children, social position, are included—the employer should pay what is necessary to recruit and to retain an efficient staff.' This principle is a keen razor in the hands of a committee seeking to cut the cost of the Civil Service, but its precision is more apparent than real. There is no direct means of measuring what is an 'efficient' staff and what is 'necessary' to keep it efficient. These things can be established only relatively and by comparison. Furthermore, the Priestley Commission insisted that public opinion now introduces ethical as well as economic considerations into all discussion about wages. Wages must be 'fair' and 'socially approved' as well as 'necessary'. 'We think that in the conduct of wage and salary negotiations concepts of fairness and of the existence of a wage and salary framework not governed solely by the "law of the market" play a large and increasing part.'[2]

So far, the Commission's argument is one which would be approved by all civil servants. The Commission's alternative doctrine of 'comparison' is not completely acceptable to the associations representing the main body of non-technical civil servants, for two main reasons: first, that grade-by-grade comparison is really impossible because there are so many jobs for which there is no true equivalent outside the Service; second, that there is no true market for clerical labour outside the Service because trade union organisation is weak, and outside employers are much affected by Civil Service rates. The Commission would have replied, not that these criticisms are wholly false but that they are over-stated and do not make comparison impossible or unfair. Moreover, the only alternative is to hitch this very large block of Civil Service salaries to some general index: either a general salaries index or a cost of living index. Officials of the staff associations, like those of other professional associations and trade unions, watch the indices of wage rates and of cost of living very closely, and use changes in them as a basis for claims, but they do not suggest seriously that Civil Service pay should be formally linked to them, and if they did they would have no chance of persuading the Treasury, since it is plain that such a formula would make for rigidity and for inflation.

The professional and technical classes, on the other hand (in so far as represented by the Institution of Professional Civil Servants),

[1] Committee on the Pay, etc., of State Servants. July 1923. Report, Para. 3.
[2] Report, Para. 94.

welcome the Commission's emphasis on fair comparison at the expense of horizontal relativities, since this sets free the salaries of specialists to follow outside rates for any class of specialists who are in short supply. They wish, however, to go even farther, by proposing that the government should use Civil Service pay to give a lead to the country: for instance, in order to encourage the training of more technologists by giving relatively large increases to technologists within the Service. This is a demand that the government should have a wages policy, and that it should use the fact that it is a very large employer as an instrument for the enforcement of its policy.

The Commission wrote as follows about wages policy: 'Wage and salary negotiations today are conducted in a social framework which, at least by implication, recognises and accepts the existence of variations in standards of living according to position in the social hierarchy. Proposed changes in this structure, that is to say narrowing or widening of variations in living standards, must raise social and, as we think in the last analysis, political considerations.'[1] If this is accepted, it follows that Civil Service pay must not be used 'to give a lead to the outside world', because this would bring the Civil Service into politics. Changes in relative rates of pay mean changes in social structure, and this is a matter on which there are profound differences between the great political parties. A general election might therefore mean an abrupt change of policy: if this change were to affect the Civil Service directly, it would create a direct relation between the interests of various classes of civil servants and the policy of different political parties. This would throw a great strain on 'the present tradition' whereby 'a non-political Civil Service carries out impartially the tasks required of it by Governments of different political complexions'. It is of overriding importance to the public that this tradition should be maintained: therefore, the government must accept certain limitations on its freedom of action as employer. Civil servants accept certain limitations in their political activity: the government must on its side avoid suspicion that politics enter into the management of the Service. This means that there must be a formal method of recruitment, an established pattern of career, a secure guarantee (in practice) of pension rights. It also means that Civil Service pay must be determined primarily by some criterion which is free even from the suspicion of party politics. This (says the Commission) is possible only if the primary principle is that of 'fair comparison'.

This theoretical argument is not wholly acceptable to the staff associations. Furthermore, it is possible, and even probable, that in

[1] Report, Para. 99.

practice the principle of 'fair comparison' will be breached here and there in the interests of social policy, or simply because it proves unworkable. But the Commission are certainly right in maintaining that a change in principle about pay would involve a change in principle about the constitutional position of the Civil Service. Certain rules are necessary if there is to be continuity of administration within a democracy of alternating parties; the existence of these rules is a factor which imposes unity on the Service, and which differentiates it from the rest of the community.

FOR REFERENCE

National Whitley Council: *Pensionability of Unestablished Civil Servants.* Report of a Committee. Cmd. 6942, 1946.

—— *Marriage Bar in the Civil Service.* Report of a Committee. Cmd. 6886, 1946.

H.M. Treasury: *Digest of Pension Law and Regulations of the Civil Service* (1952).

Report and Minutes of Evidence, Royal Commission on the Civil Service 1953-55 (Priestley). Cmd. 9613, 1956.

Introductory Factual Memorandum and Supplement presented to the Commission by the Treasury (H.M.S.O.).

For progress of negotiations between the Official and Staff Sides of the National Whitley Council on the recommendations of the Priestley Commission, see *Whitley Bulletin* for 1956 (Vol. XXXVI).

J. NIXON: *The Authentic History of Civil Service Superannuation* (1930).

CHAPTER SIX

THE GENERAL CLASSES

> Waring said, 'Look, Sammy. You may reckon that you're a great big scientist and that I'm just a commercial stooge, but the plain fact is that if you people on the technical side make a mess, I have to clear it up. I don't mind that. It's my job. But don't start being patronising about it, for God's sake.'
> I said, 'Right. And the equally plain fact is that the stuff you build a reputation on comes chiefly out of my head. I'm not a politician or a salesman, thank God. But neither am I a kid of ten.'
> Waring looked at me for a moment in silence. Then he suddenly broke into a broad grin, and said, 'Not ten, Sammy, eight. Ten's what you are when you are not cross.'—NIGEL BALCHIN: *The Small Back Room*, ch. x.

1. INTRODUCTORY

IT is natural to begin an account of Civil Service classes with an explanation of the three great general classes—Administrative, Executive, and Clerical; and they take the first place here as in most books about the Civil Service. This emphasis is disproportionate to their numbers—little more than one-third of the non-industrial Civil Service; to their responsibility—nearly two-thirds of the 'Higher Civil Service' as defined in Table IX belong to the specialist classes; to their education and social standing—since they include a comparatively small proportion of graduates and others with qualifications recognised professionally outside the Service. The skill of specialists is now of at least equal importance in the making and execution of policy.

Nevertheless, it is right to emphasise the general classes because they still determine much of the character and organisation of the Service. Their interrelation defines the framework of organisation in each Department, and the work of the specialist is done within this organisation. General arguments about the Service are still arguments about the position of these classes, about their relation to the community, and about their relation to the rest of the administration.

The phrase 'general classes' is not, as we use it here, a technical term: but it serves to define roughly the civil servants who come into the Service without specialised training for the work which they are to do, and who fill posts which are similar in all Departments and constitute the main structure or skeleton of the Service. It is impossible in grouping classes to follow these two points precisely: any rigid definition is impracticable and unrealistic. In a sense, the most useful practical grouping is that adopted in the structure of Civil Service trade unions, explained briefly in Chapter 9.

More specifically, this chapter is concerned with the Administrative, Executive and Clerical Classes, the Class of Clerical Assistants, the Typing grades and the Machine Operating Class, the Messengerial Classes, and the General Service Class of Cleaners. There are temporary civil servants in each of these categories, and there are also related Departmental classes, some of them of great importance. We add a brief note on the parallel arrangements in the Foreign and Oversea Services, which are largely outside the scope of this book.

2. Historical Development

A hundred years ago the Civil Service, after the first stages of reform, consisted mainly of three very different elements: first, a small number of senior clerks, who were the responsible assistants to Ministers in Whitehall; secondly, the officials, mainly civilian, who managed the accounting and supply services of the Navy and Army; thirdly, the relatively large staffs employed by the three great Revenue Departments, the Post Office, the Board of Customs, and the Board of Inland Revenue. The modern Civil Service has grown from these elements without breach of continuity, and its structure bears many marks of its history.

In Whitehall the staple work was that of copying and keeping papers. Practically all entrants were engaged for years on such work, and the capacity to write a good hand was the only qualification absolutely essential. In every office there were those who worked conscientiously and became expert in business: from copying they would rise to the preparation of simple drafts, and ultimately to the position of influence which comes to the man who knows the past history of every subject and the proper form of words for every letter. These important men could properly be described as 'Principal Clerks'; and often one of them would rise to be Under Secretary (also called Assistant Secretary) at the head of the office. But Ministers might well fill a vacancy at the top with a man from outside on whom they could rely in personal matters: and they would generally bring with them a rising young man to act as private secretary, who might perhaps secure a permanent post before the departure of his Minister.

This system was not inefficient in relation to the needs of its time, but it provided no basis for an expansion to the new scale of government required by industrial England. This expansion took place piecemeal, and the form of the Service is not wholly logical even now; but two main attempts were made to impose logic.

The first stage was the slow reorganisation which followed the acceptance of the principle of recruitment by examination. The Revenue Departments went their own way, so that the Post Office, Inland Revenue, and Customs and Excise still have service structures adapted to their own needs and not completely adjusted to the main structure of the Service. Other Departments gradually adopted a pattern in which the main elements were First Division clerks recruited in principle from University graduates, Second Division clerks recruited from boys with a tested knowledge of reading, writing and arithmetic, copying clerks, messengers, and cleaners.

This was still a service of clerks: the sort of work expected of a University graduate entering the Civil Service at home was not comparable in dignity or responsibility to what he might expect in the Indian Civil Service. But he could now avoid the long apprenticeship of hackwork: he would from the outset meet work of some interest and intellectual difficulty: and he stood a much better chance than his predecessors of learning how to speak to Ministers as a social equal and of finding his way to the top posts. Even for the Second Division clerks there was the chance of advancement to posts of considerable responsibility in an expanding Service. The weakest point lay in the position of the copying clerks and other ancillary staff.

These principles became obsolete before they had been fully established, as there was a complex revolution in office organisation between 1880 and 1914. One very important change was the invention of the typewriter, which in the end replaced the male copying clerk by the lady typist and altered the whole aspect of official papers. It was also important (especially after 1906) that the Civil Service began to assume responsibilities for management as distinct from 'clerking'. The Labour Exchange scheme of 1909 and the National Health Insurance scheme of 1911 were the first new nation-wide organisations set up outside the ancient framework of the Revenue Departments. This meant work of a new kind, and staff of a new kind. The position in the Admiralty and War Office also began to change, as equipment grew in complexity and in rate of development and the cost of the armed Services increased.

During the same period was created the system of grammar school education as we know it. Some of the old grammar schools chose to become, not public boarding schools, but civic day schools, and new independent grammar schools were founded. From the 1890s local authorities edged their way into the same field, without legal authority till the Education Act of 1902 set them free. 'Provincial' Universities became a stable reality and began to break the monopoly held by Oxford and Cambridge, London, and the Scottish Universities. At the same time it began to be recognised generally that the permanent official was a person of importance in his own right, that the Civil Service is a part of the British Constitution, and that one of the main problems of government in the twentieth century would be to secure effective central administration, and yet avoid bureaucracy.

All these tendencies were exaggerated by experience during the war of 1914-18, and in 1920 agreement was reached within the Service on a form of reorganisation which went much beyond anything contemplated by the MacDonnell Commission, which sat from 1910 until 1914 and was aware of the complexity that the problem had assumed even then. The main Report of the Reorganisation Committee of the National Whitley Council is a brief document, certainly equal in importance to the Trevelyan-Northcote Report. Its chief merit was that it found a clear but flexible formula for the development of the Service in its next phase. There were thus created three great 'general' classes, Clerical, Executive and Administrative, the duties of which the Report defines as follows:

The *Clerical Class* was to be a class: 'dealing with particular cases in accordance with well-defined regulations, instructions, or general practice; preparing material for returns, accounts, and statistics in prescribed forms; undertaking simple drafting and précis-work; and collecting material on which judgements can be formed'.

The *Executive Class*, in its more junior ranks, would undertake: 'the critical examination of particular cases of lesser importance not clearly within the scope of approved regulations or general decisions, initial investigations into matters of higher importance, and the immediate direction of small blocks of business'.

In its upper ranks, it would be 'concerned with matters of internal organisation and control, with the settlement of broad questions arising out of business in hand or in contemplation, and with the responsible conduct of important operations'.

The duties of the *Administrative Class* were 'those concerned with the formation of policy, with the co-ordination and improvement of Government machinery, and with the general administration and control of the Departments of the public service'.

It will be necessary to say more of these formulae in later sections: here we need only note their virtue as unifying principles. The main points are these:

(i) The formulae grew naturally out of the early structure of the Service and were flexible enough not to arouse anxiety about excessive standardisation.

(ii) The three classes (and the related Departmental classes) fitted naturally into the structure of education and society as understood in 1918.

(iii) The formula for the Administrative Class marks a step of some importance in constitutional theory: the Civil Service now has its recognised place in the making of policy for a democracy.

(iv) The formula for the Executive Class is in some ways awkwardly drafted: its advantage is that it can be stretched readily to include miscellaneous work in many different Departments, much of it of great importance although outside the scope of the Administrative Class formula.

(v) The classes thus constituted could be used in different combinations in different administrative situations. Departments (or different sections within one Department) might be administrative-clerical, executive-clerical, administrative-specialist-clerical, administrative-Army officer-clerical, occasionally specialist-clerical or Army officer-clerical. The Clerical Class is present in virtually all patterns, the Administrative Class is present at most points which are of strategic importance for politics and policy: but it is not possible to generalise further. Order is combined with flexibility, and there is room for empirical adaptation.

The vicissitudes of the Service have changed the situation greatly since 1920, and there have also been changes in the social and educational structure on which it is based. On the whole, the three formulae have proved flexible enough to absorb these developments, and no one has proposed any radical change in organisation. Nevertheless, the three-class system is now very different from that originally envisaged.

3. The Administrative Class

Numbers

The figures for the Administrative Class (Established and Permanent Unestablished) on 1 July 1955 are shown in Table XI.

TABLE XI

The Administrative Class (Home) at 1 July 1955
(Source: Civil Service Staff Statistics)

	Men	Women	Total
Permanent Secretaries	33	—	33
Deputy Secretaries	62	1[1]	63
Under Secretaries	209	5	214
Principal Assistant Secretaries[2]	2	—	2
Assistant Secretaries	644	29	673
Principals	1,143	116	1,259
Assistant Principals	245	42	287
Other Posts	63	2	65
Total	2,401	195	2,596

[1] Shortly afterwards Dame Evelyn Sharp became a Permanent Secretary, the first woman to reach that rank.
[2] A grade now obsolete.

In addition, there were about 165 temporary civil servants, some part-time, and if one includes these and Branch A of the Foreign Service the total is about 3,500. The corresponding figure given for 1914 is 450, perhaps calculated on a rather narrower basis: in 1931 it was 1,100, by 1938 1,500. The largest number reached during the war was about 4,900.

Recruitment

The tradition of the Class is still that expressed by Macaulay's famous dictum that 'the youth who does best what all the ablest and most ambitious youths about him are trying to do well, will generally prove a superior man'. It is in principle recruited from University graduates of high quality by a written examination which gives much the same value to all non-professional subjects studied in Universities. But the principle has been modified in two ways, which are together of great importance:

(i) *Assessment of Personality.* The most rigorous form of the principle gave no weight to previous record, testimonials, or interview: the result was decided solely by marks awarded on written work by examiners who did not know the candidate. This was a system designed primarily to exclude jobbery or the suspicion of jobbery; there was always opposition to it, on the ground that a successful candidate might prove quite unsuitable for his chosen career because of his personality or social background, and in fact the principle was never literally and comprehensively applied. The Home Office did not come into line until the 1880s. Until 1919 the Foreign Office required that all entrants to the examination should receive a nomination from the head of the Department, and should give proof of a substantial private income; the Board of Education made its own selection for the grade of Assistant Examiner, the normal entry to administrative work in that Department. In any event, the more influential Departments were safeguarded because they could take their pick from among the successful candidates.

After 1919 almost all special arrangements for selection by Departments disappeared; but Departments still have some room for manœuvre in selecting their entrants from the list of those successful, and it is now established practice that no one should enter the Administrative Class (or any other senior class) on the basis of written examination only. The most usual supplementary test is that of interview by a Board of civil servants and of people drawn from other walks of life, under the chairmanship of one of the Civil Service Commissioners. For the Administrative Class the maximum possible marks for interview (Method I only) is 300 out of a total maximum of 1,100. The verdict of the Board is therefore decisive for all candidates who are near the borderline on their written work.

During the 1939 war the need to select large numbers of candidates for commissions in the armed forces, particularly the Army, led to the development of organised tests of personal capacity much more elaborate than the simple interview. The War Office Selection Boards (W.O.S.B.s) assembled candidates for a period of two or three days, and submitted them to a variety of tests: some of these involved psychological measurement of capacity, others were tests of common sense and physical stamina related to situations that an officer might have to face. These tests were followed by an 'officer quality' interview with the President of the Board alone, and the Board then collectively assessed the 'grading' of the candidate, which might range from 'outstanding' to 'rejected'.

In the years after 1945 (as in the years after 1918) the Civil Service Commissioners were faced with the problems of making good a gap in recruitment to the Administrative Class and of comparing candidates who had missed University education through war service with others who had managed to complete full or shortened degree courses. The answer to this problem was the institution of the Civil Service Selection Board (C.S.S.B.), modelled on War Office practice with suitable modifications. Their main establishment was in a beautiful old house at Stoke D'Abernon: hence the name 'country-house', which seems to have stuck, although the tests are now carried out at an office in the West End of London.

Gossip about the 'country-house' suggested (as critics of the W.O.S.B. system had suggested) that it was primarily a 'knife and fork' test, designed to select those with social poise and a gift for small talk. This is emphatically not the object of C.S.S.B., and there is no evidence that it is biased in this way. Candidates are selected on the basis of a preliminary written examination of a general kind, designed primarily to eliminate those who do not have the capacity for paper work required in the higher levels of the Service. The C.S.S.B. tests are best regarded as a form of extended interview. It may be possible to reach agreement about outstanding candidates in a brief interview, but luck is important in doubtful cases: the candidate may spoil his chance by nervousness, or may make a bad impression through some accident in the sequence of questions. The longer the interview, the less room there is for chance. A week-end organised so as to include several different kinds of tests and situations gives the best possible chance to secure objectivity in assessing character. The C.S.S.B. tests raise no issue of principle not present in the decision to give weight to the interview, and there is no doubt that they provide a better sort of interview at a higher cost. The controversial question is whether any weight at all should be given to this sort of assessment.

Much has been written on this topic—perhaps more than it deserves—and the case may be summarised briefly as follows:

It is argued on the one hand that, as between two candidates equally good on paper, assessment of personality will tend to give the advantage to the one who has had the greatest advantages in early life. To take extreme cases: the son of professional people, educated at a preparatory school and a great public school, holder of an open scholarship at Oxford or Cambridge, a commissioned officer in the forces, is likely to make a better impression than the son of an artisan who has always lived at home, working his way through the local grammar school and the local University, and who has not even done National Service before he comes for interview. Obviously there is much truth in this, and statistics seem to confirm it. If it is accepted as fact, it may be argued that it is socially bad because of class bias, that it is unfair to individuals, and that it leads to the rejection of candidates who would be a better long-term investment than some of those who are accepted.

The case on the other side is sometimes spoiled by advocates who insist too much on the substantial number of candidates with no advantage of birth who secure places in the Administrative Class. This proves nothing. The number is substantial, but without the interview it might be even higher. The substance of the argument is that a written examination alone cannot be trusted to eliminate candidates quite unsuitable for posts of responsibility: in fact, that Macaulay's test is not to be accepted alone for the Civil Service, as it is not accepted alone for the Oversea Service, or for commissions in the forces. It is necessary to have some direct test of non-academic qualities, such as pleasantness of manner, control of nerves and temper, readiness of speech, capacity to grasp a complicated situation and to respond quickly. Personality assessment would be justified if it eliminated a fair number of useless candidates, even though it also eliminated a smaller number who might in the end do well.

The weight of official opinion is on this side of the argument, and the only question not settled in practice is whether the C.S.S.B. is so much better an instrument than the ordinary interview as to justify the extra expense involved. Since normal examinations for the Home Civil Service were resumed in 1948, candidates have had the right to choose either Method I (full examination and interview) or Method II (qualifying examination, C.S.S.B., and interview), and between a quarter and a half of the vacancies each year are filled by Method II. For the Foreign Service Method II is used in all cases, a practice introduced when Mr. Bevin was Foreign Secretary. The use of Method II is still regarded as experimental, and an attempt is being made by follow-up studies to compare the results of the two methods.

(ii) *Limited Competition, Promotion, and Transfer.* Recruitment into the Class is by no means confined to ordinary competition entrants and to candidates of University standard who entered by special competitions in the two post-war periods. Of the 2,531 members of the Administrative Class at 1 July 1955,[1] 1,156 (slightly less than half) entered it from another class, by promotion, limited competition, or transfer. This is due partly to rapid expansion during the two wars, which meant that there were sudden increases in the opportunities for promotion; partly to the gradual change in the role of central government, the needs of which have always been greater than could be met from the regular planned intake into the Class; partly to pressure from staff associations representing the other classes, anxious to secure opportunities of promotion for their members.

[1] That is, excluding the 65 members of the Class in 'other posts' (see Table XI). (Source: *Whitley Bulletin*, Vol. XXXVI, p. 97.)

The methods used are as follows:

(a) There is an annual competition for entry as Assistant Principal limited to established members of other classes between the ages of 21 and 28. The usual form of competition is Method II: qualifying examination, C.S.S.B., and interview; but as an experiment candidates are now allowed to take Method I (or both) if they wish, and the requirement that they must first have been nominated by their Department has been suspended. The policy agreed with the staff associations is that 20 per cent. of the places annually available should be offered in this way: but the Commissioners are not bound to fill this quota if they do not think that there are enough good candidates. In recent years the quota has usually been filled, but in 1955 only four candidates were declared successful though thirteen posts were offered.

(b) Candidates may make two attempts at entry by limited competition: if they fail, there remains the possibility of later promotion to the grade of Principal, but not before the age of 33. The procedure is based on individual recommendation by the Department and approval by the Treasury. It is difficult to see how this can be avoided, but the result is that prospects vary a good deal from one Department to another. Since the beginning of 1952, Departments have been invited to include a member of the Civil Service Commission on their promotion board, but there is great reluctance to do so. The scheme was designed to secure greater uniformity of promotion standards rather than to improve prospects, and if the Commissioners considered a candidate unsuitable for 'the wider duties of the Class', that is, for varied duties in Departments other than his own, they could advise the Treasury to reject him.

Most promotions are at the level of Principal, but some are at the level of Assistant Secretary. In 1955 the figures were (respectively) eighteen and one.

(c) Transfers between classes of equal standing are much rarer than promotions. The Administrative Class does take in a certain number of people on transfer from the Legal Class, from the Foreign Service, the old Indian Civil Service, and the Oversea Service, but each case is dealt with individually on its merits, and there is no standardised procedure. A good deal has been written about the desirability of arranging a flow of transfers from the specialist classes to the Administrative Class, and also about the desirability of transfers of experienced people from other branches of public service, such as local government or nationalised industries, or even from industry and academic life. The possibilities exist on paper, but except in time of war and emergency there is so much difference between

THE GENERAL CLASSES

the structure of different careers that transfer is very difficult for individuals, and it rarely occurs.

Table XII gives details of entry into the two most important grades over a period of years.

TABLE XII

Promotions in the Administrative Class, 1948-1955

(Source: Tables published in this form in the *Whitley Bulletin*)

(1) *To Assistant Secretary*

Grade prior to promotion	1948	49	50	51	52	53	54	55
1. Principal:								
(a) Ordinary Competition	37	31	42	29	19	24	27	46
(b) (i) Limited Competition	—	1	—	—	1	—	1	3
(ii) By promotion	28	26	24	23	30	16	12	20
2. General Executive Class	4	4	3	6	1	2	3	1
3. Departmental Executive Classes	2	2	4	1	3	1	1	—
4. Transfer from other classes	3	5	1	2	1	1	—	—
Total	74	69	74	61	55	44	44	70

(2) *To Principal*

Grade prior to promotion	1948	49	50	51	52	53	54	55
1. Assistant Principal:								
(a) Ordinary Competition	55	76	69	49	48	34	42	52
(b) Limited Competition	28	54	53	21	9	14	11	9
2. General Executive Class	12	39	29	22	13	14	18	14
3. Departmental Executive Classes	1	7	4	4	—	2	2	4
4. Transfer from other Classes	4	5	7	4	—	2	6	2
Total	100	181	162	100	70	66	79	81

The Structure of the Class

The result of these different methods of entry and of the events of the last forty years is that the structure of the Class is in practice somewhat complex. All pre-1914 entrants by examination have now passed the normal retiring age, and so have most of the Second Division clerks who were promoted to reinforce them during the expansion of the First World War. There follows a gap, due partly to the loss of men killed or disabled in war, partly to boom and slump after 1918. Some of those taken in after demobilisation are still in the Service and are near the top, but there is a gap in age between them and the first regular competition entrants of 1925. Until about 1933 the number taken in annually was quite small (ten was the lowest, thirty the highest, after 1925), and in these years of depression competition was severe. There is therefore a very able group of civil servants of that vintage, many of whom were promoted rapidly during the period from about 1935 to 1950, which threw great strain on a Service not then conspicuously strong in its higher ranks.

This period of expansion and of strain also involved a good deal of promotion from other classes, and it left a gap in regular recruitment which had to be made good after 1945 by the special Reconstruction competitions. Regular competitions were not resumed until 1948 (a few Reconstruction examinations ran over until 1952), and since then the pattern of entry into the Class has been relatively stable from year to year. But stability following a period of expansion has led to an inconvenient age-structure and to something of a promotion block in the middle ranks, some of the effects of which may be seen in the rate of promotion to Assistant Secretary as shown in Table XII. It is probable that in the same period there was an even greater decline in promotion above that level.

These general factors are present to some extent in all Departments, since the Treasury has a view of the situation as a whole, and is able to take some steps to secure equality of opportunity. But Departments differ, and the careers of individuals still depend a good deal on the 'luck of the draw'.

The Character of the Class

The complexity of its structure makes it somewhat dangerous to generalise about the character of the Class. Perhaps the only things which stamp a single pattern on its members are that they spend most of their working lives as Londoners of the middle class, and that their jobs are done almost entirely at the headquarters of central administration in London. Even to this there are exceptions. There are some Administrative Class civil servants in head offices in Edinburgh and Cardiff and a few serve as Regional Officers elsewhere; at any moment quite a substantial number are with British missions of one sort or another overseas; an attempt is made in some of the offices with large executive organisations to give Assistant Principals some experience of work in the field.

It has been argued that the Class bears too conspicuously the social stamp of the upper middle class. This scarcely applies to those recruited into it by promotion or limited competition, most of whom left school at 16 or 18 after no more than a grammar school education. The other half of the Class, the ordinary competition entrants, are drawn to the extent of about 75 per cent. from the Universities of Oxford and Cambridge, and carry with them afterwards the associations and friendships they have made there. This is of some importance to their place in the community, as the men whom they know best among their contemporaries are scattered in the Universities, the professions, finance, commerce, and journalism rather than in industry or local government. This stamp is in practice more important than their social origins, which are diverse, since they are a fair cross-section of those who win scholarships and grants for university education. In the past a high proportion of scholarship winners at Oxford and Cambridge came from the traditional public schools: but the share taken by direct grant grammar schools and local authority grammar schools is steadily increasing, and Civil Service competitions reflect the shifting structure of the educational system. In any case, the Home Civil Service has never been (like the Foreign Service) a 'snob' service: no one enters it for reasons of prestige, but for a salary and a job. It would be rare to find an Administrative Class civil servant who has a substantial income apart from his own and his wife's earnings. Most members of the Class are, or become, typical Londoners of the middle income groups, harassed by familiar problems of housing, daily travel, education for their children, jobs for their wives, annual holidays, and so on.

It is perhaps more important that the Class is stamped professionally by the fact that it is a headquarters service, living and working close to the centre of public life. The formula of 1920 describes a small body of exceptionally able people whose job is to act as the right hand of Ministers in matters of high policy. The Class is to be detached from party politics, and yet 'political' in the sense that it is to brief the Minister on all the implications of policy, as head or deputy head of a Department, as private secretary, or as the official in charge of an important Bill or of some other large piece of business. To do this effectively an Administrative Class civil servant must take at least as broad a view as the Minister himself, and he must be able to talk on equal terms, socially and intellectually, with everyone, however wealthy or eminent, who is concerned with the business of his Department.

This ideal picture of a group of Platonic guardians was not and could not be realised, but it was at one time a fair standard by which to judge the Administrative Class. It may be that the situation is changing as a result of increases in the size of the Class, in the variety of Departmental work, and in the scope of central administration as a whole. The numbers of the Class have increased about three-fold in the last forty years; this is not due to a dilution of the quality of the work done but to an increase in its scope. On the one hand, there is an increased need for people capable of handling matters of policy arising from subjects which are large in themselves and yet small in relation to the whole field of administration supervised by a Minister. On the other hand, there has been an increase in the responsibility of the Civil Service for the management of large organisations; these 'top management' jobs require acute awareness of policy, but they also require other qualities not so essential to the old Administrative Class. It is not in jobs of these two types so easy to find a clear line between policy and execution as it was in the earlier organisation.

This general blurring of what was once clear makes it impossible to draw sharp distinctions within the Class. But it is now possible to contrast two types of career, both essential to the work of the Class, but calling for different talents and imprinting rather a different professional stamp. On the one hand, a young man (or woman) soon after becoming an Assistant Principal (and this is much more likely to happen with a University entrant than with a limited competition entrant) may show talents for neat and tactful drafting, good manners, presence of mind in conversation, general good sense, some flair for politics. This is the sort of person who is likely to succeed in a junior post as private secretary, and if he succeeds there, the ladder leads through one of the more politically important sections of the Department, perhaps to a job as private secretary to the Minister, or to the Treasury or the Cabinet Office; and then perhaps, after promotion, to a Department of which he has no previous experience. This type of career produces the 'general man', and is the source from which come many (though by no means all) of the heads of the Service.

It is equally possible to 'grow up' within a single Department. A man may join the Administrative Class as Principal or as Assistant Secretary because he has become extremely valuable to his Department in managing a particular block of work, involving a large number of junior staff; or a University entrant may be given more to scholarship than to politics, and may be best placed not on the telephone in the Minister's private office but in some section where a large and confusing mass of detail has to be reduced to order. These lines of advance, as 'manager' and as 'specialist', tend to stop short at about the level of Assistant Secretary. But they are now the 'bread and butter' of the Class, and occupy a large number of its members. Among them are some who impress themselves on their colleagues (and on the Treasury) as being men bigger than their jobs, deserving promotion for their own sakes, and in the general interest of the Service. In this way a good many leaders of the Service rise within their own offices, becoming famous in Whitehall as outstanding authorities in their own field. If they are to rise to the top they must also show the capacity to collaborate with their Minister and with other Departments, in a word, to 'know their place' in central administration: but this general capacity is equally necessary for those who attain the highest posts in specialist classes and in the Executive Class, and is not the prerogative of the Administrative Class.

It is certainly not true today that the general tone of the Administrative Class is set by the political and intellectual society of the Pall Mall clubs. The Class lives under the shadow of Parliament, and no member of the Class can do his job unless he understands what this involves. But there are three possible types of Administrative civil servant, not one only: there is the right-hand man of Ministers, the political adviser, the slightly cynical guardian of the State, so well sketched by the late Mr. H. E. Dale; there is the academic man, devoured by the craving to get the facts straight and present them tidily and objectively; there is the manager, the best type of executive, the man who likes and understands large organisations and has the capacity to keep his own organisation moving. The success of the Class depends on its capacity to find, train, blend, and use civil servants who possess these very different characteristics; the men at the top ought ideally to have something of them all.

4. The Executive and Related Classes

Numbers

The figures for the General Executive Class (Established and Permanent Unestablished) on 1 July 1955 are set out in Table XIII. To this must be added the corresponding Departmental classes, for which the total of Established and Permanent Unestablished civil servants at the same date was 28,432 (including 2,889 women). The number of temporary and part-time employees was relatively small (3,558): taking these into account (part-time counted as half), the total involved is 67,483 (including 10,675 women).

The salary range for the Class is from £365 on entry as an Executive Officer at the age of 18 to £2,000 as Senior Chief Executive Officer.[1] The Priestley Commission were impressed 'with the high level of responsibility' carried by posts above this level, in view of 'the inter-

---

[1] Higher posts are paid a flat rate.

Table XIII

The General Service Executive Class at 1 July 1955
(Source: Civil Service Staff Statistics)

	Men	Women	Total
Heads of major establishments	28	—	28
Principal Executive Officer	110	—	110
Senior Chief Executive Officer	251	3	254
Chief Executive Officer	688	23	711
Senior Executive Officer	2,525	166	2,691
Higher Executive Officer	7,279	1,349	8,628
Executive Officer	17,313	5,675	22,988
Other posts	79	4	83
Total	28,273	7,220	35,493

locking of managerial and policy work', and they recommended salaries proportionate to those of Assistant Secretaries and Under Secretaries in the Administrative Class. At each stage salary scales are not far behind those of the higher class. An Assistant Principal on entry at the age of about 24 will receive £605, and by that age the Executive Officer will have reached £595. The starting salary of a Senior Executive Officer (£1,285) is slightly below that of Principal (£1,375), and about one in nine of the General Service Class are at or above this level. Assuming a similar proportion in the Departmental classes, there are about 7,000 Executive Class civil servants whose salaries run parallel with those of about 2,250 in the corresponding grades of the Administrative Class. The proportion of women in the lower grades is much larger than in the Administrative Class: in the higher grades it is much the same, presumably because of the incidence of retirement on marriage.

These figures are sufficient to illustrate the importance of the Class. This is by far the largest block of civil servants with executive responsibility for important decisions affecting members of the public as individuals.

Recruitment

The different methods of entry into the Class are illustrated in Table XIV.

Table XIV

Entry into Basic Grades of the General Service and Departmental Executive Classes, 1954

(Source: Priestley Commission Report and Central Staff Records Division, H.M. Treasury)

	Percentage of Vacancies Filled	Number
(1) *Open Competition:*		
(a) Young People:		
(i) School-leavers }	18·6	337
(ii) Serving civil servants }		
(b) University graduates	1·2	22
(c) Ex-National Service	2·7	48
(d) Ex-Regular	4·0	72
(2) *Limited Competition*	12·4	225
(3) *Promotion*	61·1	1,108
Total	100%	1,812

There is a sense in which the standard of the Class is still set by the open competition for 'young people' between the ages of 17½ and 19. This is an examination based on the work for the Advanced Level of the General Certificate of Education, normally taken after two years in the Sixth form of a grammar school. Two-thirds of the places are filled by those who do best in the written examination; below this level all those still in the running are interviewed, and places are offered on the combined mark for written examination and interview—a method which has in practice much the same effect as the addition of the interview to the written work in Method I for the Administrative Class.

Since the Priestley Commission reported, a number of places in the Class have been set aside for school-leavers on the basis of their performance in the General Certificate of Education at Advanced Level. Candidates who reach the standard required are interviewed by a Selection Board, but there is no further written examination. It is hoped to fill about 100 places a year in this way.

Entry by open competition is also available to young people who left school at 15 or 16 to enter the Service and who have prepared for it by part-time study. Serving civil servants have three further chances by limited competition between the ages of 21 and 28. This is a competition by written examination of a rather less academic kind and by interview. Ex-National Servicemen and ex-Regulars take an examination described as 'non-academic' and are interviewed. Even though these examinations are not set on an academic syllabus, it is fair to assume that the standard required in English and in general knowledge is that of a good Sixth-former.

The recruitment of University graduates was begun in 1923 for the Inland Revenue Tax Inspectorate and was subsequently extended to the 'Cadet' grade of the Ministry of Labour, to that of Assistant Postal Controller in the Post Office, and to Grade III Officers in the Joint Intelligence Branch, Ministry of Defence. The examination is the same as that for the Administrative Class (Method I or II), and candidates for the four grades compete against one another. They may state a preference for a particular Departmental class, but a successful candidate may not come high enough on the list to secure a place in the Department of his choice. These classes (which are not included in Table XIV) together took about 50 University graduates in 1954-55, mostly good Arts graduates who did not quite reach the standard of the Administrative Class. In 1946 there was added a separate competition (by Method I only) for a small number of places in the General Service Executive Class and analogous grades in the Departmental classes, including Tax Officer (Higher Grade) in Inland Revenue and Assistant Naval Store Officer. These are shown in Table XIV. A reasonably high standard has been maintained, but the numbers involved are small, and the effect on the classes as a whole is negligible.

All these forms of competition together provide little more than a third of the entrants to the Class. The remainder enter it by promotion over the age of 28, mainly from the Clerical Class. Promotion is a matter for decision by the Department concerned, but the Treasury operates a 'pool' for promotion to Higher Clerical Officer and Executive Officer in an attempt to even out disparities of opportunity.

The proportion recruited by promotion was greatly increased by the decision of 1947 which in effect placed the Executive Class 'end on' to the Clerical Class. Previously the latter included, above the basic grade of Clerical Officer, the higher grades of Higher Clerical Officer, Staff Officer, Senior Staff Officer, and Principal (or Chief) Staff Officer. All these have been merged with the corresponding executive grades, except that of Higher Clerical Officer, and this is retained only for work which is purely supervisory and without an element of executive responsibility. There are now only about 2,300 Higher Clerical Officers in a group of classes numbering about

190,000; a promising Clerical Officer now almost always goes forward by promotion into the Executive Class.

This is, however, not the only reason for increased dependence on promotion as a means of maintaining the strength of the Class. It has traditionally relied on its capacity to attract people of good Sixth-form standard, either direct from the grammar schools or by recruiting those who left school early to enter other classes of the Service. The number of school-leavers required is quite small in proportion to the output of the schools, since at least 10 per cent. of the school population are capable of reaching the standard required. But these young people have now greater opportunities, and are under greater pressure, to continue in full-time education beyond the age of 18. As is explained below, the Civil Service Commissioners have in recent years found it impossible to meet their requirement for entrants into the Clerical Class from school at 15 or 16, and an important source of recruitment to the Executive Class is thus diminishing. Until 1954 it was possible to find all entrants from school suitable for the Executive Class, but the number of qualified applicants in excess of requirements has gradually fallen, and in 1955 there was for the first time a deficiency. We are entering on a period when the size of the groups leaving school each year will increase, because of the high birth-rate since 1942, and it is possible that the trend will be reversed. If the decline continues in spite of increased numbers, some action may be necessary to increase the share of recruitment from the Universities: but the problem is not yet a pressing one, as the Class can live 'on its hump' for some time to come.

Structure and Character

It is as dangerous to generalise about the Executive as about the Administrative Class.

There are great differences in career structure between different Departments. The Treasury operates a 'promotion pool' for promotion from Executive Officer (and Higher Clerical Officer) to higher grades in the Class, and Departments which have in recent years been enjoying more than their 'fair share' of promotions are asked to contribute some of their Higher Executive Officer vacancies to the pool: a 'quota' is calculated for each Department each year.[1] This safety-valve allows some equalisation of levels of opportunity between Departments, and probably most able members of the Class entering it early in their careers can expect eventual promotion at least to Higher Executive Officer, at £1,055 to £1,255

[1] Treasury E.C. 2/56.

a year. But opportunities of rising above that level or of promotion into the Administrative Class are affected by the structure of individual Departments. Some Departments are largely 'executive', in others Executive Class civil servants 'underpin' (the Treasury's word) the Administrative Class. Clearly chances of promotion out of the Class are better in the latter Departments: but there are also important variations between the 'executive' Departments according to the shape of the hierarchy and the ratio of more senior posts.

The work of the Class also varies very greatly. It is said that about 10 per cent. of the Class (say 3,500) is in administrative divisions 'underpinning' the work of the Administrative Class. This work naturally varies as does that of the Administrative Class, but whatever its specialist content it has certain common features since it is all 'headquarters' work. Beyond this point one can proceed only by examples. At headquarters there are such jobs as those of officer in charge of the Registry, accounts officer in charge of the internal accounting and audit of the Ministry, contracts officer in charge of large blocks of important contracts, manager of a large section of a highly mechanised office such as that of the Ministry of Pensions and National Insurance, general supervisor of office management, including such matters as buildings, communications, and transport. Outside the head offices there are more specialised posts: auditor in the office of the Comptroller and Auditor-General, tax inspector in the Inland Revenue Department or the equivalent in the Customs and Excise Department, manager of a local office of the National Assistance Board, house manager and 'bursar' of one of the innumerable research and development establishments scattered about the country.

In one sense this is a random collection of different jobs, and not a single job: as has been said earlier, the formula drafted in 1920 to cover all posts of these different types is so vague that it can scarcely be called a definition. These are middle-level jobs with considerable responsibility, or top-level jobs of great importance but not involving much direct dealing with Ministers. They generally require both exact knowledge of a particular field and general ability as a manager: but the two qualities may be blended in very different proportions in different work.

Common elements are perhaps to be found rather in the career than in the job. These officials are all civil servants subject to the general conditions of the Service: and there are a number of these conditions which are worth specifying here because they are particularly important at this level.

(i) This is still largely a class of old grammar-school boys (and girls). It would be unusual to find a public-school boy, and the proportion of University graduates is negligible. Many have attained promotion with no more than elementary or secondary modern education, but they will take the prevailing colour of the Class. The social pattern of entry into grammar schools is changing, as is that of entry into Universities, and the ladder from a working-class home to the Executive Class is easy to climb for a competent boy or girl with the necessary backing from his family. But the ladder leads through the local grammar school, where the environment and contacts are still essentially middle class.

(ii) More will be said in Chapter 16 of the 'localisation' of the Civil Service, but it must be mentioned here because it is of particular importance to the Executive Class. An officer is expected to be mobile according to the exigencies of the Service, and a very high proportion of the Class works outside the London area. The situation varies from one Department to another, and there are some areas (like South-East Lancashire) where there is a fairly large concentration of civil servants and there are local opportunities for promotion. But on the whole the executive officer who wishes to accept promotion as it comes will have to move house two or three times in his career. This tends to break local connections and to emphasise the solidarity of the Class, at least in its upper ranks, as members of a national service.

(iii) The prospects offered to the young entrant are respectable but not brilliant. Many of the Administrative Class come from this source, but its intake is small in relation to the number of Executive Class officers, and the chances of promotion or of success in a limited competition do not look very large to the ordinary entrant. Promotion to an average 'suburban' salary within the Class is certain but slow: and it is doubtful whether the division of the Class internally into a large number of grades (as shown in Table XIII) is encouraging to the ordinary officer. The case for it is that merit can only be recognised by accelerated promotion from grade to grade: the larger the number of grades the greater the opportunity for recognising merit. The case against it is that there is no clearly marked difference between the level of responsibility in each grade, and with so many grades it is hard to offer a really adequate differential on promotion. A differential may be particularly important as an incentive, since promotion may be accompanied by transfer: and in the absence of high differentials executive officers may become cynical about the value of hard work and enterprise beyond the ordinary requirements of the Department.

A great deal in British administration depends on the solid ability and the absolute integrity of the Executive Class. The public has become so accustomed to these things that it has no idea what their absence would mean. We have perhaps had some experience of incompetence in the Civil Service during the process of dilution during two wars, which meant that much executive work had to be done by inexperienced people, whose energy did not always compensate for their ignorance. But we have had no real experience of dishonesty, and we are almost unable to conceive what administration is like where corruption is the rule. Regulations are ineffectual unless standards are maintained by the Service itself, and these standards are perhaps the most important mark of the Executive Class. It is impeccable, but somewhat rigid in its ways, and in consequence some ability is wasted within it through lack of opportunity. These limitations depend as much on the structure of the Service as on the character of the Class: they are perhaps the price that must be paid for securing absolute stability at the foundation of the Service.

5. The Clerical Class, the Clerical Assistant Class, and the Class of Temporary Clerks

Numbers

These three classes must be taken together, as the organisation of clerical work in the Civil Service depends on the relation between them. The figures for Established and Permanent Unestablished staffs and Temporary Clerks at 1 July 1955 are given in Table XV. To these must be added 21,271 men and 8,994 women in Established and Permanent Unestablished posts in Departmental classes, and about 4,000 other temporaries. A little is said in Chapter 7 about the special circumstances of the Post Office: but it is worth including here the main Post Office 'clerical' grade, that of Postal and Telegraph Officer, 21,741 in all, including 6,303 women.

The total figure for civil servants in all these categories is therefore about 207,000. This is a large part of the Civil Service: about one-third of the whole non-industrial Service including the Post Office, about one-half if it is excluded. This is by far the biggest block of civil servants employed in similar work on uniform terms of service: there can be no substantial reduction in the numbers (as distinct from the power and responsibility) of the Civil Service except by substantial cuts here.

This is also a large part of the whole field of clerical employment.[1]

---

[1] Total clerical employment in Great Britain about $2\frac{1}{4}$ million (Source: Census of Population, 1951). Of these, probably about $\frac{3}{4}$ million are in manufacturing industry.

Table XV

The General Service Clerical Classes and the Class of Temporary Clerks at 1 July 1955

(Source: Priestley, Report and Civil Service Staff Statistics)

	Men	Women	Total
The Clerical Class:			
(i) Higher Clerical Officers	1,474	864	2,338
(ii) Clerical Officers	49,779	25,639	75,418
(iii) Clerical Officers (Secretary)	21	1,421	1,442
(iv) Others	—	2	2
The Clerical Assistant Class:			
(i) Clerical Assistant	15,917	19,307	35,224
(ii) Others	383	2	385
Temporary Clerks:			
(i) Grade I	28	16	44
(ii) Grade II	5,372	4,499	9,871
(iii) Grade III	10,069	16,605	26,674
Total	83,043	68,355	151,398

The figures are much disputed, because of the difficulty of definition and the prevalence of temporary and part-time clerical work, but clerical civil servants are certainly the largest organised group of clerical workers in the country, those organised by the National and Local Government Officers Association are certainly the second largest.[1] The relation between these associations and public employers does much to affect the whole character of clerical employment. There are here social problems of great importance which have not attracted much attention either from the public or from research workers.

Duties

The work of the clerical and 'sub-clerical' classes is done in many different settings: as part of large organisations dealing with a great deal of routine business, such as the National Insurance Records Office at Newcastle; on routine work in smaller organisations, such as local tax offices; as counter clerks dealing with the public in local offices of the Ministry of Labour and the Ministry of Pensions and National Insurance; as personal assistants to individual officers in

---

[1] N.A.L.G.O. (230,000) has a larger membership than the C.S.C.A. (150,000), but includes many men and women who are in 'non-clerical' jobs.

the middle ranks of the general and specialist classes; on registry work and the keeping of papers in large offices; on routine accounting.

In this sense the work varies greatly, but it has a relatively small element of special knowledge—much smaller than in the Executive Class. Most of the jobs could be done adequately by someone with the right qualifications after six months' experience, and some of them could be grasped even more quickly. The problem is one of basic rather than of special qualifications.

There are perhaps three main requirements:

(i) Exactness, neatness, thoroughness, and speed in dealing with papers and figures: a clerk must be able to grasp the point of written communications on office business at his own level, to draft business-like replies on simple points, to collect and summarise figures accurately. In a sense, this requires no more than literacy, and the clerk tends now to lose the special position which he enjoyed when many people were illiterate, and which he still enjoys in underdeveloped countries. But our general standards of literacy in this country are not very high, and a dilution of skill at clerical level may be reflected in inefficiency, delay, and frustration all through the Service.

(ii) Friendliness, tact, and patience in dealing with the public. Private business selects with some care those of its clerical employees who deal direct with the public, and gives them special training and special pay, as so much depends on the impression which they make. The central administration has not the same incentive to put its best goods in the shop window, and the job of counter clerk is not treated as a specialised one. It is a rough generalisation to say that large public and private organisations have dealings with the Administrative Class, businesses of medium size have dealings with the Executive Class, the individual citizen meets only the clerical classes. Counter clerks in most offices are given some special training, but they are selected almost by chance from the clerical classes as a whole and are not treated separately for pay or for any other purpose.

(iii) Discipline, or natural aptitude for routine. The central administration is a very large organisation which attempts to follow a consistent policy, and it can only do so if those at the lowest level of operations obey instructions promptly, literally, and precisely. An order is to be obeyed in the Civil Service as in a military organisation: individual initiative at the lowest level is more likely to cause confusion than to advance business. It is practically never right for a subordinate civil servant to go against the regulations. This precision can only be combined with flexibility if the junior knows when to act and when to report to his superior: a difficult judgement, possible only within an experienced Service familiar with the implications of its work.

This combination of qualities is an impossible ideal. In a prosperous and mobile society people who are precise and careful workers and who also have gifts for personal relations do not stay long in situations where initiative is impossible to them. The traditional notion of the clerk finds a place only in a Victorian picture of a stratified society, in which there is a special class of people (immortalised in the character of Mr. Pooter, in George and Weedon Grossmith's *The Diary of a Nobody*)—some of them very able and good people—who are fixed socially at this level. The notion of a clerical class as defined in 1920, with its own avenue of promotion to higher levels, originates in this idea of a clerical type of man. It was rightly abandoned in 1947, when the main Clerical Class was placed 'end on' to the Executive Class: but the resulting structure is complicated and perhaps unstable.

Recruitment and Structure

It may be convenient to deal first with the position of Temporary Clerks and of Clerical Assistants, since the Clerical Class now rests largely on this foundation.

Large numbers of men and women were recruited by Departments as Temporary Clerks during the war years, when regular competitions for entry were suspended, and many of these have now been established by Departmental selection and by written examinations of various kinds. Up to 1955 about 41,000 had been established in this way as Clerical Officers and about 32,000 as Clerical Assistants. Some of these competitions were specifically for older people over 40 or over 45, others had no limit of age, but the general effect has been to recruit a large block of older people, both men and women, who have not much prospect of rising farther in the Service.

A 'reservoir' of temporary civil servants is essential to the Service because of seasonal work in many offices, and so as to allow some reduction of numbers quickly if policy makes this possible. But the margin has been reduced greatly, and is probably not much above a working minimum. Older men and women are still being recruited as Temporary Clerks, but there is no deliberate intention that they should become 'permanent temporary' staff, as there are now regular opportunities for establishment either on Departmental recommendation or by competition. It is regarded as being in the national interest that the Service should recruit older people and disabled persons who find it relatively difficult to get private employment: and this is in any case necessary at present in order to maintain the strength of these classes. The salary for a Clerical Officer over 40 is £690, for a Clerical Assistant it is about £10 a week. These are not unattractive rates for 'general' clerks, in combination with pension rights, and hitherto there has been no real difficulty in recruiting older people except in a limited number of areas. But too much recruitment of this kind would upset the balance of the Service. The age-distribution in the clerical classes already shows a considerable 'bulge' in the groups over 50.

The class of Clerical Assistants consists largely of Temporary Clerks who have been established. But it has also a regular intake of girls between 15 and 20, at a level at which the good Secondary Modern School girl would stand a fair chance of success. In the London area there is a competition every two or three weeks, consisting of 'simple tests in common sense, accuracy and arithmetic'. In the provinces girls are in the first instance recruited by Departments as Temporary Clerks grade III, and there is a similar competition for establishment once a year.

The pattern of recruitment to the Clerical Class itself and to the related Departmental classes can be seen from Table XVI. It omits vacancies filled by the establishment of Temporary Clerks as Clerical Officers, a large proportion in the years after the war but now dwindling. It does, however, include Temporary Clerks previously established as Clerical Assistants, and now coming forward by promotion.

TABLE XVI

Recruitment to the Clerical Class and Related Departmental Classes, 1954

(Source: Priestley Commission Report and Central Staff Records Division, H.M. Treasury)

Method	Percentage of Vacancies Filled	Number
(1) *Open Competition:*		
(a) Young People	30·8	1,564
(b) Ex-National Service	1·7	85
(c) Ex-Regular	5·9	303
(d) G.C.E. entrants	2·2	112
(e) 'Near-miss' executives	1·8	92
(2) *Limited Competition*	5·5	279
(3) *Promotion*	52·1	2,645
Total	100%	5,080

The position here is closely comparable to that of entry into the Executive Class. The standard is set by the 'young people's' examination, which is an academic examination at the Ordinary Level of the General Certificate of Education, designed for boys and girls in grammar schools who wish to leave school at 16. The standard has always been pretty good, and most of those selected would be capable of taking G.C.E. at Advanced Level. But schools and parents are exerting more and more pressure for higher education, and the field of good school-leavers at 16 is dwindling. Before the war the Civil Service Commission generally had twice as many acceptable candidates as it could place: in 1953 and 1954 it could only fill half the vacancies offered. The position is made worse because those selected must agree to work away from home: the greatest shortage of staff is in the London area, and most provincial entrants must be prepared to live in London from the beginning, which is alarming to parents, and also expensive.

The traditional competition has been eked out by other expedients, such as less academic examinations for those leaving the armed forces, selection on G.C.E. results without examination, and the offer of places to those who do not quite reach the standard of entry in the Executive Class examination at 18. These schemes produce over 10 per cent. of the total entrants, a valuable contribution, and one which cannot be increased at present without lowering the traditional standard.

Limited competition is open to those holding posts (established or unestablished) in various minor and manipulative grades, between the ages of 25 and 30 (22 and 30 in the Post Office). Clerical assistants and typists are excluded, and the field of those capable of reaching the required educational standard is therefore not very large.

Promotion, on the other hand (which is by Departmental selection without any sort of 'pool'), draws mainly from the Clerical Assistant and established Typing grades, and to a very limited extent from 'manipulative' and Departmental 'sub-clerical' grades. It tends to produce Clerical Officers of two quite different types: girls entering from school who are sufficiently able and keen to wish to go farther than their basic grade, and older people recruited originally as Temporary Clerks. Very few from either source are likely to go farther up the ladder into the Executive Class.

The effect of all this is that a simple structure of grades and salaries covers many different circumstances, and the position is not one that can be set out in figures. Indeed, in the clerical classes (even when they are called 'general' classes) there is very little movement between Departments, and each Department has special problems of its own.

There are very large differences between the 'shape' of a career in (for instance) the Commonwealth Relations Office, a small London office in which the clerks are mainly assistants in office work; in the National Insurance Records Office at Newcastle, where there is a very large block of routine work, done mainly by some 5,000 girls locally recruited; in a Department with many local offices, in which the good clerical entrant has an excellent chance (if he is mobile) of rising to 'managerial' work.

Subject to these reserves, it is perhaps fair to break the problem into three smaller problems:

(i) The possibility of entering the Civil Service at 16 as a Clerical Officer (or 'a Second Division Clerk' as it was known before 1914) was once very attractive to families at a particular level of society. The prospects offered are perhaps better now than ever before, since an able young Clerical Officer is almost certain of promotion to the Executive Class, and may even reach there the salary of a Principal, though he has only a small chance of promotion into the Administrative Class itself. This excellent tradition still sets the standard of work in the Class: but the old source of recruitment is drying up, and is not likely to renew itself unless there is an unforeseen reversal of the trends towards technological subjects and later school leaving. The alternatives are to drop the standard of entry at this age: or to make the deficit good by other forms of recruitment: or both together.

(ii) The Service has always been troubled by the problem of the simplest kinds of office work, which used to be performed by copying clerks and writing assistants on very unsatisfactory terms of service. The arrangements for taking girls in as Clerical Assistants avoid most of the old difficulties: most of the girls recruited resign on marriage during their twenties, and a good career is open to those who stay. But other employers have also discovered the advantages of recruiting girls at this age, and offer work which sounds more interesting than that of the Civil Service. Here too recruitment is inadequate, and it can scarcely be improved except by the sort of competitive bidding in which the Service cannot engage.

(iii) There has not hitherto been much difficulty in filling the gap by recruiting older people: men of reasonably good education who have not achieved success in other lines of life, married women, widows, and others set free to take employment in their forties and fifties. Many of these people fit the requirements of clerical work in the Civil Service extremely well, perhaps better than bright young recruits. But it is uncertain whether this source of supply will continue in a period of full employment, in which private business faces the same problems of recruitment as does the Service. If it does continue, it will mean a reversal of trends in Civil Service organisation.

The pattern of 1920 is that of entry at three (or perhaps four) levels from different stages of the educational system. The staff associations have pressed for adequate opportunities of promotion from each level, and this has been conceded generously, so that nearly 60 per cent. of the Clerical Class comes from below, over 60 per cent. of the Executive Class, and nearly 50 per cent. of the Administrative Class. A career from the bottom of the Service to the top is now feasible for the able entrant: but the stream of able entrants at the bottom is likely to dry up. The Service cannot react by putting up pay on entry at 16, because this would run counter to the whole course of policy in education: but it cannot live without its share of able entrants at the beginning of their career. In the end, therefore, it may be forced to pay a high price for able entrants between 18 and 25, and to recruit the clerical classes primarily in less regular ways. But the implications of a trend work out slowly in a large and complex service, and there is no likelihood of any immediate or dramatic change of policy.

6. The Typing Grades and the Machine Operating Class

The Machine Operating Class can be dismissed briefly, as its work is done mainly in specialised organisations or sections, and does not greatly affect the general organisation of the Service. In July 1953 (the latest date for which figures are available) the Class numbered rather under 4,000, almost all women, and in addition there were about 1,000 duplicator operators. These are mainly girls recruited through the procedure for Clerical Assistants and given special training within the Service.

The problem of typing and shorthand, on the other hand, is one which influences the whole conduct of business. At 1 July 1955 there were 16,475 established and permanent unestablished, and 11,061 whole-time and part-time unestablished shorthand and copy typists, almost all women (98 per cent.). There is no figure for the number who would be recruited if they were available, but it is certainly much larger. The rates of pay include very substantial bonuses for proficiency, and there is an avenue of promotion into the supervisory grades (about 1,000 posts) as well as into the Clerical Class.

Recruitment is on a temporary basis in the first instance, most frequently through local employment exchanges. Subsequent establishment depends upon Departmental nomination (which will only be made if the required standard of proficiency in typing or in shorthand is achieved) and the passing of a simple examination. Some thirty Departmental training schools in London and the provinces provide training for applicants with no knowledge of typing and for those whose proficiency does not reach the minimum standard required for permanent employment in a government office.

Since the war, increases in pay have been relatively greater for proficient typists than for other clerical grades: but recruitment remains difficult and wastage is high. The result is a continuous shortage of facilities for shorthand and typing, and great efforts to secure economy in the use of typists. When the shortage was worst in London immediately after the war, it became the practice to draft non-urgent letters in longhand and send them out to provincial offices to be typed and returned for signature. This practice is not now general, but two devices are a permanent part of the system:

(i) No official below the level of Assistant Secretary or Senior Chief Executive Officer or their equivalents has a secretary of his own: shorthand typists are to be used for shorthand and typing, and are not to spend time on the miscellaneous duties of a secretary, such as answering the telephone, taking messages, receiving callers, finding relevant papers, and generally keeping track of business. In the middle ranks officials must do such jobs themselves, or get them done by a clerical assistant who cannot type, or leave them undone.

(ii) Shorthand typists allocated as secretaries are promoted to the grade of Clerical Officer (see Table XV), and may in the end reach the Executive Class. Virtually all others are organised in typing pools, serving sections of a Department but not individuals. This economises the use of typists, but not the time of individual officers, because time is wasted in dictating to girls not familiar with the business in hand and the style of the person dictating, and often extra drafts are required in consequence. The use of dictating machines is increasing, but it is scarcely the solution of the difficulty.

Economy of typists means that girls in the Civil Service have a more boring and less varied job than they might find in private business, and they tend to leave the Service or to avoid entering it. But shortage makes economy all the more necessary, and this helps to perpetuate shortage. This means much frustration and waste of time for people in responsible positions in the Service, and so indirectly for the public. It is in some ways a merit that civil servants should be discouraged from producing typescript as freely as do some other organisations: but the results sometimes seem archaic. Much drafting is still done in longhand, and that attractive figure of the business world, the efficient personal secretary, is almost unknown. This affects higher officials who are specialists or managers just as much as it does the Administrative and Executive Classes.

7. The Messengerial Classes and the General Service Class of Cleaners

These two classes do much to give government offices their special atmosphere and character. There are about 7,500 messengers and 'paper keepers' on the permanent staff, almost all men. Women were recruited temporarily during the war, but there has now been a reversion to the pre-war practice of recruitment by Departments from men who are over 38 or disabled, with special preference for ex-Regular soldiers.

The job of 'messenger' is a vague and traditional one, which has spread round the world with British practices of government, and is to be found in most colonial and ex-colonial territories. At its worst the job is a piece of patronage at a miserably low level of pay: at his best the messenger is a valuable odd-job man, the best type of old soldier. In most offices in this country messengers do the work usually done by commissionaires and lift-men, and also the office-boy jobs of carrying messages, seeing to the mail—and making tea. The government provides uniforms, but not very smart ones; it gives some opportunities of promotion, but not many; and (on the whole) it leaves the system as it found it.

There are about 1,500 full-time cleaners and about 14,000 part-time cleaners—the army of good ladies who arrive before the rest of the office and set things straight: the modern counterparts of the 'necessary women' who appear in the records of government offices since the seventeenth century and perhaps earlier. The job of office-cleaner is organised in much the same way in government offices as in other offices, and indeed some government cleaning is done by private firms under contract. The differences lie mainly in standards of staffing; government offices have so small a complement that they are rarely very clean, and there is a familiar high-water mark on the walls which marks the limits of the cleaners' regular responsibility. There is a rota for more general cleaning and a rota for redecoration, but neither is very generous.

Anyone who works in a government office knows the messengers and cleaners, and hopes to have good friends among them. The public sees a good deal of them and of their work. The impression it gets is not one of 'spit and polish'; whatever its other faults, there is no 'bull' in the Civil Service.

8. THE FOREIGN SERVICE

The Foreign Service lies largely outside the scope of this book: it has already been mentioned briefly, but it may be wise to insert a further note about it here, so as to set out its position in relation to the general classes of the Home Civil Service, with which it is often confused.

The four 'Branches' (A, B, C, and D) of the Foreign Service were referred to in Chapter 3. They are linked to form a single Service, in principle distinct from the Home Civil Service. This principle is largely a matter of corporate spirit and prestige, but it has three important practical consequences:

(i) One of the Secretaries of the Treasury is Head of the Home Civil Service but he is not head of the Foreign Service. This means in practice that the Treasury has no responsibility either for higher appointments in the Foreign Office and in Missions overseas, or for the careers of more junior officials in Branch A. The former are managed by a Senior Promotions Board, under the chairmanship of the Permanent Secretary of the Foreign Office, who is himself appointed by the Foreign Secretary with the consent of the Prime Minister; the latter are the responsibility of the Personnel Department of the Foreign Office.

(ii) A certificate from the Civil Service Commissioners is required for establishment, just as in the Home Civil Service, and the Commissioners conduct all examinations for entry. But these examinations are managed separately from those for the Home Civil Service, and their rules (though in most respects similar) are not quite the same. For instance, there is now no examination in academic subjects for Branch A of the Foreign Service: entry is by a qualifying general examination, C.S.S.B. tests, and interview.

(iii) Foreign Service officers serving temporarily in London are not treated simply as members of the Home Civil Service. Their basic salaries are much the same, grade for grade, but they are given allowances in recognition of the fact that their living expenses cannot be reduced to the same level as those of one who lives permanently in London.

The Service is small in relation to the non-industrial Civil Service as a whole, as will be seen from Table XVII.

Table XVII

The Foreign Service at 1 July 1955

(Source: Central Staff Records Division, H.M. Treasury.
Figures are for *permanent* staff only)

	Men	Women	Total
Branch A	646	10	656
Branch B	1,020	597	1,617
Branch C	—	176	176
Branch D	77	—	77
Total	1,743	783	2,526

To this total of 2,526 permanent civil servants must be added several thousand staff locally recruited at Missions overseas, and many of the junior staff of the Foreign Office in London, who are members of the Home Civil Service. About 5,700 civil servants worked for the Foreign Office in 1955, and less than a third of these belonged to the Foreign Service.

This emphasises the dual role of the Foreign Office; on the one hand it directs and focuses the work of Embassies, Legations, and Consulates, on the other hand it is itself part of the central administration within Great Britain. Its routine office work in London is done by the Home Civil Service: services are provided for it by the Ministry of Works, the Post Office, and other common service Departments: it works like other Departments within the framework of co-operation described in Part III of this book.

9. The Oversea Civil Service

The position of the Colonial Office also requires some explanation. It is managed (and is largely staffed) by members of the Home Civil Service belonging to classes described in this chapter and in the next. The costs of the Office are borne wholly on the British Budget, and are subject to normal Treasury control: its officials are recruited through the Civil Service Commission. But each of the Colonies, Protectorates, and other Territories supervised by the Office has its own budget and is expected to pay for its own civil service. The oldest tradition is that there is not one 'oversea' civil service, but a great many: these are completely outside the jurisdiction of the

British Civil Service Commission, though many of them now have Civil Service Commissions of their own.

These local administrations have always been staffed partly by local recruits, partly by people sent out from this country. The latter were at first appointed on local terms, in the full spirit of patronage; but standardisation and centralisation have been in progress for at least a century. In 1930 and the years that followed, these 'expatriate' civil servants were drawn together into a limited number of groups, each of which was recognised in all Territories—the Colonial Administrative Service, Medical Service, Agricultural Service, Education Service, Police Service, and so on. A member of one of these Services would be paid from a local budget; but he was recruited centrally by the Colonial Office, was given preliminary training in England, and (within limits) might be asked to serve at roughly the same rate of pay in any Territory.

At the same time the Civil Service Commission was brought in, without breach of the principle that constitutional responsibility rests with the Colonial Secretary. A Colonial Service Appointments Board is appointed by the Secretary of State on the nomination of the First Civil Service Commissioner, who is himself chairman of the Board *ex officio*, and this body exercises general supervision over all recruitment.

Most of the colonies are now in transition to self-government, and wish to gain full power over all staff serving in their territory. It has been suggested that to meet this situation much of the old Colonial Service should be converted into a central service, paid from the British Budget and lent as necessary to territories wishing to have expert assistance and advice. This has not been done, but on 1 October 1954 the Service became the 'Oversea Civil Service', a name which recognises that its members do not serve only in colonies but in all sorts of territories overseas, some of them self-governing, some of them not within the jurisdiction of the Colonial Office at all.

The Colonial Office usually has on its staff a number of retired members of the Oversea Service (including its present Permanent Secretary, Sir John Macpherson); and there is quite frequent exchange of staff on secondment between the Office and territories overseas. But problems of the Oversea Service are outside the scope of this book, although the Office which manages it has an important place as a Department within the central administration.

FOR REFERENCE

Report of a Committee to consider the Scheme of Examination for Class I of the Civil Service (Leathes). Cd. 8657, 1917.

Reports of the Reorganisation Committee of the National Whitley Council, 7 February 1920 and 28 January 1921.

Recruitment to Established Posts in the Civil Service during the Reconstruction Period. Cmd. 6567, November 1944.

9th Report and Minutes of Evidence from the Select Committee on Estimates, Session 1947-48: The Civil Service Commission. H.C. 203, 205. (Deals at length with the Civil Service Selection Board.)

Civil Service Commission: *The Administrative Class of the Home Civil Service* (1950).

Memorandum by the Civil Service Commission on the Use of the Civil Service Selection Board in the Reconstruction Competitions (H.M.S.O. 1951).

86th Report of H.M. Civil Service Commissioners for the Reconstruction Period 1945-1952. 1954.

Report of the Royal Commission on the Civil Service (Priestley). Cmd. 9613, 1955. Chs. X, XI, XII.

Introductory Factual Memorandum submitted by H.M. Treasury, 1954. Chs. 13, 16, 20, 22, 23, 24, 25, 28, 29.

Proposals for the Reform of the Foreign Service. Cmd. 6420, 1943.

Reorganisation of the Colonial Service. Colonial No. 306, 1954.

CHAPTER SEVEN

THE SPECIALIST CLASSES

The Minister looked round with a very nice, rather practised-looking smile and said, 'These are the back-room boys, eh?'
'Yes,' the Old Man said, beaming round at us paternally. 'This is where all the work's done.'
We simpered.
The Minister looked round the room. 'Not very luxurious quarters, are they?'
' No,' said Mair. 'I'm afraid not. They were the best we could get.'
'Ah, well,' said the Minister. 'I always find the best work's done in the barest rooms.'—NIGEL BALCHIN: *The Small Back Room*, ch. iii.

1. INTRODUCTORY

ENOUGH has been said in the preceding chapter to indicate that there is a certain artificiality in the distinction between 'general' and 'specialist' civil servants. The 'general' classes include many who have by long experience become highly skilled in the work of one Department. They also include men and women with specific training of an advanced kind which gives them an 'internal' qualification at least as hard to obtain as the corresponding qualifications in professions outside the Service. This is true, for instance, of the higher staff of the Comptroller and Auditor-General's Office, and also for the Tax Inspectorate and other branches of the Inland Revenue, and for the Customs and Excise Service.

The distinction is therefore one imposed for administrative reasons on a situation which is much more flexible than the distinction would suggest. Nevertheless, it does correspond to a broad cleavage in the English social tradition between general education and specialist education or training, which leads to a corresponding cleavage in methods of recruitment and in the grounds of argument about pay and conditions of service. The organisation which represents many of the specialist classes is called the Institution of Professional Civil Servants, and by this it implies that the members of the specialist classes are in the first place members of a recognised profession or craft, then in the second place members of the Civil Service. Perhaps members of the 'general' classes are more truly 'professional civil

THE SPECIALIST CLASSES

servants', since few of them owe allegiance to any profession except the Civil Service and their skills do not give professional standing outside the Service.

This distinction too is blurred in practice. There are some professions (for example, that of meteorologist or Naval Constructor) which offer little chance of outside employment, and some specialist civil servants become so adept in a particular line of Departmental business that their original qualification ceases to be of much importance. Nevertheless, the general point is an important one. In 1955 there were probably about 20,000 civil servants in grades earning a minimum of £1,200 a year or more, and about half of these belonged to the professional classes. The latter recognise the standards of their own professions, read their technical literature, attend their conferences, keep up their old contacts, may quite readily contemplate moving to jobs outside the Civil Service. Their existence greatly extends the range of contact and vision of the Service: it also increases the administrative difficulties of maintaining its unity.

Earlier in this book (Chapter 3, p. 21) we estimated the number of specialist classes to be about 180: but this is a very rough approximation because some specialist grades are too small to constitute a separate class and there are many marginal cases. A more accurate (if less illuminating) picture is obtained by counting the number of specialist grades separately coded by the Central Records Branch of the Treasury. On this reckoning there are about 550 separate grades (excluding the Post Office) which seem worthy of the name 'specialist': and there are about 90 more grades in the Inspectorates. It is clearly impossible to deal with such diversity here. We can, however, make a rough classification on the basis of place in the general organisation of the Service, and exemplify it by describing some important examples in each group.

Logically (and often in practice) the process of creating a new class of specialists begins when a Department decides that there is a job which cannot be done either by training a 'general' civil servant or by paying a fee for professional assistance from outside the Service. This will lead to one or two personal appointments of persons with special qualifications: if the work grows within a Department there will in time be a small group of specialists requiring formal recognition as a 'Departmental class'. Some of these classes have become fairly large, while remaining Departmental; but it often happens that different Departments have moved separately on parallel lines, or that there are Departments which use one or two specialists of a type employed in quite large numbers by some other Department.

This sets up a situation in which Treasury policy looks towards the creation either of 'linked Departmental classes' or of a new general service class. Standardisation is tidier than departmentalism, and economises time spent on negotiation; it may also be more equitable. Departments may stand out against it for a time, pleading the need for flexibility and the existence of special circumstances; but the Treasury is in the end irresistible, and on the whole the Civil Service unions see advantages in its policy. There is therefore a continuous trend towards the creation of new Treasury classes of specialists: but many of these classes are largely employed by one Ministry or group of Ministries, with relatively few 'outlying' members elsewhere in the Service. It is rare to find a specialist class which is present in the structure of all Ministries and is important in all.

This chapter will follow the process in the reverse order, proceeding from widespread classes to those which are narrowly Departmental. It concludes with a brief description of the structure of the Post Office, which presents remarkable features of its own.

2. CLASSES GENERALLY PRESENT

There are only two specialist classes of this type, both small in numbers, but of great importance in central administration. These are the lawyers and the statisticians.

(i) *The Government Legal Service*

In all the countries of Western Europe except Britain it has been the tradition for centuries that the most important posts in central administration should be filled by men trained in the Law Faculties of the Universities. There are exceptions to this, since some important positions are held by technical administrators, and the monopoly of the Law Faculties does not go without challenge by Arts and Social Studies; it should be added that (partly because of this administrative tradition) Law Faculties on the continent teach a wider range of subjects than do their counterparts in Britain. Nevertheless, a fair contrast can be drawn between the position of lawyers in British bureaucracy and in that of Western Europe. In the former they are advisers to the administration, in the latter they are the administration itself.

Continental practice has the disadvantage that it tends to increase formality and to inculcate a certain narrowness: it has the advantage that administrators and judges are trained to talk the same language, there is less sterile controversy about their conflicts, and there is perhaps more effective observance of forms of procedure designed to hold the balance between the administration and the citizen. A good deal of trouble has arisen in Britain because of the gap between the Civil Service and the legal profession, a matter in which there have been faults on both sides; and the House of Commons, strong in lawyers, has generally been readier to adopt the lawyers' point of view.

Reference will be made later to responsibility for the organisation of the judicial system in England and Wales, which is divided between the Home Office, the Lord Chancellor's Department, and the office of the Lord Chief Justice. The problem here is that of responsibility for day-to-day advice to the administration about legal powers and duties, about forms of procedure, and about legislative drafting, jobs for which those in the main line of administration are not technically qualified.

The traditional arrangements were of a rather rudimentary kind[1]:

(a) The legal advisers to the Cabinet are the Attorney-General and Solicitor-General, holders of political office, who give legal advice in their personal capacity and conduct important cases on behalf of the Crown. They have a very small full-time staff, and obtain most of the assistance they need from Standing Counsel to the Treasury. These are practising barristers, not in government service, who are paid fees for work in court or for advising, mainly on matters of criminal proceedings. Such posts are 'plums' in the career of a barrister, and may lead to high political or judicial office.

(b) Government Bills are drafted by Parliamentary Counsel to the Treasury, the 'Parliamentary Draftsmen'. This became a full-time permanent post in 1869, at the time when the government was becoming responsible for a regular legislative programme, and when there were justifiable complaints about the amateurishness of the drafting of government Bills. The office of First Parliamentary Counsel has been held by a series of very distinguished lawyers, beginning with Lord Thring and Sir Henry Jenkyns. Recruitment is from barristers of first-rate ability who have decided to abandon private practice, and there is a long period of training under the guidance of the more senior Counsel. In spite of expansion (there are now sixteen draftsmen in the office) the standard is very high. The Office is centralised, but individual members of it are allotted to Departments from time to time for the conduct of particular Bills, and they do to some extent specialise.

(c) Another small office of central importance (dating from 1891)

---

[1] To simplify matters we do not here refer to the arrangements for Scotland, which are similar in principle, but are separately organised because of the existence of a separate system of Scots law.

G

is the Statutory Publications Office, formerly known as the Office of the Editor of Statutes Revised and Statutory Rules and Orders. It has been described as the 'handmaiden' of the Statute Law Committee, a committee of Ministers, civil servants, judges, and lawyers which is responsible for keeping the Statute Book in good order, superintending the indexing of Statutes and Statutory Instruments, and drawing attention to technical flaws requiring legislation for amendment; it is not expected to raise points of substance. The Statutory Publications Office prepares new editions of the Statutes Revised, the annual volumes of Statutory Instruments, Indexes, and Tables. It is a central point of reference on matters of form (as distinct from substance) in the layout and publication of delegated legislation made under statute, and has played an important part in improving procedure.

(*d*) The work of day-to-day legal advice to Departments has traditionally been divided between the office of the Treasury Solicitor (who is also the Queen's Proctor) and the separate Departments. The Treasury Solicitor acts for the Treasury, and for those Departments which have no legal staffs. About fourteen major Departments and half a dozen minor Departments now have their own legal advisers, and make their own arrangements about the conduct of proceedings in court, legal distraint, and so on. Among the major Departments which have no legal branch of their own are the Ministry of Transport and Civil Aviation, the Ministry of Supply, the Ministry of Fuel and Power, and the Ministry of Works. The Service Departments have their own experts on naval, military, and air force law, but are advised by the Treasury Solicitor on civil matters. A few Departments such as the Home Office and the Ministry of Health have always had sufficient legal work of interest and importance to attract first-rate lawyers, some of whom have played a large part in administration. But their staff of assistants used to be small, and often not of very high quality. Between 1877 and 1888 all the existing legal offices were 'disestablished', and the legal advisers to Departments were given annual lump sums 'for the hire of clerks'. In 1919, legal staffs were established once more in the Civil Service, and common salary scales and standard grades were introduced, but Departments continued to recruit for themselves. This was not very successful in making the career attractive, and a further reorganisation took place in 1946, when a general service class was formally constituted as 'the Government Legal Service'. (This does not include Parliamentary Counsel, who are recruited individually, nor the legal staffs of certain other Departments such as the Foreign Office.) The Class numbered just under 600 in 1955: only

32 of them received salaries above the maximum for an Assistant Secretary. Recruitment is between the ages of 26 and 40, by competitive interview, from qualified barristers or solicitors. Experience in practice is useful, and recruits are often those who incur family commitments and see no prospect of security or advancement in private practice; so that the average age of entry is about 30. Recently, there have been up to 60 vacancies a year, and it has not been possible to secure enough entrants of the right quality to fill them all; a reflection perhaps of temporarily favourable conditions in private practice, which may already be passing.

It is impossible to say whether the Government Legal Service has much corporate influence as a 'general service class'. It is probable that most lawyers still make their career in one Department, and the possibility of transfer comes into play only for exceptional men, or in the event of an awkward Departmental promotion block. Much of the business done at the lower levels is of a fairly standardised kind, and does not involve much influence on policy. Yet the organisation of the Legal Service strengthens the relative position of trained lawyers, and has perhaps played its part in improving standards.

(ii) *The Statistician Class*

There is a distinguished tradition of statistical work in the British public service associated with such men as Porter and Giffen at the Board of Trade, Farr at the General Register Office, Stamp at the Inland Revenue. Most of these men, however, worked within their own sphere in their own Departments with small staffs trained by themselves: each Department was master in its own house, collected such statistics as it thought fit for its own purposes, and processed them for itself. This system, or lack of system, had been criticised for many years, and a consultative committee was set up in 1920 for co-ordination between Departments. But effective co-operation was enforced only by experience in the war of 1939.

There were two reasons for this. One was that division of opinion at Cabinet level frequently turned on questions about production figures and about priorities, involving statistics for different types of armament, equipment, and commodities, and it was impossible to discuss policy coherently so long as there were discrepancies between figures presented by different Departments. The other was the growth of interest in the control of war-time inflation, and in the possibility of economic planning after the war. Progress in these fields depends largely on success in obtaining an adequate statistical picture of the economy as a whole.

There were three parallel developments: first, the Statistical Section of the Prime Minister's Office, a special investigating section under Lord Cherwell (Professor Lindemann as he then was), which was effective only because of the personal relationship between Sir Winston Churchill and 'the Prof', and did not become a permanent part of the machine; secondly, the creation of 'economic staffs' in the Treasury and in the Cabinet Office, and the appointment of economic advisers in most of the Departments concerned with the economy; and thirdly, the creation of the Central Statistical Office within the Cabinet Office.

The work of these organisations will be discussed later: the important point in this context is that in 1946, during the Reconstruction period, it was decided to create a specialist class of statisticians but not a specialist class of economists. The machinery for economic advice has been kept in being, but the posts within it are filled by personal appointment, and interchange with the Universities is encouraged. Some economists enter the Administrative Class by the ordinary channels and are generally appointed to Departments concerned with economic affairs: but they are not treated as specialists. It is argued that economic policy is too central a matter to be left to specialists. On the other hand, there was considerable pressure from outside the Service to have statistics, the basis of economic policy, recognised as a technical subject, and a Statistician Class was created to provide staff for the Central Statistical Office and for the statistical sections of the Departments.

The total number of the Class was 71 in 1955 (permanent staff only). It is one of the few specialist classes recruited by examination: all candidates for ordinary entry between the ages of $20\frac{1}{2}$ and 24 (with allowance for National Service, and for approved 'experience' up to three years) must take Method I of the Administrative Class examination with compulsory papers in Statistics, and either in Mathematics or in Economics. There are only about half a dozen vacancies to be filled each year, but the demand for statisticians has increased in other spheres quite as rapidly as in government service, and it is not easy to find recruits of the quality required. It is not unusual, moreover, for successful candidates to enter the Administrative Class in preference to the Statistician Class. This means that in practice a good many vacancies have to be filled by older people: and also that statistical work of some importance is still done by Executive Class civil servants. In fact, the creation of a unified class has not radically transformed the previous situation. There has undoubtedly been a general improvement in the presentation and use of British official statistics since 1939, but this may be due as much to the influence of a small group of able individuals in the Central Statistical Office and other organisations as to changes in conditions of entry to the Service.

3. CLASSES CONCENTRATED IN A FEW DEPARTMENTS

There are a number of other classes and grades of specialists which are organised on a 'general service' basis. But their position is different from that of lawyers and statisticians who play an important part in all administration: these other 'general service' classes and grades are important in some Departments and not in others, since their work is related (it might be said) to content and not to form. We deal here with the Scientific Civil Service (the most striking single instance), the Works Group, the Medical Officer Class, and the Professional Accountant Class. Other smaller 'general service' classes and grades of the same kind are (for instance) the Actuary Class, psychologists, pharmacists.

(i) *The Scientific Civil Service*

This is a very large and important group of a complex kind. The creation of some unity of organisation for the group was one of the most important pieces of Civil Service reorganisation in the period after 1945, and its broad lines are clear, though the practical effects are difficult to trace satisfactorily.

The statistics of the position as it was in 1953 are given in Table XVIII. It will be seen that there are three linked classes, the Scientific Officer Class, the Experimental Officer Class, and the Assistant (Scientific) Class; these are organised in a way which corresponds to the organisation of the three general classes, Administrative, Executive, and Clerical, and this idea of parallelism influences all discussion about scientists in the Civil Service.

The standard is set from the top. The Administrative Class is, in principle, recruited from graduates (in fact, as we have seen, there is a very large element of promotion), and the Administrative Class examinations are largely taken by Arts graduates—they are open to scientists, but really good scientists rarely compete. The Scientific Officer Class is recruited by competitive interview largely from graduates in science, engineering, or mathematics, for work in fields in which no additional professional qualification is necessary. Successful candidates liable to National Service are given deferment, which amounts in practice to exemption. The largest groups are those of graduates in physics and chemistry. There are a good many mathematicians and graduate engineers, a smaller number

TABLE XVIII

The Scientific Civil Service

(Source: Priestley Commission, Report and Minutes of Evidence)

(i) *Numbers at 1 April 1953*

	Established	Temporary	Total
Scientific Officer Class	3,127[1]	594	3,721
Experimental Officer Class	5,356	1,380	6,736
Assistant (Scientific) Class	2,734[1]	2,936	5,670
Total	11,217	4,910	16,127

(ii) *Distribution of Scientific Officer Class between Departments at 1 April 1953*

	Established	Temporary	Total
Admiralty	466	63	529
Agriculture and Food (and Scottish Dept. of Agriculture)	117	7	124
Air Ministry	203	13	216
British Museum	60	3	63
Colonial Office	23	1	24
Defence	13	5	18
Fuel and Power	37	8	45
Government Chemist	53	—	53
Home Office and Scottish Home Dept.	55	8	63
Post Office	35	3	38
D.S.I.R.	552	27	579
Supply	1,465	449	1,914
War Office	26	5	31
Other Departments[2] with less than 10 each	22	2	24
Total	3,127	594	3,721

[1] The figures quoted in Chapter 3 (p. 27) are for 1 July 1955: 1953 figures are used here because none are available as at 1 July 1955 for '(ii) Distribution of Scientific Officer Class between Departments'.

[2] Civil Service Commission, Ministry of Materials, National Gallery, Royal Mint, Transport and Civil Aviation, Treasury, Works.

of biologists, and a few graduates in narrower fields such as geology or metallurgy. Their educational career has therefore run parallel to that of their colleagues in the Administrative Class, and is rather different from that of many other specialists in the Service who would colloquially be referred to as 'scientists', although they are primarily members of professions rather than holders of degrees. It is perhaps also relevant that there is a much higher proportion of Oxford and Cambridge men among University entrants to the Administrative Class than to the Scientific Officer Class. This is due mainly not to social preferences but to differences in output from the Universities: in 1954 Oxford and Cambridge together produced a third of all British graduates in Arts, a quarter of those in science, an eighth of those in technology.

This background may help to explain why discussion about the Scientific Civil Service is often given a social or theoretical twist, and appears to be concerned as much with badges of status as with cash values. A debate about the place of particular groups of scientists in a particular organisation tends to become entangled with a much more general debate about the place of the University-trained scientist in the modern world. The central administration is the largest employer of scientific graduates in the country, and the precedents which it sets are of great importance.

There are two main points of controversy. The first is that of *relativities* between the scientific classes and the general classes. The proposals of the Barlow Committee, accepted without much modification in 1945, gave the scientific classes a structure closely parallel to that of the Administrative, Executive, and Clerical classes.

(*a*) The Scientific Officer Class is recruited from first- and second-class Honours graduates in a scientific subject (including engineering) or in mathematics.[1] The normal age-limits are 21 to 28, with the usual allowance for service in the forces; to allow for the fact that most good scientists now spend a period of post-graduate work in the Universities there is the possibility of recruitment to the second grade, that of Senior Scientific Officer, between 26 and 31. There is a 'continuous open competition', which means that candidates can apply at any time, and that their applications will be dealt with in groups throughout the year, on their record and after interview. On the whole, the Civil Service seems to have satisfied its enormous demand pretty well in this way.

(*b*) The Experimental Officer Class is recruited mainly at the

[1] Candidates not so qualified may be admitted at the discretion of the Civil Service Commissioners 'if they have high professional attainments' (Priestley Report, Para. 536).

Advanced Level of the G.C.E., with age-limits of 18 to 28 for the first grade, 26 to 31 for the second; since 1951 graduate scientists have been eligible, and a limited number of the less able graduates have been accepted. There is also provision for men with qualifications such as a Higher National Certificate.

(c) The Assistant (Scientific) Class is in principle recruited between the ages of $17\frac{1}{2}$ and 26, normally at the Ordinary Level of G.C.E., but with power to make exceptions for specialist experience or skill.

There are avenues of promotion from class to class, provided that the candidate can acquire the necessary qualifications by part-time study, and can also prove himself competent in the work of his Department. But entrants to each class by promotion are relatively much less numerous than in the general classes; this is almost inevitable, as the pyramid of the Scientific Civil Service has a much narrower base. Out of an intake of about 200 Scientific Officers a year only 20 come from the Experimental Officer Class.

There is no objective means of deciding whether the 3,700 officers of the Scientific Officer Class have greater or less responsibility and ability than the 2,600 officers of the Administrative Class. The only possible answer is the common-sense one that the two classes deserve much the same rating, and conditions of service are based on this assumption as well as on comparison with rates of pay outside the Service. Unfortunately the Treasury is rather apt to deal with the classes in what can only be construed as an order of prestige. For instance, its Memorandum for the Priestley Commission on the Civil Service sets out (in this order) details about 'the Administrative Class', 'the Scientific Officer Class', 'the Works Group of Professional Classes' (the other professional classes are not set out in the Memorandum): then come the 'Executive Class', the 'Experimental Officer Class', the 'Technical Works Engineering and Allied Classes', and so on. A little tact in these matters would be judicious, since the Treasury is run by the Administrative Class and other classes are suspicious of its unspoken assumptions.

There is, however, one problem which cannot be escaped so easily. The bulk of the scientific classes work in research establishments, not in Departments, and in these out-stations they rarely see members of the Administrative Class. The head of the establishment is a scientist, and on the non-scientific side responsibility for daily management rests (generally) with a member of the Executive Class, who works under the command of the head of the establishment, although he carries some personal responsibility for seeing that procedure for accountancy, contracts, and so on is properly observed. Within Departments, on the other hand, general responsibility for management is in the hands of the Administrative Class. There are a limited number of important exceptions (the D.S.I.R. and to a certain extent the Service Departments), but the main framework of all other Departments is that of Administrative Class officers—Permanent Secretary, Deputy Secretary, Under Secretaries. Scientists are generally organised in separate technical sections, often looking to a Chief Scientific Officer as their head within the Ministry. The exact chain of command is not always easy to define, and certainly a leading scientific official would never be excluded from direct access to the Minister on grounds of the hierarchical superiority of the Administrative Class. Yet it is a fixed principle in British organisation (this will be discussed more fully later) that the Permanent Secretary is the senior official of the Department, and seniority carries with it a badge in the form of a small 'lead' in pay (insignificant after deduction of tax) over any other official in his Department. The arguments for this relativity are hard to resist, except by rejecting one of the presuppositions of the system, and the Priestley Commission accept the proposition that no official should be paid more than the Permanent Secretary. But they suggest that this is not important lower in the hierarchy. It is pointless to argue (for instance) about differences of responsibility between directors of important scientific sections at headquarters, Under Secretaries and heads of major research establishments. If this is generally accepted, it may be possible to avoid (or at least to reduce) anxiety about the symbolic importance of small differentials in pay.

The second point of controversy is that of *career structure*. It can be shown statistically that the average member of the Scientific Officer Class will, over his whole career, earn less than the average member of the Administrative Class, even though the relativities between each grade are reasonable at each level. This follows from the nature of the work. A member of the Administrative Class works in an administrative hierarchy, a pyramid which widens fairly evenly from top to bottom. It has a corresponding distribution of work suitable for officers with varying degrees of experience, and the bottom of the pyramid is kept fairly narrow by the nature of the relation with the Executive Class. Scientific officers, on the other hand, work mainly in research, and this produces a pyramid of a different shape. Research is essentially a matter of individual initiative, not of administrative organisation and direction: a research establishment does not (if it is working well) have many jobs in management at the top. A scientist may well do his best and most important work in leading quite a small research team when he is between 30 and 40. If a man continues to do brilliant and original work of this kind later in life, he can be given special promotion to the grade of Senior Principal Scientific Officer and above (roughly equivalent to Assistant Secretary) without loading him with administrative work. But such men are exceptional, and the average competent scientist cannot look for promotion to jobs in the higher management of research. It would be fatal to create such jobs in order to create a career for scientists. Nor is there much scope for relief in the suggestion that scientists should be transferred more freely to the Administrative Class. Active research scientists in their thirties do not wish to transfer: in their forties it is as a rule too late for them to learn the general work of the Administrative Class in such a way as to hold their own with those who have grown up in that class.

These two difficulties—about relativities at the top, and about career structure—are perhaps logically insoluble within the British pattern of Departmental organisation. The best that can be said is that they are of very little importance if the picture of scientific work for government is looked at as a whole. It is, however, extremely difficult to achieve this wider view of problems of scientific organisation. The work of scientists is affected by considerations of security even more than is that of the Administrative Class, and in any case its technicality makes it difficult to assess. Besides, there is great diversity between forms of organisation in different technical environments. Hence it is difficult even to begin to discuss the common problems of organisations as different in their character as the Atomic Energy Research Establishment at Harwell (now transferred to the autonomous Atomic Energy Authority), the National Physical Laboratory at Teddington, the Road Research Laboratory at West Drayton, the Plant Pathology Laboratory at Harpenden, the Assay Department of the Royal Mint. There are of course some simple generalities which seem to hold good about all human organisations, but these are of no help in assessing the effectiveness of government scientific organisation in all its diversity. Assessment of efficiency in each field depends in the last resort on the opinion of experts in that field; this opinion is not readily available to the layman; and a lay summary of it is of necessity so vague as to be almost meaningless. The total effort expended on government research in Britain is tremendous, exceeded only in the U.S.A. and the U.S.S.R.; the best work is superlatively good; there is a good deal of work of a less exciting kind which is necessary and competent; there is also work at a lower level, ineffectual not because of incompetence but because of lack of speed and originality. How far can this lower level be raised by improvements in organisation?

Certain suggestions were made recently by a Committee which inquired into the work of the Department of Scientific and Industrial Research,[1] and this led to the D.S.I.R. Act of 1956. But the material on which the Committee's Report was based remained confidential, and debates on it in Parliament did very little to throw light on organisational problems of great and increasing importance.

(ii) *The Works Group of Professional Classes*

The Scientific Civil Service now includes most of those civil servants who have followed the normal scientific curriculum through school and University and who are engaged on work specifically related to their education. There are still some Departmental classes for those engaged in rather narrow fields of specialisation; but their conditions of service are largely determined by precedents set for the group as a whole.

The position of the Works Group is somewhat similar, but its organisation is looser. Officially it includes eight 'general service' classes: architects, maintenance surveyors, quantity surveyors, estate surveyors and land officers, civil engineers, mechanical and electrical engineers, structural engineers, and sanitary engineers; but there are a number of closely related Departmental variants of these classes, for instance, Ship Surveyor in the Ministry of Transport, Farm Buildings Advisory Officer in the Ministry of Agriculture, and Valuer in the Board of Inland Revenue and in the Treasury. Some of the members of these professions hold University degrees as well as professional qualifications; conversely, some professional engineers are included in the Scientific Officer Class. But there is a broad distinction between the University scientists on the one hand and the professional men on the other: their training, attitudes, and professional organisation are different. There is also a broad distinction between types of work, subject to similar exceptions. The main concentration of Works Group officers is in Departments concerned with the construction and maintenance of buildings and plant, and with the supervision of similar work carried out by other bodies; the main concentration of the scientific classes is in Departments concerned with research, such as the Ministry of Supply, the D.S.I.R., and the Admiralty. This is illustrated in Table XIX.

With the Works Group go the 'Technical Works, Engineering and Allied Classes' and the 'linked Departmental classes of Architectural and Engineering Draughtsmen': groups of technicians of rather diverse kinds who fit into the structure at about the level of the Executive Class and the Experimental Officer Class. In April 1953

[1] Jephcott Report: Cmd. 9734, 1956.

there were about 19,000 in the ancillary technical classes, 8,200 in the draughtsmen classes, apart from smaller related groups. The total number involved is therefore substantially greater than on the 'scientific' side.

TABLE XIX

Distribution of the Works Group and Related Classes at 1 April 1953

(Source: Priestley Commission, Minutes of Evidence)

Admiralty	648
Agriculture (including Scotland)	408
Air Ministry	950
Central Land Board	566
Education	31
Forestry Commission	287
Fuel and Power	282
Housing and Local Government (including Scotland)	371
Home Office (including Scotland)	26
Inland Revenue	2,269
Post Office	1,360
D.S.I.R.	25
Supply	2,708
Transport and Civil Aviation	577
War Office	403
Works	1,553
Other Departments[1] with less than 20 each	65
Total	12,529[2]

[1] Colonial Office, Crown Lands, Labour, Prison Commission, Public Trustee, Royal Mint, Scottish Land Court, Board of Trade, Treasury.
[2] Works Group about 4,800, Related Classes about 7,700.

The whole group of classes was reorganised in 1946, and its organisation was again reviewed in 1951 by a Treasury Committee under the chairmanship of Sir Thomas Gardiner. The reorganisation has given rise to various controversies about pay and status, which differ in many ways from the problems of the scientific classes. The members of the engineering classes 'know their place' as professional men, and there is not the same asperity about their relations with the Administrative Class or about their status within the organisation. In one relationship they are in the recognised position of advisers to clients on professional matters: in another relationship the engineers are themselves managers of projects with unchallenged executive responsibility within their own sphere. These matters are quite well understood, and raise no general issues about the structure of the Service. That is not to say that these classes are more contented with their lot than are other civil servants.

Recruitment is largely by open competition between the ages of 25 and 35, on the basis of record and interview. Men already in junior technical classes may enter for open competition if they can obtain the necessary qualifications, and there is some opportunity for promotion even after the age of 35; but entry is primarily from men who have recently completed their training outside the Service. There is a scarcity of trained men in many (though not all) of these professions, so that there is at that stage direct competition with outside employers.

Entry is into what is called 'the basic grade', and the problems of 'career structure' are indicated in Table XX, which shows the position at 1 April 1955.

TABLE XX

The Works Group of Professional Classes

(Source: Priestley Commission, Report)

	Established	Temporary	Total
Directing posts at salaries over £2,350	23	3	26
Other directing posts	136	1	137
Superintending grade	457	8	465
Senior grade	1,571	85	1,656
Main grade	3,405	933	4,338
Basic grade	3,896	1,650	5,546
Total	9,488	2,680	12,168

Two-fifths of the group are in the entry grade, which has a relatively long scale, extending from £765 (at the age of 25) to £1,190. This is rather high pay on entry as compared with that of the Assistant Principal or the Scientific Officer, who would enter at £605: and the pay is specifically related to age (up to the age of 34), so that increments are in effect given for experience outside the Service. On the other hand, prospects are rather poorer than in either of the other classes. As we have seen, a competent Administrative Class officer has a fair chance of reaching the grade of Assistant Secretary, at £2,000 to £2,600: a Scientific Officer is somewhat handicapped by the structure of the class, but is given special opportunities of rising to that level if he is an outstanding research worker: the professional man has a career with relatively few opportunities either for large administrative responsibility or for distinction in research, and he cannot expect, without quite special ability or good luck, to go beyond the top of the Principal's scale. To put this statistically, 39 per cent. of the Administrative Class are in posts with a minimum salary of £2,000 a year, 17 per cent. of the Scientific Civil Service, but only 5 per cent. of the Works Group; or (in less objective terms) the government pays high to recruit young professional men in a competitive market, but keeps salaries down at the stage when recruits are settled in the Service and are unlikely to leave.

The Priestley Commission were bound by their own principles to accept this situation, since there is direct comparison on entry with outside employment, and there is no evidence that pay at later stages is out of line with average pay in outside employment. They recognised, however, that in business the exceptional man has a better chance of rising than in the Civil Service, and they recommended palliatives in the form of special merit awards and perhaps an increase in the number of directing posts. This is not likely to have much effect on the debate, which is complicated by allegations against the Treasury of deliberate bad faith in interpreting an important but ambiguous passage in the report of the Gardiner Committee.

That Committee mentioned that there has also been some friction at the lower levels of administration, both between non-specialist and professional staffs and between different groups of professionals working in a division dominated by one of them. There is no way of assessing these problems in general terms, since the Works Group is in many respects a rather loose association of different specialists employed in different Departments. Conditions are even more diverse than in the scientific classes, since the group includes (for instance) Inland Revenue Valuers, architects helping to decide school building policy, civil engineers on airfield work for the Air Ministry, ship surveyors under the Ministry of Transport: indeed, the only obvious generalisation is a question. Is it really necessary that such diverse groups should be brought together for purposes of negotiation?

(iii) *The Medical Officer Class*

The number of doctors employed by the central administration is comparatively small, but they have a wide range of duties, some of which are important in the making and execution of policy. The most recent figures for the distribution of doctors between Departments are those given to a committee of inquiry in 1951,[1] shown in Table XXI.

[1] Report of the Committee on the Pay and Organisation of Civil Service Medical Staffs (Howitt), 1951.

Table XXI

Established Medical Posts, April 1951

(Source: Howitt Committee, Report)

Pensions and National Insurance	170
Health (including Scotland)	129
Board of Control (i.e. mental health administration) (including Scotland)	17
Home Department (including Scotland)	16
Prison Commission	53
Supply	24
Treasury Medical Service	16
Labour	17
Education	8
Others	16
Total	466

In addition, there were about 150 temporary appointments, and about 80 appointments under the Board of Control and in hospitals under the Ministry of Pensions and National Insurance, which are remunerated at National Health Service rates.

Apart from these hospital appointments there is now no difference in conditions of service between doctors engaged largely on clinical duties (as for instance prison doctors and psychiatrists, doctors carrying out clinical examinations for the Ministry of Pensions and National Insurance, or factory doctors in Ministry of Supply establishments) and those engaged largely in the making and execution of policy. The latter are few in number, but have been of great importance in the growth of public administration. The tradition began during the public health movement of the mid-nineteenth century, in which a great part was played by Sir John Simon, first as adviser to the Privy Council Committee on Public Health, and then after 1871 at the Local Government Board. It has continued to be important in the development of the National Health Service, one of whose earliest prophets was Sir George Newman, the first Chief Medical Officer at the Ministry of Health. This post now links together many of these responsibilities, since its occupant is also Chief Medical Officer to the Ministry of Education and to the Home Office, and is unequivocally the leading doctor in central administration. But these services are separately organised in Scotland, and there are also some medical posts under other Departments which carry considerable responsibility for policy, for instance under the

Factory Acts and the National Insurance Acts, and in the control of dangerous drugs, health in mines, and vivisection.

In the old days of the Local Government Board there was some open warfare between medical and lay administrators, but there is no recent record of such difficulties. The chief problem is that of conditions of service, and this arises out of the special conditions of the medical profession outside the Civil Service. Most of the profession are now engaged in public practice within the National Health Service, and are remunerated largely by capitation fees calculated so as to produce a reasonable average net income. What is deemed 'reasonable' is affected partly by the traditions of private practice, which still offers high rewards for special distinction, partly by the strain and expense of general practice conducted from the doctor's own home. Conditions of service are settled by negotiation with the Ministry of Health, but recourse has been had more than once to special independent inquiries, and the results of these inquiries have not been subject to effective Treasury control. In consequence, medical remuneration outside the Civil Service remains rather above the rate of earnings in other middle class professions; and there is a natural desire among Civil Service doctors to relate their rates of pay to those of the National Health Service—to those of consultants in the higher ranks, to those of the average general practitioner in the basic grade of Medical Officer. The Treasury would argue against this that salaries should be related to those of the few salaried doctors who are in private employment, since this should reflect both the attractions of National Health Service rates and the advantages of escaping from it into less strenuous conditions. The conclusion recommended by the Priestley Commission was in effect a compromise. The acceptance of this compromise means that the basic grade of Medical Officer rises to a point well above that of its 'opposite numbers' in the scientific and works classes, but not as high as that of an Assistant Secretary. At 1 April 1955 only 26 per cent. of the class were above the grade of Medical Officer; this looks a favourable proportion, but entry is relatively late (generally above the age of 35), so that the average career is shorter than in other classes, and the ratio of higher posts is not strictly comparable.

Government also employs people from other professions associated with health, such as dentists, nurses, and various medical auxiliaries, and some of these are engaged in administrative work. But the numbers involved are small and the problems are in general similar to those of the doctors, since employment in these classes is also primarily comparable with employment in the National Health Service.

(iv) *The Professional Accountant Class*

As has been explained in Chapter 6, internal accounting and auditing in central administration is done almost entirely by members of the Executive Class and the related Departmental classes. Some of these groups are given specialised training within the Service, but they have no professionally recognised qualification, and the central administration does not in its ordinary business make much use of the accounting profession, which plays such a large part in the administration of commerce and industry. Nor does it use members of the Institute of Municipal Treasurers and Accountants, who are prominent in the work of local authorities and other public bodies. This is of a good deal of importance in the tradition of public accounting and also in shaping the character of the Executive Class and its associated classes.

Nevertheless, there are various branches of the administration which require expert knowledge of commercial accounting: for instance, in the taxation Departments, and in Departments concerned with price controls and with the placing of bulk contracts for supplies, which involve argument about the profitability of business at different price levels. The Inland Revenue provides for its own requirements largely by training its own men, but this does not produce all it requires, and other Departments have no similar provision for training. The need was in part met, to begin with, by employing firms of commercial accountants, a useful way of obtaining impartial advice about levels of profitability, and this is still done. But it has also been necessary to recruit qualified accountants individually, and they were grouped into a small 'general service' class in 1946.

In 1953 there were 415 of them, of whom 295 were established. Most of them were in the Ministry of Food, the Ministry of Supply, the Board of Trade, and the Inland Revenue Department. Their salary scales at 10 January 1953 were:

Director	£2,100 (£1,600-£2,000 in Ministry of Food)
Assistant Director	£1,485-£1,700
Chief Accountant	£1,270-£1,500
Senior Accountant	£900-£1,220
Accountant	£650-£900

This is one instance in which the doctrine of fair comparison is simple to apply, since there is an open market for professional accountants outside the Service, and there can be fairly free movement in and out. There are, however, difficulties which arise from the nature of the work. It does not include much straightforward accountancy and auditing, since this is done by non-specialist civil servants who also take executive responsibility for large blocks of work; nor does it lead to posts of high responsibility at the policy level, since Departments do not require chief advisers on commercial accounting as they need chief legal advisers, and (in some cases) chief medical advisers. Commercial accountants are needed mainly as technical advisers within a limited sphere, at a middle level of responsibility. This poses awkward problems about the career structure of the Class, for which there is no obvious solution.

4. DEPARTMENTAL CLASSES

The specialists dealt with so far are all grouped into 'general service' classes and have functions not limited to a single Department. This process of grouping and standardisation goes on all the time, but it is still possible to find many cases of important specialist classes which are in their nature tied to a single service and so to a single Department: for instance, the Civil Hydrographic Officers and the Corps of Naval Constructors under the Admiralty; Veterinary Officers, Agricultural Advisory Officers of various types, and Agricultural Land Commissioners at the Ministry of Agriculture, Fisheries, and Food; the Inspectorate of the Ministry of Education; the officers of the Forestry Commission; the Mines Inspectors of the Ministry of Fuel and Power; the Dangerous Drugs Inspectors, the Explosives Inspectors, and other inspectorates at the Home Office; and so on.

The efficiency of each service depends largely on the skill and *morale* of the group of experts concerned with it. A number of these groups have traditions older than those of the Civil Service in its modern form, and the history of the service is largely the history of the men who made it. Bodies like the Corps of Naval Constructors, the Factory Inspectorate, and the Education Inspectorate have set standards throughout the world, and they are much more than instruments of policy held in the hands of administrators. Their most eminent members are advisers on policy whose advice it is perilous to reject: and each group contributes to policy as a whole because it has corporate experience and opinion, which expresses itself in day-to-day action quite as much as in formal advice.

This sort of organisation resists classification and is full of marginal cases. For instance, meteorologists, who work virtually as a self-contained service, are classified as members of the Scientific Civil Service; some of the Inspectorates rank as separate classes, often quite small ones, even though their members have specialist qualifications appropriate to a more general class; there is a very narrow line between specialists trained within the Service who belong to specialist classes (like the Naval Constructors) and those (like the District Auditors of the Ministry of Housing and Local Government) who belong to non-specialist classes. This confusion represents on the one hand the accidents of history, on the other hand the extreme complexity of modern administration. Its effects could only be illustrated by tracing in detail the recruitment, work, and careers of a number of specialist groups: a fairly wide selection would be necessary to give an idea of the range of different circumstances, and considerations of space make this impossible here.

Nevertheless, there are two general points which may be worth making:

First, each group has its own staff association, and is entitled to negotiate separately about its conditions of service in the light of its special circumstances. The complexities of these circumstances are a matter in the first place for the Establishments division of the Department most closely concerned. Tradition and personality have some chance to play a part here, but there are strong forces making for standardisation. Civil Service salaries are a matter of public knowledge, and individuals are bound to find analogies between themselves and others whom they regard as more or less their equals in skill and responsibility. The associations of the smaller classes generally affiliate for their own protection to one or other of the large staff associations described in Chapter 9; and the discussion of analogies is institutionalised in these larger bodies and in the machinery of Whitley Councils. Analogies are also attractive to the Treasury, since it can best exercise an influence upon the maze of separate specialisations by watching how their conditions are related to one another. Hence there is steady pressure for assimilation, on the one hand to the great non-specialist classes, on the other hand to the larger groups of specialists described earlier in this chapter.

Secondly, there is some tendency to recognise another general category, that of the Inspectorates, alongside the general classes and the specialist classes. There are about fifty of these, with staffs ranging from several hundred to less than half a dozen: they cover many different professions, and their terms of service and careers vary a great deal. Nevertheless, they are grouped together in the Civil Service Staff Statistics (2,893 of them at 1 July 1955), and there is good reason for this, because the device of Inspectorates is a characteristic of the British system, perhaps the most definite mark left by the administrative theories of the Benthamite period.

Inspectors may deal either with other public authorities (mainly local authorities) or with private firms, voluntary associations, and private persons, or with all of them. In all cases they have large powers of entry and of access to documents; these are given by statute for limited purposes, but are often couched in very general terms. They also have effective sanctions at their disposal, through their influence on central grants to local authorities and their power to recommend the prosecution of private individuals in the courts. The great Inspectorates have used this authority for a century and more almost without suspicion that they could in any circumstances be a danger to civil liberty. Most of them have created a tradition that in some sense they stand between the public and the central Departments. To the public—private persons and local authorities— they are advisers on how to work satisfactorily (and to improve standards) within regulations which often seem absurdly rigid. For the central Departments they are often the most effective point of contact with the problems of a service in operation. Some services are now organised by Departments themselves through the Executive Class, but many are still provided through other authorities or by regulating employers of labour and other private persons. In that case the burden of responsibility is divided between a headquarters service, an Inspectorate, and the operating person or authority. There are advantages in this awkward arrangement, which is related on the one hand to the special co-ordinating role of the Administrative Class, on the other hand to the traditions of private enterprise and local government. But it is a clumsy form of administration, which can be made to work only if the Inspectorates are successful in keeping a foot in all camps, central and local, public and private.

5. The Post Office

This account of the structure of Service classes would be incomplete without some reference to the Post Office, since it employs some 327,000 people (apart from 22,000 sub-postmasters) of whom 248,000 are 'non-industrial' civil servants. The statistics for 1 July 1954 are given in Table XXII (the figures for 1 July 1955 are not available). It will be seen that a very large part of this huge staff are in classes peculiar to the Post Office, and there is little interchange with the rest of the Service.

The peculiarities of Post Office organisation arise from the fact that it combines three different functions. It is one of the ancient Revenue Departments, and has a long tradition of its own as a Crown

THE SPECIALIST CLASSES 117

service: it provides a great variety of common services for other Departments: and it runs three rather different industries—a letter and parcels delivery service, a telecommunications service, and a Savings Bank. A little will be said of the second function in Chapter 17; but the rest is outside our present scope, and it is therefore impossible to give a balanced account of the staff problems of the Post Office. We wish only to refer to a number of points where these problems are linked with problems of the Service as a whole.

TABLE XXII

Post Office Staff at 1 July 1954

(Source: Post Office Memorandum to Priestley Commission: Evidence, 20th Day)

Treasury Classes (general and specialist)	36,000
Small Departmental grades	5,000
Manipulative grades	207,500
Engineering, supplies, and motor transport grades	72,500
	321,000[1]

[1] To which must be added about 6,000 industrial employees not within the Commission's terms of reference.

The 'engineering, etc., *rank-and-file* grades' consist largely of men recruited without outside qualifications and trained within the Department. There are various grades according to skill, but the top level, that of Technical Officer, might perhaps be rated as equivalent in pay and status to that of foreman in a highly skilled trade. Promotion beyond this is somewhat restricted, but there is limited competition for entry to the supervising grade of Assistant Engineer, and Post Office men have a chance in the open competition for the basic *professional* grade of Executive Engineer. This grade ranks with the basic grade of the Works Group, and from it are largely drawn the engineers who run Post Office telecommunications, with the Engineer-in-Chief of the Post Office at their head. There is thus a line of promotion from the bottom to the top of the Department on the technical side, but it is a very narrow one, since only five Executive Engineers came from the Department out of thirty-five appointed in 1953. This is a situation which has given rise to a good deal of friction between staff associations, at the critical point where the rank-and-file grades meet and overlap with the directing staff.

The so-called *manipulative* grades fall into a number of categories, each of which has its own problems. Postmen, sorters, and male telephone operators (about 115,000) are normally recruited relatively late in life after doing some other job—there is a special preference for ex-Regulars—and are granted establishment on the basis of efficiency in the job and simple tests. Women (mainly young women) are recruited as telephone operators (about 38,000), and are trained within the Department for a job comparable in status and prospects to that of shorthand typist. Boys used to be recruited as telegraph boys, and one of the old problems of the Post Office was that of finding a decent career for them after 18. The Post Office 'messenger boy' is now almost extinct, but there is still competitive entry to the grade of Postal and Telegraph Officer (about 22,000); this grade does most of the clerical work of the Department, both in local Post Offices and in large central establishments. 25 per cent. of the places are filled by open competition between 16 and 18 at about the Ordinary Level of G.C.E., 75 per cent. go to entrants from other manipulative grades, up to the age of 45.

Each of these 'manipulative' groups has supervising grades for jobs carrying considerable local responsibility, up to the level of about £1,000 a year, but promotion is slow, and the most difficult questions (here as on the technical side) are about the possibility of advance within the Department. The Postal and Telegraph Officers enter at about the same standard of education as do Clerical Officers, and resent the suggestion that they are to be classified with cleaners and messengers as 'manipulative'. More substantially, they find a slight but marked differential in favour of the Clerical Class, a fact which proves embarrassing, since a number of Clerical Officers are taken into the Post Office for work in sections dealing with establishments, accommodation, audit, and so on, and in large central offices they may be working alongside Postal and Telegraph Officers on jobs which seem similar. Finally, there is the problem of further promotion, which leads through the Executive Class. The managing staff of the Post Office on this side of the business carry titles peculiar to the Department—Telephone Manager, Postal Controller, Head Postmaster, and so on—and they have almost all grown up in its service. But the Departmental class to which they belong is closely linked to the general Executive Class, and their posts fit into the hierarchy of that class. So does the process of recruitment, which is partly by open or limited competition, partly by promotion; and the lower ranks include general Executive as well as Departmental class officers. An ambitious young man may go a long way up this hierarchy, since the Executive Class handle jobs of great responsibility in local management and have a fair chance of promotion to top jobs at headquarters.

At present (in 1957) the Director-General of the Post Office (its Permanent Secretary) is an engineer, but the directing Board includes eight Administrative Class civil servants as well as three other engineers, and promotion into these high Administrative Class posts is open to members of the Executive Class who have grown up in the service of the Post Office. Some University Arts graduates pass direct into the Office as Assistant Principals, a few more enter in the Executive grade of Assistant Postal Controller, and their opportunities of promotion are good. But there is a general shortage of men able to carry the burden of what are in effect jobs of business management, and there is a career open to talent both on the lay and on the engineering sides of the Department. In some respects the Post Office is a self-contained empire, a profession in itself.

FOR REFERENCE

Institution of Professional Civil Servants: *Post War Reconstruction* (1944).
The Scientific Civil Service: Reorganisation and Recruitment during the Reconstruction Period. Cmd. 6679, 1945. (Includes the Report of the Barlow Committee.)
Report of the Committee on the Organisation, Remuneration and Conditions of Service of Officers employed in Government Legal Departments (Barlow). 1944. (Not published by H.M.S.O. until 1949.)
Reports of Committees on the Organisation, Structure, and Remuneration of:
    (1) *the Works Group of Professional Civil Servants* (Gardiner). 1951.
    (2) *the Civil Service Medical Staffs* (Howitt). 1951.
    (3) *the Professional Accountant Class* (Gardiner). 1952.
Supplement to Introductory Factual Memorandum on the Civil Service (Medical and Legal Staffs) (presented by the Treasury to the Priestley Commission). H.M.S.O. June 1954.
Royal Commission on the Civil Service 1953-55 (Priestley). Report. Cmd. 9613, 1955. Chs. XIII and XIV, and Minutes of Evidence, *passim.*
Royal Commission on the Civil Service 1953-55 (Priestley). Memoranda submitted by Institution of Professional Civil Servants and Society of Technical Civil Servants (Evidence, 12th and 13th Days).
H.M. Treasury: *Government Statistical Services* (1953).

Books on the origins of the system of Inspectorates include:
    J. LEESE: *Personalities and Power in English Education* (1950).
    M. W. THOMAS: *Early Factory Legislation* (1948).

On the working of present-day inspection, see:
    J. HARRIS: *Government Inspection Services in Great Britain* (1956).

CHAPTER EIGHT

PROMOTION AND TRAINING

The hope, and not the fact, of advancement is the spur to industry.
... Public servants therefore, like racehorses, should be well-fed with
reward, but not to fatness.—Sir HENRY TAYLOR: *The Statesman.*

1. INTRODUCTORY

THE instinct of the administrator is to seek a free hand in the selection, training, remuneration, and promotion of his staff. He must have confidence in his own skill in selecting recruits from those who offer themselves, in shaping this raw material to fit its tasks, in offering the right inducements for extra effort, and in choosing men for further advancement: and skill is of no value without power to act.

We have seen in preceding chapters the limits imposed on selection and on remuneration by the general character of the Civil Service: and there are also limits on the negative power to enforce improvement by sanctions, as will be seen in Chapter 9. These restrictions increase the importance of efficiency in training and in promotion, and a great deal of thought has been given to both these subjects. But here too the organisers of the Civil Service work within limits set by the nature of their organisation.

2. PROMOTION

It will be convenient to deal first with promotion, since its problems and procedure are similar throughout the Service and can be explained briefly. The creation of a 'career service' in any field of activity implies a kind of bargain between the employer and his staff, and the bargain is much the same whether the career is in administration or in a fighting service, in private business, in teaching, or even in the Church. The employee literally devotes his life to the service: he is wholly committed to it, effectively excludes himself from the possibility of other employment, undertakes to give loyal and competent work. The employer on his side guarantees security and adequate reward for faithful and competent service: he must treat the service as a whole, and must balance the advantages of giving incentives to special merit against the danger of causing discontent and inefficiency among those who are not promoted.[1]

This balance of considerations leads to the vague but important conception of the 'average career', which is prominent in all argument and negotiation about Civil Service organisation. The conception is of particular importance where staff associations are strong and vocal, as in Britain, since associations represent the average man rather than the exceptions, and are mainly interested in securing the best 'average career': but it arises everywhere, since there is always strong corporate feeling among a 'career' staff, even when this is not expressed in formal organisation. Against this corporate feeling there pulls the desire of those at the top to promote the men whom they think will best advance their policy and the long-term interests of the Service. This is what Admiral Lord Fisher, a famous First Sea Lord, meant by saying that 'favouritism is the secret of successful administration'; but favouritism, the selection for promotion of men as individuals, is only successful if it does not destroy the corporate loyalty of the Service.

The general principles of Civil Service procedure are laid down in two reports of the Promotions Committee of the National Whitley Council (1922 and 1938), further modified in March 1954. These agreements are not mandatory, and there is considerable variation in detail from one Department to another; but the general position may be summed up under four heads:

(i) *Staff Reporting.* If promotion in a large service is to be otherwise than by pure seniority, there must be some means of standardising reports about the work of individuals, since there can be no fair choice except on a basis of fair comparison. Standardised reporting was introduced for the first time in 1922; its basis is that a controlling officer should report each year on all those immediately subordinate to him, under a limited number of headings such as Knowledge, Personality, Force of Character, Judgement, Power of taking Responsibility, and so on. Under each heading there are a number of grades, and if an individual is given a rating in the lowest grade it is usual to inform him, so that he may have an opportunity to protest or to mend his ways. Reports are countersigned by the officer one grade senior to the reporting officer, and then go to the Establishments division concerned, which puts them with the indivi-

[1] As Trollope (a career civil servant in the Post Office) put it: '*Detur digno* is a maxim which will make men do their best to merit rewards; every man can find courage within his heart to be worthy; but *detur digniori* is a fearful law for such a profession as the Civil Service. What worth can make a man safe against the possible greater worth which will come treading on his heels?' (*The Three Clerks*, 1858.)

dual's personal file, so that they are available for consideration by a Promotion Board or when a posting is being considered.

Senior staff are exempt from this procedure, but the appropriate salary level for exemption is determined by each Department in consultation with the Staff Side. In any event, promotion reports are of substantial importance only for the main grades in which there are large numbers of officers. Promotion for the minor and manipulative grades depends in practice largely on seniority: at higher levels officers being considered for promotion are well known personally to those who take the decisions, and standardised reporting cannot prevail against direct acquaintance.

The form of report still varies a good deal between Departments and classes, but it is the same for all officers in one class in one Department. This does not go far to solve the problem of standardisation, since there is no certain means of assessing performance objectively in work above the level of mechanical routine. Some allowance can, however, be made for the idiosyncrasies of individual reporting officers, since these become well known to Establishments divisions; and allowance can also be made for the general tendency to 'bunch' assessments round the average, avoiding exceptionally good or bad marks.

(ii) *The highest administrative posts* (except in the Foreign Office) are filled by the Minister concerned with the consent of the Prime Minister, who acts on the advice of the Head of the Home Civil Service (see Chapter 4). Much of the responsibility rests in practice on the last-named, but it is safe to say that he would not dream of acting about the appointment of a new Permanent Secretary without consulting the political head of the Department concerned through the existing Permanent Secretary, or about a lesser appointment without consulting the Permanent Secretary. Appointments are also limited by the traditions of the Service: it is rare now to appoint anyone to a high post from outside the Service, and weight is given to seniority, if other things are equal. The Head of the Home Civil Service has great power over its future, but exercises this power under the eye of a critical (though discreet) Civil Service public.

(iii) *Posts at the level of Assistant Secretary and above* in all classes, including specialist classes, are filled by the Minister of the Department concerned on the advice of his Permanent Secretary. The latter acts informally, as part of his responsibility for the good management of his Department: but he consults his Principal Establishments Officer, and in making specialist appointments he usually takes the advice of the senior member of that particular class within his Department. For instance, in promotions to senior posts in the Education Inspectorate the Permanent Secretary of the Ministry of Education is much in the hands of the Chief Inspector of Education. Some weight is always given to relative seniority, but the decision about this lies in each case within the discretion of the appointing officer.

(iv) *Promotion Boards.* There is no individual responsibility for promotion below this level, and the great mass of cases are dealt with by Departmental Promotion Boards. The composition of the Board depends on the seniority of the appointment being dealt with; usually the Principal Establishments Officer or his representative is in the chair, assisted by two other senior members of the staff, one of whom is concerned with the grade of staff in question, and the other is independent. The Staff Side is not represented on the Board: the policy of the staff associations is to refuse to discuss the merits of individual claims to promotion, but Staff Side representatives have the right to appear before the Board to ensure that agreed general rules have been strictly observed, a matter to which they attach considerable importance.

Procedure varies between Departments and between classes, but is normally somewhat as follows. A promotion can be made only when vacancies occur, and the candidates eligible are all those within a 'range of promotion' which is defined on grounds of seniority. The choice may be made solely on reports and records: or the candidates may also be interviewed. It is in some Departments the rule that if a candidate within the range of promotion has been passed over a number of times (for instance three times) he is not considered again. Generally, there is a procedure for appeal by which a candidate who feels himself aggrieved may put his case either before a special Board or before the next meeting of the ordinary Promotion Board.

Opportunities of promotion are naturally affected by the number of vacancies which occur in a Department taken in relation to the number of candidates of given seniority. One object of the creation of 'general service' classes is to give the Treasury a chance to even out these inequalities. No Department would promote an Executive Class officer to an administrative post without consulting the Treasury: and informal arrangements appear to exist for reviewing promotions at the higher levels in the 'general service' classes of specialists. Promotion 'pooling' for the advancement of Clerical Officers into the Executive Class has been discussed in Chapter 6.

There is some general pattern in these arrangements. The higher the post, the wider the discretion in promotion: and the greater the attention paid to the interests of the Service as a whole rather than to those of one Department. At the lowest levels promotion is Departmental and automatic: at the highest it is national and selective. There is room for criticism of the system as it operates for particular individuals and Departments, but on the whole it is defensible (and must be defended) because there is no alternative. It is, however, a remediable defect that in normal times it favours those who secure early promotion out of the lower classes: if a man or woman fails to set foot on the promotion ladder early, his later progress may be slow and frustrating because it is determined by rather strict rules, which concede nothing to those who mature late. The Service is bound to operate under the rule expressed by the Priestley Commission, that 'outstanding individual merit can be recognised only by accelerated promotion': but it is difficult to accelerate promotion, and there is certainly talent in the middle ranks which does not find its full scope within the Service.

3. Training

It is less easy to find a pattern in Civil Service training, partly because it varies greatly according to Department and class, partly because it has been less controversial and has not therefore been standardised through a process of negotiation. This is the latest of the staff functions to be given a central organisation in the Treasury; it would have been almost impossible before 1939 to say that there was a general policy about training at all. Some Departments, such as the Post Office and the Inland Revenue, had very strong training organisations, others provided virtually no training except by experience on the job. Training became an issue of importance during the war, partly because outside critics brought experience of personnel management to bear on the Civil Service, and partly because the Service itself soon realised the value of well-organised training as an instrument for assimilating great numbers of not very competent amateurs, and for switching staff quickly from one job to another. This change of atmosphere led to the appointment in February 1943 of a committee under the chairmanship of the Financial Secretary to the Treasury, and its report, the Assheton Committee Report, has been the basis of policy since the war. Its recommendations are unexciting and even platitudinous, but they represent a substantial common measure of agreement within the Service, and have largely been implemented within the limits set by demands for economy. Training is particularly vulnerable to cuts, since its results are not always measurable or immediate.

Training Organisation

There are three main elements in the organisation for training:

First, there has since 1946 been a Training and Education Division in the Treasury headed either by a Principal or by an Assistant Secretary (at present an Assistant Secretary is in charge) and linked with the Organisation and Methods Division under an Under Secretary, one of three Under Secretaries concerned with Establishments and Machinery of Government. The main job of the division is to co-ordinate and direct the training activities of Departments, and financial proposals for expenditure on new training schemes come to it in the first instance for approval. It is thus in a better position to control than to encourage: but it can do a great deal to stimulate Departments, when the climate of opinion is favourable, by means of personal contacts and the circulation of general information about training methods. It is itself responsible for running a limited number of training courses: these include conferences for officials holding 'managerial' positions, the 'induction' of new Assistant Principals, courses in teaching methods for Departmental instructors, and courses for groups of staff (such as superintendents of typists, personal secretaries, messengers, welfare officers) who are not numerous enough in any single Department to justify separate Departmental courses.

Secondly, all the more important Departments now have Training Sections, usually directed by a Principal or by an Executive Class officer of about the same standing, and controlled by the Principal Establishments Officer. In smaller Departments the job may only justify the full-time appointment of a H.E.O.; or it may be combined with other work. These Training Sections are primarily responsible for running Departmental training schools and for providing teaching material as required by the changing needs of their Departments. Departments with large staffs outside headquarters may also have regional training officers, who look after regional training schools and supervise training on the job.

Thirdly, in some Departments with large technical and industrial staffs, such as the Post Office, the Admiralty, and the Ministry of Supply, there are technical divisions which provide their own training officers. This is particularly important where technical innovation is rapid, since there is a regular need for revision courses to accompany the introduction of new equipment. This sort of course is generally outside the scope of Departmental Training Sections, which are primarily concerned with the training of non-specialists.

There is co-operation with the staff through the Joint Committee on Training of the National Whitley Council, on which the Treasury Training Officer sits as Official Side Secretary: and the Whitley Councils of the larger Departments generally have training committees of their own. The Civil Service Council for Further Education is a 'semi-official' body set up in 1920 under the auspices of the National Whitley Council and reconstituted at the end of the Second World War. It has a governing council consisting of representatives of the Official and Staff Sides of the National Whitley Council, with co-opted members representing the Universities, the W.E.A., and local education authorities; and it is served by a full-time National Secretary, a seconded civil servant, whose salary and office expenses are met from public funds. There are corresponding Regional Committees in each 'standard' region (see Chapter 16), and each of these has its own secretary. This is an elaborate organisation, but its role is somewhat limited, as it does not provide educational or training facilities itself, and has no funds with which to subsidise the activities of other bodies or to assist civil servants who participate in them. Its main function is to serve as a forum for discussion with Universities, the W.E.A., local education authorities, and others about the sort of facilities for part-time specialist or general education which would be of value to civil servants; to encourage new ventures and to give publicity within the Service about educational opportunities; and to see that the way is smoothed for individual civil servants to take full advantage of special assistance given by their Departments towards education outside the Service.

The staff associations take some part in training on their own account by sponsoring training in trade union work for their officers (full-time and part-time) and by maintaining relations with such bodies as the W.E.A. and the adult residential colleges. A few of them give more specific assistance in preparation for Departmental examinations: for instance, the Inland Revenue Staff Federation provides correspondence courses and publishes text-books on the work of the Department. But this is exceptional: the associations are mainly concerned to press quietly and steadily, through the Whitley machinery, for the provision of adequate training facilities by Departments for individuals who wish to take advantage of them.

Forms of Training

Form cannot satisfactorily be separated from content, and this is baffling in its variety. The Assheton Committee's classification into vocational training, background training, and further education (which is that generally adopted) is not very convenient as a framework for a brief summary; and the heads chosen here are Orientation, Operations, Specialisation, and General Education. There is some overlapping between these categories, but they serve to illustrate the great range and variety of problems covered by the word 'training'.

(i) *Orientation.* To do his job well an official must have some notion of its place in a larger context. This is true even at the level of routine: some clerical operations may be so simple as to require only mechanical skill in performance, yet they will be done better if those concerned have some picture of themselves as part of an organisation seeking larger ends. This matter of *morale* is particularly important in the Civil Service, since no way has been found of introducing piece-work rates or incentive bonuses for non-industrial civil servants.

The most obvious place for this sort of training is on first entry into the Service or into a particular class or Department. Practice still varies a good deal between classes and from one Department to another: but it is now usual for some training to be given on 'induction'. In its simplest form this may be no more than the issue of the Treasury's *Handbook for the New Civil Servant*, with a brief talk, followed by an initial period of planned work under supervision. For clerical and executive entrants there are rather more elaborate courses in most Departments, including some general explanation of the history and work of the office and its place in government, as well as a period of supervised work. Assistant Principals entering the Administrative Class are on probation for two years, and an attempt is made to treat this seriously as a period of training: the appointment is not confirmed unless the Central Probation Board of the Civil Service Commission is satisfied with the entrant's progress during this period. In fact, very few Assistant Principals fail to obtain confirmation of appointment; a rather larger number decide that they have chosen the wrong career and withdraw during probation. Entrants go first to the Department in which they are to serve, and the Department is primarily responsible for planning a period which will give them effective training in the job by systematic movement from one division to another within the office. After about three months they are gathered together for a fortnight's course, called the Junior Administrative Course, which is run under the auspices of the Treasury. A group of about twenty students is assembled, and an effort is made to mix open competition and limited competition entrants with a few scientific officers and others. The course consists partly of seminar work and projects designed to bring members of the course together in discussion: partly of talks and visits covering a variety of topics related to the work of government. This is a very limited experiment compared with the two-year period of intensive training provided by the French *École Nationale d'Administration* for similar entrants; those in authority have always refused to accept proposals for the creation of a Civil Service Staff College, largely on the strong ground that it would tend to emphasise the isolation of the Service from the rest of national life. Nevertheless the Junior Administrative Course represents a break with the tradition of informal induction to the class mainly responsible for co-ordination within the Service, a tradition of 'sink or swim' which was adequate in a period where the pace was slower and administration less complex.

Civil servants are not as persistent attenders at conferences as are members of some other professions; opportunities vary a good deal according to the nature of the job, and leading officials find it difficult to speak freely at public gatherings lest they may be thought to commit their Departments. But in most Departments there are plenty of opportunities for those who are interested to meet for general discussions of problems affecting their work. Departments generally prefer not to sponsor such conferences themselves, but they support outside bodies such as the Royal Institute of Public Administration, and the Treasury has conducted one or two experimental gatherings to give an opportunity for senior administrators of various branches of the Service to discuss topics of general interest in a methodical way.

The Assheton Committee strongly recommended that one of the best ways to prepare a young administrator for the top posts in the Service was to give a 'sabbatical year' in the period between 30 and 40, so that he might make a complete break with Civil Service work and gain experience of academic research, or of different forms of public and private administration in this country, or of government in the Commonwealth and in foreign countries. This is accepted by the Treasury, and probably about a dozen Administrative Class civil servants are absent in this way each year. The number is not larger mainly because of factors which make it difficult for a man at this stage of his career to leave his family and the work of his Department.

(ii) *Operations.* The war of 1939-45 was a period in which large numbers of people were uprooted from their usual jobs and trained hastily for some other employment, in the armed forces or in production. The result was that an enormous impetus was given to the study of training: administrators became familiar with the idea that complicated operations could be broken down into simpler component parts, and that these components could be methodically taught in a surprisingly short time. The Civil Service was relatively slow in seeing the application of this to office work, but it found in the end that the combination of work study with training was an essential tool in managing large numbers of inexperienced clerks in jobs where there were frequent changes of policy and procedure.

It is mainly in this field that training has become an established tool of administration with its own technicalities and expertise. Its earliest applications were in the Post Office, and in dealing with controls such as food rationing, which involved handling very large numbers of individual cases; but it has been extended to other large-scale jobs in Departments such as the Ministry of Pensions and National Insurance and the Ministry of Labour and National Service. Training of this kind may be used to equip a group of officers for work in contact with the public in the Post Office or other local offices; or in the opening of a new service, very well described by Mr. H. V. Rhodes, Director of Establishments and Organisation at the Ministry of National Insurance, in his book *Setting up a New Government Department*; or in preparing an office to move smoothly from an old procedure to a new one.

At a higher level there are courses for supervisors, inspired by the Training Within Industry (T.W.I.) scheme. These are sometimes provided by the Department, sometimes by the Treasury, which has now accumulated a good deal of knowledge about the use of training in day-to-day operations.

(iii) *Specialisation.* In Chapter 7 we noticed how the structure of the Service has been affected by the fact that the British government has traditionally hired its specialists in the open market. Most European countries took the initiative in setting up schools to train specialists for government service and for the several needs of the country, either through the Universities (most of which are state institutions) or through separate technical schools. British government has not created great state institutions like the *École des Mines* or the *École des Ponts et Chaussées* in France, although it has (ever since the Great Exhibition of 1851) done a good deal to encourage private and local initiative in training technologists.

This general principle admits various exceptions:

(*a*) There are a few specialist classes which take in entrants without a special qualification, but require that they should obtain one in order to be eligible for establishment or promotion. For instance, actuaries must qualify as Fellows of the Institute of Actuaries or of the Faculty of Actuaries; Estate Duty Examiners must obtain an LL.B. degree; at a much lower level, photographers must obtain the appropriate technical qualification. In some Departments, for instance in the D.S.I.R. and in the planning grades of the Ministry of Housing and Local Government, outside training for young entrants is encouraged though it is not compulsory. In other classes a man may require a degree or other certificate to enable him to compete for entry to the class above: for instance, to rise from Experimental Officer to Scientific Officer. In the first two cases, Departments are usually generous in paying fees and granting day release with pay in order to attend classes; in the third case, official aid is limited to granting release with pay to sit for examinations and the opportunity to leave early to attend evening lectures. In each case the Department must be satisfied that the qualification is specifically relevant to the work of the Department and is likely to increase the officer's efficiency.

(b) There are some cases, mainly concerned with social work, in which the Department concerned goes somewhat farther than this, by arranging the award of grants or scholarships to people intending to pursue a particular line of work, for instance as probation officers, child-care workers, psychiatric social workers, or hospital almoners. Arrangements vary in each instance: but in general there is a division of responsibility for training between the Department and some outside body such as a University. Of those trained in this way a few become civil servants, but most are employed by other bodies, such as local authorities, which are not in a position to provide adequate training facilities themselves.

(c) More commonly, the Department trains its own men and submits them to stiff examinations for promotion. On the technical side, there are the Post Office Engineers, the Royal Corps of Naval Constructors, the Cartographic Draughtsmen; among classes linked to the Executive Class there are the Tax Inspectors, the Valuers and the Collectors of the Board of Inland Revenue, the higher staff of the Board of Customs and Excise, the District Auditors under the Ministry of Housing and Local Government. All these examinations are severe intellectual tests of a rather narrow kind; those who have passed them earn respect outside the Service, but Departmental training schools are not open to outside students, and confer no recognised professional qualification. (As usual there is an exception: a few private students are admitted on payment of fees to the Naval Constructors course at the Royal Naval College, Greenwich.)

(d) There are other Departments, such as the Ministry of Pensions and National Insurance, the National Assistance Board, and the Ministry of Labour, which require from officers at executive level a certain amount of specialised knowledge. It is important that they should have an exact grasp of Departmental regulations and practice over a fairly wide field: but the content of this special study is nothing like as great as is required in the Departments which have promotion examinations. For instance, a newly appointed National Insurance Inspector (who has generally had some previous experience in the Department) is given special training for eight or nine weeks; Ministry of Labour officers have shorter periods in Departmental training schools at various stages of their careers. Departments of this type are largely concerned with the social services, and one of their most difficult problems is to give their officers an adequate background of knowledge about the structure of the services and about social problems in general. A full training in social work, such as is given in the Universities, is certainly not necessary, but it is essential that local officers who carry a good deal of independent responsibility should be able to see their own work in perspective. There is no doubt that such teaching can best be done by people outside the Service, and most of these Departments have at different times invited Universities to arrange special courses for groups of officers and have arranged day release for attendance at classes. These classes have over a period included quite a high proportion of the officials in the grades concerned: a much smaller number of officials have been given release with full pay to take a complete course in social work as University students. This procedure is experimental, but suggests that it may be possible to organise the social service Ministries so that each has on its staff a few officials specially trained as social workers, and a much larger number who have a more general knowledge of the field as a whole.

(iv) *General Education.* This experiment leads naturally to the question of facilities for general education, a matter on which policy is still somewhat uncertain. In principle, the Treasury is prepared to authorise day release with pay, and payment of fees, for training specifically related to the work of a Department; it recognises the relevance of background training if it has specific vocational value for a particular job or for work in particular Departments; it encourages but will not spend public money on the general education of civil servants. For instance, it encourages young men and women to attend local authority classes in their own time to prepare themselves for promotion examinations and to take external degrees or other general courses. If a young civil servant secures an award which will enable him to attend a University full-time for three or four years, most Departments are generous in granting release without pay and reinstatement afterwards without loss of seniority. But the Treasury is not prepared to subsidise such education as Civil Service training; and it is anxious to ensure that formal qualifications so acquired should be given no weight in promotion except through the regular machinery of competitive examination.

There is much to be said for this policy, but it leads to some anomalies because the idea of general education is very vague and raises large questions. It is not easy to distinguish between general education and the sort of 'orientation' which is valuable to those in the upper ranks of the Service: for instance, the Treasury sends about twenty to thirty civil servants a year (of the rank of Principal and its equivalent) to the Administrative Staff College at Henley, which prides itself on giving general education by mixing students of different types, and does not give special training in administrative techniques. It is equally difficult to distinguish between general education and the sort of general knowledge of political economy and social organisation which is essential for the making of policy in certain Departments. There is therefore some pressure on the Treasury either to induce it to be more generous in supporting general education or to recognise as 'special' (in the sense of being relevant to Departmental work) the sort of general education about the contemporary world which is given in University courses on economics, political science, sociology, public and social administration. The cost of a more generous policy would be trivial, but the point of principle is of some importance to the structure of the Service. The tradition has been, and still is, that a man who has been educated in classics or mathematics or English or modern languages or any other first-rate University subject can (if he has sufficient ability) pick up for himself all the knowledge that he needs about the contemporary world. Students trained in social studies have an equal chance, but no better chance than others, in the examinations for the Administrative and Executive classes. A change in policy about general education would imply reconsideration of these more fundamental questions.

FOR REFERENCE

Reports of the Promotions Committee of the National Whitley Council, 1922 (Treasury Circular 11/22, 26 April 1922), and 1938 (Treasury Circular 22/38, 28 September 1938).

Report of the Committee on the Training of Civil Servants (Assheton). Cmd. 6525, 1944.

Regulations relating to the Granting of Financial and other Assistance for External Training. Treasury Establishments Circular E.O.C. 104/47, 1947.

H. WALKER: *Training Public Employees in Great Britain* (New York, 1935).

Royal Institute of Public Administration: (*a*) *Staff Reports in the Public Services* (1936). (*b*) *Training Managers in the Public Services* (1955).
R. MENZIES and E. ANSTEY: *Staff Reporting* (1949).
F. J. TICHNER: *Modern Staff Training* (1952).
E. ANSTEY and E. MERCER: *Interviewing for the Selection of Staff* (1956).
S. A. BAILEY: 'Training the Technician in Administrative Practices', *Public Administration*, Vol. XXXIII, p. 375.

CHAPTER NINE

STAFF ASSOCIATIONS AND NEGOTIATING PROCEDURE

In government, it is good to use men of one rank equally; for to countenance some extraordinarily is to make them insolent, and the most discontented, because they may claim a due.—BACON: *Of Followers and Friends.*

1. INTRODUCTORY

THE matters discussed in this and in the following chapter are closely interrelated. As servants of the Crown, civil servants are subject to a number of disabilities, and many important matters concerning their rights are determined by their official superiors and not by judicial procedure. Their position is, however, much stronger in practice than in law, since they are organised in strong and well-staffed associations, which are recognised as effective and responsible spokesmen for their members, and since all general matters affecting conditions of service are negotiated through an elaborate procedure which ensures consultation with representatives of every grade of staff affected.

2. STAFF ASSOCIATIONS

The first effective Civil Service trade unions were those founded in the Post Office in the 1880s and 1890s, including the Postal Telegraph Clerks' Association (1881), the Postal Clerks' Association (1887), and the Postmen's Federation (1891). Departments were at first reluctant to grant staff the right to act jointly in negotiation with their employer, the Crown, and there was some victimisation of organisers in the early days. After much friction the right of collective bargaining was conceded in the Post Office by Sir Austen Chamberlain when he was Postmaster General in 1902, and by his successor Sydney Buxton in 1906, and this precedent was gradually followed by other Departments. This was the formative period of trade union organisation for 'white-collar' workers in all the public services, and associations grew largely through the federation of smaller and weaker unions. For instance, the National Association of Local Government Officers[1] was founded in this way in 1905, the Civil Service Clerical Association (known originally as the Assistant Clerks' Association) in 1903, the Clerical and Administrative Workers' Union in 1906, the Institution of Professional Civil Servants in 1919.

At first the Civil Service staff associations were weaker than their ambitious titles might suggest, and senior officials in the Departments regarded them with some suspicion even when recognition was formally conceded. The 'Whitley' machinery for joint consultation, which is described below, was established in 1919 largely through a skilful manœuvre by the staff leaders, who shamed the government into accepting for its own staff the prescription which it was recommending to other employers as the remedy for industrial strife. There has been no break in the continued existence of Civil Service Whitley machinery since 1919 (as there has been in that of the negotiating machinery for officials in local government), but the procedure was at first very formal and the gain to the associations was more in prestige than in the practice of joint consultation.

Official suspicion continued during the period of industrial disputes which culminated in the General Strike of 1926, and the Trades Disputes Act of 1927 introduced legal limitations on Civil Service staff organisation somewhat similar to those imposed on police organisation by the Police Act of 1919. The 1927 Act made it illegal for any established civil servant (industrial or non-industrial) to join an organisation concerned with conditions of service, unless it was confined to Crown servants, was not associated with any organisation outside the Service, was not concerned with any political object, and was not affiliated to any political party. Detailed regulations were to be made by the Treasury, and the penalty for a breach of them was to be first a warning, then dismissal.

These provisions disappeared entirely when the Trades Disputes Act was repealed in 1946, and there are now no restrictions except those imposed by the good sense of civil servants. Seven Civil Service unions with a total membership of 428,000 belong to the T.U.C., and one of them (the Union of Post Office Workers) is affiliated to the Labour Party. In addition, established civil servants working in industrial jobs are now eligible to join the union appropriate to their trade (unestablished industrials were never debarred). Many of them do so, but no separate record is kept of the number involved.

The complexity of Civil Service trade unionism corresponds to the complexity of the system of classes and grades, and no summary can do it justice. It may be fair to say that at first there was a tendency

[1] In 1948 renamed the National and Local Government Officers Association.

for each class, and for each grade in a class, and for the section of that grade in each Department, to form an association to represent the joint interests of its members; that this multiplicity of small organisations was a source of weakness in negotiation; that there has therefore been a steady movement towards larger associations and federations with full-time staff and adequate financial resources; and that this consolidation has played an important part in the integration of the Service as a whole. Some brief information about a few of the most important associations will illustrate these points.

(i) *Non-specialist classes:* The *Administrative Class* act in day-to-day negotiation as the 'employers' of the rest of the Civil Service. Members of the Class constitute the main body of the 'Official' Side as against the 'Staff' Side on the National Whitley Council and in most Departmental Whitley Councils, representing 'Establishments' in the Treasury and in each Department, and they carry the principal burden of responsibility for advising Ministers about Civil Service pay and conditions. In consequence, they have been slow to organise themselves effectively for negotiation on their own behalf, and the 'First Division Association' (as it is still called) is even today a relatively weak body. It has about 3,000 members, a rather small income, and no full-time officers. It now takes its place on the Staff Side in negotiations, but it does not play a leading part.

The most important organisation of *the Executive Class* is the Society of Civil Servants, which has about 38,500 members drawn from the main Executive Class and from some of the smaller Departmental classes related to it, and includes also some Higher Clerical Officers. It has an income of about £100,000 a year, and has seven full-time officers. It is not affiliated to the T.U.C. or to the Labour Party, but a former General Secretary, Mr. E. C. Redhead, was returned to Parliament in February 1956 as Labour member for West Walthamstow, without financial support from the Society.

The Society works closely with organisations representing Departmental Executive classes. The Inland Revenue Staff Federation is a strong body with over 35,000 members, grouping smaller associations which represent various levels of staff, and over Executive Class business it collaborates with the Society. It is affiliated to the T.U.C., but not to the Labour Party: but its General Secretary, Mr. Douglas Houghton, has been Labour M.P. for Sowerby since 1950, without financial support from his association. The corresponding grades in Customs and Excise are similarly organised in the 'Customs and Excise Group of Departmental Associations' (about 7,000 strong), which includes the Customs and Excise Federation, the Customs and Excise Controlling Grade Association, and some others; but this group tends to go its own way in negotiation, on the ground that its working conditions are very unlike those in other 'executive' Departments. The Ministry of Labour, another large 'executive' Department, has no staff federation: the higher grades are represented by the Association of Officers of the Ministry of Labour (2,900 members), working closely with the Society of Civil Servants, the lower grades by the Ministry of Labour Staff Association. There is some overlap between the scope of the two associations: the latter is naturally the larger (11,600 members), and it is affiliated to the T.U.C.

Much the largest of these non-specialist associations is the Civil Service Clerical Association, with nearly 150,000 members, an income of some £200,000 a year, and about a dozen full-time officials (apart from clerical staff). This represents the main *Clerical Class* and some small Departmental classes, and shares representation of Higher Clerical Officers with the Society of Civil Servants. It is affiliated to the T.U.C., but not to the Labour Party; none of its officials has a seat in Parliament at present. Behind this statement lies the controversial history of Mr. W. J. Brown, its General Secretary for twenty-six years, the first to hold that post, and the most notable personality in the history of trade unionism in the Civil Service. Mr. Brown was Labour M.P. for West Wolverhampton from 1929 to 1931, and during that time he fell out of sympathy with the Labour Party on many issues. He left it in 1931, and his changed political opinions cost him the support of a section of his association. A long struggle for his removal followed, and in 1942, when he re-entered Parliament as Independent Member for Rugby, he was moved to one side by making him the association's Parliamentary Secretary and appointing a new General Secretary. In 1946 a fresh quarrel broke out between Mr. Brown and his association over the line he had taken in Parliament after his re-election at Rugby in 1945, and an attempt was made to withdraw his emoluments. Mr. Brown appealed to the House of Commons, and the Report of the Committee of Privileges on his case and the debate which followed laid down important rules about the position of M.P.s drawing financial support from outside bodies. In the same period, and as part of the same dispute, there was an allegation (not wholly without substance) that some officials of the association were taking an ostentatiously 'Russian' line in politics, and a campaign was launched inside the association to displace them. This campaign was not strikingly successful, but compromise and good sense prevailed, and the internal politics of the association have ceased to attract much attention.

The C.S.C.A. is a member of the Civil Service Alliance, which groups with the C.S.C.A., the County Court Officers' Association, the Inland Revenue Staff Federation, and the Ministry of Labour Staff Association. The Alliance also acts as representative of the weakly organised grades, largely of women and of temporary staff: Clerical Assistants, Typing grades, Machine Operating grades, and Temporary Clerks. This gives it a total constituency of about 200,000 people: but naturally there are conflicts of interest and policy within so large and diverse a body.

Finally, there is the Civil Service Union, representing the *messengers and cleaners* and certain other grades: a rather weak union with only a small staff, which is affiliated to the T.U.C.

(ii) *Specialist Classes*. The field here is dominated by the Institution of Professional Civil Servants, with a membership of 47,000 and an annual expenditure of about £90,000. It has about a dozen full-time officers, and its General Secretary, Mr. Stanley Mayne, is a vigorous public advocate of the interests of scientists and technologists inside and outside the Civil Service. The Institution is not affiliated to the T.U.C., and has no special connection, direct or indirect, with the Labour Party. The Institution is strongest as representative of the Scientific Civil Service and of the Works Group, which are relatively coherent bodies. But even here the allegiance of each individual is divided between three bodies of rather different types: his professional association which links him with colleagues outside the Civil Service in such organisations as the Royal Institute of British Architects and the great Engineering Institutes; the smaller and less formal association which links him to fellow-specialists in his own Department and to others within the Service; and the Institution itself. Taking the Service as a whole, the picture is even more confusing. Some specialist classes (for instance, the Legal Civil Service and many of the Inspectorates) remain outside the Institution and negotiate separately. Professional engineers in the Post Office belong to the Institution, their subordinate staff do not. Salary claims for Civil Service Medical Staffs are presented by a Joint Committee which links together the British Medical Association and the I.P.C.S. for this particular purpose. At a lower level of professional skill, the draughtsmen are separately organised in the Society of Technical Civil Servants, which joins with the Institution in negotiation for limited purposes. The S.T.C.S. is itself linked with other smaller associations in the Federation of Civil Service Professional and Technical Staffs which includes some 13,000 specialist civil servants.

(iii) *The Post Office* includes (besides the professional Engineers) a good many civil servants who belong to one or other of the associations already mentioned, and these associations have therefore a position in the negotiating machinery for the Post Office. But most employees of the Post Office are grouped in two great unions, the Union of Post Office Workers and the Post Office Engineering Union, bodies with long traditions of their own, which stand somewhat apart from the rest of the Civil Service associations. The former was established in 1920 by amalgamation, and has now about 150,000 members drawn from the 'rank-and-file' grades on the non-technical side of Post Office work. There are some 15,000 civil servants in the supervising grades, represented by the Association of Post Office Controlling Officers (10,800) and by one or two smaller associations; but the Union of Post Office Workers is the sole representative of the 'rank-and-file' grades, apart from two small associations which represent male telephone operators and cable-room telegraphists. Its income is about £180,000 a year, and it has some ten full-time officers. The union has always played an important part in trade union politics as an exponent of workers' control in nationalised industry and in the Post Office itself. Apart from the break from 1927 to 1946 it has been affiliated to the T.U.C. and to the Labour Party since its formation. Its General Secretary, Mr. C. J. Geddes, has been a member of the General Council of the T.U.C. since 1947, and was Chairman of that body in 1954-55. The union has two members in the House of Commons and casts a block vote of around 147,000 at the Labour Party Conference, a strength exceeded by only six other unions; but it is not represented on the National Executive Committee of the Labour Party, though its strength might be held to give it the right to a seat.

On the engineering side, supervisory staff are organised in the Society of Telecommunications Engineers (5,000), apart from factory supervisors, who belong to the Association of Post Office Controlling Officers. For the rest of the engineering staff the only recognised association is the Post Office Engineering Union, 69,000 strong, an influential body, but one somewhat less militant than the U.P.O.W. It is affiliated to the T.U.C. but not to the Labour Party, and it does not sponsor any Parliamentary candidates. A former General Secretary, Mr. John Edwards (who is M.P. for Brighouse and Spenborough), continues to take an active interest in the union's affairs, but he receives no salary or expenses for his services.

The union's negotiating position is somewhat weakened by the wide range of grades which it covers, from labourers to skilled technicians not far short of professional status, and some of the higher grades have sought recognition for associations of their own. These claims received some support from individual Conservative politicians, and rather acrimonious argument was temporarily ended by the report of an independent committee in 1952, which recommended against recognition.

3. MEANS OF PRESSURE

This may be enough to indicate what is involved in Civil Service trade unionism. There is a great range of organisations, from large amalgamations with strong staffs, like the C.S.C.A., the S.C.S., the I.P.C.S., and the U.P.O.W.; through associations such as the First Division Association, the Civil Service Legal Society, and the Association of Post Office Controlling Officers, which are less professional in their methods but derive much influence from the ability and official prestige of their members; down to the small associations which represent the smaller groups of staff, often within a larger federation, and to bodies such as the Council of Women Civil Servants, the National Association of Women Civil Servants, and the Association of Ex-Service Civil Servants, whose membership cuts across grades and classes, and whose aims are wider and less precisely formulated. The combined influence of these bodies is very great, but much of it derives not directly from their power to bring pressure to bear on the government, but indirectly from their position as representatives authorised to speak for government servants whom the government wishes to keep loyal and contented. The main weapon of the associations is their power to make their arguments heard and to demonstrate that these arguments are widely accepted within the Service. They are heard partly through the formal machinery described below and partly through other channels. One of these channels is that of direct representation in the House of Commons. In 1956 there were only two M.P.s who were directly sponsored by associations of civil servants, with some financial support, but at least a dozen others had close relations with particular associations, either as former union officials or in other ways. It is becoming less common for leading officials to combine their duties with membership of the House: there were eight such cases in 1929, seven in 1945, but now only Mr. Douglas Houghton remains, and the current tendency is illustrated by the case of Mr. E. C. Redhead, who resigned from his post of General Secretary of the Society of Civil Servants on election to Parliament in 1956. The reason may be that the burden of an M.P.s work has increased: or that the associations find it embarrassing to be too closely associated with the Labour Party, to which all their M.P.s belong. But the presence of former officials of the associations in the House of Commons gives them a friendly access to politicians, and similarly affiliation to the

T.U.C. means that they have some personal contacts with the representatives of workers in industry.

If acute controversy arises over a claim, it is usual to organise meetings of civil servants up and down the country, so as to demonstrate their unity behind their representatives. Occasionally, there are processions down Whitehall and deputations to the Lobby of the House of Commons. But any demonstration of this sort has to be kept within bounds, since the public as a whole (and the popular press in particular) is not very sympathetic to the claims of civil servants, and is easily alarmed by any hint of improper pressure on the government.

These tactical considerations are also the main restraint upon the right to strike. In general, civil servants have in law as much right to strike as any other body of employees. The Trades Disputes Act of 1927 made it plainly illegal for them, as for other trade unionists, to take part in a general strike designed to coerce the government: and the repeal of the Act in 1946 put the law about general strikes back into its previous state of uncertainty. This did not affect either the employees' right to strike in dispute over conditions of employment, or the government's right to take disciplinary action against an employee contravening the regulations of the Service by absenting himself without excuse on a working day. This conflict of rights causes little difficulty because the legal position has not much relevance to practice. No civil servants took part in the General Strike of 1926, although rather injudicious advice against volunteering for extra duty was issued on behalf of the Staff Side of the National Whitley Council; there have been one or two brief unofficial strikes involving groups of subordinate employees; but there has never been any official strike of civil servants organised by one of the recognised staff associations. It is difficult to imagine circumstances in which it would be good tactics to attempt to further a claim in this way.

4. Negotiation

Recognition

The basis of procedure for the settlement of conditions of service is negotiation between the appropriate staff associations and the appropriate Establishments division; but an association cannot negotiate on behalf of a particular grade or class unless it is formally 'recognised' by the Department or the Treasury as 'fully representative'.

The independent committee which investigated 'break away'

associations in the Post Office in 1951 recommended that no association should be recognised unless it could satisfy the Minister that the existing 'recognised' association had failed to look after the interests of the grade concerned, since it is undesirable to have more than one union representing a grade or group of grades. Outside the Post Office the official criterion of numerical strength implies in theory that recognition of an association may be withdrawn if its membership falls. This is in practice unlikely, since official support helps to stabilise the existing framework of associations. All new members of the Service are encouraged to join associations, and facilities are given generously to civil servants engaged on association business.

'National' recognition, which is given by the Treasury, permits the association to take part in negotiations on matters affecting more than one Department (for instance, the pay of a 'general service' grade). Departmental recognition permits negotiation on matters concerning that Department only, whether on behalf of a 'general service' or a Departmental grade. Ten associations are 'nationally' recognised. 'National' negotiations are conducted with the appropriate Establishments division of the Treasury (see Chapter 4), Departmental negotiations with the senior Establishments staff of the appropriate Department. But behind the latter stand the Permanent Secretary and the Minister, and behind them the Treasury and the Cabinet. Staff associations frequently complain that negotiation with Departmental representatives is futile, because the latter are puppets in the hands of the Treasury. Such complaints are particularly strong in the Post Office, since Departmental classes and associations there are very important and may set precedents for the whole Service, so that the Treasury is much interested in Post Office negotiations.

Whitleyism

The final appeal in negotiation is to the Civil Service Arbitration Tribunal, and cases may come to it either as a result of direct negotiation or as a result of negotiation through the machinery of Whitley Councils. As has been indicated earlier, the latter were launched in rather inauspicious circumstances between the wars, and the system only came to maturity during the Second World War. There is a National Whitley Council, and about ninety Departmental Councils, one for each Department except the Post Office, which has two, one for engineering staff and one for the rest. In some of the more scattered Departments there are local Whitley Committees as well. Some of these have only delegated authority and are required to report all their proceedings to the main Council for ratification.

In principle, these are meeting-places for the discussion of matters of common concern within an organisation, and the question of appeal up a hierarchy does not arise. The National Whitley Council deals with questions affecting the whole of the Service, the Departmental Councils are free to deal with all matters affecting their own Department, so long as they do not contravene more general principles agreed by the National Council. It is in line with this theory that Departmental Councils no longer include representatives of the Treasury.

It is necessary only to give some account of the National Council, since others follow the same pattern of organisation. There are four points to be made:

(i) *Terms of Reference.* The original form of words, which has never been amended, is as follows: 'to secure the greatest measure of co-operation between the State in its capacity as employer, and the general body of civil servants in matters affecting the Civil Service with a view to increased efficiency in the public service combined with the well-being of those employed: to provide machinery for dealing with grievances, and generally to bring together the experience and different points of view of representatives of the administrative, clerical and manipulative Civil Service'. There is very little that this excludes, and the scope of the Council has depended largely on the general state of feeling in the Service. At the outset, the Official Side were lukewarm, and the Staff Side aggressive, so that most of the business arose from grievances stated by the staff. During the Second World War the government began once more to urge upon employers the importance of joint consultation in the interests of industrial efficiency, and it took the lead itself by bringing more business to the Whitley Councils. It is common now for the Official Side (either in the National Council or in a Departmental Council) to bring up any important matter which might affect the staff before taking a final decision on action.

(ii) *Membership.* The Head of the Home Civil Service is at present Chairman of the National Whitley Council, and this is probably now the established convention. The Vice-Chairman is a member of the Staff Side, but in the absence of the Chairman a member of the Official Side always takes the chair, so that the title is purely honorary. The Council consists of 54 members (including four secretaries), divided equally between the two Sides. On the Official Side there is a substantial block of Treasury representatives (in 1955 there were eight and the First Civil Service Commissioner), and most of the other members are permanent heads of Departments. On the Staff Side the balance of representation was then: U.P.O.W., 6; P.O.E.U., 2; Post Office Controlling Officers, 1; other Post Office Associations, 1; C.S.C.A., 3; Inland Revenue Staff Federation, 2; Ministry of Labour Staff Association, 1; Society of Civil Servants, 2; Customs and Excise Federation, 1; Ministry of Labour Officers, 1; H.M. Inspector of Taxes, 1; First Division Association, 1; I.P.C.S., 3; Society of Technical Civil Servants, 1; Civil Service Union, 1.

Places on the Staff Side are allocated between associations by agreement between the associations themselves, and this may be a matter of importance since each side acts as a single 'block'. There is no individual voting in the Council, but a separate meeting of the Staff Side may decide how the Staff Side as a whole is to act. It is possible for an association to be represented on a Whitley Council though not 'recognised' for purposes of negotiation: conversely, a recognised association may not obtain (or may not claim) membership on all relevant Whitley Councils.

(iii) *Staff*. The Staff Side of the National Whitley Council at the end of 1955 included representatives of 584,000 civil servants, virtually the whole of the non-industrial Civil Service, and for many purposes it acts as a sort of loose federation of staff associations. Between 1947 and 1956 the Chairman was a permanent whole-time official, but this was a special arrangement to suit the wishes of Sir Albert Day, who had held the post continuously since 1939. On his retirement, a full-time Secretary-General was appointed, and the Chairman will in future be elected every two years. It is probable that the office will rotate among the secretaries of the leading associations. The Secretary-General has a small permanent staff housed in non-official premises (in Parliament Mansions), and the expenses of the secretariat are borne by the affiliated associations. This permanent organisation (together with the full-time officials of Departmental Councils) now plays an important part in the affairs of the Service, since much depends in negotiation on success in presenting a common front reached by compromise between the claims of various groups, and such matters are settled either by the National Staff Side meeting privately or by a joint negotiating committee appointed for a particular dispute. The character and ability of the Chairman of the National Staff Side and of the Secretary-General may therefore exercise much influence on the course of events.

(iv) *Procedure*. There was, to begin with, much argument between the staff and heads of Departments as to whether the Whitley Councils should be restricted to consultation, or should have power to decide. The Constitution of the National Whitley Council states that: 'the decisions of the Council shall be arrived at by agreement between the two Sides, shall be signed by the Chairman and the Vice-Chairman, shall be reported to the Cabinet, and thereupon shall become operative'. This was condemned by the Tomlin Commission (1929-1931) as 'a misstatement of the (constitutional) position', on the ground that the National Whitley Council could have no power to commit the Cabinet in advance. But the debate was little more than a screen for a fundamental disagreement about the purpose of the Whitley system, and with the growth of mutual trust a practical compromise was found. This was that the Official Side should always negotiate within the framework of policy previously agreed by Ministers (and if necessary by the Cabinet). Within this framework there is give and take, but officials have no authority to go outside it, and the final settlement is thus one which can be deemed to have the approval of the Cabinet in advance, though it goes forward as a decision of the National Whitley Council. In fact, so much minor business is now dealt with by the Council that the procedure of report to the Cabinet is rarely followed.

The National Whitley Council met as a body only once between 1939 and 1945, and only twice between 1945 and 1956, in spite of the intense activity in negotiation during these periods. Much business is done by committees, or less formally by personal contacts within a small group, which contains, on one side, the leading officials in the Establishments divisions of the Treasury, on the other, the Chairman of the National Staff Side, the Secretary-General, and the officials of the most important associations. So far as possible the Staff Side acts together, but it has no power to insist on agreement between the staff associations, since any recognised staff association may force a reference to arbitration.

Arbitration

There were arbitration arrangements in the Civil Service between 1917 and 1923, but the present system is based on a National Whitley Council Agreement of 1925. Since that date a breakdown in negotiation may be referred by either party to a Tribunal which has the power of final decision. The powers of the Tribunal are wide, but the Agreement excludes from them certain matters which were considered by the Treasury to be matters of 'management': superannuation, 'established' status, times of attendance, numbers and complements of staff. It also excludes grades above a certain level of salary (which was in 1956 £1,450 a year) unless the Treasury otherwise authorises.

Dispute may arise because these provisions are interpreted by the parties and not by the Tribunal, and one party (in practice the Treasury) may block reference to arbitration by maintaining that the matter is one outside the terms of reference of the Tribunal. In general this is a matter of 'case-law', but there are some issues which cause a good deal of dispute. For instance, how far can the Tribunal deal with 'grading', which is held to be a matter of 'management', yet is intimately related to pay? The Tribunal deals with 'classes' of civil servants (meaning here 'categories', not classes in the technical sense), and not with individual cases: but what for this purpose constitutes a 'class'? Furthermore, the government reserves the right (rarely exercised) to refuse to go to arbitration on major issues of policy, on the ground that it would be unconstitutional for it to tie its own hands in advance.

Cases under the 1925 agreement were at first taken to the Industrial Court, set up by the Industrial Courts Act of 1919, but in 1936 there was constituted a separate Civil Service Arbitration Tribunal. It consists of three persons: an 'independent' Chairman, who is a practising barrister experienced in industrial arbitration, engaged only part-time on Civil Service work, but in the chair at all meetings of the Tribunal; one member selected for each sitting of the Tribunal from the 'Chancellor of the Exchequer's Panel', and one from the 'Staff Side Panel'. Both Panels are appointed by the Minister of Labour, and both exclude all serving civil servants and all officials of Civil Service staff associations. They both consist of men and women with experience in a variety of walks of life, and with no marked bias: but one Panel is appointed in consultation with the Official Side, the other in consultation with the Staff Side, and the Chairman is appointed with the agreement of both Sides.

The Arbitration Tribunal does not give reasons for its decisions, and it is therefore hard to comment on the body of principles which it has built up. Its decisions (which are published) consist of a formal record of the arguments put before it, followed by an award. The pattern of argument is well established, and it is to be presumed that the Treasury, the Departments, and the associations are familiar with the sort of reasoning which carries weight. The appointment of a Royal Commission in 1953 was not due to any complaint against the Tribunal, but (in part at least) it was a response to a feeling that the Tribunal was working within a framework of argument established before 1939, and that a new and more general appraisal was necessary if the Tribunal were to work satisfactorily. In fact, the mechanism of the Tribunal serves excellently to make adjustments from year to year: it is inadequate for any general overhaul of conditions, and may virtually break down in a period of inflation when claims come forward at very short intervals. The staff associations may then suspect that it acts partly as a delaying mechanism in the hands of the Treasury.

The Higher Civil Service

The Treasury have always maintained (and on the whole the staff agree) that it would be embarrassing if civil servants in managerial positions could take the government to compulsory arbitration. The result is that there is not (as in local government) arbitration about posts in the highest ranges of salary, and it is possible that this is one reason among others why increases of pay in the higher Civil Service have lagged behind those given to other professions. The Priestley Commission accepted this argument, and recommended that there should be compulsory arbitration up to £2,000 a year, the bottom of the recommended Assistant Secretary scale, and that above that level there should in future be some standing arrangements for salary revision. Their proposal (which has been implemented by the government) was that there should be an Advisory Committee of about five members appointed by the Prime Minister from various walks of life. It is the duty of the Committee to advise the government about the salaries of the higher Civil Service, either at the government's request or on its own initiative.

5. Conclusion

The most obvious comment on this system is that it is an extremely stable one, within which the Treasury supports the associations and the associations co-operate in the Treasury's task of managing the Service as a whole. The threads of the whole huge organisation are drawn together in the hands of a small group of officials on the two Sides of the National Whitley Council, who understand the 'rules of the game' very well, and who appreciate an opponent's difficulties even while attempting to outwit him. The system is also remarkably flexible, in that neither group, neither the Treasury nor the large associations, has any comprehensive power of discipline. There is a maze of Departmental particularity within which each Department and each association has some freedom of manœuvre.

In spite of these merits the system does less than might be expected to raise the corporate morale of the Civil Service in face of an unsympathetic public. Perhaps the most important difficulties arise from the remoteness of the Treasury, which remains a hostile mystery to the average civil servant in the lower grades; the capacity for delay inherent in the system, which in a period of inflation tells against the interests of the staff, and leads to allegations that the Treasury deliberately plays for time; the inconclusive nature of arbitration procedure (as distinct from judicial procedure), which continually elicits arguments from the parties and never concludes them by a reasoned decision; the lack of any machinery for reaching agreement on the work and structure of the Service as a whole, except by the cumbrous device of an occasional Royal Commission. It is not easy to think of machinery which would put these matters right; but the atmosphere might be improved if the Prime Minister and other Ministers gave more frequent indications of personal interest in the Civil Service and its problems.

FOR REFERENCE

A major source of information on this subject is the *Whitley Bulletin* (the official monthly publication of the National Staff Side). See especially articles in Vol. 33, p. 100 and p. 116, and Vol. 36, p. 52.

Report of a Committee appointed to advise on the application of the Whitley Report to the Administrative Departments of the Civil Service (Ramsay-Bunning). Cmd. 198, 1919.

W. J. BROWN: *Whitleyism on its Trial* (Undated ? 1921).

MACRAE GIBSON: *The Whitley System in the Civil Service* (1922).

G. M. STUART-BUNNING: 'The Origins of Whitleyism', *Civil Service Argus*, January 1945.

W. J. BROWN: *So Far* (An autobiography) (1943).

BERNARD NEWMAN: *Yours for Action* (A history of the C.S.C.A.) (1953).

JAMES CALLAGHAN: *Whitleyism* (Fabian Research Series No. 159) (1954).

L. D. WHITE: *Whitley Councils in the British Civil Service* (Chicago, 1932).

E. N. GLADDEN: *Civil Service Staff Relationships* (1943)—a revised version is in course of preparation.

H.M. Treasury: *Staff Relations in the Civil Service* (2nd Edn., 1955). H.M.S.O.

Report from the Committee of Privileges. H.C. 118, 1947. (Brown's case.)

Report of the Post Office (Departmental Classes) Recognition Committee (Terrington). Cmd. 8470, 1952, and H.L. Deb. 30 July 1953, Col. 1170.

CHAPTER TEN

PROFESSIONAL STANDARDS OF CONDUCT

Stand ye in the ways, and see, and ask for the old paths, where is the good way, and walk therein, and ye shall find rest for your souls.
Jeremiah, vi, 16.

1. Disciplinary Procedure

It was explained in Chapter 2 that the internal affairs of the Civil Service are governed by regulations derived mainly from the prerogative powers of the Crown, not from enactment by Parliament. These regulations may be regarded either as law or as the basis of a contract between the Crown and its civilian servants: they are not in either case the 'ordinary law of the land', and it has been held repeatedly by the ordinary courts that they have no jurisdiction over any matter arising out of them.

A similar situation in the armed forces has led to the evolution of the system of courts-martial, which are specialised tribunals possessing great powers, but following a fairly strict judicial procedure of their own and subject to supervision through a process of appeal to a Courts Martial Appeal Court, and, on a point of law of exceptional public importance, to the House of Lords. In many civil services abroad, particularly in Europe, there has arisen in the same way a system of administrative courts, part of whose function is to deal with offences against discipline in the civil service. In the British Civil Service matters of this sort are dealt with entirely through the usual channels of command, and the final authority in each Department is the Minister himself, advised by the Permanent Secretary. Penalties imposed may be reprimand, transfer to a less attractive post, demotion, suspension from duty (with or without pay), dismissal. The absence of judicial procedure may be held to involve a risk of arbitrary action by superiors and of inconsistency in standards: but this is reduced by many safeguards, formal and informal.

It is true that disciplinary action is often initiated by an official's immediate superior, but there are rules which require that certain offences be reported to the appropriate Establishments division before a penalty is imposed. At this stage (unless there is a possibility of criminal proceedings) the officer must be informed as precisely as possible of the complaint against him, and must be given an opportunity of replying to it in writing. As will be seen below, it may on grounds of security be thought impossible to give the person concerned full details of the exact charge and of the evidence on which it is based: and in such a case he has no right to insist. Lesser penalties may be within the jurisdiction of the Establishments division, greater ones must go to the Permanent Secretary. The officer has always the right to appear personally before the disciplinary authority to state his case (though the right is frequently waived), and in so doing he is allowed the assistance of a friend, who may be a staff association official. But there is no 'adversary' procedure between prosecutor and accused, and there is no appeal beyond the head of the Department.

The less formal safeguards depend mainly upon the system of staff associations. Individual cases cannot be raised at Whitley Council meetings or in arbitration, but one of the most important duties of a staff association is to act on behalf of individual members accused of some breach of regulations. The association can be relied on to know the regulations, to be familiar with previous cases, and to advise on the best method of proceeding. In the last resort, the association (or the individual concerned) may make the matter a political one by raising it in Parliament through a sympathetic M.P.

The result of these safeguards is perhaps that formal disciplinary procedure is used too little rather than too much. It is difficult to find authenticated cases of serious miscarriage of justice: but the procedure is ponderous, it causes a good deal of personal strain, and it may leave bitterness behind in the Department. The instinct of a cautious superior is therefore not to invoke formal discipline for minor offences: a habit which leads to a certain slackness of attitude, and to a situation in which the standing of a civil servant in the Department depends more on general opinion about him than on what is formally stated in his record.

The offences which may be the subject of discipline include much that needs no explanation here, such as failure to obey orders, wilful or gross carelessness (including loss of official property), absence without leave, persistent lateness, waste of time during office hours, and so on. These are offences which must be punished in any large organisation: there are, however, three matters of special importance to the Civil Service, not because they give rise to a large proportion of disciplinary cases but because they are significant as marks of the character of the Service. These may be labelled briefly probity, security, and political activity.

2. Probity

A civil servant may be prosecuted in an ordinary court for any form of theft, direct or indirect: for instance, if he makes false claims for travelling expenses. It is an offence at common law to accept bribes for following a particular course of action in an official capacity: and the law was strengthened by the Prevention of Corruption Act, 1906, which makes it an offence for a civil servant 'corruptly to accept any gift or consideration as an inducement or reward for doing or refraining from doing anything in his official capacity, or showing favour or disfavour to any person in his official capacity'.

Cases in court involving civil servants are rare in proportion to the number of civil servants, and in fact the Service attempts to set a standard higher than that enforceable by strict judicial procedure. The formula which expresses this was set out in the report of a Board of Inquiry, consisting of three civil servants, which was set up in 1928 under the chairmanship of Sir Warren Fisher, then Permanent Secretary of the Treasury. The inquiry was concerned with a case in which it was alleged that three senior officials at the Foreign Office had enriched themselves by speculating in foreign currency, on the basis of information available to them as officials. It was not established that they had committed any offence, or even that they had in fact profited by the use of inside knowledge. A long passage of the report was incorporated in a Treasury Circular of March 1928, which is brought to the notice of all recruits to the higher classes of the Civil Service. This is too long to quote in full, but perhaps the key sentences are these: 'To say that [a civil servant] is not to subordinate his duty to his private interests, nor to make use of his official position to further those interests, is to say no more than that he must behave with common honesty. The Service exacts from itself a higher standard, because it recognises that the State is entitled to demand that its servants shall not only be honest in fact, but beyond the reach of suspicion of dishonesty.'

This 'Caesar's wife' standard is of great importance in maintaining the reputation of the Service, on which so much of British government depends. Much of our policy in regard to taxation, industrial controls, government contracts, social services is only possible because there is complete confidence that the officials (whatever their other human failings) are not lining their own pockets at the public expense, and are not acting so as to favour one interest at the expense of another. The principle extends from great matters to very small ones. A high official must not discuss with a business magnate the possibility of a job after retirement, if the magnate's business is in any way the concern of the official's Department; nor may he accept such a post within two years after his retirement unless he obtains the permission of his former Minister and the Treasury. Inspectors of Taxes and Contracts Officers must be extremely circumspect in their personal relations with anyone who does business with their office. Even the junior staff of the Customs and Excise must not do part-time clerical work for football pool firms, since their Department is responsible for the administration of the betting tax.

This standard of behaviour is enforced entirely by the Civil Service itself. It goes beyond anything that could be established by evidence in a court of law: and a corollary of this is that if a civil servant suffers a penalty through Departmental discipline he has no means of forcing the Department to prosecute in court. The result may be apparent injustice to an individual; in a recent case an official was prosecuted and was acquitted by a court, but the Department refused to withdraw the penalty imposed departmentally, presumably because it was satisfied that the man had offended against the standards of the Service in a way with which the court was not concerned. Puritanical standards and a certain ruthlessness in defence of them are of extreme importance to the reputation of the Service: this is perhaps a more fundamental matter than the questions of security and political activity, which are more debated partly because there is less agreement about them within the Service.

3. Security

The present law of official secrets was built up in the period of tension which led to the First World War, and is embodied in the Official Secrets Acts 1889 to 1920. These Acts are drafted in extremely wide terms, and bring within the scope of criminal prosecution virtually any dealing with an official document (even a non-confidential one) which is not within the scope of official business. Except in certain Departments, which have their own more stringent arrangements, based on statutes other than the Official Secrets Acts, the relevant sections of the Acts are shown to all new civil servants, and they must sign a form of words to indicate that they have read them and taken note of them. A civil servant also runs the risk of severe penalties, up to dismissal, if he discloses official information 'without authority and contrary to the public interest', even though he has not infringed the Acts.

The total number of cases of trafficking in official secrets is as small as the number of cases of dishonesty, but the problem was given a new form by the general alarm over Communist penetration in the years after 1945. Enormous publicity was given to the cases of three nuclear physicists, Dr. Nunn May, Dr. Klaus Fuchs, and Dr. Bruno Pontecorvo, and of two Foreign Office officials, Guy Burgess and Donald Maclean, all of whom became involved in espionage for ideological reasons. May and Fuchs were convicted under the Official Secrets Acts, the other three escaped to Russia to avoid prosecution; but all cases pointed the moral that the Acts can be used only after the secrets have been betrayed, and that it may then be too late. Two conclusions might be drawn: first, the authorities must have power to act on suspicion, and on evidence which is known to be incomplete; secondly, they must be in a position to collect evidence unhampered by the ordinary rules of police procedure. These principles are the basis of the police state: it is fair to say that the authorities have been extremely reluctant to invoke them, and that they have acted with moderation in spite of much political agitation in this country and in the U.S.A.

It has always been within the power of the authorities to transfer or dismiss a civil servant on suspicion and without cause stated, but the power has been greatly restricted in practice, and its use is further complicated by the fact that a civil servant is free to join any political party which is not illegal. The Communist Party is not illegal in Britain, and it would have been contrary to usage to penalise a civil servant for membership or connection with the Party. Of course, Departments have always used discretion in posting fanatical Party members—as they would in posting fanatical Conservatives. Fanaticism of any kind limits the utility of a civil servant.

This principle of the equivalence of all legal parties was formally broken by a decision announced in March 1948 that certain posts should on security grounds be ranked as 'sensitive', and that Communists, Fascists, and 'persons associated with these parties in such a way as to raise legitimate doubts about their reliability' might be removed from such posts. This means that if the official concerned is an established civil servant an effort must be made to find another post for him in the same Department or in another: if he refuses transfer he may resign without official discredit. Only in the last resort will he be dismissed. This procedure amounts to imposing a penalty for an action which is not even now regarded as being in itself an offence against discipline, and the penalty may be imposed on the basis of evidence which cannot be produced publicly for examination. The best that can be said is that the authorities have done much to introduce safeguards, and that the number of cases involved is very small.

An independent advisory committee was set up in 1948, consisting of two retired civil servants and a trade union official, to which any individual case may be taken on appeal from the Departmental authorities. The committee sees all the evidence, but security authorities may refuse to disclose some or all of it to the person accused, and the latter, though he may appear before the committee in person, cannot be assisted by a trade union official or other representative. Proceedings are informal and there is no judicial hearing: nevertheless, the committee seems to have been prepared to take its own line in opposition to the security authorities. From March 1948 to March 1957 the total number of cases involved was 159, with the following results:

Transferred	81
Resigned	23
Dismissed	24
Reinstated after inquiry	30
Pending	1

There has undoubtedly also been an extension of the practice of private inquiry into the political affiliations and private lives of civil servants in 'sensitive' posts. The details are secret, but publicity was given to the introduction in March 1952 of a special 'screening' procedure for all those then engaged in atomic energy establishments (about 11,000) and for about 10,000 others. It was intended that some further extension of this procedure should follow the Report of the Conference of seven Privy Councillors, which was appointed in November 1955 to 'examine the security procedures now applied in the public services and to consider whether any further precautions are called for and should be taken'.

This report was not published in full, but a summary of it appeared in a White Paper (Cmd. 9715) which was issued in March 1956. The White Paper stressed the duty of Departmental authorities 'to inform themselves of serious failings such as drunkenness, addiction to drugs, homosexuality, or any loose living that may seriously affect a man's reliability'; and stated that the Conference had recommended that such defects might, in themselves, be 'the determining factor in a decision to dismiss a particular individual or to transfer him to other work'. Membership of the Communist Party might 'in some Departments have an unfavourable effect on prospects of promotion' as well as leading to transfer from secret work; and such transfers might be made, not only when the civil servant himself was suspected of Communist sympathies, but also where doubts existed about the political reliability of his wife or other close relatives.

These measures seem to the outside observer to be somewhat out of proportion to the disease. Certainly there has been feeling in the Service as a whole that much inconvenience has been caused to everyone for the sake of a few unbalanced intellectuals in the higher ranks of the Service, administrative and scientific. The rank-and-file have scarcely been touched by the currents of world politics, which have led to much less strain in British government than in any other Western administration.

4. Political Activity

The general rules about the political activity of civil servants have nothing to do with the danger of involvement in subversive activities. They originated in the eighteenth century, when the holders of various offices under the Crown were excluded from the House of Commons in order to prevent the Ministry in power from using patronage to corrupt Members of Parliament, and when minor public servants were disfranchised so that the Ministry could not gain by its control of their votes at elections. Its present justification lies in the theory of the two-party system and the neutral Civil Service. The electorate is to choose between a limited number of great parties, and the party chosen is to supply the Ministers who head Departments. A general election may change the party in power and eject all Ministers from office together. If this system of periodical changes by the electorate is to be compatible with orderly government there must be a permanent administration which can be handed on from one set of Ministers to the next, without fundamental change. The electorate is at liberty to eject Ministers, provided Ministers are not free to eject civil servants. Such self-limitation on the part of Ministers is possible only if leading civil servants refrain scrupulously from identifying themselves publicly with any of the competing parties: and party supporters in the country are not likely to accept Ministerial forbearance unless they see that the minor civil servants whom they meet in daily business are equally impartial.

From the eighteenth-century tradition is derived the confused body of statute law which deals with eligibility for membership of the House of Commons. This has caused much difficulty because it depends on the interpretation of the phrase 'office or place of profit under the Crown', which has been held to exclude many people who have accepted appointments on committees and tribunals of one sort or another. A Select Committee reported on the whole subject in 1942, and it seemed in 1956 as if amending legislation might at last be passed. There is, however, no ambiguity which affects any full-time member of the Civil Service: he cannot take his seat as a member of the House without first resigning his post.

There is no further statutory restriction on political activity. The rest of the discussion concerns the internal regulation of the Service, and can most readily be explained in terms of development since 1945. At that date there were no restrictions on industrial civil servants except that most of them were not permitted to accept nomination as Parliamentary candidates: that is to say, they must resign from the Service before becoming candidates. Even this limitation did not apply to industrial civil servants employed by the Service Departments, and there were some other exemptions. On the other hand, all non-industrial civil servants, however humble their position, were subject to this restriction, under an Order-in-Council of 1927. In addition, there was a long-standing staff rule in the Treasury that its officials were 'expected to maintain at all times a reserve in political matters', and this rule was widely copied in the staff rules of other Departments: its interpretation varied with circumstances, but there was probably more variation than these circumstances could justify. Indeed, the lines between industrial and non-industrial civil servants, and between one Department and another, were so arbitrarily drawn that the staff associations had excellent grounds for requesting revision of the rules.

Their pressure led to the appointment in 1948 of a Departmental committee under the chairmanship of Mr. J. C. Masterman. The inquiry was limited by a government statement that the government was 'totally opposed to any radical change in the non-political status of the Civil Service', and the Committee whole-heartedly endorsed this view, remarking that 'any weakening of the existing tradition of political impartiality would be the first step towards the creation of a political Civil Service'. Its report was therefore cautious in tone, and did not squarely meet the staff associations' argument that Treasury rules would be ineffective unless the tradition were safeguarded by the Service itself, and that the influence of the rules in a few marginal cases is not sufficient excuse for subjecting a large section of the electorate to deprivation of political rights. The Committee made a valuable survey of the situation and recommended the removal of its obvious anomalies. All industrial civil servants were to be entirely freed from restrictions, except those imposed by statute (for instance, the Official Secrets Acts), and to them were to be added non-industrial staff in the minor and manipulative grades, with a few exceptions: for example, the Committee were divided about including the Post Office supervisory manipulative grades, and were unanimous in excluding Service Department

Constabularies. Above this level they refused to draw any distinctions: the remainder were all to be subject to the existing rules. Since Departmental practice in the past had frequently been more liberal than the rules, this recommendation was interpreted by the staff associations to mean that the privileges of many non-industrial civil servants 'above the line' were to be still further curtailed.

The first part of the recommendations was put into effect in January 1950; the second part was quite unacceptable to the staff associations, and there was a long period of further negotiation through a Joint Committee representing both Sides of the National Whitley Council. This led to a compromise, which was embodied in a White Paper published in March 1953 and was put into force by a Treasury Circular in August of that year.[1]

The essence of this compromise is to divide the Civil Service into three sections:[2]

(i) Those who are freed from all restriction on political activity except the general statutory restrictions: this category includes all industrial civil servants, and about 270,000 non-industrial civil servants—roughly the same number as was suggested by the Masterman Committee.

(ii) An intermediate group, subject to the rule forbidding Parliamentary candidature but permitted to engage in other political activities at the discretion of their Departments, which are to make general rules affecting substantial blocks of staff. Political activity is defined so as to include at the national level (apart from Parliamentary candidature) holding office in national party organisations, speaking and writing on matters of national political controversy, and canvassing at Parliamentary elections; at the local level, candidature for a local election, co-option to a local authority, speaking, writing, and canvassing in local politics. The intermediate category includes Clerical Officers, Clerical Assistants, and typists, the analogous grades in other classes, and grades parallel to (but not including) the 'general Service' grade of Executive Officer: 280,000 in all.

If there is a case for restriction it certainly applies to many officers in this category who represent the Civil Service to the public in many important local activities. The Treasury recognises this, and Departments are advised to 'grant permission or refuse it mainly according to the degree and nature of the contact with the public involved by the duties of the officer concerned, and the extent to which his political activities are likely to be known... as those of a civil servant

[1] E.C. 26/53, 14 August 1953.
[2] The number of staff in each category relates to 1st January 1954. Later figures not available.

whose official duties involve his taking decisions . . . affecting the personal well-being of the Department's clients'. This is taken to exclude from national politics, for instance, clerks in local insurance offices, national assistance offices, and local employment offices, and from local politics, clerks in the Ministry of Housing and Local Government. Those 'de-restricted' are to be formally reminded that in the interests of the Service they should act decorously and express themselves with moderation.

(iii) A restricted group, which in effect includes the Administrative and Executive Classes, the corresponding Departmental Classes, and those of equivalent status to the administrative and higher executive grades in the scientific, professional, and technical Civil Service: about 120,000. They are entitled as citizens to exercise the franchise in Parliamentary elections, and this is held to include the right to belong to any political party which is not illegal, but they are debarred from all other public activity in national politics. They may apply individually to their Departments for permission to take a public part in local affairs, and this should be granted 'to the maximum extent consistent with the maintenance of the Civil Service's reputation for political impartiality'.

These changes remove many indefensible anomalies, and also represent some relaxation of the old system. The increase in the size of the Civil Service makes it impossible to treat it any longer as a class apart, and the difficulty of special treatment is increased by the general absence of formal restrictions in the rest of the public service; employees of local authorities and other public bodies are subject to rules of common sense, but not to written rules as are civil servants,[1] even when doing very similar jobs. There is still some discontent, especially in the Executive Class, and it is possible that relaxation may be carried farther. But at some point a balance must be struck between opposing considerations, unless there is to be a complete change in the constitutional position of the Civil Service. On the one hand, no responsible civil servant cares to endanger the effectiveness of his own work by indulging in public controversy about politics; and if in his youth he does not understand that these things are connected his elders soon put him right. Civil servants generally keep quiet about many matters of controversy—theological, ideological, social—from which they are not held back by Treasury or Departmental rules. On the other hand, in matters of this kind foolish acts by one or two unimportant individuals may do the

---

[1] Except that a local government officer may not sit as a councillor or alderman on the council of the local authority which employs him (Local Government Act 1933, Sec. 59 (1)).

Service much harm. The political position of the Civil Service rests on a sort of confidence trick, and a few cases dramatised by malicious reporting may have much more influence on public confidence than the solid merit of the Service as a whole. It is not unreasonable to ask that in its own interest the Service should submit to formal rules for the sake of the small number of civil servants who do not know or who disregard the standards set by the Service itself.

FOR REFERENCE

Probity:

Report of a Board of Inquiry to Investigate Certain Statements affecting Civil Servants made during the Case of Ironmonger and Co. v. Dyne (the 'Gregory' case). Cmd. 3037, 1928. (This report was the subject of a Treasury Circular T.C. 5/28 of March 1928, addressed to all Departments.)

Order-in-Council, 10 January 1910 (Clause 17 relates to the acceptance by civil servants of posts in private business).

Report of the Board of Inquiry Appointed by the Prime Minister to Investigate Certain Discussions engaged in by the Permanent Secretary to the Air Ministry (the 'Bullock' case). Cmd. 5254, 1936. *Minute by the Prime Minister* (on the above Report). Cmd. 5255, 1936.

Memorandum on Acceptance by Civil Servants of Outside Occupations after Resignation or Retirement. Cmd. 5517, 1937.

Report of the Committee on Intermediaries (Herbert). Cmd. 7904, 1950.

Report of a Tribunal Appointed to Inquire into Allegations Reflecting on the Conduct of Ministers of the Crown and Other Public Servants (Lynskey). Cmd. 7616, 1949.

Report of a Public Inquiry into the Disposal of Land at Crichel Down (Clark). Cmd. 9176, 1954.

Report of a Committee to Advise Whether Certain Civil Servants should be Transferred to Other Duties (Woods). Cmd. 9220, 1954.

Security:

Statements by the Prime Minister on security arrangements, 15 March 1948 (H.C. Deb. 448, Cols. 1703-8), and 25 March 1948 (H.C. Deb. 448, Cols. 3389-426).

Treasury Establishment Circular E.C. 21/52 of January 1952. (Security procedure for assessing the reliability of staff employed on exceptionally secret work.)

Report on the Disappearance of Two Foreign Office Officials. Cmd. 9577, 1955.

Statement on the Findings of the Conference of Privy Councillors on Security. Cmd. 9715, 1956.

Political Activity:

The position prior to the Masterman Report is summarised in the *Whitley Bulletin.* April 1938.

Report of the Committee on the Political Activities of Civil Servants (Masterman). Cmd. 7718, 1949.
White Paper on the Political Activities of Civil Servants. Cmd. 8783, 1953.
Treasury Establishments Circulars E.C. 3/50 of 16 January 1950, E.C. 9/50 of 25 January 1950, and E.C. 26/53 of 14 August 1953.

On Parliamentary candidature see:

Report from the Select Committee on Offices or Places of Profit under the Crown. H.C. 120, 1941.
Special Report from the Select Committee on the House of Commons Disqualification Bill, and Minutes of Evidence. H.C. 349, 1956.

II
THE ORGANISATION OF DEPARTMENTS

INTRODUCTORY

> But if the force of custom simple and separate be great, the force of custom copulate and conjoined and collegiate is far greater. For there example teacheth, company comforteth, emulation quickeneth, glory raiseth: so as in such places the force of custom is in his exaltation.—BACON: *On Custom and Education.*

IN Part I we have been concerned with people in central administration, and with their problems of pay, status, and personal position in relation to their contemporaries outside the Service. These people are the bricks out of which the administrative structure is built. They may be adapted to changing needs by reorganisation, by training, and by recruiting new types of expert from outside, and the Civil Service is changing continually in all these ways. But this is a slow process except in times of national crisis, when civil servants like other people become adaptable under great pressure. On the whole, administration must work with civil servants as they exist, using their strength and counterbalancing their weaknesses.

Part II is concerned with the internal organisation of Departments, and there is a somewhat similar balance here between rigidity and adaptation to need. In one sense, Departments must be understood as individuals, products of a historical process which has gone on without breach of continuity since Norman or even pre-Norman times. This book is not concerned with the history of central administration, yet it is impossible to grasp the nature of and relations between the existing Departments without some knowledge of their ancestry. Civil servants are on the whole not well informed about Departmental history, and the mythology of Departments is often quite different from the reality. Nevertheless, traditions are very strong, and are important to the dignity and morale of each Department. Many Departments have a sense of personality and of self-confidence as strong as that of an ancient school or college, and there is a certain hierarchy of prestige between Departments, which owes as much to history as to their relative importance today.

These factors are in a sense extraneous to administrative organisation, but they are not subjective or imaginary. Good administration must take account of them and use them, and it is appropriate to begin this Part with a very brief account of the historical origins of the present structure (Chapter 11). We proceed then to its physical setting, a matter as important as tradition in marking the colour and individuality of an organisation (Chapter 12); to the main elements of organisation which are common to all Departments (Chapter 13); and to the standard forms of procedure (Chapter 14).

These are all matters which depend a good deal on habit and tradition. It is with them as with a language: a language can be spoken or written at various levels of subtlety and precision, but it serves its purpose well enough so long as it ensures a measure of mutual comprehension, so long as those who use it understand it quickly and in the same sense. There are, however, also more specific problems of organisation within Departments. Each Department has a highly individual task or combination of tasks, and these change from time to time, sometimes abruptly, sometimes by imperceptible gradations. The criterion of administration here is its success in finding means to combine the individuals and groups who make up the Civil Service, within a familiar pattern of organisation, so as to produce the particular structure best suited to a particular job at a particular time. In this respect the system is highly adaptable, and not a year passes without important changes. There would be little point in attempting to give a complete account here of the administrative structure of all Departments, because it would be out of date before it could be printed, and in any case it would be far too long for a book of this kind. We therefore proceed in Chapter 15 by taking a selection of Departments, chosen somewhat at random, to illustrate some of the many ways in which administrative builders can combine the bricks at their disposal. A number of other Departments, such as the Treasury and the 'common service' Departments, are discussed separately in later chapters.

At each stage the problems of Departmental organisation throw up problems of co-ordination between Departments, and it is never in practice possible to isolate questions internal to a Department from questions about its place in 'Whitehall'. The present Part therefore necessarily refers forward continually to Part III, which deals with co-ordination: and this is particularly obvious in Chapter 16, which deals with the local and regional organisation of Departments. The Departments which possess local organisations developed them at first in isolation from other Departments; but considerations of economy, efficiency, and convenience to the public raise the issue of local co-ordination, and this illustrates in a relatively simple form some of the problems of co-ordination at the centre.

CHAPTER ELEVEN

THE HISTORICAL TRADITION

One star differeth from another star in glory.—1 *Corinthians*, xv, 41.

1. Introductory

CIVIL servants are (in the main) those who serve the great officers of state, and the history of Departmental organisation is largely the history of certain offices which have retained unbroken continuity over a very long period. It is also the history of those who have worked under these officers from one generation to another, have carried great responsibilities, and have had personal alliances, ambitions, and feuds outside the range of political history. But 'Departmental history' in this latter sense remains to be written: all that can be given here is a summary of changes in form.

The Normans established at the outset of their conquest the tradition that there should be a single chief officer of state under the King, the Justiciar, who also represented the King in his absence abroad, and a strong local administration through men owing their offices directly to the Crown. This pattern of government has frequently been obscured in periods of civil confusion, when power at the centre has been divided between various authorities, and power in the countryside has fallen into the hands of local magnates each aspiring to a share in national power. But it has never disappeared, and British government must be thought of in terms of a balance between one man's power and a division of power at the centre, between national authority and local interests in the country.

2. The King's Justices

The Justiciar had disappeared by the end of Henry III's reign, in the middle of the thirteenth century, and the other Justices of the old King's Council, the Curia Regis, were then moving gradually from the position of executive officers of the King to that of impartial interpreters of the common law. The three traditional courts of common law, the King's Bench, the Exchequer, and the Common

Pleas, had reached a fairly well settled form, and at the same time there were emerging the corporations of professional lawyers grouped around these courts and sustaining them. The rule of law was already established, in the sense that the late thirteenth-century jurists held the King to be not above the law, but 'under God and the law', and the judges ceased to be part of the administration.

Even today, however, there are traces of the tradition that the King's judges (those of the King's Bench in particular, now the Queen's Bench Division of the High Court of Justice) are charged not only with stating the law in particular cases, but (in the phrase of the Constitution of the United States of America) with taking 'care that the laws be faithfully executed'. The administration of the judicial system is largely a matter for the Lord Chancellor's Department, but in a number of matters the Chancellor cannot act without the consent of the Lord Chief Justice of England, and there are many other matters about which it is usual to consult the latter. Issues concerning the administration of justice cannot come before the Queen's Bench Division except as they arise from individual cases, but there are at least two types of case in which the High Court takes a wide view of its powers. A variety of issues of what might be called administrative discipline can be raised before it through the traditional prerogative writs, *mandamus*, prohibition, and *certiorari*. The Court has in recent years tended to leave a wide sphere of discretion to administrative officers, but it accepts general responsibility for the proper conduct of judicial proceedings in all subordinate courts throughout England and Wales, and can under the writ of *certiorari* assert effective control of any person whom it holds to be acting in a judicial capacity. In addition, appeals on points of law from the magistrates' courts lie to a Divisional Court of the Queen's Bench Division, and in hearing appeals the Court considers the general efficiency of the magistrates, and issues judgements in a way intended to give instruction to all benches of magistrates throughout the country about such matters as the relative heinousness of different offences, severity of sentences, and methods of procedure.

3. THE GREAT OFFICERS OF STATE

The high executive officers of the Crown in the Middle Ages were the Lord Chancellor, the King's Treasurer (who became Lord High Treasurer under Henry VIII), the Lord Great Chamberlain, and the Lord High Constable, and there followed slightly later the Lord Privy Seal, the Lord High Admiral, the Principal Secretary of State, and the Lord President of the Council.

(i) *The Lord Chancellor*

The Chancellors of the later Middle Ages were usually great churchmen, 'keepers of the king's conscience' and founders of the Courts of equity, as well as political advisers and magnates of the realm. Wolsey was the last and perhaps the greatest of these medieval Chancellors: since his fall no Lord Chancellor has been sole First Minister, but the office has never lost its political importance. The Lord Chancellor is still a judge, and presides over the final court of appeal, the judicial members of the House of Lords sitting alone as a court of law. He still acts for the Crown as chairman of the House of Lords, which is the lineal descendant of the medieval council of magnates: to preside over it he need not himself be a peer, since he sits on the floor of the House, on the 'woolsack' before the empty throne, and conducts business with due deference to the Lords, who maintain order in their own House. He is also head of a small Department with large responsibilities: its permanent head, a civil servant, is Clerk of the Crown in Chancery, and his staff look after a large variety of miscellaneous work relating to the administration of the law. In particular, the Lord Chancellor is directly responsible for the appointment of High Court judges, Chairmen of Quarter Sessions, Recorders, and Stipendiary Magistrates, and he advises the Prime Minister on higher appointments such as those of legal members of the House of Lords, Lord Justice of Appeal, and Lord Chief Justice. His staff deal with a very large number of minor appointments, above all those of Justices of the Peace; and his Ecclesiastical Secretary has to find incumbents for some 650 'livings' in the Church of England, quite a large proportion of all benefices. Since 1955 he has also been the Minister responsible for the Public Record Office. The Lord Chancellor's office is perhaps the extreme case in British administration of a Department combining functions logically separate, an arrangement indefensible on any principle except that of historical continuity.

(ii) *The Lord High Treasurer*

The office of the Lord High Treasurer has also survived, but in a form which illustrates a later phase of administrative history. The earliest basis of administration was the personal and individual responsibility of a great lord to his master the king. But the great lords from the first shared responsibility as members of the King's Council, and there grew up fairly early a system of collegiate administration through various councils, boards, and committees. This happened at various levels of dignity. The Great Council of the

Realm gave place to the Privy Council, and the Privy Council used committees for various purposes. A great office might for some reason be left vacant and put 'in commission', so that its functions were discharged by a group of dignitaries acting together. A committee or board might be set up for a special purpose, under the chairmanship of a high officer, but including also some lesser persons who were primarily experts in the work of the office; and for many purposes there were boards consisting wholly of relatively junior officials, who contrived to remain in office for long periods in spite of the vicissitudes of politics. This system had certain advantages in its time, such as political compromise and a check on the overmighty, mutual supervision through separation of powers, continuity in much of the administration even in troubled times. But one of the axioms of administrative theory propounded by Bentham was that 'boards are screens', and the fashion of the nineteenth century demanded individual responsibility and clarity of definition. Many ancient committees and boards were abolished, others survived in name only, and their powers were exercised by a single man. This fashion never prevailed in local government; in central government there was a counter-tendency even in the nineteenth century, and this has recently become very marked, as can be seen in the creation of such bodies as the Forestry Commission, the National Assistance Board, and a great number of 'public corporations'. On the whole, this reversal of trend has not affected the main structure of central administration. The overriding principle is still that of the individual responsibility of the Minister for his Department, but nomenclature preserves much of the earlier tradition.

All this is exemplified in the history of the Treasury. The Treasury is now in practice a unified Department under a single head, the Chancellor of the Exchequer, but its forms of business embalm quite a different theory. The office of Lord High Treasurer was first put into commission on the death of Robert Cecil, Earl of Salisbury, in 1612, and has been in commission without a break since 1714; since that date its duties have been discharged by 'The Lords Commissioners of the Treasury'. The chairman of the Board is the First Lord of the Treasury, an office so important that since Walpole's time its holder has almost always been regarded as Prime Minister. The last exception to this rule was from 1895 to 1902, when the Marquess of Salisbury as Prime Minister was first Foreign Secretary, then Lord Privy Seal, while his nephew, A. J. Balfour, was First Lord of the Treasury and Leader of the House of Commons. The Ministers of the Crown Act, 1937, links the posts of Prime Minister and First Lord of the Treasury together for purposes of salary, and this perhaps gives legal force to a very strong convention. It remains possible (of course) for a Prime Minister to accumulate offices, and to be (as Sir Winston Churchill at various times was) First Lord of the Treasury and also Minister of Defence, or acting Foreign Secretary.

The very great importance of the First Lord threw an increasing burden of Treasury work, even in the eighteenth century, on the second Lord, the Chancellor of the Exchequer, who has always been an important person since the time of the younger Pitt. Formal decisions are still recorded in 'Treasury Minutes' signed by at least two Lords Commissioners; but the junior Lords (who are junior government Whips) have no duties in the Treasury except to attend and sign when requested to do so. The Chancellor is sole master, but the structure of the Department still includes some subordinate boards. The oldest of these was the Exchequer itself, and the earliest of all treatises on British administration is the *Dialogus de Scaccario*, which treats of financial procedure in the twelfth century. The Barons of the Exchequer gradually became judges, and their judicial work has been absorbed into the structure of the High Court of Justice. The Lord Chancellor's clerk, who became 'Chancellor of the Exchequer', gradually lost judicial and gained administrative functions. But his functions were concerned mainly with the consideration and execution of financial policy: he has never been directly responsible for the two great branches of financial administration, the keeping and auditing of accounts and the collection of revenue.

The function of audit was, from the reign of Henry VIII until near the end of the eighteenth century, in the hands of the Auditors of Imprest, who were paid by fees and did their work by deputy. The business was so badly done and the arrears of work were so large that in 1785 they were abolished and replaced by the Audit Board. This was much more efficient than its predecessor, but a gradual centralisation of function led to the system completed by the Exchequer and Audit Act of 1866. On the one hand this gave final responsibility for audit to the Comptroller and Auditor-General, an officer of the House of Commons, working closely with the Treasury but not responsible to it: on the other hand, responsibility for the regular maintenance of accounts, and for internal audit, was placed squarely on each Department, through its Accounting Officer, advised and supervised by the Treasury Officers of Accounts.

The collection of revenue still remains in the hands of two great boards, the Board of Inland Revenue (set up in its present form in 1849) and the Board of Customs and Excise (set up as the Board of Customs in 1671 and last reorganised in 1909), both being amalgamations of boards created earlier for the collection of particular taxes. These Departments have their offices outside the Treasury, on traditional sites in Somerset House and in Mark Lane in the City of London; and they are not in any sense run by the Treasury. But their boards consist entirely of civil servants, and are subject to the authority of the Chancellor of the Exchequer through their chairmen, who rank as Permanent Secretaries.

The offices of Lord High Steward and Lord High Constable survive only as ceremonial posts without political or administrative importance. So does that of the Lord High Chamberlain; and it is not necessary to trouble here with the Lord Great Chamberlain, who looks after the Palace of Westminster, or with the Lord Chamberlain, who censors plays. But the fate of the Lord High Admiral is of general interest.

(iii) *The Lord High Admiral*

The last to hold that office was the Duke of Clarence (later William IV) in 1828, and it had frequently been 'in commission' before this. It is now always exercised by Lords Commissioners under the chairmanship of the First Lord, who is a politician. Two of the junior Lords hold political office; apart from them, the Board now consists of seven admirals and one civil servant, the Permanent Secretary of the Admiralty. Together, they control all the business of the Navy, a position not reached until comparatively recently. During the rise of British naval power in the seventeenth and eighteenth centuries responsibility was widely diffused. Operations were sometimes directed by a Secretary of State, sometimes by the Board of Admiralty; supply was handled partly by the Navy Board (which was also responsible for pay) and partly by the Victualling Board, and there was a separate office of the Treasurer of the Navy, who paid over the sums the Navy Board directed. This incredible system worked miracles, and only gradually gave place to an ordinary Departmental structure: even now the Board of Admiralty is more like a real board than is the Treasury. The First Lord is in practice responsible for recommending the appointment or dismissal of his colleagues (who are in fact appointed by the Cabinet) and he has in the last resort the power to overrule the Board, even though he is in the minority of one. But one politician is not likely to overrule seven admirals except on matters (such as recruiting) where a civilian's opinion is as authoritative as theirs; and (in any case) his powers are limited by the right of 'the First Sea Lord and Chief of Naval Staff' to record his dissent from decisions, and to bring his dissent to the notice of the Cabinet.

The history of the 'senior service' is particularly important because this model was adopted for the other service Departments. The modern War Office, directed by an Army Council, was created in 1904, after the gradual disappearance of a number of offices as confusing as those which ran the Navy. The Air Council was constructed from its beginning in January 1918 on the same model.

4. THE PRIVY COUNCIL

The office of Lord President of the Council also lies at the centre of a structure of nominal committees. The Lord President was not until recently charged with important Departmental duties. Indeed, the office has in the main been one of high dignity rather than of great power, and its authority has depended largely on the personality of its holder. But the Privy Council—of which the Lord President would be chairman if it ever met in the absence of the monarch or the monarch's personal representative, and today it never does so—has been the begetter of Departments through committees, in two phases.

The first phase is that of seventeenth-century and early eighteenth-century administration. Before the emergence of the Cabinet as the greatest of all committees of the Privy Council, the King did much of his business not in full Council (a very unwieldy body even then) but in various committees presided over by himself or his trusted servants. Many of these committees were transitory, some became virtually permanent. The one which has the longest history is the Committee of the Council for Trade and Plantations, first set up as two separate committees in 1660. Its tangled history over the next 200 years need not be explained here, but the tradition of collegiate responsibility was so strong that it was maintained even when the Board of Trade was formally constituted as a Department by statute in 1862. The Board of Trade remains in being, a large body of rather unlikely people, including for instance the Archbishop of Canterbury (who signifies in his person the Committee's former interest in colonial bishoprics) and the Speaker of the House of Commons; but the President does not require the Board's authority for any of his actions. It never meets, and has even disappeared from the *Imperial Calendar*.

The Board of Trade was till quite recently one of several Departments presided over by titular boards, most of which had some connection with the Privy Council. The Ministry of Education acquired the name of 'Ministry' in 1944, but it is descended from the Committee of the Privy Council for Education (1839), which had from 1856 a Vice-President of the Council as its Minister, and from the Board of Education (1899). The Ministry of Agriculture and Fisheries (1919) administers responsibilities first gathered together under a Committee of the Privy Council in 1883, and then given in 1889 to a statutory board with its own Minister. It was amalgamated with the Ministry of Food (1939) in 1955. It also inherited general responsibility for the work of the Commissioners of Woods and Forests (1810), restyled 'Commissioners of Crown Lands' in 1923 when part of their duties passed to the Forestry Commission: the adoption in 1955 of the report of a Committee of Inquiry has resulted in a further change of style and form (see Chapter 15, p. 253). The Ministry of Works (1945) has inherited through many vicissitudes the duties of the old Board of Works (1851), a Department under a First (and sole) Commissioner who was a Minister. The Ministry of Health and the Ministry of Housing and Local Government are less directly descended from the Privy Council, but their history has passed through similar stages: from the Poor Law Board (1834), the first Board of Health (1848-54), the second Board of Health (1854-58), and the Committee of the Privy Council for Health (1859), to the Local Government Board of 1871, a titular board directed by a Minister of some importance, and so to the first Ministry of Health in 1919.

As this first progeny of committees grew to maturity as Departments, a second generation began to take its place. This second phase in the history of the office of Lord President begins with the creation of the Development Commission in 1909 and the Medical Research Committee of the National Health Insurance Commissioners in 1913. These bodies, though not themselves Committees of the Privy Council, can claim to be the parents of four such Committees: the Privy Council Committees for Scientific and Industrial Research (1915), for Medical Research (1920), for Agriculture (1931), and for Nature Conservancy (1956). Each of these bodies is in form a committee of holders of high political office (though they meet very seldom as a body) under the chairmanship of the Lord President: each has at least one working committee of men distinguished in various walks of life, who take considerable responsibility for advice on priorities affecting research—the Executive Council of the Department of Scientific and Industrial Research, the Medical Research Council, the Agricultural Research Council, and the Nature Conservancy. The internal organisation is not quite the same in each case, for the Department of Scientific and Industrial Research is a government Department staffed throughout by civil servants, whereas the others are corporate bodies existing by virtue of Royal Charter[1]; but each organisation is headed by a distinguished administrator who is also a scientist, and for all of them the Lord President of the Council acts as political head and spokesman in Parliament. The Lord President is not likely to attempt to guide research policy, but these Departments are now important spending Departments, disbursing annually more than £14 million, and issues of very great importance arise out of their work; some of these may be referred to the Advisory Council on Scientific Policy, which links these organisations to one another and to the Defence Research Policy Committee. The office of Lord President is no longer a sinecure: his responsibility for the progress of scientific research encompasses the great field of research into nuclear energy, which is at present wholly financed from national taxation and is conducted under close ministerial control by the Atomic Energy Authority. For these duties the Lord President is assisted by a small sub-Department called the Atomic Energy Office, with premises at Richmond Terrace, in Whitehall.[2]

5. Secretaries of State and Ministers

The office of Secretary of State was the last in the series of offices which originated from procedure for authenticating the King's commands. The Great Seal of the Realm was (and is) imposed by the authority of the Lord Chancellor, and this was the main symbol of the Chancellor's power in the later Middle Ages. The Great Seal was set in motion by the Privy Seal, held in the custody of the Lord Privy Seal; the Privy Seal was set in motion by the Signet, held by the Principal Secretary of State.

The Lord Privy Seal has for long been an officer enjoying considerable prestige, but never quite of the first rank, except when Thomas Cromwell was the main agent of Henry VIII's policy from 1531 to 1540, and when Salisbury was Prime Minister and Lord Privy Seal from 1900 to 1902. The office has never acquired a Department, and remains today a post which the Prime Minister can use to introduce into the government a man who is needed for purposes other than Departmental work. The Chancellor of the Duchy of Lancaster, custodian of the separate seal which belongs to Lancashire as a County Palatine, is in almost the same position.

The Secretary of State, however, was never displaced from his

---

[1] The Agricultural Research Council is staffed by civil servants at headquarters but not elsewhere.
[2] Since the beginning of 1957 responsibility for the development of nuclear power has been divided between the Prime Minister and the newly created Minister of Power.

position as the officer primarily responsible for royal correspondence with foreign powers and with officers responsible for government within the United Kingdom. The office reached the first rank under Elizabeth I, when the policy of the kingdom, internal and external, was directed by Sir William Cecil, afterwards Lord Burleigh, and his successor, Sir Francis Walsingham. Perhaps no Secretaries of State were afterwards so powerful, but the office never degenerated into formality, and from it sprang many Departments which were under individual direction from the first. The new office of Private Secretary to the Monarch did not arise until the tradition of constitutional monarchy was solidly established, and it has remained a personal appointment, one of crucial importance but outside the main framework of central administration.

The office of Principal Secretary of State is still in a sense a single office. For many formal purposes 'Her Majesty's Principal Secretaries of State' are interchangeable, and the allocation of duties between them has varied a great deal in course of time. It was not until 1782 that for temporary and personal reasons duties were sorted out so that one Secretary of State was responsible for home affairs and colonies, the other for foreign affairs. A third Secretary of State had been appointed fairly frequently in the eighteenth century to relieve the burden in difficult times, and it was natural to return to this expedient in the crisis of 1794, when Henry Dundas, Viscount Melville, was appointed Secretary of State for War and Colonies. These special arrangements became permanent, and small staffs grew into Departments. The Home Office and Foreign Office have existed continuously since 1782, the office of the Secretary of State for War since 1794. The Colonial Office can claim equal antiquity, but it did not have its own Secretary of State until 1854. The India Office (later the India Office and Burma Office) was created in 1858; the former disappeared in 1947, the latter in 1948, when the two countries achieved independence. The Secretary of State for Air was added to the other service Ministers in 1917; the Scottish Office (which had been given a Secretary in 1885) attained the status of a Secretaryship of State in 1926 for the first time since 1746; the Colonial Office in 1925 lost its responsibility for relations with independent members of the Commonwealth, now handled by the Commonwealth Relations Office, which was from 1925 to 1947 the Dominions Office.

These Offices were at first secretariats but gradually became Departments, preserving continuity of policy under different political heads. This sentiment was certainly strong at the Colonial Office as early as the 1840s, even before the Office had its own Secretary of State, and the India Office took over an existing tradition when it was created in 1858. But foreign affairs were largely handled by the Foreign Secretary himself till the retirement of Lord Salisbury from that post in 1900; the War Office was not a substantial Department until the reorganisation of 1904. It was perhaps logical that at this stage the term 'Ministry' should displace the term 'Office'. In 1889, Lord Salisbury's government had opposed the creation of a 'Ministry' of Education, on the ground that this would be an 'undesirable innovation in official phraseology', and had preferred to create a phantom board with a single Minister. The precedent was set by the war-time Ministry of Munitions in 1915, and was followed by other war organisations, one of which, the Air Ministry, has become permanent under that name, even though its head is a Secretary of State. Since the Ministry of Health was created in 1919 this has become the common title for all Departments not created (like the Commonwealth Relations Office) by the subdivision of an existing 'office'.

Since 1900 some twenty-five new Ministries have been created, and many have disappeared by amalgamation or complete abolition. But there has been no further change in the pattern of Departmental organisation. The new fashion of collegiate responsibility, an old fashion revived, has been most readily followed in bodies which are only on the fringes of central administration—commissions, marketing boards, hospital boards, public utility corporations, which are largely outside the scope of this book. Historical development does not therefore impose variety in practice on central administration, but it creates variety of status. The historical order of precedence between Departments, which is given in a note appended to this chapter, bears some relation to their ranking in the social scale of Whitehall.

FOR REFERENCE

(i) The history of certain Departments is recorded briefly, conveniently, and on the whole accurately in the volumes of the Whitehall Series, which are as follows:

Old Series

Sir E. TROUP: *The Home Office* (1925).
Sir M. SETON: *The India Office* (1925).
Sir A. NEWSHOLME: *The Ministry of Health* (1925).
Sir G. V. FIDDES: *The Dominions and Colonial Offices* (1926).
Sir T. HEATH: *The Treasury* (1927).
Sir F. L. C. FLOUDE: *The Ministry of Agriculture and Fisheries* (1927).

176 THE ORGANISATION OF DEPARTMENTS

Sir E. MURRAY: *The Post Office* (1927).
Sir H. LLEWELLYN SMITH: *The Board of Trade* (1928).
Sir J. TILLEY and Sir S. GASELEE: *The Foreign Office* (1933).
Sir J. MOYLAN: *Scotland Yard and the Metropolitan Police* (Revised Edn., 1934).
Sir L. A. SELBY-BIGGE: *The Board of Education* (2nd Edn., 1934).
H. GORDON: *The War Office* (1935).
See also Sir OSWYN MURRAY: *The Admiralty* (unfinished), published in part in *Mariner's Mirror*, 1937-39.

New Series

Sir F. NEWSAM: *The Home Office* (1954).
LORD STRANG and others: *The Foreign Office* (1955).
Sir CHARLES JEFFERIES: *The Colonial Office* (1956).
Sir HAROLD EMMERSON: *The Ministry of Works* (1956).
(Other volumes in preparation)

(ii) See also:
D. KILMUIR (1st Viscount): The Office of Lord Chancellor, *Parliamentary Affairs*, Spring 1956, at p. 132.

(iii) A great deal of material is to be found in the work of professional historians, in text-books of constitutional history, and in the biographies and autobiographies of distinguished civil servants, but there is no scholarly work covering the administration of any major Department for a long period of its career. The following are the most convenient books for reference and as further guides to bibliography:

Sir WILLIAM ANSON: *The Law and Custom of the Constitution*, Vol. II, Parts I and II (The Crown) (4th Edn. by Sir A. B. Keith, 1935).
Sir JOHN CRAIG: *A History of Red Tape—An Account of the Origin and Development of the Civil Service* (1955). A careful summary, by a former Deputy Master of the Royal Mint, of much of the relevant published material.
K. B. SMELLIE: *A Hundred Years of English Government (1832-1949)* (2nd Edn., 1950).

APPENDIX II

Ministerial Departments existing in 1956, with date of origin of the Department or its main constituent

Admiralty, fourteenth century.
Treasury, *c.* 1572 (as an Office separate from the Exchequer).
Post Office, sixteenth century.
Foreign Office, 1782.
Home Office, 1782.
Board of Trade, 1784 (given statutory form in 1862).
War Office, 1794.
Colonial Office, 1801.

Works, 1851.
Scottish Office, 1885.
Agriculture, Fisheries, and Food, 1889 (Food, 1917-1921 and 1939-1955).
Education, 1899 (Education Department under the Privy Council from 1856).
Labour, 1916.
Air Ministry, 1917.
Pensions, 1917 (and National Insurance, 1946).
Health, 1919.
Transport, 1919 (and Civil Aviation, 1945).
Commonwealth Relations, 1925.
Supply, 1939.
Fuel and Power, 1942.
Defence, 1946.
Housing and Local Government, 1950 (as 'Local Government and Planning').

CHAPTER TWELVE

THE PHYSICAL SETTING

Laudabunt alii claram Rhodon aut Mytilenen
aut Epheson bimarisvi Corinthi
moenia. . . .

HORACE.

UNTIL recently the proverbial contrast between Whitehall and Westminster was a thing which could be seen plainly as a fact of administrative geography. The Palace of Westminster has been one of the King's principal palaces since Saxon times and is still administered on his behalf by the Lord Great Chamberlain. The House of Lords met there regularly from the time when it emerged from the old Curia Regis; the Commons met at first in the Chapter House of Westminster Abbey close by, and they were granted the use of St. Stephen's Chapel, the site of their present chamber, in 1547. A little earlier, after Wolsey's fall, the King had moved into Wolsey's Palace, York Place, two or three hundred yards farther down the river, and had renamed it Whitehall (beyond it was a line of noblemen's houses on the river bank, between the King's residence at Westminster and the gates of the City of London at Temple Bar). The judges remained behind in Westminster Hall for another 300 years: but other royal officers went with the King to his new Court, and this was the centre of administration until the final ejection of the Stuarts in 1688. A good many minor offices grew up outside Whitehall during this period, largely in the City of London: the Customs House in Mark Lane, the Post Office in Bishopsgate,[1] the old Navy Office (where Pepys worked) in Seething Lane and Crutched Friars. But officials were not numerous, and William III probably left the old Palace not because he was squeezed out by his staff, but because of a disastrous fire and the unlucky association of Whitehall with a fallen dynasty. The King's London residences since that time have been St. James's Palace, and later Buckingham Palace; Whitehall was left to his Ministers and their staffs, placed appropriately between the Court on the one hand and Parliament on the other.

Central administration therefore began to grow up in the eight-

[1] The Post Office was not established in St. Martins-le-Grand until 1829.

eenth century in the cramped area bounded by Westminster, St. James's, the river, and the great houses eastwards from Northumberland House, just by Charing Cross. Most of the old Palace disappeared in the fire, and the buildings first used (many of them are still there) served both as official residences and as offices. This style is still maintained at the centre of the whole system, in Downing Street itself. The street was built as a speculation by Sir George Downing, Secretary to the Treasury from 1667 to 1671, an unscrupulous politician but an able organiser of Treasury business. The Treasury was already using buildings on the site of the old Cock-Pit close by, and it was convenient in 1732 for Walpole, as First Lord of the Treasury, to move into No. 10 Downing Street; No. 11 became at the same time the residence and office of the Chancellor of the Exchequer; 'No. 12' (not a house but a sort of outbuilding) was put up much later to house that important person the Patronage Secretary of the Treasury, who is also the Chief Whip. Other houses were built or acquired from time to time: the First Lord of the Admiralty's house, built about 1725, is the nucleus of the present Admiralty building. Dover House and Gwydyr House, which were acquired in the nineteenth century, still stand. Montague House, the first offices of the Ministry of Labour, was demolished quite recently to make way for a new building.

These arrangements were in some ways elegant and convenient, but scarcely suitable to the dignity of Britain in the age of palaces such as Versailles, Schönbrunn, and Potsdam, and the process of clearance and rebuilding began quite early in the eighteenth century. A relatively small but elegant building designed by William Kent was put up for the Treasury on the old Cock-Pit site in the 1730s, the Horse Guards' was built in 1760 for the Commander-in-Chief, then responsible for much of the military administration, and it completes with the Treasury and the back of Downing Street two sides of the Horse Guards' Parade. What is now the Whitehall frontage of the Privy Council Offices and the Treasury was begun in 1824, when Sir John Soane designed a building meant at first for the Board of Trade. This was redesigned and expanded later, but still retains a flavour of eighteenth-century Whitehall.

The next stage was clearance of sites and the erection of public offices on a much larger scale in the Victorian age, a process which has gradually converted Whitehall into an area of office blocks. The Secretaries of State never secured official residences in the eighteenth century, and the old Foreign Office was in some ramshackle buildings opposite No. 10 Downing Street, from which the younger clerks were apt to 'insult' the passers-by with 'peashooters and water-spouts'.

This site was cleared in the 1850s, and a huge Italianate quadrangle (Palmerston forbade Gothic) was put up to house the Home Office, the Foreign Office, the Colonial Office, and the India Office. The Metropolitan Police acquired a new building on the Embankment behind New Scotland Yard in 1891, the Admiralty was extended behind the First Lord's house, the War Office established itself in a new building opposite the Horse Guards', with the Board of Agriculture in a much more modest (but still monumental) building near by. In 1900 a long-delayed clearance scheme was at last completed, and Whitehall was rounded off by a new bastion looking across Parliament Square towards Westminster; this is still known as the New Public Offices, and it was completed in 1907 to house the Board of Education, the Board of Trade, the Local Government Board, and the Office of Works.

This was still the setting of central administration in 1939. The transition from private house to office block was in practice complete, but the private houses were still there, the offices were all grouped very closely together, and the environment preserved a flavour of the old tradition, that this was where the King's servants lived and worked, in rather shabby conditions but at the heart of things, between his palace and his Parliament. Since 1939 the physical transformation has been so great that it almost submerges the tradition.

In the first place, Departments are being squeezed out of Whitehall. This has happened partly because of the growth of the co-ordinating machinery, which itself requires extra space. During the war the basement of the New Public Offices was reinforced with great quantities of steel and concrete, and this became with other 'fortresses' a sort of war headquarters. Even after the war the Treasury, the Ministry of Defence, and other central agencies maintained their hold and kept out the older inhabitants of the building. But the main factors are the increase in the number of Departments, and the lack of building sites. Almost all the possible sites have been cleared; a new Air Ministry building has gone up behind the Banqueting Hall, a new Colonial Office opposite the Abbey awaits financial approval. Other Departments are spreading over the West End of London, in new buildings or in adapted office blocks—the Ministry of Health in Savile Row, the Ministry of Education in Curzon Street, the Ministry of Labour in St. James's Square, the Ministry of Transport and Civil Aviation in Berkeley Square, the Ministry of Supply in the Strand, the Ministry of Works beyond Lambeth Bridge, and so on. The offices are no longer within strolling distance of one another, of Parliament, and of the political and social clubs in Pall Mall and St. James's.

THE PHYSICAL SETTING

Secondly, many Departments have grown so large that they have not been able to get near the centre of government at all except by accepting a division of their headquarters staff. There are still a few small but important Departments which can be housed under one roof, but most big Departments now have several headquarters buildings. Some of the separate buildings are in more distant parts of central London (like the new Air Ministry buildings in Theobald's Road); some are in London suburbs; some are in provincial centres, where it is easier to obtain staff for routine operations (like the National Insurance Records Office, employing a staff of about 6,500, at Newcastle-upon-Tyne). In addition, the Scottish Departments have for different reasons moved more and more of their staff to headquarters in Edinburgh, and a number of Departments have subsidiary offices in Cardiff, for instance those of the Welsh Board of Health and the Welsh Department of the Ministry of Education. No Department can afford to be without an office close to the centre of government for the Minister, the Permanent Secretary, and their personal staff. The size of Ministries means that this is impossible except by sacrificing the speed of communication and ease of informal relations which are possible if an organisation lives together under one roof. Here is a very simple instance of how the size of an administrative organisation changes conditions of work and may limit efficiency.

In the third place, it has already been mentioned that the proportion of government servants in detached offices and establishments has steadily grown, a matter dealt with more fully in Chapter 16. The only local offices with a long history are those of the Revenue Departments: to these have been added everywhere offices of the Ministry of Labour, the Ministry of Pensions and National Insurance, and the National Assistance Board. In addition, many Departments (like the Ministry of Agriculture) have offices in areas which specially concern them, and virtually all Departments have regional offices. This national network has grown up at random, in a period when priority for government building was low; office accommodation is often very bad, and slow progress is made with ambitious plans for 'local Whitehalls'. The situation is gradually improving, but many provincial offices are still in temporary accommodation not conveniently placed for the staff or for the public. In addition to administrative offices, there are a large number of separate establishments for research, development, and production, which have also grown haphazard and are usually housed in some sort of temporary accommodation.

At first sight, therefore, there is now little common background.

A civil servant may work in a historic building in that blend of dignity and fustiness which is the atmosphere of the Treasury itself; or in the rather vulgar splendour of new office buildings, like those of the Air Ministry and the Ministry of Health; or in the tidy but bare accommodation of newly built Employment Exchanges or National Insurance offices; or in a complete new town such as was built for the Atomic Energy Research Establishment at Harwell, then run by the Civil Service; or in a ramshackle collection of huts erected as temporary buildings in 1916. Nevertheless, common organisation stamps its mark on these different environments. The layout of the office always has certain familiar features. At the top of the scale there is the group of offices of those who direct the Department: the Minister's own office and his private office, the Permanent Secretary's office and private office, a central conference room, the adjacent offices of Parliamentary Secretaries and Deputy Secretaries. At the other extreme are the offices of messengers, office-keepers, registry, typing pools, and so on, also interrelated in a recognisable way. Common services also contribute to the atmosphere. The hand of the Ministry of Works is to be seen everywhere, in architecture, furniture, painting, the lettering of placards: that of the Stationery Office in the style of printed notices, letter-heads, writing-paper, and forms. (It is these two organisations which give the Civil Service such visible status symbols as it possesses, by adjusting scales of furniture and stationery with some precision to the rank of the user.) Similarly, the internal services, like those of messengers and cleaners, do not vary much from one office to another: they can quickly contrive to make any building whatever look like a government office, stamped as something quite unlike the office of a business enterprise, or a local authority, or a public corporation.

FOR REFERENCE

Some information on this topic will be found in the volumes of the (old) Whitehall Series (see references to Chapter 11); but the most convenient reference book on the topography of Whitehall is:

G. S. DUGDALE: *Whitehall Through the Centuries* (1950).

For a review of problems of accommodation—mainly for clerical staff—in government offices, see:

Working Conditions in the Civil Service—Report of a Study Group appointed by H.M. Treasury (H.M.S.O. 1947).

On Sir George Downing's influence at the Treasury see:

STEPHEN B. BAXTER: *The Development of the Treasury 1660-1702* (1957) pp. 168-9, 177-81.

CHAPTER THIRTEEN

THE PATTERN OF ORGANISATION

O! when degree is shak'd,
Which is the ladder to all high designs,
The enterprise is sick.
SHAKESPEARE: *Troilus and Cressida*, I, iii, 101-3.

1. INTRODUCTORY

THE object of this chapter is to describe the elements of structure which are common to all Departments, the next chapter similarly describes common elements of practice. It is necessary first to explain what is meant by a Department as a unit of administration.

2. THE DEPARTMENT

Departments may be classified into Ministries (or 'major' Departments) and non-ministerial (or 'minor') Departments. There were in 1956 twenty-four Ministries, about a hundred other Departments.

A Ministry is directly under the control of a Minister, who is responsible to Parliament for the conduct of his Department and is almost invariably a member of one of the Houses. There is a clear line between 'Departmental Ministers' and 'junior Ministers', who have no administrative duties except by delegation from the political head of the Department. But there are gradations within the former group. Some Ministers are members of the Cabinet, others have the same status (in so far as status is measured by salary) but are not members of the Cabinet, the rest have a rather lower salary and status.

A non-ministerial Department might be defined as a central agency staffed by civil servants but not directly under the control of a Minister. Nevertheless, there is always some Minister who is ultimately responsible to Parliament for its work. If this were not so, it could not be regarded as part of the central administration, since constitutional principle requires that the whole of this should be under Parliamentary control through responsible Ministers. Some non-ministerial Departments are small, but some are very large: for instance, the Board of Inland Revenue with a staff of about 50,000, the Board of Customs and Excise with about 15,000, the National Assistance Board with about 10,000.

Although for constitutional reasons the notion of a Ministry is dominant in central administration, and all Departments fall under the aegis of some Ministry, the minor Departments are independent in the sense that they have a complete administrative structure of their own, and do not fit into the hierarchical organisation of the supervising Ministry. Many of them present their own Estimates.

It is hard to draw a line satisfactorily between a minor Department as here defined and an independent public body appointed and financed by the central government. A few examples will illustrate the difficulties. The Civil Service Commission is best regarded as a minor Department under the aegis of the Treasury, and it has its own Estimates. The University Grants Committee, through whose hands passes (in the form of separate grants-in-aid) the largest part of government financial assistance to Universities, has a staff of civil servants with their own administrative structure and separate Estimates for the cost of running the office, under the general supervision of the Treasury. It is perhaps a 'minor Department'. The British Council, which has large responsibilities for 'cultural' propaganda, is not staffed by civil servants and is entirely financed by grant-in-aid, and cannot therefore be regarded as a Department; but it has an internal structure very like that of a Department, its Estimates are submitted annually to Parliament by the Foreign Secretary, and he accepts responsibility in the sense that he is prepared to answer Parliamentary questions about its work. The Exchequer and Audit Department, directed by the Comptroller and Auditor-General, is staffed by civil servants, and its Estimates are presented annually to Parliament by the Treasury. It is therefore usual to regard it as a Department: but the Comptroller and Auditor-General himself is a servant of the House of Commons, and no Minister is responsible for him (the other officials of the two Houses are in a somewhat similar position but are not regarded as civil servants.[1] Perhaps the safest clue through this maze is to regard a body as a government Department (as a matter of practical observation) if it is staffed wholly by civil servants, and is financed directly by the normal processes of Parliamentary grant (and not by grant-in-aid).

It is equally hard to say why some functions are performed by Ministries, some by non-ministerial Departments, and some by public bodies which are not Departments although they derive

[1] Orlo Cyprian Williams: *The Clerical Organisation of the House of Commons, 1661-1850* (1954), p. 44.

most of their revenue from central funds. The explanation of particular arrangements is often merely that they have existed for a long time and that there has never been any particular reason to disturb them. If the question becomes one for debate, there are perhaps two alternative reasons for shifting responsibility from a Ministry to a minor Department: first, that the work to be done is self-contained and causes very little political controversy, so that it is convenient to reduce the scope of the main ministerial organisation by setting this function on one side; secondly, that the matter is one of some delicacy, which requires control at the centre, but ought to be outside party controversy. It is simple to find examples to fit the first reason, such as the great Revenue Boards, or the British Museum, or (on a smaller scale) the offices of the Registrar-General, the Public Trustee, the Registrar of Friendly Societies, and the Government Actuary. Perhaps the strongest examples of the second reason are the Civil Service Commission and the National Assistance Board: this tendency also acts frequently to create bodies which are perhaps just outside the scope of central administration, like the British Council, the Arts Council, or the Royal Fine Art Commission.

3. The Permanent Secretary

The senior civil servant in a Ministry is the Permanent Secretary, a member of the Administrative Class at the highest grade of that class, except for the special position held by Permanent Secretaries of the Treasury, who stand in isolation one rung higher on the ladder. There may on occasion be two joint Permanent Secretaries, as at the Treasury for a period before the First World War, and at the present time, and as at the Ministry of Supply from the end of 1955 to July 1956; or even three, as at the Treasury in 1918. But these exceptions are not numerous enough to affect the principle of a single head.[1]

The Permanent Secretary is almost always appointed by the Treasury to be the Accounting Officer for his Department. This means that he is personally responsible for ensuring that money is not spent by the Department except in accordance with the Estimates voted by the House of Commons. It is he and not the Minister who appears before the Public Accounts Committee of the House of Commons to answer any criticisms arising out of the audit of the Department's accounts by the Comptroller and Auditor-General. This is constitutionally correct, because the issues which arise are in

---

[1] The First Permanent Secretary at the Ministry of Supply (Sir James Helmore) had a slight 'lead' in pay.

theory not issues of policy (which involve the Minister) but issues of procedure in carrying out approved policy. As Accounting Officer, the Permanent Secretary is under a duty to intervene if he observes any breach of financial procedure even by the Minister himself; but he is not Finance Officer, and he has no similar responsibility for the preparation of Estimates, since the last word on policy lies with the Minister. Nevertheless, the Permanent Secretary is intimately concerned with all financial decisions, and therefore with the whole policy of the Department as well as with economy and efficiency in its organisation.

He is also specially concerned with the Parliamentary business of the Department. He and his main subordinates in the Administrative Class are primarily responsible for briefing the Minister in Parliamentary debates, for preparing Bills and helping the Minister to see them through Parliament, and for dealing with Parliamentary questions addressed to the Minister. On policy the Minister is supreme, but Parliamentary business brings the Permanent Secretary into virtually all matters of policy; and indeed he is generally involved in all Cabinet business as well as in all Parliamentary business.

This does not mean that he is the sole channel of communication between the Minister and the Department on matters of policy. He will be wise, even in a Department without specialist staff, to encourage the Minister to deal directly with civil servants responsible for large sections of work, and most Departments now contain specialist officers who rank as high in their own field as the Permanent Secretary does in his. The strongest example is that of the service Departments, in which the Chief of Staff is the Minister's principal adviser on all service matters, and is primarily responsible for the preparation of papers for the Chiefs of Staff Committee, which deals with fundamental issues of defence policy in preparation for submission to the Defence Committee of the Cabinet and to the Cabinet itself. But there are equally distinguished specialists in other fields, such as the Chief Medical Officer of the Ministry of Health, the Chief Inspector at the Ministry of Education, and the Chief Scientist at the Ministry of Supply; and it would be absurd to suggest that they are shut out by the Administrative Class from direct access to the Minister. Indeed, some Ministries are run in such a way that their organisation is in practice many-headed rather than single-headed: but even in these Ministries there is one man (and only one man) besides the Minister so placed that he can survey the business of the Ministry as a whole. Such a man can be of great value to his specialist colleagues if he fully commands their confidence, and if they understand what his function is.

There are one or two small Ministries where the permanent head does not rank as a Permanent Secretary: in the Lord President's Office he is an Under Secretary; in the Paymaster-General's Office he is an Assistant Secretary; and this is common in the non-ministerial Departments (H.M. Stationery Office, for instance, has a Deputy Secretary, the Crown Estates Office has either an Under Secretary or a Deputy Secretary). But what has been said here is applicable, and so is much of what follows, subject to appropriate scaling-down of the ranks involved.

4. THE MAIN STRUCTURE

The Permanent Secretary is generally assisted by one or two Deputy Secretaries, who may be in charge of a particular block of work or may act as general deputies. On the next rung are several Under Secretaries, each controlling several Assistant Secretaries. Nomenclature varies, but usually an Assistant Secretary is at the head of a 'division', consisting of a number of branches or sections, each under a Principal or a Chief Executive Officer. This structure of 'non-specialists' can be combined in a great variety of ways with a hierarchy or hierarchies of specialists, so as to form a mixed organisation in which specialists play a large part, and some of these ways will be indicated in the next chapter. There are, however, two blocks of business which are always directed by members of the Administrative Class.

(i) *Finance*

In almost every major Department there is an Under Secretary who acts as chief adviser to the Permanent Secretary about matters of finance and to whom the latter delegates his detailed work as Accounting Officer. His title varies: to take some examples at random, in the Ministry of Agriculture he is Principal Finance Officer, in the Ministries of Education and Health he is Under Secretary for Finance and Accountant-General, in the Ministry of Works he is Under Secretary, Finance Division. The divisions under his charge vary according to the nature of the Department; but one usually finds:

(*a*) A division (under an Assistant Secretary) which is responsible for the preparation of the annual Estimates, for Supplementary Estimates, and for general questions involving finance. This is the main point of liaison with the Treasury on day-to-day questions of financial policy and financial priorities: its head must be a civil servant of general experience and balanced judgement, but he need not have an expert knowledge of accounting procedure.

(b) A Directorate of Accounts, under a high ranking Executive Class officer who will have had much experience in public accounts. The division has general responsibility for all questions of accounting procedure and internal audit; it is staffed mainly by Executive Class officers who are virtually specialists, and those doing accounting work elsewhere in the Ministry look to it for guidance. This is the main point of liaison with the auditors of the Comptroller and Auditor-General's Department; and also with Officers of Accounts in the Treasury.

(ii) *Establishments*

There is also an Under Secretary designated as Establishments Officer. Most Permanent Secretaries take a keen personal interest in promotion and postings at the top levels of the Department, and keep in general touch with the staff position as a whole. But no Permanent Secretary can expect to establish a position of personal ascendancy in his Department, or to maintain a very wide range of personal contacts. The Permanent Secretary is at the top of the organisation, but he is not its master. Leading civil servants (like other administrators) generally have a small 'connection' of junior men whom they trust and whom they like to see in posts round them. But all Permanent Secretaries, and especially those appointed from outside the Department, must pay respect to established habits and personalities. A Departmental head who has 'grown up' inside the Department will have a more thorough knowledge of its ways, and may be able to exercise greater influence in matters of personnel. But it is quite unusual for a Permanent Secretary to attempt to stamp his personality on his Department. Personnel administration in the Civil Service is for many reasons less personal and more formal than in other organisations: this tradition rules at the Treasury, among Permanent Secretaries, and also among Establishments Officers.

Nevertheless, a good Establishments Officer is not a mechanical device for the interpretation of regulations. The efficiency of the Department depends greatly on his reputation for fair and open dealing, since he deals with so many matters which involve imponderables. He is responsible for promotion boards, for disciplinary cases, for Whitley Council business, for postings, and for any Departmental instructions regulating leave, promotion, postings, and conditions of service generally, within the framework set by Treasury regulations. Most of these matters are closely supervised by the

Treasury, and he is the chief point of liaison with it. In addition, he is responsible for settling the 'establishment', in the sense of the number and grading of 'bodies' to be allocated for particular blocks of work. This involves close association with the Finance Officer in the preparation of Estimates. Finance and Establishments tend to interlock within Departments, as they do at the Treasury.

The Establishments Officer normally has under him an Assistant Secretary in charge of all these matters as they affect non-industrial staff: if the Department has a large block of industrial staff this may require a separate division; and there may be other subdivisions. All these posts are filled by Administrative Class civil servants except in very small Departments.

The Establishments Officer also controls other sections not so traditional in the Service. If a Department has a large number of junior staff, it generally has a staff welfare officer: and there is a central point of reference in the Treasury Welfare Adviser and her Assistant. But it is never clear to other sections of the Department what 'welfare' is, and the influence of the welfare officer depends more on individual tact and persistence than on official duties. Similarly, the status of the training officer varies from one Department to another according to circumstances and personality: in principle, every Department has an officer responsible for questions affecting staff training, and there is a central point of reference in the Training and Education Division of the Treasury.

There has been an 'office investigation' branch in the Treasury since 1919, but it was for twenty years concerned mainly with the use of office machinery of various kinds, and it was not till the Second World War that much attention was paid to the idea (already current in business) that the analytic study of organisation could be a practical instrument of administration. The new fashion, which has made the letters 'O. & M.'[1] familiar outside the Civil Service, was partly due to a passing phase of political interest in administrative techniques; but it was also a practical response to the problems of an organisation which had been expanded suddenly in very difficult conditions. Conditions have become a good deal easier since the war, and there has lately been less public interest in O. & M. But the scale of organisation is still such that there is a place for continuous analysis of its operation, and O. & M. can now be regarded as a normal part of central administration.

The practice of O. & M. continues to be based largely on the need for people with expert knowledge of business machines and their place in office organisation. The Civil Service has discouraged the

[1] Organisation and Methods.

evolution from this of high-flown ideas about 'scientific' administration. The case for special studies of organisation is based by the strongest supporters of O. & M. on the value of bringing in outside observers, uncommitted to the controversies of the Department or division, experienced in problems of organisation, and trained to use common sense methodically so as to establish beyond controversy what is really happening, and why it happens. At first, business efficiency experts were brought in from outside: but the trend of policy has been for the O. & M. Division of the Treasury to train civil servants for the work. Training courses are short (generally about five to six weeks), there is no pretence that they produce specialists, and it is intended that most of those who take them should return to ordinary Departmental duties after a period of O. & M. work in the Treasury or in their own Department.

The O. & M. Division of the Treasury is organised in sections, each responsible for a group of Departments. In addition, there is a Training Section and an Office Machinery Section, and an Assistant Secretary has recently been appointed to investigate the application of electronics to Civil Service work, largely for the further mechanisation of routine operations. A number of major Departments have strong O. & M. divisions of their own; others have smaller sections or none at all, and rely on assistance from the Treasury.

In most Departments, since 1946, the Establishments Officer has also been Organisation Officer. Where this is so he generally has a Principal or a senior Executive Class officer as head of his O. & M. branch, responsible for liaison, when required, with the O. & M. Division of the Treasury (which issues a small monthly bulletin on O. & M. experience); for handling the Departmental end of any inquiry made at the request of the Department by Treasury Organisation Officers; and for conducting investigations within the Department himself, through his own Organisation Officers, who will normally have passed through a Treasury course. These officers come largely from the Executive Class, and their main work is done at that level, in improving the smooth flow of business in routine operations. It is rarely possible for Organisation Officers to do useful work on the higher organisation of the Department: that is a matter for the Establishments Officer himself, and his contribution depends largely on his personality and experience.

The Establishments Officer is also chief housekeeper to the Department. Generally, there is an Assistant Secretary in charge of a division which maintains contact with the Ministry of Works about buildings and furniture, and about the 'pool' of cars for use on official business, with the Stationery Office about the large range of

THE PATTERN OF ORGANISATION 191

supplies for which it is responsible, with the Post Office about telecommunications equipment and switchboards (which are manned by Post Office staff); and he is also responsible for sorting out conflicting demands within the Department. This is one of the most thankless jobs in the Civil Service, and has little to do with policy; but a good deal depends on the competence and imperturbability of the man concerned.

The Establishments Officer is also responsible (directly or through one of his divisions) for those important persons, the Controller of Typists, who is responsible for the economical provision of shorthand, typing, and duplicating facilities; the Officer Keeper, responsible for the service of doorkeepers and messengers; and the Officer in charge of the Registry, a point of central importance which will be referred to again in Chapter 14.

5. PRIVATE SECRETARIES

The Minister, the Parliamentary Secretary (or Secretaries), and the most important of the officials each has a private secretary, and 'the private secretary network' plays an important part in administration. The 'private secretary' is a character peculiar to the British Civil Service, and it is difficult to explain him except in negative terms. He is not like the *Chef du Cabinet* of a French Minister, nor like the personal staff officer of a high officer in the armed forces, nor like the personal assistants of the American President, nor like the personal secretary of an industrial manager. The office grew out of an upper class tradition: a nineteenth-century Minister often brought with him into his Department a young man of good social position who could be trusted to handle tactfully and confidentially all business personal to the Minister. As the scale of business grew, the importance of private secretaries grew: men like Disraeli's Montague Corry, Gladstone's Arthur Godley and Algernon West, A. J. Balfour's J. S. Sandars, were very able people who acquired a high standing in their own right. Some of these Victorian private secretaries—Sir Algernon West, for example (who described himself as 'the last clerk that ever entered the public service without any examination whatever'), and Sir Edward Hamilton—had been civil servants before appointment, and remained civil servants after their Ministers had left office. Others, like Gladstone's Stafford Northcote, went on to make a career in politics.

An exceptional but characteristic example of the Victorian private secretary was Reginald Baliol Brett (afterwards Viscount Esher), a well-connected young man who was private secretary to the Marquess of Hartington from 1878 to 1885, first in opposition, then successively as Secretary of State for India and Secretary of State for War. In 1895 Rosebery made him Permanent Secretary of the Office of Works, a post which was attractive to him because it enabled him to work closely with the Queen's personal circle, of which he was already a member. As administrator he organised the Queen's funeral and the Coronation of Edward VII with great success, and he was offered more senior Departments, such as the Colonial Office and War Office, which he refused. He is remembered now chiefly as political diarist, expert on Army politics, and personal friend of two kings.

Perhaps the most famous private secretary of this century was Sir Edward Marsh, art collector and translator of Latin and French verse, who entered the Colonial Office by examination as a 'Second Class Clerk' in 1896 (after an education at Westminster School he graduated in classics at Trinity College, Cambridge). In 1900 he became assistant private secretary to Joseph Chamberlain, then Colonial Secretary, and was Churchill's private secretary in various posts from 1905 till 1921, and again from 1924 to 1929. He remained a 'professional' private secretary until his retirement in 1937. This also was exceptional: but 'Eddy' Marsh became a legend in his lifetime and might almost be regarded as the patron saint of private secretaries hereafter.

The rapid promotion of some of these private secretaries—Arthur Godley (later Lord Kilbracken) was private secretary to Mr. Gladstone at 25, Permanent Secretary at the India Office at 36—caused a good deal of ill-feeling in the early days of entry by examination. But the habit of appointing private secretaries from outside the Service had gone before 1914, leaving only the aristocratic tradition of a post which combines personal and official relationships in an unusual way. A private secretary is an official: his future career lies in the Department, and he has an overriding sense of loyalty to it. But he will be unsuccessful as an official unless he can establish a personal relationship with his 'master' which is not far short of friendship.

The formal arrangements are easy to describe. The Minister's private secretary is occasionally an Assistant Secretary, more often a Principal, marked out for promotion: a tested man (or woman), probably about 35. He generally also has at least one Assistant Private Secretary, an Assistant Principal who has completed probation and has acquired a good general knowledge of the Department and of the Service. There is also a Parliamentary Private Secretary, a back-bench M.P. of the Minister's party, who has a desk in the

Ministry: his work mainly lies in the House of Commons (where the Minister has a private room), as personal and political liaison officer for the Minister. There are one or two competent clerks in charge of the Minister's papers, and an allocation of stenographers much more generous than is usual in the Civil Service. This small group constitutes the Private Office.

No one else in the Ministry has so large a personal staff, but there are similar groups lower down in the hierarchy. Each of the Permanent Secretaries to the Treasury has a Principal as his private secretary. Other Permanent Secretaries have one (or perhaps two) private secretaries at the Assistant Principal level, and one or two personal clerks and typists. If there is any specialist officer at this level he has a similar establishment. The private secretary to the Deputy Secretary is generally an Assistant Principal, but may be a promising Executive Officer. Under Secretaries and Assistant Secretaries are served by a Clerical Officer promoted from the shorthand typing class, and permitted (the only instance in the Service) to combine the jobs of secretary, clerk, and shorthand typist.

There is a sense, therefore, in which the group of chief officials is shadowed by a group of private secretaries, which has its own hierarchy from the Private Secretary to the Prime Minister (who is an Under Secretary) to the Personal Assistants to Under Secretaries. There are at present about 150 Administrative Class officers in such posts, receiving special allowances of up to £250 a year.

Good private secretaries are easily recognised; bad ones do not last long. But perhaps not even a private secretary could set out general rules for success except in negative terms. A private secretary need not know everything, but must know how to find out everything: he must not offend anyone, on the telephone or in the 'outer office', but he must not let the wrong people in; he must not smother the Minister in paper, but must see that a paper is always there when wanted: he must not threaten the Minister with the consequences of failing to follow routine, but must see that public business is not delayed because work accumulates in the Minister's 'pending' tray; he must not come between the Minister and the Permanent Secretary, but must not let the Minister feel that he serves only the Permanent Secretary. It might be suggested that it is his business to see that the Minister understands the Department and that the Department understands the Minister, and to do both as inconspicuously as possible.

Experience as a private secretary remains one of the avenues of promotion. The talents required are not plentiful, and almost all promising Assistant Principals have their chance. The best of them may become P.S. to the Minister later in their career, and those who succeed there cannot fail to go higher. It is a guess (but a fairly safe one) that almost all Permanent Secretaries who entered as Assistant Principal went through this mill at some stage in their career: the attitudes and experience of the Private Office are very important in moulding the Service as a whole.[1]

6. CENTRAL SERVICES

The structure of Departments does not easily accommodate a central 'brains trust' or 'planning staff'. The organisation is one in which the planning of policy is linked closely with its execution, an arrangement which promotes realism but discourages Departments from looking very far ahead. Various attempts have been made to remedy this by including special 'thinking' sections in the headquarters of a Department, but there have been some conspicuous failures and no conspicuous successes. The lesson of experience seems to be that civil administration differs in one fundamental respect from military administration. The latter moves abruptly from passivity to action. Its operation in time of peace is dominated by the contingency of war; even in time of war while one operation is in progress another (or several alternatives) is being prepared, so that the organisation moves 'in bounds', and there is a working line of demarcation between Operations and Plans. Civil administration on the other hand is continuous, there is no natural division of responsibility, and if an attempt is made to draw a distinction the result is that either the planning section is left 'out on a limb' and exerts no influence, or it succeeds so well that it begins to direct operations. A Department can (in general) be given greater foresight only by giving those in the line of command greater opportunity and incentive to think ahead.

There are obvious exceptions. Some Departments (for example, Civil Defence) are in structure and function unusually like military organisations. Others are concerned with production programmes, a specialised activity which has been confused with 'planning' in the wider sense, because of Russian talk about Five-Year Plans, and because of the economists' controversy over 'planning'. A production Ministry must have a central programmes division: its primary function is not to plan production—that is done by those in opera-

[1] There is a superb account of the role of the private secretary in Thomas Jones, *A Diary with Letters, 1931-1950* (1954), pp. xix-xxi. Curiously enough, Tom Jones was never himself a private secretary, though as Assistant Secretary (later Deputy Secretary) to the Cabinet he was the personal confidant and assistant of several Prime Ministers.

tional control of production—but to know what all the different production plans are, and to keep a central record of them, accepted by all as reliable. This is an indispensable instrument for securing coherence between plans, since it exposes inconsistencies and impossibilities, and a programmes division if well run may be very important in the process of thinking ahead. But it is not a Planning Staff. Civil Departments do not have Planning Staffs, and one of the difficulties about the idea of a Civil General Staff (to which we refer further in Chapter 19) is that such a central organisation would have no natural points of contact outside the line of command except in the service Departments.

We have already referred in Chapter 7 to the position of the statistician class. Virtually all Departments now have a statistical section, organised as a central service for the whole Department, and these sections have a natural point of reference in the Central Statistical Office. Their importance in relation to policy varies a good deal from one Department to another. Reference has also been made to the Legal Class, and to the position of the Legal Adviser. Other central services are of less importance, but contribute to the pattern of organisation.

All Departments possess a library, and the Librarian and his staff generally provide some sort of reference service for officials seeking general information. Some libraries are used very little except for general reading; others may be of substantial importance as points of reference, and even as centres of learned work.

There is also in every Department a press officer or information officer or public relations officer. His job is mainly one of liaison with the press and with other organs of 'mass communication' such as radio, television, and films, and much of it consists of seeing that Departmental 'hand-outs' are well prepared and are issued quickly to the proper people, that press questions are answered as courteously and frankly as possible, and that correspondents and other privileged inquirers are properly looked after. It is unwise to do too much to propagate the Department's point of view: a free press is suspicious of the official 'line', and politicians are ready to attack anything which seems to be an expenditure of public money on advertisement of the Minister and his party. Much of the more interesting work is now grouped together in the Central Office of Information (Chapter 17), which deals with the more technical aspects of 'producing' publicity material, such as brochures and films.

There is nothing very exciting about the job of Departmental information officer, but it takes its place in a network which links central administration to all the organs of publicity in this country and abroad. On one side are the press, the B.B.C. and other radio and television services, and the cinema; on the other is a network of information officers ranging from the Public Relations Adviser to the Prime Minister, the Head of the Information Division of the Treasury, the Head of the News Department of the Foreign Office, the large Information Divisions of the service Departments, to individual officers acting part-time in small Departments. For some purposes (but not for all) the Central Office of Information acts as a point of reference for the whole system.

Information Officers from all Departments have since 1949 been grouped together to form a 'general service' class with its own grades running parallel to those of the Executive Class up to the level of Principal Executive Officer, and including a few higher posts. (The class numbered 266[1] on 1 July 1955.) It is too early to say whether this arrangement will prove permanent. At present the origins of members of the class are very diverse, including working journalists, graduates qualified as research workers and writers, and technicians in various branches of 'production'.

These four services—statistics, legal advice, library, and public information—may for administrative convenience be attached to one or other of the main groups of work under an Under Secretary: or some or all of them may be grouped together under some sort of central secretariat division reporting direct to the Permanent Secretary. But they do not fit neatly into the main structure of the organisation.

Another device used freely to provide services to the organisation as a whole is the appointment of specialist 'advisers' at a high level. Reference will be made later to the place of the Economic Section of the Treasury in general economic planning; for some time after the war other Departments concerned with economic affairs also had a full-time economic adviser on their staff. Similarly, Departments which are concerned with technical matters but do not conduct research themselves have a scientific adviser. This sort of appointment is essentially a one-man job: the man appointed must discover problems for himself, and must find things to say about them which are sufficiently important to the Department to command interest and support. There has at least been enough success to establish the practice as normal, and it offers a possible compromise in the dilemma posed by the idea of a specialist planning staff. An 'adviser' generally has a career of his own outside the Service. Hence, if his advice is disregarded, he can withdraw with honour; if it is taken, he

[1] Permanent staff only. (Source: Central Staff Records Division, H.M. Treasury.)

THE PATTERN OF ORGANISATION 197

does not threaten the influence of those in the direct line of command. The device in fact has some of the merits of the system of permanent and temporary advisory bodies, to which reference is made in Chapter 24.

FOR REFERENCE

(i) *Departments*

It is not clear what definition is used by the editors of the *Civil Service Calendar*, but at least they include all Departments, ministerial and non-ministerial, as well as a number of other public bodies. Nor is there complete agreement among academic writers. For some examples of the narrow line which divides minor non-ministerial Departments from independent public bodies, see:

D. N. CHESTER: 'The Classification of Administrative Bodies', *Political Studies*, Vol. I, p. 34 (bibliography in footnotes).

J. W. GROVE: 'Grants-in-Aid to Public Bodies', *Public Administration*, Vol. XXX, p. 299.

F. M. G. WILLSON: 'Ministries and Boards: Some Aspects of Administrative Development since 1832', *Public Administration*, Vol. XXXIII, p. 43.

Sir ARTHUR STREET: 'Quasi-Governmental Bodies', in *British Government since 1918* (1950), p. 157.

(ii) *The Main Structure*

There is more published material on 'Organisation and Methods' than on any other part of Establishments work. See, for example:

16th Report from the Select Committee on National Expenditure 1941-42 ('The Organisation and Control of the Civil Service'). H.C. 120, 1942.

5th Report from the Select Committee on Estimates, Session 1946-47 ('Organisation and Methods'). H.C. 143, 1947.

O. & M. Bulletin. Published monthly by the O. & M. Division, H.M. Treasury.

H. O. DOVEY: *A Handbook of Organisation and Methods* (1951).

Pamphlets issued by the O. & M. Division of the Treasury:

Suggestion Schemes (1949).
The Practice of O. & M. (1954).
Organisation Charts and Lists of Duties (1954).
Procedure Records (1950).
The Design of Forms (1950).
Machines and Appliances in Government Offices (1954).
Office Machines and Appliances—Processes of Dominant Reproduction (1950).

On Accounting Officers, Principal Finance Officers, and Principal Establishments Officers, see Treasury Memorandum printed as an Appendix to the *4th Report from the Committee of Public Accounts, Session 1950-51*. H.C. 241-1, 1951.

H. V. RHODES: 'The Director of Establishments and Organisation' (in the Ministry of National Insurance), *Public Administration*, Vol. XXX, p. 139.

(iii) *Private Secretaries* are well dealt with in:

H. E. DALE: *The Higher Civil Service* (1941).
THOMAS JONES: *A Diary with Letters, 1931-1950* (1954).
Sir HAROLD NICOLSON: *Private Faces* (a novel) (1929).
Parliamentary Papers, 1890, Vol. LVIII, p. 163, contains a statement about Civil Service appointments obtained by former private secretaries from 1869 to that date.

(iv) *Central Services*

For planning and programming, see:

E. DEVONS: *Planning in Practice* (1950).

For statistical services, see:

E. DEVONS: *An Introduction to British Economic Statistics* (1956).

CHAPTER FOURTEEN

HOW BUSINESS IS DONE

A man cannot methodise the subject matter of his business without at the same time methodising his own mind.—Sir HENRY TAYLOR: *The Statesman.*

1. INTRODUCTORY

THE title of this chapter is presumptuous: even a civil servant with a lifetime of experience could not write it adequately, and those outside the Service are bound to impose crudity and simplification on delicate matters. But civil servants have theorised very little about their own practice, and an attempt to formalise may be of some service even if it requires amendment. It should be clear that what we are looking for are the formal elements in procedure which are common to different technical spheres. This risks some misapprehension, because business is always done within some technical setting, and different settings modify procedure in different ways.

The procedure we have in mind is that of headquarters in 'Whitehall': there are doubtless variations at lower levels in the provinces, sometimes making for great strictness, sometimes for informality. No one knows all these in detail, but it is not possible for them to vary except within limits set by the general practice of the Service.

The bureaucratic style of organisation is one that is universal in the modern world, Communist or Western, in public or in private administration. It combines three elements which might be found separately.

First, there is the hierarchical order which has been universal in military organisation since the latter was first invented. The 'genealogical tree' of organisation:

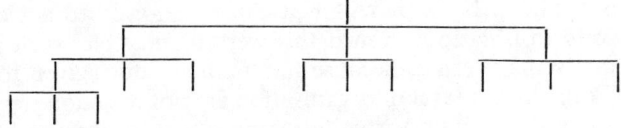

and so on, was as characteristic of Greek and Roman armies as it is of modern bureaucracies.

Secondly, there is specialisation. In simple organisations each unit at the same level is interchangeable: but armies soon see the merit of distribution of duties (even if only between infantry, cavalry, and artillery). Instead of:

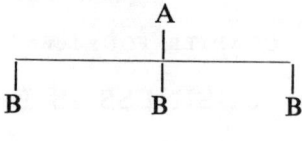

one gets:

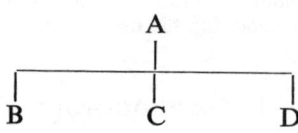

This can be continued down the line so as to secure a very high degree of specialisation, as is done in most modern armies and in all bureaucracies.

Thirdly, a bureaucracy is an office organisation, not a field service. It is harder than one might think to draw a precise distinction between a field organisation like an army at war and an office organisation like a government Department. All modern armies have an elaborate headquarters which is doing an 'office' job even when the army is on the move. All (or almost all) Ministries have some field organisation, and are not enclosed wholly within the walls of an office. The difference is one of atmosphere rather than of theory, but it is psychologically of great importance. A bureaucracy (or for that matter an army at rest) is likely to lack 'fresh air'.

The perfect bureaucracy is one in which 'every pigeon has his pigeon hole': for any imaginable piece of business there is an official (one official only) who is primarily responsible. All organisations of this type have a defined chain of command, expressed in the familiar organisation chart: they also have a defined 'distribution of duties', showing precisely the work allocated to each unit in the chart. But this is a static description. Such an organisation must solve two other problems if it is to be capable of action.

The first problem arises because the organisation is designed to move as a whole. No unit within it can be allowed to act on the outer world in isolation: even if this were permissible, such action would rarely make sense, because the 'units' of duty given to individuals at the lowest level of organisation are not in action separable from other units of duty. Virtually every piece of business is done by a combination of units. Some types of business become 'routine', in the sense that the same combination of units repeats itself over and over again. But the organisation is incapable of action at a higher level unless it can contrive different combinations of units as different pieces of business require them. Such kaleidoscopic combination requires 'communication' within the organisation: a piece of business must first get to an individual who is responsible for initiating action, and then that individual must be able to link up with other individuals in regular and understood ways, so as to produce by their interaction the recognised and 'official' decision of the organisation, from which action flows.

The second problem is that the outer world does not remain static, and therefore the structure of the organisation cannot remain static either. If it is to maintain effective specialisation it must ceaselessly adapt itself. The 'distribution of duties' is in process of modification all the time. It is doubtless best that someone should modify it consciously and systematically, promulgating the changes to all concerned. But if this is not done, the organisation will somehow contrive to modify itself. It is as common in a Ministry as in other walks of life to find that what a man really does bears little relation to what the book says he is to do.

These are problems which face all large organisations, but there are different ways of solving or of attempting to solve them. What follows is intended to bring out some special features in the practice of British central administration, and we have chosen four headings: files, levels, procedure for communications, and allocation of duties. To complete our argument there should be a fifth section here to deal with accounting, since all official business is done within the framework prescribed by the rather peculiar system of government accounting. But it is not easy to separate this from the larger question of Treasury control over income and expenditure as a whole, and we have preferred to deal with it in Chapter 18. This may serve as a reminder that the A B C of procedure within Departments also serves to link Departments together, in that it is common to all of them.

2. Files

A Department derives its administrative unity largely from its filing system. The operation of this depends on the work of the Registry, which is at once a telephone exchange for paper and a Departmental memory. One of the penalties of growth is that the largest Departments now have various subordinate Registries and subordinate filing systems, but it may be best for exposition to take a case much simpler than could be found in practice. Suppose a Department which exists before business has begun: the first communication comes to the Ministry from outside, it is delivered to the Registry, opened by a clerk, and passed by him to the section which he thinks should deal with it in the first instance. He may send it to the wrong section; but even the wrong section is under an obligation to act, either by sending the letter back to the Registry, or by referring it through the Registry to what the section thinks is the right place. Unless the purpose of the letter is very obvious, it may take a little time to reach anyone competent to act. But most correspondence falls into some familiar channel, and the novel cases are few enough to secure special attention.

When the communication reaches its billet, the official concerned ought to ask Registry to open a file. (Practice may vary: sometimes Registry opens files itself for new lines of business, sometimes files are opened only on requisition from a section.) A 'virgin' Registry might attempt before business began to imagine some general layout for an index of files to cover the business of the Department. This would be difficult, and it is reasonably easy to handle at least the first file without it. The letter is placed in a folder, secured by that important instrument of government, a 'Treasury tag', the folder is given a title and a number, Registry records the title, the number, and the destination of the file, and passes it back to the section concerned for action.

The layout of files varies from one Department to another: but their essential nature is to include both documents and internal communications about them. One simple form is to have on the left-hand side a minute-sheet, on the right-hand side the papers as they accumulate. The minute-sheet should contain a note of each paper placed on the file, and is also used for communications from branch to branch and for noting conversations. A file thus builds up a complete history of the piece of business as presented to the Department from outside and as handled within it. Files ought in theory to contain all papers relevant to one line of business. What is more, files should pass from one branch to another only through Registry, so that Registry may mark on the relevant card the whereabouts of the file to which the card refers. The system is simple enough in theory, but there are a great number of difficulties in practice.

To begin with, there is the sheer volume of business. It is estimated that files to be preserved (after much ephemeral business has been discarded) will pass to the Public Record Office at the rate of 14,000 feet of shelving—nearly three miles—each year. The Foreign Office at present registers over half a million incoming papers a year, and the Colonial Office about ninety thousand from overseas territories alone. A large Registry is a big organisation, and has to be highly specialised internally. The process is broken down into stages, each handled by separate clerks; the card-indexes and racks of files are enormous. The Registry itself begins to throw up problems of large-scale organisation.

One of these is that the Registry work fails to attract the more enterprising and able clerks. It is natural to attempt to simplify the routine work of a Registry by breaking it down into elementary operations; but a Registry cannot be mechanised, and the adoption of a mechanical routine may defeat its own purpose, since the most important problems are the unexpected ones. Special officers may be detailed to deal with difficult cases, but this will only work if the routine operators have sufficient conception of what the Department is doing to know which cases are difficult. The more highly organised the Registry, the less attractive is its routine, and the harder it is to find intelligent staff for the difficult and interesting part of the work.

Even good Registry clerks cannot be expected to have a full knowledge of the changing structure of a modern Ministry, and it may be useful to have within the Ministry a limited number of branches which can act as subsidiary 'paper exchanges'. Sometimes this happens informally, sometimes a branch (or the private secretary of a leading official) is explicitly made the point of reference for a considerable range of business.

Another difficulty is that of keeping some order in the filing system. It is very hard to keep a 'concordance' so complete that new files do not overlap with old ones. Two files may get into circulation separately on closely related pieces of business; the Registry may fail to produce a relevant file when asked for the past history of a transaction; or it may obscure counsel and waste time by attaching a bundle of irrelevant files. These things are with patience remediable, but if by accident a paper becomes attached to a file with which it has no connection it vanishes without trace, and will never be found except by accident.

The faults of Registries generate impatience in divisions and branches, which break rules and create further confusion. One tendency is to 'walk' files with urgent business from one branch to another, by-passing Registry, so that Registry no longer has a record of where the file is. Another is to hoard papers which are particularly useful to the branch, lest they be put on a file by Registry, and then spirited away to another branch which needs the file for some quite different purpose. A third (the worst of all) is to begin doing business in 'branch folders', so that the branch has in effect a private Registry of its own kept amateurishly in its own cupboard. One of us has been guilty of all these sins, for what seemed good and sufficient reasons at the time; but he has also had the experience of attempting to write the history of a war-time organisation which had no central Registry at all. That experience was enough to teach the lesson that any Registry, however bad, is better than none. It is hard to imagine how government business could be done except on this system. Files to some slight extent delay action because their subject can only be in action at one place at any one time: but they make possible a relatively complete record of action, and it is on this that the cohesion and continuity of the Department depends. Officials change, by a continuous process of posting: the record remains, and successors can take up the business where it was left without serious breach of continuity.

This is a convenient point at which to insert a note on an alarming problem created by the strictness and efficiency (in general) of the system of Departmental records. The ultimate fate of these records is still regulated by the Public Record Office Acts of 1877 and 1898, Acts mainly concerned with safeguards against improper destruction, which had been very common in earlier centuries. A Committee on Departmental Records (the Grigg Committee) recommended in 1954 that these Acts should be repealed and a simplified procedure substituted. Its Report has been accepted and will be put into effect, but at present if any Department wishes to destroy any documents in its possession (apart from duplicates) it must (first) nominate an officer to draw up a Destruction Schedule, then (secondly) submit the Schedule with samples of the documents to a Committee of Inspecting Officers, including the Deputy Keeper of the Records, an Assistant Keeper, and a barrister of not less than seven years' standing. The Schedule must then be approved (thirdly) by the Permanent Head of the Department and (fourthly) by the Lord Chancellor, and must (fifthly) lie for four weeks on the table of each House of Parliament. Departmental officials must then (sixthly) go through all files within the classes approved by the Schedule, decide which files are to be destroyed and arrange for their destruction, and (seventhly) go through the files to be preserved and weed out all valueless documents before sending the files to the Public Record Office.

It need hardly be said that the result of these precautions is that papers are not destroyed, since it is easier to keep them in storage than to find staff to sift them. The situation described in the Report of the Committee is that the Public Record Office (which is ultimately responsible for the custody of these papers) already has records occupying 40 miles of shelving. It is estimated that Departments hold records which ought to be preserved (apart from records to be destroyed) occupying another 120 miles of shelving, and that they are adding to this at the rate of about 3 miles a year. These mountains of paper are held partly in the Departments, partly in a repository at Hounslow appropriately referred to as Limbo, where Departments keep old papers not yet sorted out into categories for destruction or preservation.

This situation is one of the reasons (not the only one) why such limited facilities are available for those who wish to work on public records of the late nineteenth and early twentieth centuries. The right of access to records is granted by the Department concerned (or its heir), and not by the Public Record Office. There is now a general understanding that the records will be opened after fifty years, but this period may be exceeded in the case of especially confidential documents.

3. LEVELS

The Civil Service is not acutely conscious of differences of rank, and there are easy and informal relations up and down the hierarchy. But co-ordination in a bureaucracy depends in the first instance on a conscientious respect for what may be called the 'doctrine of levels'. This is most easily explained in terms of an organisation chart:

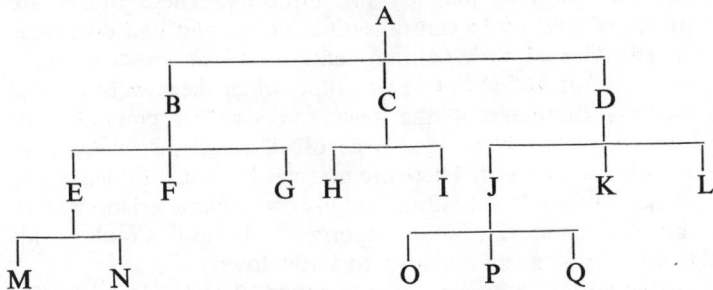

A diagram like this might portray a Ministry from the level of Permanent Secretary down to that of Assistant Secretary, or a sub-department with an Under Secretary at the top. The principle is the same irrespective of 'level'. Suppose a piece of business comes to M, either from Registry or by reference down the line from his superiors. He looks at it and decides that it involves consultation with some of the people under D. This happens all the time, on almost all matters of substantial importance: it happens so often that all business would be clogged if the line of hierarchy were followed, so that the business to be co-ordinated went up the line again through E and B to A, and down through D and J to P. The correct procedure is for M to clear matters so far as he can 'on his own level'. This means that he must take responsibility for dealing with P direct, perhaps after a brief preliminary word with E, who is in the next room. Exactly how he communicates with P depends on the relative urgency of the matter: it may be by a minute on the file, or by telephone, or by walking round to see him. The essential point is that the matter should be taken as far as possible at each level: the responsibility is thrown upon P to clear the matter if he can, in the light of his own precedents, without more than a word with J to see that there are no unexpected difficulties. The happy conclusion of the business is for M to be able to minute E (or say to E): 'I have cleared this with P, and it is obvious that you should act as follows . . .'. That is one piece of business concluded, since all that E need do is to make an occasional check in order to be sure that M is not in the habit of slipping.

It is this very simple mechanism which decides the relative speed and efficiency of Departments. In a bad Department E is unwilling to let M settle the matter at his level, perhaps because of a general feeling of uncertainty generated higher up the line; or perhaps M does not know P well enough to deal easily with him, because of frequent postings or rawness of staff; or P may fear to take responsibility because the head of his sub-department is known to guard his interests closely and to magnify his authority. These things are cumulative, and add up to centralisation, delay, and bad decisions. The opposite vice of rash commitments on lower levels is much rarer, but was not unfamiliar in war-time, when there were a good many bustling characters in the lower ranks with a contempt for procedure and a confident ignorance of all problems larger than those of their own section. There are no rules by which to decide the happy mean; but each individual has his own characteristic way of doing business, and this soon becomes well understood in his Department, if it is given a chance to settle down.

This explanation has been given in terms of the Administrative Class in one Department. It applies also between Departments, and between the Administrative Class, the corresponding specialist classes, and serving officers in the armed forces filling posts in administration. It is not always very easy to settle what the appropriate level is between classes; but some answer has to be found, and the answer evolved in practice may lead to embarrassment because levels of decision do not always correspond to levels of pay.

There is nothing peculiarly British about this system. It is only by working arrangements of this kind that big bureaucratic organisations can be set in motion at all. One short answer to hierarchical delays is to attach a special body of 'progress chasers' (as they are called in industry) to the head of a department or sub-department. It is then possible to hustle a piece of business through the machine by setting one of the 'chasers' to pursue it irrespective of level, acting at all levels in the name of the head of the Department. This is apparently familiar in industry; it is also one of the functions of the *Cabinet* of a French Minister; and from various symptoms one suspects that it is common in Russia. It is not practised in British Departments except in real emergency (as for instance when Lord Beaverbrook took over the Ministry of Aircraft Production in May 1940), and there is a tendency to doubt its efficacy even in these cases. One piece of business may be hustled through, but at the expense of more than equivalent delay in others. Mutual confidence in the Department may break down, so that there ensues a state of nervous centralisation and incoherence.

One of the greatest traditional merits of the Administrative Class is that its members are so selected and trained as to be able to work together flexibly but correctly. Socially, there is no gap between a Permanent Secretary and an Assistant Principal; officially, each speaks only on his own level or in the direct line of command to immediate superior or subordinate. One small but important exception to this rule lies in the position of a private secretary: a P.S. speaks with the voice of his master, and may operate judiciously at all levels up to his master's level. He may even 'chase'; but rarely, and with some show of apology.

The 'doctrine of levels' has been set out here in terms of people performing assigned duties, because this is on the whole the way it appears in practice. It could, however, be set out also in terms of regulations and precedents. A Department is a hierarchy of people; it is also a hierarchy of principles. All its activities are delimited by general rules of policy contained in Cabinet decisions and by general rules of law contained in Acts of Parliament. The Minister cannot change these rules except by going to Cabinet and to Parliament: within the rules he can act freely, by making subordinate rules and by deciding individual cases in such a way as to set precedents. His action (advised by his senior officials) narrows discretion for those one level down the hierarchy, because the Minister may vary his own rules and precedents and retain discretion outside them. The next level in turn retains some discretion for itself and delegates limited authority to its subordinates, subject to rules and precedents. And so down the line to the lowest level of action, where the job (as defined by the Reorganisation Committee of 1920) is that of 'dealing with particular cases in accordance with well-defined regulations, instructions or general practice'.

It is this combination of levels of duty with levels of generality which leads some writers to speak of bureaucratic organisation as the most 'rational' form of human organisation. It also explains the awe (the very proper awe) inspired within the Service by regulations and precedents: every civil servant should know the regulations, and the files should be so organised as to bring forward the right precedents. These abstractions become dangerous if regarded as something higher than the working rules of an organisation; but the organisation cannot live at all without working rules. 'Red tape' in this sense is a mark of efficiency.

4. Communications

This is a field which can be divided fairly simply into written and spoken, internal and external. Written communication within a Department is by minute, between Departments it is by letter[1]: spoken communication in each case is either *tête-à-tête* or in a more or less formal meeting.

(i) *Minutes*

The classical form of communication within a Department is by minute on a file. In principle a whole Department is unified by its files, which travel freely throughout the headquarters of the Department (outside establishments and branch offices being excluded). The principle has worn thin because of the existence of divided headquarters, with the result that some groups of files circulate only within one headquarters building. Even so, policy files circulate all round the Department at the appropriate level, and a subordinate or local file may always be called up to a higher level if it gives rise to a *cause célèbre*. Communications between headquarters and outstations are in effect letters: but are generally cast in the form of memoranda, much the same form as that of a minute.

The tradition of minute-writing grows and changes from Department to Department and from year to year. The art perhaps reached its highest form in late Victorian times, when a minute at a high level might be a succinct and polished essay, summarising all the issues of fact, precedent, and policy relevant to some large piece of business, and presenting them to the Permanent Secretary or to the Minister, so that a verdict might be recorded on the file for the guidance of

---

[1] We disregard here the rather specialised lore of communication by telegram to Departmental representatives overseas.

future generations. Such essays are still written occasionally; but it is now uncommon for a minute to run beyond one foolscap sheet. More use is made now of informal conferences, and business which would once have been done by minute on a file is now presented as a paper to a meeting, which reaches a decision recorded in its minutes. The art of writing a good minute has been merged with the art of writing a good committee paper, a difference which is not fundamental.

The shorter minutes now in vogue remain extremely important. A rough classification might be into minutes to subordinates, equals, and superiors. A minute to a subordinate would characteristically be of the form: 'Please look into the matter indicated by the papers on this file. Consult A, B, and C, and clear the matter with them if you can. Let me have your recommendations.' It might well bear also some mark of relative priority: in war-time these ranged from the Prime Minister's special tags 'Action this Day' (Sir Winston's Memoirs contain an admirable series of minutes to subordinates), through red 'Immediate' labels and green 'Important' labels, down to unmarked files which would go at the end of the queue, somewhere in the 'pending' sections of that characteristic Civil Service device, the paper tray, which stands on all desks in the middle ranks of the Service.

A minute to an equal would typically be of the form: 'So far as my section is concerned, I think the Department ought to act as follows. Will you consider the matter and comment from your point of view?' This may lead to a slow process of minuting back and forward before agreement is reached on the file. If the matter is urgent the writer can (and should) first telephone to the recipient and reach rough agreement as to what is possible. He can then put his minute on the file, and send it for confirmation in writing, with a good chance that the file will come back with an agreed answer. It may be possible to combine several branches in this way, by a circular minute passed to all of them, and requiring only their initials by way of confirmation. But the larger the number of branches the greater the risk of side-issues, cross-currents, and delay. At some point it becomes more economical of time to arrange a meeting than to try to settle matters on the file.

A minute to a superior will give most satisfaction to the writer if it is a neat demonstration that all loose ends have been tied up and that all the superior need do is to sign the draft provided. But it is equally important that the writer should have a sense of what his limits are. A minute is no less efficient if it is of the form: 'I have consulted A, B, and C, and the following points are clear.... Before

o

we can proceed further we must have guidance on the following matter. . . . This has not been raised before, so far as I can trace, and seems to involve important issues of policy.' The writer might well go on to make modest recommendations about these unsettled questions: but the important thing is to see that the right questions get to the right levels. The hierarchy should act both as funnel and sieve, so that vital questions, and no others, go forward for decision at the top.

Minutes ought to be on files, and it is worth some delay to secure this. But it may be necessary in haste to send a 'loose minute' for action in one place while the file is in action in another. If so, it is essential to reunite the 'loose minute' to its file as soon as possible, lest business proceed on two separate and diverging lines.

'Loose minutes' are not safe except when used 'for information only', and minutes on files may also be used for information. It may be wise to minute A 'through B', or 'copies for information to B, C, and D'. On the whole, this sort of circulation conveys more practical information than all that can be done in the way of circulating 'background notes' or 'policy guidance', which are apt to come too late to be of use and to lie unread in a remote 'pending tray'. This means that each section is responsible for keeping all others 'in the picture'; no central 'guidance' section can act as substitute for this.

(ii) *Letters*

Letters are in principle used not for communication within a Department but for correspondence with other Departments and public bodies and with the public. Any letter written or typed on the Department's notepaper and posted 'O.H.M.S.' will appear to the recipient to be official: it may in some circumstances bind the Department legally. In any event, a Department is extremely reluctant to repudiate as unauthorised anything embodied in a letter signed by one of its officials. There are therefore in all Departments strict rules about the signing and dispatch of letters.

Two categories of letters can be distinguished:

(*a*) *Official Letters*. These may be '*Top Hat*' *Letters*. A number of the older Departments have very formal styles of address for their most important letters: 'To the Secretary of the Admiralty: Sir, I have laid before The Lords Commissioners of Her Majesty's Treasury Mr. X. Y.'s letter of . . ., in which he states . . . In reply My Lords direct me to request The Lords Commissioners of the Admiralty . . .' and so on, in elaborate periphrases. Newer Departments have simpler forms of address even at this level, but in all Departments there is a special type of letter reserved for important matters of policy. Such a letter is always signed by an official of the Administrative Class, rarely below the level of Assistant Secretary.

Official letters may also be *'Directed' Letters*—'I am directed by the Minister to say . . .' A great deal of ordinary business is done in this form, and some of it is important: but 'directed' letters do not generally deal with big questions of policy, and may be signed at fairly low levels, varying according to circumstances. Sometimes the writer 'directs' himself: but it is usual for a superior to agree and sign such a letter.

(b) *'Demi-official' Letters*[1]: in which the form of address is, between civil servants, 'Dear Smith . . . Yours sincerely, John Brown', or to a member of the public, 'Dear Sir' (or 'Dear Mr. A.') . . . 'Yours faithfully'. The demi-official letter has gained ground steadily at the expense of the official letter until it is now the main working form of communication between Departments. Business is carried forward by telephone, interview, and demi-official letter: and official letters are used only to mark important stages in the argument, or to record final agreement or disagreement. In consequence, 'd/o' letters are generally weighed carefully, and tend to become formal in the sense that it is common for a 'd/o' letter to be drafted by a subordinate for a superior to send 'on his level'—and this may be any level up to that of the Minister himself. A 'd/o' letter is emphatically a document 'on the record'. Even if it were not binding in law, it would be embarrassing, indeed impossible, for the Department to repudiate it, and it is therefore customary for the writer of a 'd/o' letter to make as plain as possible what the limits of his authority are.

These rather vague usages are well understood by the Administrative Class: are less familiar to the professional and technical classes: and may be puzzling to the outside public. To take an actual example: a local authority committee is justifiably upset if the Minister releases to the press a 'd/o' letter from a Ministry official to one of the committee's officials, which the latter took to be personal and 'off the record'. There is also some risk of confusion in the practice encouraged in the name of 'Plain English' of writing to the public as 'man to man' without official periphrases. A 'directed letter' may be an artificial device, but the recipient is left in no doubt that it is an official letter.

Style in letter writing is an inexhaustible topic. On the whole, style in the Civil Service is no worse, perhaps rather better, than style in business correspondence. Some of the difficulties are due to

---

[1] The word 'semi-official' is better English and seems to be prevailing over 'demi-official': but the common abbreviation is still 'd/o'.

inadequate command of English, and this can be mended only by vigilance and criticism. This is a different question from that of tricks of style and jargon which are clear and convenient to colleagues (the jargon of 'levels' is an example of this), but may mislead those unfamiliar with Service practice.

(iii) *Personal Discussion*

As has been explained above, one object of Civil Service procedure is to build up a record of decisions and of the reasons for them, so as to constitute a Departmental memory and a defence against public criticism of action in individual cases. Business hierarchies and military hierarchies are not so much affected by these considerations, and therefore word-of-mouth communication is there relatively more important than it is in the Civil Service. But it is worth remembering that even in war it is important to put as much as possible in writing in an exact and unambiguous form, lest commands be misunderstood. The rule for Civil Service administration is that word of mouth should be used wherever possible to accelerate and clarify business, but not to the prejudice of the written records.

Conversations face to face (or by telephone) call perhaps for three comments only:

(*a*) It is not self-evident that it is quicker to talk than to write. It may take some time to make contact with a man on the telephone if the switch-board is incompetent or if he has left his telephone with no one to answer it; and it will take even longer to go and talk to him. It might be possible, in the time spent in trying to catch him, to do four or five pieces of business in writing, by minutes on the files. A file may take twenty-four hours to reach the next man who will handle it, but work on paper (if properly done) goes on in a steady flow, and more may be settled in this way in a given time than by methods which have an air of hustle.

(*b*) Conversations within the Civil Service are generally preparatory to confirmation in writing on the file. The formality of the record makes it easier to be informal in conversation, and on most occasions civil servants can talk freely about the background of business, knowing that what they say is not to be set down in minutes or letters as part of the record. This is an excellent system within the Civil Service: but may lead to some confusion in dealing with those outside it, as the conventions of a Civil Service conversation are rather different from those of a business one.

(*c*) The art of 'coffee-housing' or the strategy of the indirect approach is not much less important in the Civil Service than in other forms of business. The habit of dropping in for a gossip, or of meeting over lunch, does something to ease the flow of business and to settle patterns of influence within an office. But it is misleading to imagine that much of the work of central administration is now done in the Pall Mall clubs, or that there is a hidden social structure underlying the official structure. Perhaps it is a pity, but the proportion of civil servants (even of higher civil servants) who can afford club membership is very small, and there is no longer much spontaneous social contact outside the office, except between small groups of friends.

(iv) *Meetings*

There is not much doubt that there has in the last thirty or forty years been an increase in the amount of business done by meetings and committees rather than by minutes and letters. One symptom of this, which acts also as a formative influence, is the enormous importance of the hierarchy of committees, ministerial, official, and mixed, which depend upon the Cabinet. Cabinet committees are a familiar topic in discussions of British government, and are touched upon further in Chapter 19. Much less is known about the proliferation and operation of committees, conferences, meetings, working-parties, study groups, and teams, which link civil servants within Departments or between Departments. Professor Wheare has made an important reconnaissance in the field of 'Government by Committee', but of necessity he has not much to say about the use of committees within central administration, and there appear to be no official handbooks. There is therefore little to be said, but the subject is too important to omit altogether.

There might in theory be a calculus as to the expediency of proceeding by round-table meeting rather than by minute and individual discussion. A meeting may enable a decision to be taken in an hour, combining the action of five or six Departments: but this requires more than an hour (because of time for assembly) of the time of each of six high officials, and (as they are busy men) there is delay in summoning the meeting unless it is given priority at the expense of other business. Of course, it is never possible to calculate whether a meeting will save time or waste it, even if one is fairly sure how the meeting will go. Nevertheless, the balance of considerations is always there in the background, and there is a natural check on the danger of "too many committees', because most officials are anxious to see their own particular piece of business through as quickly as possible.

An *ad hoc* meeting to deal with one piece of business may be the genesis of a standing committee, meeting regularly to dispatch business requiring particular forms of co-operation. Such committees at the higher levels will require discussion in Part III, where we deal with committees to co-ordinate. It need only be said here that the most effective of these committees are generated by the experience of *ad hoc* meetings; and that most of them in due time outlive their usefulness—and are then difficult to abolish, because they have become a habit.

Here we are considering committees for the dispatch of ordinary Departmental business, not negotiating committees like Whitley Councils, nor quasi-judicial committees like promotion boards. In the dispatch of business the function of a committee is to bring together a number of people at the same level, so as to make progress by interchange of views. Normally, such a committee is convened by the Department primarily responsible for action, and the chair is taken by a man from that Department. The Chairman may be an official one level above that of other participants: for instance, an Under Secretary might convene a meeting at Assistant Secretary level on a piece of business which is in the hands of one of his own Assistant Secretaries. This has some advantages, but is not universal. The main point is that it is the Chairman's part not to push his own views but to get the business settled as quickly and thoroughly as possible.

This generally requires careful preparation, in particular of a clear and logical agenda paper, documented (probably) by papers circulated in advance which summarise shortly the origin of the business, the agreed facts, the open questions, and the possible solutions. If this is not done, someone may come to the meeting 'unbriefed', without authority to state his Department's case—and if one member of the meeting is put out of action in this way the whole proceedings may be a waste of time.

The preparation of business is a matter primarily for the man (probably junior to the level of the meeting) who is detailed to act as secretary. The chairman will naturally wish to make sure beforehand that the preparatory work is well done, and also to check the minutes of the meeting before circulation. But the minutes are primarily the responsibility of the secretary, and in a sense the object of the meeting is to enable him to prepare an effective set of minutes. The criterion of good minutes is not that they should be an exact record of what was said but that they should advance the business. For this, what is needed is a clear statement of facts, points of view and arguments, and an equally clear statement of conclusions, with a specific allocation of responsibility for action on each conclusion. It is the chairman's business to secure these things at the meeting, but no harm is done if the secretary's record makes the discussion seem clearer than it really was, because the minutes become effective as a record only when approved by the participants.

The record of the meeting so secured becomes in effect a minute on each of the files concerned in the different co-operating divisions and Departments, and each file is then 'in action' with the person concerned. If all has gone well, matters in each separate line of action are advanced to a point of decision which could not have been reached so quickly, or at all, in any other way; but once the meeting is over, action is back in the normal channels. The meeting has no continuing or collective responsibility. The secretary may act as 'chaser' on behalf of the initiating Department, to see that responsibilities have not been side-tracked or forgotten; but no committee (except the Cabinet itself or its main committees acting in its name) can break through the hierarchical order and issue general directions in its collective capacity.

5. ALLOCATION AND REVIEW OF DUTIES

So far, we have written of the organisation as if its structure were itself static, something created *de novo* by an inventor, embodied in a memorandum on the distribution of duties, and left to operate undisturbed. This is far from the truth, but it may be convenient for exposition to deal separately with the structure as static and the structure as changing.

(i) *Allocation of Duties*

The former presents relatively few problems, but there are three which deserve separate mention:

(*a*) In principle, the Crown is solely responsible for the organisation of the administration. That is to say, it is for the Cabinet to decide on the creation of new Departments and on the distribution of duties between Departments, and for each Minister to decide on the organisation of his own Department. Parliament is not concerned: this is a matter between the Crown and its servants. There are a number of exceptions, in that some Ministries and non-ministerial Departments have been constituted by statute: partly in order to give them a legal personality separate from that of the Crown (which is convenient both to the Department and to those who have dealings with it, even though the Department as a legal entity is still in law a servant of the Crown); partly as incident to a statute prescribing the service which the Department is to administer. But even these statutes rarely say anything about the internal organisation of the statutory Department; and in any case even statutory Departments may be divided, amalgamated, or abolished by Order-in-Council, under the Ministers of the Crown (Transfer of Functions) Act of 1946. An Order transferring functions becomes operative if neither House moves a Prayer to annul it within forty days. An Order amalgamating or dividing Departments requires an Affirmative Resolution of both Houses.

In this way the British executive has great freedom in handling its own organisation. Nominally its freedom is limited by the necessity of submitting for approval to the House of Commons annual Estimates which show the organisation of each Department in some detail; but there is no detailed debate on these Estimates, and voting on them is controlled by the Government Whips. They have no significance in this context except that they give the Estimates Committee of the House of Commons an excuse for inquiring into matters of Departmental organisation in some detail, with power to harass but without power to decide.

(b) Any discussion about the allocation of duties, whether between Departments or between sections within a Department, tends to raise issues of administrative principle. How many subordinates can a man effectively control? Is it better to accept the difficulties of a pyramid of many levels (a 'tall' organisation) rather than those of an extended span of control (a 'wide' organisation)? What rules should be followed in grouping functions together in divisions? How far should certain functions be centralised or decentralised within a Department? When does a Department or a division within it reach the point at which subdivision is essential? The only rule about these matters in British central administration is that there are no rules. Certain fixed points on the administrative framework have been explained in Chapter 13: beyond these, there is flexibility and empiricism. The higher Civil Service is not particularly well informed about controversies over administrative theory: if it were, it would certainly take the side of those who think that no generalisations are absolute, that in any difficult situation there are rules which conflict, and that administrative organisation must adapt itself as best it can to technical and political considerations.

(c) The technical aspect of distribution of duties consists rather in formal matters of description than in special principles of the art. The O. & M. Division at the Treasury have had the advantage of studying a very large number of lists of distribution of duties from all sorts of organisations inside and outside central administration, and they have promulgated a standardised form of layout which is in general use. It is admirably clear and compact, and has the additional advantage that the distribution of duties in different Departments is mutually intelligible and to some extent comparable. But similarity of layout on paper may be quite different from similarity in practice.

(ii) *Review of Duties*

The responsibility for maintaining and issuing the Departmental distribution of duties list is generally part of the job of a fairly junior officer in the Establishments Division. The intervals at which the list is revised may vary, but it would be normal to issue a complete new list once a year, and to issue amendment sheets from time to time. Lists are never up to date, even when newly issued. There is a time-lag between collection of information, compilation, printing, and issue, and during the interval there are changes. Branches are reorganised, new duties are added, officers are promoted and posted. The system is in continuous movement, and the movement is never without controversy.

This movement may be analysed, a little arbitrarily, into four different kinds of situation:

(*a*) The principle runs from the top of the administration to the bottom that a man is himself primarily responsible for the organisation of his own section of work. However small the section involved, it is proper that the initiative in changes of organisation internal to it should be taken by the section head, and that they should be accepted on his recommendation unless there are good reasons to the contrary. If the matter is a minor one it may be possible to settle it on this basis between the section head, his immediate superior, and the Establishments Division. But the Establishments Division must be notified and must give its approval before any reorganisation can be officially recognised by promulgation in the distribution of duties list, and there are many grounds on which it may object. The proposal may involve some conflict with rules about the duties of a particular class of civil servants; or it may introduce a layout which is different from that of other similar sections in the Department and which is therefore a possible source of confusion; or it may be embarrassing because some other discussion is going on about reorganisation on a larger scale.

All this means that the discretion of the section head is much narrower in practice than in theory. The obstacles are such that it may be simplest in small matters to have a friendly unofficial re-arrangement within the section, without bothering about official promulgation. But in theory the man who takes an interest in tidiness of organisation is officially approved; above all, if his reorganisation involves a reduction of staff.

(b) The matter becomes more serious if his reorganisation requires an increase of staff. It is his business to say how many staff he needs to do the job, but if they are more than he required last year he will have to fight hard and ingeniously to get them, taking advantage of such spells of sunny political weather as there may be. An increase in staff involves an increase in the Estimates: the Department's Finance Division is involved as well as the Establishments Division, and in the background is the Treasury. To apply for an increase in staff at the lower levels is to invite an investigation by O. & M.: not always the best use of O. & M., as it puts them in the position of acting not as impartial analysts but as the men with power to influence the answer to a request made by a responsible official who is not their subordinate. O. & M. may thus tend to become a factor in Departmental 'politics', another instrument of delay in the rearguard action which is continually fought by all Finance and Establishments Officers.

(c) There is a sardonic theorem known as 'Parkinson's Law', which lays down that all bureaucratic organisations tend naturally to grow in size at an annual rate predictable if certain factors are known. The theorem is a joke (rather a good joke), but it reflects substantial truth. There are always section heads who can use more staff, not because of personal ambition but because they see what the job needs. They are a restless and pushing force in the organisation, and there is no similar force pushing in the opposite direction. The size of the organisation as a whole tends to climb slowly but persistently, as if on a ratchet which prevents a slip back. The financial forces which demand retrenchment are weakly represented in the organisation as a whole, and their main strength is outside it. Hence all experience suggests that the best method of control is organised rearguard action interrupted by occasional sharp counter-attacks. Counter-attacks take the form of demands for block cuts or percentage cuts in the Estimates, which throw on each Department the onus of organising cuts in its own organisation or of proving its case for exemption. Cuts so imposed mean that the Department must look critically at its organisation as a whole; the initiative is no longer with the man responsible for the job. How a Department reacts to these tactics depends largely on the temperaments of its Minister and of its leading officials. It is possible to absorb a cut without much effort of thought by distributing it equally over all sections; but it may also be used more constructively as an instrument to enforce general reorganisation of an allocation of duties which has fallen out of line with reality.

(d) The continuous process is also interrupted from time to time by public controversy over the efficiency of the organisation, and these major 'rows' generally end in some formal inquiry. The controversy generally arises either out of a 'scandal' which has been given publicity in Parliament and in the press, or out of some issue of Departmental 'politics' between services or professions.

Among the latter the most conspicuous are fights between Departments, particularly between service Departments, like the long Fleet Air Arm controversy between the Admiralty and the Air Ministry; but there are less publicised cases between professions within Departments: for instance, the separation of the Animal Health (or Veterinary) Division of the Ministry of Agriculture from the National Agricultural Advisory Service. Such disputes are well known within the Service and have long histories, but they seldom erupt into open warfare except when one of the parties chooses to take the offensive.

'Scandals', on the other hand, seem unpredictable; higher civil servants must take such precautions as they can and must be ready to handle them coolly when they come. The most usual reaction is to concede a public inquiry, which may take various forms. There is sometimes a Tribunal of Inquiry, consisting of one or more independent persons, to elucidate the facts of the case, and thereafter a Departmental committee if the inquiry has suggested that the organisation is at fault; more frequently, the matter is referred directly to a Departmental committee. Such committees may consist wholly of people from outside the Service, or partly of civil servants and partly of laymen.

It is difficult to separate the political from the administrative aspects of these inquiries. There is no doubt about their political value. In a cynical sense, they serve to tide matters over until the edge of controversy has been blunted by delay, and also to soften the impact of the doctrine of ministerial responsibility, since the Minister shuffles off on to a committee some of his own responsibility for the proper conduct of his Department. Less cynically, it is undoubtedly right and proper that civil servants should be reminded from time to time that they are and should remain 'humble and obedient servants' of the public, and (conversely) it may be helpful to a Department to have a chance to put its problems clearly before an influential committee and before the (usually small) public who read the reports of such committees.

But a major attack from outside provokes defensive reactions, and controversy between Departments may darken counsel. It may also happen that a committee is appointed rather because its members command confidence among politicians and among the special publics concerned than because they have any knowledge of Departmental administration. The value of public inquiries into organisation would be greatly enhanced if they could be detached from an atmosphere of crisis and scandal, and if there could be more continuity of experience among those who take part in them. There are some signs of a trend in this direction, in the appointment of such bodies as the Ryan Committee, which investigated the organisation of the Ministry of Agriculture in 1950 before there was any question of a Crichel Down 'scandal'. It is also advantageous that the Estimates Committee of the House of Commons now seeks out subjects of inquiry which are of topical interest but not in any way 'scandalous', and that it often deals out praise and encouragement as well as blame. But on the whole the instrument of independent inquiry and recommendation is still a clumsy one, often of more value to outside students than to the administration itself.

FOR REFERENCE

The best general explanations are in:
H. E. DALE: *The Higher Civil Service* (1941).
G. CAMPBELL: *The Civil Service in Britain* (1955).
F. DUNNILL: *The Civil Service: Some Human Aspects* (1956).

Files, 'Levels', and Communication

These matters are very well dealt with in an American text-book on administrative theory:
H. A. SIMON, D. SMITHBURG, and V. THOMPSON: *Public Administration* (New York, 1950).

Correspondence, Minutes, etc.

Sir ERNEST GOWERS: *The Complete Plain Words* (1954).
R. W. BELL: *Write What You Mean* (1953).
G.P.O.: *No Idle Words: hints on the use of English in the Post Office: a training handbook* (1951).
W. C. TRICKER: 'The Classification of Political Papers: a weighty problem in the Foreign Office', *O. & M. Bulletin*, June 1951.
L. M. BUNKER: *Fundamentals of Office Method and Forms Design* (1945).

Allocation and Review of Duties

For a standardised form of presentation of distribution of duties lists, see:
Treasury O. & M. Division: *Organisation Charts and Lists of Duties* (1954).

The following are examples of procedure by public inquiry:

(a) *Estimates Committee of the House of Commons*

6th Report from the Select Committee on Estimates, Session 1953-54: Regional Organisations of Government Departments. H.C. 233, 1954.

A less successful investigation by this Committee (which illustrates its limitations) is:

7th Report from the Select Committee on Estimates, Session 1953-54: The Foreign Service. H.C. 290, 1954. The controversy which followed is to be found in *Comments on the 7th Report* . . . etc. (the Foreign Office reply, published as a White Paper), Cmd. 9377, 1955; and *2nd Special Report from the Select Committee on Estimates, Session 1954-55.*

(b) *Departmental Committees of Inquiry*

Report of a Committee Appointed to Review the Provincial and Regional Organisation of the Ministry of Agriculture (Wilson). Cmd. 9732, 1956.

Report of a Committee of Inquiry into the Department of Scientific and Industrial Research (Jephcott). Cmd. 9734, 1956.

'Parkinson's Law' was enunciated by an anonymous writer in *The Economist*, 19 November 1955.

CHAPTER FIFTEEN

TYPES OF DEPARTMENT

An administration, so checkered and speckled . . . a piece of joinery, so crossly indented and whimsically dovetailed; a cabinet so variously inlaid; such a piece of diversified mosaic.—BURKE: *Speech on American Taxation.*

1. INTRODUCTORY

ONE can get some idea of the scale of the organisation with which we are dealing here by thinking of it in terms of the descriptive volumes in the new 'Whitehall Series'. Each volume is to deal with one major Department in about two hundred pages. There would be (if the series were completed) some twenty-five volumes of this length. Each of these volumes is highly compressed. For instance, Sir Frank Newsam's book on the Home Office can afford only twenty-one pages for the prison system, only sixteen pages for the work of the Children's Department: Sir Charles Jefferies' book on the Colonial Office gives thirteen pages to the Oversea Civil Service in all its branches, seven to social development in all the colonies put together. That is to say, it is impossible even on this extended scale to give an adequate idea of what Departments do: each provides many services, and each of these services is a world in itself, sufficient to absorb the lives of many able men and women. It would be absurd even to attempt to outline here what the central administration does.

Instead, we propose in this chapter to take six Departments somewhat at random and to explain briefly how their organisation is put together out of the elements which we have already described. From one point of view, one can regard the system of central administration as a box of components, rather like a toy building-set. The number of components is limited: the methods of fitting them together are fairly simple: but an immense number of different models can be constructed out of this material. This is not the whole truth about the organisation of Departments: we have already emphasised the importance of their individual character, and the way in which the 'components' themselves, the men and women who make up the organisation, are adaptable by training and selection. Nevertheless, it is illuminating to look for a little at the organisation as if it were a series of different machines screwed together out of one box of components.

No Department exactly resembles any other, but those which we have chosen can stand to some extent in a representative capacity.

(i) *The Commonwealth Relations Office* is mainly an organisation for conducting relations with independent states. Its work is therefore rather like that of the Foreign Office, though on a much smaller scale: the Colonial Office, once mainly concerned with direct administration, is gradually assuming the same character.

(ii) *The Home Office* is concerned almost entirely with civilian services in the United Kingdom, and it is a large and complex organisation. But most of its services are provided not direct but through other authorities (principally local authorities) which it supervises. In this respect its organisation has something in common with that of the Ministries of Education, Health, and Housing and Local Government.

(iii) *The Air Ministry* is a Department directly responsible for the administration of a large fighting service, and may in this respect represent the Admiralty and War Office, although each service Ministry has its own special problems of organisation.

(iv) *The Ministry of Pensions and National Insurance* is an example of direct administrative responsibility for a civilian service. The Ministry of Labour and National Service and the National Assistance Board have similar field services: so (in a different sphere) have the Boards of Inland Revenue and of Customs and Excise.

(v) *The Board of Trade* is the principal example of a Department concerned with trade and industry which acts mainly as regulator and sponsor of private industry and not as purchasing agent for government service or as supervisor of nationalised industry. Other Departments act in a similar capacity for particular industries (for instance, the Ministry of Supply for the aircraft industry and the electronics industry, the Ministry of Works for the building and building materials industries, the Ministry of Power for the oil and steel industries); but none of these have anything like the same range of general responsibility as the Board of Trade.

(vi) *The Ministry of Agriculture and Fisheries* (now linked with the Ministry of Food) might perhaps be regarded as an organisation which exists to regulate and sponsor a single industry. But agriculture has so little in common with other industries that it is a paradox to give it that name: its Ministry is a special case of adaptation to need.

2. THE COMMONWEALTH RELATIONS OFFICE

> Which, softness' self, is yet the stuff,
> To hold fast where a steel chain snaps.
> BROWNING: 'Waring'.

The Commonwealth Relations Office was created in 1925 by subdividing the old Colonial Office, a change which symbolised the emancipation of the equal members of the Commonwealth from colonial status. It was given its present name in July 1947, because the name 'Dominions' Office, which it took at first, was thought to have some flavour of subjection; the United Kingdom, though it is an equal member of the Commonwealth, is certainly not a Dominion.

The Office is responsible for the conduct of relations with the eight independent members of the Commonwealth (Canada, Australia, New Zealand, South Africa, India, Pakistan, Ceylon and Ghana), with the 'junior member', Southern Rhodesia, and with the Republic of Ireland, which is for many purposes treated as a member of the Commonwealth, although it is not one. The work of the Office is like that of the Foreign Office, in that it deals with relations with independent states, through a system of High Commissioners who resemble Ambassadors. It is also closely associated with the Colonial Office, since many colonial territories which are on their way to independence will become the responsibility of the Commonwealth Relations Office when accepted as equals by existing members of the Commonwealth. In particular, the Office shares with the Colonial Office responsibility for the Central African Federation, which includes Southern Rhodesia (a 'quasi-Dominion') and two colonial territories, Northern Rhodesia and Nyasaland; and it is solely responsible for the administration of the three 'High Commissioner Territories', Bechuanaland, Basutoland, and Swaziland, which abut on South Africa, and are important in relations with the South African government. The Office has virtually no other executive responsibilities: its work is to maintain an even background of good relations, to negotiate on many intricate matters, generally involving technical issues within the scope of other Departments, and to advise the Secretary of State and the Cabinet on large matters of policy affecting the future of the Commonwealth.

The senior staff required for this purpose can be summarised briefly from the *Imperial Calendar* and the Civil Estimates for 1955-56.

Table XXIII

Senior Staff in the Commonwealth Relations Office

	In Whitehall	Overseas
Administrative Class		
Permanent Secretary	1	—
Deputy Secretary	1	—
Representatives ranked as Deputy Secretary (or above)	—	9
Assistant Under Secretaries	5	4
Assistant Secretaries	18	18
Principals	35	25
Assistant Principals	10	9
Executive Class		
Principal Executive Officer	1	—
Senior Chief Executive Officer	1	—
Chief Executive Officers	5	—
Senior Executive Officers	13	4
Higher Executive Officers	41	17
Specialist Class—Information Officers		
Chief Information Officers	—	3
Principal Information Officers	2	5
Senior Information Officers	1	13
Information Officers	1	5
Total	135	112

The work of the Legal Adviser and of the Librarian is important, but they are not included in Table XXIII as they are shared with the Colonial Office; the very valuable Library of the old India Office is at present managed by the C.R.O. The staff list includes three military officers: one of them is Principal Staff Officer to the Secretary of State, one is Liaison Officer with the Ministry of Defence, and one is Ceremonial and Reception Secretary to the Secretary of State; and there is a medical board staffed by two retired medical officers from the Indian Army. That is all, apart from the clerical and ancillary staff required for 'housekeeping'. The size of the Office is thus not much greater than was usual in the Victorian age, and internal organisation though complex is somewhat informal.

There are two fixed points in this Department, as in all others. An Assistant Under Secretary is appointed as 'Director of Establishments and Organisation', and he has to assist him an Assistant Secretary in charge of establishments, office services, and accommodation. The Director of Establishments and another Assistant Under Secretary are jointly responsible for all questions of finance, including the Estimates and accounts of the Department, but the second Under Secretary has a special responsibility for pensions. They are assisted by an Accountant-General, a high-ranking Executive Class officer who is in charge of all routine business: the keeping of accounts, the payment of salaries and travelling expenses, the award and payment of pensions, and so on. In the C.R.O. the staff required for establishments, services, and finance is not very large: but the structure is the same as in the largest Departments, and so is the system of liaison with the Treasury. The two branches require the services of only five of the sixty-eight members of the Administrative Class in London below the level of Deputy Under Secretary.

The distribution of duties (outside these two branches) exemplifies the methods of dividing up the work of an office responsible for a large sphere of business outside London. There are two simple alternatives: to divide up the business by area, making for instance one section responsible for everything concerned with Canada, another for Australia, and so on: or to divide it by subject, making for instance one section responsible for all economic questions, another for all defence questions, a third for all constitutional questions, wherever they crop up. Each simple alternative raises difficulties if the office is a large one. If the office is organised only by territories, the staff tend to become spokesmen of local interests, even if there is frequent posting between sections: if it is divided only by subject, the men 'in the field' in each territorial area may feel lost and disappointed because there is no one in the office whose specific business it is to understand the problems of each of them. The usual answer, therefore, is a compromise, which includes in the same office both territorial divisions and functional divisions. There is a simple form of compromise in the Foreign Office and the Colonial Office, and it certainly does not work quite without friction in either case. In the Departments concerned with local government in England and Wales there is another and more complicated compromise, which will be described in Chapter 22; this seems to work smoothly, in spite of its complexity, but the Departments concerned are fairly small.

The C.R.O. is even smaller, and, with one exception, adopts the principle of functional organisation. The 'functional' divisions are the Foreign Affairs Division, the Economic Division, and the Political Division: the exception is the 'Africa' Division, which is responsible for all matters relating to Basutoland, the Bechuanaland Protectorate, and Swaziland, and for the political affairs only of the Central African Federation. Each of the three main divisions has an

TYPES OF DEPARTMENT

Assistant Under Secretary in charge: the head of the 'Africa' Division is an Assistant Secretary, but he reports to the Assistant Under Secretary who shares responsibility for finance.

The Foreign Affairs Division deals with the external relations of Commonwealth countries, and divides up territorially not the Commonwealth but the countries with which its members deal, into a Far Eastern Department, a Western and United Nations Department, and a South Asia and Middle East Department. The Defence Department and the Principal Staff Officer's Department belong to this division, and from the point of view of Whitehall organisation the division has its principal 'opposite numbers' in the Foreign Office and the Defence Ministries. *The Economic Division* divides economic business into two territorial Departments, one for Australia, New Zealand, Canada, South Africa, the Central African Federation, and Eire; the other for India, Pakistan, Ceylon, and a variety of United Nations agencies. But there are also two other Departments, one for the Colombo Plan, which links members of the Commonwealth across territorial divisions, the other (the Economic Policy Department) for sterling area finance, defence expenditure, and a great variety of miscellaneous financial business. The natural points of liaison in Whitehall are with the economic Departments, principally the Treasury and the Board of Trade. Finally, there is *the Political Division*, which is virtually a division for 'miscellaneous' business. It includes the Constitutional Department, which handles (in consultation with the Legal Adviser) extremely important business about nationality and citizenship, the constitutional development of the Commonwealth, and political relations between its members; the Protocol Department, dealing with ceremonial matters which often have serious political bearings; the Communications Department, dealing with communications by sea, air, post, cable, and wireless within the Commonwealth; and a General Department.

It will be seen that there would be little point in going to the C.R.O. and asking to see 'the man who deals with Australia'; any serious piece of business affecting Australia's position in the Commonwealth would bring in all these 'administrative' divisions. The complexity of this is not a serious obstacle so long as the organisation involved is small. It is quite easy for everyone in the Administrative Class in the C.R.O. to know the others personally, and to keep in touch with the general course of business throughout the Commonwealth. It is also at least relatively easy to maintain fresh and lively contacts with what is going on in the Commonwealth countries, because there is a continual interchange by posting between head-

228   THE ORGANISATION OF DEPARTMENTS

quarters in Whitehall and the offices of the High Commissioners overseas. A High Commissioner and his staff can keep close personal touch with individuals in the office at home: and can tell Commonwealth representatives exactly how to handle their business at a 'semi-official' level.

3. THE HOME OFFICE

> 'And now, Mr. Oldeschole, if you have had leisure to consider the question more fully, perhaps you can define to us what is the—hum-hm—the use—hm-hm—the exact use of the Internal Navigation Office?'—TROLLOPE: *The Three Clerks.*

The Home Office is at once an aristocrat and a maid of all work. By tradition it is an 'Administrative Class' office, and its social standing has always been high, since it stands close to the Throne. For a long time after it began to draw recruits from the ordinary Administrative Class examination it could count on being placed high in order of preference by some of the best candidates. This assumption of superiority is justified by the duties of the Department as defined by its Permanent Under Secretary, Sir Frank Newsam: 'it is still the Home Secretary's duty as it was centuries ago to advise the Sovereign on the exercise of many of her Prerogative powers, to be the channel of communication between the Sovereign and her subjects, to maintain the Queen's Peace, and to discharge the Crown's ultimate responsibility for the internal safety of the realm'.[1]

These sonorous constitutional formulae cover a great deal of miscellaneous business, some of it extremely humdrum. Anything that concerns the good order and convenience of this country and its people belongs to the Home Office if it has not been allocated to some other Department. Sir Frank Newsam lists the functions which have in the past eighty years been transferred to newly created Departments, such as the Scottish Office, the Ministries of Fuel and Power,[2] Health, Housing and Local Government, Labour and National Service, Agriculture, Fisheries and Food, Pensions and National Insurance. But (he says) 'although the Home Office from time to time surrenders to other Departments some of its functions it remains, like the widow's cruse, always full'.

The pattern, therefore, is that of a traditional organisation adapting itself to an unending variety of new business, and in the process

---
[1] Sir F. Newsam: *The Home Office* (1954), p. 26.
[2] Now Ministry of Power.

expanding and growing more complex. The C.R.O. occupies 4½ columns of the *Imperial Calendar* for 1956, the Home Office occupies 17. The C.R.O. employs virtually no specialists except for its Information Officers, the Home Office employs (taking them as they come in the *Imperial Calendar*) a Legal Adviser; a Chief Scientific Adviser; a Chief Architect; a Senior Quantity Surveyor; a Senior Wireless Engineer; a Chief Inspector, Dangerous Drugs Branch; a Chief Inspector, Explosives Branch; a Chief Inspector under the Vivisection Acts; a Chief Information Officer; a General Manager of the public houses of Carlisle and District (as well as a Head Brewer); a Chief Inspector, Immigration Branch; a Chief Inspector, Children's Department; a full General (retired) who is Director-General of Civil Defence; a Chief Fire Service Inspector; a number of Inspectors of Constabulary and Directors of Forensic Science Laboratories; a Principal Probation Inspector; and a Chief Administrator of the Women's Voluntary Services. Each of these specialists is the head of a group of specialist staff, and these groups, though generally small, are too numerous to set out in tabular form here.

Yet the main structure of the Department is formed by members of the general classes of the Service. The total for 1956 was: 1 Permanent Under Secretary, 1 Deputy Under Secretary, 8 Assistant Under Secretaries, 24 Assistant Secretaries, 61 Principals, and 15 Assistant Principals. In addition there are about 260 members of the Executive Class of the rank of H.E.O. or above. There are therefore 110 members of the Administrative Class in Whitehall as against 70 in the C.R.O., 260 Executives of some seniority (including many in 'out-stations') as against about 60. These form the scaffolding and the main channels of communication: their guiding principle is that referred to by Sir Frank Newsam in his book, that 'no unit should appear to itself to become isolated from the main body'. In this sense they are custodians of the traditions of the Department: but its policy, or rather 'policies', covers so many technical subjects that it is impossible to suppose that it is made by the 'general' civil servants.

The organisation as set out by Sir Frank Newsam is relatively simple. There is (as usual) an Assistant Under Secretary responsible for finance (including the Accounts Branch), and there is the Establishments Division (including Training, Welfare, and O. & M.), under a different Assistant Under Secretary. There are three 'high-level' specialists with very small staffs who report direct to the Permanent Under Secretary: the Chief Scientific Adviser, the Legal Adviser, and the Medical Adviser, who is the senior medical man in government service and is also Chief Medical Officer of the Ministry of Health and of the Ministry of Education. There is a Deputy Under Secretary, who works with the Director-General of Civil Defence at the head of the large and relatively self-contained Civil Defence Department, which would in an emergency act as framework for an enormously expanded organisation, as it did between 1939 and 1945. Its responsibilities in peace-time cover research, training, supplies, and their interrelation: and the Home Office provides the chairman of two interdepartmental committees, the Civil Defence Joint Planning Staff and the Civil Defence Joint Supply Staff, which link the organisation to that of the Chiefs of Staff and the Defence Committee.

The rest of the work of the Department is organised under five Assistant Under Secretaries. One of them has some internal responsibilities, but his main duty is to act (in effect) as the Home Office's own Foreign Office. One result of the growth of international organisations is that almost all Departments are involved in foreign affairs: and the Home Office has extensive 'external relations' regarding control of aliens and immigration, extradition, international police work, the war against the drug traffic, and so on. Each Home Office Department has to make its own policy in these matters, but they are linked together by one small division, which is the main point of liaison with the Foreign Office and the main representative of the Department in international business. Other Departments which meet the same problem generally adopt a similar solution.

There is a second Under Secretary, the Principal Establishments Officer, who perhaps might also be described as 'Assistant Under Secretary (General Department)'. His divisions include responsibility for the Isle of Man, the Channel Islands, and perhaps eventually for Malta; for liaison with the government of Northern Ireland; for supervision of local by-laws and Private Bill legislation; for the prevention of cruelty to animals; for dangerous drugs and for explosives; for enforcement of the permitted hours of opening for shops, forl iquor licences, and for the state public houses in Carlisle; for the conduct of elections; and for ceremonial occasions. He is also the residuary legatee of internal business: statistics, public relations, and so on. It is clearly the policy of the Department to concentrate miscellaneous business (perhaps under a man whose temperament it suits), so as to keep the rest of the work in coherent blocks. Of the other Assistant Under Secretaries, one is in charge of the large organisation dealing with aliens, immigration, naturalisation, and nationality; one of police and prisons; and one of the 'social work' of the Department: deprived children, juvenile delinquency, and probation.

The location of many of these divisions may serve as an example of what happens in a Department of moderate size. The old Home Office building in Whitehall contains the Secretary of State, the Permanent Secretary, their immediate entourage, and other very senior officials such as the Legal Adviser and the Scientific Adviser. There is also room for the Under Secretary in charge of finance, the Principal Establishments Officer and some of the 'general' divisions for which he is responsible, and the Under Secretary in charge of the police and criminal division with most of his staff. There is a second headquarters building in Horseferry Road, about a mile away, which houses the headquarters of the Civil Defence Department, the Fire Service Division, and the Children's Department (but the other 'social service' work is in Whitehall); and a third headquarters building is farther off in High Holborn, with the Aliens and Nationality Branches and those related to them, the Architects' Branch, and the office of the London Civil Defence Region. Headquarters is completed by an 'out-station' on the Kingston By-pass, near Surbiton, which houses Statistics, Supply, and Transport. Probably there are more officials outside London than in these four buildings together: one can reckon ten civil defence regional headquarters, with training establishments, depots, and stores, six forensic science laboratories, various police wireless and training stations, six regional offices of the Children's Department inspectorate, and the Carlisle state management district.

The Home Office has a staff of nearly 6,000 civil servants, 3,500 non-industrial and 2,500 industrial, but this gives no idea of the number of people for whom it is responsible. It is in charge of a number of central services provided by minor Departments, in particular by the Metropolitan Police Offices, which run a force of 16,000 men and women; and by the Prison Commission, which is responsible for all prisons in England and Wales and has a staff of about 6,700. The Office also supervises, but is not directly responsible for, a number of important local authority services, of which the largest are police (60,000), fire services (33,000), and civil defence (320,000, mainly part-time). The Children's Departments of local authorities have about 60,000 children in care at any one time, there are about 48,000 people under the care of the Probation Service. These local authority services are 'managed' through the old system of inspectorates, of which we shall have more to say in Chapter 22.

4. THE AIR MINISTRY

> He closed his eyes wearily and said, 'It's a thousand pities that the Services are allowed to interfere in matters they don't understand. If they would concentrate on their fighting and leave the thinking to us, we should get on a good deal quicker.'
> 'Maurice hates the Service people,' said the girl Gillian brightly.
> 'Still, you can hardly blame them for being *interested*,' I said sarcastically. 'After all, they have to use the stuff.'—NIGEL BALCHIN: *The Small Back Room*, ch. iii.

The Commonwealth Relations Office is concerned largely with high policy, but manages directly only the affairs of its own small staff at home and overseas. The Home Office also makes policy; it manages a larger office directly, and controls other services indirectly through minor Departments and local authorities. When we come to the Air Ministry a further dimension is added: not so much because this is a service Department concerned with defence policy, as because the Ministry is directly responsible for the administration of a very large body of Crown servants, the Royal Air Force (about 240,000 strong in 1956), and for the provision of their extremely expensive equipment. The Estimates of the C.R.O. for 1955-56 amounted to a little under £2 m., with a further £2 m. for 'Commonwealth Services and Overseas Settlement' (payments to the British Council, technical assistance, research, and assisted passages for emigrants); the Estimates of the Home Office amounted to £70 m. (including grants for police, fire services, civil defence, prisons, and child care, but excluding the state public houses, which are self-financing); those of the Air Ministry amounted to over £500 m., excluding equipment for the R.A.F. borne on the Estimates of the Ministry of Supply. The C.R.O. required $4\frac{1}{2}$ columns of the *Imperial Calendar* for 1956, the Home Office 17, the Air Ministry 30. Yet it is not easy to say with assurance that the Air Ministry's responsibilities are larger than those of the other Departments.

The present pattern of organisation in the service Departments was created at the end of the nineteenth century after there had been much controversy about the proper form of Army administration. The result was a compromise between the traditional organisation of the British Admiralty and that of the Prussian General Staff, both proved by success over many generations. A Minister is responsible to Parliament for the work of each of the service Departments. His responsibility is not in theory diminished either by the existence of the Defence Committee of the Cabinet, the Chiefs of Staff Committee, and the Ministry of Defence, or by the fact that the Minister is always (or almost always) a layman directing professionals of

TYPES OF DEPARTMENT

great authority. In practice, the position within the Air Ministry (and probably within the other service Departments) is that the Minister's authority is decisive only in his own professional sphere, which is that of Parliamentary politics, and in matters where technical arguments are nicely balanced and an uncommitted layman may be the best person to give a verdict. This range of business is much greater than might be thought: a good Secretary of State for Air is far more than the mouthpiece of his Air Marshals.

The special position of the lay head of a service Department is recognised by the fact that the titular head of the Air Ministry is not the Secretary of State but the Air Council. The Secretary of State is the Council's chairman and may in principle take a decision in its name even though he is in a minority of one: but formal action on most business proceeds under the authority of the Air Council, which corresponds to the Board of Admiralty and the Army Council.

The Air Council consists primarily of the heads of the great departments of the Air Ministry: the Chief of the Air Staff (and his deputy the Vice-Chief of the Air Staff), directing the Air Staff; the Air Member for Personnel, directing all matters of recruitment, conditions of service and ancillary personal services; the Air Member for Supply and Organisation, in charge of the provision and maintenance of aircraft and all other supplies, and the construction of airfields and buildings; the Permanent Under Secretary, responsible for finance, establishments, and a number of miscellaneous services.

Up to 1940 there was a fourth Air Member, responsible for research, development, and production. This department was transferred to the Ministry of Aircraft Production when it was set up in 1940; the corresponding department of the War Office had been transferred to the Ministry of Supply in 1939, and the two Supply Ministries have now been combined. But through all vicissitudes since 1940 the old structure remains recognisable, and the Air Ministry still has a special relation with the Air Division of the Ministry of Supply, and with the Controller of Aircraft there, a serving Air Chief Marshal, who is also an 'Additional Member' of the Air Council. Similarly, the War Office must contrive to work very closely with the Munitions Department of the Ministry of Supply, headed by a Lieutenant-General. The Admiralty has retained control of its own organisation for research, development, and production in many fields, but is wholly dependent on the Ministry of Supply for aircraft and all kinds of aircraft equipment and armament.

The main lines of the organisation are as follows. There are four large departments, the Air Staff, the departments of the Air Members for Personnel (A.M.P.) and for Supply and Organisation (A.M.S.O.), and that of the Permanent Under Secretary (P.U.S.). The Chief of the Air Staff (C.A.S.) is also a member of the Defence Committee and of the Chiefs of Staff, sharing general responsibility for defence as a whole, and he has a special position as the holder of the highest post in the R.A.F. and chief representative of the service. It is therefore essential that he should have assistance in directing the Air Staff, and this is given by two high officers with wide responsibilities, the V.C.A.S. and the D.C.A.S., who are members of the Air Council. The Air Staff is divided into seven large sections, six of them under Assistant Chiefs of the Air Staff, for Policy, Operations, Intelligence, Training, Operational Requirements, and Signals. The seventh section is that of the Commandant-General of the R.A.F. Regiment, which is primarily responsible for the defence of R.A.F. installations against ground attack.

A.M.S.O.'s department consists of two large blocks of work under serving officers, the Director-General of Organisation and the Controller of Engineering and Equipment, and of the largely civilian department of the Director-General of Works. A.M.P.'s department consists simply of two large subdivisions, each under a Director-General.

The Permanent Under Secretary is assisted by a Deputy and five Under Secretaries: one for Finance, one for Establishments and Organisation, and one for each of the three 'Air' departments. He is responsible for a limited range of central services, such as the Central Statistical Branch, the Air Historical Branch (which is linked with the Library), and the Information Division. The Meteorological Office (which was before the First World War an independent organisation financed by a grant-in-aid) has been attached to the Air Ministry since 1919. It is supervised by an interdepartmental committee which includes representatives from the three service Departments (though the Admiralty has its own Naval Weather Service), but the Permanent Secretary is generally responsible for it.

The Scientific Adviser to the Air Ministry, who ranks with the Under Secretaries and has quite a large department under him, is placed for purposes of administration in the Air Staff. There is a Directorate of Legal Services in the A.M.P.'s department, but this deals with matters of military law: the Air Ministry is one of the Departments which use the Treasury Solicitor as adviser on ordinary law.

The departments answerable to the Air Members of Council are staffed primarily by serving officers of the R.A.F., but depend on civilians for all office services. Some of the branches deal with a good deal of routine work, and are staffed at this level by civilian clerks;

TYPES OF DEPARTMENT

but so far as possible the routine work of R.A.F. pay, records, and stores is removed from the Air Ministry to R.A.F. Commands, and to specialised units like the R.A.F. Record Office. The only big civilian organisation under the direct control of an Air Member is that of the Director-General of Works in A.M.S.O.'s department. At its peak during the war of 1939-45 the Air Ministry Works Directorate was responsible for one of the largest constructional organisations in the world, and the organisation is large even in peace-time. There is a staff of about 270 in the higher grades of the Works Group of civil servants (over £1,000 a year): and this is the headquarters organisation for a very much larger staff at R.A.F. Commands.

Similarly, the sections answerable to the Permanent Under Secretary are civilian, headed almost entirely by members of the Administrative Class. There are 87 members of the Administrative Class: 1 Permanent Secretary, 2 Deputy Secretaries, 5 Under Secretaries, 26 Assistant Secretaries, 41 Principals, and 12 Assistant Principals. The senior men have almost all had long experience of the Department, and there is a fair proportion (up to the rank of Under Secretary) of men promoted from the Executive Class.

This is an organisation in which there is more Executive Class work than in the Commonwealth Relations Office, but it is not one of the great executive organisations. There is a considerable block of executive work in the Directorate of Accounts, and there is also a substantial amount of contracts work. But a great deal of routine accounting is done by service personnel in Commands, and most of the contracts for aircraft and their equipment are now handled by the Ministry of Supply.

The main lines of the organisation have remained essentially the same for a long time through periods of expansion and contraction, but a number of problems common to the service Departments are exemplified here. The most important of these is the problem of shaping a single policy for national defence, but there are three narrower problems which deserve reference at this point.

The first difficulty is that of relations between the Air Ministry and R.A.F. Commands. The Commanders-in-Chief are very great men, responsible only to the Air Council. There are therefore in a sense two chains of command, that described above, which is the chain of command from top to bottom within the Air Ministry, and the operational chain of command, leading straight from the Air Council collectively through Commanders-in-Chief to the smallest units of the R.A.F. This duality offers much scope for friction, and there may be further complications if (as happened during the war of 1939-45) a R.A.F. Commander-in-Chief is responsible to an Allied Supreme Commander, who is responsible in turn to the political leaders of a grand alliance acting together. The formula of reconciliation is a classical instance of the principle of Line and Staff. The line of command leads through Commanders-in-Chief; the whole Air Ministry (not only the Air Staff) is a staff organisation. Most sections within the Air Ministry have 'opposite numbers' in the R.A.F. Commands, whether the subject be operational (as with Operations and Intelligence), or technical (as with Signals or Works), or organisational (as with Organisation, Equipment, and Works), or concerned with officers and men (as with Personal Services and Postings). Each Air Ministry division or section is expected to act as brains-trust, father confessor, and London office for its opposite numbers at each level in Commands, but it has no authority to dictate to them, and may not have power to do so, since orders (as distinct from suggestions) can be given only from the top by the Air Council itself, which need not always accept the advice of its own technical staff. All this is familiar in text-books of administration: but it is worth emphasising it here, because the use of Line and Staff is uncommon in British central administration and the civilian Departments are largely unfamiliar with its advantages and difficulties. In the defence Departments it works well on the whole, perhaps with no more friction than is inherent in the system. The organisation is worked by people who have been familiar with it all their lives, and who know one another well: but even so, there are occasional public rows, and more frequent domestic ones.

Secondly, there is the problem of relations between civilian and military staff. Difficulties may arise partly from differences of tradition and temperament, but the worst danger is that there may be persistent friction and misunderstanding because in a defence organisation the chief role of the civilians (apart from engineers and scientists) is to say 'No'. This happens most often in matters of money, since it is the Permanent Secretary who bears the main responsibility for framing the Estimates, for negotiating with the Treasury about them, and for enforcing strict procedure in accounting. But it may also arise over matters of establishments and organisation, since it is the Permanent Secretary who is primarily responsible for the effectiveness of the Ministry (as distinct from the R.A.F.) as an organisation. It may even arise over matters of service policy, since recruitment (especially by conscription) and personnel policy raise many issues outside the scope of professional airmen. The Air Ministry solution is to involve civilian staff in policy on as wide a front as possible. The Administrative Class supplies private secretaries to the Air Members of Council as well as to the Secretary of State and the Permanent Secretary; and it also provides staff for what are known colloquially as 'bedded-out' secretariat branches. This is an application of the Line and Staff principle within a Ministry which is itself a Staff organisation. Each department of an Air Member has attached to it a Secretariat division under an Assistant Secretary, responsible to the Air Member for secretariat work in that department. Each Secretariat serves its Air Member, not the Permanent Under Secretary, but it draws experience and contacts from other civilian divisions, and its staff pass later to posts elsewhere in the Ministry. This seems to secure an easier mixing of civilian and service views than is achieved in the other defence Departments, which are differently organised. But the organisation itself partly reflects the greater flexibility of a new service.

The third formidable difficulty is that of liaison between serving officers, Administrative Class civil servants, and those engaged in research and development. One of the strongest arguments against the creation of a separate Ministry of Aircraft Production was that research and development must as a matter of organisation go with production, and that it is disastrous to break the close link between scientists and airmen. The decision of 14 May 1940 may well have been right at a time when all emphasis was on short-term production: it is not so certain that it is right in peace-time.

The gap is bridged by formal organisation of three kinds:

(i) The Air Staff includes several branches manned largely by technically trained officers, under A.C.A.S. (Operational Requirements) and A.C.A.S. (Signals). These branches are primarily concerned with defining 'operational requirements', a process which involves balancing considerations of intelligence (about the equipment of other powers) and of strategy (the time scale of threatening dangers) against considerations of the technical developments possible in a given time and the fighting capacity which they promise. This affects equipment of all types. So far as aircraft are concerned, the crucial decisions are the decisions when to issue specifications for the development of aircraft of particular types, and when to ask the Ministry of Supply to put an aircraft into series production so as to re-equip squadrons. These are perhaps the gravest decisions to be taken by the Air Ministry in time of peace: the shape of things to come was settled long before 1939 by decisions about single-seater fighters, about heavy bombers, and about radar, and since 1947 the 'balance of power' in the world has depended to some extent on the stage reached by each great power in re-equipping with new aircraft.

(ii) These Directorates in the Air Staff are matched by corresponding Directorates in the Ministry of Supply, dealing with research and development under various heads, and dependent on a variety of specialised establishments and on work done in private firms. This organisation is mainly civilian, but includes some service officers. In theory it provides a series of links between pure scientific research and squadron service: there should be no break anywhere in the chain between pure science, applied science, development, production, introduction into squadron service, and use in battle; and experience in service ought to 'feed back' promptly along the chain. It is better to have overlapping responsibility than a breakdown in contact, and the links are kept strong by interchange of staff and by shared interest in technicalities of a most absorbing kind.

(iii) After the construction of the Ministry of Aircraft Production the Air Ministry was left with virtually no research organisation of its own, and it was soon found both in London and in the Commands that it was almost impossible to get on from day to day without someone at hand to advise on scientific problems. This was not a matter of cutting across the responsibility of the research organisations, but of helping laymen to grasp and discuss the issues involved. A Scientific Adviser to the Air Council was appointed during the war, with a very small staff; there was also for some time a special post of Scientific Adviser on Telecommunications. These were personal appointments, at a very high level. As a more permanent arrangement, these have been linked with another development, that of operational research sections at Commands. These were created first because radar was being introduced into squadron service in great haste at a very early stage of development, and it was essential for the research workers to study performance under service conditions, so as to prevent mistakes in use and to secure prompt and accurate reporting back about needs for further research. Experience soon showed that 'boffins' were valuable for a variety of other reasons. Expert knowledge gave them a special prestige, and civilian status enabled them to speak relatively freely even to the 'top brass'. There were many problems besides those of electronic equipment which could be handled well by men with fresh minds and a scientific sense of how to use evidence: lively and tactful men in charge of operational research sections made great contributions to operational policy.

From this developed a new type of scientific advice. Each Command 'grew' its operational research section, and so much depended on the evaluation of their reports that a corresponding organisation was required in the Air Staff. There is therefore under the C.A.S. a

Scientific Adviser's Branch, which links together the research done in Commands, contributes some research of its own, and (even more important) has a range of contacts in the scientific world which enables the Air Staff to hold up its head in scientific argument. The Ministry of Supply is the only formal source of scientific advice to the Air Ministry on matters within the sphere of the former, and the organisation would break down if it provoked a conflict between experts. But it is in the nature of science that boundaries cannot be demarcated clearly: and even on matters within the sphere of the Ministry of Supply business is likely to proceed better if the Air Staff has its own informal briefing about the nature of the problems and the snags involved in different lines of solution. The organisation is rather delicately balanced, and may break down on questions of personality: but it represents an experimental solution which has on the whole worked well.

5. THE MINISTRY OF PENSIONS AND NATIONAL INSURANCE

Constans et perpetua voluntas ius suum cuique tribuendi.—ULPIAN.

The Ministry of Pensions and National Insurance serves here as an example of a great Executive and Clerical Class Department. In 1956 it had, for a total staff of 37,000, only 68 members of the Administrative Class, the same number as the Commonwealth Relations Office with a total staff of under 1,000. The Ministry was created in 1954 by merging the old-established Ministry of Pensions (1917) with the youngest of the 'social service' Departments, the Ministry of National Insurance (1944). The suggestion that there should be a single Ministry of Social Security has never been taken very seriously in Whitehall, though it has had powerful advocates, among them Lord Beveridge himself. The present Ministry is not a Ministry of Social Security, for it has comparatively few 'welfare' functions (these are divided between a number of Ministries and non-ministerial Departments), but its responsibilities are very wide. It is, in one respect, like a very large publicly-owned insurance company or friendly society (except that certain benefits are paid without premium), and this is reflected in its internal organisation. Its duties comprise the management of a national programme of social insurance against sickness, old age, death, industrial injury, and other contingencies; the administration of family allowances and maternity benefits; and the payment of war pensions to the disabled ex-Service men of two world wars, their dependents, and certain war-disabled civilians.

In its insurance work, the Department is almost entirely concerned with the collection of contributions and with the assessment and payment of cash benefits according to detailed regulations made under the authority of statute; it has much less responsibility for the general welfare of the recipients than has (for instance) the National Assistance Board. It is not, however, entirely without responsibilities of this broader kind: its pensions work includes not only the assessment of disability and the payment of pensions but also the general care of the disabled pensioner and his dependents and the care and guardianship of war orphans. For the latter task it employs some fifty children's officers, who perform duties not unlike those of social workers in the children's departments of local authorities.

But the bulk of its work consists of routine and the management of routine: an immense number of records must be kept (some $25\frac{1}{2}$ million insurance contribution records, for example), payment of contributions must be enforced, and hundreds of thousands of claims for benefit must be assessed, checked, and paid each year. The organisation must be flexible enough to deal quickly with seasonal rushes of work (for instance, claims for sickness benefit in the mid-winter months), leaving less urgent business to 'take up the slack' in quieter periods. There is a relatively small staff at headquarters in London (about 1,500), mainly concerned with policy-making, organisation (including training), and finance. The work falls compactly into two main compartments: Pensions, and Insurance, with a Deputy Secretary responsible for each. Also reporting direct to the Permanent Secretary are the head of the Finance Division (an Under Secretary), the Solicitor in charge of the Legal Division (ranking as Deputy Secretary), the Under Secretary in charge of Establishments and Organisation, and the Chief Medical Officer. These divisions are spread about London: in the Strand, in Millbank, in Grosvenor Gardens, and in the Euston Road.

A feature of headquarters organisation is its two large out-stations: one for pensions at Blackpool, and one for insurance at Newcastle-upon-Tyne. These account for a quarter of the staff of the Ministry: about 3,000 at Blackpool and about 6,500 at Newcastle. On the pensions side, a small staff under an Under Secretary operates in London, dealing with pensions policy and the welfare and rehabilitation of war pensioners, but the bulk of the executive work—the assessment, award, and issue of pensions—is done at Blackpool. This central office is under a Controller, a high-ranking Executive Class officer. On the insurance side, four Under Secretaries assisted by a small number of Administrative and Executive Class officials deal, in London, with insurance policy, the drafting of regulations, and the issue to local staffs of detailed codes of instructions about the administration of industrial injuries and national insurance benefits, contributions, family allowances, and other matters. Records are kept centrally at Newcastle. This office is housed in a specially designed single-storey office block covering some 64 acres, an area larger than the whole of Whitehall. Most of the staff are girls recruited on Tyneside and are not expected to be 'mobile'. The work is highly mechanised, and though it is largely routine it calls for great accuracy and precision. Every day some 50,000 references arising out of benefit claims and similar matters are made to the $25\frac{1}{2}$ million individual contribution records, and over half of these references require a search in the alphabetical index of insured persons containing 35 million cards.

Much of the detailed executive work is carried out in regional and local offices, which in 1956 employed about 26,000 people, more than two-thirds of the total staff of the Ministry. There are 'Central Offices' for Scotland and Wales, and 10 regional offices of similar status for England, the standard 'London' region being divided into two.[1] Each Regional Controller ranks as an 'executive assistant secretary', and is assisted by a Deputy Regional Controller (roughly S.C.E.O.) and three or four Assistant Controllers (C.E.O.s). The regional offices are principally concerned with organisation and management, including the proper staffing of local offices, training, the arrangement of work, and periodic inspection of work in progress; but they take decisions on matters which cannot be dealt with locally; and they administer certain functions, such as welfare, which require special staff and can be more efficiently and economically concentrated at regional level.

Grouped under the regional offices, there are about 30 local war pensions offices and 900 local insurance offices. These offices receive some 20 million calls each year from members of the public. The manager of a local office is normally an H.E.O., though in large offices he may be an S.E.O., but the men and women the public most frequently meet are clerical officers.

One of the features of the national insurance legislation is that responsibility for deciding on claims to benefit rests with 'officers appointed by the Minister',[2] called local Insurance Officers. They are, in fact, ordinary Executive Class officers but are given a special status, and there is at least one Insurance Officer in each local office.

---

[1] The areas of the standard regions are shown on the map at the end of Chapter 16.
[2] National Insurance Act, 1946, Sec. 43.

Difficult cases may be referred for advice up the hierarchy to regional Insurance Officers, and to the Chief Insurance Officer at headquarters if necessary, but the final decision rests formally with the local Insurance Officer. Appeals from his decisions lie to a local appeal tribunal and from there to the National Insurance Commissioner (a barrister appointed by the Crown on the advice of the Lord Chancellor). There are separate local appeals tribunals for war pension cases, and several important national tribunals for special purposes. In addition, the Minister makes extensive use of national and local advisory committees, one of the most important of which is the National Insurance Advisory Committee. This statutory Committee advises the Minister on all draft Statutory Instruments before they are submitted to Parliament.

There is a large legal branch (employing some 50 lawyers), for an important side of the Ministry's legal work (quite apart from the work of drafting Bills and Statutory Instruments) concerns the enforcement of contributions and the prosecution of fraudulent claimants. Cases are prepared initially by 'enforcement officers', who are ordinary Executive Class civil servants, and the legal branch advises on procedure and on the conduct of cases in court.

The Chief Medical Officer's department is staffed by about 150 doctors. About a dozen of these are employed at headquarters, mainly advising on policy. The remainder are out-stationed at various provincial centres, and their duties are almost entirely clinical: examining pensions and industrial injuries cases, advising on claims for sickness and other benefits, advising on the medical problems of pensioners. They also serve on Pneumoconiosis and Byssinosis Medical Boards. The medical boards for war pensions and industrial injuries cases are for the most part composed of general practitioners selected from local panels, but cases are examined in the first instance by a Ministry doctor.

In an organisation as large as this, matters of staffing, work organisation, and office management bulk large, and there is considerable scope for the Organisation and Methods Section. O. & M. played a big part in the design of the original Ministry between 1944 and 1946, one of its first tasks being to advise on the creation of a Central Registry; and it has advised on many problems arising out of the amalgamation of the two Departments, including the unification of their work processes, which has made possible fairly considerable reductions in staff.

Another problem of a large Executive and Clerical Class Department is to recruit and transfer staff to fill vacancies occurring in local offices all over the country. Established civil servants have an obligation to serve anywhere in Great Britain, but housing difficulties now make this particularly onerous. The creation of this new Ministry involved the very considerable task of transferring to Newcastle and to the network of local offices some 20,000 civil servants who had been employed previously in London and in wartime evacuated offices in Blackpool. The position is now relatively stable, though there are still difficulties in filling posts in some parts of the country, notably in the Midlands and the North, to which there are no longer any staff wishing to return. Staff are now normally transferred on the basis of priorities determined by the degree of hardship involved. An officer may claim to be moved, or may object to compulsory transfer (which is normal only on promotion), on grounds of hardship, and, as far as possible, a vacancy is filled either by an officer suffering the greatest hardship in his existing post, or by an officer who will suffer least from the transfer.

The M.P.N.I. serves also to illustrate the exchange of services between Departments on an agency basis. We have singled out in Chapter 17 a number of Departments as 'common service' Departments *par excellence*, but each Department serves others when it is convenient so to arrange matters, or simply because it is an established practice. The M.P.N.I. acts for the Ministry of Health in issuing the documents which entitle children and expectant mothers to 'welfare foods' free or at reduced prices. Conversely, unemployment benefit is paid on behalf of the M.P.N.I. at the local offices of the Ministry of Labour; other cash benefits are paid by various vouchers which can be cashed at Post Offices; and Post Offices also collect revenue on behalf of the M.P.N.I. by the sale of insurance stamps.

6. The Board of Trade

Monstrum horrendum, informe, ingens, cui lumen ademptum.—VERGIL: *Aeneid.*

A recent Permanent Secretary of the Board of Trade has likened its organisation to Milton's vision of

> The other shape, if shape it might be called
> That shape had none.

Its traditional responsibility is for 'improving the trade and manufactures of these Our Kingdoms', and it rests upon the Order-in-Council of 1786 which constituted a Committee of the Privy Council 'for the consideration of all matters relating to trade and foreign plantations'. Its situation thus in some respects resembles that of the Home Office, since it has been the begetter of other Departments and now retains wide responsibility combined with an untidy list of specific functions. The Ministry of Power, the Ministry of Labour, the Ministry of Transport and Civil Aviation all began as Departments of the Board of Trade. The Department of Overseas Trade, the Ministry of Economic Warfare, and the Ministry of Materials were reunited to it after separation.

In spite of the extent of its terms of reference, the Board of Trade does not act as a 'super-Ministry' or co-ordinating Department except in limited fields specifically entrusted to it. There is no co-ordinating Department for 'trade and manufactures'. A separate Minister of Economic Affairs with a small staff was appointed for this purpose in September 1947, but this became part of the Treasury after only a few weeks of life. But its scope was narrowed and not extended by amalgamation: the Treasury could not and does not try to 'co-ordinate' production and distribution.

During the war the Board of Trade was in charge of a number of 'Controls' each of which managed the allocation of materials, labour, and other scarce resources for a specified industry. At the period of greatest expansion there were more than a dozen such Controls in the Board of Trade, and there were others in other Departments. Their organisation often took a rather 'syndical' form, as it was usual to bring an eminent man from the industry into the Department to run the Control, to staff it with other experienced men from outside (with a few permanent civil servants as 'scaffolding'), and to act in close concert with the trade associations concerned. The Department at its time of greatest expansion in 1947 had a staff of 15,000; by 1956 it had sunk to about 7,200, and the organisation had entered what appears to be a period of relative stability.

The framework of organisation is provided by a relatively large Administrative Class staff, backed by the Executive Class. In 1956 there were 169 members of the Administrative Class in the Department: 1 Permanent Secretary, 3 Deputy Secretaries, 14 Under Secretaries, 50 Assistant Secretaries, 85 Principals, 16 Assistant Principals. There were also about 190 Executive Class officers above the rank of Higher Executive Officer, that is to say overlapping the salary range of the Principal: rather a high proportion of them were engaged on the sort of work which the Treasury describes as 'underpinning the Administrative Class' in administrative divisions.

The Board of Trade is one of the Departments which maintains an overseas service of its own. There are 50 members of the Administrative Class in Trade Commissioner Offices, and these officials are in principle interchangeable with officials serving at headquarters (there are no data about the practice of this theory, which presents certain difficulties). These officers are mainly in countries which are members of the Commonwealth, but there are a few in the colonies. There are none in foreign countries, and this arrangement has a long history. Briefly, British exporters have for generations complained about the lack of understanding of their problems shown by the Foreign Office, its diplomatic missions and its consuls, and have pressed for separate commercial representation overseas. The Foreign Office has (rightly, from its own point of view) objected strongly to any division of the responsibility for the British official representatives in a foreign country, and a series of compromises have been tried. From 1880 to 1917 there were a limited number of Commercial Attachés at the larger British missions abroad. From 1917 to 1946 there was a separate Department of Overseas Trade, with a political Secretary of its own responsible to the Foreign Secretary and the President of the Board of Trade acting jointly. Since 1946 the Foreign Service has made a resolute attempt to widen its own outlook, and there are now a large number of members (about 120) of the 'Commercial Diplomatic' branch of the Service. But this arrangement naturally does not apply within the Commonwealth, and the Commonwealth Relations Office has not set up a similar service of its own. The Board of Trade provides its own representatives there: and its Commercial Relations and Exports Department is in effect a headquarters both for them and for commercial officers in the Foreign Service.

The Department can best be described in terms of central services, main framework, and ancillary departments; perhaps its most striking feature is the proliferation of ancillary agencies of various sorts.

It need hardly be said that *central services* include a Principal Finance Officer and a Principal Establishments and Organisation Officer, both Under Secretaries. There is an unusually important Statistics Division, with a Director who ranks as an Under Secretary. There is a strong Solicitor's Department, the head of which ranks as a Deputy Secretary, and is responsible for all legal matters arising out of the enforcement of controls, as well as for 'Administration of Enemy Property', a result of 'economic warfare' in two world wars, which still presents a good deal of technical difficulty. The Board of Trade is one of the main employers of the specialist accountant class referred to in Chapter 7; and there is a part-time Accountant Adviser, and a strong Accountants Division, concerned with various aspects of commercial costing, not with the internal accounting of the Department. There is also one of the larger Information Divisions, the head of which also looks after Exhibitions and Trade Fairs; and a

Parliamentary Branch under a Chief Executive Officer, whose main business is to see that Parliamentary Questions move swiftly through the mazes of the organisation.

The *main framework* is subdivided in a way which is relatively simple at the top, extremely confusing in the lower levels, where the Department has to match the complexity of the business world. There is one Deputy Secretary in charge of the Commercial Relations and Exports Department, with half a dozen Under Secretaries and an economist (who ranks as Under Secretary) to act as 'Commercial' Adviser. Another Deputy Secretary is in charge of the Distribution of Industries Division and the Industries and Manufactures Department, which has five divisions each with an Under Secretary: Engineering Industries, and four numbered divisions, two covering general subjects and two dealing with particular industries for which the Board is responsible. The division of work between these four divisions may be roughly described as follows: first, imports and tariffs; secondly, general industrial policy and administration (this division is also responsible for the hotel and tourist industry and for the regulation of monopolies and restrictive practices); thirdly, textiles, timber, and a wide range of consumer goods industries; and, fourthly, the chemical and related industries.[1]

The third Deputy Secretary takes charge of the remainder of the Departmental business; this includes the Insurance and Companies Department and the Bankruptcy Department, both dealing with highly technical matters important to the business world; and he is also in charge of most of the central services described above, presumably because his department throws up fewer urgent problems of policy than those which come to the other Deputy Secretaries.

The officials so far referred to almost all belong to the non-specialist classes, though they are backed by lawyers, statisticians, information officers, and accountants. The sort of specialist work which in the Home Office is done by Inspectors supervising independent public authorities is in the Board of Trade done by a great variety of *ancillary organisations*. These can be roughly classified as follows:

(i) There are a number of divisions and sub-departments which are part of the Board of Trade but are relatively self-contained. There are, for instance, the Export Licensing Branch, the Import Licensing Branch, and the Export Services Branch, all run largely by the Executive Class; the Standards Department (with its own technical staff); the Companies Registration Office; the Companies

[1] Until the creation, at the beginning of 1957, of the Ministry of Power, this division was also responsible for the iron and steel industry.

(Winding-up) Department; the Bankruptcy (High Court) Department. Above all, there is the Patent Office and Industrial Property Department, a very large office with its own Departmental class of Patents Examiners and Receivers.

(ii) Still within the Department, but in a rather different category, are the surviving industrial Controls. There appear in 1956 to be only the Dyestuffs Office in Manchester, the Jute Control in Dundee, and the Directorate of Home Flax Production, which has headquarters in London and local offices in the main producing areas.

(iii) Thirdly, there is the Export Credits Guarantee Department, a minor Department under the aegis of the Board, headed by a Comptroller-General (Under Secretary), which is in effect a large insurance business, backed by government credit, which helps exporters by offering insurance against bad debts overseas on payment of premiums which are expected to cover the Department's costs.

(iv) The Board 'sponsors' in various ways a great many bodies of a 'semi-public' character. These include, for example, Industrial Development Councils which were set up for various industries under the Industrial Organisation and Development Acts of 1947 and 1953. These Councils were designed to induce industries to develop some sense of corporate responsibility for running their own affairs, and to provide the government with a single point of reference not dominated by the selfish point of view of any one section of the industry. There are also the Regional Boards for Industry, one in each of the 'standard' regions, consisting of representatives of employers' organisations and trade unions with an independent chairman; each acts as a local forum for discussion and advice on production matters and industrial conditions in the region, and they have from time to time been given minor executive functions. There are the Industrial Estates Companies, set up under the Distribution of Industry Acts, 1945 and 1950, to manage factories and trading estates in the development areas in accordance with Board of Trade policy: these are non-profit-making companies limited by guarantee, and the directors are appointed by the President of the Board of Trade. There is the National Film Finance Corporation which gives financial assistance to the British film industry.

There are also a number of bodies not connected with one particular industry or region which the government wishes to encourage as agencies of self-help. The most effective way in which it can act is by grant-in-aid, often matching contributions from industry, or intended to set going an activity which industry may later finance for itself. Typical cases are the British Travel and Holidays Association, the Council of Industrial Design and the Industrial Design Centres, the British Institute of Management, the British Standards Institution, the Dollar Exports Council, and the British Productivity Council.

(v) The machinery for regulating monopoly and restrictive practices in industry must be put in a category by itself. The Monopolies and Restrictive Practices Act of 1948, which set up a Monopolies Commission, was a tentative first step in dealing with one of the thorniest problems of industrial organisation. It is not easy for a Department which is for some purposes urging industry to combine in effective associations also to take responsibility for repressing industrial association which is deemed to go too far. The experiment of 1948 was in effect that there should be an independent tribunal with a small staff (including seconded civil servants) which should hear cases referred to it by the Board of Trade about abuses of industrial organisation, and should report on the answer to certain specific questions contained in the reference. The form of reference was decided by the Board of Trade, often after representations had been received from the public: action on the reports of the Commission was a matter for the Department responsible for the industry.

The scope of the Monopolies Commission was much reduced by the Restrictive Trade Practices Act of 1956, which provided for the appointment of a Registrar of Restrictive Trading Agreements to take proceedings against offenders before a special Division of the High Court. The Registrar is an independent officer of the Crown, but acts in close consultation with the Board of Trade.

7. The Ministry of Agriculture, Fisheries, and Food

O fortunatos nimium, sua si bona norint,
Agricolas.
VERGIL: *Georgics.*

The Board of Agriculture and Fisheries came into existence under that name in 1903, when the Fisheries Department of the Board of Trade (1886) was merged with the Board of Agriculture (1889). It became a Ministry in 1919. Its responsibility is for England and Wales only, not for Scotland or Northern Ireland. The Ministry of Food, on the other hand, was responsible for all four countries. It was an emergency organisation which existed under that name from

1916 to 1921, and was set up again in 1939. The two Ministries were amalgamated in 1955, without change of responsibilities.

Both organisations have come in for a good deal of political criticism, much of it unfair, since their difficulties have arisen mainly from the complexity of their problems and from the fact that they touch sensitive political nerves. Farmers and fishermen make themselves effectively heard in a good many constituencies, and all voters can be appealed to through their stomachs. There have been many inquiries into the organisation of the two Ministries; their headquarters layout has been frequently changed; and it is at present once more in transition as a result of the attempt to combine them in such a way as to secure economy and co-ordination without sacrificing politically important interests.

The only stable elements in their headquarters organisation at present are those familiar from earlier examples, and we therefore propose to use the Ministry primarily to illustrate the extraordinary variety of ancillary organisations through which the central administration works. Each type of agency set out below has its parallels in other fields, but no other Ministry possesses so complete a collection. One of its special difficulties is that these ancillary agencies exist and have vested interests which cannot be brushed aside, so that headquarters must somehow contrive for itself a scheme of divisions adopted to the complexity of its subordinate bodies.

Of the Ministry as a whole it is necessary to say only that it is of medium size (17,594 on 1 July 1955); that many of these officials are scattered about the country, so that headquarters contains only about 8,000 of them; and that these consist of a relatively large number of members of the Administrative Class, backed by a small section of the Executive Class and by many small groups drawn from a great variety of specialist classes. In 1956, after the amalgamation, there were about 150 members of the Administrative Class in the combined Department: including 1 Permanent Secretary, 4 Deputy Secretaries, 15 Under Secretaries, 36 Assistant Secretaries, 85 Principals, and 17 Assistant Principals.

The list of organisations which follows is not comprehensive, and there is room for difference of opinion about how to classify them. But it is useful to have some classification, and the headings we offer are: self-contained Ministry 'services' within the Departmental organisation; Ministry services outside the Departmental organisation; minor Departments controlled by the Ministry or closely related to it; public corporations; marketing boards; sponsored 'voluntary' co-operation; local organisations outside the structure of these services; and finally the National Farmers' Union itself.

(i) *Ministry Services within the Departmental Organisation*

There are four important Agricultural Services and a number of minor ones. The main services are:

(*a*) *The Veterinary Service*, which is staffed by qualified veterinary surgeons and technical assistants (about 500 in all) and has its own regional and divisional organisation. The Animal Health Division (which is at Surbiton in Surrey) acts as its head office: it manages a number of veterinary laboratories and a special veterinary investigating service, which are primarily disease control organisations, and have analogues in the public health field.

(*b*) *The National Agricultural Advisory Service*, which is staffed largely by graduates in agriculture (about 1,700 at present, with a plan for ultimate expansion to 2,000) and is primarily responsible for 'husbandry' in all its aspects. These include animal husbandry, which is scarcely separable from animal health, but this organisation is staffed by people without veterinary qualifications and is separate from the veterinary organisation at every level up to that of Under Secretary. The local areas of the N.A.A.S. are the administrative counties (except that some small counties are grouped together): each of them has a County Agricultural Officer responsible for co-ordinating the various experts within the Advisory Service, and there is a 'provincial' (i.e. regional) organisation intermediate between the county organisation and headquarters. At headquarters the Service is grouped with 'Education' in the Education and Advisory Services Division, which has an office of its own in Horseferry Road. The Service runs a number of 'experimental farms' (not 'research stations', for 'research' is conducted either by the Agricultural Research Council or by 'independent' Research Institutes), and a Plant Pathology Laboratory, which is in principle concerned with disease control.

(*c*) *The Agricultural Land Service* (about 300 strong), which is staffed mainly by people with professional qualifications in estate management and in surveying. The A.L.S. is needed primarily because the Ministry is the chief adviser to the government on the use of agricultural land, and has many problems involving the market value of land, the condition of farm buildings, and the development of estates. Its headquarters is with that of the N.A.A.S. in Horseferry Road; in the country it has its own organisation of Agricultural Land Commissioners, but its Provinces are the same as those of the N.A.A.S.

(*d*) *The Agricultural Economics Advisory Service* perhaps does not belong strictly to this group, since its staff (about 150 in all) are employed under a peculiar system by which they are the servants not of the Ministry but of a number of chosen Universities. These Universities obtain from the Ministry a grant to cover the salaries and expenses of the Advisory Service in full, but maintain with their own funds small University departments for teaching and research in agricultural economics, and these are closely associated with the Service. The main objects of the Service are (on the one hand) to obtain objective information about costs of production for the use of the Ministry; on the other hand, to advise farmers about the profitability of alternative courses of action. The device adopted is intended to emphasise the independence of the Service, as well as to encourage the study of agricultural economics in the Universities. It is by no means wholly unsuccessful, though it causes a good deal of confusion to all concerned, and this confusion has been increased because the N.A.A.S. has recently been given responsibility for advice about profitability, on less specialised lines. The Economics Advisory Service reports to headquarters through the Economics Division and the Statistics Division.

The minor services include a number of inspectorates which have functions of control: the National Milk Testing Service (with about 350 staff), the Seeds Inspectorate, the Rodent and Insects Inspectorate, and the Agricultural Machinery Inspectorate. Perhaps one should also place here the Agricultural Lime Department ('out-stationed' at Lytham St. Annes in Lancashire), which operates the statutory financial arrangements for grants in aid of liming and fertilisers; and the National Stud, a stud of thoroughbred horses which the government acquired by gift in 1916 and which it has run on a commercial basis ever since (this is a nationalised enterprise which has returned a small but consistent profit).

The trading divisions and Controls of the Ministry of Food have gradually been dismantled, and by 1956 what was once an enormous enterprise had virtually ceased to exist. The Controls were run by civil servants, generally assisted by men from the trade concerned, acting as temporary officials or as part-time advisers. Each organisation was administratively a part of the Ministry, but its trading accounts were segregated from the Departmental accounts so that a profit or loss could be shown. The accounting problems which arose from this system were complex, and the history of these organisations is a world in itself.

(ii) *Ministry Services not within the Departmental Organisation*

It seems to be an accident that certain bodies which are for practical purposes Departments have been brought within the general control of the Ministry for matters of finance and establishments and are consequently borne on the Ministry's Vote. The most important of these are:

(a) *The Royal Botanic Gardens* at Kew, under its own Director: a world-famous organisation much senior to the Ministry, for it was founded in 1762.

(b) *The Agricultural Land Commission*, a body of five part-time members, with a separate Welsh Sub-Commission, both of them set up by the Agriculture Act of 1947. Their functions are to manage agricultural estates vested in the Minister or made over to him by another Department, and they may either let these estates to tenants or farm them themselves. They also advise the Minister about compulsory purchase and about the management of agricultural land generally. Their operations are substantial, as they were responsible for 227,648 acres of land in England and Wales at the time of their last annual report, though they farmed directly only 7,000 acres. The Commission and Sub-Commission are staffed almost entirely by members of the Agricultural Land Service.

(c) *The Wheat Commission* is in a curious position. It is the survivor of several 'commodity commissions' which were set up in the inter-war years to administer subsidies and levies. Established in 1932, the Commission is appointed by the Minister to represent wheat growers, flour millers and importers, consumers, and other interests. Its executive functions were suspended in 1940 and its staff (who were not then civil servants) were merged with the Ministry. Its present Secretary is Director of the Ministry's Home Grown Cereals Marketing Division. Since 1940 it has remained in existence as an advisory body pending government action about long-term marketing arrangements for cereals.

(iii) *Minor Departments*

There are three minor Departments fully within the scope of the Ministry. These are:

(a) *The Ordnance Survey* (also much older than the Ministry itself), the organisation responsible for mapping the United Kingdom. The work was begun in the reign of Elizabeth I by the Surveyor of Wards and Liveries, but passed after 1747 to the engineers of the Ordnance (presumably because they were the best body of surveyors at the government's disposal). It remained under the Master-General of Ordnance, and later the Secretary of State for War, until 1870, and was then for thirty-three years in the Office of Works. It passed to the Board of Agriculture in 1903, but it is still staffed by officers of the Royal Engineers, and its Director-General is a Major-General.

(In the U.S.A., the Federal Corps of Army Engineers has obtained even larger civilian functions.)

(b) *The Forestry Commission*, a body of part-time Commissioners, acting through a Director-General. It was set up by the Forestry Act of 1919, under which it enjoyed a large measure of administrative autonomy; the Minister had no power to issue directions to it, its funds were obtained by a grant-in-aid from the Treasury, and it was represented in Parliament by the same back-bench Member whichever party was in power. This weakened rather than strengthened the position of the Commission, since its planting programme was an obvious target in times of economy; and the strength of the organisation seems to have been increased by the Forestry Act of 1945, which gave the Minister of Agriculture wide powers to issue directions. It is staffed entirely by civil servants, non-industrial and industrial.

(c) *The Commissioners of Crown Lands* were the direct descendants of the officers responsible for managing the estates of the Crown in the Middle Ages. Since 1760 the revenues of these estates have always passed into the Consolidated Fund, a partial offset against the grant of a Civil List to the Monarch: but Crown lands are still administered as a single 'trust estate', with a capital value of at least £50 m., a unit quite separate from the lands managed by the Agricultural Land Commission. At one time (1832-1851) the Commission was headed by a junior Minister, but its effective head has for many years been the Permanent Commissioner, an Administrative Class civil servant.

In June 1955 the government announced that it had accepted the recommendation of a Committee of Inquiry (the Trustram Eve Committee) that the Commission should be replaced by a statutory Board of Trustees. This was one of the results of the Crichel Down episode, which led to much criticism of the isolated position of the Permanent Commissioner.

The Ministry has a good deal to do with various agencies which are responsible to Parliament through other Ministers. The most important of these are the Committees of the Privy Council for Agricultural Research and Nature Conservation, which act through two working committees, the Agricultural Research Council and the Nature Conservancy, and are responsible to Parliament through the Lord President of the Council; and the National Parks Commission, a body which acts largely through local planning authorities (in effect the county councils), and reports to the Minister of Housing and Local Government in virtue of his responsibility for decisions about land use.

(iv) *Public Corporations*

Another undemarcated frontier divides the minor Departments from a number of public bodies which are not staffed by civil servants. These include:

(*a*) *The Herring Industry Board*, set up in 1935 (under the Herring Industry Act of 1933) with responsibility for all four countries. It consists of three part-time members, jointly appointed by the Minister of Agriculture, Fisheries, and Food, the Secretary of State for Scotland, and the Home Secretary (who is responsible for the industry in Northern Ireland).

(*b*) *The White Fish Authority*, set up in 1951 under the Sea Fish Industry Act of that year to replace an earlier body, the White Fish Commission (1938). Its position is in most respects parallel to that of the Herring Industry Board.

(*c*) *The Sugar Board*, set up by the Sugar Act of 1956 to purchase and sell Commonwealth sugar on behalf of the Minister.

These bodies resemble Marketing Boards more than they do the bodies which run coal, electricity, gas, and transport; they are trading but not producing organisations, they can finance themselves in part by levies on producers, and they differ from Marketing Boards mainly because none of their members is elected by producers.

(v) *The Marketing Boards*

These are an easier category to handle because they all owe their existence to the Agricultural Marketing Acts, 1931 to 1949, which might be described as an experiment in enforcing producers' co-operation. The immensely complicated financial arrangements for the maintenance of British agriculture depend partly on direct control of imports, partly on tariffs, partly on control of domestic production through the organisation of producers, and partly on subsidies, which are largely channelled through the Boards and the other organisations analogous to them. In some respects the Boards bear the brunt of the battle, since they are elected by producers and have real powers of enforcement only so long as an overwhelming majority of producers support them. The Ministers appoint only one member to a Board for every four elected members.

During the Second World War a number of Boards were suspended or were kept in being only as direct agents of the government. Some of these have been revived and one or two additional Boards have been or are being created. There are now: the Milk Marketing Board, the Potato Marketing Board, the Hops Marketing Board, the Tomato and Cucumber Marketing Board, and the British Wool

Marketing Board (all except the last being responsible for England and Wales only). The Pig Marketing Board, Bacon Marketing Board, and Bacon Development Board are still suspended pending a final decision on permanent marketing arrangements: at present they act (rather like the Wheat Commission) as advisory bodies to the Minister, in consultation with the National Farmers' Union. The latter's proposals for a Marketing Board to deal in pork and bacon pigs were rejected by a committee (the Bosanquet Committee) appointed by the Minister of Agriculture, which reported in July 1956. An Egg Marketing Board was proposed in 1956 and will shortly be set up.

(vi) *Sponsored Co-operation*

We have seen how the Board of Trade fosters what are technically private bodies through official encouragement, including grants-in-aid. The Ministry of Agriculture acts in the same way to support a large number of independent bodies which provide facilities for research and training in agriculture and fisheries; it is in general terms a supporter of agricultural co-operation; and it makes small grants to allotment societies, the National Federation of Young Farmers' Clubs, and similar bodies.

The Fatstock Marketing Corporation requires special mention: a body which had in 1955 a turnover of £107 m., and which has no legal existence except as a private company. It owes its creation to the combined ingenuity of the Ministry and of the National Farmers' Union, anxious to dismantle official controls of meat marketing without losing their advantages.

This body has some affinities to *the British Sugar Corporation*, set up by the Sugar Industry (Reorganisation) Act of 1936[1] to purchase home-grown beet for manufacture into sugar. The Corporation is a company limited by shares and registered under the Companies Acts but carries certain Treasury guarantees. It acts in close co-operation with the Sugar Board.

Another body of this kind is *the Agricultural Mortgage Corporation* (there is a corresponding though smaller body for Scotland), which was set up by the principal joint-stock banks in 1928, under statutory authority, to provide farmers with medium and long-term loans. It receives a grant from the Ministry, and there is a Treasury representative on the Board of Directors.

(vii) *Local Organisation*

Many of the bodies so far referred to have local organisations of

[1] Repealed by the Sugar Act, 1956.

their own. There are also more general local organisations of two kinds:

(a) *Local Authorities*, primarily counties and county boroughs, are responsible for a number of functions in the field of the Ministry, and it acts with and through them by means of grants and supervision much as is done by other Departments (this is summed up in Chapter 22). Perhaps the most important urban functions are those of meat inspection and the control of slaughter-houses (the main responsibility for the standards and hygiene of most other foods has since 1955 been vested in the Minister of Health). The local education authorities are responsible for all agricultural education below University level: in practice, the counties are the important authorities in this field, and supervision is primarily (but not wholly) a matter for the Ministry of Education. It is not at all easy to ensure proper co-ordination between these activities in the field of 'education' and that of the N.A.A.S. in the field of 'advice'.

The local authorities are also land drainage authorities, and they are represented on the River Boards, which are very large *ad hoc* authorities appointed by the Minister and supervised by drainage engineers in the Ministry. Authorities on the sea-coast of England and Wales jointly form eleven Sea-Fisheries Committees, primarily responsible for the making of by-laws for the control of fisheries within territorial waters.

(b) *Specially Appointed Bodies.* At the beginning of the war of 1939 the Ministry had to contemplate the imposition of controls in the interests of crop production much more stringent than any which would be possible in time of peace, and it did not seem that the problem of enforcement was one which could be handled by officials sent out from the centre. The Ministry therefore proceeded by appointing in each administrative county a County War Agricultural Executive Committee. These bodies consisted primarily of local farmers; they employed their own officers, and they had considerable autonomy in enforcing the Ministry's policy on the farmers in their area, who were in a sense their constituents, since members were nominated on a basis of their standing in the locality. This system worked remarkably well during the time of crisis: cropping programmes were, in general, conscientiously followed; the C.W.A.E.C.s showed themselves to be stern with farmers who wasted the resources of the land by incompetence; and they provided a good many services at cost price, such as the use of agricultural machinery and of labour gangs.

Such enthusiasm could scarcely be expected in time of peace; and in any case the need for a strict policy gradually diminished. Nevertheless, there is still a good deal for the Committees to do. They still provide some 'pooled' services, and they are still the agents responsible for acting against bad farming, an invidious job, which has earned some criticism in the courts, but which can scarcely be done at all except by a body representing the public opinion of good farmers. To recognise their permanent value the Committees were established on a statutory basis in 1947 as County Agricultural Executive Committees; they were brought more closely within the official hierarchy of the Ministry, and their officials were absorbed into the Civil Service (they are now mainly drawn from the National Agricultural Advisory Service). The Committees' formal functions declined fairly rapidly after 1950 and are now relatively small, but their position remains important because they are the only sounding-board organised by the Ministry to represent the opinion of local farmers, and the only local organisation of the Ministry which can properly act as a focus for agricultural services as a whole.

The Wilson Committee (which was appointed to review the local and provincial organisation of the Ministry, and reported in April 1956) recommended that the Committees' work should be limited to advising the Minister on policy, promoting technical and development services in the counties in conjunction with the N.A.A.S., and hearing appeals. This recommendation has apparently been rejected, at least for the present.

(viii) *The National Farmers' Union for England and Wales*

This point leads naturally to a consideration of the N.F.U. for England and Wales (there are separate N.F.U.s for Scotland and for Northern Ireland), which is sometimes regarded as a hand pulling strings on which the Minister of Agriculture dances. This is much too simple a view of a complicated situation; the N.F.U. is undoubtedly in one sense a political body, but it is also a good deal more.

This section has enumerated about thirty separate central agencies in more or less close relationship to the Ministry, apart from local organisations. It is no wonder that there is talk sometimes about 'hordes of officials' in the countryside; but there is a strong, indeed unanswerable, case for each service taken by itself. Of course, these services do not all impinge on each section of the farming world; on the other hand, they are only one part of the formal organisation of agriculture, and a fuller study would also describe a large number of voluntary agricultural societies of many different kinds, such as the Royal Society for Agriculture, the agricultural co-operatives, and the various 'breed' societies. The Ministry looked at from one point of view is that part of the government which is the focus for all this range of activity; the Ministry's organisation has to parallel its complexity, and to attempt to control it in so far as government policy requires. The N.F.U. is also a central point, a focus of rather a different kind; its strength and its peculiar contribution is that in the countryside all activities must come to a single point in the actions of each farmer on each farm. Within an area the number of farmers is limited, and they know one another well; the farming community has in most areas a natural unity up to the level of the county, and within the county its leaders constitute a 'stage army' who reappear in different capacities on many bodies, as J.P.s, as County Councillors and District Councillors, as members of the C.A.E.C.s, as members of Marketing Boards, as members of co-operatives, as members of various other area organisations—and above all as members of local committees of the N.F.U. It is not easy to see who within this system is effective governor or originator of action: but close links bind the Ministry to the farmers (as well as to the fishermen and to the food trades), and mutual response is swift although not certain.

FOR REFERENCE

1. *General:*

The Imperial Calendar and Civil Service List.
Civil Estimates.

2. *Commonwealth Relations Office:*

The Commonwealth Relations Office List.
Europa Publications: *The British Commonwealth, 1956* (1956). (A new annual reference book. This issue contains an essay by N. Mansergh on the work of the C.R.O. and the Colonial Office.)

3. *Home Office:*

Sir FRANK NEWSAM: *The Home Office* (1954).

4. *Air Ministry:*

C. G. GREY: *A History of the Air Ministry* (1940).
W. RALEIGH and H. A. JONES: *The War in the Air*, Vol. I (1922).

5. *Ministry of Pensions and National Insurance:*

Annual Reports.
H. V. RHODES: *Setting up a New Government Department* (British Institute of Management Occasional Papers, 1949).
Royal Commission on Scottish Affairs. *Memoranda*, Vol. I (1953).

6. *Board of Trade:*
Sir H. LLEWELLYN SMITH: *The Board of Trade* (1928).
Royal Commission on Scottish Affairs. *Memoranda*, Vol. II (1953).
H.M. Treasury: *The Regional Boards for Industry* (1951).
The Board of Trade Journal.

7. *Ministry of Agriculture, Fisheries, and Food:*
Report of a Committee on the Agricultural Education and Advisory Services (Luxmoore). Cmd. 6433, 1943.
Report of a Committee on the Working of the Agricultural Marketing Acts (M.A.F.F. Economic Series No. 48. 1947).
Report of a Committee on the Organisation of the Ministry of Agriculture and Fisheries (Ryan) (H.M.S.O. 1950).
Report of a Working Party on Co-operation between Local Education Authorities and the N.A.A.S. (Carrington). December 1953.
5th Report from the Select Committee on Estimates, Session 1953-54 ('Agricultural Research'). H.C. 218.
Report on the N.A.A.S. 1946-1954 (H.M.S.O. 1955).
Report of the Committee on National Stud Policy and Methods of Operation (Loraine) (H.M.S.O. 1955).
Monograph on *Governmental Services to the Sea Fish Industry of Great Britain.* Prepared by F. M. G. Willson under the auspices of the Royal Institute of Public Administration for Food and Agriculture Organisation (United Nations) (December 1955).
Report of a Committee on Crown Lands (Trustram Eve). Cmd. 9483, 1955.
Report of the Committee appointed to Review the Provincial and Local Organisation and Procedures of the M.A.F.F. (Arton Wilson). Cmd. 9732, 1956.
Annual Reports of Agricultural Land Commission and Forestry Commission.
History of the Second World War, Civil Series:
  R. J. HAMMOND: *Food: The Growth of Policy* (1951).
  K. A. H. MURRAY: *Agriculture* (1955).

CHAPTER SIXTEEN

LOCAL AND REGIONAL ORGANISATION

He is the very model of a modern major-general.
W. S. GILBERT: *The Pirates of Penzance.*

1. INTRODUCTORY

A VERY high proportion of the Civil Service works outside 'Whitehall', however widely that term may be construed. Official statistics do not draw this non-technical distinction between 'Whitehall' and the rest, but the figures for established non-industrial civil servants in Table XXIV give some indication of proportions.

TABLE XXIV

Geographical Location of Established Non-Industrial Civil Servants (Home and Foreign) at 1 July 1954

(Source: Civil Service Staff Statistics. Figures for 1 July 1955 not available)

London area (including the S.E. Region)	196,715[1]
Northern Region	21,450
East and West Ridings	24,146
North Midland Region	18,873
Eastern Region	17,694
Southern Region	33,264
South West Region	31,281
Midland Region	25,571
North West Region	47,096
Wales	19,558
Scotland	41,661
Northern Ireland	5,834
Overseas	6,670
Total	489,813

[1] The number of established non-industrial staff on 'London' rates of pay at the same date was 164,604.

There is no reason to believe that the distribution of unestablished non-industrial civil servants is very different, and the picture is therefore that only about two-fifths of the servants of the central administration work in London and the Home Counties. Many of these are employed in local offices, so that the proportion actually employed at headquarters is even smaller.[2]

Two minor notes on these figures. The number of civil servants in Northern Ireland is relatively small, because Northern Ireland is for some purposes self-governing and has a local Civil Service of its own —a complication which is not within the scope of this book. The civil servants overseas include the Foreign Service, Trade Commissioners, works and accountancy staff belonging to the service Departments, and a few 'home' civil servants filling posts in the Oversea Civil Service.

Civil servants outside 'Whitehall' can be divided into four categories, between which broad distinctions can be drawn.

(i) The majority are to be found in local offices which deal directly with the public on behalf of one or other of the large national Departments—the Post Office, the Board of Inland Revenue, the Ministry of Labour, the Ministry of Pensions and National Insurance, the National Assistance Board, and the Board of Customs and Excise.

(ii) Many Departments now interpose a level of organisation, generally called 'regional', between headquarters and their local offices. The number of civil servants working in such 'regional' offices at the beginning of 1954 is shown in Table XXV.

TABLE XXV

Non-Industrial Staff in Regional Offices at 1 January 1954

(Source: Treasury Table supplied to Select Committee on Estimates: see *6th Report 1953-54*, p. 169. Figures for 1 July 1955 not available)

Admiralty	43
Agriculture and Fisheries	1,028[1]
Central Land Board	1,325
Education	44
Food	1,428
Fuel and Power	780
Home Office	181
Housing and Local Government	933
Central Office of Information	87
Labour and National Service	2,814
National Assistance Board	349
Pensions and National Insurance	2,358
Post Office	4,305[1]
Supply	197
Trade	625
Transport and Civil Aviation	413
Works	1,928
	18,838

[1] Do not conform to the 'Standard' regions.

[2] About 93,000 (Emmerson: *The Ministry of Works* (1956), p. 26.

There has been much discussion of the geography of administrative regions, the grouping of the regional offices of various Departments into local 'Whitehalls', and the extent of the discretion which can be delegated to this level. Such 'delegation' has gone in Northern Ireland to the point of constituting a local Parliament and a local administration. Scotland and Wales have a number of Departments concerned purely with their affairs, so that it would be formally accurate (though a little unrealistic) to say that the Scottish Office has its headquarters in Edinburgh, the Welsh Board of Education in Cardiff, and that they have 'out-stations' in 'Whitehall'. In addition, practically all other Departments treat Scotland and Wales each as a single 'region', and have offices there which they call by some name less offensive to national sentiment than is the word 'region', such as 'Central Office for Scotland' and 'Central Office for Wales'.

(iii) Reference has already been made to 'out-stations of Headquarters', offices such as the Central Records Office of the Ministry of Pensions and National Insurance at Newcastle-upon-Tyne and its Central Pensions Office at Blackpool, mentioned in Chapter 15. There is no difference in principle between such offices and those portions of 'Whitehall' which have been widely dispersed in the London suburbs for much the same reasons: for instance (to take a few cases at random), the Infestation Control Division of the Ministry of Agriculture at Surbiton, the Health Services Superannuation Division of the Ministry of Health at Stanmore, the Establishments and Finance Divisions of the National Assistance Board on the Kingston By-Pass, the Statistics Department of the Ministry of Labour at Watford.

(iv) There are also a large number of specialised 'establishments' of one sort or another, engaged on relatively self-contained tasks. These 'establishments' are of extreme importance in the life of one section of the Civil Service, that concerned with scientific research and development. The great atomic energy establishments, now transferred to the autonomous Atomic Energy Authority, are the example most familiar to the public, but there are dozens of other such 'stations' within the orbits of the Departments concerned with research. This is the normal 'habitat' of the scientific civil servant.

These last two categories present problems which have hardly been explored at all outside the Service. 'Out-stations' of headquarters are organisations, often largely staffed by locally recruited routine workers, which are rather different in character from the head offices to which they nominally belong. Some of the 'establishments' (for instance the Royal Aircraft Establishment at Farnborough) may be so large that they are the centre of scientific worlds of their own;

LOCAL AND REGIONAL ORGANISATION 263

and in other cases isolation has been sought deliberately for reasons of security or in order to find convenient conditions of work. But isolated institutions do not on the whole offer a very suitable environment for first-rate scientific work, which flourishes best where there are wide contacts and an easy exchange of ideas.

These matters deserve study, but cannot be pursued here. The object of this chapter is to discuss the first two forms of dispersal, to local offices and to regional offices, and a word is necessary about terminology, as it has caused a good deal of confusion. We prefer to use the word 'decentralisation' for the growth of local and regional offices of central Departments, 'deconcentration' for the dispersal of headquarters, and 'devolution' for the introduction of a separate 'regional' government such as is to be found in Northern Ireland.

2. ENGLAND AND WALES

In England and Wales the idea of central administration 'decentralised' to local offices is largely modern. In the Middle Ages, in quite different conditions, there were certainly various forms of decentralised government, but most of these had vanished or had changed their nature by the seventeenth and eighteenth centuries. In the earlier part of the nineteenth century the current maxim was that of John Stuart Mill that 'it is but a small portion of the public business of a country that can be well-done or safely attempted by the central authorities': a maxim which contrasted English 'local self-government' with the 'centralisation' of continental bureaucracies. Where no locally elected body existed to carry out a service new bodies were created, such as the Boards of Guardians, the Local Boards of Health, and (later) the School Boards.

Local self-government did not even then mean local autonomy. Departments such as the Poor Law Board had wide powers to make rules for the conduct of a service, and to enforce them by inspection; and these powers became still greater when the central government began to give grants on a substantial scale in order to secure uniformity of standards between rich and poor areas and to shift part of the cost from local rates to national taxation. Economy, efficiency, and political pressure have frequently taken the process a stage farther, and English administrative history is full of instances of services begun by local authorities and eventually taken over by civil servants.

The history of the Board of Inland Revenue is a good example, because it is now quite uncontroversial. The collection of the land-tax and of stamp duties on certain kinds of documents (grants of probate, for instance), both of which originated in the time of

William III, was placed in the hands of local unpaid bodies of justices of the peace and substantial merchants who were known as 'commissioners'. These commissioners in turn appointed local assessors and collectors who were also usually unpaid. When William Pitt imposed the first income tax to help pay for the Napoleonic Wars he used this machinery, but introduced for the first time a Crown officer, a 'Surveyor' (or as we now say 'Inspector') of Taxes, who was responsible for overseeing the work of the local commissioners, assessors, and collectors in his area. This system was retained until the present century, and it was not until after the First World War that the amateur assessors, and a little later the collectors, were entirely replaced by civil servants in the Board of Inland Revenue. Thus, the decentralised organisation of the Board has been built up around the old local, amateur system, and indeed the 'General Commissioners of Income Tax' still retain a few functions, such as the hearing of appeals against tax assessments.

The administration of the poor law is perhaps less securely settled even now. Formerly an autonomous function of the parish, it was transferred in 1834 to more suitable local *ad hoc* bodies: the Boards of Guardians for Unions of parishes, subject to central inspection by a body of Assistant Commissioners. In course of time, during which the poor law has been 'broken up', the functions of the Guardians have been in part absorbed into other services provided by local authorities subject to central control, and in part have passed to officials of the central Departments.

These are examples of the way in which 'local self-government' can pass into 'decentralisation', a relatively recent phase. There are some services in which 'decentralisation' has a longer history. The Board of Customs and Excise, for instance, has collected the revenue through local districts, known as 'Collections', since the seventeenth century. The Post Office long possessed officials known as 'Provincial Surveyors of Posts' whose job it was to act as the Postmaster-General's chief local representative, overseeing the work of the postmasters and the carriage of the mails. When Anthony Trollope was appointed Surveyor's clerk in Ireland in 1841, there were (as he tells us in his *Autobiography*) 'seven Surveyors in England, two in Scotland, and three in Ireland'. This system remained virtually unchanged for generations, and was not finally abolished until the reform of Post Office organisation which followed the report of the Bridgeman Committee in 1932.

The Revenue Departments were, however, exceptions to the general rule: at the close of the nineteenth century the bulk of the work of central administration was still carried on in London, and local administration was largely a matter for local bodies. During the century a large number of central inspectorates were created, among them the Inspectors of Factories and Inspectors of Education (in 1833), the Assistant Commissioners of Poor Law (in 1834), the Inspectors of Prisons (in 1835), the Inspectors of Constabulary (in 1856), the District Auditors (in 1879), and many others. Some of these inspectorates had no one permanently stationed in the provinces, and the inspectors travelled out (as indeed some still do) from Whitehall. It was not until the beginning of the present century that local offices of the central Departments began to appear in any number in the country at large.

One of the first experiments in the decentralisation of central functions was the creation of Naval 'Commands' in the mid-nineteenth century, and the system proved so successful that in 1904 it was extended (on the recommendation of the Esher Committee on War Office Reconstruction) to the Army at home. Previously, the Army had been a combination of a small centralised regular force, subdivided regimentally, and a county militia, though a step towards a general territorial subdivision had been taken as part of the Cardwell reforms of 1870. The Esher Committee recommended that the country should be divided into a number of large areas, each under a high-ranking officer, who would have charge of the administration and training of the troops in his area. These recommendations were accepted, a sign of the changing climate of opinion, since they owed much to French and Prussian models; the War Office and the newly created Army Council maintained contact with Home Commands by means of an Inspector-General of the Forces. Much executive and administrative work hitherto centralised in the War Office was now decentralised to the new Commands.

Another step was taken in 1909 when the Labour Exchange system was introduced. It would have been possible to set up this service in the traditional way by leaving it to local authorities (as was done in Germany), assisted by grants from the central government, and subject to central control. Indeed, a number of English local authorities had already established such a service.

This possibility was explored by the framers of the Labour Exchange Act of 1909, but it was eventually decided to make a new departure, and the administration of the service became the direct responsibility of a sub-department within the Board of Trade. The country was divided into 'labour exchange areas', and the areas, served by local offices under labour exchange managers, were grouped into six 'Divisions'. Each Division had a senior official in charge who was responsible for overseeing the work of the local exchanges. This hierarchical structure on three levels became the model for other large 'social service' Departments such as the Unemployment Assistance Board of 1934 (now the National Assistance Board) and the Ministry of Pensions and National Insurance.

These were important changes. Even as late as 1899 a Parliamentary Select Committee rejected a system of old age pensions on the ground that 'if the State is to provide the means for the cost of pensions, the State, it seems to us, must necessarily administer the scheme, and that is a proposition which we are unable to support'. Moreover, the Labour Exchange service was a highly personal one, and required the exercise of a good deal of local discretion and adaptability, qualities not hitherto expected from civil servants.

The tradition was not, however, entirely abandoned. Each labour exchange was given a local advisory committee, which was at first expected to have large functions. When the National Health Insurance system was introduced in 1911, it was administered (at least so far as the individual contributor was concerned) by voluntary 'Approved' Societies, and by specially created 'local insurance committees', based on existing local authority areas, and subject to inspection by a central body, the National Health Insurance Commission. War pensions were similarly administered (from 1916 to 1919) by *ad hoc* 'local pensions committees' supervised by the central Department, the Ministry of Pensions. Even the war-time Food Control (1916) made extensive use of local food committees set up by local authorities.

This tradition of using *ad hoc* local bodies wherever possible is not completely dead even today. The 'local food committees' of the Second World War were at first given important executive functions, though they were always performed under the supervision of regional officials of the Ministry of Food. And until very recently an important part of the local executive functions of the Ministry of Agriculture was carried out by the *ad hoc* County Agricultural Executive Committees referred to in Chapter 15. There is a tendency, however, for most local committees of this sort to lose their executive functions to civil servants after a time and to be reduced to the status of advisory bodies. We deal with this topic again in Chapter 24.

The First World War provided the incentive for a more rapid development of 'decentralisation'. The Ministry of Munitions (1915), the Ministry of Food (1916), and the Ministry of National Service (1917) all had local organisations. They also gave wider currency to the idea of 'administrative regions', adopted by the War Office in 1904 and by the Labour Exchange Department of the Board of Trade in 1909, the Ministry of Munitions with its division of the country into ten 'Areas', each under a Munitions Controller, providing the model for the rest to follow. These were responses to administrative needs, and it is curious that they coincided with the first general interest in 'regionalism' in a wider sense. Sir Halford Mackinder, Professor Fawcett, and others laid the foundations of regional geography, and began the definition of 'regions' within England. At the same time, one of the political responses to the demand for Home Rule for Ireland was talk about 'Home Rule all round' or 'Back to the Heptarchy', a rather frivolous exercise in constitution-making of which no more was heard after the Irish Free State was set up in 1922.

Much of the administrative development of decentralisation disappeared after 1918; the Ministry of Labour (1916) alone among the new Departments retained and strengthened the full-scale 'regional' system and the local organisation of labour exchanges which it had inherited from the Board of Trade. There were a few short-lived experiments by new Ministries. In 1920 the Ministry of Pensions took a particularly bold line. Following the report of a Departmental Committee, the pensions organisation was reconstructed and the local committees became little more than advisory bodies. Regional offices, with a full range of staff, were established to reproduce headquarters organisation on a small scale. General control and major policy-making were reserved to headquarters, but all the executive work was performed in the regional offices. In 1919 the new Ministry of Health divided the country into 15 Housing Regions each controlled by a Commissioner with wide powers. The scheme was abandoned by the middle of 1922, killed by the economic depression and the Geddes Axe; and in 1926 the Ministry of Pensions greatly reduced its regional organisation, though it did not abolish it entirely, nor did it restore the powers of the local pensions committees.

One or two other decentralised organisations were set up between the wars: for instance, those of the Office of Works in 1930, and of the Unemployment Assistance Board in 1934; but on the whole new services were carried out either by the traditional method of execution by local authorities and supervision by inspectorates (such as the child care inspectors of the Home Office (1933), and the provincial lands service of the Ministry of Agriculture (1919); or by the first of the new public corporations, such as the Forestry Commission in its original form (1919), the Central Electricity Board (1926), and the London Passenger Transport Board (1934); or by quasi-judicial bodies like the Licensing Authorities of the Ministry of Transport under the Road Traffic Acts of 1930 and 1933.

Up to this stage, except in the Ministry of Labour, decentralised organisations within Departments worked to their own geographical areas and reported direct up their own hierarchy to headquarters: there was no co-ordination, even for 'housekeeping' purposes, at an intermediate level. The reform of the Post Office, which took place between 1932 and 1939, led to renewed interest both in the large-scale decentralisation of functions and in the idea of an 'administrative regionalism' that would collect together the scattered decentralised activities of a Department into a single organisation based on a common set of areas. The Post Office had a large decentralised organisation before 1932, but there was little co-ordination between the postal, the telecommunications, and the engineering services. The reforms (which were not completed until after the outbreak of war) brought all the services in each area into a single regional organisation. But many of these services were highly technical, and they were much more closely interrelated than the range of services provided by the average Department, so that Post Office reorganisation did not offer a model for imitation in detail by other Departments.

It was, however, obvious by the 1930s that something like 'regional government' would be inevitable if Britain had to face a modern war. Emergencies had provoked a similar response in the past: Cromwell had divided the whole country into eleven 'Districts', each commanded by a Major-General, to supervise the militia, collect taxes from Royalist estates, and look after public order and morals; a similar subdivision of the country, this time into twelve 'Districts', had been made in 1803, against a possible invasion by the French army.

During the period of industrial unrest which followed the Armistice in 1918, successive governments maintained an Emergency Transport Scheme on a regional basis to meet the threat of national strikes. The scheme was hastily improvised in 1919 on the directions of the Coalition Government, but it had been considerably improved before being put to the test in the General Strike of 1926. The pivot of the whole organisation in each region was the 'Road Commissioner' and his staff from the Ministry of Transport, but a number of other Departments, including the Mines Department, the Post Office, and the Board of Trade, appointed emergency regional staffs. The whole system was co-ordinated in each region by a Regional Commissioner: an M.P. appointed by the government of the day.

A system of Regional Commissioners formed part of the Civil Defence plan for the Second World War, and most of its features, including (with slight modifications) the areas of the regions used, were borrowed from the emergency transport and feeding organisation of 1926. By an odd coincidence the system adopted in 1939 was also linked with Cromwell's: the area of the South Western Region corresponded closely to his, and the first Regional Commissioner for the Northern Region bore the name of one of his Major-Generals (Lambert).

The system involved, first, a general decentralisation on a much greater scale than before, with a larger number of more senior officials stationed in each region. Some Departments were reluctant to accept this; regional offices were not established by the Ministry of Aircraft Production or by the Ministry of Supply, for example, until the war was well advanced, and even then they agreed only with great reluctance to grant them any real powers. In time, however, almost all the major Departments established a regional organisation of some sort.

Secondly, the system required a measure of co-ordination by the Regional Commissioner of the work of all the Departments in the region. This was strictly limited in practice; the formal reserve powers of the Commissioner were immense, but the Departments remained their own masters, and their Regional Officers were primarily responsible to their own headquarters and not to the Regional Commissioner. There were, however, a large number of regional inter-departmental co-ordinating committees, and the Commissioner served as a focus, helping to integrate the activities of government staffs with those of local authorities in the region.

Thirdly, the system gave a further impetus to discussion of 'administrative regionalism'. This came about partly through the *esprit de corps* and strong local ties which were developed by large numbers of civil servants working under very great stress and confronted with common tasks and problems, often of great complexity, and partly because almost all Departments adopted a common set of 'standard' (civil defence) regions each with its 'regional capital town'. Almost the only exception to this was the Post Office, whose regions were based on the technical requirements of postal circulation and the layout of the telephone system.

The system of Regional Commissioners was for a time extremely unpopular with local authorities, which foresaw a development of elected regional bodies after the war which might endanger their own position, and the Commissioners were quickly withdrawn when the emergency was over. 'Regionalism', however, remained; the regions and their 'capital towns' were retained in slightly modified form as standards to which all Departments were encouraged to conform (these are shown on a map at the end of this chapter); and decentralisation of functions on a fairly large scale was common practice in the immediate post-war period. All the major Departments except the Treasury now possessed some form of local and regional organisation, and even the Treasury was for a time responsible for a series of regional advisory committees (the Regional Boards for Industry).[1]

Much of this post-war decentralisation was temporary: there were arrears of work to be overtaken when war ended, and shortages of commodities and raw materials required the retention of controls and licensing systems, most of which could only be operated in the field. But the Labour Government was committed to the permanent retention of some controls as instruments of national planning, and made plain its intention also to retain the main structure of regional administration.

A review of the working of this system under the 1945 Labour Government suggests that there were considerable variations between Departments in the status of their Regional Officers, the powers they possessed, and their authority in their regions. Decentralisation had proceeded farthest in those Departments which administered detailed regulatory statutes, or performed a great deal of routine work that could be reduced to written codes of procedure. Other Departments found it harder to define the scope of their regional organisations, but said that they regarded them as important. The Regional Officers were often described officially as 'ambassadors of Whitehall' and, sometimes, as 'the eyes and ears of headquarters'. In this respect they differed little from the old Surveyors of Posts, of whom Anthony Trollope had written: 'A great expense is often incurred for a very small object, but the system works well on the whole as confidence is engendered, and a feeling is produced in the country that the Department has eyes of its own and does keep them open. . . .' This general function included a wide variety of specific tasks, varying from one Department to another: advice, supervision, interpretation of headquarters policy and its application to the region, inspection, and liaison with local bodies on specific problems delegated by headquarters.

The advantages of these rather vague arrangements entailed corresponding disadvantages. Local authorities differ greatly in strength, and political leaders and heads of departments in the largest of them are apt to regard even Assistant Secretaries as rather small fry. The more powerful local authorities have tended therefore to by-pass Regional Officers and to go direct to Whitehall; and large businesses with interests spread over the whole country (above all, the nationalised industries) have usually adopted the same tactics. The Regional Officer (unless he is an exceptional personality) may slip into the

---

[1] These have since passed to the Board of Trade (see p. 247).

position that he is partly a 'post office', partly a man who deals only with minor cases within his Region, and not with his Region as a whole. If this happens, it encourages the natural tendency of any headquarters organisation to draw in responsibility to itself, so as to limit the risks of mistakes and divergencies in the application of policy.

These considerations scarcely apply to the Revenue Departments, including the Post Office, or to the 'social service' Departments, and their combination of local and regional offices can be regarded as fairly stable. In other Departments, local and regional offices have gone somewhat out of fashion since 1951, partly because of a change of economic climate, partly because of a change of government, and partly because the administrative problems have become more familiar. Some Departments have abolished their local and regional organisation altogether; others have reduced their 'field' staffs either by recentralising certain functions or by amalgamating regional or local offices as the work load has lightened; the Board of Trade and the Ministry of Supply actually combined their regional offices for a time under one Regional Officer with one staff instead of two.

An attempt was also made, in 1953, to amalgamate a number of local offices of the Ministry of Labour, the Ministry of Pensions and National Insurance, and the National Assistance Board: a scheme which promised economy in staff and overheads and also an increase in convenience to the public, who would be able to find what they needed under one roof. But there were thought to be serious difficulties in administering a single local office from three head offices; no one was prepared to contemplate the creation of a single enormous Ministry in London; and the Departments were unable to agree that one of them should run the whole scheme on an agency basis. In addition, there was apparently friction within the local offices between staff drawn from different Departments who were unfamiliar with one another's duties. The scheme was therefore dropped after about a year's trial.

Up to 1 April 1956 the Departments shown in Table XXV had succeeded in reducing their regional office staffs by about 3,000 (from 18,838 to 15,759), and there were some further reductions, notably in the Ministry of Housing and Local Government (see p. 409), later that year. After this period of scrutiny it is probable that local and regional organisations have been cut to the lowest point consistent with the convenient provision of the existing services. The organisation now differs from that of 1938 in scope rather than in kind. The principle that the central government should take responsibility for certain social services has been reaffirmed and extended, and there has been a corresponding increase in the number of civil servants administering these services in the regions and in local communities. There has also been a considerable growth in the number and range of government advisory and regulatory services and technical inspectorates. The Ministry of Agriculture is perhaps the most striking example of this. In general, however, there have been no major innovations in the decentralisation of central functions since the Second World War. The reasons are fairly clear, and no new extension of the powers of regional and local officials is likely except in the event of a new emergency threatening communications. Indeed, the tendency to limit the powers of officials outside 'Whitehall' is to some extent self-perpetuating, because it is important to have a similar degree of decentralisation among Departments which have to consult together frequently on common problems. One of the advantages of a decentralised system is lost if one Department insists on referring to headquarters problems which the others settle locally, and this comes to mean that all must conform to the practice of the most cautious.

3. Wales and Monmouthshire

Up to this point we have written of 'England and Wales' together, as the Kingdom of England and the Principality of Wales were for centuries treated as a single administrative unit, and there was little or no divergence of practice until the revival of Welsh national feeling in the latter part of the nineteenth century. This feeling was from the first of considerable political importance, and it is this political element which differentiates the position of Wales, Scotland, and Northern Ireland from that of the English 'regions', though much of their administrative organisation has had a common source.

The earliest important divergence between England and Wales was in the field of education. In 1896 a Central Welsh Board was created for the inspection and examination of schools.[1] The Education Act of 1902 was much disliked in Wales, and an attempt was made in 1906 to create a special 'Council for Wales' which would deal with all education including agricultural education. The Welsh Department of the Board of Education was set up, partly in response to this pressure, in 1907. It has no statutory position, and its chief officials work mainly in London. But its head ranks as an Under Secretary, a rather unusual Under Secretary who is called 'Permanent Secretary' and often obtains a knighthood, and it has for many years been the practice to appoint a Welsh-speaking Welshman.

[1] Following the Welsh Intermediate Education Act of 1889.

There has since 1920 been a Welsh Department of Agriculture at Aberystwyth, under an Under Secretary, which took over the office of the Agricultural Commissioner for Wales set up in 1912. The Department has formal powers not very different from those of a regional office; but in practice its position is very different, since officials dealing with Welsh farmers are of necessity largely Welshmen, and members of the various Ministry of Agriculture services are not wholly interchangeable between Wales and England.

There is also a Welsh Board of Health in Cardiff, which is an independent statutory body appointed under Section 5 of the Ministry of Health Act, 1919, and which (though again within delegated limits) acts in relation to Wales as the Minister of Health in relation to England. The functions of the Welsh Board of Health were affected by the reorganisation of the Ministry of Health in 1950, and in consequence the Welsh Office of the Ministry of Housing and Local Government has come to occupy a rather peculiar position. It has inherited functions and powers in relation to housing and local government formerly possessed by the Welsh Board of Health, and it performs these (like the Board before it) as a largely self-contained headquarters, not as a dependent 'regional office'. A further delegation of authority was made in January 1956, so that almost all the functions of the Ministry of Housing and Local Government relating to Wales are now carried out in Wales. Both Offices are headed (like the Welsh Departments of Education and Agriculture) by Under Secretaries.

The Welsh Offices of other Departments are of the same status and have the same powers as English regional offices, though in some cases the use of the word 'regional' is avoided. All government Departments treat Wales as a single region,[1] in spite of difficulties of communication between different parts of the country. Wales is not a convenient administrative unit, and in spite of Welsh protests some public organisations (for instance, the Central Electricity Authority and the Area Electricity Boards) have preferred to adopt regions following the 'catchment areas' of their services.

There is no completely independent 'Welsh Office', and there is no separate 'Minister for Wales'.[2] Wales to this extent lags behind Scotland in devolution, but in October 1951 the Home Secretary was given the additional title of 'Minister for Welsh Affairs', and a second Parliamentary Secretary was appointed with some general responsi-

[1] The Post Office tacks on to it, for convenience, certain Border counties in England.
[2] The Council for Wales and Monmouthshire recommended, in 1957, the creation of a Secretary of State for Wales with Cabinet rank, and a Welsh Office with four Departments of State on the Scottish model. (*Third Memorandum by the Council on its Activities*, Cmnd. 53, 1957.)

bility for sponsoring Welsh interests.[1] There has also existed since 1949 a nominated 'Council for Wales and Monmouthshire', but its functions are purely advisory. It is assisted by all the Regional Officers in Wales meeting as the 'Conference of Heads of Government Offices in Wales'. This Conference has apparently met quarterly since 1946 'to review the general execution of Government policy in Wales as a whole, and to advise Ministers on questions of general administration'.

4. SCOTLAND

A Royal Commission on Scottish Affairs, which presented a cautious report in 1954, stated as a general principle that 'in the absence of convincing evidence of advantage to the contrary the machinery of government should be designed to dispose of Scottish business in Scotland'. To a large extent this has been the rule since 1925, when the post of Secretary for Scotland was raised to the rank of Principal Secretary of State, and more particularly since 1939, when the administrative machinery for Scotland was reorganised. Since that date, 'Scotland's Minister' has had charge of four Departments (Health, Education, Home, and Agriculture) now employing about 5,000 people and working from St. Andrew's House in Edinburgh. Since 1951 he has had the assistance of a Minister of State (who spends most of his time in Scotland), and three Parliamentary Under Secretaries. The four Departments perform work for Scotland which in England is divided between six Ministries. Their responsibilities include agriculture, education, housing, health, town and country planning, local government affairs, public order, fisheries, and oversight of the supply of electricity by the Scottish Electricity Boards. In these matters, the authority of the Scottish Departments is complete, subject only to the overriding control of the Cabinet.

In addition, a number of the high offices of the Kingdom of Scotland have maintained their continuity since the Union of the Kingdoms in 1603. Perhaps the most important in practice is the independent system of courts, headed by the Court of Session and the High Court of Justiciary, which interpret the law of Scotland. There is general uniformity of law in many respects, and the House of Lords in its judicial capacity is a final Court of Appeal in civil matters for both Kingdoms, but the symbolic importance of the maintenance of Scots law as a separate system is very great. Among the other officers are the Keeper of the Great Seal of Scotland (an office now held by the

[1] In 1957, Wales was transferred from the Home Secretary to the Minister of Housing and Local Government, who took the additional title 'Minister for Welsh Affairs'.

Secretary of State for Scotland); the Lord Clerk Register, who is formally responsible for the General Register House in Edinburgh; the Lord Advocate and the Solicitor-General, the two law officers for Scotland; the Crown Agent for Scotland; the Queen's and Lord Treasurer's Remembrancer (who performs *inter alia* the functions of Registrar of Companies and Assistant Paymaster-General); and the Commissioners of Northern Lighthouses.

These are the trappings of an independent Kingdom, but in other respects the government of Scotland is carried on from Whitehall, except in so far as powers have been delegated to Scottish 'regional' offices. It is these arrangements that have been most sharply criticised by sections of Scottish opinion. The criticism is particularly directed against the Departments concerned with economic affairs (Trade, Transport, Supply, and so on) which, it is said, take decisions affecting Scotland without knowledge of local conditions and regardless of Scottish views, and fail to delegate sufficient powers to their 'regional' representatives on the spot. As the Royal Commission pointed out, when the State's interference with the individual was insignificant, it mattered little to the Scotsman whether this came from Whitehall or Edinburgh; but now that this is no longer the case, it is natural that the Scotsman should resent what he, perhaps wrongly, regards as insensitive 'English' government. They thought that there were good grounds for conferring a status on the Scottish Officers higher than that of their English regional counterparts; that the term 'region' should never be used; that appointment as Scottish Officer should be regarded 'as a mark of preference rather than a form of exile'; and that the appointment should be made normally from officers of good quality, namely those 'likely to reach the grade of Under Secretary and above'.

The Treasury had already in June 1946 issued a rather cautious memorandum to Departments on the subject of the status, organisation, and staffing of Scottish Regional Offices. It stated that 'Departments with a strong regional organisation throughout Great Britain should devolve upon their Scottish Representatives sufficient authority for business to be settled on the spot'. In other Departments, 'the stationing in Edinburgh of an administrative official, with suitable staff, should be considered in all proper cases', even though 'it may not be possible for so much administrative responsibility to be devolved'. The memorandum went on to suggest, however, that the official in charge should 'have sufficient standing to make his advice valuable', and that he 'should visit London frequently in order to share in the formulation of general policy'. Departments were therefore recommended to strengthen their Scottish offices 'even if the result is an official or an organisation of greater weight and standing than on ordinary staffing canons would be thought appropriate'.

The extent to which this advice has been heeded is limited. Some Departments now refer to their 'Scottish Office'. One or two, like the Ministry of Works, have even upgraded their Scottish Officer to the rank of Under Secretary. But with these exceptions, the Scottish Officers are normally of the same grade as their English regional counterparts.

Since the introduction in 1907 of the present system of Standing Committees of the House of Commons,[1] recognition has been given to the special political position of Scotland by the reference of all Bills dealing purely with Scotland for their 'committee' stage to a Scottish Grand Committee consisting of all the Scottish M.P.s with ten to fifteen English M.P.s added. This concession was taken a step farther in 1948 by the decision that the Scottish Grand Committee should meet to discuss the Estimates of the Scottish Departments, and should thus be in a position to debate Scottish affairs in general terms. But the idea that this body might occasionally meet in Edinburgh has been discouraged, and political devolution has gone no farther.

5. NORTHERN IRELAND

Northern Ireland (on the other hand) has had its own government at Stormont since 1920. Under the Government of Ireland Act of that year, general legislative and executive powers were delegated to a local Parliament and Cabinet subject to the reservation of certain important powers to the United Kingdom Parliament: these included issues touching the Crown and the succession, peace and war, the armed services, foreign affairs, foreign trade, navigation, post office, coinage, and certain other matters. The services transferred were assigned to Northern Ireland Departments by formal Notification of the Lord Lieutenant on 7 June 1921. Since then Ministries have been established for Finance, Home Affairs, Agriculture, Education, Commerce, Labour and National Insurance, and Health and Local Government. The Government of Northern Ireland has its own Civil Service Commission, Exchequer and Audit Department, and its own National Assistance Board. In addition to performing the very extensive duties which now arise out of the 'transferred' powers, these Departments act in some cases as agents for U.K. Departments in matters not transferred. Other U.K. Departments have

[1] Two Standing Committees were set up in 1883, and were provided for in Standing Orders of the House in 1888, but they were committees to deal with specialist subjects, and were not at all like the present Standing Committees. It was rare for an important Bill to be referred to them.

LOCAL AND REGIONAL ORGANISATION

their own offices in Belfast and elsewhere (for example, the Ministry of Pensions and National Insurance and the Board of Trade). The Governor of Northern Ireland represents the Queen there, and there is an Agent of the Northern Ireland Government in London.

This special status works reasonably well, but naturally gives rise to a number of puzzling problems of collaboration between governments and between officials. It is a paradox that it should have been thrust upon Northern Ireland against its will, through the failure of an attempt at a compromise solution of the problem of 'Home Rule' for Ireland as a whole.

6. The Channel Islands and the Isle of Man

These are of much less substantial importance, but their position is a curiosity worth mentioning. Both have governments of their own, and the formal links with the Crown are the Lieutenant-Governors appointed by the Queen. The Channel Islands consist of the Bailiwick of Jersey and the Bailiwick of Guernsey (which includes Alderney and Sark). Their dependence on the British Crown dates from 1066, when their ruler, the Duke of Normandy, conquered England. Normandy was later lost, but they have remained loyal to this day. The claim of the English Crown to the island of Man was established in the reign of Henry IV, after a century or more of dispute between the Kings of England and Scotland. The local governments of these islands assert their ancient independence in many matters: they have their own legislative assemblies and administrative and judicial systems, and their traditional rights and privileges are stoutly maintained. The House of Keys of the Isle of Man claims to be one of the oldest legislative assemblies in the world. Acts of the United Kingdom Parliament do not apply to them, except by express provision or necessary implication, but their domestic laws require ratification by the English Crown, which is rarely refused.

Originally they were treated as colonies, but in 1801 (when the Home Office lost its colonial functions) they were not transferred. Consequently the Home Secretary is the Minister chiefly responsible for matters relating to them. In regard to the Channel Islands, he advises the Queen on certain appointments (the Lieutenant-Governors, the Bailiffs, and the Law Officers) and on local legislation which is submitted for ratification to the Queen-in-Council. He acts as the main channel of communication between the Islands and the United Kingdom government. His constitutional position and functions are much the same in regard to the Isle of Man, except that the Lieutenant-Governor has certain executive powers not possessed by his counterparts in Jersey and Guernsey.

FOR REFERENCE

Historical Development: England and Wales:

MAY L. DHONAU: *Decentralisation of Government Departments* (1938).
J. W. GROVE: 'Some Recent Experiments in the Decentralisation of Government Departments', *Australian Journal of Public Administration*, Vol. X, p. 481.
GEORGE GLASGOW: *General Strikes and Road Transport* (1926). (A little-known account of the Emergency Organisation.)
T. H. O'BRIEN: *Civil Defence* (History of the Second World War, Civil Series) (1955). (On the origins and workings of the Regional Commissioner system.)
E. HARRISON: 'Local Advisory Committees,' *Public Administration*, Vol. XXXI, p. 65.
Report of a Committee of Inquiry on the Post Office (Bridgeman). Cmd. 4149, 1932.
Report of a Committee on Regional Boards (Citrine). Cmd. 6360, 1942.
Sir D. J. LIDBURY: *Post Office Regionalisation* (1937).
R. WOLMER (1st Viscount): *Post Office Reform* (1932).

The 'Regional Geographers':

C. B. FAWCETT: 'Natural Divisions of England', *Geographical Journal*, Vol. XLIX, p. 121. 1917.
—— *Provinces of England* (1919).
E. W. GILBERT: 'The Geographical Aspects of Regional Planning', *Geographical Journal*, Vol. XCIX, p. 61. 1942.
—— 'Practical Regionalism in England and Wales', *Geographical Journal*, Vol. XCIV, p. 29. 1939.
V. D. LIPMAN: *Local Government Areas 1834-1945* (1949).

'Devolution' and 'Home Rule':

Conference on Devolution: Letter from Mr. Speaker to the Prime Minister (with Appendices). Cmd. 692, 1920.
F. H. NEWARK and others: *Devolution of Government—The Experiment in Northern Ireland* (1953).
R. J. LAWRENCE: 'Devolution Reconsidered', *Political Studies*, Vol. IV, p. 1 (and a reply by A. H. BIRCH, *Political Studies*, Vol. IV, p. 310).
T. WILSON (Ed.): *Ulster under Home Rule* (1955).

Regional and Local Organisation of Central Departments since 1945:

J. W. GROVE: *English Regional Government: A Study of the North West* (1950). Introduction by W. J. M. Mackenzie.
West Midlands Study Group: *Local Government and Central Control* (1956). Chs. VI and VII.
6th Report and Minutes of Evidence from the Select Committee on Estimates (Sub-Committee D), Session 1953-54. H.C. 233, 1954. ('Regional Organisations.')

2nd Report of the Local Government Manpower Committee. Cmd. 8421, 1951. Appendix VIII.

H. T. WOOLSTON: 'The Joint Local Office Experiment', *Public Administration*, Vol. XXXIII, p. 197.

General Post Office: *Report of a Working Party on the Present System of Regionalisation in the Post Office.* 1951.

Scotland:

Scottish Office: *Committee on Scottish Administration.* Cmd. 5563, 1937.
Scottish Affairs. Cmd. 7308, 1948.
Report of the Royal Commission on Scottish Affairs. Cmd. 9212, 1954. And *Minutes of Evidence.*
Memorandum presented to the Royal Commission on Scottish Affairs by the Scottish Departments. Memoranda, Vol. I. 1953.

Wales and Monmouth:

Wales and Monmouthshire: A Summary of Government Action, 1946. Cmd. 6938, 1946.
Wales and Monmouthshire, 1949. Cmd. 7820, 1949.
3rd Memorandum by the Council for Wales and Monmouthshire on its Activities. Cmnd. 53, 1957.
E. L. CHAPPELL: *The Government of Wales* (1943).

Northern Ireland:

Memorandum by the Northern Ireland Departments presented to the Royal Commission on Scottish Affairs. Memoranda, Vol. IV. 1953.

III
CENTRAL CONTROL OF ADMINISTRATION

INTRODUCTORY

And if they were all one member, where were the body?
But now are they many members, yet but one body.
1 *Corinthians*, xii, 19-20.

IN one sense the Department is the true unit of government. For most civil servants their Department is the focus of loyalty and tradition: most civil servants understand the policy of their Departments, few understand the relation between Departments and the structure of central administration as a whole. This is our justification for attempting in Part II to explain the work of central administration in terms of Departmental procedure and organisation. Yet it will be obvious from much that has been said earlier that a Department taken in isolation is no more than a convenient abstraction. Its staff are employed on conditions determined for the Service as a whole. There are 'levels' of organisation which run horizontally through all Departments, so that there is no ambiguity about the relative status of officials in different Departments, except in a fairly small number of cases affecting relations between lay civil servants, professional civil servants, and members of other Crown services. There are common factors in the internal organisation of Departments, and these unify the whole system in that they help officials in one Department to see problems in the same way as do their 'opposite numbers' in another. All this means that co-operation between Departments is easier than co-operation between a Department on the one side, a public corporation, a private business, or a local authority on the other. But it would generally be assumed that unity in administration requires not only co-operation but central direction.

Direction is required by the forms of the constitution, which postulate that there is a single political organ, the Cabinet, executing through the administration a policy approved by the electorate through their representatives in the House of Commons. It is also required by the logic of administration: a Department is an administrative, not a political, organisation: it exists to further purposes given to it, not to choose purposes for itself, and it is to be judged primarily for its efficiency in executing a task given to it by higher authority. But constitutional and administrative logic must not be taken too literally. It is a common theme that no single mind or single organisation can attain to a completely comprehensive view of policy, or shape an administrative organisation so that it is directed with complete unity of purpose to a single end; and the form of British Departments owes at least as much to historical accident as to deliberate invention. They were not constructed, they grew.

An adequate theory of the place of administration in democratic politics would have to take account of both sides of this contrast between direction and spontaneity, and to combine them coherently. This is extremely difficult to do; but such theoretical puzzles cause little difficulty in practice. The problem of unity in administration is solved partly by the structure of the system, which gives administrators at working levels a simple 'drill' for co-operation, as well as incentives for conforming to it; partly by rules giving specific powers of direction to specific organs of government.

Part III is concerned with this system of co-ordination through direction, and we group the rules under three headings: the position of the 'common service' Departments, which have, in effect, powers of direction for a variety of 'housekeeping' services; the system of accounting and financial control, at the apex of which stands the Treasury; and the authority of the Cabinet, the ultimate, often tacit, source of all administrative rules, as it is also the source of legislation.

This classification is not completely realistic. The 'common service' Departments are not in a very different position from others, because each Department in a sense makes rules within its own determined sphere. All questions of office buildings concern the Ministry of Works; similarly, all questions of our relations with foreign powers concern the Foreign Office, all questions of the care of deprived children concern the Home Office; and each of these Departments is prepared to invoke higher authority in order to ensure that it is consulted and that its views are given full weight. Since the administration has unity as a system, in a sense all Departments are 'common service' Departments. Furthermore, it is a little paradoxical to treat as being *in pari materia* the operations of the Stationery Office in acting on requisitions about office machinery; the operations of the Treasury in the continuous supervision of a complex financial system; and the operations of the Cabinet in settling from day to day a great variety of specific questions of extreme urgency. In spite of these paradoxes, our classification seems to be the one that comes most naturally to mind in discussions about the central control of administration; its headings represent three categories intelligible to the plain man and the ordinary politician—economy in overheads, effective supervision of current expenditure, resolute central direction.

CHAPTER SEVENTEEN

COMMON SERVICES

Servus servorum Dei.
POPE GREGORY I

1. INTRODUCTORY

As we have just indicated, there is a rather empty sense in which each Department serves all other Departments by doing the work assigned to it. In practice, however, it is simple enough to distinguish services carried out by one Department for another from services which it provides as part of its duty to serve the public—subject, of course, to occasional debate about difficult marginal cases. We are concerned here with the former, and they may be identified by the procedure for accounting for their cost.

Practice embodies two principles laid down in a Treasury Minute in 1882. In the first place, 'each Department should show and account for its own cost': that is to say, if a Department employs as its agent another Department for some service, the cost should fall on the Vote of the Department receiving the service and not on that of the Department providing it. The receiving Department will therefore 'pay' for the service by a book transfer from one set of accounts to the other. Secondly, 'double-counting' should be avoided: that is to say, an item of expenditure should not be shown twice, once in the Vote and Appropriation Account of the Department providing the service and again in the Vote and Appropriation Account of the Department receiving it. If this were done, the total cost of the public services would be fictitiously inflated. The providing Department is therefore to treat the book transfer 'payment' as an 'appropriation-in-aid', and its Vote is to be reduced by that amount. Yet if these principles were followed by Departments whose main business it is to provide services to other Departments, a great deal of additional 'book-keeping' would be required. For this reason it is customary for such Departments to provide their services 'free', in the sense that the cost of the service does not appear in the Vote or accounts of the Department which receives it, except as a note for the information of the House of Commons.

This is the distinction in central government accounting between 'Allied' (or 'free') Services and 'Agency' (or 'repayment') Services. The Departments providing 'Allied' Services on a large scale are thought of primarily as 'common service' Departments, though the expression 'common services' is not a term of art in British central administration. These services are the main subject of the present chapter, but we deal first with 'Agency' Services, which raise comparatively few general issues.

2. AGENCY SERVICES

The theory of Agency Services is that they are arranged by agreement between independent and friendly parties. The Department seeking a service has (at least notionally) a choice between hiring staff for itself and opening new offices, or making arrangements with a private contractor, or using another Department as its agent. But in practice the Treasury may have something to say about this, and Departments frequently complain that the Treasury will not agree to their using outside contractors even though they are dissatisfied with the service they are receiving from the 'agent' Department.

A Department asked to render a service can in theory agree, or refuse, or bargain about terms (though, again, the Treasury may intervene). The bargain between the parties is affected by various factors which do not apply to commercial transactions: but it is handled rather as if it were a commercial transaction, and the complicated problems which arise have nothing in particular to do with central control of administration. They turn (as in other types of bargain) partly on the specification of the service (including promptness in performance) and partly on its cost. The cost is calculated on the basis of actual expense incurred, but the system of accounting in use is not such as to make it easy to assess this unambiguously, and there is room for a good deal of negotiation.

Some examples have already been quoted in passing, but it may be worth adding to them here to illustrate how widespread the practice is. They can be analysed roughly into four types:

(i) *Purchasing Services.* The Departments rendering Allied Services often act also as purchasing agents for other Departments, and this is dealt with more fully below. But they are not the only Departments to do so: for instance, the Ministry of Health purchases medical equipment and stores, the Ministry of Supply purchases motor vehicles required by other Departments. The general practice is for the Department which is the largest user of the commodity to act as 'agent' for the rest.

(ii) *Buildings and Works.* The Ministry of Works not only erects and maintains government buildings as an Allied Service, it is also ready to erect buildings for any Department which requires them for the use of authorities controlled by it. The building of schools, hostels, factories, research establishments, barracks, military housing, and so on, is sometimes put out to tender by the Department concerned, sometimes it is done for it by the Ministry of Works on a repayment basis. Similarly, the Directorate of Works at the Air Ministry constructs and maintains civil aerodromes for the Ministry of Transport and Civil Aviation.

(iii) *Counter Services* used to be provided by the very few traditional Departments which had local offices. The Post Office acquired some functions of its own (such as the management of a Savings Bank) primarily for this reason: it also acts for a great variety of other Departments. It pays pensions and allowances, it sells insurance stamps, it issues motor vehicle licences, it issues and repays National Savings Certificates. The Ministry of Labour pays unemployment benefit for the M.P.N.I., and assistance allowances for the N.A.B., and it has recently begun to issue passports as agent for the Foreign Office.

(iv) *Investigating and Regulatory Work.* The N.A.B. may be asked to follow up individual cases for the M.P.N.I., and for Departments which have no local offices of their own, such as the Ministry of Health. The Board of Customs and Excise dealt with non-contributory pensions until 1946. It still performs a great variety of services at the ports for other Departments exercising import and export controls of various kinds: it supervises horses and other livestock for the Ministry of Agriculture, dangerous drugs for the Home Office, quarantine for the Ministry of Health, and so on.

3. ALLIED SERVICES: THEIR SCOPE

In principle, an Allied Service is paid for by the Department rendering it, and the Department receiving it shows the cost only as a footnote in its own Estimates. This serves to strengthen the hands of the providing Department and of the Treasury. As usual, this part of the system owes more to history than to planning; but it has been justified, and new services have been added to it, primarily on the plea that centralisation would introduce economies in overheads by extending the scale of operations. The providing Departments are in this sense agents of the Treasury (and of the Public Accounts Committee) as well as of the Departments for which they work; and their allegiance to the former prevails in case of conflict, because it is the providing Departments which must account for the expenditure through the procedure of Treasury and Parliamentary control. In the last resort, an Allied Service Department backed by the Treasury can make and enforce its own rules about the standard of service which it provides. Such sanctions rarely come into play, and most things are done by agreement and gentle persistence; in this more gradual process the Treasury puts pressure on the providing Departments to keep down their Estimates, and this pressure is transmitted by them throughout the Service.

It will be best, before saying anything further about the effects of this system, to explain briefly what its scope is. This can be set out under three headings, of which the first is much the most important.

(i) *Housekeeping Services*

There are four services of this type: 'works services', the government car pool, 'stationery', and telecommunications, and they are associated with three offices which are 'common service' Departments *par excellence*.

(*a*) *The Ministry of Works.* The Department did not come into existence in its present form until 1945, but it has had a long history. The Office of His Majesty's Surveyor-General of Works was already highly organised by the beginning of the seventeenth century, but it was not until 1814 that it became responsible for all government buildings as well as for royal palaces. In 1832 the Office was merged, as an economy measure, with the Board of Woods and Forests, and from 1832 until 1851 there were three 'Commissioners of Woods, Forests, Land Revenues, Works and Buildings', one of whom sat in Parliament and was regarded as a Departmental Minister of the second rank. In 1851 the Department was divided: 'Woods and Forests' became a non-ministerial Department, ancestor of the present Crown Estates Office; 'Works' became the Department of the First Commissioner of Works, a politician who was sometimes in the Cabinet, but who generally earned many kicks and little glory. The Department had some prestige, since it was 'close to the Throne' through its management of great public occasions such as coronations and state funerals (it was a later Minister of Works who remarked after a coronation that he had had a wonderfully good leading lady), and of royal parks and palaces: but it was also the butt of wits in the Civil Service and outside, and though the fun was sometimes sympathetic (as over Mr. George Lansbury's 'Lido' in Hyde Park), it was sometimes rather sour.

The position of the Office changed a good deal during the war, as a result of public control of all building: in 1940 it became a full

Ministry ('Works and Buildings'), in effect the Ministry for the construction industry, and for a few months in 1942 and 1943 it was also responsible for Town and Country Planning, but lost this function for purely personal reasons. Its functions as 'sponsoring' Ministry have dwindled a good deal with the disappearance of controls from 1950 onwards, but it is still a 'production' Department, as well as a 'common service' Department, and this combination of functions is not likely to be upset. We are not concerned here with its economic functions; they are important, but the staff solely concerned with them is now relatively small.

The Ministry is one of the larger Departments, with a non-industrial staff of over 12,000 (nearly one-third of whom work outside London), an industrial staff of about 15,000, and an annual salary and wage bill of £10 m. A very high proportion of the non-industrial staff are qualified architects, surveyors, engineers, and other technical and professional people. There are only about 70 members of the Administrative Class at headquarters; an Under Secretary is in charge of the Ministry's Scottish Office, and there are 7 Regional Directors who rank as Assistant Secretaries.

The Ministry is responsible for the purchase and lease of sites, the construction of new office blocks, and the purchase and lease of existing buildings and their conversion for government use. The cost is borne on the Ministry of Works Vote, and was about £26 m. in 1955-56. Most of the work of construction and alteration of buildings is done by contractors, but the Ministry places the contracts and supervises the design, layout, construction, and decoration of the buildings in co-operation with the 'user' Department. Many of its industrial workers are employed not on construction but on maintenance, on gardening, on running services (such as office heating and lifts), and as custodians in historic buildings, royal parks, and ancient monuments.

Once a building is in use by a government Department, the Ministry is responsible for repairs and maintenance, for providing fuel, gas, electricity, and water, and for carrying out alterations and extensions. It is also responsible for arranging major cleaning and redecoration: offices are redecorated once in about eight years, and are washed once in three.

Standards of accommodation, decoration, lighting, room temperatures, and so on, are laid down by the Ministry in conjunction with the Treasury, and are the subject of national negotiations with the Staff Side. Since 1945 the Ministry has endeavoured to 'squeeze up' staff (and cut down office space) so as to make room for civil servants evacuated during the war and to release requisitioned premises. This has been a constant topic of discussion between Staff and Official Sides.

The Ministry provides most of the fittings, furniture, carpets, curtains, and other equipment needed in government offices, and it is a very large bulk-purchaser of many types of supplies: tools, fire appliances, protective clothing, hardware, canteen equipment (for the Ministry provides staff restaurants as well as offices), and many other items. Furnishing standards are carefully graded according to the rank of the officer. Thus an Under Secretary is entitled to (but will not necessarily get) a Wilton carpet, but must do without the pastel flat oil paint which decorates the Deputy Secretary's walls. The Assistant Secretary's mirror is to be without a frame, unlike that of the Under Secretary, and his bookcase will be smaller, but he will have Axminster carpet, whilst his Principals must make do with haircord. A P.E.O. has the same standard of furnishing as an Assistant Secretary, and a C.E.O. as a Principal, but 'if rooms are shared with junior officers (S.E.O.s and under) all furniture will be supplied in light oak' instead of mahogany.

The main divisions of the Ministry concerned with supply to government Departments are: the Directorate of Works, under the Director-General of Works (a very large division, employing about 4,000, the majority of whom are professional and technical officers), which covers every aspect of the professional side of the Ministry's building work; the Directorate of Lands and Accommodation (about 300, mainly technical), which manages the Ministry's land and property, negotiates leases, purchases land and buildings, allocates space to the Departments; the Supplies Division (about 1,000, approximately half of whom are technical officers and storekeepers) under a Controller, which designs, purchases, supplies, and repairs a great variety of stores; and the Contracts Directorate (about 100: mainly Executive and Clerical Officers, but including a few professional accountants employed on contract costing).

These technical divisions are controlled by a number of administrative divisions (about 350 people, half of whom are clerical and typing staff, which are responsible for considering and deciding on the requirements of 'user' Departments. They act on the advice of the specialist divisions after negotiation with the Department concerned, and where necessary in consultation with the Treasury.

The Ministry has a 'strong' regional organisation,[1] and considerable authority over accommodation, works, and supply within the regions is delegated, within prescribed financial limits, to the Regional Directors.

[1] Though some of the regional offices have recently been amalgamated.

(b) *The Official Car Pool.* The sight of Ministers and civil servants riding in official cars causes public indignation quite out of proportion to the cost, and official transport is always a vulnerable target in economy campaigns. Since 1946 all passenger cars used by headquarters in the London area have been concentrated in a single 'pool'. This is in a sense a 'taxi rank' or 'central garage', but cars are only sent out on request through the proper channels and subject to strict rules of economy. The service was operated until 1952 by the Ministry of Supply, and is now run by the Ministry of Works: its total cost as shown in the Ministry's Estimates is now £340,000 a year.

This does not prevent Departments from having their own vehicles for the maintenance of a service, as distinct from the occasional transport of Ministers and officials, but the Ministry of Supply buys motor vehicles for all except a few Departments like the Post Office, which have very large fleets of their own.

(c) *Her Majesty's Stationery Office,* one of the minor Departments, was set up in 1786 as an economy measure, to purchase vellum and parchment and to undertake (or put out to contract) all binding and printing required by the Departments. Its Controller holds the ancient office of Queen's Printer of Acts of Parliament, but it has never had a political head of its own. Its responsibility is to the Treasury, but it has in practice a good deal of independence.

The Stationery Office has a monopoly of all government printing, and of the supply of paper and writing materials. Of course this has never been completely enforced; much printing has always been put out to contract, and before the invention of typewriters, carbon paper, and duplicating machines, printing was the only way to duplicate a document conveniently for internal circulation, so that the Foreign Office and some of the other Departments had their own office printers. But since the end of the eighteenth century the hand of the Stationery Office has been visible in most of the immense series of official papers, published and unpublished, and the mechanisation of offices has extended its scope even farther.

Office supplies and equipment are the concern both of the Ministry of Works and of the Stationery Office. Broadly speaking, the Ministry of Works provides all office furniture and large equipment, the Stationery Office provides printing services, stationery, office requisites, and office machinery. Thus the desk at which the Clerical Officer sits is put there by the Ministry of Works, but the pencil with which he writes and the date stamp which he uses are supplied by the Stationery Office. There are some curious divisions of responsibility: the punched card machines are provided by the Stationery

Office, the equipment for storing the cards by the Ministry of Works; the addressograph stencils and metal plates are provided by the Stationery Office, their containers by the Ministry; time-recording clocks are supplied by the Ministry, but the cards which go in the clocks are provided by the Stationery Office.

In theory, and for the most part in practice, no Department obtains office supplies except through the Stationery Office, though small items are sometimes bought from office petty cash. But the Stationery Office does much more than provide printed matter and supplies. It gives Departments advice on the layout and format of circulars and forms, on duplicating processes, and on office machinery, and it trains duplicator operators for other Departments. It collects and disposes of all government waste paper (including secret and confidential documents, which have to be specially treated), repairs office machines, and disposes of a great variety of surplus office stores.

Its staff of about 7,000 includes some 4,000 industrial workers, and about 900 non-industrials employed in the regions in stores, depots, and the government bookshops which sell publications to the general public. Except for the Controller, who is an Administrative Class official, the Office is run entirely by Executive Class officers and supervisory technical officers. It employs roughly equal numbers of non-specialists and of technicians.

(*d*) *The Post Office*. Maintenance of administrative lines of communication is one of the first necessities of all government, and governments have provided a 'Royal Mail' for their own use at least since the time of the Persian Empire in the seventh century B.C. This was the original function of the British Post Office, but it has in course of time become a 'common carrier', a banker, and so on, and provides various counter services as agent in its local offices.

The carriage of mail for a charge has been a Post Office monopoly since the beginning of the seventeenth century, and can be enforced against any private enterprise in this field. The monopoly does not hold against other government Departments, so long as they do not open their dispatch services to the public and do not allow them to be used by officials for their own private correspondence; and some Departments do run services of their own, such as messenger vans between offices, dispatch riders for the service Departments, Queen's Messengers. But they have to pay for such services from their own Vote, whereas Post Office mail services are borne on the Post Office Estimates; and in practice an overwhelming proportion of government mail is carried by the Post Office even between detached sections of one headquarters.

The telegraph service was nationalised (by Mr. Gladstone's government) in 1869; the telephone service (except for the service provided by the city of Hull) was taken over at the beginning of 1912. The process of 'nationalising' overseas telecommunications was begun before the First World War and was completed in 1950 when the assets of Cable and Wireless Ltd. were acquired by the Post Office (all the shares in this public company were taken over by the government in 1946 and vested in Treasury nominees).

In addition, the Post Office has an ultimate responsibility of a rather more delicate kind for the communications aspects of radio broadcasting and television.

This monopoly of telecommunications holds against government Departments as against the public, with a few obvious exceptions: the armed services use their own channels for active operations and in training for operations (but not for much routine administrative business); the police radio network is provided jointly by the Home Office and the local police authorities. A great deal of the traffic is carried on lines or radio channels used also for other purposes (cypher or scrambling equipment being used if necessary); but the Post Office provides special channels when required. It is also responsible for the maintenance of administrative communications during invasion, heavy bombing, or civil disturbance, so that the Post Office is involved in some very important matters of civil defence. The Post Office also provides the telecommunications staff who work within other Departments. The most familiar instance is that of the switchboards in Whitehall, which are manned by Post Office girls; but of course it also means the provision of skilled engineers at various levels.

Postal services are provided 'free' to Departments, the total expenditure falling on the Post Office Vote, but the Estimates of each Department contain a note allocating the approximate cost. Since 1 April 1956 (after some pressure by the Estimates Committee and the Post Office itself) all Departments 'pay' (by book transfers) for their telephone and telegraph services, the receipts being treated by the Post Office as revenue: the resulting increase in Departmental Estimates for 1956-57 was of the order of £2½ m.

(ii) *Minor Services*

As we have seen, a number of specialist and technical services are provided within Departments by small specialist classes, most of which have some focal point in a particular Department; others are provided (for the most part free of charge as Allied Services) by minor 'common service' Departments, partly through historical accident, partly because of special reasons of convenience in each case. Such Departments generally have a monopoly of the service which they render. We have already mentioned the Ordnance Survey, attached first to the War Office and latterly to the Ministry of Agriculture, which has a virtual monopoly in its own field; and the Meteorological Office, attached to the Air Ministry, which serves all Departments except the Admiralty. The Valuation Office of the Board of Inland Revenue serves a large number of other Departments; the Government Actuary was first appointed when National Health Insurance was introduced in 1911, but now acts as general adviser on national insurance and on many matters of superannuation and mortality; the Government Chemist's Department grew out of the analysis of food and drugs, but now has a variety of other functions.

(iii) *The Central Office of Information*

We draw attention to these minor services here largely because they offer an analogy for the creation of the Central Office of Information, a Department which has attracted a good deal of political controversy. Very large questions may be raised about the extent to which the government should use the taxpayers' money to explain to the taxpayer the excellence of government services. In a party system politicians in opposition are naturally suspicious of any expenditure on publicity by the party in office: not without reason, because one aspect of dictatorship is that the government uses the resources of the public to perpetuate itself by propaganda. The question of the place of 'propaganda' or 'information' services in British government has never been free from controversy since the problem first became a practical one during the First World War; and a paradoxical result of these arguments is that the only central organisation concerned with them has to be classified with such offices as those of the Government Actuary and the Government Chemist.

During the First World War there existed for a short time a Ministry of Information, as well as a separate organisation for propaganda to enemy countries. The question did not arise again until the 1930s, and there was then created (in 1934) an organisation for British cultural propaganda overseas, the British Council. This was not then, and (as we have already observed) still is not, a government Department within our definition; it is in many respects treated as a Department, but its officials are not civil servants, a distinction which is presumed to have some virtue in keeping the British Council free from contamination by an official 'line'. During the Second

World War, responsibility for overseas propaganda was divided in a confused way between the British Council, the B.B.C., an organisation called the Political Warfare Executive, and the Ministry of Information. Only the last of these concerns us here, since the British Council and the B.B.C. are not government Departments, and P.W.E. disappeared at the end of the war. In its early days the Ministry of Information was a great joke in Fleet Street: some of the attacks on it were malicious, but many were well-deserved, and the Ministry was an extremely 'hot seat' for any politician. The problems of organisation for overseas propaganda were never completely solved, but by the end of the war the Ministry had come to fill a modest but necessary place in the work of public relations at home. This was based mainly on three functions. The Ministry was a central point of reference for the press in all matters of government press releases and of censorship, which was on a 'voluntary' basis and needed much tactful handling; it was the main specialist Department (though it had no monopoly) in the techniques of 'mass communication' apart from radio—such matters as film production, advertising display, and the conduct of publicity campaigns; and it had considerable experience in using the technique of 'sample surveys' in testing public reactions to administrative action. The Minister's personal scope extended rather beyond this, and he could in some minor respects be called a 'mouthpiece' for the government, and adviser on home propaganda; but his position was not strong, except through the personality of Mr. Brendan Bracken.

At its period of greatest expansion the Ministry had a staff of about 5,000 at home and overseas. Such an establishment could not be justified in time of peace, and in any case even the existence of a Ministry of Information was a symbol of war government. It was therefore for a time possible that the organisation might be disbanded completely; but it was defended on the plea of economies of scale and the advantages of the 'common service' system. The compromise reached was the creation in 1946 of the Central Office of Information as a non-ministerial Department under the aegis of the Lord President of the Council, then Mr. Herbert Morrison. Responsibility for administrative matters affecting the C.O.I. was transferred in 1949 to the Financial Secretary to the Treasury and in 1957 to the Chancellor of the Duchy of Lancaster, who answers Parliamentary Questions about the work of the Office and is, in addition, responsible for 'the coordination of Government information services at home and abroad'.

The Office has its own Vote, which amounted to about £1½ m. in 1955-56. In addition, a White Paper is published annually which gives (in round figures) total expenditure on government information services, allocating the cost of C.O.I. services between Departments and adding the cost of their own services. The total is about £2¼ m. for home services, £10½ m. for overseas services. Among the home services are such large blocks of expenditure as War Office £360,000, National Savings Committee £277,000, Air Ministry £246,000, Ministry of Agriculture £103,000. The unallocated cost of the Central Office of Information amounts only to about £117,000 under both heads, home and overseas together.

The Office began in 1947-48 with a staff of about 1,700, and economy cuts had by 1956 brought this down to about 700 in London and 90 in the regions. Its Director-General ranks as a Deputy Secretary, and a number of heads of divisions are Assistant Secretaries; but the Office is run primarily by Executive Class civil servants, and by members of the 'general service' class of Information Officers, specialists in a variety of branches of their subject. The regional organisation was at one time substantial, but has now been reduced to a skeleton service, which is no more than a point of reference for the various local operations of the Office.

The Office has no responsibility either for government tactics in handling the press or for the content of any publicity material which it issues. It may exercise influence by virtue of its experience, but it can only do so by accepting policy and suggesting better ways of promoting it.

Its services can be summed up briefly as follows:

(*a*) Government press releases are centralised in a C.O.I. office in Queen Anne's Gate, and a 'dispatch rider' service distributes them to the London press and news agencies.

(*b*) The C.O.I. is the channel for almost all press and poster advertising, and usually handles it through commercial advertising agents.

(*c*) It is the chief adviser to Departments on the conduct of publicity campaigns, and it prepares all kinds of publicity material at the request of Departments (it has no monopoly of this).

(*d*) It is an agency for the production (and in some cases distribution) of films by private contractors for official purposes.

(*e*) It prepares (but has no monopoly of) exhibitions for official publicity.

(*f*) It shares with the British Council the responsibility for 'conducted tours' by sponsored visitors from overseas.

(*g*) It runs the government Social Survey (a sampling organisation similar in some respects to those maintained by commercial advertising agencies in order to test market reactions), which plays a part of some importance in reporting on possible requirements for particular services.

It would be unsafe to say that this organisation has yet made a permanent place for itself. It would be administratively possible without much loss to break up its functions and distribute them among other Departments. But it is unlikely that this would lead to significant saving and it might lead to an increase in costs; it would in any case dissipate an organisation which has some value as a basis for expansion in emergency. The Ministry of Information would have escaped many troubles if a working nucleus had existed before 1939.

4. COMMON SERVICES: PROCEDURE AND CONTROVERSIES

The procedure and its effects can be illustrated by a relatively simple case. The Stationery Office receives about 200 demands a week for new 'office machines' from the whole of the central administration. Most of these are for relatively simple items such as typewriters, duplicators, and desk calculating machines; but quite large installations of 'business machinery' will be required from time to time. In September each year, when it begins to make up its Estimates, the Stationery Office sends out to all Departments an inquiry about their requirements for office machinery (*inter alia*) during the next financial year. Its Estimates will include a total for office machinery based partly on these figures, partly on past expenditure, and partly on knowledge about the trend of costs. The Estimates do not break this total down by 'user' Departments, but the Stationery Office naturally has in mind a provisional allocation of the total allowed, and an estimate of the rate at which it may safely be used in the earlier part of the year. If the allocation is expended too soon, it is the Stationery Office which has to ask for a Supplementary Estimate.

If a division requires a new piece of office machinery, its head must first convince the official in charge (usually a Higher Executive Officer) within the Department; it is the latter's business to see that the case is *prima facie* reasonable and that the requirement cannot be met by using equipment available elsewhere in the Department. It is now the practice to bring the Departmental O. & M. Branch into consultation if the machinery specified is in any way out of the ordinary. A requisition thus cleared within the Department must be signed by a more senior official for transmission to the Stationery Office. If the type of equipment is one covered by precedents, and if the Department's total requirements are within expectations, the

Stationery Office can proceed to action without much further trouble. But if there are difficulties it is bound to discuss them closely. Is this particular type of machine really necessary? Can a cheaper substitute be found? Can the demand be postponed? Can existing machinery be used through some arrangement for pooling? The Stationery Office acts partly as expert adviser, partly as a subordinate agent of financial control, partly as legislator by precedent for the types of equipment to be used within the Service for particular purposes.

The example chosen is one in the middle range. For small items of equipment the element of standardisation is paramount: the Stationery Office virtually makes binding rules about such matters as types of stationery and of office equipment, and the rules are automatically applied by junior officials. At the other extreme, in such matters as the provision of a new office building by the Ministry of Works, rules are of some importance, because a good deal depends on permitted scales of accommodation, but there is much scope for negotiation at a high level, involving both the question of cost and the skill of engineers and architects in designing a building worthy of its public purpose and convenient to users.

The case for the extension of this procedure was made by the Haldane Committee, in proposing the creation of a Ministry of Supplies to obtain *all* supplies required by the government, 'in order

'(a) to eliminate competition between Departments for labour, materials, and the services of individual firms;

'(b) to ensure that the prices paid and the conditions imposed under Government contracts for various classes of work should so far as possible be arranged on uniform lines;

'(c) to secure economies in the use of technical staffs (such as contracting, accounting, costing, and inspecting sections).'[1]

These objects could be secured by 'common services' provided either on an Agency basis or as Allied Services. The Committee did not enter into this, but the trend of their argument is towards the extension of Allied Services. The case against this development is partly a matter of natural independence and conservatism; as the Haldane Committee acknowledge: 'it cannot be expected that difficulties will not be raised by Departments desirous of retaining their existing powers and functions'. But there are also practical limits to the useful extension of standardisation and routine procedure. 'Common service' Departments strive to meet the individual needs of their clients, and are on the whole very efficient and co-operative organisations. But there is certain to be controversy about what needs are

[1] Cd. 9230, p. 50.

truly individual; within the Allied Service system the presumption is against departure from precedent unless a case has been made, and precedents ranging over the whole Service are extensive and somewhat discouraging to those who seek colour and enterprise. These substantial arguments, allied to the spirit of departmentalism, keep the growth of 'common services' in check, in spite of the pressures which support them.

FOR REFERENCE

E. C. R. HADFIELD: 'Common Service Organisation in the Central Government', *Public Administration*, Vol. XXVIII, p. 305.

Sir ROBERT FRASER: 'The Virtues and Vices of Common Services', *Public Administration*, Vol. XXXII, p. 253.

Royal Commission on Scottish Affairs: *Memoranda submitted by the Ministry of Works, Post Office and Stationery Office* (H.M.S.O. 1953).

Annual Reports of the Ministry of Works and Central Office of Information.

Annual Statement of Estimated Expenditure on the Government Information Services (published as a Command Paper).

The *O. & M. Bulletin* (published by H.M. Treasury) contains a number of articles on various aspects of the work of Common Service Departments. See, for instance:

    Vol. 6, No. 3, p. 32 ⎫
    Vol. 6, No. 4, p. 11 ⎬ *H.M.S.O.*
    Vol. 7, No. 1, p. 32 ⎭
    Vol. 3, No. 3, p. 31—*The Government Chemist*.

Report of the Committee on the Cost of the Home Information Services (French). Cmd. 7836, 1949.

Report of the Committee on the Overseas Information Services (Drogheda). Cmd. 9138, 1954.

CHAPTER EIGHTEEN

ACCOUNTING AND FINANCIAL CONTROL

> But help it I cannot, I cannot help thinking
> How pleasant it is to have money, heigh-ho!
> How pleasant it is to have money.
>   A. H. CLOUGH: *Spectator ab extra.*

1. INTRODUCTORY

FOR the whole of central administration there is one style of accounts and a single code of financial procedure. These forms are the result of a long process of evolution, and have acquired an importance of their own not directly related to their practical effects. They were designed originally to give effect to the constitutional supremacy of the House of Commons in all financial matters, and to establish the especial sanctity of 'public money'. The financial supremacy of the House of Commons is now a myth rather than a reality: but it is a myth which affects practice in two respects. It is important (first) in moulding the attitude of civil servants towards elected persons, through the whole cycle of financial procedure and in particular through the influence of the two financial committees of the House of Commons, the Public Accounts Committee and the Estimates Committee (a matter dealt with in Chapter 20). It is important (secondly) because all business is done within a set framework of accounting practice, which brings the finance officers of the Departments and of the Treasury into consultation at critical points in the process of administration.

These formalities do not constitute 'Treasury control', but they make it possible; and Treasury control lies at the centre of administrative co-ordination and of government influence over the national economy. We therefore begin by setting out the framework of financial routine and explain the main organisations involved: the Paymaster-General's Office, the Audit Office, the finance divisions of the Departments, and the Treasury itself. This makes it possible to explain the cycle of business in the financial year, within which Treasury control is exercised in four ways: Estimates, Budget-making, running control, and accountancy and audit. These are technical matters which require a text-book to themselves, but it is only within this technical setting that it is possible to understand the practical effects of established procedure.

2. THE HANDLING OF PUBLIC MONEY

The Consolidated Fund

At the centre of the system is the Consolidated Fund, a device introduced by William Pitt in 1787. This might be described somewhat crudely as the Crown's current account with the Bank of England. (The Bank of England has since 1946 been a public corporation, directed by a Board of Governors appointed by the Crown on the advice of the Treasury; but this change has made no difference to the traditional procedure.)

The income of the central administration (apart from occasional windfalls, such as reparations, gifts, and legacies) consists of four elements, the proceeds of taxation, of loans, and of trading profits, and the hereditary revenues of the Crown (which are not the same as the private fortune of the Queen and her relatives). In principle, all income flows into the Consolidated Fund (the Exchequer Account at the Bank of England) and all expenditure is met from it. Exceptions have increasingly been made in recent years, allowing the creation of subordinate funds, such as the National Insurance Fund and the Exchequer Equalisation Fund. In addition, the Treasury has two relatively small funds on which it can draw in an emergency without formal authorisation till after the event: the Treasury Chest Fund for disbursements at distant stations overseas, and the Civil Contingencies Fund for unexpected civil expenditure at home. But behind all these separate funds stands the Consolidated Fund, and the Treasury will, if necessary, 'claw back' subordinate balances in order to replenish it. The Treasury may sometimes require the express authority of Parliament to enable it to 'raid' a subordinate fund set up originally by statute, but it is inconceivable that this should be refused if asked with the authority of the Cabinet behind the request.

Income

All taxation requires the authority of statute: the only exception to this is the rule made statutory in 1913,[1] that in order to avoid inconvenience the Crown may collect revenue on the authority of the House of Commons alone, provided that the appropriate resolutions of the House of Commons are approved by statute within four months. This is the explanation of the 'Budget Resolutions' passed

[1] Provisional Collection of Taxes Act, 3 Geo. 5, c. 3.

by the Commons at the end of the first day of the debate on the Budget. These authorise the Chancellor of the Exchequer to act at once on his proposals regarding taxation, subject to confirmation by a subsequent Finance Act. Other forms of income (loans, trading sales, and hereditary revenues) do not rest on specific Parliamentary sanction in each case—the Crown can up to a point exercise the powers of an ordinary legal person; but the disposal of the money is limited by statute, principally by the Exchequer Act of 1834 and the Exchequer and Audit Departments Acts of 1866 and 1921, which direct that (subject to the limited exceptions referred to above) all receipts are to be paid into the Consolidated Fund.

Expenditure

No money can be paid out of the Consolidated Fund without the express authority of Parliament, and conformity to statute is ensured by the vigilance of the Comptroller and Auditor-General. Payments are of three types:

(i) *'Consolidated Fund Services'*, recurrent charges which are authorised by permanent legislation, such as the interest on the National Debt, the Civil List of the monarch, and the salaries and pensions of officers outside the control of the central administration, such as judges of the superior courts and the Comptroller and Auditor-General.

(ii) *'Supply Services'*, for which monies are granted annually by Parliament after the formal presentation of Estimates: authority for payment is given by Appropriation Acts and Consolidated Fund Acts.

(iii) *Capital Payments*, such as loans to local authorities and other public bodies. In such cases Parliament generally gives discretion to make loans within a specified total, which may be large; the expenditure incurred is (at least in theory) recoverable, and is shown as a matter of form outside the annual revenue accounts presented to Parliament, as 'expenditure below the line'.

To take a recent instance, in 1954-55 expenditure on Consolidated Fund Services was about £670 m., on Supply Services about £3,880 m., 'below the line' was about £390 m. net. Supply Services are thus dominant; expenditure in the other categories is constitutionally and politically important, but accounting procedure is settled primarily for Supply Services.

The formal scheme is as follows. Statute grants money to the Crown. The Crown acts by Royal Warrant (under the royal Sign Manual subscribed by two Lords of the Treasury) to put the money at the disposal of the Treasury, permitting the Lords of the Treasury

ACCOUNTING AND FINANCIAL CONTROL

to draw from the Exchequer Account up to the sum authorised by statute. General statutes (the Exchequer and Audit Acts, 1866-1921) prohibit the Treasury from drawing money except on requisition countersigned by the Comptroller and Auditor-General. Money so released is transferred from the Exchequer Account to the account of the Paymaster-General, also held at the Bank of England, and the Paymaster-General in turn acts as banker for each separate Department.[1]

Receipts by Departments

The largest collectors of money for the Crown are the three great Revenue Departments, the Board of Inland Revenue (in 1954 about £2,550 m.), the Board of Customs and Excise (about £1,900 m.), and the Post Office (about £270 m.); but most Departments have receipts of some sort from various sources.

There are two principles of public accounting which determine how these receipts are to be treated. On the one hand, all money received must ultimately be accounted for in the Exchequer Account; on the other hand, it is traditional that money should if possible be used where it comes to hand, so as to avoid unnecessary book-keeping transactions, but not so as to leave large idle balances in the hands of Departments.

The practical application of these principles is as follows. The Revenue Departments are permitted to retain out of the money they collect sufficient to meet their own expenses: unlike the 'spending' Departments, they do not draw upon the Paymaster-General for their requirements. Local offices of the Revenue Departments generally receive money either by cheque or in cash, and money so received is paid into a local account with a branch of the Bank of England or with a commercial bank. The local collectors are authorised to draw on their accounts within stated limits for local expenditure; balances not required for this purpose are transferred daily to the respective accounts of the Departments at the Bank of England and are paid over by the Bank to the Exchequer Account. Periodically (at present once a month) the Revenue Departments submit statements of their expenditure to the Treasury, which then authorises a notional issue from the Consolidated Fund covering these amounts, and the Departments make a notional repayment, so that all receipts and issues are eventually accounted for in the Exchequer Account.

All receipts by the 'spending' Departments are paid over daily to the Paymaster-General's cash account at the Bank of England, and

---

[1] Except the Revenue Departments, on which see below.

are used by him as a general cash balance to make whatever payments may be required by the spending Departments for the public service. He is also supplied day by day with additional issues from the Consolidated Fund (requested by the Treasury and duly authorised by the Comptroller-General) according to his needs. The Paymaster-General's general cash balance is adjusted frequently, so that he is never in possession of much larger sums than are needed to meet his immediate requirements, and notional issues and repayments are made to bring the Consolidated Fund into balance.

There is thus a rather intricate compromise. In principle there is a single account, the Exchequer Account; as a matter of convenience this is broken up into various subordinate accounts. At any moment only net receipts are flowing into the Account, but eventually all receipts are credited and all issues are authorised by a general adjustment of balances.

Payments by Departments

Each Department is responsible for keeping the Treasury informed periodically of the amounts it requires for the public service in order to keep a proper balance in its accounts, and these requests (formally authorised by the Treasury) enable the Department to draw upon the Paymaster-General as necessary, subject only to the ordinary processes of audit. It does so in three ways:

(i) *By Payable Orders*. These are in effect cheques drawn by the Department on the Paymaster-General, and are handled much like cheques drawn on an ordinary bank. Payable orders flow back to the Pay Office from commercial banks, are authorised for payment (after checking against schedules of orders issued by the Department), and are met by instructions from the Pay Office to the Bank of England debiting the Pay Office account and crediting the accounts of the banks into which orders have been paid. At the end of each month the Pay Office sends each Department a schedule of payments made along with the discharged payable orders, and there is a further check.

(ii) *By 'Write-off'*. This is an adaptation of the usual commercial method of making regular periodical payments. The creditor asks that payment (of salary for instance) should be made regularly to his own bank. The Department completes a schedule of regular monthly payments to each commercial bank, and action in the Pay Office follows from this, subject to the usual checks.

(iii) *By 'Imprest'*. All Departments require some money for payments in cash (e.g. weekly wages), and in some cases (for instance in the service Departments) the sums required are very large and have

ACCOUNTING AND FINANCIAL CONTROL 305

to be disbursed through a great many scattered offices. Practice is complicated, the principles are simple. A local imprest can be opened only on the authority of a finance division. Once opened, the imprest is replenished periodically by payable orders drawn on the Pay Office and cashable at a local bank. Such drawings are made only by authorised officials and are subject to careful scrutiny.

3. THE ORGANISATIONS INVOLVED

This procedure involves four main agencies: the Paymaster-General's Office (in Scotland, the Office of the Queen's and Lord Treasurer's Remembrancer), the Comptroller and Auditor-General's Office, the finance divisions of the Departments, and the Treasury. Financial procedure and financial control depend primarily on the staff of these agencies: the ordinary civil servant must conform scrupulously to the procedure which they have evolved, but need not understand the reasons for it.

(i) *The Pay Office*

The present Pay Office was created by statutes of 1835 and 1848[1] to replace a number of ancient offices which had become remunerative sinecures. The Paymaster-General is in effect a Minister without Portfolio, and takes no part in the work of the Office, which ranks as a subordinate Department of the Treasury (its Estimates are included in the Treasury's Vote) and is directed by the Assistant Paymaster-General, at present an Assistant Secretary, who is granted powers of attorney by his Minister. He is assisted by a Senior Chief Executive Officer and two Chief Executive Officers, and has a staff of about 600, of whom about 130 are drawn from the Executive Class. The Office is directly responsible for the payment of most civil pensions (including the pensions of former civil servants, other than those employed in the Revenue and service Departments, and the pensions of their dependents: about £40 m. a year). Interest payments on the National Debt (which form the major part of the issues on 'Consolidated Fund Services', about £600 m. out of £670 m. in 1954-55) are authorised by the Treasury and are paid by the Bank of England; but the Pay Office makes most of the other Consolidated Fund payments, including such items as judges' salaries. It also acts, as has been described above, as paying agent for all except the Revenue Departments, and this part of its work corresponds to the routine work of a very large bank. None of the work allows of discretion except in the management of staff and the improvement of

[1] 5/6 Will. IV, c. 35, and 11/12 Vict., c. 25.

procedure; it calls, however, for complete accuracy and fidelity. Little special knowledge is required apart from knowledge of the routine of the Office, and the staff are ordinary 'general' civil servants trained by experience on the job.

(ii) *The Exchequer and Audit Department*

This is a Department not much larger than the Pay Office, but its responsibilities involve much greater exercise of discretion (it has thirteen officers of the rank of Principal Executive Officer or above, a rank equivalent to that of the head of the Pay Office). Its head is the Comptroller and Auditor-General, who ranks as a Permanent Secretary. He and his staff are civil servants in the sense of the definition used in this book, but their position is peculiar: although they are servants of the Crown, their main duty is to serve the House of Commons.[1] The salary of the Comptroller and Auditor-General is borne on the Consolidated Fund, the rest of the cost of the Department (about £470,000 a year) is borne on a separate Vote in the Annual Estimates. (The Comptroller and Auditor-General is the Accounting Officer, and the Appropriation Account is audited in the Treasury and is signed by the Auditor of the Civil List—one of the two Permanent Secretaries to the Treasury). The Comptroller and Auditor-General is appointed by the Crown (by Letters Patent) on the nomination of the Prime Minister, advised by the Head of the Home Civil Service; he is always an Administrative Class civil servant of mature experience (and quite frequently is an ex-Treasury official) who will end his career in this post, and therefore does not look elsewhere for promotion. Levels of pay within the Department correspond to those of the Civil Service as a whole, and men may (in theory) be transferred from it to other Departments, but it is left very much to itself in its internal affairs.

The Department is in form two offices, the Exchequer Office and the Audit Office, but Exchequer business has dwindled until it is no more than a constitutional formality. The signature of the Comptroller of the Receipt and Issue of Her Majesty's Exchequer is still necessary to confirm a requisition by the Treasury transferring money from the Exchequer Account to the Paymaster-General's Account. Such requisitions are signed almost every day, and involve very large sums, but the work of checking them employs only two clerks for about an hour each afternoon.

The real business of the Department is that of the Auditor-General of Public Accounts, a post evolved by a gradual process of abolishing

---

[1] Cp. the position of the Clerks at the Table and other officials of the House of Commons, p. 184 above.

and amalgamating older offices, until this simple and effective centralisation was achieved by the Exchequer and Audit Departments Act of 1866. The office is divided into nine sections each under a Director of Audit: one of these deals with internal matters of establishments and finance, the others divide the field of business between them in more or less equal blocks of work. They now audit the accounts of all government Departments (including the accounts of receipts by the Revenue Departments), and of a number of public bodies financed by large grants-in-aid, such as the Arts Council, the British Council, and the Medical Research Council. They audit the consolidated accounts of the National Health Service (the accounts of individual local health authorities, Regional Hospital Boards, and so on, are audited either by the District Audit or by the Ministry of Health Hospital Audit); but their responsibility for the accounts of the nationalised industries is limited to advising the Public Accounts Committee about the published commercial accounts. There are special arrangements by which they audit the accounts of a number of public bodies quite outside the sphere of central administration, such as the Church Commissioners, the governments of the Channel Islands and the Isle of Man, and U.N.E.S.C.O.

The total annual audited expenditure has increased from about £66 m. in 1865 to about £4,500 m. in 1956, but during the same period the staff of auditors has increased only from 113 to 435. Expenditure since 1939 has increased five-fold, and the audit staff has only increased by about a half. This economy of overheads is possible because of decentralisation of the process of audit, and the method of 'test checks'.

A great part of the work is done in the Departments: indeed all the large Departments have a number of the Auditor-General's staff permanently in the building engaged on a running audit, and (ideally) these men are at any moment auditing the accounts made up during the previous month or six weeks. Errors in the accounts are corrected on the spot after discussion between the auditor and the Departmental accounts officers.

Because of the huge volume of work, the office relies increasingly on test checks to uncover instances of waste or extravagance or lack of control over expenditure. It is these which find their way into the Comptroller and Auditor-General's Reports to Parliament, which are published each year with the relevant Appropriation Accounts, and are the basis of the work of the Public Accounts Committee. The auditors (like the District Auditors in local government) give particular attention to the adequacy of arrangements for Departmental accounting and internal audit, and adjustments are frequently made on their advice without the need for more formal action. The sanction behind this informal control is the possibility of report to the Public Accounts Committee, which can cause acute discomfort to the Accounting Officer of a Department found to be at fault, and can in the last resort propose to the House of Commons that it hold him personally responsible for defalcation. Nevertheless, the effective working of the system depends primarily on the position of audit staff within Departments.

These auditors are recruited in the main from school-leavers by the ordinary Executive Class examination. It is uncertain how individual entrants come into this Department rather than another: partly perhaps a matter of choice, based on knowledge through personal connections, partly a matter of official selection. The quality of entrants (about 30 a year at present) has traditionally been high, and on entry to the office they are given an intensive course of training lasting three years. This consists partly of book work in courses organised by the office, partly of desk-training under supervision, and partly of external courses in law and accountancy taken at the City of London College, or, where the recruit is stationed outside London, by correspondence with the School of Accountancy. This training may be regarded as equivalent to the period of articles served by a commercial accountant, and the standard expected is considered to be at least as high as that of the District Auditors, the other important 'corps' of official auditors.

During training an entrant ranks as Assistant Auditor; and his avenue of promotion thereafter lies generally within the Department, through a hierarchy of Auditor, Senior Auditor, Deputy Director, and Director, corresponding to the Executive Class hierarchy up to Principal Executive Officer. The highest posts filled from within the Department are those of Secretary and Deputy Secretary, which are specially graded executive posts. A man is moved during his career from one group of Departments to another, and there are a few posts overseas. An auditor is rarely kept for more than five years on one block of business, so as to safeguard independence and to secure that experience at the top is general rather than specific.

(iii) *The Finance Divisions of the Departments*

There is a good deal of variation in practice between Departments, and generalisation is not altogether safe. Nevertheless, there are three elements in the situation which are in some form present in all Departments: the Accounting Officer, the routine management of accounts, and the administrative sections concerned with finance.

(a) *The Accounting Officer.* The post of Accounting Officer, with 'personal and pecuniary liability' for all financial matters, was created by administrative action under the authority of the Exchequer and Audit Act of 1866, which permitted the Treasury to nominate an officer to prepare the Appropriation Accounts in each Department. The functions of the Accounting Officer were first defined in a Treasury Minute of 14 August 1872, which made it clear that the Treasury would wherever possible nominate the Permanent Secretary of the Department. The proposal was for many years resisted by some of the larger Departments, on the not very convincing ground that the Permanent Secretary was already fully occupied with his administrative duties. The job was frequently assigned to a subordinate officer of relatively junior rank, with the result that the financial implications of policy were ignored, and the finance division became isolated from the rest of the Department and regarded as an outpost of the Treasury.

The present system dates from the report of a Council of Financial Officers presided over by Mr. Baldwin when he was Financial Secretary to the Treasury in 1920. Its implementation was largely the work of Sir Warren Fisher, Permanent Secretary to the Treasury from 1919 to 1939. Under Fisher the number of important Departments in which the Permanent Secretary was designated Accounting Officer rose from 6 in 1920 to 20 out of 24 in 1931.

The formal importance of these changes is obvious. The permanent head of the Department is expected to assume personal responsibility for the correctness of its accounts, and also for general economy in administration. The standard Treasury letter (last revised in 1953) by which these appointments are made draws the attention of Accounting Officers to the fact that the Comptroller and Auditor-General is 'specifically encouraged to bring to the notice of the Public Accounts Committee any cases of apparent waste and extravagance', and not merely to ensure that every Departmental payment is covered by statutory authority. The object of the changes was to raise the status of finance within the Departments, and to dissipate the nineteenth-century tradition of hostility between the Treasury and the other Departments by shifting some of the Treasury's burden of control to the shoulders of civil servants within the Departments themselves. The effectiveness of the scheme in practice depends on how matters are handled there, since the Permanent Secretary cannot discharge in person the duties for which he is responsible.

(b) *The Accounts Branch.* Responsibility for accounting practice within a Department usually rests in the first instance upon an official known as the Director of Accounts (or by some similar title). The post is in a large Department filled by an experienced Executive Class officer ranking slightly above the level of Principal Executive Officer. The shape of the accounting organisation depends on the shape of the Department. It may be concentrated in the hands of officers of the Directorate of Accounts, or divided among officers within sections; it may be done largely at headquarters, or distributed among many establishments at home and overseas. The technical aspects of efficiency in public accounting are largely concerned with this problem of flexibility in adapting accounting organisation to fit administrative organisation; but in spite of flexibility there are certain common factors.

Much routine business is concerned with payments to staff: the calculation and authorisation of monthly salaries and weekly wages, allowances, overtime, and travelling claims; staff superannuation; and the computation and deduction of income tax. Other sections may be necessary to deal with collection of monies owed to the Department, payment for goods supplied and services rendered by contractors, checking bills, writing off losses and bad debts, settling claims, or paying grants to local authorities and other bodies.

The accounts sections of the finance division maintain the cash accounts, and possibly (depending on the nature of the Department) stores accounts, cost accounts, and trading profit and loss accounts. All items of Departmental expenditure and income must be allocated to the appropriate sub-heads of the Appropriation Account and payments must be carefully checked to ensure that there is no overspending without Treasury authority and that the necessary Parliamentary sanction has been obtained. There may be other sections employed on the internal audit of accounts, books, and vouchers, and there is usually a separate cashier's section for cash payments and for the preparation of schedules for payments made by the Paymaster-General on the Department's behalf.

The exact form of accounts (other than the Appropriation Accounts) is a matter for the Department, but the two Treasury Officers of Accounts are available to give general advice. The senior Treasury Officer of Accounts is the Under Secretary (or sometimes the Third Secretary) in charge of one of the finance divisions of the Treasury (see below); the second Treasury Officer of Accounts is an Assistant Secretary; and they have a small staff of Executive Class officers. Their principal functions are to advise on the organisation of accounts branches, systems of accounting, contract methods and procedure, and similar matters, and they have a statutory duty to

ACCOUNTING AND FINANCIAL CONTROL

supervise the form of public accounts, in particular of the Appropriation Accounts.

In the largest Departments accounting employs a large staff of clerical officers, clerical assistants, and machine operators, and it is usually highly mechanised. On all questions of accounting machines and other office machinery these Departments can draw on the considerable body of expert knowledge built up by the Office Machines section of the Treasury O. & M. Division since its inception in 1919, and Departmental O. & M. teams may also be called in to help the finance division when new machines are being installed or accounting procedures redesigned.

Executive Class officers are responsible for the higher levels of supervision and for the management and organisation of routine business, as well as for devising the procedure needed to meet the particular requirements of their Department. They are also employed on the more difficult processes of accounting and audit. Many of their external contacts are with officers of their own rank in the Paymaster-General's Office, and with the Comptroller and Auditor-General's staff who work alongside them within the Department.

Departments may provide introductory courses of their own for officers posted for the first time to accounting sections: and some of them may acquire qualifications for themselves outside the Service. But in principle training is 'on the job', promotion depends on seniority and on good work, and there is no special 'trade' of public accounting. The burden of this highly technical and responsible work rests on ordinary members of the Executive Class, and efficiency from day to day depends on their probity and skill.

(c) *The Principal Finance Officer.* To give reality to the responsibilities of the Accounting Officer there must be an administrative link between him and the routine financial business of the Department. This is provided by the Principal Finance Officer, an important Administrative Class official of whom we have already said something in Chapter 13. In those Departments in which the 'Fisher system' is fully applied, the Principal Finance Officer has direct access to the Permanent Secretary and to the Minister, and his division stands in relation to the administrative divisions as the finance divisions of the Treasury stand in relation to the Departments as a whole. The division is the channel for all formal communications to and from the Treasury about finance. It is its business to watch the rate of expenditure so as to give early warning to the Department and to the Treasury that the whole Estimate or a sub-head may be exceeded unless spending can be checked; to discuss with the appropriate

Treasury officers matters requiring their approval; and (most important of all) to decide when the Treasury should be consulted. There are certain matters (not very precisely defined) on which the Treasury must be consulted; there are others where the Treasury has delegated specific authority to Departments to act within prescribed financial limits without its approval; but there remains a large and undefined area in which the Principal Finance Officer must use his discretion. His relations with the Treasury are necessarily a good deal closer than those of his colleagues, and his contacts more frequent. A close and friendly relationship with Treasury officials is essential, and the less formal this is the better the system will work.

The Principal Finance Officer is usually assisted by quite a small number of other Administrative Class officers, Assistant Secretaries and Principals. Sometimes the finance division is organised in sections, each under an Administrative Class officer, which reflect the administrative organisation of the Department as the Treasury reflects the whole organisation of the central administration. Sometimes financial responsibility is pushed down to the Administrative Class officials in charge of particular services. In all cases the key points in financial policy are held by members of the Administrative Class, and it is the business of the Principal Finance Officer to feel the movement of the situation and to advise the Accounting Officer and the Minister himself.

He also has a rather special relation to the Principal Establishments Officer, which is best illustrated by describing the organisation of the Treasury itself.

(iv) *The Treasury*

Something was said in Chapter 4 to indicate the position of the Establishments Divisions within the Treasury. It is now necessary to set these in relation to the organisation as a whole. There is a continuous process of reorganisation, and the Department has not yet fully adapted itself to the changes made at the top on the retirement of Sir Edward Bridges and Sir Bernard Gilbert in October 1956; but the main framework is not likely to be altered as it is bound up with the working of the system as a whole.

The Treasury's Ministers are: the First Lord, who is now always Prime Minister; the Chancellor of the Exchequer, who is Second Lord and for most purposes the working head of the Department; a Parliamentary Secretary, who is the government's Chief Whip, is still called colloquially by the traditional title of 'Patronage Secretary' and who takes no part in the ordinary business of the

ACCOUNTING AND FINANCIAL CONTROL

office[1]; the Financial Secretary and the Economic Secretary, whose duties will be referred to in passing later; and five junior Lords, who are junior government Whips and, together with the First and Second Lords, constitute the Lords Commissioners who (in form) exercise the powers of the Lord High Treasurer. The junior Lords have no official business in the office nowadays except to sign their names when properly requested to do so.

The official heads of the Department are now two Permanent Secretaries of the Treasury, ranking one rung above other Permanent Secretaries, of whom there are three in the Treasury. As has been explained, one of the Secretaries is Head of the Home Civil Service and Secretary to the Cabinet; in these capacities he has much business to do with the Prime Minister directly, but his Treasury business is not clearly marked off from other Treasury business, as will be seen from the description below. He is assisted by two officials: a Second Secretary ranking as Permanent Secretary in charge of the Establishments and Machinery of Government business in the Treasury, and a Deputy Secretary to the Cabinet who holds the same rank as a Third Secretary in the Treasury. The other Secretary of the Treasury works almost entirely for the Chancellor of the Exchequer; he is assisted by two officials ranking as Permanent Secretary, each in charge of a large block of financial and economic business.

At the next level there are at present six groups of divisions, each under a Third Secretary, with the rank of Deputy Secretary. In addition there is an Economic Section directed by the Economic Adviser to the government, whose standing is about equivalent to (or a little above) that of a Third Secretary, and an Economic Information Division (under a Third Secretary) which is the Treasury's own public relations branch.

We have already dealt in Chapter 4 with the various *Establishments Divisions*. These are grouped under a Third Secretary, who is also Establishments Officer for the Treasury itself. Associated with these divisions under the same Second Secretary are the O. & M. Division, the Training and Education Division, and the Treasury Medical Service, which gives professional advice to most Departments on the medical aspects of the layout of buildings and of conditions of work, and on individual cases of sick leave, retirement or transfer for reasons of health, and suitability for foreign service.

---

[1] The Prime Minister, principally in his capacity as First Lord of the Treasury, is still responsible for a great deal of 'patronage', ranging from the appointment of Archbishops and Lords of Appeal to Regius Professors and the incumbents of small livings. There is now a separate official in the Prime Minister's private office, the Secretary for Appointments, who looks after such business; so far as is known, he is not guided by the Patronage Secretary of the Treasury.

The Establishments Divisions are closely associated in the control of Departmental expenditure with two other groups of divisions, the *Supply Divisions* and the *Mixed Supply and Establishments Divisions*. The former deal with expenditure on social services, on trade and industry, on defence, and on agriculture, fisheries, and food, *except* for expenditure on staff, which is handled by two Establishments Divisions, Establishments (Departmental) and Defence (Personnel). The latter (which were mentioned in Chapter 4) deal with *all* questions of expenditure, *including* staff, for three groups of Departments: 'Government and Allied Services' (which includes the Post Office and other 'common service' Departments); 'Imperial and Foreign' (including besides the Foreign Office, Colonial Office, and Commonwealth Relations Office, the British Council, colonial development, and international organisations); and 'Law and Order' (the Home Office, the Law Departments, and some others).

This rather intricate division of responsibilities is of long standing, and is perhaps not very likely to be upset; it may be confusing to students, but it serves a purpose by promoting the interlocking of business within the Treasury. So long as it exists there can be no 'clean cut' between the responsibilities of the two Secretaries of the Treasury. The Head of the Home Civil Service is directly responsible for the Establishments Divisions; but these cannot be separated in operation from the Supply Divisions and the Mixed Supply and Establishments Divisions; and these in turn cannot be separated from the *Home Finance* Divisions.

Home Finance includes two important divisions. The first of these is responsible, in liaison with the Revenue Departments, for the revenue side of the Budget, and also for general advice on taxation policy. The same division is the main channel for dealing with the Bank of England on matters of currency and banking and for the day-to-day decisions about government operations in the money market. The second division is responsible for the control of capital investment, which involves liaison with the Bank of England, the City of London, and the Capital Issues Committee about capital issues, and (through the Investment Programmes Committee) with each Department about the investment programmes of the industries and public bodies in its sphere.

The Home Finance group also includes the Accounts Branch, not to be confused with the Treasury Officers of Accounts. The former is in two sections: one of these is the Treasury's own finance division, prepares the Estimates for which the Treasury is responsible (about twenty of them), and does the routine accounting business of the Department; the other deals with the Pay Office and the Exchequer

ACCOUNTING AND FINANCIAL CONTROL 315

Office about issues from the Exchequer (described above) and prepares the daily balance sheet of Exchequer transactions. It also audits the accounts of the Civil List and (as already explained) the accounts of the Exchequer and Audit Department.

Also in this group are the two Treasury Officers of Accounts, and the Estimate Clerk, a Principal who is responsible for the mechanics of gathering the Estimates and Supplementary Estimates from all the Civil and Revenue Departments at the proper time, and for advising them and other Treasury divisions on Estimates procedure generally; he also watches the Treasury's interest in all Public and Private Bills and in the proceedings of the Statutory Instruments Committee.

Another narrow line separates this group of divisions from the sphere of the *Overseas Finance Group* and the *Economic Co-ordination Group*. The former deals with exchange control, import and export policies, the balance of payments, mutual aid, problems of Commonwealth financial and economic policy, international financial statistics, and related matters. Some of the divisions in this group are organised on the basis of function, others by territory (e.g. Europe west of the Iron Curtain, the Commonwealth). The Economic Co-ordination group has perhaps been more subject to the vicissitudes of politics and of economic crises than any other part of the organisation. At present (1957) its main constituent is a section known as the Home and Overseas Planning Staff. This is a descendant of the Central Economic Planning Staff, which was set up by the Labour government in July 1947 (we refer to this again in Chapter 19). It was originally headed by Sir Edwin Plowden, a business man with wartime experience of central administration, who was brought back into government service at a salary higher than that of the Permanent Secretary of the Treasury. Sir Edwin was given the designation of Chief Planning Officer, and at first he reported to the Lord President of the Council. When Sir Stafford Cripps became Minister for Economic Affairs (see Chapter 19, p. 348) in September 1947, he assumed responsibility for the Central Economic Planning Staff, and he took this responsibility with him to the Treasury a few weeks later when he succeeded Mr. Dalton as Chancellor of the Exchequer. When Sir Edwin Plowden left government service in 1953 the post of Chief Planning Officer was abolished, and special responsibility for economic co-ordination was given to Sir Bernard Gilbert, a Second Secretary at the Treasury, who acted as Deputy to the Permanent Secretary in the field of economic and financial affairs. A little later the Central Economic Planning Staff was renamed the Home and Overseas Planning Staff.

It consists of two main sections, each under an Under Secretary:

one of these is particularly concerned with problems of investment and of the economic effects of the defence programme, the other with more general problems, in particular the problems of the balance of payments. There is also a small 'Overseas Co-ordinating Section', which is primarily the secretariat of two inter-departmental committees, one dealing with commercial and financial negotiations, the other with N.A.T.O., O.E.E.C., and E.C.E.

The Economic Adviser to the government moved from the Cabinet Office to the Treasury in 1953; and brought with him the *Economic Section*, a group of professional economists without administrative responsibility who work closely with the Economic Co-ordination group.

Outside these groups there are a number of offices of a specialised kind: the Ceremonial Officer, who assists the Head of the Home Civil Service in advising the Prime Minister about the award of honours and decorations, and who is Secretary to the Political Honours Scrutiny Committee; and the Government Hospitality Fund Office, a small 'common service' Department which manages the fund set aside for the entertainment of foreign guests.

These complete the organisation of the Treasury itself, but within its orbit are a number of offices (some of great importance) for which it prepares Estimates and which are included in its Vote: the Cabinet Office, the Office of the Lord President, the Office of Parliamentary Counsel, the University Grants Committee, and the Capital Issues Committee; and some which present their own Estimates, in particular the two great Revenue Boards, the Civil Service Commission, and the Central Land Board and War Damage Commission.

In spite of its span of influence the Treasury is not a large Department: the main administrative divisions employ about 1,100 and various specialist sections add about 120 more, half of whom are in the O. & M. Division. These figures are somewhat misleading, however, as the total includes about 170 members of the Administrative Class, with a high proportion of 'top brass'. Numbers have increased a good deal since 1939, and the Treasury is no longer under one roof. A nucleus remains in the rambling office which extends from Soane's frontage on Whitehall to Kent's Treasury, built on the Cock-Pit site, and on through devious corridors to Nos. 10 and 11 Downing Street. But the most important base now is in the New Public Offices in Great George Street, which also house the Cabinet Office and the Ministry of Defence.

In spite of this expansion the Department retains a certain atmosphere of intimacy and informality, of casual rather than bureaucratic efficiency. Each division is relatively small, the work of divisions is closely related, many of the staff have worked together for years through many vicissitudes and through many fashions in economic and political theory. Additional staff are obtained partly by secondment from other Departments, partly from new entrants into the Administrative Class. Apart from retirement, there are some who leave the Treasury for high appointments in business or in other Departments, but the annual turn-over of staff is quite small. It was at one time, during Sir Warren Fisher's reign, felt in the Service that the best route to promotion lay through the Treasury; but in recent years Treasury men have certainly not had so high a share of top posts as to create ill-feeling. The 23 most important Departments (including the Cabinet Office) employed, at the beginning of 1956, 24 Permanent Secretaries (the Ministry of Supply then had 2) and 40 Deputy Secretaries. Of these, 6 Permanent Secretaries and 4 Deputy Secretaries had served in the Treasury at some time during their careers.

Since the 'Keynesian revolution', formally accepted by the Treasury in Sir Kingsley Wood's speech introducing the Budget for 1941, the Treasury has become a 'planning' Department, not merely a 'finance' Department. Economic planning in Britain depends largely on the structure and functions of the Treasury, and on the attitudes and capacity of its officials. Many other factors are involved, such as political influences shaping the climate of opinion, the effectiveness or otherwise of the organisation of other Departments, the pressure exercised by competing groups of interests through various channels; but the Treasury stands at the centre of things, responding to the whole range of factors involved, and perhaps to a limited extent controlling some of them. These modern functions have been grafted on to a much more ancient stock, and we believe that the administrative aspects of central planning in time of peace are only intelligible in relation to the annual cycle of financial business. This was largely created in the latter part of the nineteenth century, when the dominant theory of Treasury business was that of 'the saving of candle-ends'; this theory has gone for ever, but perhaps it tends even now to swing the mind of the Treasury away from considerations of 'planning' to considerations of finance. But such effectiveness as the Treasury possesses as a planning organisation depends on the existence of this regular, traditional framework of business. Much of it is routine business, but the effect of rules for formal control is to bring Treasury officials into continuous contact with the officials of other Departments throughout the year, and also to weld together the Treasury itself into a single organisation, in spite of its vast range of interests. Virtually every division in the Treasury is concerned in the preparation of the Budget and in the continuous process of financial negotiation which lies behind it. 'Policy', as has been said, 'is secreted in the interstices of routine.'

4. The Financial Cycle and the Process of Control

We therefore make no apology for basing our account on the formal cycle of business, using as an example the financial year 1954-55. The Estimates come to the House of Commons in February; in 1954 they were presented as follows:

Air Estimates	9 February 1954
Navy Estimates	10 February 1954
Army Estimates	11 February 1954
Ministry of Defence Estimates	15 February 1954
Civil Estimates and Estimates for the Revenue Departments	23 February 1954

Since the Estimates are not embodied in a statute until the Appropriation Act is passed four months after the beginning of the financial year, Parliament must authorise the issue of a provisional sum from the Consolidated Fund to cover interim expenditure. This it does in a Consolidated Fund Act which is passed just before the new financial year begins (in this case it was 26 March 1954), and this Act also authorises sums to cover Supplementary Estimates for the financial year just ending (in this case for 1953-54). In some (calendar) years more than one Consolidated Fund Act may be required, but in that year there was only one.

The next stage is the Budget, which the Chancellor of the Exchequer normally introduces in April (in that year Budget Day was 6 April), and which is the formal presentation of his proposals for changes in taxation for the coming year and for the renewal of taxes, such as income tax, which must be annually approved. To prevent tax evasion, all but one of the Budget Resolutions are passed immediately the Chancellor finishes his speech: the exception ('That it is expedient to alter the law relating to the National Debt') is adjourned to keep the debate open on subsequent days (in this case, 7, 8, and 12 April).

The Budget proposals are provisional until the Finance Bill receives the Royal Assent in July (30 July 1954), just as Supply is not fully granted until the passage of the Appropriation Bill in the same month (30 July 1954). The Finance Act enacts the details of the

ACCOUNTING AND FINANCIAL CONTROL

Budget Resolutions, the Appropriation Act authorises the total sums to be granted to each Department.

Meanwhile, the Finance Accounts for the financial year just ended (1953-54), showing the details of issues and receipts of the Consolidated Fund, are presented to the House of Commons by the Treasury (21 June 1954). These Accounts do not show how the money issued has been used, and Departments are at this stage completing the making up of their Appropriation Accounts (for 1953-54), a long job which is never completed for all Departments until near the end of the calendar year. Before the work is finished the Treasury calls (on 1 October 1954) for the Estimates for the next financial year (in this case for 1955-56).

The completed Appropriation Accounts, together with the reports which the Comptroller and Auditor-General makes on them, are presented to the House, usually during the period from November to January: the dates for those of the financial year 1953-54 were:

Appropriation Accounts of Revenue Departments	8 November 1954
Trading Accounts	16 November 1954
Commercial Accounts of Post Office	22 November 1954
Civil Appropriation Accounts	16 December 1954
Ministry of Defence Appropriation Accounts	20 December 1954
Navy Appropriation Accounts	27 January 1955
Air Force Appropriation Accounts	27 January 1955
Army Appropriation Accounts	1 February 1955

The Public Accounts Committee begins its examination of these Accounts soon after they are laid before the House of Commons (usually about December) and continues its work until the following July. Thus the Committee began to examine the accounts for 1953-54 in December 1954, and finished on 21 July 1955. It issued three Reports on the Accounts: on 21 June, 30 June, and 17 November 1955.

Meanwhile, Supplementary Estimates for the year 1954-55 were coming in during the last months of 1954 and the first months of 1955, and issues from the Consolidated Fund for these, and a provisional sum for the public service in 1955-56, were authorised by the Consolidated Fund Act, 1955 (March 1955), thus completing the cycle.

The work of the Treasury is of extreme importance in four stages of this cycle, with which we will now deal in turn: Estimates, the

Budget, running control during the year, accounting at the end of the year.

(i) *The Estimates*

The printed Estimates are presented to Parliament in six volumes: for the Army, the Navy, the Air Force, the Ministry of Defence, the Revenue Departments, and the Civil Estimates (i.e. all other Departments). The Civil Estimates are at present divided into ten 'Classes' grouped according to their subject matter. The classification is rough and ready; the arrangement changes as Departments are amalgamated or divided; and it is revised and simplified occasionally, on the initiative of the Treasury or of the Departments themselves or at the request of the Estimates Committee.

The Department's Estimate, approved in its final form by the Treasury and later embodied in the Appropriation Act, is the 'budget' of the Department for the coming year. Part I of the Estimate (or 'Vote' as it becomes after enactment by Parliament) provides the statutory description of the purposes for which supply is granted: this is the 'Ambit' of the Vote (a Department may have several Votes). The 'Ambit' is usually very widely drawn, for example: 'Estimate of the amount required in the year ending 31 March 1955 for the salaries and expenses of the Ministry of Transport and Civil Aviation, including the salaries and expenses of the Coastguard, the Transport and Transport Arbitration Tribunals, and the Air Transport Advisory Council, and sundry other services: Seven million, one hundred and ninety-three thousand pounds.'

The 'Ambit' is explained in much greater detail in Parts II and III of the Vote, which have no legal force. Part III is purely for the information of Parliament; Part II details the sub-heads under which the Treasury (acting under the authority of Sec. 23 of the Exchquer and Audit Departments Act, 1866) requires Departments to account for expenditure. The Estimates were first divided into sub-heads in 1867 on the recommendation of the Public Accounts Committee, when it was agreed that they should 'correspond with the divisions in the departmental ledgers'.

The sub-heads are arranged according to the subject or nature of the expenditure (e.g. Salaries, Works, Purchase of Materials, etc.) and not according to its object or purpose (e.g. Housing, Research, Information). The system is simple to operate, but it is not easy to deduce from it the actual cost of a particular 'object' of expenditure, especially when (as is frequently the case) the services of more than one Department are needed to achieve it. For this reason the Departments sometimes provide 'Appendices' to the Estimates (where these are specifically requested by the Estimates Committee) showing the expenditure on particular objects.

Treasury control of the Estimates is traditional (though it was not until 1861 that the House of Commons required that the Estimates of all Departments should be submitted to the Treasury before being presented to Parliament). This tradition is reinforced by the Exchequer and Audit Departments Act, 1866, which gives the Treasury the power to prescribe the form of the Appropriation Accounts. The Estimate has been called 'the precursor and foundation of the Account': it must be in the same form as the Account if there is to be proper accountability to Parliament. A Treasury Minute of 1885 laid it down formally that no changes are to be made in the form of the Estimates without Treasury consent. It is usual for the Treasury to consult the Public Accounts Committee before authorising changes, since the Committee is ultimately responsible to the House of Commons for matters of audit. As a matter of courtesy it may also ask the opinion of the Estimates Committee, which is empowered by its terms of reference (*inter alia*) 'to suggest the form in which the Estimates shall be presented'.

It follows from the form of the Appropriation Accounts (and this in turn follows from the nature of Parliamentary control over issues from the Exchequer) that the Estimates are made up in what has been rudely called 'the penny exercise-book system' of accounting. They are designed to show the estimated cash payments of Departments during the year. No attempt is made to assess the value of assets and liabilities at the beginning and end of the period and to bring the difference into account; nor to distinguish between capital investment and recurrent annual expenditure. Services rendered free by one Department to another ('Allied Services') are included (as we have seen, Chapter 17) in the Estimates of the former and not of the latter, though the latter now append a rough assessment for the information of the House of Commons. The result of this is that the Estimates are not in themselves of much use for discussion of the 'true' or 'economic' cost of government services.

Procedure is formally initiated by Notes sent out to Departments by the Estimates Clerk at the Treasury over the signature of the Financial Secretary. These Notes (which, as we have seen, go out on 1 October) require, in a rather menacing way, the submission of Estimates by about 1 December. The main work on Estimates within the Departments is done in October and November each year, but this brings to a conclusion much preparatory work begun long before the Treasury Note is received. The total Estimate is built up by the finance division through discussion and negotiation within the

x

Department; the finance division is responsible for most of the actual figures, but the discussion involves a review of the Department's policy and prospects up to a date eighteen months or two years ahead. In October and November 1954 the Department settles provisionally what it hopes to do up to the end of March 1956. There is not at this stage formal consultation with the Treasury, but many items have a long previous history, and it is for the Principal Finance Officer to advise his colleagues in the light of past experience of Treasury practice.

The rules of the game are well understood, though they are not all written down. The Treasury acts by the known policy of the government of the day, and in particular by the policy of its own Minister, the Chancellor of the Exchequer. The Departments know that there are some matters on which it is useless to proceed beyond a certain point until the Treasury has been consulted. Matters are discussed informally between Departmental officials and their opposite numbers in the Treasury and are agreed before any formal action is taken. Mistakes do occur, but the wise Departmental official abides by the rule (expressed in a Treasury Minute of 1886 and many times repeated) that a Department should consult the Treasury whenever it is in doubt.

The final draft Estimates begin to reach the Treasury about the middle of November, and 'Estimates Time' lasts from then till about the middle of February, when all the Estimates have been agreed by the Chancellor of the Exchequer, and formally approved by the Cabinet. They are then presented to Parliament (together with a Financial Memorandum) by the Financial Secretary to the Treasury, and are printed as House of Commons Sessional Papers. This is a busy time for the Treasury divisions concerned, but it does not involve in practice a fresh scrutiny of every item each year. In the first place, much expenditure follows almost automatically from continuing discussions about policy (for instance on such matters as National Insurance rates), and secondly there are very many items which have been specifically approved by the Treasury in advance of the Estimates procedure.

The list of items which require specific Treasury sanction is long, and it has been growing with the years: the basic document is a Treasury Minute of 1868, which (like most such documents in British history) gives formal expression to what was even then longstanding practice. This Minute states that 'sanction should be required for any increase of establishment, of salary, or of cost of a service, or for any additional works or new services which have not been specifically provided for in the grants of Parliament'.

'Increases in establishment' are now a matter in which the Departments possess considerable discretion. Until 1939, Treasury authority was required for the employment of every additional clerk. Current practice (based on a Treasury Circular of 29 July 1949) is that the Treasury fixes 'ceilings' at six-monthly intervals for each grade of staff, and sometimes for particular sections of a Department. These are maxima which the Department cannot exceed without approval, but within these limits Principal Establishments Officers are free to determine their own staffing requirements. Salaries and gradings are also matters of great interest to the Treasury, but its authority is now exercised, as we have seen in Chapter 9, through its central position in the machinery of joint negotiation.

In principle, specific Treasury approval must now be sought for the following: (i) all new projects, whether or not they involve an increase in the total expenditure of a Department; (ii) all proposals to increase expenditure on projects which the Treasury has already approved; (iii) long-term projects which commit the government to expenditure over a period of years; and (iv) projects presenting particular features of novelty and difficulty. These rules are modified by the current practice of delegating authority to the Departments to incur expenditure without approval on certain specified types of project up to a fixed maximum.

Treasury approval of Estimates, or of specific proposals outside them, does not relieve the Department's Accounting Officer of his responsibility. There have been occasions, such as the inception of the National Health Service, when it has been decided as a matter of policy to go ahead, even though accurate estimating was at first impossible. There has also been difficulty about the cost of capital projects during a period of inflation, when price changes often make even good estimates obsolete very quickly. The Accounting Officer has to face cross-examination by the Public Accounts Committee on matters of this kind, which are outside his effective control, as well as on matters of bad estimating and weak supervision.

The Estimates as approved by the Treasury are formally sanctioned by the House of Commons by resolutions in Committee of Supply, but the House now makes no attempt to scrutinise them in detail: it uses 'Supply Days' (except those on which Supplementary Estimates and Excess Votes are under consideration) to debate general issues. The debates on the Estimates for 1954-55 which took place during March 1954 dealt, for example, with the general industrial situation, the growing of crops on airfields, civil aviation, National Service, and conditions in the Suez Canal Zone. The twenty-six days allotted for 'Supply' each Session begin before the Estimates for the financial year are presented (often in November of the preceding calendar year) and do not end until after the financial year has begun (they must finish by 5 August). On the last two Supply days large numbers of Estimates are voted without any debate at all, and Members spend several hours in tramping through the Lobbies.

The Estimates Committee of the House (further referred to in Chapter 20) is not much better equipped than the House itself for a detailed scrutiny of all Supply; but it succeeds each year in turning a beam of light on perhaps a dozen major items of expenditure, which it investigates in some detail (in the four Sessions 1946-49, for instance, it presented forty-six Reports).

(ii) *The Budget*

The work of controlling the Estimates does not proceed in isolation from the other work of the Treasury. It is for the Chancellor of the Exchequer to put before the Committee of Ways and Means in April his plans for finding the money during the ensuing year. In practice, discussion of the relation between revenue and expenditure goes on continuously throughout the year, and in particular during the time when Estimates are being compiled. The Treasury's views about revenue are based partly on current reports about the trends of expenditure and the out-turn of taxes, partly on the political and economic climate of the time. If policy calls for reduction of taxation and borrowing (or the refusal of increases in time of inflation), this is reflected at once in the Treasury's attitude to Estimates. It may be expressed by a direct instruction to Departments that no additional funds will be provided during the ensuing year even for increases in expenditure (such as salary increases) which are outside their control, or by an explicit demand for an x per cent. cut all round. Both steps have the effect of throwing back upon Departments the onus of determining where to cut their own services; and there will follow a period of internal stress and of pressure for special exemptions, perhaps backed by interest groups dependent on the Department concerned.

The process of 'balancing the Budget' is thus a continuous one: both sides of the account are present to the collective mind of the Treasury throughout the year. There are, however, decisions of special importance to be taken about how the sum required is to be raised; how it is to be shared between borrowing and taxation, between different forms of borrowing, and between different forms of taxation. In these matters there is no clear line between the Treasury's responsibility for the financial operations of the central administration and its responsibility for the management of the national economy as a whole.

The Treasury's line of action was fairly clear so long as economic orthodoxy laid it down that its main obligations were to keep taxes low, and to shift the burden as far as possible from indirect to direct taxation. But this fortress is now in ruins, destroyed, first, by the use of progressive taxation from about the 1890s as an instrument for the redistribution of income between individuals; secondly, by the reintroduction of tariffs in the 1920s and 1930s, which meant that decisions about taxation became decisions to encourage or not to encourage particular industries, as they had not been since the 1840s; and, thirdly, by Keynesian economics and the experience of the Second World War, which emphasised in theory and practice the possibility and limits of direct planning of the economy by the central administration. There have been minor shifts from year to year in fashions and attitudes about these matters, and it is impossible to say that central administration has yet evolved a satisfactory way of handling them. But it is common ground that the traditional form of government accounts is almost useless as a basis for general discussion about the management of the economy, and since 1941 a number of new documents have established themselves as part of the annual cycle of discussion.

These are, first, the National Income White Paper, first issued in 1941, and prepared by the Central Statistical Office, which is generally published at the end of March, and now contains only brief 'preliminary' estimates of national income and expenditure over the past five or six years; secondly, the National Income Blue Book, which has since 1953 covered the same ground in much greater detail and is published later in the year (usually in August); thirdly, the annual Economic Survey, which appears at the same time as the White Paper (it was first published in 1947 and attempted to lay down general lines of economic development for the coming year; now it merely reviews the progress of the economy over the past year in the light of the statistics available up to that time); and fourthly, the Balance of Payments White Paper, first issued in 1948, which deals with the external financial position. These documents, which are technical in form and are generally very cautiously expressed, are the visible part of a huge iceberg of discussion, involving the Home Finance, Overseas Finance, and Economic Co-ordination groups of Treasury officials, as well as the Economic Section, the Revenue Departments, and economic staffs in other Departments. All this discussion feeds into the process of preparation for the Budget, which is now both a financial plan and an economic plan for the ensuing year.

After the Budget follow the Budget Resolutions and other formalities to which we have already referred. There is nothing in any of these which involves discussion of policy.

(iii) *Running Control*

The Budget is the most dramatic event of the financial year, but it is easy to recognise that modern Budgets are merely points in a continuous process. The Chancellor attempts to halt the stream of events for a moment, so that he can present a static picture of interrelated factors and find firm ground for decisions about policy; but events move so fast that Budgets may become out of date while they are being discussed. For administrative reasons taxation policy cannot be altered on short notice, and a second 'Budget' is so inconvenient that it is introduced only as a sign of crisis. But in its control of Departmental expenditure and of the money market a government can move much more freely, so that day-to-day decisions throughout the year are at least as important as the formal resolutions put to the Committee of Supply and the Committee of Ways and Means.

The Treasury exercises running control in three ways: by calling on each Department for periodic reports on the progress of its expenditure; through its power to grant or withhold *virement* (that is, authority to spend savings on one sub-head on objects included in another sub-head: or, in the case of the Defence Departments only, transfer between Votes); and by its control over cash advances to Departments and its power to 'short-issue'. These formal devices are important, but not so important as the informal contacts between Treasury officials and their 'opposite numbers' in the Departments, since these enable them to keep in constant touch with the way in which things are going.

Periodic returns of particular classes of expenditure (for example, capital works) must be provided, and the Departmental finance divisions supply monthly and three-monthly forecasts of their total requirements. Whenever it appears probable that expenditure on a sub-head may be exceeded, the Department is expected to provide advance warning and to apply to the Treasury for authority for the excess.

If the excess is detected soon enough, the Treasury may either agree to *virement*, or tell the Department to cut its expenditure on certain items in the sub-head, or allow the Department to continue operating on the understanding that it will have to go to Parliament for a Supplementary Estimate. The number of formal refusals of *virement* in a year is small, but the Treasury tries to prevent the

ACCOUNTING AND FINANCIAL CONTROL

excess if it can. In any case, Departments understand that authority for *virement* is not given automatically, and refusal means that a Supplementary Estimate must be sought. Supplementaries are not popular, for they reflect upon the Department's financial administration. There are some occasions, however, when they cannot be avoided: for instance, when a new service is begun which is not within the Ambit of the Vote (for this is the only way in which a new sub-head can be opened).

The Treasury's reserve power to refuse *virement* between sub-heads is a check on overspending, and it encourages Departments to watch carefully for potential excesses. But the power has never been expressly granted by Parliament: it is regarded as a necessary consequence of Appropriation procedure, and it has traditionally been supported by the Public Accounts Committee, which may nevertheless criticise its use in particular instances. The Comptroller and Auditor-General has formal authority to call upon the Department to show that Treasury approval has been obtained, and the existence of this power (though it is rarely exercised) is a further reinforcement of Treasury control.

There is no power of *virement* between the Votes of Civil Departments, and if a Vote is likely to be exceeded a Supplementary Estimate must be put in. The annual appropriation Act authorises *virement* between the Votes of a Defence Department, but the total sum provided for in all the Department's Votes must not be exceeded. Treasury sanction of *virement* between Votes is provisional and must be confirmed by Parliament.

Excesses on Votes rarely occur and are regarded as a grave financial crime when they do, for Supplementary Estimates should have been presented. An Excess Vote is considered by the Public Accounts Committee and is reported to the House of Commons. A Department is forbidden to avoid an Excess Vote by postponing payments due (though this has happened), but is encouraged to avoid it by putting off commitments to further expenditure if this is possible.

Finally, as we saw earlier in this chapter, Treasury authority is required for cash advances made to Departments by the Paymaster-General, and these are carefully related to the needs of the Department from month to month, so that a Department is never in possession of a larger balance than is absolutely necessary. In this (almost literal) sense the Treasury does hold the purse-strings, for the Parliamentary grant vests in the Treasury and not in the Department, and may be spent only at the Treasury's discretion.

(iv) *Framing of Accounts and Audit*

As soon as possible after the end of the financial year the Departmental finance division must close its books and make up the Appropriation Account. This must correspond in form to Part II of the Estimate: that is, the money must be accounted for under the sub-heads of the Parliamentary grant, and these (as we have seen) must correspond to 'the divisions in the departmental ledgers'. The Account, as presented to Parliament, shows the total grant under each sub-head with any Supplementaries, the total expenditure, the amount by which the expenditure exceeds or falls short of the grant, and the reasons for the difference. The Account is signed by the Accounting Officer, is countersigned by the Comptroller and Auditor-General, and is presented to Parliament with the Comptroller and Auditor-General's Report. It is then examined, and if necessary reported on, by the Public Accounts Committee, following the timetable already described.

The form of the Appropriation Account largely determines the forms and procedures of government accounting generally. The accounts are designed to show how the payments actually made by a Department accord with the cash grants authorised by Parliament for the year, yet they ought, ideally, to serve a number of other purposes. They ought to provide, in the words of the Committee on the Form of the Government Accounts,[1] 'a comprehensive and comprehensible statement of the volume and variety of all the operations of the central administration'; they ought to provide Parliament and the public with the essential facts about the state of the national finances; they should provide the raw material for an expert assessment of current and future economic trends; they should enable Parliament, the Treasury, and the Departments to judge whether any particular service is being provided with maximum economy and efficiency; and, finally, they should provide a guide to the formulation of policy. These are all ends which the most modern commercial accounting forms and procedures are designed to secure; but they cannot be attained so long as the accounts are framed only on a cash basis.

There has been much criticism of the government accounts on these grounds, and a number of proposals for alternative forms have been put forward. Some have been tried and have broken down, usually because of the complexity and labour of the process of keeping the accounts in two separate forms, one for Parliamentary control, the other for purposes of business management. Neverthe-

---

[1] Cmd. 7969, 1950.

ACCOUNTING AND FINANCIAL CONTROL 329

less, the Post Office and certain other Departments which run large commercial services do provide separate Trading Accounts. Elsewhere, no solution has been found except to put large blocks of public business entirely outside the Parliamentary system of accounting, by devices such as the use of public corporations and other independent bodies.

Once the accounts are made up they are formally ready for audit, but in practice (since it is carried on continuously) the audit is almost complete when the financial year ends. The audit has three objects. First, there is the normal accounting audit, which is largely a matter of arithmetical checking. All large Departments have a system of internal audit, and these checks may by statute be accepted by the Comptroller and Auditor-General at his discretion. His auditors make a careful examination of the books, but do not follow matters up in detail unless they notice something unusual or irregular. Secondly, the auditors look for instances of waste and extravagance, and (as explained) they proceed by test checks. Thirdly, the audit is a test of legality: a scrutiny to ascertain whether any monies have been applied contrary to the expressed intentions of Parliament, whether (in the Comptroller and Auditor-General's judgement) the Treasury has exercised *virement* correctly, whether expenditure falls within the Ambit of the Vote, and so on.

The Comptroller and Auditor-General cannot (as can his counterpart in the United States) disallow expenditure, nor sanction it before it is made. The power of disallowance (involving 'surcharge' of those responsible) is reserved to Parliament; it is rarely exercised in practice, but the House of Commons through the Public Accounts Committee may show disapproval in other ways.

Having completed his audit, the Comptroller and Auditor-General certifies the Accounts correct (subject to any comments he has to make) and prepares his Reports, which then form the basis on which the Public Accounts Committee proceeds. The Committee's programme is worked out by its Chairman in conjunction with the Comptroller and Auditor-General. Most of the Accounts are passed without comment; but each year a number are selected for detailed examination, including some of those on which the Comptroller and Auditor-General has reported adversely.

The Accounting Officer, supported by his Principal Finance Officer and other officials, appears to give evidence. One or both of the Treasury Officers of Accounts attend with the Comptroller and Auditor-General, but they are normally silent unless particular points are referred to them. In due course the Committee makes its Report, which is then published together with the Minutes of

Evidence. The Treasury replies formally to most of the Committee's comments in a series of Treasury Minutes, which are prepared by the Treasury Officers of Accounts, and these are also published. The Committee Reports and Treasury Minutes constitute a large volume of 'case law', and the Epitomes which are published from time to time are the technical handbooks of financial procedure.

5. The Characteristics of the System

Our description has contained much comment, and it is unnecessary to do more than summarise this in conclusion.

First, it is relatively easy to see in this sphere the justification for a division of the general service classes into two main levels, administrative and executive. There are two rather different spheres of financial procedure: the executive, which is concerned mainly with the form of accounts, and the administrative, which is concerned mainly with their content. The distinction is not absolute (for instance, criticism by the Comptroller and Auditor-General and his executive staff often comes close to matters of policy), but part of the strength of the system is that it breeds its own race of semi-professional public accountants. This 'class' (though it does not officially exist as a class) interlocks throughout the administration, and sets for itself and others very high standards of care and integrity. Promotion from it to the administrative level is not frequent enough even now to constitute a career.

Secondly, the form of the accounts is very well adapted to serve financial control on behalf of Parliament at this level. It is not so well adapted either for control of internal efficiency or for the assessment of alternatives at the level of policy. Much thought has been spent on this problem, but it has been impossible to propose seriously either that more sophisticated accounting methods should replace the forms hallowed by constitutional practice, or that accounts should (as a general practice) be kept twice over, in different forms for different purposes. The National Income White Paper, the Economic Survey, and other such documents only touch the fringes of the problem.

Thirdly, in spite of its limitations as a device for measurement, the system serves extremely well as a device for administrative liaison. The procedure enforces continuous informal contact between Departments and the Treasury; yet the Treasury even now is small enough to have a 'collective mind' which can to some extent grasp the administration as a whole and judge considerations of revenue and of economic policy at the same time as considerations of expenditure. There is, however, an important reservation. There are a good many important matters (for instance, in foreign policy and colonial policy) which do not involve the Treasury in their early stages because no immediate expenditure is involved. Thus the Treasury may be dragged along with decisions in which it did not participate, and in conditions of war or extreme crisis its position as co-ordinator is weakened. This is indicated by the fact that long-term financial planning through the Estimates then becomes impossible; issues from the Consolidated Fund are authorised by Votes of Credit, without detailed appropriation; the machinery of audit survives, but forward planning is carried out only in physical terms with no effective financial 'yardstick'. These limitations are important; but in normal times the Treasury is better placed than is any other Department to judge what is 'imperative' (it was a former Permanent Secretary of the Treasury, Lord Welby, who enunciated the greatest of all administrative platitudes or proverbs, 'the imperative ought to have preference'), because it is at the meeting-place of many different lines of communication, and no adequate alternative has been found to replace this system when it is pushed aside by the exigencies of war. It was partly because of the extreme convenience of the old procedure that the Treasury gradually regained after 1945 much of the influence which it lost in the period of 'physical planning'.

Fourthly, in spite of this, the Treasury is not in any constitutional sense the 'superior' of other Departments. Procedure is devised so far as possible to throw back upon Departments the responsibility for considering the financial aspects of policy, for adjusting their own priorities, for securing internal efficiency, and for defending themselves against criticism in the House of Commons and its Committees. This perhaps gives the 'Treasury mind' a touch of remoteness from daily reality, and certainly does not add to its popularity within the Service: but it is hard to see how so much could be achieved in any other way without inducing congestion at the centre.

Finally, the ultimate strength of the system is that behind the Treasury stand the House of Commons and the Cabinet. So far as policy is concerned, the main role of the Commons is to support the Cabinet; but its attitudes and procedure continue to be of great importance in enforcing strictness of control below the level of policy, and much depends on this. The Cabinet and its committees are expected to take final responsibility for the broadest decisions of policy, and the Treasury is one of the main channels through which matters reach them for decision. From about 1920 until 1939 there was a Cabinet instruction, apparently renewed by successive

Cabinets, that no proposal involving finance should be circulated without the Chancellor's prior sanction. This has now been replaced by a general instruction that no proposal affecting more than one Department shall be submitted to the Cabinet until it has been thoroughly discussed at the official level, and if necessary between Ministers. These provisions merely give form to the existing implications of the system. The Chancellor of the Exchequer can force discussion by the Cabinet of the decisions of any other Minister in any matter which touches his sphere. His sphere is wide, and his authority is great: an attack on the Chancellor in Cabinet cannot succeed without great danger to the stability of the government. Hence much is settled by his approval without any Cabinet discussion at all.

FOR REFERENCE

(i) *Official Documents:*

Epitome of the Reports from the Committees of Public Accounts 1857 to 1937 with Treasury Minutes Thereon. H.C. 154, 1938.

Supplementary Epitome 1938 to 1950. H.C. 155, 1952.

4th *Report from the Select Committee on Estimates (Sub-Committee E), Session 1946-47,* and *Minutes of Evidence:* 'The Form of the Estimates'.

Final Report of the Committee on the Form of Government Accounts. Cmd. 7969, 1950.

(See also 7th *Report from Select Committee on National Expenditure.* H.C. 98, 1918. 'The Form of Public Accounts'.)

4th *Report from the Committee of Public Accounts, Session 1950-51, Memoranda and Minutes of Evidence:* 'Treasury Control'. H.C. 241-1.

3rd *Report from the Committee of Public Accounts, Session 1951-52, Minutes of Evidence,* H.C. 253, p. 152 ff.: 'The Functions of the Comptroller and Auditor-General' (Witness: Sir Frank Tribe). (For history of the Office up to 1896 see *Epitome 1857-1937,* pp. 398-9, and up to 1916, *Memorandum Prepared by the Comptroller and Auditor-General for the Information of the Committee of Public Accounts.* Cd. 8337, 1916.)

Reports and Minutes of Evidence of the Select Committee on Procedure on Public Business. H.C. 161, 1930-31; and H.C. 129, 1931-32.

3rd *Report and Minutes of Evidence from the Select Committee on Procedure, 1945-46.* H.C. 189-1.

H.M. Treasury: *Notes for the Use of Accounts Branches of Government Departments* (H.M.S.O. 1947).

Comptroller and Auditor-General: *Memorandum on the British Government's System of Auditing Public Accounts* (1949).

H.M. Treasury: *Memorandum on Financial Control* (1949).

H.M. Treasury: *The Statutes governing the Relation between the Treasury and Other Departments* (1949).

(ii) *Books and Articles:*

The standard works on the system of public accounts are:

A. J. V. DURELL: *Principles and Practice of the System of Control over Parliamentary Grants* (1917).

E. HILTON-YOUNG (Lord Kennet): *The System of National Finance* (3rd Edn., 1936).

See also:

R. G. HAWTREY: *The Exchequer and the Control of Expenditure* (1921).

J. R. HICKS: *The Problem of Budgetary Reform* (1948).

F. S. BRAY and R. STONE: *The Presentation of the Central Government Accounts* (1948).

The standard work on the Public Accounts Committees and Estimates Committees is:

B. CHUBB: *The Control of Public Expenditure* (1952).

On Treasury Control, see:

S. BEER: *Treasury Control* (1956). And an article under the same title in the *American Political Science Review*, Vol. XLIX, p. 144. See also a review of Professor Beer's book by D. N. CHESTER in *Public Administration*, Vol. XXXV, p. 15.

Sir EDWARD BRIDGES: *Treasury Control* (1950; revised, 1956).

Sir JOHN WOODS: 'Treasury Control' (in W. A. Robson (Ed.): *The Civil Service in Britain and France* (1956)).

Other useful books and articles are:

Sir FRANK TRIBE: 'Parliamentary Control of Public Expenditure', *Public Administration*, Vol. XXXII, p. 363.

Sir HORACE HAMILTON: 'Treasury Control in the Eighties', *Public Administration*, Vol. XXXIII, p. 13.

A. H. HANSON: 'The Select Committee on Estimates, 1945-50', *Yorkshire Bulletin of Economic and Social Research*, Vol. 3, p. 103.

Articles in *Public Administration* on Sir Richard Hopkins (in Vol. XXXIV, p. 115), and on Sir Warren Fisher (in Vol. XXIX, p.3).

Royal Institute of Public Administration: *Financial Control, Its Place in Management* (1950).

Anon: ' The Treasury', articles in the *Midland Bank Review*, August and November 1956.

B. St. J. TREND: 'The formation of Economic and Financial Policy: Great Britain', *International Social Science Bulletin*, Vol. VIII, p. 239.

CHAPTER NINETEEN

THE ADMINISTRATIVE FUNCTIONS OF THE CABINET

For if the trumpet give an uncertain sound, who shall prepare himself to the battle?—1 *Corinthians*, xiv, 8.

1. INTRODUCTORY

IT is necessary but difficult to include in a study of British central administration some explanation of the part played by the Cabinet. It is necessary because the Cabinet is in various senses the heart of the system; it is difficult because the Cabinet has many functions outside the scope of administration. Indeed its fundamental function, in the familiar words of Bagehot, is that it is 'the hyphen which joins, the buckle which fastens' the administrative system to the political system.

The Cabinet is the heart of the system in three senses. First, there is the constitutional sense: the administration derives its authority from the Cabinet, which collectively derives its authority from the House of Commons, which derives its authority from the electorate. There is more than a touch of myth about such a theory, but myths are constitutional realities; the system could not work as it does if this assumption were not held as common ground by the participants. Secondly, there is the hierarchical sense: a Minute recording a decision of the Cabinet outranks all other administrative documents, the Cabinet stands at the pinnacle of the administrative hierarchy. This contains also an element of mythology; because of limits of time and human reason the Cabinet can never in practice intervene at more than an infinitesimally small proportion of points at which decisions are required. But it is a very practical point in establishing unity of administration that there exists in all matters a court of appeal to give decisions which are final and unchallenged until altered by the same authority. Cabinet decisions may be evaded or whittled away: they cannot be ignored. Thirdly, there is the sense which is in some ways simplest and most practical, but which evades generalisation: the Cabinet (and Committees endowed with authority by it) do from week to week take an immense number of decisions,

THE ADMINISTRATIVE FUNCTIONS OF THE CABINET

which are not foregone conclusions before they are taken, which are taken not for the sake of constitutional or administrative form, but because someone must give the answer to pressing questions, and which lead to chains of action spreading out through the central administration to the whole country. This part of the matter will scarcely be understood fully until it is possible to make a thorough and realistic analysis of the Minutes of the Cabinet and its Committees; and that will not be for many years.

An attempt to set on one side for analysis the administrative functions of the Cabinet suggests four headings: its role as co-ordinator, as director, as planner, and as supervisor of organisation. These are headings natural in discussing the work of the head of an administrative organisation, and they fit the work of the Cabinet quite well. An administrative head is usually also (some would say 'primarily') responsible for the selection and promotion of the top levels of subordinate staff; it will be obvious from much that has already been said that this is not the business of the Cabinet at all. It is in part the business of the Prime Minister, to a smaller extent of other Ministers individually; and this suggests one difficulty in discussing the work of the Cabinet, that it is not easy to separate its collective operation from individual action by its chairman, the Prime Minister, and its other members.

The other great difficulty is that presented by the political functions of the Cabinet. Its business is to govern not the Civil Service but the nation. It is largely a group of party leaders, with the strength and weakness of party leaders: it represents different interests within its party, the party as a whole is sensitive to the danger of failure at the next election, public opinion in its various forms presses upon the Cabinet all the time. These political functions cannot be described here, yet they colour all the relations of the Cabinet to the administration; above all, they determine the success or failure of the Cabinet in its role as buckle or hyphen.

Our problem is therefore insoluble within our own terms of reference, and we do not attempt to give our answer an unreal precision. We begin by dealing in formal terms with membership of the Cabinet and the organisation of Cabinet business, in so far as they affect the central administration. We then consider, in a somewhat discursive way, the four types of possible intervention in administration by the Cabinet: co-ordination, direction, planning, and the supervision of organisation. Our conclusions are that the Cabinet in its present form is admirably contrived as an organ of co-ordination; that it can act effectively as a final court of appeal in specific controversies about organisation, but can do little to lay down in general terms forms of organisation for the administration as a whole; that controversies about 'resolute central direction' and about 'planning' are somewhat confused by ambiguity in discussion, and that on the whole the Cabinet's part in practice (however it may be organised) is not to direct or plan, but to encourage or discourage individual Ministers and officials who seek to act as directors and planners. Sir Winston Churchill's remark, that 'at the top there are great simplifications',[1] can be applied more readily to individual than to collective leadership.

2. Membership of the Cabinet

The matter of Cabinet membership embraces two rather different questions: What individuals belong to the Cabinet? What Departments are represented in the Cabinet?

The former belongs almost wholly to the sphere of party politics and political history. There are, however, two ways in which it may affect administrative organisation:

(i) A Minister's knowledge of the Department which he is to direct may be intimate or it may be almost negligible. There are exceptional cases in which an eminent person (very occasionally a civil servant) is brought into Parliament and into the Cabinet to give an impetus to the work of some Department which he knows very well. At the other extreme, a rising politician may attain Cabinet office because he is influential with a section of the party and is a good spokesman in one of the Houses. Such men have to be provided for somehow in the allotment of offices and may know next to nothing about their job when they take it over. The position is generally between these extremes. Some politicians (like Sir Anthony Eden) choose to follow one line of interest throughout their career, and are successful enough to command appointment to the Ministry of their choice; others have had experience as 'shadow' Ministers in opposition before taking over a Department when their party comes into power. The average Minister has a reasonably good idea of the work of his Department and of how business is done in it, though he does not come to it as an expert.

(ii) The internal structure of the Cabinet is partly determined by administrative convenience, but it also reflects the situation within the party in power. There may sometimes be one outstanding man who dominates others by experience and personality, as did Sir Winston Churchill after the first and most difficult period of his war

[1] *The Second World War*, Vol. II, p. 15.

government. Sometimes there may be three or four men head and shoulders above the rest, sometimes the balance of interests and personalities within the party is so delicate that influence is diffused among a wider group. These political considerations always affect the structure of the Cabinet, and on the whole it is so flexible that it easily adapts itself to them. There is no fixed point within it except the office of Prime Minister, and even that office, great though its powers are, varies in influence according to situation and personality.

It is a much more straightforward matter to say which Departments are represented in the Cabinet. Since July 1945, when the Churchill 'Caretaker' government came to an end, the size of Cabinets has varied within the narrow limits of sixteen to twenty, including the Prime Minister. Pre-war Cabinets were sometimes larger because they included automatically a number of Great Officers of State and the heads of all Departments of the first rank, those who under the Ministers of the Crown Act of 1937 enjoyed salaries of £5,000 a year. But the number of such Departments increased greatly during the war (there were 30 at the time of greatest expansion), and the practice of the War Cabinet made familiar the idea that there were Ministers 'of Cabinet rank' who were not members of the Cabinet. The term 'Ministers of Cabinet rank' has now been officially abandoned, and has no proper constitutional meaning. Ministers not invited to join the Cabinet remain individually responsible to Parliament for the conduct of their Departments. They are entitled to be summoned to Cabinet meetings when the business of their Departments is discussed, but it is not clear to what extent they share responsibility for decisions taken by the Cabinet.

Since 1946 the holders of the following offices have *always* been members of the Cabinet:

> Lord President of the Council
> Lord Chancellor
> Lord Privy Seal
> Chancellor of the Exchequer
> Minister of Defence
> Foreign Secretary
> Home Secretary
> Secretary of State for Commonwealth Relations
> Colonial Secretary
> Secretary of State for Scotland
> President of the Board of Trade
> Minister of Labour and National Service.

The following have been in the Cabinet for varying periods:
   Chancellor of the Duchy of Lancaster
   Paymaster-General
   Minister of Education
   Minister of Health
   Minister of Agriculture and Fisheries (now Agriculture, Fisheries, and Food)
   Minister of Fuel and Power (now Power)
   Minister of Town and Country Planning
   Minister of Local Government and Planning
   Minister of Housing and Local Government
   Minister of Pensions and National Insurance
   Minister of Food
   Minister of Materials
   Secretary of State for the Co-ordination of Transport, Fuel, and Power.

There is thus a nucleus of offices which are as a rule 'Cabinet' offices, either because they are posts of dignity given only to very senior men, or because the work of the Departments is always of great national importance (the Treasury or the Foreign Office, for instance), or because a political outcry would be caused by their omission (the Scottish Office). Other offices come into the Cabinet from time to time because of the special position of their holders or of public business at the time. Other major Departments with large administrative responsibilities are not now represented in the Cabinet.

3. Cabinet Procedure and the Cabinet Secretariat

Later sections of this chapter deal with controversial matters in which it is not easy to separate fact from opinion, and it may be convenient next to set out certain fixed points about the way in which business is done.

The Cabinet meets only on the summons of the Prime Minister or of a recognised deputy acting for him at his request. In peace-time it usually assembles in the Cabinet room at No. 10 Downing Street, looking out on the garden behind the house, but it is for the Prime Minister to call the Cabinet to meet where he chooses: it may, for instance, meet in the Prime Minister's room at the House of Commons. In recent years there have normally been meetings twice a week throughout most of the year, with occasional emergency meetings. Meetings seem generally to last about two hours. The fact of a meeting is announced to the press, but no information about the details of discussions or decisions is given officially, and leakages (though not unknown) are remarkably rare.

It is for the Prime Minister to decide what shall be on the agenda, and it would be improper (except in very unusual circumstances) to raise any matter without prior notice. If a Minister (including a Departmental Minister not in the Cabinet) wishes to put an item on the agenda the Prime Minister is unlikely to refuse, but he and his advisers try to ensure that nothing comes to the Cabinet without proper preparation. Much of the business is done on the basis of Cabinet papers circulated in advance, and it is a rule that all Departments concerned must see a paper in draft and have a chance to comment before it is circulated. As we have seen, this brings the Treasury into most business at an early stage. Even if a paper is not circulated, the Prime Minister may try to ensure prior consultation, and may perhaps secure decision by agreement without reference to the Cabinet.

It was suggested in Chapter 14 that the art of drafting papers for the Cabinet and its Committees has replaced the art of minute-writing as the most important technical skill of the administrative civil servant. The object is to produce a document which is clear, relevant, incontrovertible, and, above all, brief. Occasionally a Minister of strong personal character (Sir Winston Churchill or Lord Beaverbrook) drafts his own Cabinet papers, in a style of his own, on the basis of material given him by his advisers; but administrators are generally responsible both for the material and for the first stages of drafting. Policy is quite often 'secreted in the interstices' of discussion between Ministers and civil servants about the drafting of Cabinet papers.

The practice of careful preparation means that much Cabinet business is now almost formal. Many items of great importance are dealt with by the presentation of a paper agreed in advance by all concerned, generally after discussion in a Cabinet Committee: the matter can then be disposed of quickly, by agreement to record the Cabinet's approval of the action recommended.

There also arise at most meetings some matters where the decision is still in real doubt, either because the Ministers concerned have still some unsettled point of disagreement, or because (as often happens in war or foreign policy) a quick and authoritative decision is needed on some point arising suddenly during a long train of events. The procedure in such cases is normally that of exposition by the Minister or Ministers concerned, a request by the Prime Minister to each of the other Ministers individually to state an opinion, and a summing up by the Prime Minister of the 'sense of the meeting'. A formal vote (as distinct from a statement of opinion by each Minister in turn) is never taken, but there is no doubt that a minority must either accept and support the decision or resign.

It is possible to speak of a stable form of procedure only since the emergence of the Cabinet Secretariat. This was established by Lloyd George for his War Cabinet in the First World War by taking over the organisation gradually built up for the Committee of Imperial Defence from 1904 onwards. The institution was not popular with the Conservative Party, which ejected Lloyd George from office in the autumn of 1922, but after considerable debate the view prevailed that the Cabinet Secretariat was a useful institution not to be rejected out of hand because of its association with Lloyd George. The essence of the difficulty was that pre-war constitutional practice regarded the Cabinet as a private meeting of political leaders, whose discussions were always (in a more modern phrase) 'off the record'. This tradition was broken by the presence of secretaries at meetings of the Cabinet and by the preparation of authoritative minutes of proceedings and decisions. The result of the change has certainly been to give greater formality to Cabinet proceedings, but there has proved to be no foundation for the fears that if the Cabinet proceedings were more formally organised the focus of decision would pass elsewhere.

The Cabinet Secretariat is a small organisation, staffed at the senior level (apart from the Secretary to the Cabinet himself) by a Deputy Secretary, two Under Secretaries, two Assistant Secretaries, and about half a dozen Principals. During the Second World War various newly created organisations were associated with it to form the Cabinet Office: but of these there now remain only the Central Statistical Office and the Historical Branch. The latter is concerned with the military and civil history of the war and is attached to the Cabinet Office simply for administrative convenience and because it makes the historians independent of any single Department.

The primary duties of the Secretariat are to prepare a draft of the Cabinet agenda for approval by the Prime Minister, to see that they are supported by the necessary papers, to issue the summons for a meeting, to attend and record the discussion, to circulate draft Minutes for concurrence or correction (they are rarely amended), and to keep in touch with the progress of action on Cabinet decisions. The Cabinet Minutes are the centre of this sphere of action: they usually record briefly the arguments used in Cabinet without attributing them to individual speakers, and state as precisely as possible what action the Cabinet has approved and who is respons-

THE ADMINISTRATIVE FUNCTIONS OF THE CABINET

ible for taking it. The Minutes preserve the constitutional fiction that the Cabinet is an unofficial body: the Cabinet never 'orders' or 'instructs', it 'takes note' or 'approves' or 'invites'. This ambiguity about the exact scope of the Cabinet's authority raises an issue to which we will recur later. Can the Cabinet act at all except as 'co-ordinator'? But whether the Cabinet 'directs', or merely 'approves', its Minutes are now the organised record of decisions by the British government on all matters of importance, and the index of the Minutes and of their supporting papers, most meticulously kept, provides a continuous record of policy decisions and of the main reasons for them, with a network of cross-references which make it fairly certain that nothing will be discussed in ignorance of action in related fields. This set of records may disappoint and even deceive political historians when ultimately they gain access to them, because they are dry in form, devoid of personality, and rarely refer to considerations of party politics. But they were designed as an instrument of administration, not as a historical record.

The Minutes and papers of the Cabinet itself are linked with those of a very large number of Cabinet Committees. The oldest and most elaborate network is that of the Defence Committee of the Cabinet (successor to the Committee of Imperial Defence), advised by the Chiefs of Staff Committee, which is in turn the apex of a network of Service committees. The Secretariat of the Chiefs of Staff and of their committees now belongs formally to the Ministry of Defence and not to the Cabinet Office; but there is within the latter a Defence Secretariat, serving the Defence Committee, and this is closely associated with the C.O.S. Secretariat, whose records are kept and indexed on the same system. Various attempts have been made, since the Second World War and even earlier, to create a similar pyramid of committees for economic affairs, but there have been more frequent breaches in continuity of policy and organisation, and the records are not so exact and comprehensive. They are probably even less complete for foreign affairs, since much is decided from day to day by minor changes of emphasis in negotiation, and the Cabinet is brought in only for major decisions to which it has sometimes been partly committed in advance. But even in these spheres the record occupies a central position. It may be imperfect, but there is nothing to take its place as a working record of decisions by the government as a whole.

Cabinet Minutes are circulated to all Cabinet Ministers and to a limited number of other people (no list is available). They bear the characteristic heading: 'This document is the property of Her Britannic Majesty's Government'. That is to say, it is improper for a Minister to take Cabinet Minutes and papers away with him when he leaves office, as he may take away his own personal correspondence even when it deals with official matters. It is the Minister's business to decide (subject to proper security precautions) what arrangements are made for taking action on Cabinet Minutes within his Department. Some Departments, such as the Treasury, the Foreign Office, and the Ministry of Defence, have business with the Cabinet very frequently, and doubtless have formal internal arrangements for the communication of decisions to those immediately concerned with action. Others have so little Cabinet business that a Cabinet Minute which concerns them is an event of some note in the office, and may be treated with slightly exaggerated reverence.

The responsibility of the Secretariat for 'following up' Cabinet decisions is limited, and can only be exercised with tact and a sense of proper occasions. It is not for mere Secretaries to suggest that a Department has been remiss in a matter which lies within its own official sphere of action.

4. CO-ORDINATION

By 'co-ordination' we mean in this context the role of the Cabinet as a final court of appeal. We discussed in Chapter 14 the 'doctrine of levels'; for most purposes in administration the Cabinet is 'the highest level', and business flows up to it from below 'through channels'. This is by no means the Cabinet's only function, but it is an essential one, and there has been much discussion about its proper organisation.

Much of the business of co-ordination between Departments is carried on in the same way at the top level as lower down in the hierarchy. There are letters of various degrees of formality, telephone conversations, meetings to discuss particular questions, informally and tête-à-tête, or more formally round a conference table. It requires great skill and experience to know when matters can be advanced by raising a question to 'ministerial level'. The issues must be defined in such a way as to pose a clear question for decision and yet leave room for compromise, and the Minister himself must have good judgement about how to allocate his time and how to approach his colleagues. In these respects an experienced Minister can contribute a great deal both to his own Department and to the administration as a whole. But there is nothing in all this that requires specialised machinery for co-ordination below Cabinet level.

The formal problem of machinery arises only because the ordinary procedure does not always lead to a decision, and appeal is made to 'the highest level', that of the Cabinet. Members of a modern Cabinet cannot find time both to sit together as a court of appeal for a large number of difficult cases and also to act individually as Departmental administrators and party politicians. The time regularly spent in Cabinet is perhaps four or five hours a week; to this must be added the time spent on reading Cabinet papers and on preliminary 'briefing'. This appears to be all the time that an ordinary Cabinet can spare for joint action, and it is quite inadequate. Hence the growth of devices for increasing the time available by introducing a 'level' between the Cabinet and the Departments.

These devices may be summed up in a formal way as follows:

(i) *Ad hoc* committees of the Cabinet.
(ii) Standing Committees of the Cabinet, each of which may be under the chairmanship of a Minister who has no other duties, so that the chairmen form together a group of senior Ministers.
(iii) The appointment of co-ordinating Ministers without Departmental staff, each of whom has authority over a range of subjects of interest to several Departments, so that for limited purposes a new 'ministerial level' is created 'above' the Ministers of those Departments.
(iv) The creation of co-ordinating Departments, in each of which there is a Minister with a fairly large staff of officials, so that the new Department has (at least in some matters) authority over a group of Departments.
(v) The amalgamation of a group of Departments, to form a single 'super-Department' under one head.

It is perhaps unnecessary to say more about Cabinet Committees in general or about the amalgamation of Departments. These are the simplest and most natural devices, but have inherent difficulties to which the others provide partial answers. An *ad hoc* committee may be successful in disposing of a single issue without troubling the whole Cabinet, but it has no continuity of experience, and each new committee has to find its own way of doing business as a group (in practice, the Secretariat and the Departments are now so experienced that a committee can find its feet fairly quickly). A 'super-Department' relieves the Cabinet merely by handing over its problem to a single Minister; there is no improvement if he is given a range of business which is too big for him to handle, as perhaps happened in the amalgamation of the Ministry of Aircraft Production with the Ministry of Supply, and of the Ministry of Food with the Ministry of Agriculture and Fisheries. The other three devices are compromises which avoid these difficulties at the cost of introducing others.

(i) *Standing Committees and 'Co-ordinators'*

The earliest reported Standing Committee of the Cabinet is the Home Affairs Committee which was set up in 1918 to relieve the War Cabinet of some of its domestic business.[1] A Committee of the same name was appointed by successive governments until 1939, but its functions appear to have been confined to the scrutiny of government Bills in draft, the consideration of drafts of speeches to be delivered by the monarch to Parliament, and the conduct of Parliamentary business for the Session. In 1940 the Committee was incorporated in the Home Policy Committee, which had wider functions. It was revived by the first post-war Labour government as the 'Legislation Committee', and a new Standing Committee, known as the 'Future Legislation Committee', was also appointed, to plan the government's legislative programme twelve months ahead.

The tradition before 1939 was that the Home Secretary should always be chairman of the Home Affairs Committee. But it does not greatly ease business if the head of a Department has to add the chairmanship of a Standing Committee to his other duties, and the (war-time) Home Policy Committee and Mr. Attlee's Legislation and Future Legislation Committees were entrusted to non-Departmental Ministers.

The most important non-Departmental Ministers are the Lord President of the Council, the Lord Privy Seal, the Chancellor of the Duchy of Lancaster, and the Paymaster-General. Any or all of them may be in the Cabinet, and if necessary their number can be increased by the addition of 'Ministers of State' or 'Ministers without Portfolio', or by the creation of a special office, as the post of Minister for the Co-ordination of Defence was created for Sir Thomas Inskip in 1936. The holders of these offices are available for any special duties that the Prime Minister may care to give them.

Sir Winston Churchill in his Memoirs has declared that they should not be used as 'exalted brooders' to form an inner ring of non-Departmental Ministers, and his policy was in general to give important Ministers charge of important Departments. 'It is easier', he says, 'to give directions than advice, and more agreeable to have the right to act . . . than the privilege to talk at large.' Nevertheless, the most successful of all co-ordinating committees was the Lord President's Committee, during the period when Sir John Anderson

---

[1] The Committee of Imperial Defence (1904) included as full members persons who were not members of the Cabinet.

(now Lord Waverley) held that office from 1941 to 1943. This was used almost as a subsidiary Cabinet for Home Affairs, and disposed of a great deal of business with dispatch and clarity. Its value, however, depended primarily on the personality and standing of its chairman, an ex-civil servant of immense experience and authority, who stood outside party politics and had the strong personal support of the Prime Minister.

In Mr. Attlee's government the situation was somewhat different. The large programme of legislation and the difficulty of the economic situation meant that co-ordination was not easy, and various experiments were tried. At the outset there was a clearly marked inner group of Ministers, including Mr. Bevin, Mr. Morrison, and Sir Stafford Cripps, with Mr. A. V. Alexander, Mr. Dalton, and Mr. Aneurin Bevan holding important but slightly less senior positions. In this phase, Mr. Attlee tended to use 'co-ordinators' rather more than Mr. Churchill had done, but he did not use them to the exclusion of other devices. Mr. Morrison, as Lord President of the Council and Deputy Prime Minister, was chairman of a large number of extremely important Cabinet Committees including the Future Legislation Committee, the Committee on the Socialisation of Industries, and the Lord President's Committee (which dealt with all questions of domestic policy not assigned to some other committee). But a co-ordinating Department was created for Defence, and its head, Mr. A. V. Alexander, was the Prime Minister's deputy as chairman of the Defence Committee of the Cabinet. For a short time in 1947 Sir Stafford Cripps was Minister for Economic Affairs, and chairman of the Cabinet Committees concerned. But after he became Chancellor of the Exchequer, late in 1947, he continued to act as 'co-ordinator' although head of a great Department; and Mr. Bevin as Foreign Secretary was always (says Mr. Morrison) 'regarded as co-ordinating Minister for overseas affairs generally'.[1]

(ii) *'Overlords'*

'Co-ordinators' were less conspicuous in Mr. Attlee's second government, partly because of the death of Mr. Bevin in 1951, the grave illness of Sir Stafford Cripps, and the lack of a coherent inner group within the Labour Party. Mr. Churchill's third government, from 1951 to 1955, is associated with the invention of 'Overlords'; the word is a witticism coined at the expense of Lord Woolton and Lord Leathers, with a side glance at Lord Cherwell. But 'Overlords' were of course not the only device used by that government.

Lord Woolton was Lord President of the Council with (*inter alia*)

[1] H. Morrison: *Government and Parliament* (1950), p. 36.

a not very clearly defined responsibility for the co-ordination of food and agricultural policy; Lord Leathers was Secretary of State 'for the Co-ordination of Transport, Fuel, and Power'. Their appointments gave rise to debate in both Houses about the exact difference between their responsibility and that of the Departmental Ministers whom they were to supervise, and it proved very difficult to give a constitutionally satisfactory answer. They were to 'co-ordinate' policy decisions, but not to interfere with the responsibility of the co-ordinated Ministers for their own Departments. Yet if they could issue directions to Ministers they deprived them of responsibility; if they could not issue directions their position was merely that of chairmen—'exalted brooders'.

The position was made no clearer when, in reply to Lord Stansgate in the course of a debate in the House of Lords, the Lord President said[1]:

> What the Secretary of State [for the Co-ordination of Transport, Fuel, and Power] is responsible for is co-ordinating transport, fuel, and power. That does not mean that he is able to give orders to the Minister of Fuel and Power or the Minister of Transport.

Mr. Churchill stated[2]:

> A Departmental Minister who is invited by a co-ordinating Minister to adjust a Departmental policy to accord with the wider interests of the Government as a whole always has access to the Cabinet.

Thus a co-ordinating Minister could only 'invite' and not 'order', and an appeal lay to the Cabinet against his 'invitation'.

In spite of these ambiguities there is no evidence that the Overlords worked badly as an administrative device. The attack on them was based mainly on constitutional grounds, in particular on the ambiguities of responsibility to Parliament, and on the fact that these two very important men (and also Lord Cherwell) were not available to answer for themselves in the House of Commons. This proved embarrassing, and the scheme was dropped when Lord Leathers resigned in 1953.

(iii) *Co-ordinating Departments*

It is constitutionally more logical to go one step farther, and to set up not only a Minister but a Ministry, with terms of reference defining where the division of responsibility lies between the new Ministry and those which it co-ordinates.

The classic case here is that of defence, where there has been

---
[1] 176 H.L. Deb., Cols. 523-7.
[2] 500 H.C. Deb., Cols. 188-96.

THE ADMINISTRATIVE FUNCTIONS OF THE CABINET 347

regular progression from the old Committee of Imperial Defence (whose work passed to the Defence Committee of the Cabinet in 1940, though the former was not formally wound up until 1946), through phases in which the chairman was at first deputy for the Prime Minister (Sir Thomas Inskip in 1936), then titular Minister (Mr. Churchill from 1940 to 1945), to the creation of an actual Ministry, by Mr. Attlee in October 1946.

The Ministry of Defence incorporated the Secretariats of the Committee of Imperial Defence, of the Chiefs of Staff Committee, and of their network of sub-committees. It therefore came into existence with experience and tradition behind it and with a body of men (both in the Ministry of Defence and in the services) who knew how to work the machinery of co-operation. This development has been marked by a gradual rise in the status of the senior officer who serves as 'co-ordinator'. At the outset the only post of this kind was the relatively junior one of Secretary to the Chiefs of Staff Committee and 'service' Secretary to the C.I.D. or to the Defence Committee of the Cabinet. During the war of 1939 there appeared the post of Chief Staff Officer to the Prime Minister, a post held first by General Sir Hastings (later Lord) Ismay, who had been Secretary to the Chiefs of Staff Committee, and who now attended all their meetings as an equal. When the Ministry of Defence was created, the post became that of Chief Staff Officer[1] at the Ministry of Defence; in 1955 the holder of it became permanent chairman of the Chiefs of Staff Committee.

In addition to its role as secretariat the Ministry of Defence was given two other functions more precisely defined.

(a) It is responsible for 'questions of general administration on which a common policy for the three services is desirable'. This involves participation in all discussions about pay and conditions of service, with considerable influence on questions where conditions are much the same for all three services (such matters as medical services and chaplains).

(b) The Ministry also became responsible for the management of a number of small but important organisations which do not belong to any one of the three services. The most important of these are the Imperial Defence College, the Joint Services Staff College, the Joint Intelligence Bureau, and the Amphibious Warfare Headquarters. In addition, the Ministry carries 'on its books' the British inter-service representatives overseas on bodies like N.A.T.O. and the U.N., and it has a special responsibility for liaison with the British element in any international high command.

[1] In 1957 redesignated 'Chief of Staff to the Minister of Defence'.

Finally, the Ministry fits into the general scheme for liaison between administration and scientific research. The Chief Scientific Adviser to the Minister of Defence is chairman of the Defence Research Policy Committee, a body which can be called into consultation by the Defence Committee of the Cabinet, and which in any case keeps under general survey all matters of scientific research bearing on national defence. The chairman is a full-time scientific civil servant who usually combines this work with other jobs of scientific administration at a high level, and he is assisted by a very small staff within the Ministry of Defence.

These functions are rather diverse, but they are reasonably precise and have grown as a result of experience of earlier organisation. The Ministry has not escaped criticism, but it seems to have worked well. Its staff is relatively small (only about twenty members of the Administrative Class, in addition to a few scientists and a rather larger number of service officers), and there is little danger that it will attempt to do again work already done by the service Departments. It thus acts along with the Defence Committee and its hierarchy of lesser committees as a filter limiting the number of issues which come to the Cabinet itself. The Ministry has not much administrative business of its own, but what it has is sufficient to give its staff a status rather different from that of a secretariat. There is certainly no general hierarchy of administration for the three services: they retain too much independence of spirit for this to be possible. But the Ministry has substantial influence so long as it does not attempt too much.

Other experiments based on the experience of the Ministry of Defence have been less successful. During the war of 1939 an attempt was made to create a Ministry of Production out of the secretariats of various committees concerned with war production, strengthened by some able permanent and temporary civil servants and headed by a very strong Minister, Mr. Oliver Lyttelton (now Lord Chandos). The experiment perhaps came too late in the development of war production. It was scarcely a failure, but it was not clear that it had achieved anything which could not have been achieved with less effort in other ways.

As we have already mentioned, a similar attempt was made to strengthen the organisation for economic planning during the period of reconstruction by the appointment of Sir Stafford Cripps as Minister for Economic Affairs in September 1947. This was in principle a personal appointment and not the creation of a new Department, but Sir Stafford drew together a number of groups which were primarily secretariats and might have welded them into something like the Ministry of Production. A few weeks later he succeeded Mr. Dalton at the Treasury, and took his new responsibilities with him. The Treasury was already beginning to emerge from a period of partial eclipse, and this development strengthened its hand still farther. When Sir Stafford became Chancellor, an additional Parliamentary Secretary, the Economic Secretary, was appointed to assist him, and this new post has been retained and has been filled by such rising politicians as Mr. John Edwards, Mr. Reginald Maudling, Sir Edward Boyle, and Mr. Nigel Birch. The result of this development has therefore been (in the end) to strengthen the greatest of all 'co-ordinating Departments', the Treasury itself.

A word should be said (finally) about the co-ordination of civil research. We mentioned earlier how the Lord President's Department, once a sinecure, has gradually accumulated responsibilities through the creation of Committees of the Privy Council for research of various kinds. The Lord President's Office is still very small, and presumably the Lord President is advised directly by the heads of the research Departments concerned, so that there is at present little administrative co-ordination of civil research. This is a policy acceptable to all concerned; but if it ever becomes necessary to create a Ministry for Civil Research there is now a nucleus from which it can grow.

5. Central Direction

So far we have written almost entirely in terms of 'co-ordination', not of 'central direction'. There is a sense in which the effective units of central administration are sub-departments and establishments dealing with relatively simple topics which can be effectively grasped by one man and his immediate assistants. A great deal of the real work of government is done 'at Assistant Secretary level', because it is at this level that there are men and women who can understand the details of one subject in all its complexity and who can also see something of the larger context in which it has to be placed. It is essential to the health and activity of the system that much of the initiative should come from low down in the hierarchy, and that the higher levels should be regarded as responsible primarily not for issuing orders to their subordinates but for providing the right conditions for their work.

This is clearly not enough in itself. One condition of good work is that the 'front line' sections should be effectively linked so that they do not frustrate one another or run blindly against obstacles outside the administrative system. This is the function of 'co-ordination', closely organised within each Department, more loosely throughout the whole system. But there are occasions which demand more than co-ordination. The War Cabinet in its Report for 1917 wrote of Asquith's Cabinet, which it displaced, that: 'It was extremely difficult for so large a body to give the resolute central direction which became more imperative the more the population and resources of the nation had to be organised for a single purpose— the defeat of German militarism.' How is the system organised for 'resolute central direction'? In other words, who is to plan the work of Departments and issue orders to them? The Cabinet is a band of equals which co-ordinates: who is to command?

There are a number of preliminary points. *First*, it is the small change of politics to attack one's opponents for lack of 'resolute central direction'. The passage quoted is by implication an attack on Asquith and his associates, who had been ousted from office by a combination in which Lloyd George was the most important figure. It is tempting to argue that the failure of one government shows that it was less effectively organised than another government which succeeded. But there are too many other variables in the situation for this to be convincing except to a political audience.

Secondly, however effectively central direction is organised it can never be comprehensive. In times of war and other emergency it may *appear* to be comprehensive because there is a real convergence of wills towards a single intelligible purpose. But the small group of individuals who make up the 'high command' and their most important advisers grasp only some of the complexities of the situation, and their success depends mainly on success in identifying key points of influence and in arousing a general sense of common purpose. Such leadership is largely political and is directed to the nation as a whole: it can affect administration directly only by limited and judicious intervention at key points.

Thirdly, it must always be remembered that at this level one is dealing with a small number of individuals closely associated in a particular historical situation. Individual character and aptitude varies, the historical situation never repeats itself. There cannot therefore be generalisations about the highest level of government in the same sense as about the management of Departments and sections within them. All that can be done is to set out the kind of devices which have proved useful in the past, and which may be used again or combined or modified in the future.

These devices can perhaps be dealt with under two headings, the organisation of the high command, and the staff of the high command.

(i) *Organisation*

It would probably be accepted as an axiom that a body of more than fifteen people cannot act jointly as a high command in a rapidly changing situation. The process of mutual comprehension and agreement is too slow and consumes too much energy. Hence there is always an element of command within the Cabinet, though it remains in theory a body of equals. This can take various forms and may or may not be recognised by specific designations. One can imagine four forms: Prime Minister alone, Prime Minister and his deputies, Prime Minister and a junta, and a junta in which the Prime Minister is no more than a chairman.

(*a*) The Prime Minister has enormous constitutional powers at his disposal. He 'hires and fires' Ministers, dissolves Parliament, can take the initiative on any matter in a way which virtually commits his Cabinet and his Party. A resolute Prime Minister has powers at least equal to those of an American President, and his position is always a somewhat lonely one. But no Prime Minister has ever attempted to assume the burden thrust upon the President by the American Constitution, of carrying final responsibility for all major decisions of policy.

(*b*) Mr. Attlee's government of 1945-1950 had a relatively large Cabinet, but it has been described as working on something like a 'three tier' system: the Prime Minister at the top, then a 'level' of men who might be regarded as Deputy Prime Ministers (there has only twice been a titular Deputy Prime Minister, Mr. Attlee in Churchill's war-time government and Mr. Herbert Morrison in the first post-war Labour government), then the 'level' of Departmental Ministers, some of whom were so important that in effect they reported direct to the Prime Minister. This is perhaps too rigid a picture of the position under Mr. Attlee; it would require some modification to make it serve as a description of the organisation under Mr. Churchill from 1940 to 1945. In practice the War Cabinet had little responsibility for the general conduct of the war, which was left in the strong hands of Mr. Churchill, acting through the Chiefs of Staff, and through various capable Ministers, some with Departments and some without. But there were many matters of home affairs and of post-war policy which Mr. Churchill left to be settled by agreement (or failure to agree) among his colleagues.

(*c*) Most large Cabinets have been dominated by an 'inner Cabinet' of three or four: in the first two Labour governments Ramsay MacDonald with Henderson, Snowden, Clynes, and J. H. Thomas; in the Chamberlain government of 1937, the Prime Minister with Lord Halifax, Sir John Simon, Sir Samuel Hoare, and Sir Kingsley Wood. In each case there was a strong and independent Prime Minister who was able to carry through his own line, with the support of a group whom he consulted much more freely and continuously than anyone else. Lloyd George's War Cabinet of 1916 was a body of the same kind, consisting of the Prime Minister, with five to seven colleagues only one of whom (Bonar Law, the Chancellor of the Exchequer) was head of a Department. This was then recognised as *the* Cabinet: the Ministers directing Departments were excluded from it, and were formally subordinate, a solution perhaps only possible in war-time. Lloyd George's War Cabinet operated continuously as a junta, meeting several days a week and dealing jointly with business as it arose. This was a time-wasting arrangement compared with procedure for decision by the Prime Minister and his deputies acting singly, each in a large area of business, but it was perhaps forced on Lloyd George by political circumstances. He had a very uneasy and quarrelsome team, and the powerful personalities involved were perhaps best combined by a process of joint decision.

(*d*) In all three of these forms the Prime Minister plays a vitally important part as initiator of business. One can think of instances in the eighteenth and nineteenth centuries of vigorous governments in which the Prime Minister was no more than a chairman. But these were in the early period of the evolution of the office, and its powers are now so great that it is as difficult to imagine a British government acting vigorously without a lead from the Prime Minister as it would be to imagine an American government acting vigorously without a lead from the President. The Prime Minister who is merely an able chairman (Balfour and Asquith were the greatest of these) can create a Cabinet which is a first-rate instrument of co-ordination, but no more.

(ii) *Staff*

It is perhaps also axiomatic that the 'high command' cannot control or direct the Departments unless it has means outside their control by which to secure information and follow up the execution of policy. A command (whether one man or a group) is no more than co-ordinator unless it has its own eyes, ears, and tentacles.

This axiom has led to demands for a 'Civil General Staff' or an 'Economic Planning Staff', as the only method of securing effective foresight and direction. The demand for a General Staff is in fact misconceived, as a result of failure to understand what the staff system really is. It has two essential components; a body of men who share a common set of 'staff doctrines' and who are capable through careful training of acting in concert even though placed at different levels and in different sections of the hierarchy; and an organisation set up on the 'line and staff' plan, so that there is a 'staff channel' (or more than one 'staff channel') parallel to the main line of command. This military invention can be and has been adapted to civilian organisation: but no one has ever seriously considered its application to British central administration. None of the Departments is organised on this system: there is no civil staff college, and it is difficult to see how one could be created, because in a democracy many fundamental points of civil planning are matters not of indoctrination but of controversy. The Administrative Class and the 'private secretary network' serve some of the purposes of a staff organisation; so do the 'general service' professional classes; to go farther in this direction would be to change the political setting of British administration.

The problem is therefore the much simpler one of providing special agencies to 'brief' the high command and to report back to it on the execution of its decisions. To a limited extent this is the responsibility of the 'private offices' of the Prime Minister and his closest colleagues; but in practice the private secretaries and their small staffs have enough to do in keeping business in good order, and have little time to act as 'chasers'. Two alternatives have been tried: extension of the Prime Minister's Office and extension of the Cabinet Office. Both are open to objection: the former because it magnifies the position of an individual in a way that is bound to cause uneasiness, the latter because a group of officials cannot serve collectively a group of Ministers acting independently of one another, except in neutral matters such as secretarial duties and the co-ordination of statistics. There have therefore been various shifting patterns since the issue was first raised, perhaps about 1904.

As has already been said, the nucleus of a central staff was first created in the Secretariat of the Committee of Imperial Defence which existed on a small scale before 1914. The 'dynamism' of Lloyd George's War Cabinet and the passionate hostility which it evoked were partly due to the creation of the organisation known as the 'Garden Suburb' or 'Kindergarten' because it was housed in huts in the garden of No. 10 Downing Street. In addition to the Secretariat of the Cabinet this included what seemed to the rest of Whitehall to be a host of personal assistants to the Prime Minister. It was the channel for all sorts of unofficial contacts, including contacts with foreign powers; the Foreign Office was particularly enraged by the action of negotiators over whom it had no control, and the whole organisation was held by the Conservative Party to be one of its grievances against Lloyd George. The Cabinet Secretariat was preserved with some difficulty after Lloyd George's fall, but eventually all other central staff disappeared.

A timid new beginning was made with the constitution of the Economic Advisory Council in 1930, which included Ministers and academic economists. It was important in that, although the full Council never met after the summer of 1931, it gave birth to the Committee of Economic Information, whose chairman was Lord Stamp. When the Economic Advisory Council was formally wound up in 1939, the Stamp Committee was replaced by a 'Survey of Economic Plans' consisting of Stamp, Sir Hubert Henderson, and Sir Henry Clay, under the aegis of the Treasury. A little later (after the outbreak of war) a Central Economic Information Service was started, and grew rapidly by the recruitment of a considerable number of exceedingly able young economists. This was officially part of the Cabinet Office, though it was housed for some time alongside the Flying Squad in a bombproof cellar in New Scotland Yard. In 1941 it was split in two, one half becoming the nucleus of the Central Statistical Office, the other the nucleus of the Economic Section of the Cabinet Secretariat. There were then certain difficulties, as the Treasury also had its economic advisers, and there was during the war and immediately after it some uncertainty as to the respective roles of the Cabinet Office and the Treasury. But controversy was never bitter, and was finally resolved in 1953 by the incorporation of the Economic Section in the Treasury.

Even at the time of greatest expansion the Cabinet Office of the Second World War never rivalled the 'garden suburb'. There was, however, a separate organisation personal to the Prime Minister which did the main work of 'chasing' on his behalf. This had various ramifications and changed from time to time, but it remained intelligible to administrators largely because of the personality of 'the Prof.', Professor Lindemann (later Lord Cherwell), whose ability and foibles coloured most of what was done. Confusion there was, but Mr. Churchill could not have exercised so much influence without the assistance of this personal staff. It was one of his many contributions to the art of government that he was able to combine the use of the Cabinet Office and of personal staff with free and confident delegation to senior colleagues.

Mr. Churchill appears to have used the same device in a modified form in his government of 1951; it was not used by Mr. Attlee, though he did have a Public Relations Adviser (and for a short time a personal Economic Adviser as well) at No. 10 Downing Street. His government used Cabinet Committees and co-ordinating Ministers, as has been described above; and it also invented or developed devices for consultation and exhortation like the National Joint Advisory Council of the Ministry of Labour, the National Production Advisory Council for Industry of the Board of Trade, and the Economic Planning Board which met under the chairmanship of the government's Chief Planning Officer.

But in the field of economic direction its principal inventions, the Minister for Economic Affairs, the Chief Planning Officer, and the Economic Planning Staff, ended in a restoration and increase of the traditional powers of the Treasury. In resolute hands the Treasury has great value as an instrument of direction, but it is an instrument not of the Cabinet as a whole but of a single Minister, the Chancellor of the Exchequer.

6. PLANNING

At least since the time of the Haldane Committee there has been talk of 'thinking as an aid to administration', and of the responsibility of the Cabinet for looking ahead in peace, just as General Staffs prepare for war. At present this line of thought is somewhat out of fashion, but it is certain to recur.

Its administrative implications are not easy to discuss because of the ambiguities involved in the word 'planning'. At least four different senses can be distinguished.

(i) *Planning as Administration.* In one sense planning is inseparable from administration. The object of administration might be roughly defined as the deliberate and rational organisation of resources to attain a defined objective, and planning is an essential part of any cycle of administrative action. The organisation is given a task; it collects relevant data; it hazards forecasts (with some estimate of their reliability) about factors outside its control; it puts forward a scheme for using the available resources in the available time to secure the defined objective—or it recommends that the objective is unattainable. The preparation of such a scheme is 'planning': the preparation of the plan passes into the execution of the plan, and execution is accompanied by continuous observation of success or failure. These observations themselves become part of the data for a new plan (or a decision to abandon the enterprise), so that the process of planning is continuous, even though marked off into stages by plans formally made and approved at turning points in the action.

(ii) *Planning as a Political Programme.* This analysis was first clearly made for the planning of military operations, and the application of the military analogy to the whole work of the State was first made in Germany. *Planwirtschaft* was a conception noised abroad in Germany at the end of the war of 1914, largely because of the gaps in German planning for war which had been revealed by experience. The idea of 'economic planning' was picked up in Russia in the 1920s as a slogan for a socialist state on the march towards communism, and 'economic and social planning' therefore became a left wing or socialist creed.

(iii) *Planning as Target*. It should be noticed that a Russian five year plan as published to the world is not in the administrative sense a plan at all, but a target. It does not set out the consecutive steps to be taken to secure an objective, it merely specifies the objective in considerable detail. Much of the Russian economy must be run by administrative planning, and good planning at that, otherwise it could not function at all. But administrative planning is something quite different from the technique of governing industry by estimating in round figures what each enterprise can achieve, adding perhaps ten per cent. for good measure, and then imposing severe penalties on those who fail to achieve 'the plan', which is actually given the force of law. This has both advantages and dangers: but it is a technique of government in general, rather than of 'planning' in any specific sense of that word.

(iv) *Planning as Responsibility for the Economy*. It is safe to say that in Britain all parties now accept the view that it is incumbent on the government to take action to see that the economy is working well, that the government should be given powers to do so, and that it will at least do better than the 'blind working of economic laws'. This is a reversal of *laissez-faire* doctrine, and has come to be referred to in general terms as 'planning'. In this sense 'we are all planners now', but there is room for much controversy about what sort of planning. One can distinguish two problems. There is the problem of objectives. What would we mean by saying that the economy is working 'well'? Is the aim to be 'productivity', or 'welfare', or 'equality', or what? And there is the problem of powers. What sort of powers does the government need, and how should it use them? Incentives or controls? Bribes or threats? There is still perhaps a tendency to attach the word 'planning' to the policy (whatever it is) chosen by the Labour Party on these issues, since 'planning' has traditionally been a favoured word on the Left, and out of favour (except in Germany) on the Right.

Much more could be said about the ambiguities of planning: but it is clear that a book of this kind is concerned only with the first of the various senses referred to above. This is the sort of planning that goes on whatever political party is in power; it goes on whatever the objectives of policy and whatever the powers held by the government. It is not a specialised topic within administration, it is a function of the whole of administration, and there is little to be said here which has not been anticipated. It may, however, be worth making three points.

First, the technique of planning varies according to subject matter. At one extreme there is the least speculative type of military planning: for instance, the making of a 'plan' to move a particular unit overseas in time of peace. This is a 'once-for-all' plan, laid out in detail as a set of instructions for movement, designed to bring men, transport, food, equipment, ammunition, fuel, and many other things together in the expected order at the expected time. At the other extreme perhaps is something like the planning of the educational system. The responsibility of the Ministry of Education is very clearly laid down in the Act of 1944: it is 'to promote the education of the people of England and Wales'. But the field is enormous, the Ministry acts through about 140 semi-autonomous authorities, the final objective is unlimited and unattainable perfection, to be reached through a succession of vicissitudes over a long period. The Ministry is not 'planless', but its general plan is very large and is a combination of much that is very vague and distant with much that is very precise and near. There may be occasions like 'HORSA'—Hutted Operations for Raising the School-leaving Age—when the Ministry can dabble in military techniques of planning; and one can think of other examples of civil planning of an 'operational' kind, such as planning for evacuation and emergency feeding, or for smaller matters like moving an office without a break in operations. But these are exceptional incidents in civil administration.

Secondly, a military organisation contains at each level a 'general staff', and the highest of these staffs has special sections for Intelligence, Planning, and Operations. It is, however, misleading to think that 'planning' is carried out only by general staffs. General staffs draw on the whole experience of the organisation: their business is to learn how to do this, and how to formulate their information in exact, relevant, and coherent terms. In a sense, the general staff is a 'bureaucracy' within a fighting organisation; its job is the sort of job that most higher civil servants do all their lives, and it is not therefore easy to find a special place for general staff organisation in a civil service.

Some Departments (for instance the Ministry of Education and the Ministry of Health) have experimented with special 'Intelligence' units, designed to gather experience from other countries and to make it available to other administrators; but these have not on the whole been very successful. The most striking example of the successful use of special 'planning' units was in organisations like the Ministry of Aircraft Production, concerned with formulating programmes for a large number of different types of equipment which were to some extent interdependent. The impression given by first-hand accounts of this process (for instance in Professor Devon's book on *Planning in Practice*) is that the basis of specialisation in this sort of work was a capacity to manipulate figures quickly and to realise their practical implications. There are few people who possess these gifts, which are not those of the ordinary civil servant or the ordinary statistician, and there is a natural place for a 'planning section' in Departments which have much work of this kind.

A convincing case has never been made out for similar specialisation within Departments which have a wider and more general responsibility for economic matters. Such Departments usually have excellent statistical sections; they often have one or two general economists who act as advisers at a high level without routine duties, but 'planning' remains the responsibility of the administrative hierarchy as a whole. This is the general model throughout the system: statistical sections, linked but not controlled by the Central Statistical Office; economic advisers, linked but not controlled by the Economic Section of the Treasury; planning as a function placed squarely on the shoulders of officials in the line of authority, acting either singly or in committee. The invention of a 'Central Economic Planning Staff' added very little to established practice.

Thirdly, there will always be disputes as to the amount of detail that should go into a plan. Some administrators insist on providing variations for all possible contingencies, lest they be caught unawares. Others trust to instinct to guarantee that the plan is generally workable, and concentrate on training subordinates to extemporise on the right lines if anything unexpected happens. The first school may seem pedantic, the second may seem imprudent. Undoubtedly the bias of the Civil Service is towards the former. Higher civil servants are on the whole promoted because of accuracy in detail, skill in drafting, and a sense of political problems, rather than because they show capacity for leadership, which is not encouraged by the atmosphere of Parliamentary control. It is perhaps true that the Civil Service when called upon to plan on a really large scale in the years before 1939 and after 1945 planned too carefully, and fell into despondency when it found that no amount of care could produce a completely accurate plan. In the years after 1940 this carefulness was married to an outburst of national energy, and the mingling of diverse characters in war-time organisation produced (amid much confusion) some very remarkable administrative successes. After 1945, national enthusiasm abated, many of the bolder spirits left central administration, and more normal conditions gradually returned.

These remarks have taken us some distance from the Cabinet, because they are directed to show that there is very little reality in discussing 'the Cabinet as planner' except in the context of administration as a whole. Administrative planning, good or bad, goes on all the time; the Cabinet can by understanding and sympathy do much to encourage those who have foresight, and make early provision for eventualities foreseen. Planning in the other senses that we have suggested raises questions of politics rather than of administration: in these matters the Cabinet sets the tone for the administration, but it does so as political leader of the nation, not as prudent administrator.

7. Supervision of the Machinery of Government

In the words of the Haldane Report, the Cabinet is (*inter alia*) responsible for 'the continuous co-ordination and delimitation of the activities of the several Departments of State'. As the quotation implies, 'co-ordination' and 'delimitation' are linked together: effective 'co-ordination' requires power to decide who is to be responsible for action. The 'sovereignty' of the Cabinet includes power to reshape the machinery of government.

In practice this is a reserve power rather than one in constant use. There are three important practical limitations. First, much of the structure is so ancient and well-established that it never comes into question at all. It would never occur to anyone to raise in Cabinet fundamental questions about the office of Lord Chancellor or of Secretary of State. The Cabinet is so busy that it could never find time to overhaul the whole machine and reconstruct it on new principles. This could happen only in a revolutionary situation, if, for instance, a party seized control of government and in effect substituted departments from its own headquarters for the Departments of State, as the Nazi Party virtually did in Germany.

Secondly, there is much that is settled at lower levels without troubling the Cabinet. Minor reorganisation is going on all the time, for convenience or because of changing needs, and little of this is reported to the Cabinet. Rather larger changes agreed between Ministers may require Cabinet approval, especially if legislation is required, or if a Statutory Instrument has to be made under the Ministers of the Crown (Transfer of Functions) Act, 1946. But agreed change requires little or no discussion.

Thirdly, at the highest levels much is done by the Prime Minister himself. The balance of power between the Prime Minister and the Cabinet varies according to circumstances and personality, and we have indicated above some of the forms which it assumes. The point here is that the Prime Minister can manage his personal powers as he pleases, delegating them to colleagues on such terms as he thinks fit. Such delegation is normally reported to the Cabinet, but it does not need Cabinet approval.

In spite of these reservations the Cabinet is the court of last appeal for disputes between Departments about jurisdiction, as about other matters; it is also the natural forum for discussion of action about any incident which casts serious doubt on the efficiency of government organisation in general. Questions of this kind may be embarrassing to the Cabinet, as they involve the prestige of its own members, and its collective desire to avoid them is a factor in retarding general change. It is not realistic to picture the Cabinet as a body which debates regularly about the machinery of government; still less to suppose that there is or could be a body of doctrine enunciated by the Cabinet as a basis for organisation. Changes are usually made *ad hoc* to meet particular circumstances, and in a sense there is no general supervision of the system at all, since no one is ever in a position to grasp and modify the whole system at once. In practice there are always at any given moment controversies 'in action' about specific matters of organisation, some of which may be taken to the Cabinet for decision; and perhaps the only realistic way to discuss the general oversight of the machinery of government is by reference to the course of such specific controversies, each arising out of particular technical problems within a particular historical setting. This is, however, impracticable here, and we limit ourselves to setting out the formal machinery which exists for settling such issues and to discussing the sort of general principles which may be involved.

(i) *Procedure*

The first point can be disposed of quite briefly. The earliest period of debate about modern administrative problems, extending from about 1780 to about 1860, has left permanent marks both on the structure of administration and on British theories about national administration in general. But at that time matters were on the whole settled by general public debate, followed by decision *ad hoc* on particular issues, such as the development of Parliamentary and Treasury control of finance, the system of audit, the Poor Law Board and the Local Government Board, the evolution of the system of providing services through local authorities, the critical decisions about the structure of the Civil Service. At this stage, the government had no machinery for considering its own organisation; changes of organisation were forced upon it, not generated from within.

At the end of the 1880s there began a period of government sponsorship of formal public inquiries into large questions of organisation, of which the most important perhaps were inquiries into organisation for defence, into social service organisation, and into the financial relations between central and local government. The inquiry was normally conducted by a Royal Commission or Departmental Committee, consisting of a cross-section of experienced persons and hearing evidence from all who wished to present it. Some of these inquiries (like that of the Poor Law Commission, which sat from 1905 to 1909) were very large in scope, and discussed principles of great generality, but none of them attempted to survey government organisation as a whole.

At the end of the 1914-18 war the Ministry of Reconstruction through various committees attempted to sum up experience and look forward into the post-war period. One of these committees, which was appointed in July 1917 and reported in December 1918, was instructed: 'to inquire into the responsibilities of the various Departments of the central executive Government, and to advise in what manner the exercise and distribution by the Government of its functions should be improved'. This was the first Machinery of Government Committee, an extremely distinguished body whose Report has influenced all subsequent discussion. But it had not the authority of the Cabinet behind it, and lacking that authority it had no direct and immediate influence in securing specific changes.

During the Second World War, in 1943, a committee with the same title was set up on a very different basis. This was a Standing Committee of the Cabinet under the chairmanship of the Lord President; it met to deal with specific points referred to it as they arose. This Ministerial Committee was served by a parallel committee of civil servants, which recommended in 1945 that the Treasury should be given official responsibility for a continuous review of the machinery of government. A small branch was set up in the Treasury in 1946, and was later incorporated in the O. & M. Division. This Machinery of Government Branch acted as secretariat to a committee of Permanent Secretaries and others, which met under the chairmanship of the Permanent Secretary to the Treasury and carried out investigations for it when required. Present Cabinet arrangements are not made public, but it is unlikely that it has been necessary to keep a Standing Committee in existence during the quieter times of the 1950s.

These formal arrangements within the Treasury represented some concession to the frequent demand (made for instance during an inquiry by the Select Committee on National Expenditure in 1943) that government should be organised at the top on 'sound principles', 'scientifically', or 'on business lines'. But the Treasury has always resisted the idea that questions at this level could be handled by the ordinary procedure of O. & M., since the Cabinet cannot be relieved of responsibility for major decisions affecting its own members. Giving evidence before the Estimates Committee in 1947, Sir Edward Bridges said:

> From one point of view it is clear that the Machinery of Government work is part of the O. & M. work in its widest sense ... [but] there is one difference ... namely that you want to bring into play not only an experience of organisation and of the operations carried out by Departments, but also, I think, experience of the handling of these questions at the higher levels, some experience of the way Ministers approach these questions of organisation and of the working of Cabinet Committees and so forth.

And again:

> At the present day there are bound to be an enormous number of points of contact between different Departments. Looked at from the outside it may often appear as though there were an overlap ... but only too often I think you find that if you made a re-arrangement you would get an even more awkward point of division somewhere else. Although I am certainly not saying that those points should not be looked at possibly more than they are to-day, I do not believe that inquiry into them would give very big results either in staff saving or in reducing the pressure on the people at the top.[1]

The most that could be claimed for the system introduced in 1946 was that it might reduce friction and help to secure consistency in decision. Controversies recur in cycles, and similar issues turn up in different contexts. It is undoubtedly helpful that responsibility for general advice should be placed squarely on the Treasury (in particular on one of the Permanent Secretaries) and that within the Treasury one branch should be responsible for maintaining records, and for setting standards of objective investigation and discussion.

---

[1] Minutes of Evidence taken before the Select Committee on Estimates (Sub-Committee D), Session 1946-47 (Q.s 1608 and 1631).

(ii) *General Principles*

The general arguments involved in such controversies perhaps fall into two groups: arguments from the logic of administration in general; arguments from British experience (and, to a very slight extent, from experience elsewhere).

The Haldane Committee attempted to find principles of organisation *a priori* by a consideration of the general nature of the problem, and suggested that on this basis there were only two alternatives. Functions could be divided between Departments *either* on the basis of 'particular classes of persons' to be served *or* on the basis of 'the particular service which the Department renders to the community as a whole'.[1] They assumed these alternatives to be exclusive, and chose the latter, from which they deduced a logical division of the functions of government into ten parts.

The Haldane Committee stated their principle as if it were self-evident. It can, however, be shown that its special value in the year 1918 was to link together a number of controversies in which members of the Committee were specially interested: about organisation for defence, justice, health, education, and relief of poverty. It is also possible to push farther their own method of analysis, so as to illustrate the difficulties of defining exactly such terms as 'classes of persons' and 'particular services', and to indicate other bases of classification. The most common division in text-books about the theory of administration is into organisation by area or unit (e.g. the Scottish Office, or the command of a ship or of a battalion); by type of client (e.g. persons over the age of 65); by service or 'function' (e.g. education); by technique or 'process' employed (e.g. the organisation and maintenance of a telephone system). Such terms are difficult to define so that they are mutually exclusive: for instance, an employment exchange service can be called a service to a particular group of clients (those seeking jobs), or a service using a particular technique (that of job placement), or a service discharging a particular function; and its lower organisation may well be organisation by areas. Some of these ambiguities might be resolved by further refinement in definition, but it is not clear that this would be of any practical value.

Criticisms of this kind tended from about the 1940s to discredit

[1] This is very like something said by Aristotle, and perhaps remembered by those members of the committee who had studied him in their youth. 'We have also to consider whether to allocate duties on the basis of the subject to be handled, or on that of the persons concerned: e.g. should we have one officer for the whole subject of the maintenance of order, or a separate officer for the class of children and another for that of women?' (Aristotle: *Politics*, Bk. IV, xv, 9, trans. Barker).

the 'logical' or 'analytical' approach to the study of administration. Various trends in sociology and psychology have combined to emphasise that an 'illogical' organisation may be as good as a 'logical' one if it proves in practice to work well. Current academic textbooks about the higher organisation of government and industry stress 'human relations' rather than 'rationality', and offer quite a different set of generalisations, emphasising particularly the importance of easy communication within the organisation, of unofficial contacts, of a stable and well-understood structure of roles and functions. The period is past when this fashion was carried to excess, and the trend in theoretical discussion now is to seek for some way of combining the old fashion with the new. This is not easy to do, but in the process there is perhaps emerging a better view of the relation between theory and practice in administrative discussion. Theory certainly cannot dictate to practice; but the practice of administration involves continuous discussion about alternative courses of action, which cannot be carried on at all without reference to general terms. Discussion might become more effective as a prelude to action if there were better general understanding of the competing 'principles' and of the limits of their application.

(iii) *British Experience*

Lessons can be learnt, in rather a different way, from the experience of British administration. Administrative history has not been much studied academically, but all senior administrators have had personal experience of controversies about Departmental organisation and there is probably some consensus of opinion within the Service about what is wise and unwise, possible and impossible. This experience is, however, difficult to sum up and to transmit, because of the great complexity of the issues involved. There are now quite a large number of 'classical' controversies about Departmental frontiers: for instance, about the responsibility for research and production for defence; about control of the Fleet Air Arm and of the Coastal Command of the R.A.F.; about the organisation of central government activities in Scotland and Wales; about the relation between education services, child health services and child care services; about the activities now divided between the Ministry of Health and the Ministry of Housing and Local Government; about the relations between the Ministry of Agriculture and the Ministry of Food. Each of these is in itself an intricate and technical story: personalities and political circumstances are involved in every change, and the general factors are difficult to disentangle. Experi-

THE ADMINISTRATIVE FUNCTIONS OF THE CABINET

ence perhaps suggests lines of thought rather than conclusions, and some of these are indicated tentatively below.

(a) It would be a useful starting-point if it were possible to reach some working agreement about a grouping of the functions of government. The Haldane Committee suggested that there were ten main divisions; experience suggests that it is more natural to work with a division into five. These are: the three traditional functions of government—law and order, external affairs, and defence; the function of finance, which now involves responsibility for the management of the country as an economic unit; and the field of social services, which are partly a matter of distribution 'to each according to his needs', partly a matter of maintaining the nation as an effective body of producers, well-educated, well-housed, and in good health. The business of the Cabinet tends (so it seems) to subdivide itself in this way. This is a usual grouping of subjects for Cabinet committees, and each group tends to attract the attention of politicians and administrators of a particular bent.

Nevertheless, the division is in practice an uneasy one, and troubles about demarcation arise where the lines between these groups are not clear. For instance, ought each Defence Department to include the relevant production and research divisions, or should these be grouped together in one or more separate Departments? Ought the Ministry of Food, responsible for social as well as for economic problems of food distribution, to be merged with the Ministry of Agriculture, responsible for production? Is the Factory Inspectorate best placed in the Home Office or in the Ministry of Labour?

(b) On many of these issues considerations one way or the other are so evenly balanced that perhaps the main public interest is that a decision should be given which will be accepted by all parties as final. If there is a strong case on both sides, as there often is, the process of argument may divert the attention of Ministers and civil servants from more important things; it may even produce a situation in which each organisation does its work partly with a view to establishing a better position in debate. Various forms of settlement have been tried: investigation and decision by the Prime Minister or by a senior Minister on his behalf; some sort of quasi-judicial procedure, like that of the Inskip judgement upon the Fleet Air Arm dispute; inquiry by a Cabinet Committee; inquiry by some independent body. It is not possible to say that one procedure has in general been more successful than another. The Prime Minister and the Permanent Secretaries of the Treasury have to hand a variety of devices for the settlement of disputes, and they must choose according to circumstances and judgement.

(c) In some countries each Department and sub-Department has its own clientèle which constitutes a strong pressure group: the clientèle and the Department interact, and any question of increasing or reducing the Department's functions at once becomes a public question. There are some traces of such a system in Britain, such as the relation of the British Legion to the old Ministry of Pensions, or of the National Farmers' Union to the Ministry of Agriculture. But Departments are in part shielded from this kind of politics by the British structure of Cabinet and Treasury control, and pressure for reorganisation is more likely to arise out of some particular incident which attracts (it may be deliberately used to attract) public attention to the failure of a public service. In the years from 1936 to 1939 the agitation for resistance to Hitler assumed in part the form of agitation for a reorganisation of defence by the creation of a Ministry of Defence and a Ministry of Supply. In 1940 the setting up of a Ministry of Aircraft Production under a dynamic Minister was a gesture of resolution in face of defeat and an indication of top priority. In 1945 an inquiry into the death of an orphan child[1] built up public support for the recommendations of a Departmental Committee[2] which was then sitting, and resulted in a reorganisation of the child care services. Since 1942 there has been a maze of reorganisation and changes of titles among the Ministries dealing with Health, Housing, Works, Town and Country Planning, and Local Government, each change representing a shift in personalities and in political emphasis.

The debates in these cases follow patterns of argument which tend to recur. A shake-up of the organisation will give a chance to get rid of dead wood and to make a fresh start with new men in key positions. But it is a pity to dislocate existing relations, familiar to all concerned, and it will take some time for a new organisation to find its feet. It is desirable to group similar functions together, for instance functions of research and production, because one can then get the right type of man at the top, and energy will not be dissipated between conflicting demands. But it is dangerous to divide producer from user. If they are separated the user gets into the habit of stating impracticable requirements, the producer ceases to respond quickly to need. It is desirable to get rid of small Departments because they are expensive in overheads and make collaboration difficult. But large Departments are slow and cumbersome, and it is impossible for a single Minister to supervise one of them or to represent it adequately in Parliament. And so on: in isolation, each of the conflicting

[1] Report by Sir W. Monckton on the O'Neill Case. Cmd. 6636, 1945.
[2] The Curtis Committee. Report, Cmd. 6922, 1946.

THE ADMINISTRATIVE FUNCTIONS OF THE CABINET 367

'proverbs' makes good sense, but they cancel out unless it is possible to relate them closely to experience, and this is difficult to do. In default of experience the matter may be settled (at least temporarily) by a combination of pressure, fashion, and tactical skill.

(d) The 'lessons of experience' are real, but are difficult to use in argument because of the nature of the evidence. It is almost impossible to produce objective or conclusive proof that any reorganisation above the level of routine has succeeded or failed, since its effects cannot be compared with what would have happened if there had been no reorganisation. There was a surge of fighter output when Lord Beaverbrook took over aircraft production from the Air Ministry. But (say his detractors) there would have been a surge in production in any case in the summer of 1940, because preparatory organisation was just coming to fruition, and there was a wave of enthusiasm in the factories. Besides (they would say), he never understood that an aircraft in the production statistics was not the same as an aircraft fit for combat, and therefore he pushed up the production of complete aircraft at the expense of the spare parts needed to keep existing aircraft in service. A stronger instance of successful change might be the reorganisation of the child care service by the Act of 1948. Here there were good theoretical arguments in favour of reorganisation, and few arguments the other way; and there has been an improvement in the service which can be measured satisfactorily by various criteria. But much more money and enthusiasm have gone into the service since its reorganisation, and at least some of the gains would have been made by putting these extra resources into the old framework. Besides, the new organisation undoubtedly creates points of overlap and friction between the child care service and the health, education, and welfare services, which become more noticeable as other difficulties decrease. Both instances suggest that at this level it is misleading to separate success in administration from success in politics. A reorganisation is a 'good' one in certain circumstances if by dramatic change it gives impetus to a particular service, even though the new organisation is not in any other sense more efficient than the old.

(e) Other instances also suggest considerations of a type more readily appreciated by politicians than by non-political administrators. The case most often argued on these lines is that of the arrangements for the organisation of justice. The responsibility for the maintenance of efficient courts administering a coherent body of law is in Britain distributed between a number of authorities, none of whom has effective control. The Victorian attempt to codify the law of England, even section by section, has broken down; the machinery for recommending changes in private law which are admitted to be necessary moves very slowly; and the organisation of magistrates' courts resists all attempts to reform it. Such evasion of responsibility can be excused only on the ground that attempts by the executive to organise the judiciary are a danger to the system of freedom under law; that the organisation of the law is autonomous and cannot be reformed except from within. Similarly it could be maintained that the character of the relations between police and public in Britain depends partly on the peculiarities of an organisation in which the government does not have legal authority to issue orders to any police force except that of the metropolis. The Home Office has sufficient sanctions at its disposal to secure efficiency and co-operation, but it shares responsibility for public order with locally elected committees throughout the country. Again, there are anomalies in the system of education. The Ministry of Education supervises the provision of schools, but it has limited authority over curricula and examinations. It has great influence over many forms of higher education through grants to students, but it is not responsible for grants to Universities. It is thus very difficult to plan, or even to understand the educational system as a whole. On the other side of the account, teachers and students are to some extent protected against sudden swings in political and educational fashion, which would be transmitted more quickly through a more centralised system.

In all these matters a change in organisation would mean more than a reallocation of duties. It would mean a change in the nature of the State. It would be a constitutional and not an administrative change if we had a Ministry of Justice which effectively supervised the organisation of the Courts, a Ministry of the Interior which controlled local authorities and police, and a Ministry of Education which directed the whole system of public instruction, or a Scottish Office which grouped together all the administrative services of the central government in Scotland. We come once again to the difficulty of disentangling the role of the Cabinet in politics from its role in administration.

FOR REFERENCE

Central Organisation for Defence. Cmd. 6923, 1946.

Sir GWILYM GIBBON: 'The Organisation of Government', *Public Administration*, Vol. XVIII, p. 7.

Sir JOHN ANDERSON (Lord Waverley): 'The Machinery of Government', *Public Administration*, Vol. XXIV, p. 147 (The *Romanes Lecture*, 1946).

THE ADMINISTRATIVE FUNCTIONS OF THE CABINET

L. S. AMERY: *Thoughts on the Constitution* (2nd Edn., 1953). (Chapter on the Machinery of Government.)
K. C. WHEARE: 'The Machinery of Government', *Public Administration*, Vol. XXIV, p. 75.
FRANCIS WILLIAMS: *The Triple Challenge* (1948).
—— 'The Office of Public Relations Adviser to the Prime Minister', *Parliamentary Affairs*, Vol. IX, No. 3.
D. N. CHESTER (Ed.): *Lessons of the British War Economy* (1951).
(See especially Introduction by Sir Richard Hopkins, 'The Central Machinery for Economic Policy' by D. N. Chester, and 'The Prime Minister's Statistical Section' by G. D. A. MacDougall.)
H. MORRISON: *Government and Parliament* (1954). (Chapters 1, 2, 3, and 13.)
Sir OLIVER FRANKS: *Central Planning and Control in War and Peace* (1947).
R. S. MILNE: 'Britain's Economic Planning Machinery', *American Political Science Review*, Vol. XLVI, p. 406.
—— 'Has Britain an Economic General Staff?', *Australian Journal of Public Administration*, Vol. XII, p. 11.
S. C. LESLIE: 'Work of the Economic Information Unit', *Public Administration*, Vol. XXVIII, p. 17.
R. J. P. HEWISON: 'The Organisation of the Cabinet Secretariat', *Public Administration*, Vol. XXX, p. 221.
E. C. WILLIAMS: 'Science and Defence,' *Public Administration*, Vol. XXXIV, p. 257.
M. P. A. HANKEY (LORD HANKEY): *Diplomacy by Conference* (1946).
—— *Government Control in War* (1945).
—— *Development of the Higher Control of the Machinery of Government* (1942).
R. MARRIS: 'The Position of Economics and Economists in the Government Machine', *Economic Journal*, Vol. 64, December 1954.
—— *The Machinery of Economic Policy* (1955). (Fabian Research Series, No. 168.)
(See also a reply to Mr. Marris by Mr. Hugh Gaitskell in *Fabian Journal*, No. 14, at p. 4.)
Political and Economic Planning (P.E.P.): 'The Machinery of Government', *Planning*, No. 173 (1941).
—— 'A Civil General Staff', *Planning*, No. 214 (1943).
Sir HENRY BUNBURY: *Governmental Planning Machinery—A Comparative Study* (Chicago, 1938).
P. GORDON-WALKER: 'On being a Cabinet Minister', *Encounter*, April 1956.
Royal Institute of Public Administration: *The Organisation of British Central Government 1914-1956, A Survey*. Edited by D. N. Chester and written by F. M. G. Willson (1957).
C. H. WILSON: Haldane the Machinery of Government (Haldane Memorial Lecture, 1956).

2 A

IV
THE PLACE OF CENTRAL ADMINISTRATION

INTRODUCTORY

WE have now traced the internal structure of the administration, treating it so far as possible in isolation from other factors in British government. This description culminates in an account of the administrative role of the Cabinet, and it might be constitutionally proper to stop there, since the Cabinet is the seat of supreme authority and the formal link between central administration and the rest of British public life. There would be some justification for this; ministerial responsibility is not a fraud but a fact of extreme importance in the working of the system. It is much truer in Britain than in most other countries that central administration looks upwards and not outwards; the British administrator is more concerned with his Minister, less concerned with the public and other public authorities, than is an administrator in France or the U.S.A. But this is no more than part of the truth. The central administration is in practice tied into British life at many points and not at one only, and our object in these concluding chapters is to indicate the nature of some of these contacts.

For the present purpose it is convenient to make a five-fold division: Parliament and the world of party politics; the law courts and the system of law; local government; public administrative bodies outside the structure of central and local government; and the public itself, especially as represented in government through a very large number of stable organisations each with its own leadership and internal politics. Each of these topics requires a text-book to itself, and it would be useless to attempt summaries here. We therefore take for granted that the reader knows something of the formal structure of each of these spheres of action, and we make no attempt to explain subjects such as the powers of Parliament and of different types of local authority. What we are concerned with is the practical relationship between these other spheres and that of the civil servant. How do they impinge on his work as administrator?

This problem is generally posed in terms of 'control'. Has Parliament adequate 'control' over the central administration? Have civil servants too great 'control' over the courts? Or too little 'control' over nationalised industry? And so on. The word 'control' has various overlapping senses; for our present purpose we distinguish two of them:

(i) 'Control' may mean 'legal authority to issue orders'. In law there is generally (but not always) a precise answer to the question 'who controls whom?' Who can issue valid orders, and by what procedure? We are not much concerned here with legal powers of control except in so far as they constitute the framework within which administration works.

(ii) 'Control' may also refer to the practical or informal aspect of the work of the administrator. These working relationships are all two-sided relationships: A affects B, and at the same time B affects A. Certain Departments 'control' local government, but only on the basis of information which comes to them largely from local government, and only after long discussions with local government associations. The law courts 'control' the administration; but the effect of their control is to produce reactions in the administration, which may then either override control by new legislation or accept it without challenge so that control by legal action does not come actively into play at all. The system as a whole is one of action and reaction: it is often difficult to say where real power lies, as distinct from legal authority. Nevertheless, there are clear cases, and we identify them when we can.

FOR REFERENCE

We give more detailed references after each chapter, but emphasise that the next four chapters are intelligible only on the basis of some technical knowledge. This might be obtained from:

Parliament:

LORD CAMPION: *Introduction to the Procedure of the House of Commons* (2nd Edn., 1947).

Sir IVOR JENNINGS: *Parliament* (1939).

Two excellent short works on this subject are:

Sir COURTENAY ILBERT: *Parliament: Its History, Constitution, and Practice* (3rd Edn., revised by Sir Cecil Carr, 1953), in the Home University Library.

ERIC TAYLOR: *The House of Commons at Work* (2nd Edn., 1955), published by Penguin Books.

Administrative Courts and Administrative Law:

J. A. G. GRIFFITH and H. STREET: *Principles of Administrative Law* (1950).
W. A. ROBSON: 'Administrative Law in England, 1919-1948' (in Campion and others: *British Government since 1918* (1950)).

Local Government:

Sir W. E. HART and W. O. HART: *An Introduction to the Law of Local Government* (5th Edn., 1952).

A good short work is:

Sir JOHN MAUD and S. E. FINER: *Local Government in England and Wales* (2nd Revised Edn., 1953).

Other Public Bodies

Sir JAMES ROSS: *The National Health Service in Great Britain* (1952).
W. A. ROBSON (Ed.): *Problems of Nationalised Industry* (1952).

CHAPTER TWENTY

POLITICS AND PARLIAMENT

'The word politics, sir,' said Mr. Pickwick, 'comprises, in itself, a difficult study of no inconsiderable magnitude.'
'Ah!' said the Count, drawing out the tablets again, 'ver good—fine words to begin a chapter. Chapter forty-seven. Poltics. The word poltic surprises by himself.'— DICKENS: *Pickwick Papers*.

1. INTRODUCTORY

THIS chapter is a short one in spite of the importance of the subject, because much of it has been foreshadowed earlier. Parties in Britain are essentially Parliamentary parties, and their influence on central administration is exercised largely through Parliament. In Chapter 10 we set out the present limitations on political activity by civil servants, and there is no doubt that these are in general observed in the spirit as well as in the letter. The Service does not on the whole attract political enthusiasts, and it is not in the interests of a civil servant's career that he should identify himself very closely with a political party, or even become socially intimate with politicians. Some reservations must be made. Civil servants differ in temperament if not in party spirit, and it may in some political circumstances be obvious that the right man for a particular job is Mr. A, who is exact and unenterprising, rather than Mr. B, who is dynamic and sometimes wayward. It may also prove valuable to an individual if an important Minister believes in him and asks for his services. But these things are largely fortuitous; there is no systematic relationship between civil servants and politicians outside 'official channels'— 'correct' relations with Ministers within the Department, 'correct' relations with Parliament outside it. We need not recapitulate what has been said in Chapter 13 about the formal position of the Minister as the highest level of administration in his Department; and in Chapter 18 about the determining influence of Parliament on the system of financial control. Our object is simply to identify the main occasions on which civil servants have to deal with politicians as individuals, and in doing so to illustrate the informal aspects of Parliamentary control over administration.

2. Correspondence and Questions

In the daily life of a Ministry there are two kinds of business which continually bear witness to the importance of Parliamentary politics: the Minister's correspondence and Parliamentary Questions. These are in form quite distinct, but both belong to a well-recognised procedure for obtaining inquiry into individual grievances. An individual aggrieved by the behaviour of a subordinate official will naturally pursue his grievance by frontal attack on the Ministry, and may secure redress by the presentation of new arguments and new facts. Or he may be advised that he has a legal remedy in the courts. If these direct methods fail, indirect methods are still open. The person aggrieved may seek publicity through the press. Alternatively (or in addition) he may gain the ear of someone who has access to the Minister in his political capacity. The most obvious person is the M.P. for the constituency in which the aggrieved person votes. Most M.P.s nowadays run 'clinics' at which they are available to discuss individual grievances, and it would be improper and unwise for an M.P. to refuse to discuss a grievance because the person concerned belonged to a different political party.

An M.P. may succeed in persuading some complainants that they have had a fair deal, and in this sense M.P.s' 'clinics' are a help to central administration. If the M.P. thinks that there is a *prima facie* case for discussion, he may be able to clear the matter by a telephone call to the local office responsible: many quite genuine grievances arise because officials and members of the public simply cannot understand one another. But local officials are often more nervous than is really appropriate in dealing with such 'political' persons as M.P.s, who may 'cause trouble' at higher levels; and M.P.s themselves do not always have time or patience to settle matters locally. It is easier to dictate a letter to the Minister, or simply to forward a constituent's letter with a request for elucidation.

M.P.s are not the only channel for inquiries of this kind: they come to the Minister from various people who have personal access to him, such as leading members of the party organisation which supports him in his constituency, leaders of interest groups in which he has been concerned, or personal friends and old colleagues. But all these may prefer to act through an M.P., since an M.P. is in a position to pursue matters farther in a public way. If he does not like the reply to his informal letter he may put down a Parliamentary Question; if he does not like the reply to his Question he may seek to raise the matter on the adjournment. These are formal ways of so handling an individual grievance that it involves the Minister's personal and political reputation in the House of Commons.

The Minister's correspondence about individual cases is handled by his Private Office, often without consulting him in the first instance. A letter which seems to deal with a minor case (if it really does concern the Department—a good many complaints come to the wrong Minister, and have to be redirected) is acknowledged, and is then put in a special folder and sent to the division or branch concerned, with a note from the Private Secretary or Assistant Private Secretary. Procedure varies somewhat in different Ministries: in general, the special folder demands reasonably high priority, but not top priority unless this is specially indicated on it. The branch concerned is expected to obtain the relevant files, to put the story together accurately and completely, and to give a succinct account of it (and usually to draft a reply) for the Minister. The folder (with files annexed) then returns to the Private Office, probably not going above the level of Assistant Secretary on the way; and the Private Secretary may be able to present the Minister with the letter of inquiry and a draft reply ready for dispatch if approved. Ministers vary greatly in the amount of trouble they are prepared to devote to individual cases; some worry, others sign confidently what is put before them.

The treatment of Parliamentary Questions is similar, but more exacting. Many Ministries have a special Parliamentary Branch under the charge of a Principal, part of whose business is to get prompt information about Questions as soon as they are put down, and who has a line of contact with the Clerks at the Table about this and other matters. The exact form of 'P.Q. Folder' varies in different Ministries: but there is always a fresh folder for each Question, with a note of extreme urgency on its cover, and the business done on that folder is limited to the preparation of a reply to that Question.

Questions may be either for oral or for written answer. The 'written answers' are printed in Hansard; there is an administrative rule that answers must be given within seven days of the Question first appearing on the Order Paper, but there is no opportunity for oral Supplementary Questions and replies do not generally attract much political attention. The Question for oral answer is a more severe test. Ministers 'take their Questions' at Question-time in rotation, and in conditions of normal business a Department's turn comes round about once every ten days while Parliament is sitting. An oral answer cannot be requested on less than forty-eight hours' notice; so the time available to prepare an answer varies from two to ten days. Even ten days is a brief period in which to prepare an answer on a complicated question; to prepare it in two days means giving absolute priority above all other business. A 'P.Q. Folder' travels by special messenger within the Ministry, is passed direct to the person concerned, its times of transit are noted on it to the minute, and it is dealt with at once—literally 'at once', not 'at the first convenient moment'.

Generally, the Parliamentary Branch first identifies the division or branch most closely concerned, then sends them the folder with a request to find material for an answer. The division may itself cast this into the form of a draft Answer, with 'Notes for the Minister' indicating the background and suggesting answers to possible Supplementary Questions; or this may be done by the Parliamentary Branch. In either case, the 'end product' is one single sheet, from which the Minister reads the reply at the dispatch box in the House of Commons. This has been considered by someone high in the hierarchy, perhaps by the Permanent Secretary himself. The draft is polished till it shines, and no one can blame the civil servants if (as has happened) the Minister, after reading the Answer, goes on absent-mindedly to read out the 'Notes for Minister' as well.

This is in its simplest form the process of 'briefing the Minister'. If a particular issue is pursued beyond Questions to a debate on the adjournment, the procedure is the same, more elaborate but perhaps less tense, because the Minister has to deal not with the risk of snap Supplementaries in a crowded House but with formal speeches generally in a thin House.

A distinguished civil servant defined the art of dealing with Questions as that of drafting an answer 'that is brief, appears to answer the question completely, if challenged can be proved to be accurate in every word, gives no opening for awkward "supplementaries", and discloses really nothing'.[1] The point of this apparent cynicism is that a civil servant in preparing an answer has the political life of his Minister in his hands. Questions are put sometimes genuinely to secure justice, sometimes to secure information or extract admissions for an ulterior purpose, sometimes as groundbait for a trap to be sprung in a Supplementary. The Minister is himself (or should be) an expert on the House of Commons; but it is the business of his civil servants to help him to defend himself,

[1] The late Mr. H. E. Dale, in *The Higher Civil Service* (1941) p. 105. A hundred years ago the procedure was the same, but civil servants played a smaller part in it. 'For why, indeed, should any gentleman sit on the Treasury Bench if he be not able, when so questioned, to give very satisfactory replies? Giving satisfactory replies to ill-natured questions is, one may say, the constitutional work of such gentlemen, who have generally well learned [sic] how to do so, and earned their present places by asking the self-same questions themselves, when seated as younger men in other parts of the House.' (Trollope, *The Three Clerks*, 1858.)

since in defending himself he is defending them. It is not an elementary exercise in politics to prepare a case which will stand examination by a critical assembly of experienced debaters. Civil servants are 'non-political': how do they acquire the 'sense of the game' required for briefing in political debate?

3. OTHER PARLIAMENTARY BUSINESS

A short answer is that few of them do acquire it, and that these few are certain of promotion to high office. There is substance in a remark by Lt.-Col. Urwick that for a civil servant in Britain 'the nobleness of life (as Antony said when he kissed Cleopatra) lies not in being the executive leader of a great department employing perhaps 20,000—or ten times that number—of human beings. It resides for the great majority, even of high civil servants, in being a trusted Chief of Staff to a succession of Ministers.'[1] The highest type of British civil servant is a secretary, rather than a manager. The Service includes many very able managers, but unless they have a sense of politics they are not safe advisers to a Minister whose life depends on success in the House of Commons. A Ministry cannot be successful if its Ministers fail. Hence the character of the House of Commons affects the character of central administration: it enforces a particular type of financial procedure and a very careful procedure for the record of individual cases, and it brings to the top men who are capable of understanding politics without becoming party politicians. How do such men gain experience?

Much experience comes in the ordinary course of business to those capable of acquiring it. Civil servants are bound to read Hansard in so far as it concerns their own branch of work, and they may read more than that. They can learn much from procedure on M.P.s' letters and on Parliamentary Questions (some Ministries circulate the relevant folders for information after action is complete); those who show promise may learn still more by working in a Private Office. But this applies only to staff at headquarters; even at headquarters few civil servants are directly concerned, and the opportunities for direct contact with the political process are so few that they are rather alarming when they come.

There are, however, three types of business which bring some civil servants more closely into contact with the House of Commons (the House of Lords is much less important, in this as in other things): the promotion of Bills; subordinate legislation; hearings before committees of the House.

[1] *The Making of an Administrator*, ed. A. Dunsire (1956).

(i) Bills

The preparation of a Bill is to some extent intelligible merely as a piece of administration. A working scheme must be prepared, with a sense of the difficulties involved and the resources available. The scheme must then be thrown into the form of sections, clauses, and schedules, and the drafting of each sentence must be carefully considered in close consultation with Parliamentary Counsel. But even the preparation of a Bill involves politics: it may originate in a party programme, and in framing it steps may have to be taken to meet the requirements of party orthodoxy, as well as to reduce opposition by a careful balance of the interests concerned. While a Bill is passing through the Commons such matters are of lively and pressing importance to the civil servants concerned.

During debates involving 'their' Minister the civil servants directly concerned with the business in hand sit in 'the box', the small and uncomfortable gallery behind the Speaker's Chair on his right, at the end of the Government benches. The Minister is on the front bench, his Parliamentary Private Secretary behind him on the second bench, so that he may act as go-between during the debate between the Minister and the officials 'in the box'. The officials may not have the answer at hand; they then have to try to get it from the Ministry, and this may mean that many officials there 'stand by' far into the night, since Parliament does not keep office hours. This may happen for a short period on big occasions, such as a Supply Day debate on the work of the Ministry or the second reading of a major Bill; it happens over long periods, generally before a less crowded House, when a large Bill is going through its Committee stage on the floor of the House. The discussion of a Bill, clause by clause, brings the civil servant very close to the small number of Members who are keen enough to follow a Bill in detail, and to the groups of experts and interests which brief them against his own briefing of the Minister. This contact is even closer if the Bill goes 'upstairs' to a Standing Committee of the House. There proceedings are still formal, and the official may not intervene, but he sits where he may be consulted by his Minister personally, and he and the other non-members concerned become more intimately part of the proceedings. This atmosphere of 'informal formality' can be felt even in the printed record of proceedings in a Standing Committee on a big Bill.

(ii) *Subordinate Legislation*

The House of Commons is keenly interested in the use of legislative powers delegated to Ministers by Act of Parliament. It is a commonplace (a very misleading one) to speak of this as a transfer of the sovereign power of legislation from Parliament to officials, and the back-benchers on both sides are generally ready to demand more thorough control by the House itself. This has always been refused by Ministers, generally with the sympathy of the 'alternative government' on the Opposition front bench, since it would greatly add to the burden of administration if each Instrument made under an Act had to be justified on its merits to the House of Commons or to one of its committees. It is an accepted constitutional principle in Britain that choice of policy within the powers given by statute is a matter for the government, not for the Commons, subject to the right of the courts to quash an illegal use of powers, and subject to the right of the Commons to express a general lack of confidence in the government, and so to dismiss it.

The control of delegated legislation is therefore in practice a matter for the courts rather than for Parliament. The powers of the Commons are limited to the right of 'praying' for the annulment of Instruments which 'lie on the Table' subject to negative resolution; and (in a restricted category of cases) of giving or withholding approval by affirmative resolution. These powers preserve the strict form of Parliamentary sovereignty over delegated legislation, but for two reasons they are not of great practical importance: first, because all Instruments are made on the authority of the government, and the government's majority is invoked to defend them; second, because over 2,000 Instruments are submitted to Parliament each year, and it is not possible to scrutinise even a very small proportion of them on the floor of the House without causing hopeless congestion of business.

On both counts, those who desire more effective practical control demand the creation of a committee of the Commons with full powers to scrutinise Statutory Instruments in draft. This is the only way in which to gain more time for the purpose, and there is a chance that the solidarity of a well-informed committee might (as has happened in other spheres) weaken the hold of the party Whips. In 1944 Mr. Churchill's government went a short distance to meet these claims, and agreed to the appointment of a Select Committee on Statutory Rules and Orders, which is reappointed each Session, now under the name of the Select Committee on Statutory Instruments, or (more colloquially) 'the Scrutiny Committee'.

The weakness of this Committee is that its terms of reference were limited from the outset and that all attempts to extend them have failed. The Committee is not of course a court of law, and cannot decide formally whether or not an Instrument has been properly made, though it can (and does frequently) seek information about the authority under which Departments claim to act. Nor is it entitled to advise the government and the House about the political merits of an Instrument. Its main task is to draw the attention of the House to any Instrument in draft which:

(*a*) imposes a charge on the public revenues;
(*b*) excludes challenge in the courts;
(*c*) purports (without statutory authority) to have retrospective effect;
(*d*) has been unjustifiably delayed in publication or laying before Parliament;
(*e*) is obscure in form or purport; *or*
(*f*) appears to make some unusual or unexpected use of the powers conferred by the parent statute.

Within this rather limited field the Committee has been very effective, largely because it was served from the outset by Sir Cecil Carr, then Counsel to Mr. Speaker, who was editor of the Statutes Revised and Statutory Rules and Orders from 1923 to 1943, and who has a unique knowledge of the whole procedure for delegated legislation. Its main influence has been in the field of procedure rather than in that of constitutional principle, and there is no doubt that it has had a real influence on Departments through direct contact with civil servants. It can demand from the Department concerned explanations of delays in publication, or of obscurity in phraseology, or of lack of proper reference to the authorising statute; and it can also take oral evidence from the civil servants personally concerned. Its business is handled quietly, and it would be an exaggeration to call it a terror of wrong-doers. Between 1944 and the beginning of 1953 it commented on only 93 Instruments out of a total of nearly 7,000 which came before it for examination. Nevertheless, it has had so much success in improving the observance of good procedure that the number of cases in which it makes complaint has diminished, and the controversy about Statutory Instruments has (for the present, at least) died away. The Committee remains in being rather as a reminder to civil servants than as a sanction in constant use.

(iii) *Other Committees of the House of Commons*

The other Committees concerned are the **Public Accounts Committee** and the **Estimates Committee**, to which reference has already been made in earlier chapters. The House of Commons has very wide powers of inquiry, and in the nineteenth century much work was done by Select Committees which would now be done by Royal Commissions or Departmental Committees. A civil servant may be called upon to give evidence before any committee of this kind, and such an appearance is necessarily an ordeal; but it is not now a common one, whereas inquiries by the Public Accounts Committee may affect a Department in any year (particularly if there is an unfavourable report by the Comptroller and Auditor-General), and those by the Estimates Committee are fairly frequent.

Enough has been said in Chapter 18 to indicate how these Committees fit into the structure of the financial system. What needs emphasis here is that it is only through these Committees that civil servants are regularly put on their defence before Members of Parliament.

An Accounting Officer appears before the Public Accounts Committee in his individual capacity. The members of the Committee are his masters, not for policy but for financial procedure, which is designed primarily to satisfy the formal requirements of the House of Commons. The Committee which enforces this control regards itself as a guardian of the Constitution, and it does not hesitate to report in very severe terms about Departments and occasionally about individuals. It is part of the atmosphere of the Committee that there is rarely business before it which enables it to say a kind word about the administration, since it proceeds to its inquiry on the basis of critical reports by the Comptroller and Auditor-General.

The Committee is not perhaps as awe-inspiring in practice as in theory. A Permanent Secretary 'on trial' appears before it supported by his Principal Finance Officer and other members of his staff. The Comptroller and Auditor-General is generally present in person, but does not conduct the examination, nor does he intervene very frequently. A Treasury Officer of Accounts is also present, but his role is generally not so much to criticise the Department as to explain the Treasury point of view. Much of the business is already more familiar to the Permanent Secretary than to those who examine him, since it comes to them only at the end of a long process of discussion within the administration. Nevertheless, the existence of the Committee affects the atmosphere of Departments, both because a Permanent Secretary must brief himself very carefully before he appears before it, and because in making day-to-day decisions about action and about procedure he is constantly aware that he may be called upon to answer in detail some two years later.

The Estimates Committee has quite different forms of procedure. It acts through fairly small sub-committees, not as a single body. It is served only by one or two members of the House of Commons staff, and has no expert service like the Audit Office at its disposal; it does not act on reports by others, but proceeds to inquire and report itself. For these reasons, and because its constitutional powers are much smaller, its relations to the administration are rather different. Its inquiries are 'fishing' expeditions. Some members of the sub-committees have hobby-horses that they wish to ride; others want publicity for the Committee and for themselves. Hence there is a real chance that if civil servants handle a sub-committee well they may get it on their side in the promotion of the Department's policy. Reports sometimes recommend cuts; but almost as frequently they recommend reorganisation, and suggest (in the name of 'true economy') greater spending on some part of the service under review.

It is perhaps too soon to generalise about the Estimates Committee, which has worked under its present forms of procedure only since 1945. One contribution which it has certainly made has been to record annually millions of words of dialogue between civil servants and Members of Parliament. The evidence is of immense interest to the student of British government, but its readers are few and the direct influence of the Committee's Reports is not great. Certainly the Committee has not yet produced the intimacy of relationship between representatives and officials which is common in the U.S.A. and in some other countries. Such intimacy is by British standards undesirable, but the curious British distinction between political and non-political rulers will only work if there is mutual comprehension, and the Committee contributes a good deal to this.

FOR REFERENCE

Report of a Select Committee on Delegated Legislation, Session 1952-53. H.C. 310-1.

Reports from the Select Committee on Statutory Instruments.

LORD CAMPION and Others: *Parliament—A Survey* (1952) (particularly chapters by H. E. Dale on 'Parliament in Relation to the Civil Service', and Sir Cecil Carr on 'Delegated Legislation').

K. C. WHEARE: *Government by Committee* (1955). (Chapters VI and VIII.)

B. CHUBB: *Control of Public Expenditure* (1952).

A. H. HANSON: 'The Select Committee on Statutory Instruments', *Public Administration*, Vol. XXVII, p. 278. See also a reply by F. A. Stacey in the same journal, Vol. XXVIII, p. 333, and a further note by Mr. Hanson, Vol. XXIX, p. 281.

E. H. BEET: 'Parliament and Delegated Legislation 1945-53', *Public Administration*, Vol. XXXIII, p. 325.

Sir CECIL CARR: 'Parliamentary Control of Delegated Legislation', *Public Law*, Vol. I, p. 200.

K. E. COUZENS: 'A Minister's Correspondence', *Public Administration*, Vol. XXXIV, p. 237.

CHAPTER TWENTY-ONE

THE COURTS OF LAW

Let no man weakly conceive that just laws and true policy have any antipathy: for they are like the spirits and sinews, that one moves with the other.—BACON: *Of Judicature*.

1. INTRODUCTORY

THERE is judicial control of the administration in a formal sense if courts of law have power to make orders which must be obeyed by civil servants. English courts can certainly make such orders, and (in laymen's language) there are three types of case in which they may do so:

(i) If it is alleged that the rules on which the Department relies are not law at all: that is to say, that the regulation involved was made without legal authority or by faulty procedure.

(ii) If it is alleged that the Department has acted on a wrong construction of the law; for instance, if under a law which permits him to enter dwelling-houses an inspector has entered what is not in law a dwelling-house (though he thought it was).

(iii) If it is alleged that the Department has in a specific matter done something which it was entitled by law to do, but only if it followed the right procedure, and it has in fact followed the wrong procedure. 'Faults in procedure' may range from narrow points of date or signature to large questions about 'the rules of natural justice'.

These formal powers of control are very wide, and it is beyond doubt that English courts use their powers with integrity and skill. But the value of formal control is questioned on various practical grounds:

First, the forms of procedure are cumbrous and expensive, so that citizens find it convenient to seek redress against Departments through political channels rather than by legal action.

Secondly, the administration influences Parliament, and therefore influences the making of the law which the courts must interpret. The Departments (politicians and civil servants acting together) are often in a position to modify law which has proved inconvenient.

Thirdly, there is not much interaction in ordinary business between civil servants and lawyers: neither wholly understands the other's point of view, and the civil servant is not as responsive to problems about law as he is to problems about politics.

This contrast between the theory and the practice of judicial control lies at the root of the controversy about the role of the courts in relation to administration, opened by Dicey's book on *The Law of the Constitution*, which went through many editions from 1885 until the author's death in 1922, and is still influential. The technical side of this controversy is too complex to summarise here: in what follows we assume elementary knowledge of the main legal questions involved. Our present purpose is to attempt to set out what the Civil Service has to do with the courts in practice, a matter which has not been much investigated, so that our account is in many ways provisional. We do this under five headings: lawyers and legal habits of mind in central administration; central administration as responsible for the management of the judicial system; civil servants as legislators; civil servants as judges and advisers to judges; civil servants before the ordinary courts.

2. Lawyers in the Civil Service

In Chapter 7 we explained briefly the organisation of the Legal Class of the Civil Service. There are about 600 members of the Class, and of these perhaps 350 rank with the grades of Principal, Senior Executive Officer, and above. There are about 2,250 officials in these grades in the Administrative Class, about 3,700 in the main Executive Class alone, apart from Departmental Classes. Entry to the Administrative Class is open to law graduates fresh from the Universities, but the number entering in this way from year to year is very small.

The organisation of the Legal Class and its expansion even to its present size have been relatively recent, and its members work largely in self-contained Departments and divisions, as advisers and not as administrators. They therefore do little to affect the general character of the administration; the ordinary civil servant is an expert—perhaps better than any professional lawyer—on the law affecting his own field, but he has had no formal training in law, and is not sensitive to general considerations about the effect of particular measures on the legal system as a whole. In this, British administration differs from that of all other European countries, and also (though not quite in the same way) from that of the United States.

Perhaps for the same reason, it is not 'judicialised' or 'legalised' internally. This appears in two respects:

(i) There are no internal disciplinary tribunals, and there is no *Statut des Fonctionnaires* giving enforceable rights to the individual civil servant; nor is there any serious demand for a change.

(ii) Matters of internal procedure are screened from any form of judicial inquiry, either by ordinary courts or by administrative courts. It is quite usual on the continent of Europe to regard the rules of internal procedure as law, so that an official act which does not conform to them is invalid, and may in some circumstances be upset by administrative courts or other judicial procedure. This 'judicialisation' is thought to protect the administration and the public against all the difficulties that arise from irregularity in procedure; probably it does not lead to much greater formalism or correctness than we have in Britain, since British civil servants are well disciplined in the ways of their Departments. The difference is as much one of method as of substance, except perhaps at the highest levels of administration; the British system certainly seems to be more flexible and less formal at the top than are systems more legal in character.

3. CENTRAL ADMINISTRATION AND THE ORGANISATION OF THE COURTS

The Haldane Committee (whose chairman was Lord Chancellor from 1912 to 1915, and again in 1924) commented on the confusion of responsibility for the management of the judicial system as a whole, and the system remains much as they described it in 1918. There are four main elements:

(i) *The Lord Chancellor's Office*. The curious position of the Lord Chancellor has already been described. He is generally a member of the Cabinet and is its chief legal adviser. He presides over the House of Lords both as chamber of the legislature (which is a formality) and as supreme court (which is a very onerous duty). He is responsible for advice on practically all appointments to high judicial office; and as President of the Supreme Court of Judicature he also has general responsibility for the management of its office arrangements. He appoints all Justices of the Peace in England and Wales (except in the County of Lancaster), and all County Court judges, and he has a great deal of other patronage of various kinds. On the other hand, he intervenes very little in the organisation of the judicial business of the Supreme Court or in its making of rules for procedure; and no Chancellor since Lord

Birkenhead has found time to exercise much influence over the important general questions of law reform which do not interest any political party.

The Lord Chancellor's 'Departments' are referred to in the plural in the Civil Service List, as if to underline the looseness of the organisation. The Permanent Secretary (whom it is usual to appoint also to the ancient dignity of Clerk of the Crown in Chancery) is directly responsible for a central office staffed by a small group of senior officials, mainly lawyers. He is also responsible in a more general way (and the exact scope of his responsibility varies) for a group of offices, including the County Courts Branch, the Central Office of the Supreme Court, the Bankruptcy and Companies (Winding-up) Office, the Land Registry, and the Office of the Public Trustee. These are staffed partly by lawyers who may act as minor judges, partly by officials roughly comparable in status to those of the Executive Class. This organisation, though loose and informal, is on a considerable scale, as it manages the most important legal business of a community of over forty million people (Scotland and Northern Ireland have separate arrangements).

(ii) *The Home Office.* The Home Office is responsible for the exercise of the prerogative of mercy, for the management of the penal system, for the general operation of the magistrates' courts and the appointment of stipendiary magistrates. The Legal Adviser is an extremely important person, but his own staff is quite small (six legally qualified officials in 1956) and the work of the Office which affects the legal system is split up between various administrative divisions. There is certainly a general Home Office policy about matters of police, punishment, and the control of crime. The Home Office has also a lively (though perhaps not continuous) interest in improving the efficiency of magistrates' courts; but it has no concern with the High Court (which is largely responsible for criminal sentences) nor with the lower civil courts.

(iii) *Other Departments.* One result of the absence of any administrative body concerned specially with arrangements for the judicial settlement of disputes is that from about the 1880s there has been a tendency for statutes introducing new controls or new services to introduce also special machinery for the settlement of disputes. The jungle of tribunals which has grown up is now a separate subject of study: Sir Carleton Allen in his book on *Administrative Jurisdiction* identifies over one hundred types of authority which might properly be called 'tribunals'. All the major civil Departments are concerned, and to these might be added the three service Departments, which have general responsibility for cases arising under naval, military, and air force law. There has, however, been some centralisation here, since in 1918 the responsibility for the conduct of judicial proceedings within the Army and R.A.F. was brought together in the joint office of Judge Advocate-General of the Forces, subject (since 1948) to the general supervision of the Lord Chancellor.

(iv) *The Treasury.* The Haldane Committee (doubtless reflecting the feelings of its chairman) complained of the indirect influence of the Treasury, through its control over matters of establishments, finance, and accounting which affect the whole judicial system. It might have been expected that the Treasury would in time accept some responsibility for the general working of the system, over which it has much indirect influence, especially as it is responsible (see Chapter 7) for two small but important legal Departments, those of Parliamentary Counsel and of H.M. Procurator-General and Treasury Solicitor. In practice, so far as can be seen by the outside observer, these Departments stick closely to their limited role, and do not act as general advisers to the Treasury; and the Treasury shows little interest in general questions of law except when stimulated by special inquiries such as those of the Donoughmore Committee, set up in 1929, and the Franks Committee, set up in 1955.

As has already been indicated in Chapter 19, these arrangements can only be justified by invoking the doctrine of the separation of powers. Some administrative arrangements there must be for the running of the judicial system; but the power of the central administration over the system as a whole is weakened, and indeed destroyed, by extreme diffusion of responsibility. The case for a Ministry of Justice as proposed by the Haldane Committee is extremely strong on grounds of rational administration: the case against it is usually based on the risk that an effective Ministry—even a Ministry staffed mainly by lawyers—would strengthen administrative control over the judiciary at the expense of judicial control over the administration.

4. Civil Servants as Legislators

Enough has been said in Chapter 7 and Chapter 20 about the procedure for making Statutory Instruments. There is no doubt that in the last thirty years difficulties between judges and administrators have diminished, and there is now little dispute about the mechanics of the system, which works well within its limits. The drafting of Instruments has improved, so has procedure for publicity and supervision, and judges show more comprehension of administrative problems. But if an Instrument is 'controlled' by a court as outside the powers of the Department, the Department can make a new and better Instrument at once, or go to Parliament for increased powers. Lawyers do not like this, but it does not destroy the effectiveness of control altogether. Departments proceed cautiously if there is a risk that they may be attacked in court (and in Parliament and the press) for exceeding their powers; and Departments cannot always obtain a grant of extra powers from Parliament when they want it. Quite apart from the risk of criticism, there is the difficulty of finding a place in the legislative programme, and most Departments have a considerable waiting-list of small amendments to statute which they would like to put through Parliament if time could be found.

This is not therefore a controversial topic at present, but a word should be added about the problem of what legal authors now call 'administrative quasi-legislation'. If a Department is given by law limited discretion about the operation of a service, it may issue a series of 'circulars' or 'practice notes' informing administrative authorities and the public of the rules it proposes to follow in using its powers. These announcements are not made with the formality of Statutory Instruments: they may be issued under statutes which confer no formal power of delegated legislation. There are even curious cases in which 'practice notes' may go rather beyond the letter of the Acts: for instance, instructions are given to income tax inspectors about 'concessions', and these are never likely to be attacked in court because tax-payers will not complain and others have no title to sue. The courts, if a case does come to them, normally refuse to treat such 'quasi-legislation' as if it were law,[1] and do not therefore recognise it as conferring or altering legal rights; but in practice for a great many purposes these Departmental 'notes' are binding until the Department decides to change them.

This is not exactly an encroachment by Departments on the sphere of the legislature and judiciary. A large administrative organisation must have rules for the guidance of subordinate staff about the exercise of discretion, and some of these rules will affect dealings with the public. The same thing happens when a large commercial organisation makes rules for the behaviour of junior members of staff in dealing with customers or suppliers, and the latter may sometimes feel the same sense of frustration about 'red tape'. The courts have assimilated the use by the Crown of its discretion to the use of discretion by any private person or firm, and have therefore put it outside their power to inquire into the making of any rule which is

[1] See Griffith and Street, *Principles of Administrative Law*, p. 63-69.

not, in the sense of a rather narrow definition, a legislative act. This limitation of the scope of judicial control over the executive is usual in other European countries, but the gap is to some extent made good there by the growth of judicial bodies within the administration itself, which supervise procedure for the use of administrative discretion in this or in other matters.

5. CIVIL SERVANTS AS JUDGES

There is a general feeling that the offices of administrator and of judge are and should be incompatible, but it is hard to give practical force to the rule because of difficulties in definition. The definition which has widest currency is that formulated by the Donoughmore Committee in 1932:

> A true judicial decision presupposes an existing dispute between two or more parties, and then involves four requisites—(1) the presentation (not necessarily orally) of their case by the parties to the dispute; (2) if the dispute between them is a question of fact, the ascertainment of the fact by means of evidence adduced by the parties to the dispute and often with the assistance of argument by or on behalf of the parties on the evidence; (3) if the dispute between them is a question of law, the submission of legal argument by the parties; and (4) a decision which disposes of the whole matter by a finding upon the facts in dispute and an application of the law of the land to the facts so found, including where required a ruling upon any disputed question of law.
>
> A quasi-judicial decision equally presupposes an existing dispute between two or more parties and involves (1) and (2), but does not necessarily involve (3), and never involves (4). The place of (4) is in fact taken by administrative action, the character of which is determined by the Minister's free choice. . . . Decisions which are purely administrative stand on a wholly different footing from quasi-judicial as well as from judicial decisions and must be distinguished accordingly. . . . In the case of the administrative decision, there is no legal obligation upon the person charged with the duty of reaching the decision to consider and weigh submissions and arguments, or to collate any evidence, or to solve any issue. The grounds upon which he acts, and the means which he takes to inform himself before acting, are left entirely to his discretion.[1]

This sharp distinction between judicial, quasi-judicial, and administrative acts has influenced the courts, but modern authorities on administrative law maintain that it does not accurately reflect their practice. 'The courts are required to determine the meaning of "judicial" in many varying contexts. . . . There is no one definition of *judicial* for these several purposes.'[2] From this it follows that a better

[1] Cmd. 4060, pp. 73-4, 81.
[2] Griffith and Street, *Principles of Administrative Law*, p. 142.

analysis can be achieved by a study of the tasks that have been laid on the administration by statute and common law, of the different devices invented to perform them, and of the extent to which the traditional courts can and do interfere to ensure legality. Such an analysis is to be found in Chapter IV of the book by Mr. Griffith and Professor Street, and it is unnecessary to repeat it. What concerns us here is the use for the purposes of central administration of a particular kind of procedure, loosely thought of as 'judicial': procedure (generally public) in which there is confrontation between parties, production of evidence, argument about fact and law. This procedure may lead either to a decision by the body conducting the procedure or to a report by that body to a higher procedure. In the former case it might be called a 'tribunal', in the latter case a 'public inquiry'. Such proceedings may be conducted either by civil servants, or by a mixture of laymen and civil servants, or by laymen advised by civil servants. For our purpose three headings will serve: tribunals, public inquiries, civil servants as advisers.

(i) *Tribunals*. The definition of a civil servant which we used in Chapter 2 explicitly excludes servants of the Crown who are 'holders of judicial offices', but this does not serve to separate judges from civil servants in practice, because there is no satisfactory definition, either legal or practical, of what constitutes a judicial office. The courts define (not without controversy) the characteristics of a judicial act, and are prepared to rule whether or not an individual was acting 'in a judicial capacity'. Their control is over judicial *procedure*, not over judicial *persons*; and it has therefore never been necessary for them to define on what conditions the exercise of the role of a judge constitutes an 'office'.

In consequence, the theoretical distinction between judicial officers and administrative officers is not convenient in describing the working of the system. Judicial procedure is used in administration in a variety of different contexts, and tribunals are constituted in a great variety of different ways.

At one extreme, there are officers who appear in the Civil Service records and statistics, but who could properly be called specialised administrative judges. A number of tribunals (such as the War Pensions Appeal Tribunals and the National Insurance Commission) are manned by lawyers appointed relatively late in life from outside the Civil Service; some of these men are chosen by the Lord Chancellor, not by the Department concerned; they all have in effect complete independence and security of tenure. Some of them serve part-time, or combine the work of various tribunals under different statutes (for instance, the Chairman of the Civil Service Arbitration

Tribunal is a member of the Industrial Court and of the Industrial Disputes Tribunal). There is here the nucleus of a group of professional judges, not differing in any essential way from their colleagues in the ordinary courts.

The Area Traffic Commissioners of the Ministry of Transport and Civil Aviation illustrate an intermediate category. There are three Commissioners in each area; one of them is a full-time civil servant, who is generally an engineer without legal qualifications, following a career in the Civil Service within his own professional class, the other two are part-time members appointed from a panel of local authority representatives for three years. The full-time Commissioner sits alone as Licensing Authority for Goods Vehicles, and an appeal lies from his decision to the Transport Tribunal, a body presided over by a lawyer who might fairly be called an 'administrative judge'. The three Commissioners sit together as Licensing Authority for Public Service Vehicles and to license drivers and conductors; for the former, appeal lies to the Minister, for the latter, to local magistrates' courts. On all these matters the 'ordinary' courts can be invoked only if there is an error in substantive law or in procedure. The full-time Commissioner in the course of his business acquires a great deal of knowledge about road transport services, and (though this is not publicly stressed) there is no doubt that the individual and collective advice of the Commissioners on practice and policy is valuable to the Department. This is perhaps an exceptionally confused instance, but it serves to illustrate the sort of compromise which is evolved to suit the various interests involved in a particular administrative problem.

Finally, there are instances in which an ordinary civil servant who is primarily an administrator acts sometimes in a judicial capacity. The most familiar instance is that of the National Insurance Acts (see Chapter 15), under which Executive Class civil servants in local offices are nominated as Insurance Officers, and act in a sense as 'courts of first instance' in deciding claims for benefit under the relevant statutes and regulations. There is no formal procedure, and it can scarcely be said that the Insurance Officer is a 'tribunal'; but he records his decision in a formal way, as a statement of facts and law, with a conclusion which is a 'decision', not merely 'advice' to his superiors. From this decision appeal lies through two channels according to the subject matter: in a few cases, up the administrative hierarchy to the Minister; in the majority of cases, through local National Insurance Tribunals (the chairmen of which are usually lawyers, the members laymen) to the National Insurance Commissioner, who is a typical 'administrative judge'. The 'ordinary' courts can in theory control all these tribunals for excess of jurisdiction or faults in procedure; but in practice the tribunals know their business, appellants are satisfied with their fairness, and 'control' from outside the administration is notional and not real. The case of the Insurance Officer is again a rather extreme one, though there are some parallels in the Revenue Departments; but it suits the character of the national insurance system, which is primarily one for the issue of benefits earned by contributions in a manner strictly in accordance with a formal code of regulations.

(ii) *Public Inquiries*. The types of public inquiry by civil servants which are most familiar to the general public are inquiries into accidents, and inquiries relating to housing and land use preparatory to some form of Ministerial direction. In both types of inquiry there is a hearing before an Inspector, and anyone concerned can appear to give evidence or state an argument. The hearing results in a report, not in a decision, and there is no appeal to a court because there is in a sense nothing to appeal against; ordinary courts can control only the forms of procedure, not its result. In accident inquiries (railway, civil aviation, and merchant shipping) the report is generally published, and is a basis for policy rather than for specific action by the Ministry. In inquiries of other types, principally about the approval of development plans and compulsory purchase orders, the Inspector makes a report to the Minister on the points at issue, and the report (which sometimes includes a recommendation for action) goes forward through the ordinary channels of the Department. There is no standard practice about the publication of Inspectors' reports, but reports relating to land use are almost always withheld. Publication is regularly demanded by aggrieved parties and by critics of administrative procedure in general. If it were the general practice it might give the public a better insight into the making of policy; but if reports were regularly used as a basis for attack on the Department the result might not be to increase public control but to lead Departments to avoid procedure by public inquiry, which is in many ways valuable as a means of satisfying all concerned that their voice has been properly heard, even though it has been disregarded.

The conduct of such inquiries is one of the traditional functions of Inspectors, and it is not easy to generalise about the small but influential bodies involved: bodies such as the Railway Inspectorate, the Inspectors of Civil Aviation, and the Housing and Planning Inspectorates. The Inspectors are generally technical experts of good standing; generally they learn how to hold public inquiries by experience and good sense, without special training in the law; generally the holding of inquiries is only part of their duties, and they act as technical advisers to the Department on any matters that concern them. It is worth mentioning, as an indication of atmosphere and tradition, that in 1951 instructions about the rules of evidence issued to Inspectors of the Ministry of Local Government and Planning (as it then was) were identical with those drafted for Poor Law Inspectors in 1850 and criticised by the Donoughmore Committee in 1932. Procedure is traditional, amateurish, and tolerably successful.

(iii) *Civil Servants as Advisers.* There is a rather narrow line between a tribunal presided over by a chairman who is technically a part-time civil servant and one which is wholly a tribunal of laymen. There are a number of 'lay' bodies, such as National Assistance Appeal Tribunals and Rent Tribunals, which have the right to take decisions (sometimes not subject to appeal) on matters affecting individuals. These bodies consist wholly of part-time members, and do not as a rule meet frequently: the chairman is sometimes but not always a lawyer. Continuity can be maintained only if these bodies are effectively advised, and there are difficulties in the position of a civil servant who knows that he must in effect make up 'his' tribunal's mind for it, by the way in which he proposes the case and by the advice which he gives about policy and about the meaning of the regulations. This may be particularly difficult if the tribunal is in effect hearing an appeal against a subordinate officer in his own Department. Such situations are not common, but experience of them indicates that in order to show that justice is done it is best to move one way or the other: either to place responsibility for decision squarely on the civil servant, perhaps assisted by a body of lay advisers, or to constitute a tribunal with sufficient strength and continuity to avoid all suspicion that it is 'in the pocket' of a Department.

One might summarise this section as follows. There are many different ways in which civil servants have become involved in the organisation of tribunals and public inquiries. These administrative devices have grown up in such a way that each of them fits easily into the structure of the service to which it belongs, and represents a degree of 'judicialisation' resulting from that service's peculiar history and balance of forces. The 'ordinary' courts rarely interfere, but the influence of the 'ordinary' system of law is nevertheless substantial. Many tribunals are now chaired by men who are in effect 'administrative judges'; all tribunals and inquiries are influenced by the traditions of British legal procedure; and the influence has behind it the possibility of interference by the 'ordinary' courts to control not policy but procedure. In spite of this, the total area of 'judicialisation' is quite limited, and many responsible civil servants go through their careers without direct experience of judicial procedure in administrative business.

6. CIVIL SERVANTS IN COURT

This is not, however, the end of the matter: there are a number of ways in which civil servants in their official capacity can become involved in ordinary legal proceedings. There is no neat way of classifying these.

(i) *Actions involving the Department.* In general, an action in court involving a Department has very little effect on the Department as a whole. The case is prepared and handled by the Treasury Solicitor or the legal adviser to the Department in consultation with the small number of officials directly concerned, and the internal affairs of the Department are protected quite effectively against judicial inquiry. Even since the Crown Proceedings Act of 1947, the ordinary litigant has little power to compel the production of documents which the Department does not wish to make public: a civil servant in the witness box can safely limit himself to matters of fact, and refuse to answer questions on matters of Departmental policy. The trend of judicial decision is still against allowing inquiry into the manner in which decisions are actually taken in the Minister's name: at present the Minister may claim privilege on the ground that disclosure would injure 'the proper functioning of the public service', and his claim must be accepted by the court.[1]

(ii) *Civil Servants as 'Policemen'.* There are a good many statutes and regulations under which civil servants have special powers to enter and search (but rarely to arrest) without obtaining a warrant from a Justice of the Peace or calling in a constable. A typical case is that of the preventive officers of Customs and Excise, whose warrant gives them very wide powers to enter on private land and premises in search of goods evading tax; but other Inspectors, such as Factory Inspectors, Explosives Inspectors, Dangerous Drugs Inspectors, Lunacy and Mental Deficiency Commissioners, have great powers for the purposes of their own service. If one makes a list of civil servants authorised to search without a warrant, the result is formidable, and suggests a collapse of the eighteenth-century rules against 'general search warrants'. If an unscrupulous government wished to find pretext for entry anywhere exempt from judicial

[1] Statement by the Lord Chancellor in the House of Lords, 6 June 1956 (H.L. Deb., Vol. 197, Cols. 741-8), which sets out certain modifications of the practice which have now been adopted. See also *The Times* leader, 7 June 1956. In Scotland, the courts have greater powers to demand the disclosure of documents.

control it would have no difficulty in finding it under one heading or another. But this problem never really arises in practice; each of these bodies has high professional standards, keeps to its terms of reference, and uses its powers cautiously. There is little doubt that the expert public opinion interested in each of these areas of administration is strongly in favour of giving effective powers to Inspectors, even though this may exclude the jurisdiction of the courts.

(iii) *Civil Servants as Prosecutors*. The next question is that of the power of the central administration to set the courts in motion, a matter which is recognised in most continental systems (and also in Scotland) by the attachment to most 'ordinary' courts of an official who is (under varying titles) the public prosecutor, charged with bringing breaches of the law to the notice of the court. English law has never wholly abandoned an earlier tradition, that of private prosecution, though most criminal cases are now in fact initiated by the local police, acting as individual 'constables' and not as agents of the administration. Breaches in principle affecting the central administration are of two kinds:

(*a*) There are certain crimes[1] for which prosecutions cannot be started without the authority of the Law Officers of the Crown or the Home Secretary. This power is exercised by the Director of Public Prosecutions, who may himself prosecute, permit a police prosecution or (very rarely) a private prosecution, or refuse leave to prosecute. The Director's Office is staffed by civil servants of the Legal Class, and on many matters he is nominally subordinate to the government of the day through the Attorney-General. But he has his own statutory powers and enjoys a high degree of independence in all matters of ordinary crime. The Attorney-General is not likely to be involved except in the rather rare cases which have some political aspect, such as treason, sedition, and breaches of the Official Secrets Acts.

(*b*) It is generally for the Department concerned with the administration of an Act of Parliament to decide whether there shall be prosecution for offences under it. There may be something in the statute which settles procedure for prosecution, but more usually the matter is left uncertain. Offences and penalties are defined, enforcement is a matter of administration. Private individuals rarely wish to take action, other public authorities leave to the Department concerned the question of tactics about enforcement: how many offenders should be let off with a warning; what risk should be

[1] Principally murder, some of the more serious statutory offences such as those falling under the Punishment of Incest Act, 1908, and certain offences against the state, under the Public Order Act, 1936, and the Official Secrets Acts.

taken of a stultifying acquittal; whether some provisions of the law should be let slip by failure to enforce them. Perhaps more civil servants are involved in the judicial system in this way than in any other: it concerns the Inland Revenue and Customs and Excise, the Post Office, Inspectorates of various kinds such as the Factory Inspectorate, the Departments which attempt to impose controls and standards, the social service Departments which are called on to check abuse of services. Practically nothing has been said or written about the practical problems of enforcement, in spite of the central position of this question in deciding the role of the administration and of the courts. So far as can be seen, Departmental practice varies greatly: at one extreme, there is centralisation of prosecutions in the legal branch, so that all decisions to prosecute are taken by lawyers, and action in court is professional; at the other extreme, there is decentralisation to the man on the spot, for instance to Factory Inspectors, who take their own decisions and appear in court themselves. It is possible to guess at the effects of different systems, but there is no direct evidence, and it is wiser not to speculate.

7. Conclusion

Perhaps enough has been said here to illustrate the importance of informal interplay between the administration and the legal system. There is contact at many points, and forms of organisation are often due to a mixture of motives, impelling administrators on the one hand to invent a system that fits the function and responds easily to direction, on the other to respect the principle that administration aims at justice as well as at efficiency. Formal controls can be evaded, and the system is sometimes shaped so as to evade them. It is also true that many civil servants go through their careers lacking both general knowledge of law and specific experience of courts of law. But the strength of the British legal tradition spreads through the administration certain vague but important ideas of just procedure, and the political presentation of individual grievances continually reinforces the instinct for justice. The system at present lacks intelligibility rather than fairness. Perhaps the main object of reform should be to evolve a system of administrative justice which the ordinary citizen can understand, as he understands in a general way the procedure of the courts.

FOR REFERENCE

(i) *Official Documents:*

Report of the Machinery of Government Committee (Haldane). Cd. 9230, 1918.

Report of the Committee on Ministers' Powers (Donoughmore). Cmd. 4060, 1932.

H.M. Treasury: *Subordinate Legislation* (May 1951). (A comprehensive handbook of procedure with appendices including specimen Statutory Instruments, the text of the Statutory Instruments Act, 1946, the Statutory Instruments Regulations, 1947, and other documents.)

Memoranda submitted by Government Departments to the Committee on Administrative Tribunals and Inquiries (Franks). (H.M.S.O. 1956.)

(ii) *Books and Articles:*

The classic attack on the powers of the central administration is:

LORD HEWART: *The New Despotism* (1929).

For a more moderate (though still hostile) view, see:

Sir CARLETON ALLEN: *Law and Orders* (2nd Edn., revised, 1956).

For a recent comprehensive survey of administrative tribunals by the same author, see:

'Administrative Jurisdiction', *Public Law*, Vol. 1, No. 1 (1956), also reprinted separately (under the same title) as a book (1956).

The work of a selected group of administrative tribunals is discussed in:

R. S. W. POLLARD (Ed.): *Administrative Tribunals at Work* (1950).

Standard works by administrative lawyers include:

Sir CECIL CARR: *Delegated Legislation* (1921).

—— *Concerning Administrative Law* (1941).

W. A. ROBSON: *Justice and Administrative Law* (3rd Edn., 1950).

Sir IVOR JENNINGS: *The Law and the Constitution* (3rd Edn., 1946).

J. A. G. GRIFFITH and H. STREET: *Principles of Administrative Law* (1952).

B. SCHWARTZ: *Law and the Executive in Britain* (New York, 1949).

See also:

W. A. ROBSON: 'Public Inquiries as an Instrument of Government', *British Journal of Administrative Law*, Vol. I, December 1954.

Sir THEOBALD MATHEW: *The Office and Duties of the Director of Public Prosecutions* (1950).

CHAPTER TWENTY-TWO

LOCAL AUTHORITIES

... to keep the mean between the two extremes, of too much stiffness in refusing, and of too much easiness in admitting any variation.—
Preface to the Book of Common Prayer.

1. INTRODUCTORY

IN Chapter 16 we explained briefly the responsibilities and organisation of central administration for the direct provision of services all over the country. It is characteristic of British practice that this is only a small part of the sphere of public activity and that those who advocate the extension of 'controls', or of 'socialism', or of 'the public sector', do not generally propose much extension of the direct provision of services by the central government. The main providers are on the one hand local authorities, on the other hand the range of *ad hoc* organisations which we have called here 'independent public bodies'.

Table XXVI gives a very rough indication of the distribution of responsibility for public services.

These figures are far from exact, since published statistics are not generally analysed in this way. Indeed it is usual to compile statistics on the basis of numbers employed in different industries and professions, not of employing bodies, and this is justifiable because there is now in this country a continuous 'spectrum' of types of organisation, extending without precise lines of division from direct central administration to the (now very limited) sphere of private enterprise untouched by considerations of 'the public interest'. But in spite of this vagueness of definition there is no real uncertainty about the main types of organisation involved, and our concern in this and the next chapter is with the practice of central administration in relation to them. So little has been written about these administrative relations that our account is necessarily provisional and incomplete, but the matter is too important to omit. In this chapter we deal, first, with the organisation and powers of the five Ministries mainly concerned with local authorities in England and Wales; then with the general influence of local government as expressed through various

Table XXVI

The Public Services (excluding the armed forces)

Central Government

Non-industrial civil servants	600,000
Industrial civil servants	400,000
Total	1,000,000

Local Authorities[1]

Education:	
(a) Teachers, and lecturers in technical colleges, etc.	350,000
(b) Clerical and other staffs (including school cleaners, etc.)	150,000
Police (including Metropolitan Police)	70,000
Fire	30,000
Water	20,000
Transport	90,000
Health and Welfare Services	140,000
Building and Civil Engineering	80,000
Restaurants, canteens (including school canteens), orchestras, amusement parks, racecourses, etc.	150,000
All other local authority services	430,000
	1,510,000

Other Public Bodies

Airways	20,000
Railways and other nationalised transport	900,000
Coal	850,000
Gas	140,000
Electricity	170,000
Atomic Energy	20,000
Hospitals	500,000
Miscellaneous (say)	150,000
Total	2,750,000

Total for Public Sector	5,260,000
Total Employed Population	24,000,000

[1] There are no completely reliable figures either for local government 'office' workers or for manual workers separately. The ('service') classification given here is based on figures in the *Ministry of Labour Gazette* for December 1956. There are probably about 150,000 'office' workers in the local government service.

associations and professional bodies; finally, with the practice of relationships between central and local government as it affects individual local authorities.

The recent history of local government in England and Wales is familiar and requires only a brief recapitulation.

(i) *Trends*

The roots of English local government are old, but the present practice of providing services throughout the country by co-operation between central and local authorities is relatively recent. It began to grow up in the 1830s, and the existing framework of local authorities dates from the 1890s. The system was constructed in the first instance by a series of compromises, and it has always been easier to advance by fresh compromises than by radical reconstruction. The present organisation is certainly very odd; the legal classification of authorities is out of line with any possible classification of types of community, and boundaries no longer define convenient administrative areas. Nevertheless, the system can generally be made to work by those familiar with it, and there is no politically influential demand for total reorganisation.

Various changes have resulted from the combination of an illogical structure with a general demand for improved and equalised national services. Some services have been 'nationalised' by removal from control by local authorities: 'major' local authorities have gained services at the expense of 'minor' local authorities; central government has accepted greater responsibility for the finance of local government, and with it has obtained greater formal powers of control. It is still an accepted principle that *all* local authorities are 'responsible bodies competent to discharge their own functions . . . [exercising] their responsibilities in their own right, not ordinarily as agents of Government Departments'[1]; but the principle can be reconciled with law and practice only by rather strained interpretation of the words 'ordinarily' and 'agent'.

(ii) *Controls*

The Departments of central government have no general status superior to that of local authorities, and they have no general powers of supervision over them. But there are various types of specific control, some of them very wide, which are combined in different ways for different services. These are briefly as follows:

(*a*) Controls over general administration: for instance, audit,

[1] 2nd Report of the Local Government Manpower Committee. Cmd. 8421.

approval of appointment and dismissal of certain officials, approval of the terms of Local Acts, confirmation of by-laws.

(b) The issue of regulations for a particular service. Usually the main code of regulations is 'made' as a Statutory Instrument, and is glossed by memoranda, circulars, manuals, and codes of practice. These supplementary instructions are a good example of 'administrative quasi-legislation' (Chapter 21, p. 392), since they have many of the practical effects of law but not its form.

(c) The requirement that local authorities must submit 'schemes' or 'development plans' for certain services. These schemes must be approved by the Department concerned. Once approved, they are binding on the local authority until amended in proper form.

(d) Inspection: some of the Inspectorates are older than the Departments to which they are now attached, and have a statutory existence independent of them.

(e) Inspection is linked with control of finance, through the power to make grants for approved purposes and to withhold sanction for loans. For some purposes an Inspector's certificate is formally required, but the standards set by Inspectors are important even without this specific sanction.

(f) Departments have a wide range of specific statutory powers to issue directions on particular matters.

(g) Departments also act, under various statutes, as a court of appeal in disputes between two or more local authorities and between a local authority and members of the public. There may be a public inquiry by an Inspector (see Chapter 21, p. 396), but the final decision is taken privately within the Department.

(iii) *Co-operation*

In spite of these powers there is substance in the commonplace that the relation between central and local government is one of co-operation, not one of principal and agent. The large local authorities have staffs whose heads are better paid and more experienced than their opposite numbers' in Whitehall. Local authorities collectively know more about 'where the shoe pinches' than can those who direct a Department, even though the latter are well served by Inspectors. Each great city and large county has considerable political influence in its own right, and the associations of local authorities have so high a standing that they cannot be disregarded. Hence the relationship between central and local authorities is one of delicate balance between co-operation and control, a balance that varies a little for each authority and each service.

2. Departmental Organisation

Responsibility for local authority services falls mainly on five major Departments:

The Ministry of Housing and Local Government has a real but limited concern for local government as a whole; it has no general powers of 'tutelage', but holds most of the specific statutory powers of general administrative control. It is also responsible for housing, town and country planning, water supplies, and a variety of minor services.

The Home Office also has certain specific powers of general control, for instance over elections, Private Bills, and a wide range of by-laws. It is responsible in particular for police, fire brigades, civil defence, and the care and protection of children, which are primarily local authority services; and also for the probation of offenders, a responsibility of the magistrates, who are closely associated with local authorities though distinct from them.

The Ministry of Health supervises the local authority health services, which form one of the three 'pillars' of the National Health Service.

The Ministry of Education is responsible for the very wide range of local authority education services, and has more limited responsibility for education not provided by local authorities.

The Ministry of Transport and Civil Aviation is responsible for highways and bridges, many of which are provided by local authorities, and for municipal aerodromes, a minor matter to which we need not refer again.

In addition, there are a number of other Departments which deal separately with local authorities about their own services. *The Ministry of Agriculture, Fisheries, and Food* is concerned with smallholdings developed by County Councils. *The Ministry of Power* uses local officials in their personal capacity to run fuel controls. *The Ministry of Labour* shares responsibility with local education authorities for the administration of the Youth Employment Service. *The National Assistance Board* uses local authorities as its agents to provide 'reception centres' for homeless and indigent persons. *The Board of Trade* is concerned with looking after the development of industry in local areas scheduled as 'Development Areas'. An account of these minor services would be rather misleading unless it were extended to cover the whole scope of central administration. Practically every Department has some dealings with local authorities; every Department is entitled to deal with a local authority direct about its own Departmental business.

We do not attempt here to explain the position in Scotland and in Northern Ireland, where powers of control are divided between United Kingdom Departments and Scottish or Northern Ireland Departments. There are no great differences in principle, but practice probably differs a good deal because of the difference of scale.

(i) *The Ministry of Housing and Local Government*

This Ministry (which has a total staff of about 3,000) deals with matters affecting the structure and organisation of local government, its financial soundness, and general standards of administration and probity. It also supervises those functions of local government which are not dealt with by any other Department. The most important of these are rating, public health and hygiene, town and country planning, housing, rent control, and water and sewerage.

The organisation is headed by a Permanent Secretary, a Deputy Secretary, and seven Under Secretaries—the Under Secretary for Finance and Accountant-General, the Director of Establishments and Organisation, and five Under Secretaries in charge of administrative divisions. These divisions are: Local Government, Housing, two Planning Divisions (one for London and the Home Counties, one for the 'Provinces'), and New Towns and Water. The Director of Establishments is in charge of a sixth administrative division, dealing with Minerals.

On the professional and technical side there are a Solicitor and Legal Adviser, a Chief Architect and Housing Consultant, a Chief Engineer, a Chief Technical Planner, and the Chief Inspector of Audit. The Solicitor and the Chief Architect are perhaps of the standing of the Deputy Secretary in their professional classes, the other three might rank as Under Secretaries.

A high proportion of the directing staff at headquarters is drawn from the professional classes: the administrative divisions principally concerned with local authorities employ about one hundred officials of the rank of S.E.O. and above; the professional and technical staffs of equivalent rank (including architects, estates officers, and technical planners) number about one hundred and fifty.

The Local Government Division is concerned with general structure, organisation, and finance, as well as with control of the miscellaneous capital expenditure of local authorities, local legislation, land transactions, public health and sanitary matters, appeals against decisions of district auditors, alteration of boundaries, statistics, by-laws, co-ordination of civil defence planning within the Department and liaison with the Civil Defence Division of the Home Office, local government superannuation questions. The work is divided between three 'branches' each under an Assistant Secretary, and each branch contains a number of sections controlled by a Principal or S.E.O.

The distribution of duties at this level is on a basis traditional in the Ministry and characteristic of the system. A division is concerned with a subject or group of subjects; this is subdivided by branches, each responsible for a subdivision of the whole field, and the branch is further subdivided into sections. A section may be responsible for a group of specialist topics (such as offensive trades, rents and rent tribunals, compulsory purchase orders, the safeguarding of agricultural land in planning schemes), *or* for all matters within the scope of the branch arising from a particular group of local authorities, *or* for a group of topics and a group of local authorities. In the Local Government Division local authorities are grouped alphabetically; in the Housing and Planning Divisions they are grouped according to the 'standard' region in which they fall.

Particular pieces of business coming forward for the first time go to one of a number of Higher Executive Officers. The H.E.O. concerned may be able to deal with matters of procedure, even fairly complicated ones, on his own or after informal consultation, but for serious business he acts as distributing agent (advised by his superior if necessary), pushing business forward either up a 'geographical' hierarchy or up a 'subject' hierarchy in his own division, or referring it to the appropriate level in some other division.

It will be obvious that this is an attempt to solve the perennial problem (to which we referred in Chapter 15, p. 226) of how to subdivide complex business which involves the management or supervision of integrated units. This solution avoids purely geographical organisation, which is bound to dilute the value of special knowledge; it avoids organisation by subjects only, which may lose sight of close links between subjects in the working units of administration; it avoids the creation of large parallel organisations, one for general administrators working geographically, the other for specialists working by subjects, a formula apt to encourage war between 'generalists' and 'specialists'. It secures these advantages at the expense of great complexity, which makes it very difficult for the outside observer to be sure who deals with what at what stage. This must be confusing to local authorities, especially to the smaller authorities whose dealings with Whitehall are infrequent. It also runs the risk of delay and confusion within the office unless the group concerned is small and coherent, working with ease and familiarity as a team. In good times this office organisation works admirably, but it may be doubted if it stands up well to dilution or rapid expansion.

The Ministry was one of those which in the post-war period greatly extended its organisation in the regions, so that in effect it had nine geographically organised branches physically located in their area, and acting as first 'filter' for much of the business from that area. In 1954, when there had already been some contraction in staff from the post-war peak, a typical regional office (Birmingham) employed 87 people: a Principal Regional Officer and Deputy, 17 professional officers (architects, technical planners, estates surveyors, research staff), 18 Executive officers, 30 Clerical officers, 16 typing and messengerial staff, and 4 draughtsmen. By the end of 1955 the regional staff of the whole Ministry had been reduced from 750 to 540, and after major reorganisation in the summer of 1956 it was further reduced to 136. There are now not more than ten or a dozen people in each region, and almost all the day-to-day executive functions have been recentralised in Whitehall.

The Housing Division is divided into four 'branches' and the work is distributed on the same principle, geographically and by major subject. One branch, for example, deals with the local housing authorities in three of the standard regions and with slum clearance policy and procedure, compulsory purchase orders, housing management, 'new tradition' housing, the sale of council houses, and housing associations; another deals with two regions, with part of a third (the Greater London area), and with housing standards and design, rents and rent tribunals, and research and development policy.

One of the two *Planning Divisions* takes all general planning matters (including Development Plans and appeals) for London and the Home Counties, the other takes the remaining regions; but certain specialist subjects are divided between them without regard to area: thus all matters relating to the control of advertisements, access to the countryside, historic buildings, and tree preservation, are dealt with by the Provinces Division; procedure for acquiring land under Town Planning legislation and New Town legislation, and general Departmental policy on land transactions (except for housing and water undertakings) come under the London Division.

The New Towns and Water Division represents a grouping of two quite distinct sets of functions under a single Under Secretary. The bulk of the work of the two New Town Branches is concerned with the Development Corporations, independent public bodies appointed by the Minister under the New Towns Act, 1946, to plan and develop new towns in areas which he designates. But since all the new towns so far designated are being built around the nucleus of an existing 'old' town, there are many matters of interest and concern to the elected local authority on which it wishes to be heard.

The Water Branches deal with all matters connected with national water supply and conservation, and are in contact not only with local authorities but also with the River Boards (see p. 256) and with the numerous statutory water companies.

Local government finance, including the settlement of grants, is handled by two large divisions: *the Accountant-General's Department* and *the Local Government Finance Division*. The former deals with housing subsidies and all other questions of housing finance, and with grants payable under Town and Country Planning, New Towns, and National Parks legislation. The work in some subjects (but not in all) is subdivided geographically, and a C.E.O. or S.E.O. is in charge of each block of work. *The Local Government Finance Division* has a wide range of duties. One branch collects and tabulates local government financial statistics, and is responsible for compiling and publishing the annual returns of 'Local Government Financial Statistics', 'Rates and Rateable Values', and other papers. A second branch calculates and authorises the payment of Exchequer Equalisation Grants and other payments to local authorities under the Local Government Act, 1948, and certain other grants under various statutes, including the Town Development Act, 1952. The Exchequer Equalisation work is subdivided by regions with a H.E.O. in charge of each group.

A third branch of this division acts as a general liaison with the work of the District Audit: it examines auditors' reports, considers appeals against surcharge, and examines local authorities' requests for permission to incur expenditure which is not specifically sanctioned by statute (once approved, this expenditure is not subject to surcharge, and about 7,500 such sanctions were given between 1950 and 1954).

A fourth (small) branch under a Principal is concerned with general problems of local authority rating and valuation.

Applications for loan sanction are approved by the Department responsible for the particular service for which the loan is required, but in recent years about 90 per cent. of the loans sanctioned have been either for schools, or for housing, water, and sewerage, so that the Ministry of Education and the Ministry of Housing and Local Government have been the main Departments concerned. The position would change if a large road-building programme were approved.

Loan sanctions are issued by a branch of the Finance Division, which is also responsible for giving consent to stock issues, examining the financial clauses of Local Bills, and dealing with a large number of general questions about local government finance including those arising out of the nationalisation of local authority gas and electricity undertakings. It is the main point of liaison with two other bodies concerned with local authority borrowing: the Capital Issues Committee and the Public Works Loans Board. The former (which is an Advisory Committee staffed by Treasury officials) considers all loan applications which are 'sponsored' by the appropriate sanctioning Department. From 1945 to 1952 local authorities could only borrow (subject to limited exceptions) from the Public Works Loan Board, but the position is now reversed and they are at present virtually forced to borrow on the open market unless they can show good cause. The smaller local authorities traditionally used the Public Works Loan Board, but in 1954 about 50 per cent. of all sanctioned borrowing was financed by the Board compared with 15 per cent. before 1939. The Board, which dates from 1817, is a minor Department independent of the Ministry of Housing and Local Government (the Treasury is generally responsible): there are twelve unpaid Commissioners with a Secretary (a Principal Executive Officer) and a staff of about 80.

The Architects' Division employs about a hundred architects and quantity surveyors. Until the reduction in the regional organisation referred to above, many of these were employed in the regional offices. The division gives advice (which amounts almost to 'quasi-legislation') on layout, design, construction, and maintenance; it examines and must approve tenders for specific projects; and it is the channel of liaison with the very large Building Research organisation of the D.S.I.R.

The Technical Planning Services Division, under the Chief Technical Planner, includes about 140 qualified architects, town planners, estate surveyors, and draughtsmen, and there is also a research staff of about 40, mainly University graduates with degrees in geography, economics, and social studies. The main business of the division is to advise local authorities about framing Development Plans and about difficult cases arising out of Development Plans, and to advise the Minister about giving or withholding his consent when it is required by statute.

These two divisions, whose joint influence on the face of Britain is enormous, are both organised on the pattern (set out above) of distribution of duties by subject and by geographical area together, so that individuals at medium levels usually have both a special subject and general responsibility for an area. Their heads have direct access to the Minister if they request it, and take a full and equal part in the discussion of policy. In routine business, however, their 'advice' goes forward for decision through the appropriate administrative division, that of Housing or one of the two Planning divisions. The decision of the Minister thus combines technical and administrative considerations; the balance between them shifts, but the former always play a large part.

There are three Inspectorates within the Ministry: *the Housing and Planning Inspectorate, the Engineering Inspectorate,* and *the Alkali Inspectorate*. The last of these consists of 10 qualified chemists, and is concerned with pollution and smoke abatement. The Housing and Planning Inspectors (about 75) are qualified architects, town planners, or engineers; the Engineering Inspectors (about 40) are mostly civil engineers, but they include one or two chemical engineers and a public cleansing Inspector. These are the officials who hold public inquiries and hearings under the Town and Country Planning, Housing, Acquisition of Land, New Towns, and other Acts.

The size of these Inspectorates indicates the large number of local inquiries which are needed. From 1950 to the end of 1954, 134 public inquiries were held to consider local authority Development Plans under the Town and Country Planning Act, and only nine Plans were approved without inquiry. Some of these inquiries occupied only one day: the largest (on the L.C.C. Plan) occupied 153 days and employed four Inspectors. The number of objections by individuals and organised bodies varied from one (on the Merioneth Plan) to more than 7,000 (Middlesex).

Between 1951 and 1954 the Ministry received 16,633 appeals against refusals by local authorities to grant planning permission under the 1947 Act; many of these were subsequently withdrawn, but for most of the 9,503 cases decided in this period it was necessary to hold a local inquiry. Shortage of suitably qualified staff was partly responsible for the large number of cases (over 2,000) which were outstanding at the end of the period, 1,400 more than at the beginning.

That extremely important body, *the District Audit,* has its headquarters in the Ministry's building in Whitehall, but it is technically a separate Department. The cost of its salaries and expenses is covered (as is required by law) by the sums collected from local authorities in stamp duties; this serves to emphasise the independent position of the audit staff, who might almost be said to act in a judicial capacity. Their exact degree of independence is a little uncertain in law, but a Minister would certainly not in practice give instructions to auditors about the interpretation of statutes. 'They are not my auditors', said Mr. Neville Chamberlain in 1927; '[they]

are a body of officers appointed by the Minister of Health[1] but they do not take directions from the Minister of Health. They are independent of him and they have duties laid upon them by statute.'[2]

There are about 400 auditors recruited by the ordinary Executive Class competition but tested by a severe internal examination (in law and accounting) before promotion to the grade of Assistant District Auditor. Some auditors also qualify themselves professionally as accountants, solicitors, or barristers, but even without this they hold their own with the very well qualified financial staff of local authorities.

The auditors are 'out-stationed' in fifteen Audit Districts (the office of the London Audit District is actually in County Hall, the headquarters of the L.C.C.), and each out-stationed office audits the accounts of the local authorities in that District. The expenditure of local authorities is about £1,500 m. a year and about three-quarters of this is subject to district audit, but the power of surcharge is rarely exercised. Between April 1950 and the end of 1954 there were 222 disallowances and surcharges involving a total of £35,375 (a remarkably small number in relation to the total annual volume of local authority transactions), and 700 recoveries of overpayments (totalling £155,000) without recourse to formal action. These are important reserve powers, but the Auditors' influence is in general exercised much less formally, by advice about interpretation of law and the form of accounts. The Auditors do not, however, act as advisers about the use of accounts as an instrument of management or budgetary control.

The Auditors also certify claims made by local authorities for grants. Authorisation of expenditure by a Department constitutes approval in principle only; it remains for the district auditor to certify that the claims are a complete and accurate statement of the expenditure actually incurred. It is, in effect, his business to certify 'subject to any adjustment finally settled by Departments, the incidence of charge of grant-aided expenditure as between rates and taxes'. The audit staff at present certify 47 different types of grant claim for 14 different Departments.

(ii) *Health*

The Ministry of Health and the Ministry of Housing and Local Government have in effect divided the inheritance of the old Ministry of Health, as it existed from 1919 to 1951, and in the process the Ministry of Health has lost much of its traditional interest in local

[1] Now by the Minister of Housing and Local Government.
[2] H.C. Deb., Vol. 207, Cols. 1024-5.

government. One division of the Ministry, *the Local Authority Services Division*, is concerned with local authority personal health and welfare services; but the work is so organised that it does not stress the importance of local authority organisation. The same division is responsible for the general practitioner services, which are managed not by the elected local authorities but by *ad hoc* bodies, the local Executive Councils and other local committees, which use the same areas; and for nursing, a profession which is important throughout the Health Service. The other local authority health services, those concerned with environment and the prevention of disease, belong not to this division but to the Local Government Division of the Ministry of Housing and Local Government. The link between the two divisions is provided by two small sections in the Ministry of Health's Local Authority Services Division, one of which deals with matters of common interest in Local Bills, the other with other joint business.

There are about 25 senior officials in the division, at the level of Principal, Senior Executive Officer, or above, but none of them is solely concerned with local government. It is difficult, for the same reason, to say how much of the time of the professional staff in *the Chief Medical Officer's Division* is devoted to local authorities' business; but a number of them have certainly had experience in local government at some time in their careers.

The Ministry of Health uses the same engineering and architectural staff as the Ministry of Housing and Local Government, and the two Departments continue to share a *Legal Branch* under a Solicitor and Legal Adviser who has an important part to play in both Ministries. There is no special Inspectorate for local authority health and welfare services, but the Ministry's regional offices include a 'public health nursing officer' and a 'welfare officer'. The Principal Regional Officers are successors to the General Inspectors of Poor Law, a once influential body who traced their descent from the Assistant Commissioners of 1834; but inspection of local authority services is now a small part of their duties, which are mainly concerned with hospitals and the general practitioner services.

(iii) *Education*

The Ministry of Education is more specifically concerned with local authority services than is the Ministry of Health: indeed, from one point of view, it is the most important single Ministry which deals with local authorities, since about 40 per cent. of their total revenue from rates and grants is now expended on education, and the expenditure on new school building is far larger than any other capital outlay except that on housing. Its organisation, however, stresses the structure of the education service rather than that of the local authority system. It is a relatively small Ministry, with about 100 senior general staff, and about 50 senior professional staff. The main 'policy' divisions are organised under Under Secretaries by subject: Schools; Special Services (this includes the School Health Service, provision for handicapped children, and School Meals); Teachers' Training and Qualifications, Salaries, and Pensions, three divisions which are grouped under one Under Secretary; and Further Education. The Awards Branch (which deals with state scholarships, local authority awards to university students, and so on) is under an Assistant Secretary reporting direct to the Permanent Secretary; and there are small branches dealing with teachers' overseas exchanges, the education of families of servicemen abroad, and U.N.E.S.C.O., for which the Principal Establishments Officer is generally responsible.

The Ministry shares its Chief Medical Officer with the Ministry of Health, but has its own Legal Adviser. Its statistical and information branches (which are of considerable importance) come under the Principal Establishments Officer. Its Architects and Buildings Branch, under an Assistant Secretary and a Chief Architect (they rank as 'joint heads of branch'), is an important organisation which greatly influences the layout and design of school buildings through 'quasi-legislation', as the corresponding divisions in the Ministry of Housing and Local Government influence housing and civic design.

In a few divisions (for example, Pensions, and Teachers' Qualifications) business is distributed functionally, but in most it is distributed both functionally and territorially. The Schools Branch has eleven sections (under Principals), four of them functional and seven geographical, each of the latter covering one or more 'regions'[1]; School Health works in seven sections, five of which are partly geographical (by regions) and partly functional, and two functional only; the Architects Branch is organised in five 'Building Teams' each responsible for a group of counties; the Awards Branch is organised in much the same way as School Health, except that the territorial division is based on Universities, not on local authorities. The effect of this somewhat complex system is that a local education authority does not find any convenient single point of reference in the Ministry, and it is not the business of any official to grasp the problems of any education authority as a whole. This gap is partly filled by the 'H.M.I.s'—*Her Majesty's Inspectorate of Schools*—a body of about

[1] Called 'divisions' in this Ministry.

550 Inspectors (including the separate Welsh Inspectorate) under a Senior Chief Inspector, who ranks fourth in the Ministry after the Deputy Secretary and the Legal Adviser. The Inspectorate (which has as distinguished a place as the Ministry itself in the history of education) is recruited by selection from men and women who have high qualifications in their own field and also have experience in teaching. It is organised in ten 'divisions' in England, the areas corresponding to the 'standard' regions, but a few Inspectors are stationed at headquarters for special advisory duties. The Divisional Inspector is in charge of a large number of Inspectors who are allocated to 'Districts'. The work of H.M.I.s is roughly three-fold: they are, in the strict sense, 'inspectors' assessing and reporting on the efficiency of schools and local education authorities; they are expert advisers on educational theory and practice; and they have a variety of functions concerned with equipment, such as the inspection of school building works, and advice on the layout and design of schools, the purchase of text-books and apparatus, and so on.

The education grant depends formally upon the Inspector's certificate, which should be given only if he is satisfied that the requirements of the Ministry have been complied with. But influence is exercised mainly through the Ministry's key position in such matters as the training and qualifications of teachers, salary negotiations, approval of development programmes, rationing of funds allowed by the Treasury for school building, and also through a stream of circulars, manuals, and reports. Sanctions are never used except in extreme cases, and then only if the Ministry is sure that the opinion of the educational world is behind it.

(iv) *Roads*

The Ministry of Transport and Civil Aviation's local highways functions are administered chiefly through *the Highways Administration Group of Divisions* and *the Engineering Staff* at headquarters, and by *the Divisional Road Engineer Organisation* in the field, but the work of a number of other divisions bears directly or indirectly on the highways and road safety duties of local authorities: in particular *the Road Safety, Traffic, and Vehicle Regulation Group*. The Department makes grants to, and supervises, local highways authorities in their work of constructing and maintaining classified roads, bridges, road lighting, etc., and it provides many services: in particular it promotes road research and road safety research through the Road Research Laboratory of the D.S.I.R., provides snow clearance and emergency bridging equipment, and makes grants towards the expenses of traffic censuses.

The Highways Administration Group of Divisions is controlled by an Under Secretary with four Assistant Secretaries in charge of Highways Policy, Highways Development, Trunk Roads, and 'Highways General'. There is a large staff of civil, electrical, and mechanical engineers employed on highways work at headquarters, and the Divisional Road Engineer Organisation employs some 200 engineers, technicians, and draughtsmen, with a further 200 Executive and Clerical officers. The Divisional Road Engineers work to their own ten regions (which follow the lines of the main trunk roads) and they are responsible for the technical supervision of local highways authorities. They scrutinise tenders and specifications, give technical advice, inspect and report on the progress of the local authority's services. There is an 'Area' Finance Office in each division (staffed by Executive Class officials) which certifies claims for grants and carries out test audits of local authority contractors' accounts, and of direct labour accounts (if grant-aided).

This is a very substantial business, involving a revenue and capital expenditure of about £50 m. a year, including that on trunk roads which are maintained at the Ministry's expense by the major local authorities: but it is a relatively small part of the Ministry's sphere, since the Ministry deals also with all road transport questions, all railway questions, and all shipping questions, as well as with civil aviation.

(v) *Police, Fire Service, Civil Defence, Children, Probation*

We have already (in Chapter 15) given some account of the organisation of the Home Office, and only three points need to be made separately here.

(a) 'Except in so far as agencies of government have special responsibilities in particular fields' (says Sir Frank Newsam)[1] the Home Secretary 'is concerned with the structure, health and well-being of society.' This is a rather extreme statement, but it is certainly true that the Home Secretary has a *general* concern with certain matters relating to local government as a whole. He is mainly responsible for the system of local lay magistrates, a system which has long historical connections with the system of local government; he is, under a great variety of statutes, concerned in the proper conduct of elections, national and local, and for the former the Registration Officers and Returning Officers are officials of local authorities, acting in their personal capacity; he issues model by-laws for 'good rule and government', and must approve by-laws made

[1] *The Home Office* (1956).

under various statutes, a power which can be related to the general principle that by-laws may create new criminal offences and therefore new problems of law enforcement.

(b) In spite of the generality of his powers, if considered in this large historical perspective, the organisation of the Home Office is conspicuously an organisation by service. All five services referred to are administered on the same general pattern: there is a small administrative headquarters; a central inspectorate; a system of Exchequer grants; a local committee; a locally employed field service.

(c) This pattern admits of wide variations according to the nature of the service. The Civil Defence organisation is largely a planning, training, and supply organisation, designed for enormous expansion in emergency. It has a relatively large Inspectorate and headquarters staff. On the other hand, there are only four 'Inspectors of Constabulary', with one woman Assistant Inspector; the number has traditionally been small, and this reflects a rather special relation between the Inspectors and the Chief Constables commanding police forces. The Fire Service Inspectorate is larger; the Children's Department Inspectorate is larger still, with over sixty Inspectors in all. This is natural, because the task of the Department has been to build up decent standards of treatment for children who have come into the care of public authorities under a great variety of conditions, previously little regulated. Each of these Inspectorates is very well acquainted with the personalities and problems of individual authorities so far as this concerns their own service; but it is not their business to compare notes or to form a general opinion about the working of any local authority as a whole.

3. LOCAL GOVERNMENT ORGANISATIONS

In the field of local government, as in other fields of administration, an enormous amount of business is done on the basis of collective representation and negotiation. Prior agreement among local authorities and their officials strengthens their collective hand in dealing with Whitehall. Whitehall may sometimes play one group off against another, but on the whole it seeks not to divide and rule but to foster organisations with which it can deal. There are about 140 Counties and County Boroughs, about 1,400 Boroughs and Districts in England and Wales. The Ministries prefer to proceed by negotiation and discussion rather than by direction, but co-operation of this kind is only possible if local authority views are defined and crystallised before discussion with the Ministries.

One type of organisation shades off into another, but three categories can be distinguished.

(i) *Associations of Authorities*

The oldest of these is the Association of Municipal Corporations, which was founded in 1873. It was followed by the County Councils Association in 1890, the Associations of Urban and Rural District Councils in 1895,[1] the Metropolitan Boroughs' Standing Joint Committee in 1912, and the Parish Councils Association in 1947.

The A.M.C. originated in a dispute between the central government and a number of boroughs over the terms of the Borough Funds Act of 1872, a piece of legislation introduced in the interests of the boroughs to rectify an anomaly in the law, but containing provisions for central control which were then much resented, though they seem inoffensive enough by modern standards. The boroughs protested that the Act was 'inconsistent with the due recognition of the principle of local self-government', and formed the Association 'more effectually to watch over and protect the interests, rights and privileges of municipal corporations'. This was the model on which the later associations were based: all the English and Welsh Boroughs are members, with the exception of the City of Westminster (which has never joined) and the Borough of Lambeth, which left after a dispute in 1953.

(ii) *Associations of Committees*

The experience of these general associations prompted the organisation of some associations concerned with particular services, some of which were once run by separate local *ad hoc* authorities dealing with one service only. Good examples of these are the Association of Education Committees and the National Association of Divisional Executives for Education.

(iii) *Associations of Officers*

Parallel with these are associations specifically limited to Chief Officers heading a service within their authority: for instance, the Society of Town Clerks, the Society of Medical Officers of Health, the Association of Chief Education Officers, the Society of County Treasurers, the Association of Children's Officers, and the Chief Constables' Association of England and Wales. A rather narrow line divides these associations of chief officers from associations and institutions of professionally qualified officials mainly or solely

[1] The Urban District Councils Association was originally constituted in 1890 as 'The Local Boards Association', and changed its name after the passage of the Local Government Act, 1894, which set up Urban District Councils.

employed in local government, such as the Local Government Legal Society, the Institute of Municipal Treasurers and Accountants, the Sanitary Inspectors Association, and the Institute of Municipal Engineers. These professional associations again shade off into associations of groups of staff who seek for professional status but can hardly be said to have attained it as yet, such as the Association of Child Care Officers, the Institute of Public Supplies Officers, the Education Welfare Officers Association, the National Association of Local Government Health and Welfare Officers (formerly the National Association of Relieving Officers), and the National Association of Bath Superintendents. All these bodies are concerned (in different proportions) with the professional work of their members, and with their members' anxieties about salaries and conditions of service. Many of their members also belong to the National and Local Government Officers Association, which now has some 230,000 members, about 150,000 of them in local government service; and N.A.L.G.O. plays a very large part in all salary negotiations. The N.U.T., which has about 220,000 members, mainly in local government service, is almost equally important.

All these bodies are linked together through interlocking membership, and also because there is a relatively small circle of paid officials and of influential chairmen of committees who are well known to one another and to officials in the Ministries. They also interlock through membership of advisory bodies appointed by Ministers, such as the Central Health Services Advisory Council, the Central Fire Brigades Advisory Council, the Central Midwives Board, the Central Council for Health Education, the Advisory Councils for Education; and through membership of unofficial bodies concerned to further the development of particular services, such as the Royal Institute of Public Health and Hygiene, the National Associations for Maternity and Child Welfare and for Mental Health, the National Housing and Town Planning Council, and the Town Planning Institute.

Civil servants in dealing with 'representations' or in sponsoring proposals of their own are usually concerned only with a particular service, and with those specifically interested in it; the associations of authorities occupy rather a special position in speaking for local government as a whole. It is true that much of their business is done through committees each dealing with a separate service, not subject to much central co-ordination; and also that on major issues the associations are often divided internally, so that they do not always constitute a very secure point of reference in discussion. Nevertheless, their status is such that it is almost officially recognised that the associations must be consulted in advance about any major proposal affecting local government. To take one instance among many, an explanatory note issued with the Civil Defence Grant Regulations (1953) begins: 'These regulations have been made after consultation with the associations of local authorities. The Ministers concerned have agreed that they will be open to review after two years and that the associations will then be free to revive any alternative proposals made by them during the consultations.'

Such consultations take place at various levels: quite informally, between officials of the Ministries and of the associations; more formally through the exchange of letters and proposals, which may be the subject of detailed negotiation. Sometimes the Minister throws responsibility almost entirely upon the associations, by offering to accept any solution (within certain limits) which the local authorities agree between themselves. It is usual to discuss the actual text of draft regulations and of many circulars; it would not be constitutionally proper to show a draft Bill to the associations before it is introduced in either House of Parliament, but Bills are drafted in the light of what is known about the associations' views, and there is often active negotiation behind the scenes while they are before Parliament.

This system of collaboration works to some extent 'at arm's length': those concerned are tough negotiators for the interests which they represent. But they have been intimately associated for long periods—the post of Secretary of the A.M.C. has had only three occupants since 1878, and the first two of these, the Pritchards, father and son, reigned from 1878 to 1944; all the moves in the game are well known to both sides, and they need one another. The Ministries have great and specific powers; the associations have equally great but less tangible ones—their long experience, their standing in the eyes of public opinion, their essential place in administration, and in the background the sanction of appeal to Parliament. A number of M.P.s and Peers are always associated with their work either as members of special committees or as Vice-Presidents. In 1954 about 50 M.P.s and about 30 Peers were Vice-Presidents of associations of authorities. The post is honorary, but a Vice-President is expected to state the association's case to Parliament if asked to do so, and often speaks from what is known by all concerned to be a brief prepared by 'his' association's officials. On a larger issue further resources can be mobilised. About a quarter of the Conservative M.P.s and half the Labour M.P.s in the 1951 House of Commons had had experience in local government. The overlap between locally and nationally elected bodies is less in Britain than in some other countries, but it is quite considerable, and local councillors are influential in local party committees. Hence the House of Commons can in a crisis be induced to take an active interest in relations between central and local authorities; but on the whole it does not do so, because business goes on reasonably well without bringing in the clumsy apparatus of political debate.

4. Individual Authorities

In the last resort a Department can coerce a local authority which defies it when it is acting within its powers. Two methods are possible. It may take the case to a court and obtain an order of *mandamus* or prohibition, instructing the authority to comply with law subject to penalties; or it may make an order to supersede an authority which is in default, by transferring its powers and duties to another authority or to the Minister.

The only important example of the use of default powers in recent years was that of Coventry in 1954. Early in that year the Coventry City Council decided (by a majority of 32 to 13) to disband its civil defence organisation in protest against what the majority regarded as inadequacies in national defence policy. After some dispute between the City authority and the Home Office, the Home Secretary made an order transferring the city's civil defence functions to a body of three Commissioners: the 75 per cent. grant was stopped, and it was announced that the full cost of the service was to be borne by the City. The Commission managed to exercise its functions for about a year before the Council reversed its decision and reconstituted its civil defence committee. But this experience suggests that the practical difficulties which face one body acting in default of another are almost insuperable unless (which is unlikely) the defaulting authority allows its officials to co-operate fully. On the other hand, the case also suggests that the financial weapon is almost certain to prevail in the long run.

Such examples serve only to show that these powers exist and may be used in extreme cases. For the most part relations go on smoothly enough from day to day; there is usually complaint on one side or the other, but this is 'part of the game', and there is very little risk of breakdown. The process varies according to service, according to Department, according to authority; and we have already indicated many of the considerations involved.

(i) *Services*

The administrative structure is different for each service, and so is the spirit in which it is run. The Inspectors of Constabulary are few in number, and the annual inspection of a local police force has something of the atmosphere of a visit from the Commanding General of an Army; the Inspector formally reviews the force on parade, talks with some of the men, briefly inspects the books, tours the offices, visits a number of police-stations. On the other hand, there are the five hundred Inspectors of Education who live in their areas, often work from their own homes, and are in contact with 'their' schools and local authorities day by day. Those who manage Civil Defence have the intractable problem of encouraging local authorities to find enthusiastic volunteers for participation in the Day of Judgement, if and when it comes; the Children's Department Inspectorate must at once encourage and control the maternalism of committees; housing, schools, and highways work in the political world of pressures and competing priorities.

(ii) *Departments*

Departmental traditions vary in this as in other things. The Ministry of Housing and Local Government has inherited from the old Ministry of Health and from its predecessor, the Local Government Board, a tradition of good relations and a reputation for cautious and tactful dealing. Other Departments have on occasion been more aggressive, not always with good results. During the war, for instance, there was a marked contrast between the methods of the Ministry of Health and those of the Home Office and its temporary offshoot, the Ministry of Home Security. This is to be explained partly in terms of the more lordly *ethos* of the Home Office; partly by the extreme gravity of the situation which it had to handle; partly by the half-military form of the police, fire, and civil defence organisation through which it worked; and partly by the inexperience of the large number of 'temporaries' whom the Ministry had to absorb very quickly. An experienced Town Clerk could certainly suggest other examples of Departmental idiosyncrasies.

(iii) *Authorities*

There is a broad distinction between the position of large local authorities and that of small ones, even when they have the same legal powers. At one extreme are the 'great' authorities: the L.C.C.; the 'five largest cities', which have permanent representation on all the important committees of the A.M.C., Birmingham, Liverpool, Manchester, Leeds, and Sheffield, and their nearest rivals, Bristol, Bradford, Newcastle-on-Tyne, Cardiff, Hull, and others; the 'great' counties such as Middlesex, Surrey, Kent, the West Riding, Lancashire, Glamorgan. At the other extreme are the small Districts and Boroughs, places with a population of perhaps 10,000 to 20,000, a limited range of services, and a staff which includes perhaps only half a dozen people who might rank with Executive Class officers in the Civil Service. Between the extremes there are no clear lines of distinction; the anomalies of the system are such that the legal distinction between 'major' and 'minor' authorities is not very important: some Boroughs and Districts carry more weight than some Counties and County Boroughs, in spite of their limited range of services.

Such differences derive directly from differences in social and economic importance, and are expressed in two ways. First, the larger authorities each have several M.P.s whom they regard as 'theirs'. British politics are not highly localised, but it is regarded as usual that the M.P.s for a Borough or County should all be prepared to speak for it on some matters regardless of party. The Town Clerk will normally brief the local M.P.s if trouble is expected about a Private Bill; letters may be sent to Ministers, questions asked in the House, all the usual methods used to stress the importance of the authority. The effectiveness of these methods may vary a little according to the political situation: a Conservative government may be less responsive than a Labour one to the claims of an authority whose area constitutes a block of safe Labour seats, and this attitude may convey itself to officials. But the variations from a norm of correctness and impartiality are very slight.

Secondly, there are wide differences between the position of officials in different places. There are Clerks whose salaries rank them with Permanent Secretaries, and other chief officers who can look down on Under Secretaries; there are some who are perhaps on the whole better paid than H.E.O.s and E.O.s, but do not differ from them in ability and scale of responsibility. Much lies between these extremes, but the central administration has attitudes derived from extreme cases which serve to explain its general line of conduct. On the one hand, it is a little frightened of the standing, particularly of the collective standing, of the great local authorities, who are led by influential men, are served by able staffs, and are quite as capable as Whitehall of looking far ahead in the development of a service. On the other hand, there are authorities which need guidance and encouragement, even coercion; where the quality of councillors is low, and the management of a department may lie becalmed for years in the charge of a man not really qualified to run it.

There is no means of tracing the consequences of these attitudes in practice. There are certainly differences in the consideration accorded to authorities of the same legal status, and it might perhaps ease administration if these differences were made even greater. Large authorities complain that they are bound by red tape which is not designed for them; those interested in particular services complain that not enough is done to bring the worst authorities up to the standard of the average.

There is a corresponding difference in attitudes on the side of the local authorities. This is shown in the divisions between associations and within associations about proposals for changes in local government areas and powers. It also appears in the views taken by local authorities about the organisation of central administration, and it is worth quoting from the views about regional administration expressed to the Estimates Committee in the session 1953-54. The County Councils Association said that they 'esteem greatly the personal contacts maintained between their senior officials and the senior civil servants who are associated with the creation of policy. The value attached to these is such that they would accept, and it is apparent that many county councils would welcome, severe contraction of the functions, and in some cases an abolition, of the regional office.' The Secretary of the Association of Municipal Corporations said in evidence: 'It does not make the same appeal to the representatives of the public to see someone regionally. . . . I do not think, even if the representative of the regional organisation was of the same rank as the officer in Whitehall, that the public's representative would have the same feeling of satisfaction.' Before the war 'they saw somebody in Whitehall at a sufficiently high level, and as a result the local authority, whether they got their point or not, at any rate were satisfied that they had had justice. . . .' On the other hand, many of the smaller local authorities liked the regional system and found it helpful. The majority of rural district councils supported the retention of the regional organisation of the Ministry of Housing and Local Government, because rural districts generally 'found it more expeditious to deal with the regional office', and the Urban District Councils Association agreed with this view. In fact, the dismantling of the regional organisation represented a gain for the larger authorities at the expense of the smaller ones,

5. Conclusion

The impression left by this account may be one of confusion. This is misleading, since the system is well understood by the relatively small number of people who occupy key positions, and its compromises have their own logic.

The centre has great powers over local government, but these powers are widely diffused. The Ministry of Housing and Local Government has a certain general responsibility for the system, and takes its responsibility seriously, but even that Ministry has to handle particular services of great importance and complexity which continually engage the attention of Ministers and officials. Other Ministries have powers over finance and policy which may be used so as to modify the system profoundly, but it is not their business to consider anything but the development of their own service. This 'separation of powers' has conservative effects on the structure of local government, and also greatly limits the powers of the central government to affect (for better or for worse) the general conduct of business in any single authority. There is no Ministry of the Interior, no prefects, no tutelage: the position of local government is in the short run very strong, but may grow weaker in the long run if it proves impossible for working compromises to make sense of a system which is obsolete in form.

The reverse of this is that, on the whole, officials in Whitehall are much more interested in services than in authorities. This is an attitude natural to technically qualified men interested in the standards of their profession; the organisation of Departments and the distribution of duties inside Departments tends to give the same bent to general civil servants. They find themselves in a Ministry concerned mainly with one or more functions; they work with professional enthusiasts and learn from them; they become qualified by experience in large parts of the field. This 'functional' organisation began in the period when it seemed natural to apply the same principle within local government, by creating separate *ad hoc* authorities for separate services, and there was no reorganisation in Whitehall when the fashion changed in favour of the creation of 'comprehensive' local authorities. This may be part of the reason for the more recent trend back from comprehensive local authorities to separate functional authorities for health and for the nationalised industries; but it reflects a characteristic which underlies this trend, the tendency for voluntary organisations to grow out of the interests of people concerned with a particular service, their interests as reformers, as professional employees, as administrators, as customers and clients. This functional organisation cuts right across the old local organisation of England and Wales; it is equally strong, but not strong enough to displace it.

The Ministries have a part to play in this framework which helps to explain their part in the 'control' of local authorities. The Minister and the group of administrators specially concerned with a service act in a sense as agents for that service within Whitehall. They are its advocates in dealing with the Treasury and the Cabinet, they must watch the current of events and try to keep ahead of it. If they fail to take this position of leadership—as they often do—they are at the mercy of shifting pressures, and have no effective control at all. But if they attempt to grasp and direct the politics of their service as a service they are bound to look at the position of local authorities functionally. New lines of policy emerge from a combination of public demand and expert opinion, both expressed partly through local authorities, but also through other channels. Civil servants as advisers on policy are bound to think primarily of 'their' service. Up to a point local authorities can be led, advised, directed, sometimes restrained in the interest of a service; but there is always some friction, and if for some reason friction is great, or vested interests weak, the needs of a service may lead to new administrative inventions outside the traditional forms of local government.

FOR REFERENCE

Imperial Calendar.
Civil Estimates.
Report of the Ministry of Housing and Local Government for the period 1950-51 to 1954. Cmd. 9559, 1955.
1st and 2nd Reports of the Local Government Manpower Committee. Cmd. 7870, 1950, and Cmd. 8421, 1951.
6th Report from the Select Committee on Estimates, Session 1953-54. H.C. 233, 1954. Regional Organisations of Government Departments.
D. N. CHESTER: *Central and Local Government* (1951).
A West Midland Study Group: *Local Government and Central Control* (1956).
C. A. CROSS: 'The Association of Municipal Corporations' (an unpublished thesis for the degree of M.A. (Econ.) in the library of Manchester University).
A. WILSON: 'The District Audit Service', *Public Administration*, Vol. XXVIII, p. 189.
JOHN S. HARRIS: *Central Government Inspection in Great Britain* (1956).
A discussion on 'Local Government in Parliament' is to be found in *Public Administration*, Vol. XXXI, p. 46 (D. E. Butler), Vol. XXXII, p. 409 (W. J. M. Mackenzie), and Vol. XXXIII, p. 207 (B Keith-Lucas).

CHAPTER TWENTY-THREE

INDEPENDENT PUBLIC BODIES

In order that the strong may serve the strong, there must be mutual respect, and in one or both of the parties a high and rare humility. . . . There must be over the efforts of both a common bond of reverence for what is greater than either.—Sir HENRY TAYLOR: *The Statesman.*

1. INTRODUCTORY

WE referred in Chapter 13 to the difficulty of finding an exact line of division in law and practice between government Departments and independent public bodies which are not local authorities. A Local Authority is defined unambiguously by the Local Government Act, 1933, as 'the council of a county, county borough, county district or rural parish'; a county district is defined as a 'non-county borough, urban district or rural district'. We chose to define a Department as an organisation wholly staffed by civil servants, and also financed directly and wholly by the normal form of Parliamentary grant and not by grant-in-aid or by any other method. This is a reasonably good practical test, but does leave somewhat ambiguous the position of bodies like the Forestry Commission (which is staffed wholly by civil servants but is financed from a special fund).[1]

Bodies not belonging to either category may be called 'independent': but which 'independent' bodies are also 'public'? The sort of bodies in which we are interested here are those which are assisted by grants from central funds; or established at the instigation of some central authority, legislative or administrative; or both. This definition is wide enough to include all that can conveniently be included in the sphere of 'public' administration, but it does not make a clean cut. There are a good many organisations (District Nursing Associations and Family Service Units for instance) which were formed originally by private initiative and are still entirely or almost entirely privately managed, but which draw much of their support from local (not central) public funds. There are voluntary

---

[1] There is also a curious ambiguity about the position of 'joint boards' consisting solely of representatives of local authorities: strictly, such a board is not itself a 'local authority', but an 'independent public body'.

bodies not supported by public funds (such as the Howard League) which occupy a special position in relation to particular Departments as 'semi-official' channels of representation. There are even private firms, operating commercially, which can scarcely be called 'independent' since their existence depends almost entirely on government business: they are found necessary by some Department, and the favour of the Department is equally necessary to them.

These complexities are implicit in the structure of British society, which cannot readily be labelled 'capitalist' or 'socialist', 'directed' or 'free'. To illustrate them, we take here two principal examples, the nationalised industries and the hospital service. Important though these services are, they represent only a part of this enormous field of organisation. As in preceding chapters, we assume a knowledge of the legal structure and responsibilities of the bodies concerned, and consider only the problems which they pose for administrators in Whitehall.

2. General Considerations

There are, however, some general points which should be made first about the classification and growth of the very large number of bodies which fall within our definition.

(i) *Voluntary Bodies*

Many independent public bodies began as voluntary associations, but for various reasons the government has come to take an active interest in their work and to exercise a measure of control over them, usually in exchange for a grant of public money. Certain conditions are as a rule attached to such grants: the appointment of some or all of the members of the governing board, the appointment of 'assessors' who 'sit in' on meetings, financial scrutiny of varying degrees of rigour.

The British Standards Institution is a good example of this process. Though it retains most of the characteristics of a voluntary association, its functions have increasingly taken on national importance, and it now receives a substantial grant from the central government. Its governing body includes civil servants representing the main interested Departments, it has a Royal Charter, and its organisation and finance have in recent years been the subject of an official inquiry. It would be difficult to deny that it is a public body.

A more extreme case is that of the British Council, to which several references have been made in earlier chapters. It began in 1934 as a voluntary body supported by private donations and a small government grant. In the course of time the grant has been increased, until today it constitutes almost the whole of its income. Pressure from Parliament for greater financial accountability, and from the Council's staff for a structure of salaries and conditions of service comparable to that of the Civil Service, have so altered the character of the organisation that it is practically indistinguishable from a government Department. Its policy is greatly influenced by the wishes of the Overseas Departments, its Executive Committee includes their representatives as well as officials from the Board of Trade and Treasury, it is subject to tight financial control by the Treasury, and its accounts are audited by the Comptroller and Auditor-General in the normal way.

(ii) *Sponsored Associations*

This situation has become so familiar from experience that it may be deliberately copied. A government Department may be interested in the development of a service, but reluctant for one reason or another to take direct responsibility for it. It may therefore suggest, and even actively promote, the formation of a 'voluntary' association; once formed, the association may be given special recognition and even assistance from public funds, though the Department often hopes to make it self-supporting through private subscriptions and fees. To this category belong, for example, many industrial research associations, the British Travel and Holidays Association, the British Institute of Management, and the Council of Industrial Design.

The British Institute of Management was set up as the result of the Report of a Committee of Inquiry (Baillieu) appointed by the President of the Board of Trade in 1945. 'While there are many existing bodies in this country concerned with questions of management which have done good work in the past', the Report said, 'they ... cannot individually provide the sort of comprehensive facilities which a central institute would offer.' The British Travel and Holidays Association (formerly 'Board') was set up by the government in 1947 'to foster and develop the tourist, catering, and holiday services'. The Council of Industrial Design was established in 1944 'to promote by all practicable means the improvement of design in the products of British industry'. These three bodies provide services which the government considers necessary, but which it hopes to persuade industry to finance for itself. This has proved difficult in practice, and nearly the whole of the income of the Council of Industrial Design, three-quarters of that of the B.T.H.A., and half of that of the B.I.M., still come from public funds.

(iii) *Statutory and Chartered Bodies*

The categories just discussed are familiar and important, but the really powerful organisations are those set up from the outset as fully public bodies, either by statute or by Royal Charter. They include national industrial corporations like the Coal Board, national research and development organisations such as the Atomic Energy Authority and the Medical and Agricultural Research Councils, traditional corporations like Universities and Colleges, national regulatory bodies such as the Independent Television Authority, regional and local corporations such as the Area Gas Boards, the New Town Development Corporations, and the Regional Hospital Boards, regulatory bodies concerned with particular industries such as the Iron and Steel Board.

In some of these instances (not by any means in all) there has been dispute between political parties about the advantages or otherwise of 'nationalisation', but there has been a good deal of agreement about administrative forms. Most of the national public corporations were set up in that form in order to avoid what were supposed to be the bad effects of direct control by central administration; the local and regional bodies were created to avoid the rather different defects of control by local authority committees, and also because of the limited financial resources of local authorities and their inconvenient areas of administration. These points are illustrated by our discussion of the nationalised industries and the hospital service.

3. THE NATIONALISED INDUSTRIES

Direct contacts between central administration and the nationalised industries are mainly confined to two major Departments: the Ministry of Power (which is responsible for the nationalised coal, electricity, and gas industries) and the Ministry of Transport and Civil Aviation (which supervises nationalised railway and road transport and their ancillary services such as hotels and restaurants, as well as the two airways corporations). The Ministry of Power is also responsible for liaison with the Atomic Energy Authority, which is both a research institution and an authority for the development of nuclear power, though it is not in charge of a 'nationalised industry' in the strict sense of the term.[1]

Many other Departments are concerned, but less directly: the Treasury, which has many formal duties under the nationalisation

[1] The Ministry of Power took over this duty from a small section in the Lord President's Office (the Atomic Energy Office) at the beginning of 1957.

Acts; the Ministry of Labour, through its general responsibility for the use of manpower; the 'economic' Departments, which are all interested in the progress of nationalised industries; and the Scottish Office, which has a special interest in their operations in Scotland.

A Minister of Power or a Minister of Transport and Civil Aviation may bring to his office considerable experience in public affairs and in the climate of public opinion about particular industries. He will certainly not lack unofficial advisers. But the main responsibility falls on quite a small group of civil servants in these two Departments.

The Ministry of Fuel and Power was in 1956 organised under a Permanent Secretary and a Deputy Secretary in five administrative divisions directed by Under Secretaries: Coal, Petroleum, Gas, Electricity, and Safety and Health; and it is unlikely that the main outlines of the organisation have been changed by the Ministry's change of name and acquisition of responsibility for iron and steel and for atomic energy. We therefore retain the present tense. There are a Chief Scientist and a Chief Inspector of Mines, who rank next to the Deputy Secretary; an Economic Adviser, who is an Under Secretary; a Chief Statistician, who is an Assistant Secretary. There are also finance and establishments divisions directed by Under Secretaries: presumably the former has a good deal to do with financial policy in relation to nationalised industry, presumably the latter acts purely in matters internal to the Department.

None of these organisations is very large (there are only 18 Assistant Secretaries in the Department, about 75 members of the Administrative Class altogether), and they are responsible for a good deal of business which would have existed independently of nationalisation: the Mines Inspectorate, the Gas Standards Branch, the Engineering Inspectorate and the Meter Examiners of the Electricity Division, the Statistics Branch, the Fuel Efficiency Branch, the Safety in Mines Research Establishment. Some of these ancillary organisations have long and distinguished records, but they do not contribute to the making of policy about the operation of the nationalised industries.

The corresponding organisation at the Ministry of Transport and Civil Aviation is more complicated because the Minister, not the airways corporations, is responsible for the provision of aerodromes and the control of air traffic, and because the Ministry's responsibilities for regulating the various forms of transport and transport undertakings were already very extensive before nationalisation. There is, in fact, a small section of the Ministry known as the 'Nationalised Industries Division', but this deals with a small part only of their affairs: with the finances of the airways corporations, and with their pensions and compensation cases and those of the British Transport Commission. Other matters fall to various general divisions in the Ministry, which is much larger than the Ministry of Power. The Permanent Secretary has four Deputy Secretaries; of these, one is concerned with airline operation and another with civil aviation ground services. On the civil aviation side (this was a separate Ministry from 1945 to 1953) an Under Secretary is head of the 'Civil Aviation Services and Civil Aviation International Relations Group', including four divisions under Assistant Secretaries which are particularly concerned with matters of policy affecting the nationalised airways. But there is also a large 'Civil Aviation Safety and General Group', there is the Accidents Investigation Branch under a Chief Inspector, and the 'Controller of Civil Aviation Ground Services' directs a very large organisation, administrative and technical. The old Ministry of Transport likewise included many services which have nothing to do with nationalised industry. We referred in Chapter 22 to the divisions which deal with highways, largely through the local authorities. The other main Groups are the Road Transport, Inland Transport Planning and International Inland Transport Group; the Railways and Inland Waterways Rates and Charges Group; the Marine Group; the Shipping Operations, Ports and Planning Group; the Shipping Policy Group; and there are the usual 'staff' divisions—finance, establishments, economics, and statistics.

It will be seen that this organisation differs a good deal from that of the Ministry of Power. It is not only much larger—about 155 members of the Administrative Class, including 44 Assistant Secretaries—but it carries a heavier burden of direct services (such as civil aviation ground services), and of supervisory services, involving such matters as safety and tariffs, which were regulated in detail long before nationalisation. Many divisions deal with a 'mixed bag' of public and private bodies: inland transport policy involves nationalised services, local authority services and licensed private companies; shipping operations and ports involve private shipping companies, nationalised railways, docks and road transport services which are run by a variety of different authorities. The Ministry is involved at so many points with the industries that it controls, that it is hard to say specifically where responsibility lies for general matters of policy about the public corporations.

The business of the two Departments in relation to the nationalised industries can be arranged roughly under three headings: to be well informed about them, to advise the Minister on the exercise of his formal powers under statute, and to act as intermediaries on behalf of the industries within the administration and also (through the Minister) before Parliament.

(i) *Information*

During the process of nationalisation all parties were agreed that the boards of the industries must be given considerable independence in the business management of production, and a good many safeguards for independence were included in the nationalisation Acts. The boards finance themselves, in the sense that they are almost wholly independent of public funds provided out of national taxation[1]; in consequence, they stand outside the ordinary system of Treasury control, and the Comptroller and Auditor-General has power only to examine and comment upon their final balance-sheets and consolidated income and expenditure accounts which are presented annually to Parliament. The House of Commons also exercises restraint in its undoubted power of general investigation, and has not yet (in spite of much discussion) established any effective procedure for the supervision of nationalised industries. A Select Committee on Nationalised Industries has been appointed each Session since 1954, originally with very restricted terms of reference; its exact scope is still uncertain and it is too early yet to say what effect it will have.

There is, however, a certain unreality about the process of taking these great national enterprises 'out of politics'. Their size and importance to the national economy are such that no government can be indifferent to them, or evade responsibility if there is a major disaster or crisis. Constitutionally, they are the creatures of Parliament, and the House of Commons remains conscious of this even when it attempts to draw a line between matters of policy, for which a Minister must be answerable to Parliament, and matters of day-to-day business, which are supposed to be exempt from Parliamentary control. Politically, they remain controversial, partly because much of what they do has a direct effect on large numbers of individuals, partly because their success or failure is continually dragged into political debate to prove a case for or against the nationalisation of other industries. The result is that the government is entangled with all the operations of the corporations, and that its informal responsibility exceeds the formal powers given to it by law, which are used

[1] This is subject to the reservation that for an experimental period of two years in the first instance (beginning in 1956) they obtain their capital direct from the Exchequer. The National Coal Board is obliged by its parent statute to obtain its capital in this way, but it is the exception: the other industries had hitherto raised capital by the issue of stock bearing a fixed rate of interest.

with great restraint. Mr. Gaitskell was certainly right when he said (as Minister of Fuel and Power, in 1949) that the Minister 'must accept responsibility for what I should describe as the general success or failure of the enterprise'.

The implication of this is that the Minister must be well informed about the affairs of the corporations for which he is responsible, but each of the nationalised industries is a vast subject in itself, and for detailed information and evaluation he must go either to the board or to his civil servants. The boards naturally provide great quantities of statistical and other data, but the Minister is entirely in their hands unless he has advisers of his own to sift and to assess what they tell him. This is perhaps the primary responsibility of the civil servants concerned, a responsibility which is always difficult, but is made rather easier if the Department also runs regulatory services and inspectorates, since these enable it to meet its industries on a fairly broad front. An experienced civil servant sitting in London may make a good guess at the trend of (for instance) labour efficiency on the railways, but he is in no position to argue his case unless it is supported by specific evidence from men in the field.

(ii) *Formal Control*

The Minister is also dependent on his principal officials for advice about the exercise of his formal powers of control. The complete list of the statutory powers of Ministers is a formidable document; schedules prepared by the Departments in 1955 for the Select Committee on Nationalised Industries included some two hundred separate items. Most of these were specific powers, and they fell into six main groups:

(*a*) Powers of approval and consent to various activities of the Boards: the most important of these relate to capital development and the general conduct of financial operations, but they also include such matters as consent to schemes of training, education, and research, and approval of particular acts, such as compulsory purchase orders, the disposal of assets, the promotion of Bills, proposals for the breaking-up of streets, and the acquisition of new undertakings.

(*b*) Powers of appointment: of the boards themselves, of consumer councils, and of auditors; and powers to determine their tenure of office, remuneration, and other matters.

(*c*) Powers to make regulations and to give specific directions on certain matters.

(*d*) Powers to hold public inquiries and to settle disputes.

(*e*) Powers to obtain information.

(*f*) Powers of co-ordination (for instance, the Minister of Power's 'general duty' to secure the 'effective and co-ordinated development of fuel and power in Great Britain').

Some of these powers the Minister would exercise whether the industries were in public ownership or not; for example, he would have power to make general 'public utility' regulations, and regulations affecting safety, health, and welfare. Other powers, such as the control of capital development, are not peculiar to nationalised industry but are applied to all public authorities including local government.

In addition to these specific powers the Minister possesses the power to give general directions, and some of his specific powers (for example, to appoint and dismiss the boards) have very wide implications. Both these matters are of crucial importance in determining the relations between the two sets of authorities.

(*a*) *General Directions.* The Minister's power to give directions of a general character is imprecisely defined: these directions may be given 'as to the exercise and performance by [the boards] of their functions in relation to matters appearing to [him] to affect the national interest'. The Minister, so it seems, is the sole judge of when to intervene, and the boards must give effect to his directions whether they agree with them or not. Few formal directions have been given, but the mere existence of the power is a formidable weapon, since almost any matter of high policy concerning the nationalised industries may be held to 'affect the national interest'.

A classic case in the early days of the nationalised electricity industry illustrates how this may work in practice. An advisory committee appointed by the Minister (under the chairmanship of Sir Andrew Clow) recommended that a surcharge should be imposed on winter tariffs for domestic electricity in an endeavour to discourage consumption at peak hours. This was opposed by the Central Electricity Authority and by all the Area Boards, though the government was clearly anxious that they should accept it. No written directive was ever issued, but the Authority and the Boards finally agreed, under protest. The history of negotiations remains obscure. It is said, on the one hand, that the Boards asked for a written directive in order to safeguard their reputation with their consumers; on the other, that they were threatened with a directive and acquiesced rather than have one issued.

(*b*) *Appointments.* The appointment, dismissal, and determination of tenure of board members imposes perhaps the heaviest burden of all on the Minister's official advisers. 'No task surpasses this in importance,' said the Report of the Committee of Inquiry into the

Electricity Industry (Herbert), 'for unless the best appointments are made the industry's efficiency must suffer. . . . The greatest care and skill is needed in making the key appointments.' This can be an extremely onerous task: the Minister of Power has over two hundred such places to fill in the coal, electricity, and gas industries. Similarly, the power of dismissal is wide, for the Minister may relieve a member of his duties if he considers him 'unable or unfit to discharge his functions', and the interpretation of 'unfitness' and 'inability' lies with the Minister alone.

(iii) *Spokesmanship*

The administration is under an ill-defined obligation not only to control the industry for which it is responsible but also to defend it. An important part of this work must be done within Whitehall, and there is not enough information available to justify comment. To take the example of capital requirements, the Ministry of Power must represent the National Coal Board, the Central Electricity Authority, the Gas Council, and (in a rather similar way) the private oil and steel companies, in dealing with the Treasury about the authorisation of investment programmes annually or for longer periods. One can only guess at the character of the many-cornered debate which ensues: it is at least certain that its complexities reach ministerial level only after a long process of defining issues and narrowing differences.

The process of spokesmanship before Parliament has been much more discussed because it is more readily documented. Bagehot remarked nearly a hundred years ago, thinking of the experience of the Poor Law Board, that 'the incessant tyranny of Parliament over public offices is prevented and can only be prevented by the appointment of a Parliamentary head, connected by close ties with the present Ministry and the ruling party in Parliament. The Parliamentary head is a protecting machine. He and the friends he brings stand between the Department and the busybodies and crotchet-makers of the House and the country.' Local authorities are elected bodies which answer for themselves before their own constituents; independent public bodies sometimes act in a representative capacity, and they often deal with matters which do not arouse much controversy. The nationalised industries come off badly in both respects: their boards owe their position solely to the Minister, and the idea of election, or even of selection in a representative capacity, has been vigorously disclaimed; and (as we have seen) they arouse both the cries of party politicians and the daily grumbles of millions of individuals. The corporations make some attempt to conduct their own defence; they employ public relations officers, maintain their own contacts with the press and with influential groups, and give especially prompt and thorough replies to questions put to them by Members of Parliament. But only the Minister, briefed by his civil servants, can deal with criticism at the centre of public debate, and the Minister is in an ambiguous position, because he must be prepared not only to defend his corporations but to defend Cabinet policy, his Department, and himself. There have already been a number of cases in which these obligations have proved incompatible.

What we have said under these three headings is no more than an indication of the kind of problem to be handled by civil servants working in this field. It is a particularly difficult one, because no firm understandings about procedure have yet been reached by the parties concerned and tested by experience. There is uncertainty about the proper constitutional relation between Parliament, the Ministers, and the corporations; in spite of a great deal of discussion, almost everything still depends on circumstances and personalities. For instance, at one period during the early summer of 1956 Sir Anthony Eden's Minister of Fuel and Power (Mr. Aubrey Jones) was defending the National Coal Board against Government back-bench criticism, while the Minister of Transport and Civil Aviation (Mr. Harold Watkinson) carried on what appeared at times to be a personal quarrel with the British Transport Commission and the British Overseas Airways Corporation, unsupported either by the Opposition or by prominent members of his own party.

There is almost equal uncertainty about the proper administrative channels for dealing with business between Ministers, civil servants, and nationalised industries. The officials responsible are 'small fry' compared with the chief officers and board members of the corporations, and there is plenty of evidence that the latter prefer to deal direct with the Minister himself. Mr. George Strauss, for instance, speaking of his relations as Minister of Supply with the heads of the newly nationalised steel industry, said: 'Every week on one morning I spent an hour or two with the Chairman and Deputy Chairman of the Corporation [the Iron and Steel Corporation of Great Britain] considering every single problem, not only of national interest, but on every conceivable detail concerning the Corporation. There was not a subject with which I was not concerned.' But this is clearly a method which is possible only in a period of crisis, when top priority is given to a single industry. It would be impracticable in ordinary times for a Minister of Power or a Minister of Transport and Civil Aviation to do all his business with 'his' corporations in person.

The continuous background of relations must be provided by officials, who will perhaps act as an extension of the Minister's 'private office' rather than as policy-makers or directors of the industry.

4. THE REGIONAL HOSPITAL BOARDS

The structure of the National Health Service has caused almost as much controversy as that of the nationalised industries, and the position of the hospitals will serve to illustrate a number of quite different points about the problems of representation and control. Hospitals are financed almost wholly by Parliamentary grants, and are managed within a framework of detailed regulations made by the Minister of Health: but they are not staffed by civil servants.

In setting up the hospital service in its present form Parliament (in effect) rejected three possible alternatives: the creation of a (grant-aided) National Hospitals Corporation organised like the gas and electricity industries with their 'Area' Boards; the setting up of a new Government Department with its own regional and local organisation, staffed by civil servants, to run the entire hospital system; and the transference of all hospitals to the local authorities. The existing structure and its pattern of control and direction by the central administration differs from all of these, yet possesses some of the features of each.

The Regional Hospital Boards are the Minister's agents in a rather specific sense. It is the Minister's statutory duty 'to promote the establishment of a comprehensive health service in England and Wales'. In this respect alone the Boards are no different from local education authorities, for the Education Act of 1944 includes a similar provision.[1] But the Boards differ from local authorities in regard to method of financing and ownership of land and property. The Boards have no independent sources of income, and all hospital buildings, land, property, and equipment belong to the Minister. Thus the hospital service is a 'national' service in a sense in which education is not. The Boards are not part of the Ministry of Health: they are legal persons with their own statutory duties and obligations. But, on the one hand, they are tied much more closely, in form and practice, than are the nationalised industries; on the other hand, they do not enjoy the same prestige as a local authority which is elected and not centrally appointed.

[1] The Minister's duty is 'to promote the education of the people of England and Wales . . . and to secure the effective direction by local authorities . . . of the national policy for providing a varied and comprehensive educational service in every area' (Education Act, 1944, Sec. 1.)

Central administration cannot escape responsibility for a service which in 1956 cost the Exchequer about £330 m.[1]: but it cannot run it as if hospitals were local offices of a Ministry. There are 438 separate units of administration in England and Wales alone (14 Regional Hospital Boards, 36 Boards of Governors of Teaching Hospitals, and 388 Hospital Management Committees); their work is extremely technical and involves delicate human relations; and the organised medical profession jealously guards its professional standards of independence. During the debates on the National Health Service Bill the government made it clear that its intention was 'to provide that the central responsibility which the House places upon the Minister . . . does not result in the service becoming too highly centralised in its administration', so that 'individuals in a locality can have as much influence as possible over the medical and hospital services'.[2]

These intentions were set out in the first circulars issued to hospital authorities by the Ministry of Health, with the unfortunate result that many of them assumed that they were to be allowed a very free hand, and that 'the hospital service (being financed by the Exchequer) would be able to call upon unlimited resources to make good its deficiencies'.[3] The steep rise in the cost of the service resulted in 1951 in a reorganisation of the formal arrangements governing the relations between the Ministry and the hospital authorities. The organisation then created was approved in general terms by the Guillebaud Committee, and it is perhaps now fairly stable. It is convenient to describe it under four main heads: policy and administration, establishments, finance, and central supplies and contracts.

(i) *Policy and Administration.* The Ministry of Health is a small Department, with about 75 Administrative Class officials (apart from regional officers) and about the same number of professional civil servants, mainly doctors. Its most important professional official is the Chief Medical Officer, who ranks next to the Permanent Secretary; he is also Chief Medical Officer to the Home Office and to the Ministry of Education, and is (informally but unambiguously) 'head' of the medical civil service. As was noted in Chapter 22, the Ministry shares a number of other specialists (lawyers, engineers, and architects) with the Ministry of Housing and Local Government; and there are also specialist advisers on aspects of hospital manage-

---

[1] Cost of the hospital service in England and Wales only, 1956-57. The cost of the whole National Health Service was about £500 m.
[2] H.C. Deb., 426, Col. 469.
[3] Report of the Committee of Inquiry into the Cost of the National Health Service (Guillebaud). Cmd. 9663, 1956.

ment such as catering, which are outside the scope of the Chief Medical Officer. Its main point of contact with the hospital service is the Hospital and Specialist Services Division. There is an Under Secretary in charge, about half a dozen Assistant Secretaries, and a dozen Principals. Each Assistant Secretary looks after two or three hospital regions. Under him the general affairs of each region are dealt with by a Principal, an H.E.O., and occasionally an Assistant Principal under training. In addition to this geographical distribution of duties (which is similar to that used in the Ministry of Housing and Local Government and described in Chapter 22) there is an allocation by particular subjects: mental health, hospital catering, venereal disease, pay beds, building and land acquisition, hospital dental services, chronic sick, and so on. Thus each Assistant Secretary takes a group of subjects and a group of regions, and every Principal and H.E.O., acting together, have one region and one or more subjects. What this means in practice is that all the business from one region, with its Regional Hospital Board, its Board of Governors of the teaching hospital, its Hospital Management Committees, comes in the first instance to two men. The Principal concerned may be able to decide some matters out of hand: if he cannot do so, he must refer them farther, either up the subject hierarchy or up the geographical hierarchy as he thinks best. The double system appears intricate, but in fact the decision lies within a small group of people working in adjoining rooms.

On policy matters the Division may have to refer to the General Practitioner and Local Authority Services Division (described in Chapter 22), and to the Chief Medical Officer's Department, which has sections dealing (for instance) with the consultant and specialist services and with hospital planning and administration.

There is a small field organisation consisting of general regional offices, under Principal Regional Officers, based on the standard regions, which keep in contact with the hospital and other health authorities; and the Chief Medical Officer has his own regional medical, dental, and auxiliary staff at various provincial centres, for the medical examination of insured persons claiming national insurance benefit, for artificial limb fitting, and for certain functions relating to the dental health service. We have mentioned in Chapter 22 the Principal Regional Officer's position in regard to local authorities: apart from this, he is concerned with liaison and advice rather than with decisions. He receives the papers of the hospital and general practitioner authorities, and has the right to attend their meetings.

It is obvious that much of this organisation was created by taking over traditional methods of dealing with local authorities, and that these did not prove to be wholly applicable. There was no established hospitals Inspectorate comparable to the old poor law Inspectorate or to the Inspectorate of the Ministry of Education, to serve as 'eyes and ears' of the Ministry. In spite of this, the central officials stuck at first to the tradition of dealing with business largely on paper, by formal letters and circulars. This is proper in handling local authorities which insist on their legal powers and independent status, and must to some extent be dealt with 'at arm's length'; but it was quite unnecessary in managing authorities which were wholly subordinate to the Minister, and it led to much exasperation among people who were not accustomed to it. There is now a tendency towards less formality, towards conferences and personal contacts, and the number of circulars issued has fallen steadily since 1950.

(ii) *Establishments.* Hospital staffs resemble local government officers in that they are not employed by a single national authority: they are not the Minister's employees, but the employees of a Regional Hospital Board, a Board of Governors, or a Hospital Management Committee. An elaborate system of joint negotiation has been developed (under statutory authority) for bargaining about pay and conditions of service, and this is linked to the Ministry through the officials of the Staffing and Remuneration Division, who provide the secretariat of the Whitley Councils. This division deals with all policy matters affecting pay, conditions of service, staff complements, and so on throughout the entire health service. Hospital establishments were at first uncontrolled, but between 1950 and 1952 the Ministry carried out a planned review (with the assistance of the Regional Hospital Boards), and on 5 December 1952 the establishment of every hospital authority was fixed. Any increase in the establishment of a Regional Hospital Board or of a Board of Governors requires the prior sanction of the Ministry: every increase in the establishment of a Hospital Management Committee requires the approval of the appropriate Regional Hospital Board. The Guillebaud Committee recommended that these controls should be relaxed 'as far and as fast as possible', since it seemed to them that 'in a well-established service with an effective budgetary control, it should not be necessary to require managing bodies to seek the approval of the next higher authority to each and every increase in staffing establishments'.

(iii) *Finance.* Financial control is very strict. The fact that almost the whole of the money comes from public funds provided out of taxation means that the hospital service must conform to Treasury and Parliamentary practice: an Annual Vote by Parliament, the restriction of expenditure to the specific purposes for which it is voted, and the return of unexpended balances to the Exchequer at the end of the financial year. Within the Ministry the detailed administration of hospital finance is the job of a special Hospital Finance Section in the Accountant-General's Division. The audit of hospital accounts is carried out (through a decentralised organisation) by teams of Executive Class officers in another section of this division. This is comparable to the District Audit of local authority accounts except that there is no provision for surcharge. The accounts are kept on an income and expenditure basis in a standard form prescribed by the Ministry (no special form of accounts is prescribed for local authorities), and cash is advanced to the hospitals on monthly requisitions. Annual financial statements, duly audited, are transmitted to the Comptroller and Auditor-General, who reports on them to the Public Accounts Committee (see Chapter 18).

Estimates procedure has been much simplified in recent years. Regional Hospital Boards and Boards of Governors of teaching hospitals are now required to submit (by the end of October in each year) general forecasts of the amount likely to be required in the financial year beginning in the following April. On the basis of these forecasts the amount to be included in the Ministry's Estimate for the whole hospital service is settled in December or January in consultation with the Treasury. The allocation of this 'global' figure is then worked out between the Ministry and the Regional Hospital Boards and Boards of Governors: a process involving some hard bargaining, which takes place each year in late January and early February.

When the totals are agreed, each Regional Hospital Board makes a corresponding allocation to its Hospital Management Committees. Within these fixed limits, the Boards of Governors, Regional Hospital Boards, and Hospital Management Committees draw up their detailed Estimates for approval. Regional Hospital Boards approve the Estimates of their Management Committees; the Ministry approves the Estimates of the Regional Hospital Boards and Boards of Governors; transfers between sub-heads of the Estimate are sanctioned at the same levels.

The annual capital expenditure on hospitals is necessarily limited by the total amount allocated to the Ministry for all purposes. The Ministry must first decide how much of this can be spent on the hospital service; having done this, it allocates capital to each Regional Hospital Board on the basis of the population of the region. Schemes costing more than a fixed amount need Ministry approval before they can be started; 'larger' schemes (more than £30,000 in 1956) require Treasury approval as well; and if the project is one of 'special interest or novelty' it requires Ministry approval whatever the cost.

(iv) *Central Purchasing*. Central contracting and bulk purchasing by the Ministry (mostly for the hospital service) cost about £6 m. annually, and the Supplies Division (under a Controller, a P.E.O.) employs a staff of about 250, mainly Executive and Clerical officers, but including some technical officers and an industrial complement of twenty. The division is responsible for placing bulk contracts on behalf of the hospitals, and itself purchases medical supplies and appliances, such as drugs and laboratory equipment, and various items of domestic stores (for instance, wax floor polish) which have been standardised.

It will be obvious from this account that central administration of the hospital service has been evolved by 'crossing' forms of control well tried in dealing with local authorities with other forms proper to the management of a Department. The latter are necessary because of the scale of expenditure involved: loose financial control would be constitutionally improper and administratively dangerous. But Parliament chose to set up the hospital service under the management of what are in our present sense 'independent public bodies'. The case is well put by Sir John Maude in a reservation to the Guillebaud Report. 'In practice [the Minister] finds his powers limited to an undefined and indefinable extent by pledges given in Parliament when the proposed legislation was before it . . . and by public opinion which would resent the idea of large bodies of men and women, who are selected for their knowledge and experience . . . and give unpaid service, being required automatically to carry out Ministerial instructions.' This is the crux of the relationship: the Ministry must deal not with paid agents, but with local bodies each widely representative of specialist and lay opinion in its own region. But the fact that they are appointed by him, and have to rely upon the central administration for the money required to carry the service on, must mean in practice that they can never be as free as an elected local authority.

5. Conclusion

It has been possible within the compass of this chapter to deal only with two of the largest and most important groups of 'independent public bodies'. But the discussion may serve to illuminate certain points of more general application. 'Independence' must be combined with safeguards for the public interest; the number of possible devices for control is limited, and they are used in much the same way (though not in the same combination or degree) for all these bodies. Every 'independent public body' has some 'parent' Department which is responsible in a general way for its welfare and progress. In some cases 'control' amounts to little more than that involved in the sponsorship of a private firm; in others it is both extensive and detailed.

The Public Accounts Committee has recommended as a general principle, that 'the degree of government control must depend on the proportion of government grant to total income'. This is much too simple a view of the matter, even if it is construed narrowly and with specific reference to the forms of Treasury control. The situation in each case is determined by a delicate balance of factors which can only be summarised (somewhat platitudinously) as follows:

(i) The *proportion* of the body's total income which is derived from funds provided out of national taxation, and the *scale* of the total amounts involved.

(ii) The nature of its functions.

(iii) The historical and political circumstances in which it was first set up, and the constitutional basis on which it rests.

(iv) The importance of its work in the national interest, and the extent to which its activities impinge on the general policy of the government.

(v) Political pressures to bring it into closer dependence on, or to give it greater freedom from, central control.

It is easy to find examples of how these factors operate. The Universities obtain most of their income by grants-in-aid, but they are relatively free from Treasury control, and the Treasury in general supports them in resisting demands by the Public Accounts Committee for more detailed financial inspection. The strength of the Universities' case lies partly in their history, as chartered corporations of a particular kind, partly in their functions, which require long-term planning and freedom from even the suspicion of interference in the interests of political parties. Somewhat similar considerations apply to the great Research Councils, and to the Arts Council of Great Britain. For quite different reasons, considerable autonomy is enjoyed by grant-aided bodies like the British Institute of Management, which were founded in the hope of stimulating self-help, and which draw only part of their revenue from public funds. At the other extreme are bodies like the British Council and the Regional Hospital Boards, which are treated almost like government Departments, though for various good reasons they have not been given the status of Departments. And in the middle are the public corporations for the nationalised industries, each with its peculiar history, constitution, and economic structure.

Many of these arrangements are formally embodied in legal documents: Acts of Parliament and Statutory Instruments; Royal Charters; the Articles of Association of limited companies and the trust deeds of voluntary bodies; the provisions of a contract between an independent public body and its sponsoring Department. But the informal understandings and conventions which govern day-to-day dealings are of much greater importance than the written document. These can only be elicited by close study of each case; their general importance is clear from the experience of old-established bodies like the B.B.C. Since the B.B.C. was set up as a public body in 1927, the government has many times intervened in particular matters of day-to-day administration although it has had no formal powers to do so. A case in point was the attempt by the B.B.C. in 1946 to merge its Western and Midland Regions, a proposal which met with such stiff political opposition inside and outside Parliament that the Corporation was forced to abandon it.

Even where the constitutional position of two bodies appears to be the same, their working relations with central administration may be very different. Indeed the outward form that the body takes may be entirely misleading. The British Council and the Arts Council are both chartered corporations and each receives the bulk of its income from a Parliamentary grant-in-aid, but the Arts Council enjoys much greater freedom.

It is pointless to multiply instances. Perhaps administrative formulae must be invented separately for each case: many different formulae have already been found, and there are no constitutional conventions to inhibit new invention. Indeed, tradition tells the other way. To quote Bagehot again, 'We love independent "local authorities", little centres of outlying authority. When the metropolitan executive most wishes to act, it cannot act effectually because these lesser bodies hesitate, deliberate, or even disobey.' This is a sentiment which always evokes sympathy for a local authority or an independent public body if it is involved in conflict with central administration, and the administration must adapt itself to it.

FOR REFERENCE

(1) *General*

D. N. CHESTER: 'Public Corporations and the Classification of Administrative Bodies', *Political Studies*, Vol. 1, p. 34, and references there cited.

Sir ARTHUR STREET: 'Quasi-Government Bodies since 1918' (in Campion and others: *British Government since 1918* (1950)).

J. W. GROVE: 'Grants-in-Aid to Public Bodies', *Public Administration*, Vol. XXX, p. 299.

2nd Report from the Select Committee on Estimates, Session 1953-54. Grants-in-Aid. H.C. 143, 1954.

(2) *Nationalised Industries*

Acton Society Trust: *The Powers of the Minister* (1952).

Administrative Staff College: *The Accountability of Public Corporations* (1955).

Special Report and Minutes of Evidence from the Select Committee on Nationalised Industries. H.C. 120, 1955.

1st Report from the Select Committee on Estimates, Session 1955-56. Civil Aerodromes and Ground Services. H.C. 128, 1955.

(3) *Hospitals*

Acton Society Trust:

Hospitals and the State: Background and Blueprint (1956).

Groups, Regions, and Committees, Part I Hospital Management Committees, and Part II, Regional Hospital Boards (1957).

Report of the Committee of Inquiry into the Cost of the National Health Service (Guillebaud). Cmd. 9663, 1956.

CHAPTER TWENTY-FOUR

PUBLICS AND THE PUBLIC

'The Department is accessible to the—Public', Mr. Barnacle was always checked a little by that word of impertinent signification, 'if the—Public approaches it according to the official forms: if the—Public does not approach it according to the official forms, the—Public has itself to blame.'—DICKENS: *Little Dorrit*.

1. INTRODUCTORY

CENTRAL administration exists to serve the public: the criterion of its excellence is that it should give good service subject to public control. This is an axiom of the system, on which everything rests, and yet it is difficult to use because it is difficult to define its terms.

A rough-and-ready check on the efficiency of a service can be obtained from statistics of productivity showing the number of postage stamps sold per annum per counter clerk, the number of claims 'processed' in a given time by the M.P.N.I., the number of patients treated in a given number of hospital beds in a year. Such figures are essential, but no one believes that they tell the whole truth about the success or failure of a public service.

The idea of public control is also a source of puzzles. The services provided by central administration are so managed because there is at least a reasonable case for central control. But control at the centre entails the sacrifice of control at the periphery; in theory, this loss should in a democracy be balanced by public control at the centre through representatives of the public. Yet such representation itself interposes one more stage between the citizen and the administrator, and it is common for the former to feel that his representatives are closer to the administration than to those whom they claim to represent. Representatives and officials together come to form an indeterminate 'they', who run things from a remote central point, and the sense of 'public' service disappears. It is hard, perhaps impossible, to find any means of measurement by which this loss of sympathy and support can be set off against the administrative advantages of unity in management; difficult decisions about centralisation are influenced by sentiment and political pressure as much as by arguments.

The public deal with the central administration either as individuals, or through voluntary organisations representing interests of various kinds, or through the constitutional processes of Cabinet and Parliament. In this chapter we are concerned with the first two of these processes, matters of enormous importance about which it is difficult to talk in precise terms, because little has been done either by official inquiries or by academic research to discover and describe what actually happens.

2. THE PUBLIC AS INDIVIDUALS

If an organisation is created to deal with an enormous volume of business involving individual cases, it follows almost geometrically that its clients rarely meet any employees except those in the lowest ranks. The National Insurance system (for instance) is an organisation in which more than 30,000 officials deal in a year with 7 m. claims for sickness benefit, $2\frac{1}{2}$ m. claims for unemployment benefit, 1 m. payments of maternity benefit, and retirement pensions for $4\frac{1}{2}$ m. pensioners. This is only possible because most of the business has been reduced to routine. There is experience of an enormous number of more or less similar cases, and most eventualities have been met or foreseen. In consequence the organisation is very broad-based: a relatively large number of junior clerks deal with individual cases in accordance with quite specific instructions, a relatively small number of higher officials manage the organisation and deal with the tiny percentage of exceptional cases which have to be referred upwards for guidance. These higher officials spend far more time on the internal affairs of the organisation than on cases affecting members of the public.

The National Insurance system is an extreme case, but this is the pattern of organisation for large Departments dealing with very large numbers of cases which affect the public as individuals: the Post Office, the Inland Revenue, the Customs and Excise, the National Assistance Board, the Ministry of Labour and National Service. Greater flexibility can be obtained only by increasing the range of discretion allowed by the rules to the officials in contact with the public; this involves the risk of divergence of standards, of favouritism (or at least of accusations of favouritism), of greater cost. The problem can partly be met by narrowing the pyramid, so that the proportion of experienced and reliable officials is higher; or by employing individuals outside the hierarchy as 'social workers', to follow up really difficult cases and give individual help. But these solutions cannot be taken very far; one of the limits of the development of central administration (and a good reason for the use of local authorities and other independent public bodies) is that on the whole the least qualified members of the Service must do one of the most difficult parts of the business, that of meeting the public as individuals.

There are two problems for discussion: how can these low-level contacts with the public be improved, and how can the hard cases be sifted out correctly for decision at a higher level?

(i) *Personal Relations*

The Assheton Committee on the Training of Civil Servants wrote in 1945 that 'the inculcation of the right attitude towards the public . . . should be one of the principal aims of civil service training. . . . Many civil servants who are brought most frequently into contact with the public know and appreciate the value of the right attitude; others must be raised to the same standard.'[1] This means above all that junior civil servants engaged on such jobs must be trained in the exact observance—and comprehension—of the regulations. Sloppiness in detail is much more inconvenient for the public than the proper use of 'red tape'. Given this basis of accuracy, the rest is a matter of courtesy and patience in discussion across the counter, simplicity and clarity in letter-writing. Such qualities are not easy to acquire, except for those to whom they come by nature, and it takes time to give junior civil servants the sort of confidence which is needed for easy public relations. Rapid turn-over of staff, rapid expansion and contraction of offices increase friction, and the public is best served in quiet times.

One of the difficulties is that some members of the public are paralysed by the sight of official paper. A good deal of thought has been given to the problem of official style and presentation by Departments dealing with large numbers of people. There is expert knowledge (canalised through O. & M. and the Stationery Office) on such matters as the design of forms, the reduction of official explanations to plain terms, the use of typography and layout to gain clarity in circulars and in public notices. Aesthetically, official printing and display suffer somewhat from standardisation and from the reduction of margins and spacings in the interest of economy; but there has been great improvement in recent years. In spite of this, there will always be many plain people who cannot grasp the rights and wrongs of their dealings with the administration unless they are helped by some intermediary: a personal friend, a social worker, a

[1] Report, Para. 17.

trade union official, or a friendly civil servant acting outside his official duty.

There are other members of the public who approach all officials with a chip on their shoulder. The 'awkward customer' may be an enterprising person who is trying by bluff to get more than his rights; he may be a man who is ready enough to appreciate (once he has had his explosion) that the civil servant is 'only doing his job'. A patient official will learn to discriminate between these types. Nevertheless, some friction with the public arises from an atmosphere created by bad publicity. Politicians and the press rarely suggest that the public has obligations as well as rights in dealing with its own officials. Candidates for election and newspapers seeking circulation can scarcely be expected to bore the public by lecturing it on its duties; and civil servants certainly cannot do it as individuals. It might perhaps ease their conditions somewhat if their staff associations collectively gave rather more thought to the problem of public relations.

(ii) *Exceptional Cases*

In a sense the whole of the administration is a machine for bringing each individual case up to the 'level' at which it can be handled adequately. In theory the rules of procedure sift out from the mass of routine those few cases in which something is about to go wrong. Things may go wrong in two ways. There may be a muddle in the office—instructions have been conflicting, papers have been lost, procedure has not been followed, there has been gross carelessness or even corruption. Or there may be a mistake in policy, with the result that careful and exact application of the rules leads to obvious injustice or absurdity.

The former case is a matter for supervision. The responsibility falls on the first-line supervisor observing his section at work, knowing its personalities, and making a sample check of work done. This has not traditionally been a strong point in the Civil Service, but the position is improving as more attention is paid to the training of supervisors and as the staff position grows more stable.

It is more difficult to improve by organisation the technique for picking up the exceptional case which is important because it shows that something is wrong with the existing policy. To some extent, a supervisor in close contact with his section can get the sense of difficulties as they arise, even though he handles relatively few cases himself; but the main responsibility lies on the routine official, who is by definition least fitted to bear it. As has been said already, 'reference up' is the most difficult of arts, because too much automatic application of the rules causes hardship and leaves the 'high command' in the dark about what is happening, too much reference up clogs the intermediate levels of the organisation. A large administration with a broad base is bound to be relatively slow in its reactions to difficulties. This is part of the price to be paid for cheap administration of large services, and it is worth paying if the service (like the National Insurance system) is one which has been well tested in practice and is likely to remain stable in its essentials for a long period.

Hence administrative need, as well as democratic theory, justifies the existence of ways by which the 'awkward customer' can get his case to a higher level without going through the official channels. Where this does not happen readily it is apparently necessary to create artificial means of picking out special cases and 'featuring' them, as is done in the U.S.S.R. through the intervention of the Communist Party and its press.

In Britain there are three main ways of taking a case farther when the process of formal appeal has been exhausted: to approach a politician; to approach the press; to appeal to a group organisation. These are not alternatives: an effective campaign (like that which led to the Crichel Down affair) involves all three. The politicians, the press, and the organisations may occasionally be interested in running a case as a 'stunt' when there has been no real hardship and the main object is to find a stick with which to beat the government. But generally it is in their interest to act as a filter, disregarding weak and trivial cases and pursuing only questions which are likely to awaken general public interest and sympathy.

From time to time it is suggested that (at a level far short of corruption) there are great advantages in having one's own personal contacts with civil servants. The most striking case of this was the affair of Mr. Sidney Stanley, who traded for some time on the claim (almost completely false) that he had valuable personal contacts within the Board of Trade. Some odd things happened during the war and its aftermath, but it would be almost impossible for such a system of influence to operate in ordinary times. The appointment and promotion of civil servants is now controlled almost entirely by civil servants: those outside the Service can find no leverage here, nor is it easy for them to approach and influence civil servants as a group, since outside their offices they are dispersed socially among the great multitude of dwellers in the suburbs.

After the Stanley case, there was a careful investigation of a much more limited development, the appearance of a small profession of 'intermediaries', known in the United States as 'five-percenters', who undertook to put applications in order and to facilitate contacts in dealing with particular Departments. Few cases were found, and some of these were fraudulent, in that payment was claimed for influence not really exercised. Others were genuine cases of former members of Departments who were able to sell useful experience of the regulations; an embarrassing development, not unlike the appearance of former Income Tax Inspectors as tax accountants. The British have great faith in 'a man who knows a man who knows a man who . . .', in the strength of the 'old boy network'. Undoubtedly there are some large private concerns which have, through personal relationships, particularly good lines of entry to the Ministries on which they depend, but this often arises out of an interlocking between a Department and the firms which serve it which is convenient to both parties, and perhaps also operates in the public interest by facilitating an easy interchange of ideas. A firm which recruits a distinguished administrative or technical civil servant gains a proved man trained for it by the government. Government gains in that it has 'placed' its own man in a key position.

3. Organised Publics

It is characteristic of the liberal democracies that the extreme complexity of their social and industrial organisation is allowed to express itself freely in voluntary organisations not closely connected with the organisation of the state. However important these organisations may be, they remain 'non-political', in the sense that they do not owe allegiance to any political party and do not believe that the support of one party would help them to achieve their ends. In so far as these organisations 'play politics' at all, it is non-party politics: in this sense their position 'outside politics' is analogous to that of the central administration itself, and this is part of their strength in dealing with it.

Such associations are not completely free from legal control even in the most liberal society. In England associations with their own rules and funds can be set up very readily under the private law of trust, and they are under no obligation to register themselves or to obtain any form of licence or charter unless they wish to obtain special legal privileges. Many associations are in fact registered in one way or another, either as limited companies under the Companies Acts or in some special category, such as those of Trade Unions and Friendly Societies. But the official control established by registration is directed more to matters of financial honesty than to the substance of activities or interests, and it is therefore of little practical importance to draw a line between different forms of group organisation according to their legal status. It may be of more service to give a rough classification according to the types of public which organisations represent.

(i) *Salary and Wage Organisations.* In the field of pay negotiations, everyone thinks first of a relatively small number of very powerful organisations: bodies like the British Medical Association (80,000 members), the N.U.T. (220,000 members), N.A.L.G.O. (230,000 members), and the great Trade Unions grouped in the T.U.C., such as the Transport and General Workers Union with 1,290,000 members and the fifteen other Unions with over 100,000 members each. The field is now dominated by these giants, but there are still 400 registered Trade Unions, many of them very small, and there are a large number of small professional or semi-professional groups which have an interest in conditions of service as well as in the standing of their members as experts.

(ii) *Expert Organisations.* There is therefore much overlap in practice, since an organised profession claims a right to maintain its standard of living, a right based on the claim that it maintains its own standard of skill. But there are organisations (the Royal Society for instance) which are clear cases of the association of experts for the pursuit of their own branch of knowledge; and there is a sense in which each branch of knowledge consists of a recognised association of experts. A government Department consults an expert for the sake of his skill as an individual; it also consults him as a 'recognised' expert, as a man of standing whose opinion will carry weight with other experts who have not studied the matter in detail. Expert knowledge of this kind may be recognised formally by letters after a man's name—A.R.I.B.A., M.R.C.P., F.Inst.P., A.M.I.C.E., and so on. Quite as frequently the recognition is informal: Professor A is *the* expert on the tsetse fly; Mr. B is widely recognised as one of the best people to consult about the latest developments of coal-cutting machinery; Dr. C is a man whose opinion carries weight in a discussion about the genetic effects of nuclear explosions. There are hundreds—perhaps thousands—of groupings of experts, some large and formal, others almost without organisation. One man or woman may belong to more than one group: but what makes the 'expert' for purposes of government is recognition by some group which is itself recognised publicly as the dominant group of experts in its own field.

(iii) *Business Organisations.* It is not in practice easy to distinguish organisations the members of which depend on success in business dealings from other types of organisation; but there is a recognisable type of organisation which may loosely be called the trade association. Trade associations generally have various purposes which overlap. In the extreme case they may create and enforce a strict system of price fixing and restriction of output, but this is exceptional. There is generally a combination of an element of competition between members with an element of mutual aid in the business in which they are all engaged. There may be standardisation of components and of finished products; co-operation in research through an industrial research association; mutual assistance in dealing with some of the problems of overseas trade; and so on. The terms of reference of such bodies vary a great deal, but in almost all cases they include responsibility for negotiation with government Departments on all general problems involving the industry. Indeed, the introduction of a general tariff in 1932, supervised by an Import Duties Advisory Committee, and the extension of government intervention in industry in more recent years, have been largely responsible for the creation of many new trade associations. It became essential to men engaged in one branch of business to have a single point of reference in their dealings with Whitehall: and Whitehall was equally concerned to find trade bodies which would represent and reconcile their members.

To some extent these business organisations are grouped together by the Federation of British Industries, the British Employers Confederation, and the National Union of Manufacturers, bodies with somewhat limited powers of action which play an important part as centres of consultation, comparable to the T.U.C. and to the associations of local authorities.

(iv) *Non-economic Organisations.* Next, there is a miscellaneous group which could be subdivided in various ways. There are Churches and other bodies interested in a particular creed, form of worship, or ideology: the Church of England, the Roman Catholic Church, the Free Churches, and many smaller bodies. There are bodies interested in reform or in social service: the National Council of Social Service is the widest of these, but there are specialist bodies in almost every field—the Council for the Preservation of Rural England, the Howard League, the United Kingdom Alliance, the Lord's Day Observance Society, the N.S.P.C.C. There are innumerable bodies interested in sports and leisure-time activities, ranging from the Jockey Club, the Royal and Ancient, the Football Association and Football League, the Automobile Association (all of them landmarks in British life) to local tennis and golf clubs, school football associations, even informal groups of people in the habit of playing together.

This is a classification which will break down if pressed hard: for instance, it is not easy to find a place in it for the associations of local authorities, the importance of which was stressed in Chapter 22; there is no place here for trading organisations like co-operatives and marketing boards; and there are special factors (explained in Chapter 9) affecting the position of the Civil Service staff associations, though in many ways they resemble other middle-class salary associations. The classification may, however, serve to indicate the substance of the discussion in this chapter, since every reader will be able to add illustrations from his own experience. It also exemplifies a characteristic of British social organisation which has important effects on the work of the administration. There are countries—including countries with an effective parliamentary democracy and rule of law—in which it is usual to find some close ties between associations belonging to separate groups in our classification. A particular religion has some special association with a particular sector of economic life; Trade Unions tend to subdivide on religious lines; so do organisations for leisure activities; and this linked complex of organisations may be associated with its own political party, returning members to Parliament and to local bodies. This sort of organisation was especially typical of the countries of the old Austro-Hungarian empire, where subdivision by language was added to subdivision by religion, and (even in democratic times) society was divided into sectors each of which was united by political organisation, by economic organisation, by religious or ideological creed, and perhaps by language too. This pattern is quite familiar in Europe, even in such old democracies as Scandinavia, Holland, and France. But in Britain, the Commonwealth, and the U.S.A. it seems alien: traces of it can be found here and there if one looks closely, but it would be assumed by most people that this sort of linking of diverse organisations is a step towards totalitarianism. It is natural to us (the reasons are outside the scope of this book) to think that religious views, political party views, economic organisation, and leisure organisation can be and should be kept separate; and this ideal is to some extent realised in society as it now exists.

What this means for the practice of administration is, first, that the administrators themselves are independent of any single group of associations or sector of society; in this respect they are supposed to behave like everyone else, except that they must be careful to avoid identifying themselves publicly with a political party. Secondly, this network of associations is largely free from party ties, and associations do not depend greatly on party politicians for influence over administration. Large associations have close contacts with a number of M.P.s on both sides of the House, and all associations in time of crisis invoke the aid of politicians and the press, just as an individual might do. But it is normal for an association to deal with a government Department direct, as one non-party organisation with another, and a great variety of business is handled in this way. The importance of political pressure through the House of Commons and the constituencies should not be underrated, but relations between Departments and group organisations grow readily out of the necessities of administration.

The job of the administrator in relation to the public concerned in his field of administration is not primarily to control it by directives, prohibitions, and sanctions. These things may be necessary in the last resort, but no policy except a purely negative one can ever be enforced against solid hostility among those concerned with its execution. It is the administrator's duty to consider enforcement: but enforcement depends on a balance of force, and the simplest way to get the balance on the official side is to reduce the force of opposition. Hence it is rare for any British Department to set out upon a new line of policy without taking careful thought about the points of view of the sections of the public directly involved. Direct public consultation is not always possible, but the administrator has two powerful inducements to seek it: first, he will wish to take a line which has been endorsed by all or most experts, since public opinion is influenced by expert testimony; secondly, he will wish to conciliate the organisations concerned, since effective opposition can be led only by organisations. These reasons are always valid as a matter of tactics; they are often valid also on grounds of public policy, since the main weight of expert opinion is often right, and organisations can often make a most effective contribution to public action. But the habit of consultation makes for caution, and slows down the process of policy-making: it may even lead to an abdication of responsibility altogether.

Various established practices and institutions have grown out of this, but they have grown haphazard, and classification is not easy. The following five heads may perhaps serve:

(i) Ad hoc *Committees to inquire and advise*

If one wishes to learn about some section of British administration one generally reads first a series of committee reports, since these are the obvious landmarks in the development of the subject. The practice of public inquiry before legislation is a very old one, but till the early part of the nineteenth century the inquiry was generally carried out by a specially appointed committee of the House of

Commons. In those days the initiative in legislation lay with private members rather than with the government, but the practice of public inquiry and report survived the change in procedure. The effect has been that since about 1850 reports on policy have generally been made by Royal Commissions or by Departmental Committees, bodies differing only in dignity and in the formalities of appointment. Departmental Committees have in recent years appeared under a variety of other names ('Working Parties', and so on), but the change of name has not involved much change of substance.

Various motives may prompt the appointment of a committee: the desire to conciliate, to delay, to confuse may often be as important as the desire to act. One of the duties of the higher administrator is to advise his Minister on committee tactics: when it is wise to appoint, what shall be the terms of reference, who shall be members, who shall be chairman. A committee is never appointed without careful thought about the organised interests concerned, and particular organisations may be asked informally to suggest names. But the Department almost always has the last word; on most topics it is limited in its choice of the types of people to be appointed, but it may have considerable freedom in naming individuals and above all in choosing the chairman, and the secretary is usually one of its own officials, an Assistant Secretary or Principal. In this way the committee may be 'blended' so as to establish at least a strong probability about the nature of its report.

(ii) *Permanent Committees to advise*

These have now become an almost equally familiar part of the framework of government. These bodies assume a rather different character according to the level at which they are appointed.

(*a*) '*Sub-Parliaments.*' There are a number of national advisory bodies with very wide terms of reference, generally meeting infrequently. The two largest of these (since the disappearance of the Councils of Agriculture for England and Wales, set up in 1920) are the National Joint Advisory Council of the Ministry of Labour and the National Production Advisory Council for Industry, presided over by the President of the Board of Trade, to which we referred briefly in Chapter 19. Such bodies are generally ineffective as advisers on policy unless they are so organised that the main committee is only the apex of a pyramid of sub-committees appointed to examine specific matters, but they may have their uses as 'sounding boards' on wide general issues.

(*b*) *Advisory Councils.* A number of Departments possess advisory councils which make important contributions to the development of policy. Some of these are appointed under statute, others are not. Their effectiveness seems to depend not on status, but on organisation, and this in turn depends on the subject matter.

The Defence Research Policy Committee of the Ministry of Defence is closely associated on the one hand with the Advisory Council on Scientific Policy, which reports to the Lord President, on the other hand with a network of specialist committees on particular aspects of defence research. The Advisory Council of the D.S.I.R. (replaced by a directing Council in 1956) perhaps transacted little business of vital importance at its full meetings, but it was a central point of reference for all the activities of the Department which are pursued in consultation both with science and with industry. The Advisory Council on Education of the Ministry of Education, reconstituted by the Education Act of 1944, has been under successive chairmen the sponsor of a series of reports (such as the Hadow Report and the Norwood Report) which have charted the course of long-term policy in education; and the Secondary Schools Examination Council, although it has no statutory powers, is in effect the policy-making body for the whole complex system of General Certificate examinations. The Central Health Services Advisory Council will perhaps in time become equally important to the Ministry of Health.

Such committees are naturally not associated with the work of Departments such as the Foreign Office or the Commonwealth Relations Office, where policy emerges from day-to-day action about individual questions, under the supervision of the Cabinet itself; and they cannot work effectively on problems which are subjects of party controversy. But they are of great value in giving some public backing to the continuous development of Departmental policy on non-political questions, and if adequately staffed they can acquire great influence. Indeed, this device has (in instances like that of the University Grants Committee, the Medical Research Council, the Agricultural Research Council, and so on) become the basis of a special type of 'independent' administrative organisation to which reference has been made in Chapter 23.

(c) *Special Advisory Committees*. There are a few instances of special advisory committees charged with definite functions under a particular Act. The best known of these is the National Insurance Advisory Committee, a body of not less than four or more than eight members, chosen more for expert knowledge than as representatives of organisations, to whom all regulations to be made under the Acts must be submitted for comment before they are laid before Parliament. The issues raised are technical in character, but frequently involve questions of fairness and public policy, and there is no doubt that this is a useful device in the making of delegated legislation. The Committee's reports are likely to be helpful both to the Ministry, as a barometer of the reactions of informal opinion, and to Parliament, as a guarantee that technical matters which mean cash to a large number of people are not wholly in the hands of the Ministry's own experts.

(*d*) *Local Advisory Committees* have been set up for a number of services: for instance, for the Employment Exchange service of the Ministry of Labour, (separately) for its Disabled Persons and Youth Employment services, for the National Assistance Board, and for the Ministry of Pensions and National Insurance. In some cases it is not easy to find work for these bodies to do, unless there has been some major crisis or change of policy. It is, however, Departmental policy to keep local advisory committees in being, as a means by which a number of local people are as individuals brought into contact with the work of the Departments; and most of them are used for reference in individual cases which the Department has found difficult. Sometimes the procedure becomes almost that of an appeal to a committee from the Department's decision. There is no judicial hearing, but the committee serves some of the purposes of an independent tribunal, since it demonstrates to the aggrieved person and to some representative members of the public that the Department does not work only behind closed doors.

(iii) *Consultation with Organisations*

There are a number of statutes which direct the Department concerned to carry out consultations with unofficial bodies before initiating action. Well-known cases are the obligation of the Minister concerned to consult 'any organisation appearing to be representative of substantial numbers of employers and workers in the industry' before setting up a Development Council for the industry[1]; and the obligation of the Minister of Agriculture and Fisheries under the Agriculture Act of 1947 to consult 'with such bodies of persons as appear to him to represent the interests of producers in the agricultural industry'. It is hard to say why statutory directions have been inserted in some Acts but not in others, and no generalisation about this is possible without a good deal of research. A first impression is that the differences are due to accidents of debate in the House of Commons, since it is the established practice that there should be full consultation in all practicable cases. A failure to consult may be made part of the case against the Minister in the

[1] Industrial Organisation and Development Act, 1947.

House of Commons, and there is therefore a good deal of ill-defined constitutional doctrine about when and how it is proper to consult. The following propositions are suggested with some diffidence:

(a) Unless there is some clear reason to the contrary, a Department should make an attempt to consult all effective organisations concerned before bringing a piece of business to the House of Commons, or taking a new step in policy.

(b) The status of organisations varies greatly. There are some bodies, like the local government associations, which have a recognised place in procedure about all general questions affecting local government. At the other extreme are weak and even disreputable organisations struggling for recognition. In doubtful cases the Department must act warily, since consultation gives recognition, and a precedent once established is difficult to break.

(c) There is a narrow line between consultation and negotiation. It is generally proper for a Department to consult, improper for it to negotiate, since the Minister has no authority to pledge either of his two titular masters, the Crown or the House of Commons. Bargains may be reached tacitly, but cannot generally be recognised 'on the record'. But it would be absurd (for instance) not to regard as negotiation the long course of discussions which preceded the introduction of the Health Service Bill in 1946.

(d) A Minister (or an official acting within his duty) can always consult individuals 'off the record', and there are often consultations outside strictly official channels about highly confidential matters, as for instance with judges, psychiatrists, and police officers about reprieving a criminal condemned to death. There may even be confidential reference to individuals holding important positions in an organisation, such as the Director-General of the Federation of British Industries, the Secretary of the Association of Municipal Corporations, the President and Secretaries of the Royal Society, and so on. Such confidential approaches arise out of the nature of the organisations concerned, but can hardly be regarded as full consultation.

(e) Full consultation may be impossible because of emergency and the need for rapid action. It may also be limited by two other considerations. First, security limits consultation in many matters of defence and foreign policy, which now have wide ramifications. It also limits consultation about matters on which inside knowledge is worth a fortune to speculators, such as details of the Budget. Taxation proposals are often (for this reason) made in a way which is administratively untidy. Representations are received by the Chancellor from a variety of bodies while he is making up his proposals: some of these are general and platitudinous, some specific, but he can do no more than acknowledge them all. New schemes of taxation are worked out entirely from experience within the Departments and from their judgement about public reactions. A cut-and-dried scheme is presented to the House of Commons in the Finance Bill; but a process of consultation then follows, and it is quite common for the Chancellor to make concessions during the finance debates.

Secondly, budget secrecy is in part due also to constitutional principle. It would be constitutionally improper that any document drafted as a basis for decision either by the Cabinet or by the House of Commons should be shown first to some outside body. Hence the text of Bills and of Cabinet papers cannot be the subject of consultation. Civil servants must be careful of the principle involved, but it affects practice relatively little. A proposal goes through many stages before it becomes a Bill or a Cabinet paper, and it is not out of order to discuss draft heads of proposals at these earlier stages. So far as can be guessed, little difficulty is found about consultation on the actual text of draft Statutory Instruments. The inexperienced 'consultant' may feel at first that civil servants are evasive at the decisive point: but those who understand the conventions have no serious difficulty in working them.

(iv) *The Creation of Organisations*

Here we need only refer back to what has been said in previous chapters.[1] There is a great range of possible cases: organisations formed spontaneously by those concerned because of the necessities of negotiation; organisations encouraged unofficially by Departments in order to ease negotiation and diffuse responsibility; organisations assisted by grants-in-aid and in some sense controlled; organisations given statutory powers subject to limited control. It is a delicate business for a civil servant to advise his Minister on such matters of administrative politics; this is one of the 'growing points' in the structure of government, and its controversies though quiet are often bitter.

(v) *Sponsorship*

The period of controls made familiar a relation between Departments and industries which was generally called 'sponsorship'. Private industry was not only 'directed', it was 'sponsored'. Each industry had its 'sponsor' in Whitehall: that Department was responsible for working certain primary controls affecting the

[1] E.g. in Chapters 15 and 23.

industry (for instance, the allocation of materials), and it was also responsible for representing the needs of the industry to other Departments. For instance, the Ministry of Works was generally responsible for the building and building materials industries, and attempted to allocate building resources between different programmes in accordance with general policy. It was at the same time necessary for it to act for the building industries in getting as much steel as possible from the Ministry of Supply, as much manpower as possible from the Ministry of Labour, as much timber as possible from the Board of Trade, and so on; and when it had secured its allocation it had to attempt to share it out intelligently and fairly. The system was largely the expression of shortages and of the attempt to control inflation by allocation of physical resources, and its scope is now much reduced. But controls still exist over capital development and the location of industry. The pattern can also be seen in the relation of the Ministry of Agriculture and Fisheries to the farmers as represented by the N.F.U. There is an annual period of hard and even bitter bargaining over guaranteed prices between the farmers and the Ministry; but in this the Ministry is recognised to be the agent of the Treasury, and in other matters (for instance, in trade negotiations, or in the protection of agricultural land) it has been the Ministry's business to act for the industry, a position perhaps modified by amalgamation with the Ministry of Food.

The relations between government and private industry vary greatly according to the structure of each industry, but perhaps the formula of 'sponsorship' embraces such factors as are common. These are, in particular:

(*a*) Primary responsibility for every branch of production is allocated to some section somewhere in Whitehall.

(*b*) These sections are linked through hierarchical organisation, committees, and informal acquaintance.

(*c*) All but the largest firms approach their sponsor through trade associations, the permanent staff of which become well known to the civil servants concerned.

(*d*) The associations are administratively necessary, because civil servants are dependent on them for a machinery of allocation which is accepted by the industry as practicable and fair.

The relationship is in many ways a peculiar one. Relatively junior civil servants occupy positions of great power, since their decisions are the source of good or ill to the industry with which they deal; but they evade responsibility by passing it, as far as possible, to the organised industry itself. This may stabilise a distribution of resources which is becoming obsolete; it may even create a vested interest in the maintenance of the *status quo*, since that is the main reason for which the trade association exists. But the system arose out of a situation in which control and allocation were necessary, and no better alternative has ever been suggested.

4. Conclusion

The system which we have described here is not ineffectual: the administration is controlled in the sense that it has no choice but to fit the general framework of public life in Britain, as sketched in this and the four preceding chapters. But this is not enough to answer the question indicated at the beginning of this chapter: does it give good service under public control? The only possible answer is a platitudinous and perhaps feeble one: yes, but it could be better service, and there could be more effective control. There are within reach of every civil servant ways in which procedure could be improved, personal quality enhanced. The public (one might say) can have such control as it is intelligent enough to assert, co-operative enough to organise. There is no lack of things that might be done to secure improvement, but there is no easy way to improvement, because it depends partly on outside events, partly on the personal spirit of those concerned. Central administration is part of the history of the country, and its effectiveness depends to some extent on the situation which it has to handle. The tempo of events and the spirit of the nation have changed again and again in the last thirty or forty years, and civil servants move with events; they are excited, tired, angry, patriotic, cynical at much the same times and seasons as other men. How could it be otherwise? They live in the same sort of houses, read the same papers, listen to the radio, look at television, face problems of schools, taxation, and travel. The central administration is not isolated from the community, but entangled in it everywhere, in office hours and out of them. If the community wishes to have a good servant it must be a good master, a task as hard as that of the administration.

FOR REFERENCE

Government and Industry: A Survey of Machinery for Consultation and Co-operation (H.M.S.O. 1948).
Report of the Committee on Intermediaries (Herbert). Cmd. 7904, 1950.
H. M. CLOKIE and J. W. ROBINSON: *Royal Commissions* (1937).
R. VERNON and N. MANSERGH: *Advisory Bodies* (1939).
Sir HENRY BUNBURY: *Officials and the Public* (1947).
J. H. BREBNER: *Public Relations and Publicity* (1949).

Royal Institute of Public Administration: *I Am, Sir, Your Obedient Servant* (1949).
Political and Economic Planning: *Government and Industry* (1950).
Trade Associations (*Planning* No. 221, May 1944 and No. 383, July 1955).
Trade Associations and Government (*Planning*, No. 240, October 1945).
Clubs, Societies, and Democracy (*Planning*, No. 263, March 1947).
Industrial Trade Associations (1957).
K. C. WHEARE: *Government by Committee* (1955), Chs. III and IV.

On local advisory committees, see:

E. HARRISON: 'Local Advisory Committees', *Public Administration*, Vol. XXXI, p. 65.
—— 'The Work of the National Insurance Advisory Committee', *Public Administration*, Vol. XXX, p. 149.
F. M. G. WILLSON: 'Departmental Reports', *Public Administration*, Vol. XXX, p. 163.
S. H. BEER: 'Pressure Groups and Parties in Britain', *American Political Science Review*, Vol. 50, p. 1.
S. E. FINER: 'The Political Power of Private Capital', *Sociological Review* Vol. 3, No. 2.
W. J. M. MACKENZIE: 'Pressure Groups in British Government', *British Journal of Sociology*, Vol. VI, No. 2, p. 133.

SELECTED BIBLIOGRAPHY

NOTES

This is not a comprehensive bibliography but a selection of general books which could not appropriately be included in the references at the end of each chapter, though they have an important bearing on our subject. We exclude biographies, novels, and memoirs, a very full list of which is to be found in R. K. Kelsall: *Higher Civil Servants in Britain* (1955).

Useful sources of reference to official papers are: E. W. Cohen, *The Growth of the British Civil Service* (1941), and two works by P. and G. Ford, *A Breviate of Parliamentary Papers 1917-1939* (1951), especially the first section, *Machinery of Government*; and *A Select List of British Parliamentary Papers 1833-1899* (1953).

Place of publication is the United Kingdom unless otherwise stated.

ALLEN, C. K.: *Bureaucracy Triumphant* (1931).
—— *Law in the Making* (5th Edition, 1951).
ANDERSON, J. (LORD WAVERLEY): *Administrative Technique in the Public Services* (1949).
Anonymous: *Letters from a Civil Servant to his Son* (1947).
BARKER, Sir ERNEST: *Development of the Public Services in Europe 1660-1930* (1944).
BERTRAM, Sir A.: *The Colonial Service* (1930).
BEVERIDGE, W. H. (LORD BEVERIDGE) and others: *The Development of the Civil Service* (1922) (lectures delivered to the Society of Civil Servants).
BRIDGES, E. (LORD BRIDGES): *Portrait of a Profession—The Civil Service Tradition* (1950).
BROWN, R. D.: *The Battle of Crichel Down* (1955).
BROWN, W. J.: *The Civil Service, Retrospect and Prospect* (1943).
BURNS, C. D.: *Whitehall* (1921).
CARR-SAUNDERS, Sir A. M., and WILSON, P. A.: *The Professions* (1933).
Central Office of Information: *The British Civil Service* (1955).
CRITCHLEY, T. A.: *The Civil Service Today* (1950).
DALE, H. E.: *The Personnel and Problems of the Higher Civil Service* (1943).
DUNSIRE, A. (Ed.): *The Making of an Administrator* (1956).
EVANS, D.: *Women and the Civil Service* (1934).
Fabian Society: *The Reform of the Higher Civil Service* (1947).
FARRER, D.: *The Sky's the Limit* (an account of Beaverbrook at M.A.P.) (undated).

SELECTED BIBLIOGRAPHY

FINER, H.: *The British Civil Service, An Introductory Essay* (1927), revised and greatly enlarged as *The British Civil Service* (1937).
FINER, S. E.: *A Primer of Public Administration* (1950).
FLYNN, Sir J. A.: *Problems of the Civil Service* (1928).
FRANKS, Sir OLIVER: *Experiences of a University Teacher in the Civil Service* (1947).
GAUDEMET, P. M.: *Le Civil Service britannique* (Paris, 1952).
GLADDEN, E. N.: *The Civil Service—Its Problems and Future* (2nd Edition, 1948).
—— *An Introduction to Public Administration* (1949).
—— *The Essentials of Public Administration* (1953).
—— *Civil Service or Bureaucracy?* (1956).
GREAVES, H. R. G.: *The Civil Service in the Changing State* (1947).
GRIFFITH, LL. WYN: *The British Civil Service 1854-1954* (1954).
HANKEY, W. P. A. (LORD HANKEY): *The Science and Art of Government* (1951).
HARRISON, W.: *The Government of Britain* (1948).
HEADLAM, Sir CUTHBERT (Chairman): Report of a Group of Conservatives, *Some Proposals for Constitutional Reform* (1946).
HEATH, F. G.: *The British Civil Service* (1915).
HOOPER, F. C.: *Management in the Public Services* (1948).
JEFFERIES, Sir CHARLES: *The Colonial Empire and its Civil Service* (1938).
JENNINGS, Sir IVOR: *Cabinet Government* (2nd Edition, 1951), Chs. 4-7, 9, 10.
JONES, Sir THOMAS: *The Unbroken Front—Ministry of Food 1916-44* (1944).
KEITH, Sir A. B.: *The British Cabinet System* (2nd Edition by N. H. GIBBS, 1952), Chs. 4, 5, 7.
KINGSLEY, J. D.: *Representative Bureaucracy: An Interpretation of the British Civil Service* (Yellow Springs, Ohio, U.S.A., 1944).
LASKI, H. J.: *Reflections on the Constitution* (1951).
LEGGE-BOURKE, H.: *Master of the Offices* (1950).
LE MAY, G.: *British Government 1914-53, Selected Documents* (1955).
LEWIS, R., and MAUDE, A. E.: *The English Middle Classes* (1949).
—— *Professional People* (1952).
Liberal Party: *Civil Service Reform* (1942).
MCKECHNIE, S.: *The Romance of the Civil Service* (1930).
MALLALIEU, J. P. W.: *Passed to You Please* (1942).
MARTINDALE, H.: *Women Servants of the State 1870-1938: a history of women in the Civil Service* (1938).
MILWARD, G. E. (Ed.): *Large Scale Organisation* (1950).
MONCK, BOSWORTH: *How the Civil Service Works* (1952).
MORANT, Sir ROBERT, and others: *The Civil Servant and his Profession* (lectures delivered to the Society of Civil Servants) (1920).
MORRIS JONES, W. H.: *Socialism and Bureaucracy* (Fabian Tract No. 277) (1949).
MUIR, RAMSAY: *Peers and Bureaucrats* (1910).
MUNRO, C. K. (pseud. C. W. K. MACMULLEN): *The Fountains in Trafalgar Square* (1952).

NIGHTINGALE, R. T.: *The Personnel of the British Foreign Office 1851-1921* (Fabian Tract No. 232) (1930).
RAWLINGS, R. W.: *The Civil Service and the People* (1945).
Reconstruction, Ministry of (1918-19): *The Business of Government:* (1) *The Central Machinery:* (2) *The Work of the Departments:* (3) *The Civil Service* (1919).
REID, Sir GEORGE: *The Origin and Development of Public Administration in England* (1913).
ROBSON, W. A.: *From Patronage to Proficiency in the Public Service* (1922).
ROBSON, W. A. (Ed.): *The Civil Service in Great Britain and France* (1956).
—— *The British Civil Servant* (1937).
Royal Institute of Public Administration: *Problems of Public Service Organisation and Management* (1952).
SKEVINGTON, L.: *The Crisis of the Bureaucracy* (1947).
STOUT, H. M.: *The Public Service in Great Britain* (New York, 1938).
—— *British Government* (New York, 1953).
TAYLOR, Sir HENRY: *The Statesman* (1832: reprinted with an Introduction by H. J. Laski, 1927).
WHEARE, K. C.: *The Civil Service in the Constitution* (1954).
WHITE, L. D., and others: *The Civil Service Abroad* (Monograph 2, *The British Civil Service*, by L. D. White) (New York, 1935).
WILLIAMS-THOMPSON, R.: *Was I Really Necessary?* (1951) (an account of public relations in central government in wartime).
WILLIS, J.: *Parliamentary Powers of English Government Departments* (Cambridge, Mass., U.S.A., 1933).

Official History of the Second World War (*Civil Series*). Published by H.M.S.O. and Longmans Green.

These volumes contain much valuable information about the organisation and operation of central Departments before 1939 and during the Second World War. The full list of volumes published to date is as follows:

British War Economy. By W. K. Hancock and M. M. Gowing (1949).
British War Production. By M. M. Postan (1952).
Problems of Social Policy. By R. M. Titmuss (1950).
Statistical Digest of the War. Prepared in the Central Statistical Office (1951).
Agriculture. By Keith A. H. Murray (1955).
Civil Defence. By T. H. O'Brien (1955).
Civil Industry and Trade. By E. L. Hargreaves and M. M. Gowing (1952).
Coal. By W. H. B. Court (1951).
Economic Blockade. By W. N. Medlicott. Vol. I (1952).
Financial Policy. By R. S. Sayers (1956).
Food. By R. J. Hammond.
    Vol. I: *The Growth of Policy* (1951).
    Vol. II: *Studies in Administration and Control* (1956).
Merchant Shipping and the Demands of War. By C. B. A. Behrens (1955).

Studies in the Social Services. By S. M. Ferguson and H. Fitzgerald (1954).
Works and Buildings. By C. M. Kohan (1952).
Administration of War Production. By J. D. Scott and Richard Hughes (1955).
Contracts and Finance. By W. Ashworth (1953).
The Control of Raw Materials. By J. Hurstfield (1953).
North American Supply. By H. Duncan Hall (1955).
Studies of Overseas Supply. By H. Duncan Hall and C. C. Wrigley (1955).

Civil Service staff association journals include:

Civil Service Argus (M.o.L. Staff Federation).
Civil Service Opinion (Society of Civil Servants).
Civil Service Whip (Civil Service Union).
Customs Journal (Customs Preventive Staff Association).
Journal of the Customs and Excise Federation.
Taxes (Inland Revenue Staff Federation).
Red Tape (Civil Service Clerical Association).
Whitley Bulletin (National Staff Side).
The Post (U.P.O.W.).
State Service (I.P.C.S.).
Journal of the Post Office Engineering Union.
Journal of the Association of Officers of the Ministry of Labour.

Academic Journals:

Public Administration (Journal of the Royal Institute of Public Administration). There is a cumulative index to 1932, annually thereafter.
Political Studies (Journal of the Political Studies Association).
British Journal of Administrative Law.
Public Law.
Political Quarterly.
Parliamentary Affairs.
Cambridge Journal (no longer published).

Occasional articles on British Central Administration are to be found in:

Revue Internationale des Sciences Administratives.
Australian Journal of Public Administration.
New Zealand Journal of Public Administration.
Public Administration Review (Journal of the American Society for Public Administration).
American Political Science Review.
Journal of Politics (American).
Western Political Science Quarterly (American).
Canadian Journal of Economics and Political Science.
International Social Science Bulletin

INDEX OF NAMES

Alexander, A. V. (Lord Alexander of Hillsborough), 345
Allen, Sir Carleton, 390
Anderson, Sir Alan, 56
Anderson, Sir John (Lord Waverley), 344
Aristotle, quoted 363n
Asquith, H. H. (Lord Oxford and Asquith), 350, 352
Attlee, C. R. (Lord Attlee), 344, 345, 346, 351, 354

Bagehot, Walter, quoted 334, 437, 446
Baldwin, Stanley (Lord Baldwin), 309
Balfour, A. J. (Lord Balfour), 168, 352
Beaverbrook, Lord, 207, 339, 367
Bevan, A., 345
Beveridge, Lord, 239
Bevin, E., 67, 345
Birch, N., 349
Birkenhead, Lord, 390
Bonar Law, A., 352
Boyle, Sir Edward, 349
Bracken, Brendan (Lord Bracken), 295
Brett, R. B. (Lord Esher), 191-2
Bridges, Sir Edward (Lord Bridges), 35, 312, quoted 362
Brook, Sir Norman, 35
Brown, W. J., 137
Burgess, Guy, 153
Burke, Edmund, 4
Buxton, Sydney, 134

Carr, Sir Cecil, 383
Cecil, Robert (Lord Salisbury), 168
Cecil, Sir Wm. (Lord Burleigh), 174
Chamberlain, Sir Austen, 134
Chamberlain, Joseph, 192
Chamberlain, Neville, 351, 412
Cherwell, Lord, 100, 345, 346, 354
Churchill, Sir Winston, 100, 169, 209, 336, 337, 339, 344, 345, quoted 346, 347, 351, 354, 382
Clarence, Duke of (William IV), 170
Clay, Sir Henry, 354
Clow, Sir Andrew, 436
Clynes, J. R., 351
Cockcroft, Sir John, 41
Corry, M. (Lord Rowton), 191
Cripps, Sir Stafford, 315, 345, 348-9
Cromwell, Oliver, 269

Dale, H. E., 73, quoted 379
Dalton, H., 315, 345, 349
Day, Sir Albert, 144
Devons, Ely, 358
Dicey, A. V., 388
Downing, Sir George, 179
Dundas, H. (Lord Melville), 174
Dunsire, A., 380n

Eden, Sir Anthony, 336, 438
Edwards, L. J., 139, 349
Elizabeth I, 252

Farr, W., 99
Fawcett, C. B., 267
Fisher, Admiral Sir John (Lord Fisher), 121
Fisher, Sir Warren, 151, 309, 317
Fuchs, K., 153

Gaitskell, H., 435
Gardiner, Sir Thomas, 108
Geddes, C. J. (Sir Charles Geddes), 139
Gilbert, Sir Bernard, 35, 312, 315
Giffen, T., 99
Gladstone, W. E., 4, 293
Godley, A. (Lord Kilbracken), 191, 192
Griffith, J. A. G., 394

Halifax, Lord, 352
Hamilton, Sir Edward, 191
Hartington, Lord (8th Duke of Devonshire), 192
Henderson, A., 351
Henderson, Sir Hubert, 354
Henry IV, 278
Hitler, A., 366
Hoare, Sir Samuel (Lord Templewood), 352
Houghton, A. L. N. D., 136, 140

Inskip, Sir Thomas (Lord Caldecote), 344, 347
Ismay, General Sir Hastings (Lord Ismay), 347

Jeffries, Sir Charles, 222
Jenkyns, Sir Henry, 97
Jones, Aubrey, 438
Jones, Thomas, 194n

INDEX OF NAMES

Kent, William, 179

Lansbury, G., 288
Leathers, Lord, 345, 346
Lloyd George, D. (Lord Lloyd George), 340, 350, 352, 353, 354
Lyttleton, O. (Lord Chandos), 348

Macaulay, T. B. (Lord Macaulay), 6, quoted 64
MacDonald, R., 351
Mackinder, Sir Halford, 267
Maclean, Donald, 153
Macpherson, Sir John, 92
Makins, Sir Roger, 35
Marsh, Sir Edward, 192
Masterman, J. C., 156
Maude, Sir John, 444
Maudling, R., 349
May, Nunn, 153
Mayne, S., 138
Mill, James, 6
Mill, John Stuart, 6, quoted 263
Monckton, Sir Walter (Lord Monckton), 366
Morrison, H., 295, 345, 351

Napoleon, 5
Newman, Sir George, 111
Newsam, Sir Frank, 222, quoted 228, 229, 417
Normandy, Duke of (William I), 278
Northcote, Sir Stafford (Lord Iddesleigh), 191

Pitt, William, 169, 264, 301
Plowden, Sir Edwin, 315
Pontecorvo, B., 153

Porter, G. R., 99
Pritchard, Sir Harry, 421

Redhead, E. C., 136, 140
Rhodes, H. V., 129
Rosebery, Lord, 192

Salisbury, Lord (3rd Marquess), 168, 175
Sandars, J. S., 191
Simon, Sir John, 111
Simon, Sir John (Lord Simon), 352
Snowden, P. (Lord Snowden), 351
Soane, Sir John, 179
Stamp, Sir Josiah (Lord Stamp), 99, 354,
Stanley, Sidney, 452
Stansgate, Lord, 346
Strauss, G., 438
Street, H., 394

Thomas, J. H., 351
Thring, Lord, 97
Trevelyan, Sir Charles, 6
Trollope, Anthony, quoted 121n, 264, 270, 379n

Urwick, L., Lieut.-Colonel, quoted 380

Walpole, Sir Robert, 168, 179
Walsingham, Sir Francis, 174
Watkinson, H., 438
Welby, Lord, 331
West, Sir Algernon, 191
Wheare, K. C., 213
William III, 264
Wolsey, Cardinal, 169
Wood, Sir Kingsley, 317, 352
Woolton, Lord, 345

INDEX OF SUBJECTS

Accountant Class, professional
  work of, 113-114
  number and salaries, 113
Accounting Officer, 169, 186, 306, 308, 328
  appointment by Treasury, 37, 185, 309
  responsibility to House of Commons, 37, 185, 323
  functions of, defined, 309
  responsibility for accurate estimating, 323
  appearance before Public Accounts Committee, 329, 384
Accounting procedures, in central government
  distinction between 'Allied,' and 'Agency' services, 285-6
  payment for Post Office services, 293
  nature of, 300-1 330
  handling of income and expenditure by Departments, 301-5, 309-11, 326-7
  audit, 328-30
Accounts, form of government, 310, 321, 328-9
Actuaries, Institute of, 129
  Faculty of, 129
Administrative Class
  careers of, Treasury interest in, 37
  duties, defined by Reorganisation Committee, 62-3
  at present time, 72-3
  number, 64
  recruitment, 64-9, 71
  interview, 65
  Civil Service Selection Board, 65-7
  Methods I and II, 67
  limited competition, promotion, transfer, 67-9
  number recruited by various methods, 67, 69
  structure of the class, 69-70
  annual intake, 1925-1933, 70
  character, 70-3
  relations with scientific classes, 103-6
    with works group, 108-9
  on Post Office Board, 119
  promotion procedure, for higher posts 122-3
  training, 127-8
  organisation for negotiation, 136

highest posts in, number attained by former Treasury Officials, 317
Administrative Staff College, Henley, 132
Administrative tribunals
  in Ministry of Pensions and National Insurance, 242, 395
  growth of, 390
  in Ministry of Transport, 395
  civil servants as advisers to, 397
Admiralty, 61, 107, 114, 125, 170, 180, 219, 223, 232, 233, 234, 265, 294
  Lords Commissioners of the, 170
  First Lord, 170, 179
Advisory Committees, use of in British central administration, 457-8
  types of, 458-60
  local, 266, 460
  Permanent:
  Statute Law Committee, 98
  on Remuneration of the Higher Civil Service, 147
  for appeals from security authorities, 154
  Advisory Council on Scientific Policy, 173, 459
  Defence Research Policy Committee, 173, 348, 459
  National Insurance Advisory Committee, 242, 459
  Political Honours Scrutiny Committee, 316
  Capital Issues Committee, 314, 316, 411
  Economic Advisory Council, 354
  National Joint Advisory Council, 355, 458
  National Production Advisory Council for Industry, 355, 458
  Central Health Services Advisory Council, 420, 459
  Central Fire Brigades Advisory Council, 420
  Central Council for Health Education, 420
  Advisory Councils for Education, 420, 459
  Import Duties Advisory Committee, 455
  Councils for Agriculture, 458

474 INDEX OF SUBJECTS

Advisory Committees—*cont.*
  Secondary Schools Examinations Council, 459
  Ad hoc:
    on the Pay, etc. of State Servants (Anderson), 56
    on the Organisation of D.S.I.R. (Jephcott), 107
    on Training (Assheton), 127
    to Investigate certain statements affecting Civil Servants (Fisher), 151
    Conference of Privy Councillors to review Security Arrangements, 154
    on the Political Activities of Civil Servants (Masterman), 156
    on Departmental Records (Grigg), 204
    on Crown Lands (Eve), 253
    on War Office Reconstruction (Esher), 265
    Council of Financial Officers (Baldwin), 309
    on the Form of Government Accounts (Crick), 328
    on the Care of Children (Curtis), 366
    on Machinery of Government (Haldane), 355, 359, 363, 365, 389, 391
    on Minister's Powers (Donoughmore), 391, 393, 397
    on Administrative Tribunals and Enquiries (Franks), 391
    on Local Government Manpower (Proctor/Playfair), 404n
    on the organisation of a Central Institute of Management (Baillieu), 430
    on the Domestic Consumption of Electricity (Clow), 436
    on the Organisation of the Electricity Industry (Herbert), 437
    on the Cost of the National Health Service (Guillebaud), 440, 444
Agency services, in Ministry of Pensions and National Insurance, 243
  nature of, 285, 286
  types of, 286-7
Agricultural Commissioner for Wales, 273
Agricultural Land Commission, 252, 253
Agricultural Marketing Boards, *see* Marketing Boards
Agricultural Mortgage Corporation, 255
Agricultural Research Council, 172, 173n, 253, 431, 445, 459
Agriculture, Board of, 172, 180, 248, 252
Agriculture, Fisheries and Food, Ministry of, 107, 114, 172, 181, 187, 219, 220, 228, 262, 266, 272, 287, 294, 343, 364, 365, 366, 463

Minister of, 338, 460
work of, 223, 248-9
origin of, 248
size of, 249
Veterinary Service, 250
N.A.A.S., 250
A.L.S., 250
Agricultural Economics, 250-1
Inspectorates, 251
Agricultural Lime Department, 251
National Stud, 251
food controls in, 251
Agricultural Land Commission, 252
minor Departments of, 252-3
and public corporations, 254
and Marketing Boards, 254-5
sponsorship of independent bodies, 255
and local authorities, 256, 406
and County Agricultural Executive Committees, 256-7
relations with National Farmers' Union, 257, 258
Air Council, 171, 233-9
Air Ministry, 110, 174, 175, 180, 181, 182, 219, 287, 294, 367
work of, 223, 232
organisation of, 232-5
relations with Royal Air Force Commands, 235-6
relations between civilian and service staff, 236-7
relations with the Scientific Civil Service, 237-9
Secretary of State for Air, 233
Aircraft Production, Ministry of, 207, 233, 237, 238, 269, 343, 358, 366
'Allied' Services (or 'Common Services')
  nature of, 285, 287-8, 321
  types of, 288-97
  procedures, 297-9
Amphibious Warfare Headquarters, 347
'Approved' Societies, 266
Archbishop of Canterbury, 171
Area Electricity Boards, 436
Area Gas Boards, 431
Armed Forces, 10, 12, 60, 67, 149, 391
Army Council, *see under* War Office
Arts Council of Great Britain, 185, 307, 445, 446
Association of Chief Education Officers, 419
Association of Child Care Officers, 420
Association of Childrens' Officers, 419
Association of Education Committees, 419
Association of Ex-Service Civil Servants, 140
Association of Municipal Corporations, 419, 423, 425
  Secretaries of, 421, 461

INDEX OF SUBJECTS

Association of Officers of the Ministry of Labour, 137, 144
Association of Post Office Controlling Officers, 139, 140
Association of Rural District Councils, 419, 425
Association of Urban District Councils, 419, 425
Associations, role of in British society, 453-4
 types of, 454-6
 consultation by Departments, 460-2
 sponsorship of, by Departments, 462-4
Atomic Energy Authority, 22, 106, 173, 182, 262, 431
Attorney-General, 97, 399
Audit Board, 169
Auditors of Imprest, 169
Automobile Association, 455

Bank of England, 301, 303, 304, 305, 314
Benthamite principles, in English administration, 5-6
Bills:
 drafting of, in office of First Parliamentary Counsel, 97, 381
 in draft, scrutiny by Cabinet Committees, 344
 civil servants' interest in, during passage through Parliament, 381
 consultation with interested organisations on, 462
Board of Control, 111
Boards of Governors of Teaching Hospitals, 440, 441, 442, 443
Boards of Guardians, 263, 264
Boards of Health, the central, 172
Boards of Health, local, 263
British Broadcasting Corporation, 196, 295, 446
British Council, 12, 184, 185, 294, 295, 296, 307, 429, 445, 446
British Employers' Confederation, 455
British Institute of Management, 248, 430, 445
British Legion, 366
British Medical Association, 138, 454
British Museum, 185
British Overseas Airways Corporation, 438
British Productivity Council, 248
British Standards Institution, 248, 429
British Sugar Corporation, 255
British Transport Commission, 22, 433, 438
British Travel and Holidays Association, 248, 430
Buckingham Palace, 178

Bureaucratic organisation, characteristics of, 199-201, 205-8

Cabinet, 14, 97, 99, 142, 170, 171, 183, 186, 207, 215, 224, 313, 427, 449, 462
 and financial control, 5, 33, 331-2
 and decisions of National Whitley Council, 145
 central place in administrative system, 334-5
 functions of, 335, 360
 membership, of 336-8
 Departments represented in, 337-8
 procedure in, 338-42
 papers, drafting of, 339
 Minutes, 340-2
 Committees of: 341, 343, 344
  Investment Programmes, 314
  Imperial Defence, 341, 344, 347, 353
  Home Affairs, 344
  Home Policy, 344
  Legislation, 344
  Future Legislation, 344, 345
  Lord President's, 344, 345
  Socialisation of Industries, 345
  Defence, 186, 232, 341, 345, 347, 348
 Machinery of Government, 361
 as co-ordinator of public business, 342-9
 and 'central direction,' 349-55
 of Mr. Attlee, 351
 of Mr. Churchill (1940-1945), 351
 of Mr. Ramsay MacDonald, 351
 of Mr. Neville Chamberlain, 351-2
 of Mr. Lloyd George, 352
 and planning machinery, 359
 and supervision of machinery of government, 359-68
Cabinet Office, 35, 72, 100, 316
 origins of, 340
 and opposition to Ll. George, 340, 353-4
 and Cabinet secrecy, 340
 organisation and duties of, 340-2, 353
 and Secretariat of the Chiefs of Staff, 341
 origins of Economic Section, 354
 transfer of Economic Section to Treasury, 354
 origins of Central Statistical Office, 354
 (see also Treasury (Economic Section), Central Statistical Office)
Cable and Wireless Ltd., 293
Career service, nature of a, 120-1
Central Economic Information Service, 354
Central Economic Planning Staff, 315, 355, 358

INDEX OF SUBJECTS

Central Electricity Authority, 273, 436, 437
Central Electricity Board, 267
Central Land Board, 316
Central Midwives Board, 420
Central Office of Information, 195, 196
  political controversy about, 294
  origins of, 294-5
  organisation and work of, 295-7
Central Statistical Office, 100, 101, 325, 340, 354, 358
Central Welsh Board (for Education), 272
Channel Islands, 278, 307
Chef du Cabinet, 191
Chief Constables' Association, 419
Chiefs of Staff Committee, 186, 232, 341, 347
Church Commissioners, 307
Church of England, 455
City of London College, 308
Civil Research, Ministry for, 349
Civil Service:
  growth of, 1-9
  dismissal from, 4, 17, 38, 52
  superannuation (pensions), 4, 6, 16, 17, 18, 50-4
  system of pay, 4, 12, 44-7, 54-8
  Parliamentary control of, 5
  origin of term, 6-7
  Trevelyan-Northcote Report on, 6
  Head of, 7, 8 (*see also* Home Civil Service, Head of)
  standards of probity, 8, 135, 141, 149-152
  scope of, 10
  law relating to, 10, 13, 14, 389
  definition of, 11-12
    industrial and non-industrial, 15-16
    established and unestablished, 16-18
  comparison with European civil services, 11, 389
  conditions of service for established staff, 17, 44-8
    for unestablished staff, 17-18, 48, 52, 83
  no contractual rights against Crown, 17
  retirement, 18, 51-52
  size of, 22, 23
  distribution between Departments, 24
  numbers :
    established, 25, 49
    unestablished, 25
    non-industrial, 22, 23, 24, 29
    industrial, 22, 24
    women, 22, 25
  percentage of women in main classes, 26
  promotion, 38, 46, 121-4
  promotion 'pools,' 38, 77
  methods of entry, 40-2
  hours of work, 47-8
  overtime, abolition of, 47-8
  leave, 48
  provincial differentiation, 49-50
  equal pay for men and women, 49
  widows' and dependents' pensions, 51
  benefits in kind, 54
  Pay Research Unit, 55
  training, 124-132
  negotiating procedure, 134-48
  right to join trade unions, 135
  right to strike, 141
  arbitration, 145-7
  disciplinary procedure, 149-50
  political activities, 152-9, 376
  geographical location of, 260-3
  relations with M.P.s, 376-85
  internal procedures not open to judicial enquiry, 389
  relations with general public, 448, 449-53
  relations with organised 'publics', 453-64
Civil Service Alliance, 137
Civil Service Arbitration Tribunal, 142, 145-6, 394
Civil Service Clerical Association, 135, 137, 140, 144
Civil Service Commissioners, 16, 17, 34, 51, 65, 85, 90, 91, 143, 184, 185, 316
  creation by Order-in-Council (1855), 6
  functions of, 6, 7, 38, 39, 42
  certificate of, 16, 34, 39
  First Commissioner, 28, 39, 41, 92
  organisation of, 38-9
  conditions under which certificate granted, 40-2
  size of staff, 39
  scale of work, 42
  difficulty of finding recruits, 77
  recruitment for Oversea Civil Service, 92
Civil Service Council for Further Education, 126
Civil Service Legal Society, 140
Civil Service Pay Research Unit, 55
Civil Service Selection Board, 41, 65-7
Civil Service Staff College, creation of resisted, 128
Civil Service Union, 138, 144
Clerical and Administrative Workers Union, 135
Clerical Classes:
  duties, defined by Reorganisation Committee, 62, at present time, 81-2
  placed 'end on' to Executive Class, 76
  obsolete grades, 76
  number of Higher Clerical Officers, 76

INDEX OF SUBJECTS

numbers, 80-1
qualities required of clerical officer, 82-3
recruitment and structure, 83-5
salaries, 84
promotion into, 85
Colonial Civil Service, *see* Oversea Service
Colonial Office, 13, 91-92, 174, 180, 202, 223, 224, 225, 226
Colonial Secretary, 337
Commissioners of Northern Lighthouses, 275
Committee of Economic Information, 354
Committees in civil service, 213-15
Common Services, *see* 'Allied' Services
Commons, House of, 11, 33, 34, 54, 97, 141, 150, 169, 178, 184, 185, 216, 306, 334, 338, 346, 421, 424, 457, 460, 461, 462
control of civil service, 5
formal supremacy in financial matters, 37, 300, 301, 302, 331
and civil service staff associations, 137-140
Estimates procedure, 318-19, 320, 322, 323-4, 327
and Budget, 318, 324, 326
and Finance Accounts, 318
and Appropriation Accounts, 318
and Parliamentary Questions, 377-80
and Bills, 381
and subordinate legislation, 381-3
Select Committees of:
  on Public Monies (1856), 5
  on House of Commons Disqualification Bill (1956), 12, 155
  of Public Accounts (Public Accounts Committee), 287, 300, 320, 323, 328, 443
    formation (1861), 5
    and accounts of nationalised industries, 307
    and Comptroller and Auditor-General, 307, 319, 329
    control of Departments, 308, 384
    and Appropriation Accounts, 319, 329-30
    and form of the Estimates, 321
    and *virement*, 327
    reports to Parliament, 329-30
    and grants-in-aid, 445
  on Estimates (Estimates Committee), 300, 362, 425
    and form of the Estimates, 320, 321
    scrutiny of Estimates, 324, 384-5
    on National Expenditure, 362

on Nationalised Industries, 434, 435
on Statutory Instruments (Scrutiny Committee), 382-3
Standing Committees of :
  Scottish Grand Committee, 276
  Standing Committees on Bills, 381
Select Committee of Privileges, Report of (Brown's case), 137
(*see also* Parliament)
Commonwealth Relations Office, 86, 174, 175, 232, 239, 245, 459
size of staff, 24
work and organisation of, 224-8
Secretary of State for, 337
Communist Party of Great Britain, 153, 154
Comptroller and Auditor-General, 39, 169, 184, 185, 319, 330, 430, 434, 443
control of Consolidated Fund, 302, 303, 304
rank and status of, 306
reports to Parliament, 307, 309, 328, 329
and *virement*, 327
and audit of accounts, 329
appearance before P.A.C., 329, 384
Conservative Party, 340, 354
Consolidated Fund, 301, 302, 303, 304, 305, 306, 318, 319, 331
Co-ordination of Defence, Minister for the, 344
Correspondence, in Civil Service, 210-12, 450
Minister's, 378
Council of Industrial Design, 248, 430
Council for the Preservation of Rural England, 455
Council for Wales, 272
Council for Wales and Monmouthshire, 273n, 274
Council of Women Civil Servants, 140
'Country House': see Civil Service Selection Board
County Agricultural Executive Committees, 257, 266
County Councils Association, 419, 425
County Court Officers' Association, 137
County War Agricultural Executive Committees, 256-7
Court of Session, 274
Courts of Law:
  ancient Common Law courts, 165-6
  power to control the administration, 387-8, 391-3, 400
  and definition of a 'judicial act', 393-4
  and of a 'judicial' office, 394
  and disclosure of official documents, 398
Coventry City Council, 422

INDEX OF SUBJECTS

Crichel Down, 220, 253, 452
Crown Agent for Scotland, 275
Crown Estates Office, 187, 288
Crown Lands, Commissioners of, 172, 253, see also Crown Estate Office
Crown, the, 3, 5, 97, 134, 165, 228, 242, 276, 278, 306, 392, 394, 461
   position of servants of, 4, 10-11, 52
   and regulation of Civil Service, 10, 13-14, 32-3, 149, 215-16
   offices of profit under, 11-12, 155
   privilege, 14, 398
   power to grant pensions, 50
   hereditary revenues and estates of, 253, 301
   and the control of public monies, 302-3
Curia Regis, 165, 178
Customs and Excise, Board of, 6, 25, 60, 61, 78, 94, 152, 169, 178, 184, 223, 261, 264, 287, 303, 316, 398, 400, 449
Customs and Excise Controlling Grade Association, 136
Customs and Excise Federation, 136, 144
Customs and Excise Group of Departmental Associations, 136

Defence, Ministry of, 76, 180, 225, 232, 341, 342, 366
   functions of, 347-8
   Minister of, 337
Department, non-ministerial
   definition of, 183-5
   grade of permanent head of, 187
Departmental classes
   defined, 18-20
   examples of, 19
   size of, 27
   of specialists, 114-16
Departmental Whitley Councils, 142, 143, 150
Departments, creation of, by statute, 34
   co-ordination between at 'Cabinet level', 342-3
   Co-ordinating, 343, 345, 346-9
   legal actions against, 398
   legal actions brought by, 399-400
Deputy Secretaries
   appointment of, 8, 37
   duties of, 187
Development Commission, 172
Dialogus de Scaccario, 169
Discussion, transaction of business by, in Civil Service, 212-13
District Auditors, 115, 130, 307, 410, 443
   organisation and duties, 412-13
   independence of Minister, 412
District Nursing Associations, 428
Dollar Exports Council, 248

Dominions Office, 174, 224
Duchy of Lancaster, Chancellor of the, 173, 295, 338, 344

East India Company, 6 (see also Indian Civil Service)
École des Mines, 129
École Nationale d'Administration, 128
Écoles des Ponts et Chaussées, 129
Economic Adviser to H.M. Government, 313, 316
Economic Advisory Council, 354
Economic Affairs, Minister for, 244, 315, 345, 348, 355
Economic Planning Board, 355
'Economic Reform', 1-5
Economic Warfare, Ministry of, 244
Economists in the Civil Service, 100
Education, Board of, 65, 172, 180
Education, Ministry of, 25, 111, 114, 123, 171, 180, 186, 187, 223, 230, 256, 357, 368, 410
   and local government, 406
   organisation and functions of, 414-16
   Minister of, 338, 439
Efficiency, measurement of in public administration, 448-9
Establishments Divisions (Departmental)
   and negotiating procedure, 141-2
   and disciplinary procedure, 150
   organisation of, 188-91
   and review of duties, 217-18
   and control of staff numbers, 323
   (see also Principal Establishments Officer)
Estacode, 33
Estimates, form of the, 320-1
Exchequer, ancient office of, 169
Exchequer and Audit Department, 78, 94, 184, 188, 305, 311, 314, 315, 329, 330
   organisation and work of, 306-308
   (see also Comptroller and Auditor-General)
Exchequer, Chancellor of, 5, 33, 35, 49, 168, 169, 170, 179, 302, 312, 313, 318, 322, 324, 326, 332, 337, 345, 355, 461, 462
Executive Classes
   duties, defined by Reorganisation Committee, 62
   at present time, 78
   numbers, 73, 74
   salary range, 73, 74
   recruitment, 75-7
   of university graduates, 76
   promotion into, 76-7
   structure and character, 77-80
   promotion pool, 77

INDEX OF SUBJECTS 479

prospects for promotion within, 78, 79
Executive Councils (N.H.S.), 414

Family Service Units, 428
Fascists, British, 153
Fatstock Marketing Corporation, 255
Federated Superannuation System for Universities, 53
Federation of British Industries, 455
  Secretary of, 461
Federation of Civil Service Professional and Technical Staffs, 138
Finance Divisions, Departmental
  organisation of, 187-188, 308-12
  methods of collecting monies, 303
  of making payments, 304
  and Estimates, 320, 321-2
  and Budget, 324
  and day-to-day control of expenditure, 326-7
  preparation of Appropriation Accounts, 328
  and audit by Auditor-General, 328-9
  (*see also* Principal Finance Officer)
Financial White Paper, Annual, 325
First Civil Service Commissioner, *see* Civil Service Commissioners
First Division Association, 136, 140, 144
First Sea Lord, 170
Food, Ministry of, 113, 172, 248, 251, 266, 343, 364, 365, 463
  Minister of, 338
Football Association, 455
Football League, 455
Foreign Office, 13, 65, 90-1, 98, 122, 151, 174, 179, 180, 196, 202, 223, 224, 226, 230, 245, 287, 291, 338, 342, 353, 459
  Foreign Secretary, 184, 337, 345
Foreign Service, 13, 16, 28, 67, 68, 71, 90-1, 261
  Commercial Diplomatic Branch, 245
Forestry Commission, 114, 168, 172, 253, 267, 428
Free Churches, the, 455
Fuel and Power, Ministry of—*see* Power, Ministry of

Gas Council, 437
'General' classes
  defined, 20-1
  examples of, 21
  size of 26
  importance of, 59
  history of, 60-3
  distinguished from specialist classes, 94-5
General Register House, 274
General Register Office, 99
Government Actuary, 185, 294

Government Chemist, 294
Government, Machinery of :
  allocation and review of duties within Departments, 215-20
  public enquiries into, 219-20, 360-8
  Haldane Report, quoted, 359, 363, 365
  Cabinet and supervision of, 359-60
  procedure for review of, in 19th century, 360-1
  appointment of Haldane Committee, 361
  Cabinet Committee on, 361
  'scientific' organisation of, 362

Health, Ministry of, 98, 111, 112, 172, 175, 180, 182, 186, 187, 223, 228, 230, 243, 256, 262, 267, 286, 287, 357, 364, 415, 423, 439
  Hospital Audit, 307, 443
  and local government, 406
  organisation and functions in relation to local government, 413-14
  relations with hospital authorities, 440-4
  organisation and functions in relation to hospital service, 440-4
  Minister of, 338
Herring Industry Board, 254
High Court of Justiciary, 274
'Higher Civil Service'
  as defined by Priestley Commission, 29
  size of, 29
  promotion procedure, 122-3
  and arbitration, 147
History of the War, 17
Home Civil Service, contrasted with Foreign and Oversea Services, 13, 71, 90, 91-92
  Head of, 35, 90, 143, 313, 314
  responsibility for advising Prime Minister on highest posts, 37, 122
  and on honours and decorations, 316
  and appointment of Auditor-General, 306
  (*see also* Civil Service, Head of)
Home Office, 25, 97, 98, 111, 114, 174, 180, 232, 243, 246, 278, 287, 293, 365, 368, 407, 422, 423
  recruitment of staff, 65
  work and organisation of, 223, 228-31
  size of, 231
  and Metropolitan Police, 231
  and Prison Commission, 231
  responsibility for judicial system, 390
  and local government, 231, 406, 417-18
Home Secretary, 254, 273, 337, 399, 417, 422
  responsible for the Channel Islands and the Isle of Man, 278

INDEX OF SUBJECTS

Home Secretary—*cont.*
as Chairman of Home Affairs Committee, 344
Home Security, Ministry of, 423
Horse Guards', 179, 180
Hospital Management Committees, 440, 441, 442, 443
Hospital Service,
audit of accounts, 307
financing of, 439, 440, 442-4
status and duties of, 439-40
relations with Ministry of Health, 440-4
Establishments (staffing), 442
central purchasing for, 444
(*see also* : Regional Hospital Boards, Hospital Management Committees, Boards of Governors)
Housing and Local Government, Ministry of, 115, 130, 158, 172, 223, 228, 253, 271, 364, 414, 415, 423, 425, 426, 440
and local government, 406
organisation and functions of, 407-12
Minister of, 338
Howard League, 429, 455

Imperial Defence College, 347
Independent public bodies:
difficulty of defining, 184-5, 428
audit of accounts, 307
provision of services by, 402
staffs employed by, 403
growth of, 429-31
'independence' assessed, 444-6
Independent Television Authority, 431
India (and Burma) Office, 174, 175, 180, 225
Indian Civil Service, 6, 61, 68
Industrial Court, 395
Industrial Design Centres, 248
Industrial Development Councils, 247, 460
Industrial Disputes Tribunal, 395
Industrial Estates Companies, 247
Information, Ministry of, 294, 295, 297
Information Officer Class, 196
Inland Revenue, Board of, 25, 60, 61, 78, 94, 99, 107, 110, 113, 124, 144, 152, 169, 184, 223, 261, 294, 303, 316, 400, 449
graduates in, 76
history of, 263-4
Inland Revenue Staff Federation, 126, 136, 138, 144
Inspectorates, Central Government:
status of, 114
numbers, 115
influence of, 115-16

growth of in 19th century, 265
in 20th century, 267, 405
work of, 123, 396-7, 412, 414, 416, 418, 423, 442
powers of, 398-9, 400, 405
Institute of Municipal Engineers, 420
Institute of Municipal Treasurers and Accountants, 113, 420
Institute of Public Supplies Officers, 420
Institution of Professional Civil Servants, 56, 94, 135, 138, 140, 144
Interior, Ministry of, 368, 426
Iron and Steel Board, 431
Iron and Steel Corporation of Great Britain, 438
Isle of Man, 278, 307

Jockey Club, the, 455
Joint Intelligence Bureau, 347
Joint Services Staff College, 347
Judicial offices, definition of, 12, 394
Justice, Ministry of, 368, 391

Keeper of the Great Seal of Scotland, 274
King's Justices, the, 165-6
Labour and National Service, Ministry of, 25, 76, 81, 129, 130, 131, 146, 179, 180, 181, 223, 228, 243, 244, 261, 262, 267, 268, 271, 287, 365, 432, 449, 463
Minister of, 337

Labour Party, 135, 136, 137, 138, 139, 140, 345
National Executive of, 139
Labour Party Conference, 139
Legal Class : transfers to Administrative Class, 68
position of lawyers in Civil Service compared with other Western countries, 96-7, 388
Departments without legal advisers, 98
size of, 98
recruitment of, 98
reorganisation as a General Service Class, 98
'administrative judges', 394-5
(*see also* Attorney-General, Solicitor General, Standing Counsel to the Treasury, Parliamentary Draftsmen, Statutory Publications Office, Treasury Solicitor, Lord Chancellor, Director of Public Prosecutions)
Levels, doctrine of, in Civil Service, 205-8, 451-3
Local Authorities, 258, 307
and Home Office, 231, 406, 417-18
and Ministry of Agriculture, 256, 406
provision of services by, 402
staffs employed by, 403

INDEX OF SUBJECTS

forms of control by central administration, 404-5, 422
relations with central Departments, 405, 422-7
and Ministry of Housing and Local Government, 406, 407-12
and Ministry of Health, 406, 413-14
and Ministry of Education, 406, 414-16
and Ministry of Transport and Civil Aviation, 406, 416-17
and other central Departments, 406
and Public Works Loan Board, 411
and District Audit, 412-13
associations of, 418-19, 420-2
use by Ministers of advisory bodies representing, 420
large and small, effect on relations with central administration, 423-5
negotiations with central Departments through associations, 420-1, 425
and through Parliament, 421-2, 424
ambiguity in legal definition of, 428
Local Government Board, 111, 112, 172, 180, 361, 423
Local Government Legal Society, 420
Local Government and Planning, Minister of, 338
Ministry of, 397
Local Government Service, 158n
compared with Civil Service, 47
distribution by categories, 403
associations of officers, 419-20
Local offices of central departments, *see* Regional and local organisations
London Passenger Transport Board, 267
Lord Chamberlain, 170
Lord Chancellor, 166, 167, 173, 204, 242, 337, 359, 391, 394
Department of, 97, 166, 167, 389-90
Lord Chief Justice, 166
Department of, 97
Lord Clerk Register, 274
Lord Great Chamberlain, 166, 170, 178
Lord High Admiral, 166, 170
Lord High Chamberlain, 170
Lord High Constable, 166, 170
Lord High Steward, 170
Lord High Treasurer, 166, 167, 168
Lord President of the Council, 166, 171, 173, 295, 315, 337, 344, 345, 459
Lord President's Office, 187, 316, 349, 431n
Lord Privy Seal, 166, 173, 337, 344
Lord's Day Observance Society, 455
Lords Commissioners of the Treasury, 168, 169
Lords, House of
as judicial body, 149, 274, 389

as legislative body, 178, 380, 389 (*see also* Parliament)

Machine Operating Class, 87
Marketing Boards, 254-5, 258
Materials, Ministry of, 244
Minister of, 338
Medical Officer Class, 110-12
number and distribution between Departments, 110-11
duties, 111
relations with lay administrators, 112
relativities with National Health Service, 112
Medical Research Committee (National Health Insurance Commission), 172
Medical Research Council, 172, 307, 431, 445, 459
Messengers and Cleaners, Class of, 89-90
Metropolitan Boroughs' Standing Joint Committee, 419
Metropolitan Police, 180, 231
Mines Department, 268
Minister for Welsh Affairs, 273
Ministers:
power to regulate their Departments, 13, 33
choice of chief advisers, 37, 122-3
'of Cabinet Rank', 337
not in Cabinet, position of, 337
those always members of Cabinet since 1946, 337
those sometimes members of Cabinet since 1946, 338
'co-ordinating', 343, 345 (*see also* 'Overlords')
non-Departmental, 344
'Overlords', 345-6
responsibility for their Departments, 373
correspondence of, 377-8
and Parliamentary Questions, 378-80
and Bills, 381
and subordinate legislation, 382
may claim privilege for official papers, 398
Ministry, origin of word as synonym for 'Office' or 'Department', 175
definition of, 183
Ministry of Labour Staff Association, 137, 138, 144
Minutes, use of in Civil Service, 208-10
Monopolies Commission, 248
Munitions, Ministry of, 175, 266

National Assistance Appeal Tribunals, 397
National Assistance Board, 25, 78, 130, 168, 181, 184, 185, 223, 240, 261, 262, 271, 287, 449

INDEX OF SUBJECTS

National Association of Bath Superintendents, 420
National Association of Divisional Executives for Education, 419
National Association of Local Government Health and Welfare Officers, 420
National Association for Maternity and Child Welfare, 420
National Association for Mental Health, 420
National Association of Women Civil Servants, 140
National Coal Board, 22, 431, 434n, 437, 438
National Council of Social Service, 455
National Farmer's Union, 249, 255, 257-258, 366, 463
National Federation of Young Farmers' Clubs, 255
National Film Finance Corporation, 247
National Health Insurance Commission, 266
National Health Service, 53, 111, 112, 307, 323, 406, 414, 439, 440n
National Housing and Town Planning Council, 420
National Insurance Commissioner, 394, 395
National Insurance Appeal Tribunals, 395
National and Local Government Officers' Association, 81, 135, 420, 454
National Parks Commission, 253
National Physical Laboratory, 106
National Service, Ministry of, 266
National Society for the Prevention of Cruelty to Children, 455
National Union of Manufacturers, 455
National Union of Teachers, 420, 454
National Whitley Council, 19, 20, 47, 49, 136, 141, 147
  creation of, 8, 135
  ambit of, 15-16
  and Civil Service Pay Research Unit, 55
  Reorganisation Committee of, 62
  Promotions Committee of, 121
  Joint Committee on Training, 125-6
  organisation of, 142-5
  official side, 143, 145, 146
  staff side, 143, 144, 146
  Joint Committee on Political Activities, 157
Nationalised industries
  accounts of, scrutiny by Comptroller and Auditor-General, 307
  political controversy over, 431
  organisation of Departments concerned with, 431-3

Ministerial functions in relation to, 433-9
Nature Conservancy, 172, 253
Navy Board, 170
Navy Office, 178
New Town Development Corporations, 409, 431
Northern Ireland Departments, 261, 262, 263, 278, 407
  relations with U.K. Departments, 276-7

Official Car Pool, 291
Orders-in-Council affecting the Civil Service: (1855), 6, 38; (1870) 7, 38; (1910), 47; (1920), 8, 33; (1921), 8; (1927), 156; (1950), 33
Ordnance Survey, 252, 294
Oversea Service, H.M., 13, 28, 67, 68, 91-2, 261
Overseas Trade, Dept. of, 244, 245

Parish Councils Association, 419
Parliament, 3, 73, 183, 186, 207, 232, 253, 276, 288, 302, 320, 321, 326, 328, 330, 336, 337, 344, 346, 351, 358, 361, 392, 421, 430, 434, 437, 438, 439, 442, 444, 449
  and control of civil service, 5, 13, 33, 215-16, 376-85
  and definition of political office, 11-12, 155
  attitude to pensions, 52
  (*see also* Commons, House of; Lords, House of)
Public Acts:
  Agricultural Marketing Acts (1931-1949), 254.
  Borough Funds Act (1872), 419
  Children Act (1948), 367
  Crown Proceedings Act (1947), 398
  Distribution of Industry Acts (1945, 1950), 247
  Education Act (1902), 62, 272
  Education Act (1944), 357, 439
  Exchequer Act (1834), 302
  Exchequer and Audit Departments Act (1866), 5, 302, 309, 320, 321
  Exchequer and Audit Departments Act (1921), 302
  Forestry Acts (1919, 1945), 253
  Government of Ireland Act (1920), 276
  Herring Industry Act (1933), 254
  Industrial Organisation and Development Acts (1947, 1953), 247
  Labour Exchange Act (1909), 265
  Local Government Act (1933), 428
  Ministers of the Crown Act (1937), 337

INDEX OF SUBJECTS 483

Ministers of the Crown (Transfer of Functions) Act (1946), 216, 360
Ministry of Health Act (1919), 273
Monopolies and Restrictive Practices Act (1948), 248
New Towns Act (1946), 409
Official Secrets Acts (1889-1920), 152, 399
Police Act (1919), 135
Prevention of Corruption Act (1906), 151
Provisional Collection of Taxes Act (1913), 301
Public Order Act (1936), 399n
Punishment of Incest Act (1908), 399n
Regency Act (1705), 11
Restrictive Trade Practices Act (1956), 248.
Sea Fish Industry Act (1951), 254
Sugar Act (1956), 254, 255n
Sugar Industry (Reorganisation) Act (1936), 255
Superannuation Act (1859), 6, 38
Trades Disputes Acts (1927, 1946), 135, 141
Welsh Intermediate Education Act (1889), 272
Parliamentary Draftsmen, 97, 98
Parliamentary Private Secretaries, 192-3
Paymaster-General, 305, 338, 344
  Pay Office, 187, 303, 304, 305, 310, 311, 314, 327
  organisation and work of, 305-6
Pensions, Ministry of, 266, 267, 366
Pensions and National Insurance, Ministry of, 23, 25, 78, 81, 86, 111, 129, 130, 181, 228, 261, 262, 266, 271, 278, 287, 448, 449
  work of, 223, 239-40, 395
  size of, 239
  organisation of, 240-2
  mobility of staff in, 242-3
  Minister of, 338
Permanent Secretaries
  appointment of, 8, 37
  as Accounting Officers, 37, 185, 309, 323, 329, 384
  salary of, 45
  occasionally more than one at head of a Department, 185
  duties of, 185-6, 188
  relations with specialist advisers, 186
Planning
  nature and ambiguities of, 355-7
  in administration, 357-9
Planning staffs, 194, 352-5
Plant Pathology Laboratory, 106
Political Warfare Executive, 295

Poor Law Board, 172, 263, 361
Post Office, 6, 23, 25, 60, 61, 76, 80, 85, 91, 124, 125, 129, 142, 178, 191, 243, 261, 264, 269, 271, 273, 287, 303, 329, 400, 449
  engineering and allied grades, 15, 117
  staff associations, 16, 134, 138-40
  temporary staff, 17
  size of, 20, 116-17
  functions, 116-17, 292-3
  manipulative grades, 117-18
  relations of P.O. classes to general administrative, executive and clerical classes, 118-19
  reforms of, 1932-1939, 268
Post Office Controlling Officers' Association, 16, 144
Post Office Engineering Union, 16, 139 140, 144
Post Office Workers' Union, 135, 139, 140, 144
Postal Clerks' Association, 135
Postal Telegraph Clerks' Association, 134
Postmen's Federation, 134
Power, Ministry of, 98, 114, 173, 223, 228, 244
  nationalised industries for which responsible, 431
  and Atomic Energy Authority, 431
  organisation, 432
  functions, 433-9
  Minister of, 338, 346, 438
Priestley Commission (Royal Commission on the Civil Service, 1953-1955) quoted
  on 'Higher Civil Service', 29
  on hours of work, 47
  on annual leave, 48
  on provincial differentiation, 50
  on Civil Service pensions, 53
  on Civil Service pay, 54-58
  impressed with responsibility of Executive Class, 73
  on salaries of Works Group, 110
  on salaries of Medical Officers, 112
Prime Minister, 33, 35, 55, 90, 122, 147, 148, 173, 306, 345, 347, 353, 354, 365
  and appointment of Permanent Secretaries, etc., 8
  as First Lord of the Treasury, 168-9, 312
  private secretary to, rank of, 193
  patronage of, 313
  his Secretary for Appointments, 313n
  award of honours, 316
  powers of, 335, 337, 338-9, 340, 344, 351, 360
  Public Relations Adviser to, 196, 354
  Economic Adviser to, 354

484 INDEX OF SUBJECTS

Principal Establishments Officer
  appointment of, 8, 36, 37
  rank of, 36
  and appointments to highest posts in Administrative Class, 122
  duties of, 125, 188-91
Principal Finance Officer
  appointment of, 8, 37
  duties of, 187, 311-12, 322
  status in Department, 311
  appearance before PAC, 329, 384
Prison Commission, 231
Private Secretary to the Monarch, 174
Private Secretaries, 45, 191-4, 353, 378
Privy Council Committees, 168, 171, 349
  on Public Health, 111
  for Trade and Plantations, 171, 243
  for Education, 171
  for Agriculture (1883), 172, 253
  for Health, 172
  for Scientific and Industrial Research, 172
  for Medical Research, 172
  for Agriculture (1931), 172
  for Nature Conservancy, 172, 253
Production, Ministry of, 348, 349
Public Corporations
  political agreement as to form of, 431
  advantages of, 431
Public enquiries, 396-7
Public Prosecutions, Director of, 399
Public Record Office, 202, 204, 205
Public Trustee, 185
Public Works Loan Board, 411

Queen's Bench, 166
Queen's and Lord Treasurer's Remembrancer, 275, 305
Queen's Printer, 291

Reconstruction, Ministry of, 361
Regional Boards for Industry, 247, 270
Regional Commissioners, origin and development of, 268-9
Regional Hospital Boards, 11, 307, 431, 439-44, 445
Regional and local organisations
  staff employed in, 260, 261
  types of, 261-3
  history of in England and Wales, 263-70
  work of regional officers assessed, 241, 270-1, 409, 414, 441
  recent developments, 271-2, 409
  in Wales and Monmouth, 272-4
  in Scotland, 274-6
  in Northern Ireland, 276-8
Registries, 201-205
Registrar of Friendly Societies, 185
Registrar-General, 185

Registrar of Restrictive Trading Agreements, 248
Rent Tribunals, 397
Revolution Settlement (1689), 33
River Boards, 256, 410
Road Research Laboratory, 106
Roman Catholic Church, 455
Royal Aircraft Establishment, 262
Royal and Ancient Society, 455
Royal Botanic Gardens, 252
Royal Commissions
  on Equal Pay, 49
  on Poor Law, 361
  on Scottish Affairs, 274, 275
  on the Civil Service
    MacDonnell (1910), 62
    Tomlin (1929), 11, 145
    Priestley (1955), see under Priestley Commission
Royal Fine Art Commission, 185
Royal Institute of British Architects, 138
Royal Institute of Public Administration, 128
Royal Institute of Public Health and Hygiene, 420
Royal Mint, 106
Royal Society, 454
  President and Secretaries of, 461
Royal Society for Agriculture, 257

St. James's Palace, 178
St. Stephen's Chapel, 178
Sanitary Inspectors Association (now Association of Public Health Officers), 420
School of Accountancy, 308
School Boards, 263
School Welfare Officers Association, 420
Scientific Classes, the
  structure and recruitment, 101-4
  numbers, 102
  distribution between Departments, 102
  relations between scientific and general classes, 103-5
  career structure, 105-6
  work of, 106-107
Scientific and Industrial Research, Department of, 37, 105, 106, 107, 130, 172, 416, 459
Scottish Office, 174, 181, 228, 261, 274, 338, 368, 407, 432
  Secretary of State for Scotland, 254, 274, 337
Sea Fisheries Committees, 256
Secretary for Scotland, 174, 274
Secretary of State, office of, 34, 166, 173, 174, 179, 359
  (see also under Home Secretary, Foreign Secretary, etc.)

INDEX OF SUBJECTS 485

Society of Civil Servants, 136, 137, 140, 144
Society of County Treasurers, 419
Society of Medical Officers of Health, 419
Society of Technical Civil Servants, 138, 144
Society of Telecommunication Engineers, 16, 139
Society of Town Clerks, 419
Solicitor-General, 97, 399
Solicitor-General for Scotland, 275
Speaker of the House of Commons, 171
Specialist classes
  defined, 20-21
  examples of, 21, Appendix I, 96-119
  size of, 27
  Treasury interest in, 37
  importance of, 59
  distinguished from general classes, 94-5
  number of classes and grades, 95
  growth of, 95
  Departmental classes, 114-16
  training of, 129-30
Staff associations
  training of officers in trade union work, 126
  part played by in training civil servants, 126
  organisation of, 135-40
  growth of, 134-5
  affiliation to T.U.C. and Labour Party, 134
  and M.P.'s, 140
  and negotiating procedure, 142-8
  and disciplinary procedure, 150
  (*see also* under names of particular staff associations)
Staff reporting, 121-2
Standing Counsel to Treasury, 97
'Stanley' Case, 452
Stationery Office (H.M.S.O.), 182, 187, 190
  origin of, 291
  work of, 291-2, 297-8
Statistician Class
  origins of, 99-100
  size and recruitment of, 100-1
Statutory Publications Office, 98
Subordinate legislation, 381-3, 391-3
Sugar Board, 254
Supplies, Ministry of, Haldane Committee's proposal for creation of, 298
Supply, Ministry of, 98, 107, 111, 113, 125, 180, 185, 186, 223, 232, 233, 235, 237, 238, 239, 269, 271, 275, 286, 291, 343, 366, 463.
  Minister of, 438

Survey of Economic Plans, 354
Surveyor of Wards and Liveries, 252

Temporary Clerks, Class of: *see* Clerical Classes
Town and Country Planning, Minister of, 338
Town Planning Institute, 420
Trade Associations, 455
Trade, Board of, 99, 113, 179, 180, 227, 255, 265, 266, 267, 268, 270, 271, 275, 278, 463
  origin of, 171-2, 243
  work of, 223, 243-4
  size of, 244
  organisation of, 244-8
  Trade Commissioners, 244-5
  Export Credits Guarantee Dept., 247
  sponsoring of independent public bodies, 247-8
  relations with Monopolies Commission, 248
  relations with Registrar of Restrictive Trading Agreements, 248
  and local authorities in Development Areas, 406
  and 'Stanley' Case, 452
  President of the, 337, 430 458
Trades Union Congress, 135, 136, 137, 138, 139, 141, 454, 455
Transport and Civil Aviation, Ministry of, 98, 107, 110, 180, 244, 267, 268, 275, 287, 320, 346
  Area Traffic Commissioners, 395
  and local government, 406
  organisation and functions in relation to local government, 416-17
  nationalised services for which responsible, 431
  organisation in relation to nationalised services, 432-3
  functions in relation to nationalised services, 433-9
  Minister of, 438
Transport, Fuel, and Power, Secretary of State for the Co-ordination of, 338, 346
Transport and General Workers Union, 454
Transport Tribunal, 395
Treasurer of the Navy, 170
Treasury, 17, 18, 19, 25, 40, 41, 42, 43, 45, 46, 51, 52, 53, 55, 56, 68, 70, 72, 76, 77, 78, 90, 91, 95, 96, 98, 100, 104, 107, 110, 112, 115, 124, 126, 127, 128, 129, 131, 132, 135, 141, 142, 143, 145, 146, 152, 156, 157, 158, 168, 170, 179, 180, 182, 184, 185, 187, 196, 201, 218, 226, 227, 244, 253, 255, 270, 275, 286, 287,

Treasury—cont.
288, 289, 290, 291, 293, 338, 339, 342, 349, 354, 355, 362, 366, 411, 416, 427, 430, 431, 434, 437, 442, 443, 445, 463
  General
    Primacy among Departments, 5, 7
    Permanent Secretaries, status and functions of, 7, 8, 35-6, 313-14
    responsibility for organisation of service recognised, 8
    size of staff in, 24, 35, 36, 316
    powers in relation to Civil Service, 32-4
    Standing Counsel to, 97
    Parliamentary Counsel to, 97, 316, 381, 391
    responsibility for promotions into Administrative Class, 123
    history of office, 167
    Ministers, 312-13
    Second and Third Secretaries, 313
    buildings, 316
    work and influence of, assessed, 316-318, 330-2
    and legal system, 391
  Treasury Control
    of Civil Service pay, 12, 322, 323
    of Oversea Service, 28
    of establishments, 33, 34-8, 322, 323
    of pensions, 50
    and negotiating procedure, 147-8
    Departmental responsibility for exercising economy, 309
    of Estimates, 320-4
    of specific objects of expenditure, 322-3
    of the Budget, 324-6
    of day-to-day expenditure, 326-7
    of *virement*, 326-7
    of cash advances, 327
  Internal Organisation
    Establishments Divisions, 34-6, 313, 314
    Home Finance and Supply Divisions, 35, 314
    Overseas Finance Divisions, 35, 315
    Organisation and Methods Division, 35, 189-90, 216-17, 311, 313, 316
    Training and Education Division, 35, 125, 313
    Establishment Officer's Branch, 35
    Machinery of Government Section, 35, 361
    Officers of Accounts, 169, 188, 310, 314, 315, 329, 330, 384
    Economic Section, 313, 316, 358
    Economic Information Division, 313
    Medical Service, 313
    Accounts Branch, 314
    Economic Co-ordination Group of Divisions, 315
    Estimate Clerk, 315, 321
    Ceremonial Officer, 316
    Subordinate Departments and Offices, 316
    Government Hospitality Fund, 316
  Treasury Circulars, quoted, 8, 36, 151, 157, 323
  Treasury Classes
    growth of, 8
    defined, 18-20
    examples of, 19
    'linked' with Departmental Classes, 20
    size of, 26-8
  Treasury, First Lord of, *see* Prime Minister
  Treasury Minutes, quoted: (1919), 8; (1882), 285; (1872), 309; (1885), 321; (1886), 322; (1868), 322.
    in reply to observations of P.A.C., 330
  Treasury Solicitor and Queen's Proctor, 37, 98, 234, 391, 398
  Trevelyan-Northcote Report, 6
  Typing Grades
    number, 87
    recruitment, 87-8
    as personal secretaries, 88
    effect on Service of shortage in, 88-9
    training schools for, 88

Unemployment Assistance Board, 266, 267
Union of Post Office Workers (*see* Post Office Workers Union)
UNESCO, 307
United Kingdom Alliance, 455
United States
  Congress, 14
  career civil service, 47
  Constitution quoted, 166
  Presidential aides, 191
  burden on President, 351
  Presidential leadership, 352
  'five percenters', 452
University Grants Committee, 184, 316, 459

Victualling Board (Navy), 170

War Office, 61, 171, 174, 175, 180, 223, 233, 265, 266, 294
  Secretary of State, 252
  Army Council, 171, 265
War Office Selection Boards, 65
War Pensions Appeal Tribunals, 394
Welsh Board of Health, 181, 273
Welsh Department of Agriculture, 273

Welsh Department, Ministry of Education, 181, 262, 272, 273
Welsh Office, Ministry of Housing and Local Government, 273
Westminster Abbey, Chapter House of, 178
Westminster, Palace of, 178
Wheat Commission, 252, 255
White Fish Authority, 254
Whitehall
   development as seat of central administration, 178
   dispersal of offices from, 180-1, 231, 240-1
'Whitleyism'—*see* Civil Service, negotiating procedure, Staff associations, National Whitley Council, Departmental Whitley Councils
Woods and Forests, Commissioners of, 172, 288

Work, methods of dividing, 226, 363-5, 408, 441
Works, Board of (also Office of), 172, 180, 252, 267, 288
Works Group of Professional Classes, the structure of, 107, 110
   reorganisation of, 108
   relations with Administrative Class, 108-9
   recruitment to, 109
   number, 109
   salaries, 109
   Priestley Commission on, 110
Works, Ministry of, 91, 98, 172, 180, 182, 187, 190, 223, 276, 287, 292, 298, 463
   organisation and duties of, 288-90, 291
   First Commissioner, 288
   Minister of, 288

York Place, 178